The Cambridge Companion to
the International Court of Justice

As international law has become more present in global policy-
making, the International Court of Justice (ICJ) has come to occupy an
essential and increasingly visible role in international relations. This
collection explores substantive developments within the ICJ and offers
critical perspectives on its historical and contemporary role. It also
examines the growing role of the ICJ in the settlement of international
disputes and assesses the impact of the ICJ's jurisprudence on the major
areas of international law, from territorial delimitation to human
rights. With contributions from a diverse range of scholars and
practitioners, the collection's contents combine a legal perspective with
institutional and sociological insights on the functions of the ICJ. By
considering the ICJ's character, jurisdiction, and effectiveness, this
collection offers a varied and holistic account of the ICJ, an institution
whose significance and influence only increase by the day.

Carlos Espósito is Professor of Public International Law at the
Universidad Autónoma de Madrid. He has taught at numerous
universities and institutions around the world, including at the Hague
Academy of International Law and as a visiting professor of law at the
Universities of California, Berkeley, and Paris-I Sorbonne. Carlos was
He has appeared as an advocate before the International Court of
Justice. Vice President of the European Society of International
Law and was formerly counsel and deputy legal advisor at the
International Law Department of the Spanish Ministry of Foreign
Affairs and Cooperation.

Kate Parlett is a barrister at Twenty Essex in London, specializing in
public international law and international arbitration. She regularly
appears as an advocate before the International Court of Justice. Kate
has taught public international law, international investment and
commercial arbitration, and international human rights law at the
University of Cambridge, Paris-II University (Panthéon-Assas), Queen
Mary University of London, Queen's University of Canada, the
University of Queensland, and the Graduate Institute in Geneva.

Cambridge Companions to Law

Cambridge Companions to Law offers thought-provoking introductions to different legal disciplines, invaluable to both the student and the scholar. Edited by world-leading academics, each offers a collection of essays which both map out the subject and allow the reader to delve deeper. Critical and enlightening, the Companions library represents legal scholarship at its best.

The Cambridge Companion to European Union Private Law
Edited by Christian Twigg-Flesner

The Cambridge Companion to International Law
Edited by James Crawford and Martti Koskenniemi

The Cambridge Companion to Comparative Law
Edited by Mauro Bussani and Ugo Mattei

The Cambridge Companion to Human Rights Law
Edited by Conor Gearty and Costas Douzinas

The Cambridge Companion to Public Law
Edited by Mark Elliott and David Feldman

The Cambridge Companion to International Criminal Law
Edited by William A. Schabas

The Cambridge Companion to Natural Law Jurisprudence
Edited by George Duke and Robert P. George

The Cambridge Companion to Comparative Family Law
Edited by Shazia Choudhry and Jonathan Herring

The Cambridge Companion to Comparative Constitutional Law
Edited by Roger Masterman and Robert Schütze

The Cambridge Companion to the First Amendment and Religious Liberty
Edited by Michael D. Breidenbach and Owen Anderson

The Cambridge Companion to the Philosophy of Law
Edited by John Tasioulas

The Cambridge Companion to

The International Court of Justice

Edited by

Carlos Espósito
Universidad Autónoma de Madrid

Kate Parlett
Twenty Essex, London

Assistant Editor

Callista Harris
University of Sydney

CAMBRIDGE
UNIVERSITY PRESS

Shaftesbury Road, Cambridge CB2 8EA, United Kingdom

One Liberty Plaza, 20th Floor, New York, NY 10006, USA

477 Williamstown Road, Port Melbourne, VIC 3207, Australia

314–321, 3rd Floor, Plot 3, Splendor Forum, Jasola District Centre, New Delhi – 110025, India

103 Penang Road, #05–06/07, Visioncrest Commercial, Singapore 238467

Cambridge University Press is part of Cambridge University Press & Assessment, a department of the University of Cambridge.

We share the University's mission to contribute to society through the pursuit of education, learning and research at the highest international levels of excellence.

www.cambridge.org
Information on this title: www.cambridge.org/9781108487252

DOI: 10.1017/9781108766241

First published 2023

A catalogue record for this publication is available from the British Library.

Library of Congress Cataloging-in-Publication Data
Names: Espósito, Carlos D., editor. | Parlett, Kate, editor.
Title: The Cambridge companion to the International Court of Justice / edited by Carlos Espósito, Universidad Autónoma de Madrid; Kate Parlett, 20 Essex Street Chambers, London ; contributors, Freya Baetens [and others].
Description: Cambridge, United Kingdom ; New York, NY : Cambridge University Press, 2023. | Series: CCLW Cambridge companions to law | Includes bibliographical references and index.
Identifiers: LCCN 2022049147 (print) | LCCN 2022049148 (ebook) | ISBN 9781108487252 (hardback) | ISBN 9781108732840 (paperback) | ISBN 9781108766241 (epub)
Subjects: LCSH: International Court of Justice.
Classification: LCC KZ6275 .C36 2023 (print) | LCC KZ6275 (ebook) | DDC 341.5/52–dc23/eng/20230105
LC record available at https://lccn.loc.gov/2022049147
LC ebook record available at https://lccn.loc.gov/2022049148

ISBN 978-1-108-48725-2 Hardback
ISBN 978-1-108-73284-0 Paperback

Contents

Contributors

Freya Baetens (*Cand. Jur./Lic. Jur.*, Ghent; LLM, Columbia; PhD, Cambridge) is Professor of Public International Law (Faculty of Law, University of Oxford), Head of Programmes at the Bonavero Institute of Human Rights, and Fellow at Mansfield College. She is also affiliated with the PluriCourts Centre (Faculty of Law, Oslo University) and the Europa Institute (Faculty of Law, Leiden University). As a member of the Brussels Bar, she regularly acts as counsel or expert in international and European disputes. She is listed on the Panel of Arbitrators and Conciliators of the International Centre for the Settlement of Investment Disputes, the South China International Economic and Trade Arbitration Commission (Shenzhen Court of International Arbitration), and the Hong Kong International Arbitration Centre. She is a general public international lawyer, with a particular interest in the law of treaties, responsibility of States and international organisations, privileges and immunities, law of the sea, human rights, WTO and investment law, energy law, and sustainable development.

Daniel Bodansky is Regents Professor at the Sandra Day O'Connor College of Law, Arizona State University (ASU). He is the author of *The Art and Craft of International Environmental Law*, which received the 2011 Sprout Award from the International Studies Association, and has coauthored *International Climate Change Law*, which received the 2018 Certificate of Merit from the American Society of International Law. Prior to joining the ASU faculty in 2010, he taught at the University of Washington from 1989 to 1999, served as Climate Change Coordinator at the US State Department from 1999 to 2001, and held the Woodruff Chair of International Law at the University of Georgia from 2002 to 2010. He is a member of the Council on Foreign Relations, served on the board of editors of the *American Journal of International Law* from 2001 to 2011, and is a graduate of Harvard (AB), Cambridge (MPhil), and Yale (JD).

Rose Cameron (LLB, Monash; LLM, Cantab) is an Australian lawyer with extensive experience in international and criminal law. She has worked as an associate legal officer to HE Judge James Crawford at the International Court of Justice and as a legal officer in the Appeals Chamber of the Special Tribunal for Lebanon. She previously worked as a barrister at the Victorian Bar and is currently a senior legal advisor to the Victorian Government in Melbourne, Australia.

Alejandro Chehtman is Professor of Law at Universidad Torcuato Di Tella (Argentina) and a fellow at the Argentine National Research Council (CONICET). He has held research and visiting positions at the LSE, University College London, Harvard Kennedy School, University of Girona, LUISS, and the University of Arizona. His main research areas are public international law, including international criminal law and international humanitarian law, and constitutional law, with special emphasis on philosophical and empirical approaches. He has published articles in leading peer-reviewed journals such as the *European Journal of International Law, Legal Theory*, the *Journal of International Criminal Justice, Law and Philosophy*, the *Leiden Journal of International Law, Utilitas*, and the *Journal of Law and Courts*. His book, *The Philosophical Foundations of Extraterritorial Punishment*, was published by Oxford University Press. He is currently working on a book project titled *A Theory of Asymmetrical* War, to be published by Oxford University Press.

Judge James Crawford (AC, SC, FBA) took up his position as a judge of the International Court of Justice (ICJ) in February 2015 and served on the bench until his untimely death in May 2021. Previously he was Whewell Professor of International Law at the University of Cambridge and a professorial fellow of Jesus College; he also held chairs at Adelaide, Sydney, and LaTrobe Universities in Australia and was Chang Jiang Distinguished Professor at Xi'an Jiaotong University, PRC. He was responsible for the International Law Commission's (ILC) work on the International Criminal Court (1994) and for the second reading of the ILC Articles on State Responsibility (2001). During his practicing career, he was involved as counsel, expert, or arbitrator in over 100 cases before the ICJ and other international tribunals. His main publications include *The Creation of States in International Law* (2nd ed., 2006), *Brownlie's Principles of Public International Law* (8th and 9th ed., 2012 and

2019), *State Responsibility: The General Part* (2013), and *Chance, Order, Change: The Course of International Law* (2014).

Jean d'Aspremont is Professor of International Law at Sciences Po Law School. He also holds the Chair of Public International Law at the University of Manchester. He is General Editor of the *Cambridge Studies in International and Comparative Law* and Director of Oxford International Organizations (OXIO). He is a member of the scientific advisory board of the *European Journal of International Law* and series editor of the *Melland Schill Studies in International Law*. He writes on questions of international law and international legal theory. His work has been translated in several languages, including Spanish, Portuguese, Hindi, Japanese, and Persian.

James Devaney is Senior Lecturer in Law and Program Convenor of the LLM in International Law at the University of Glasgow, Scotland. He also teaches in a visiting capacity at the Universities of Sydney, Australia, and Kobe, Japan. His research interests relate primarily to international courts and tribunals and legal reasoning, although he has published on a range of areas of international law. His monograph *Fact-Finding before the International Court of Justice*, which focuses on the use of evidence before international courts and tribunals, including the adjudicative bodies of the WTO and inter-State arbitration, was published by Cambridge University Press and nominated for the Peter Birks Book Prize for Outstanding Legal Scholarship. He is also a member of the Bar of the State of New York.

Carlos Espósito is Chair Professor of Public International Law at the Universidad Autónoma de Madrid. Carlos has taught at numerous universities and institutions around the world, including the Hague Academy of International Law and as a visiting professor of law at the Law School of the University of California, Berkeley, and Paris-I Sorbonne. Carlos, who is admitted to the Madrid Bar, has had a considerable professional practice as a counsel and deputy legal advisor at the International Law Department of the Spanish Ministry of Foreign Affairs and Cooperation (2001–2004). He has also been a counsel to States and international organizations, and has appeared as an advocate before the International Court of Justice. Carlos studied law at the University of Buenos Aires (Argentina) and earned his PhD from the Universidad Autónoma de Madrid (Spain) in 1995 with a thesis on the advisory jurisdiction of the International Court of Justice (*La jurisdicción consultiva de la Corte Internacional de Justicia*). He is a life member of Clare Hall College, University of Cambridge, and holds an honorary doctorate degree from the Universidad de Mendoza (Argentina).

Rotem Giladi is a senior lecturer at the Law School, Faculty of Business and Law, University of Roehampton, and an adjunct professor at the Law Faculty of the Hebrew University of Jerusalem. He also taught international law at the Universities of Helsinki, Leipzig, and Edinburgh. Between 2001 and 2007, he was the senior legal and policy advisor for the International Committee of the Red Cross delegation to Israel/the Occupied Palestinian Territories. His current research focuses on the history of the laws of war as well as the meeting points between Jewish history and the history of international law.

Tom Ginsburg is Leo Spitz Professor of International Law at the University of Chicago, where he also holds an appointment in the Political Science Department. He is also a research professor at the American Bar Foundation. He holds BA, JD, and PhD degrees from the University of California, Berkeley, and codirects the Comparative Constitutions Project, a dataset cataloguing the world's constitutions since 1789, that runs the award-winning Constitute website. His latest book is *Democracies and International Law* (2021). Before entering law teaching, he served as a legal advisor at the Iran–US Claims Tribunal, and he currently serves as a senior advisor on constitution building to International IDEA.

Callista Harris is a consultant in public international law and international arbitration. She acts as counsel in disputes before domestic and international courts and tribunals, including the International Court of Justice, the International Tribunal for the Law of the Sea and UNCLOS Annex VII tribunals. Callista recently completed a PhD at the University of Sydney, where her research focuses on international dispute settlement. She also holds an LLM from the University of Cambridge.

Mamadou Hébié is Associate Professor of International Law at the Grotius Centre for International Legal Studies (Leiden University). Before rejoining Leiden University as Associate Professor in 2021, Dr. Hébié was Legal Officer and Special Assistant to the President of the International Court of Justice HE Judge Abdulqawi A. Yusuf. His PhD thesis, 'Souveraineté territoriale par traité: une étude des accords entre puissances coloniales et entités politiques locales' (Paris: PUF, 2015), was awarded the Paul Guggenheim Prize in International Law in 2016. Mamadou Hébié acted as advisor to the Argentine Republic in the *ARA Libertad* case before the International Tribunal for the Law of the Sea. He is admitted to practice law in New York.

Sir Kenneth Keith studied law at the University of Auckland, Victoria University of Wellington (VUW), and Harvard Law School. He worked as a lawyer in the New Zealand Department of External Affairs and the Office of Legal Affairs in the UN Secretariat. He was a member of the Law Faculty at VUW for over twenty years in which he is now Professor Emeritus. In New Zealand he was a member in a number of law and constitutional reform bodies and led the New Zealand delegation to the sessions of the diplomatic conference that prepared the Additional Protocols of 1977 to the Geneva Conventions of 1949. He was a member of the legal team that brought proceedings in the ICJ against France about its nuclear testing in the Pacific in 1973, 1974, and 1995. He was a judge of the New Zealand Court of Appeal and the Supreme Court from 1996 to 2006 and a judge of the ICJ from 2006 to 2015.

Jan Klabbers is Professor of International Law at the University of Helsinki, having earlier taught at the University of Amsterdam. He has held invited visiting positions at New York University, Sorbonne, and the Graduate Institute, among others, and is the author of a large number of books and articles on the law of international organisations. These include *An Introduction to International Organizations Law* (4th ed., 2022), *Treaty Conflict and the European Union* (2008), and the *Cambridge Companion to International Organizations Law* (editor, 2022). Having recently completed a project on global ethics (*Virtue in Global Governance: Discretion and Judgment*, 2022), he is currently working on a research project on international organisations and the private sector.

Marcelo Kohen has been Professor of International Law at the Graduate Institute of International and Development Studies in Geneva since 1995. He has also been a member of the Institut de Droit International and its Secretary-General since 2015 and counsel and advocate for a number of States of four continents before the ICJ, the ITLOS, and other tribunals. He also acts as an international arbitrator. He has been Rapporteur for the International Law Association, the Council of Europe, and the Institut de

Droit International. He is the author of more than a hundred publications in the field of international law in English, French, and Spanish. He was awarded the Paul Guggenheim Prize in 1997 for his book *Possession contestée et souveraineté territoriale.*

Robert Kolb has been Professor of Public International Law at the Law Faculty, University of Geneva, since 2007. He is a leading expert in international law and international humanitarian law and has published several books and articles on these topics in English, French, German, and Italian. In 2011, he acted as a counsel for the German government in the *Jurisdictional Immunities* (*Germany* v. *Italy*) case at the ICJ. Prior to 2007, Professor Kolb worked as a legal advisor to the International Committee of the Red Cross and Swiss Federal Department of Foreign Affairs. He was also Secretary of the Institute of International Law and a member of the board of directors of the University Centre for International Humanitarian Law, which became the Geneva Academy in 2007. He was Lecturer in Public International Law at the Graduate Institute of International and Development Studies, Associate Professor at the University of Bern, and Adjunct Professor at the University of Neuchatel. He also taught at the Catholic University of the Sacred Heart, Milan.

Roger O'Keefe is Professor of International Law at Bocconi University, Milan, and Honorary Professor of Law at University College London. He is joint general editor of the *Oxford Monographs in International Law* series. He has written and spoken widely on canonical topics of public international law, such as the sources of international law, the law of treaties, the relationship between international and domestic law, statehood and admission to the United Nations, title to territory, jurisdiction and immunities, and State responsibility, as well as on topics in the subfields of international criminal law, international humanitarian law, international human rights law, and international cultural heritage law. His many publications on jurisdictional immunities under international law include *The United Nations Convention on Jurisdictional Immunities of States and Their Property: A Commentary* (Oxford University Press, 2013), co-edited with Christian J. Tams.

Nilüfer Oral is Director of the Centre of International Law at the National University of Singapore, member of the UN International Law Commission and co-chair of the Study Group on sea-level rise in relation to international law. She was a legal advisor and climate change negotiator for the Turkish Foreign Ministry. She was a member of the law faculty at Istanbul Bilgi University. She has appeared before the International Tribunal for the Law of the Sea. She is a Distinguished Fellow of the Law of the Sea Institute at Berkeley Law, University of California and a Senior Fellow of the National University of Singapore Law School. She is also a member of the Committee of Legal Experts of the Commission of Small Island States on Climate Change and International Law, and a member of the Steering Committee of the IUCN World Commission on Environmental Law.

Federica Paddeu is Derek Bowett Fellow in Law at Queens' College Cambridge, where she also directs studies. She is a fellow of the Lauterpacht Centre for International Law, a member of the International Law Advisory Panel of the British Institute of International and Comparative Law, the Director of Studies of the British Branch of the International Law Association, and a member of the academic research panel of Blackstone Chambers. Federica is a general international lawyer, with particular interest in the law of State responsibility, the law on the use of force, and the theory and role of exceptions in the various fields of international law, most prominently international investment law. Her research has been published in leading journals, including the *British Yearbook of International Law*, the *American Journal of International Law*, and the *European Journal of International Law*. Federica's monograph, *Justification and Excuse in International Law: Concept and Theory of General Defences*, which was based on her PhD dissertation, was published by Cambridge University Press in 2018. Federica holds a law degree (*cum laude*) from Universidad Católica Andrés Bello, Caracas, and an LLM and PhD in international law from the University of Cambridge and is admitted to practice in Venezuela as a member of the Caracas (Distrito Federal) bar.

Kate Parlett is a barrister at Twenty Essex in London. She acts for States and private entities on disputes in relation to land and maritime boundaries, investment treaties and contracts, international trade law, human rights, law of the sea, State responsibility, treaty obligations, immunities, transboundary environmental harm, and sanctions. Kate regularly appears as an advocate before the International Court of Justice and other international tribunals and also sits as arbitrator. Kate has taught public international law, international investment and commercial arbitration, and international human rights law at the University of Cambridge, Paris-II University (Panthéon-Assas), Queen Mary University of London, Queen's University of Canada, the University of Queensland, and the Graduate Institute in Geneva.

Antonio Remiro Brotóns is Emeritus Professor of International Law of the Faculty of Law at the Universidad Autónoma de Madrid and a member of the Institute of International Law. He is a member of the Permanent Court of Arbitration and a counsel and advocate of States before the International Court of Justice and international arbitrations. His extensive list of publications includes a classic study on the law of treaties in Spanish: *Derecho de los Tratados* (1987).

Amy Sander is a barrister at Essex Court Chambers (London). She has developed a significant practice in public international law (which she previously taught at Cambridge University), with extensive advocacy experience, before the English courts and in international forums, including the ICJ. Amy is on the A Panel of Junior Counsel to the Crown (the Attorney General's Public International Law Panel), and she is recommended in the legal directories (the Chambers and Partners Global Guide, and the Legal 500) as a leading junior (band 1) for public international law. Amy is a board member of the YPILG and a member of the BIICL PIL Advisory Panel. She is coauthor (with Professor Vaughan Lowe QC and Professor Robin Churchill) of the fourth edition of *The Law of the Sea*. Amy also supports 'Be Her Lead', an organization dedicated to supporting young girls in schools.

Yuval Shany is Hersch Lauterpacht Chair in International Law and formerly Dean of the Law Faculty at the Hebrew University of Jerusalem. He was a member of the UN Human Rights Committee from 2013 to 2020 and served as its chair for one year during that time. He is also a senior research fellow at the Israel Democracy Institute, the chair of the academic committee of Hebrew University's Minerva Center for Human Rights, the codirector of the Faculty's International Law Forum and transitional justice program, and Head of the CyberLaw program of the Hebrew University Federmann CyberSecurity Research Center. Among his research areas are international courts and tribunals, international human rights law, international humanitarian law, and international law in cyberspace.

Jean-Marc Thouvenin is Professor of International Law at the University Paris Nanterre, Secretary General of The Hague Academy of International Law, Associate Member of the Institut de Droit International, and a member of the board of the French Society of International Law. He has published extensively on international law, including the law of the sea and international sanctions. As a practitioner, he appears regularly before international courts and tribunals and has represented or is representing States before the ICJ, the PCA, the ITLOS, the ECJ, and the IACHR.

Dire Tladi (BLC; LLB, Pretoria; LLM, Connecticut; PhD, Erasmus) is Professor of International Law and a holder of the NRF SARChI Chair in International Constitutional Law at the University of Pretoria. He is a member of the UN International Law Commission and its Special Rapporteur on Peremptory Norms of General International Law (*Jus Cogens*). He is also a member of the Institut de Droit International. He was formerly Special Advisor to the South African Foreign Minister. He had also been a legal advisor to the South African Foreign Ministry and a legal counsel of the South African Mission to the United Nations in New York. Tladi has appeared as counsel before the International Criminal Court.

Philippa Webb is Professor of Public International Law at King's College London and a barrister at Twenty Essex. She writes on a wide range of international law issues and represents States, companies, and individuals in international and domestic courts, including the International Court of Justice, the European Court of Human Rights, and the UK Supreme Court. Previously, Philippa served as a special assistant and legal officer to Judge Higgins GBE QC during her presidency of the International Court of Justice and held positions in the International Criminal Court and UN headquarters. Her publications include *The Right to a Fair Trial in International Law* (2020, with Amal Clooney) with the accompanying *travaux préparatoires* to Article 14 of the ICCPR (2021), *Oppenheim's International Law: United Nations* (2017, with Rosalyn Higgins, Dapo Akande, Sandy Sivakumaran, and James Sloan), *International Judicial Integration and Fragmentation* (2015), and *The Law of State Immunity* (2015, with Lady Hazel Fox QC).

Samuel Wordsworth KC is a barrister at Essex Court Chambers in London and specializes in public international law and international arbitration.

He has been regularly instructed by governments in international law cases and has appeared before numerous international tribunals, including the International Court of Justice and tribunals constituted with respect to the law of the sea. He is a visiting professor teaching investment arbitration at Kings College, London. He has also been instructed as counsel in multiple investment treaty disputes and occasionally sits as arbitrator.

Preface

The first words of appreciation go to the outstanding group of contributors to the *Cambridge Companion to the International Court of Justice*. The authors have shown patience and understanding as this project adapted to the vicissitudes of the pandemic.

We are grateful to Cambridge University Press, and particularly to Marianne Nield for her invaluable support. Thanks are also due to Finola O'Sullivan, former executive publisher at Cambridge University Press, who played an instrumental role in the birth of the project. Finally, we are indebted to Callista Harris for her helpful contribution as assistant editor of the book.

The manuscript was finished before the Russian invasion of Ukraine on February 24, 2022. The Court adopted provisional measures in the case concerning the *Allegations of Genocide under the Convention on the Prevention and Punishment of the Crime of Genocide* (*Ukraine* v. *Russian Federation*) on 16 March 2022, including that 'the Russian Federation shall immediately suspend the military operations that it commenced on 24 February 2022 in the territory of Ukraine'.

It is our hope that this book will help the readers to understand and assess the proper role of the Court in the settlement of disputes and the development of international law and its place in the maintenance of international peace.

The book is dedicated to the memory of the late Judge James Crawford, our beloved friend and precious mentor.

Introduction

Professor Carlos Espósito and Dr Kate Parlett

The International Court of Justice held its first sitting on 18 April 1946 and heard its first two cases in 1948: it heard preliminary objections in *The Corfu Channel Case* from late February to early March, and it held hearings in the advisory opinion on *Conditions of Admission of a State to Membership in the United Nations (Article 4 of the Charter)* in late April. Those first two cases were emblematic of the kinds of disputes that the Court would eventually hear and resolve as part of its ordinary caseload: they both dealt with practical issues, with significant political implications, and were an opportunity for the Court to provide guidance to the broader international community on disputed issues of international law. They provided the Court with scope to fulfil its mandate as the principal judicial organ of the United Nations; to function as a prominent interpreter of international law, as it is used and applied in practice. As international law has become more present in global policy-making and in academic and journalistic commentary, the International Court has come to occupy an essential and increasingly visible role in international relations, and has exercised jurisdiction over a significant number of international disputes addressing the same matters as are being wrestled with in the halls of the United Nations, and in ministries of foreign affairs across the world, and are being discussed as leading stories in international newspapers.

Some seventy years on from the Court's first hearings, we offer a timely, thorough, reflective and critical study of the role of the ICJ, its practice and the impact of its jurisprudence. It is with this in mind that we proposed the inclusion of this Companion into the series of *Cambridge Companions*, a decade after Professor James Crawford and Professor Martti Koskenniemi edited the *Cambridge Companion to International Law (2012)*, an intellectually ambitious project which provided thought-provoking fodder for the most senior of specialists, and at the same time, an accessible introduction for the non-specialist student and those with a more general interest in international affairs. We hope that this *Cambridge Companion to the*

International Court of Justice might go some way to opening up the work of this important judicial body for the non-specialist, while also giving those of us who practice, teach and research across the field of international dispute settlement some food for thought.

The *Companion* is structured in three parts, each of which is intended to cover substantive developments as well as critical perspectives.

The first (Part I) looks at the historical and contemporary role of the ICJ, including its various functions, history and context, jurisdiction (both theoretical and as it has been practically exercised), and its effectiveness as a dispute settlement body and as contributing to the development of international law and to international peace and security within the UN system.

It is fitting that the *Companion* commences with a chapter co-authored by Judge James Crawford, together with Professor Freya Baetens and Rose Cameron, on the functions of the ICJ. Chapter 1 was finalised a few months before James's untimely death. James was a towering presence at Cambridge, and one of the world's most experienced practitioners and academics on matters related to the Court, as well as many other aspects of international law. He was to us also a good friend and mentor. He is and will be much missed on the Bench and elsewhere. The chapter traces the origins of the ICJ in its predecessor, the PCIJ, and then considers the Court's core functions: deciding the disputes submitted to it and exercising its advisory functions. It also critically examines the Court's functions in finding and developing the law, and in maintaining international peace and security.

Sir Kenneth Keith, former judge of the ICJ, contributed Chapter 2 on 'The Role of an ICJ Judge', considering first the process of nomination and election of judges, as well as their qualifications and the outcomes of the election process. He then examines the way in which the Court engages as a judicial body with the parties, with specific reference to the Court's exercise of its advisory jurisdiction. Finally, he discusses the process of decision-making, before drawing conclusions on the outcomes of that process – the judgments and opinions of the Court.

In Chapter 3 Professor Dire Tladi looks in more depth at the role of the ICJ in the development of international law, from both a doctrinal and a practical perspective. He considers concrete examples of the way in which the Court's judgments and opinions have had an influence on the development of international law, and he concludes that the Court has in practice had a significant impact on the development of international law, even though that goes beyond its core mandate.

The institutional context of the Court is then examined by Professor Tom Ginsburg. Chapter 4 focuses first on the Court's function as a court, that is, as the principal judicial organ of the United Nations. He then considers the Court's relations with States, as an *international* court. Finally, he considers the Court's institutional grounding as an organ of the United Nations, and examines its relationship with the United Nations. Professor Ginsburg discovers that there is a gap between the Court's formal institutional structures and its actual operation in practice, and he emphasises in particular the way in which the Court has taken a central role in the development of international law.

The final chapter in Part I, Chapter 5, by Professors Rotem Giladi and Yuval Shany, assesses the effectiveness of the ICJ. They first set out an evaluative framework for assessing the Court's effectiveness, adopting a goals-based analysis. They identify the ICJ's goals, and then consider the structural features of the Court that assist and hinder it from achieving those goals. By reference to specific examples, the authors then consider whether the ICJ has achieved its goals in practice, concluding that its record of achievement produces mixed results, but highlighting the Court's success in preserving confidence in international adjudication.

The second part of the book (Part II) examines the role of the ICJ in the settlement of international disputes. It commences with Chapter 6 by Professor Jean-Marc Thouvenin on the jurisdiction of the Court. He addresses the Court's jurisdiction in contentious cases and its jurisdiction in advisory opinions, using specific examples from the Court's judgments and opinions. He considers whether a novel approach is needed to confer on the Court compulsory jurisdiction across a wider range of disputes.

Professor Kolb's Chapter 7 on provisional measures provides a thorough and timely analysis of the Court's jurisdiction to order provisional measures. He identifies an evolution in the Court's practice on provisional measures, with the Court most recently developing specific conditions for the indication of provisional measures. He examines those conditions and their elaboration through the Court's caselaw, together with the Court's findings as to the binding effect of its provisional measures orders. He also addresses issues of procedure. From this survey, he concludes that provisional measures continue to evolve in significant ways, that the law on provisional measures has been fleshed out and is relatively complex, and that the Court's jurisprudence has had a strong influence on the approach of other international courts and tribunals.

Then follows Chapter 8 on the ICJ 'as the master of the sources' by Professor Jean d'Aspremont. It commences with some preliminary remarks on the Court's significant role as the master of the sources of international law. It then considers the repressive dimension of Article 38, before turning to consider the ways in which the Court has concretely used its role in respect of the sources of international law. Finally, he critically examines how repression and mastery can often work together in international legal thought.

Dr James Devaney's Chapter 9 on fact-finding and expert evidence considers how the Court has treated competing evidentiary claims, and how it engages in a fact-finding process, looking at the evolution of the Court's process in this regard. He evaluates the significant criticism that has been directed against the Court in respect of its approach to fact-finding and the ways in which the Court has begun to address those criticisms. His chapter concludes with some further practical suggestions as to how the Court could increase confidence in its fact-finding processes.

In Chapter 10 Professor Philippa Webb then considers the ICJ's relationship with other courts and tribunals through the dual prism of integration and fragmentation. She argues that three factors influence the degree of the Court's integration or fragmentation: the identity of the court, the substance of the law, and the procedures employed. She selects three legal issues that have been considered by the ICJ and other courts and tribunals in recent years: jurisdiction over issues of immunity involving treaties that do not expressly refer to immunity; inferring specific intent for genocide; and the nature of consular assistance as a treaty obligation, individual right or human right. These issues provide insight into the way that identity, area of law and procedure influence integration or fragmentation among international courts

The working practices of the Court are critically examined by Callista Harris in Chapter 11. She looks at the framework for these practices and then considers how they operate in practice, as cases proceed through the Court's dispute-resolution process. She notes that reforms have been made to the Court's working practices to increase the speed of cases, as well as to improve the processes. She notes that the Court has demonstrated significant agility in its more recent amendments to the Rules to take account of the worldwide pandemic, and argues that there is evidence to suggest that the Court is becoming more assertive, moving away from its traditionally high level of deference to States.

Specific aspects of the Court's procedure in contentious cases are examined in Chapter 12 by Dr Kate Parlett and Amy Sander. They focus on the key features of procedure: the institution of proceedings; provisional measures; preliminary objections; intervention; and non-appearance. For each of these aspects of procedure, the authors set out the current rules and practice, commenting on the way in which they have evolved, and making some suggestions for further innovation by the Court. They note that there have been recent calls urging the Court to codify aspects of its practice on procedural issues into generally applicable rules. While this might seem an attractive approach, the authors argue that this has the potential to unduly restrict the way in which the Court addresses cases – each of which may have its own particular procedural needs. They emphasise the need for the Court not to be overly prescriptive, but to make certain that it retains power to ensure a fair and just outcome in each particular case.

The second part concludes with Chapter 13 on effective advocacy before the ICJ, by Samuel Wordsworth QC and Kate Parlett. It examines both written and oral advocacy before the Court, with the fundamental objective of the advocate in all cases being to persuade, making it essential to consider what will be of most utility to the judges when they come to reach a decision on the case. They also emphasise the significant role the advocate has to play in the pre-litigation stage and in early procedural exchanges: she or he must bear in mind that they have a dual function of presenting the best case for the client to the Court, while also persuading the client as to the most effective way in which to do that.

The final part of the book (Part III) assesses the impact of the ICJ's jurisprudence, with a focus on the principal substantive areas of international law which have been the subject of the Court's cases. Each chapter provides an overview of the Court's contribution to the development of the law by reference to its jurisprudence and taking account of broader developments in international law-making.

Professor Antonio Remiro Brotóns examines the law of treaties in the jurisprudence of the ICJ in Chapter 14. He highlights the Court's position on key selected issues of interpretation: specifically the language of the treaty; time and treaty interpretation; and the role of policy. He also examines the issues of systemic integration, hierarchy and concurrence of rules.

In Chapter 15 Professors Marcelo Kohen and Mamadou Hébié look at the ICJ and territorial disputes, which is an area where the Court has had significant scope to consider the applicable law in multiple cases. They identify three areas in which the Court has made a significant contribution to the law on territorial disputes: first, the reconceptualisation of the rules of international law governing the acquisition of territorial sovereignty; second, the clarification of the territorial implications of the fundamental principles of international law; and finally, the elaboration of a clear and coherent method for the legal settlement of territorial disputes, the core of which rests on respect for the principle of legality.

Professor Nilufer Oral, in Chapter 16, considers the contribution of the ICJ to the law of the sea, highlighting four areas where the Court has made a key contribution to the development of the law: maritime delimitation cases, the status of islands and rocks, navigational rights in straits and lastly, the conservation of natural resources. She notes that the Court's influence is not equal in all of these areas, but emphasises the significant rule that the Court has played in developing the principles and rules of international law applicable to maritime boundary delimitations.

The ICJ's influence on international environmental law is addressed by Professor Daniel Bodansky in Chapter 17. Drawing on concrete examples, he identifies six ways in which the Court's jurisprudence has contributed to environmental law: by articulating foundational principles; by acting as a gatekeeper for customary international law; by elaborating existing principles; by interpreting environmental agreements; by valuing environmental harms; and by incorporating environmental considerations into other areas of international law. He reflects on potential future evolutions of the Court's role in the international environmental law space, given the increasing number of disputes that the Court has addressed in this field in recent years.

Dr Federica Paddeu's Chapter 18 considers the ICJ's contribution to the law of State responsibility, looking back to the Court's contribution to the codification of that law by the ILC; looking at the Court's current attitude to the ILC's Articles on State Responsibility; and looking to the future, addressing one of the main challenges facing the Court in this field, that of multilateral disputes. She concludes that the Court has been an important player in this field of international law, and it has made a significant contribution to vesting the ILC Articles with the authority they have today. She emphasises that the Court has an important role to play going forwards in the growth and development of community interest litigation for the enforcement of *erga omnes* obligations.

The ICJ's contribution to the law on jurisdictional immunities is elucidated by Professor Roger O'Keefe in Chapter 19. He argues that, through its case law in this area, the ICJ has affirmed basic aspects of the international law of jurisdictional immunities, clarified a few more specific points, and variously crystallised, consolidated, and catalysed the further development of important customary rules on controversial issues in relation to civil and criminal proceedings respectively. Through its work in this field, the Court has reasserted an orthodox, possibly conservative vision of the role of jurisdictional immunities in the international legal order.

In Chapter 20 Professor Alejandro Chehtman examines the ICJ's contribution to the law on the use of force. He considers the Court's case law on the prohibition of the use of force and its potential exceptions, most notably the law on individual and collective self-defence. He identifies the main conceptualisations, inconsistencies, disagreements, and limitations of the Court's opinions, arguing that although the Court initially had a significant influence, it has faded significantly over the years as a result of what appears to be a conscious or strategic decision of its judges.

The contribution of the ICJ to the law of international organisations is assessed by Professor Jan Klabbers in Chapter 21. He emphasises the limited role of the Court in this field, setting out the multiple reasons for this: parts of the law were developed before the Court commenced its work; and the Court has only had intermittent opportunities to consider it through its cases. He argues that the Court's approach reflects a more general ambivalence of classic international law when it comes to international institutions: that it emphasises the centrality of States in the international legal system, notwithstanding the steps that have been taken by States to institutionalise significant areas of international law.

In Chapter 22, Professor Carlos Espósito deals with the ICJ and human rights. He argues that, while the Court is not and will never be a specialised human rights court, it has a significant role in the protection and development of human rights. He first explains some structural obstacles and impediments to the engagement of the Court with human rights, and then offers some instances of substantial incorporation of human rights into the fabric of general international law through interpretation and legal concepts encompassing international community interests. In other words, the chapter suggests that structural disengagement in the sense of norms allowing only States to litigate before the Court does not impede substantial incorporation which may depend on other factors, including the changing attitudes of the ICJ judges and lawyers before the Court.

This overview of the contents of the *Companion* reveals its ambition to explain and discuss all aspects of the ICJ's law and practice in a handy volume. The logical structure of the book requires no further elucidation: it is based on the institutional relevance of the Court in the international legal system and stems from the main functions of this principal judicial organ of the United Nations – that is, to decide in accordance with international law such disputes as are submitted to it, and to contribute to the development of international law. These basic roles of the Court are present throughout the chapters in all varieties, with both comprehensive descriptive internal and external analysis, and rich normative discussions.

Regarding the *dispute settlement role* of the Court, the contents of the *Companion* recognise consent as the linchpin of its jurisdiction and States as the main clients of the Court, as established by the Statute. Consent is a key element of the system, a premise of any analysis of the contentious jurisdiction of the Court. Its fundamental importance, to give just one example, has recently been underlined by President Donoghue addressing the United Nations General Assembly on the occasion of its seventy-sixth session, on 28 October 2021. She declared that the Court 'is mindful that its authority hinges, among other things, on the unwavering respect for the boundaries of its jurisdiction, since the ICJ Statute made consent a corner-stone of the jurisdictional framework'. Consent, however, is not necessary for the advisory jurisdiction of the Court, which requires only a legal question – 'any legal question' – asked by the Security Council or the General Assembly. Other organs or specialised agencies authorised by the General Assembly may request such advisory opinions on legal questions arising within the scope of their activities. Many chapters of the *Companion*, including those of Judge Keith and the late Judge Crawford together with Baetens and Cameron, underscore the importance of the advisory function of the Court for the development and clarification of international law. In relation with consent it is interesting to mark in particular the comments by Thouvenin referring to the impact of the *Chagos* advisory opinion as viewed from the Special Chamber of the ITLOS, which considered the opinion of the Court as putting an end to the bilateral sovereign dispute between the UK and Mauritius, notwithstanding the fact that the UK never consented to have the dispute resolved by the ICJ.

The *Companion* offers analysis and commentary on the key elements of the Court's dispute settlement role after jurisdiction is established. The sources of law, of course, are a fundamental element of the law and practice of the Court as explained by D'Aspremont, who argues that the obligation to decide the disputes as are submitted to it applying the sources of international law, as provided for in Article 38 of the Statute, is a command that has not impeded the Court to become 'the master of the sources of international law'. Another fundamental element of the judicial function of the Court is the establishment of the facts. Devaney argues that 'any failure to establish the facts could lead to the application of the wrong rule, or of the right rule in the wrong manner', with disastrous consequences to the authority of the judgment and the very function of the Court as a judicial body. He also comments on the efforts of the Court to introduce best practices with regard to fact-finding and expert evidence. This appreciation coincides with Parlett and Sander's conclusion on the will of the Court to evolve its procedure 'to ensure it adapts in a flexible and pragmatic manner to the needs of its users and the objective of ensuring a fair and just outcome'. An objective that can only be achieved with competent advocacy, as Wordsworth and Parlett argue in their chapter. The functioning rules and methods of the Court are explained by Harris, who signals the will of the judges to improve and innovate 'the machine of the Court' through the constant review of its rules and methods of work, as shown by the new practices needed to deal with the cases during the pandemic or the new ad hoc committee to monitor the implementation of provisional measures. These measures, which have posed important humanitarian challenges to the Court, have been addressed deftly by Kolb, unveiling their complexity and constant evolution.

With regard to the contribution to the *development of the law*, the chapters of the *Companion* explicitly or implicitly recognise the 'tangible contribution of the Court to the development and clarification of the rules and principles of international law', as Sir Hersch Lauterpacht put it in his classic book on *The Development of International Law by the International Court*, published in 1958. The authors of the *Companion* are well aware that the Court is not a legislator, but give full credit to the law development function as much more than simply a by-product of the Court's judicial function. For instance, Tladi speaks of 'an immense impact on the development of the law', which can hardly be denied as an empirical fact and is relevant both in specific rules and in the 'more methodological aspects of the identification of rules' that may have a more systemic impact in the international legal system. Ginsburg suggests that, given the institutional design of the Court and the international system in which it operates, 'its most important contributions have been in the development of the law, a task not formally assigned to the Court at all'. Shany and Giladi affirm that the Court, as principal judicial organ of the United Nations world institution, 'is expected to *develop* international law, not merely engage in law-application'. Part III of the *Companion* is filled with specific considerations of the development of international law by the Court. Some of these fields of international law have been fully specified by the Court, as it happens with the international law governing territorial disputes. There are other fields in which the Court has had a less determinant role, such as international environmental law or human rights law. All the international legal fields considered in Part III have benefitted from some degree of development and clarification by the Court, which, as Judge Crawford has suggested, provides 'a centre of gravity' in international law.

The Court, the principal judicial organ of the United Nations, is *an instrument for maintaining international peace*. It performs its contribution to the maintenance of international peace primarily through the settlement of international disputes in accordance with international law, using fair procedures and issuing high quality judgments. The Court also contributes to the maintenance of international peace through the development and clarification of the law and principles of international law, providing more certainty in the law, fostering a culture of respect for the rule of law and legitimising the role of law in international relations. The potential of the Court as an instrument of peace is, of course, conditioned both by the inherent limits of the law for securing peace, the will of States to abide by the rule of law and the state of international society at a given time. Whatever its limitations, the Court is a central, essential and established institution for the peaceful settlement of international disputes and the advancement of the international rule of law.

Recommended General Further Reading

Kolb, R., *The International Court of Justice* (Elgar, 2013).

Lauterpacht, H., *The Development of International Law by the International Court* (London: Stevens & Sons, 1958).

Shaw, M. N., *Rosenne's Law and Practice of the International Court: 1920–2015* (vols. I–IV, 5th ed., Nijhoff: Brill, 2016).

Tams, C. and R. Sloan, *The Development of International Law by the International Court of Justice* (Oxford University Press, 2013).

Zimmerman, A. and C. Tams (eds.), *Statute of the International Court of Justice: A Commentary* (3rd ed., Oxford University Press, 2018).

Part I

The Role of the ICJ

Functions of the International Court of Justice   1

Judge James Crawford, Freya Baetens, and Rose Cameron

I Introduction

This chapter first examines the origins of the International Court of Justice ('ICJ' or 'the Court'): starting with the Permanent Court of International Justice ('PCIJ') and its functions, it outlines the establishment of the ICJ and its composition. Subsequently, the chapter explores the core functions of the Court: deciding 'such disputes as are submitted to it' pursuant to Article 38 of the ICJ Statute (with a particular focus on the subject-matter of cases before the Court and the geographical distribution of its caseload) and exercising its advisory function under Article 65 of the ICJ Statute (focusing on the aim of the advisory function and comparing the Court's advisory function to its function in contentious proceedings). Next, the chapter analyses the ICJ's functions beyond its core activities in terms of finding and developing the law, as well as the maintenance of peace and security, followed by some brief conclusions.

II Origins

A The Permanent Court of International Justice and Its Functions

During the Paris Peace Conference of 1919, at which the Covenant of the League of Nations was negotiated, a proposal was put forward to include a court amongst the organs of the League.[1] Although the institutionalisation

---

[1] S. Rosenne, 'Permanent Court of International Justice' (2006) in R. Wolfrum (ed.), *Max Planck Encyclopedia of Public International Law* (online ed., Oxford University Press), para. 4; *see also* A. Pellet, 'Competence of the Court, Article 38' in A. Zimmermann and C. Tams (eds.), *Statute of the International Court of Justice. A Commentary* (Oxford University Press, 3rd ed. 2018), para. 17; M. O. Hudson, 'Permanent Court of

of a Permanent Court for inter-State disputes was not finalised at the conference,[2] Article 14 of the Covenant required the Council of the League to 'formulate and submit to the Members of the League for adoption plans for the establishment of a Permanent Court of International Justice'.[3] Article 14 also provided a 'rudimentary guide'[4] to the twofold functions of the future Permanent Court. First, the Court was to be 'competent to hear and determine any dispute of an international character which the parties thereto submit to it'. Second, the Court could 'give an advisory opinion upon any dispute or question referred to it by the Council or by the Assembly'.[5]

In February 1920, the Council of the League of Nations established a committee, called the Advisory Committee of Jurists, to work out plans for the new court.[6] Following amendment of those plans by the Council of the League[7] and the Assembly of the League,[8] the Statute of the new court, the PCIJ, was approved in December 1920.[9] Unsurprisingly given the unprecedented character of the PCIJ as the first permanent international court at the public international level,[10] the functions of the Court, as set out in broad terms in Article 14 of the Covenant of the League, gave rise to controversy. This impacted both the contentious and advisory proceedings of the PCIJ.

International Justice' *Harvard Law Review*, Vol 35 No 3 (1921–1922), pp. 245–275, at 246–247; M. Shaw (ed.), *S Rosenne's Law and Practice of the International Court 1920–2015* (Brill Nijhoff, 2016).

[2] Rosenne, 'Permanent Court of International Justice', para. 4.

[3] Covenant of the League of Nations, 28 June 1919, 225 CTS 195, Art. 14.

[4] Pellet, 'Competence of the Court, Article 38', para. 18.

[5] Covenant of the League of Nations, Art. 14; *see* O. Spiermann, 'Historical Introduction' in Zimmermann and Tams, *Statute of the International Court of Justice*, para. 5.

[6] *Procès-verbaux of the proceedings of the committee*, June 16th–July 24th 1920 (Van Langenhuysen Brothers, The Hague, 1920), Preface, p. III.

[7] Rosenne, 'Permanent Court of International Justice', paras. 5–6; *see also* M. O. Hudson, *The Permanent Court of International Justice (1920–1942)*, (Macmillan, 1943), pp. 118–119.

[8] Article 14 of the Covenant of the League does not mention the Assembly of the League of Nations, but rather its Members. Hudson noted in this regard that 'it was clearly open to the Members of the League to employ [the Assembly] in connection with their . . . adoption of the plans formulated' and this is what occurred: Hudson, *The Permanent Court of International Justice (1920–1942)*, 104.

[9] Rosenne, 'Permanent Court of International Justice', para. 7; Hudson, *The Permanent Court of International Justice (1920–1942)*, 119–123.

[10] J. Crawford, 'Continuity and Discontinuity in International Dispute Settlement,' 1(1) *JIDS* (2010) 3 at p. 13.

In relation to contentious proceedings, the Statute of the PCIJ introduced the innovation of the unilateral initiation of legal proceedings by
one State against the other.[11] Prior to the establishment of the PCIJ,
disputing States primarily had recourse to ad hoc arbitral tribunals to
resolve their differences. Arbitral tribunals were constituted with the consent of the States involved, their members were appointed to resolve the
particular dispute and they generally applied the law as agreed upon by the
litigants.[12] During the elaboration of the PCIJ's Statute, there was much
debate as to whether the Court should be endowed with compulsory
jurisdiction, which would, inter alia, enable it to be seised by one party.[13]
Ultimately a compromise was reached whereby an applicant State could
seise the court by way of an Application, as long as all parties had already
indicated their consent through a compromissory clause in a treaty or by
making a declaration accepting the jurisdiction of the Court.[14] The jurisdiction of the Court is discussed in further detail in Chapter 6 of this
volume. The unilateral submission to the Court of a dispute was often
strongly opposed by respondent States before the PCIJ and resulted in the
development of the procedure of preliminary objections.[15]

---

[11] Rosenne, 'Permanent Court of International Justice', para. 26.

[12] Pellet, 'Competence of the Court, Article 38', para. 4.

[13] Hudson, *The Permanent Court of International Justice (1920–1942)*, 191–192; Spiermann,
'Historical Introduction', paras. 11–17. *See for example*, Advisory Committee of Jurists,
Documents Presented to the Committee Relating to Existing Plans for the Establishment of
a Permanent Court of International Justice, p. 113; *Procès-verbaux of the proceedings of the
committee*, June 16th–July 24th 1920 (Van Langenhuysen Brothers, The Hague, 1920),
Ann. 6, Note read by Baron Deschamps, pp. 46–47. The Committee of Jurists recommended
that the future court be endowed with compulsory jurisdiction over disputes of an international character (which would enable the unilateral seizure of the court by one State in all
disputes within the jurisdiction of the court). However, the Council did not support compulsory jurisdiction under pressure from the Great Powers: Rosenne, 'Permanent Court of
International Justice', paras. 5–6, 30. One concern of those in favour of obligatory jurisdiction was that the lack of compulsory jurisdiction would render the court 'merely an arbitration tribunal': Hudson, *The Permanent Court of International Justice (1920–1942)*, 192,
relaying the concern of the Argentine delegation in the First Assembly.

[14] Article 36 of the PCIJ Statute embodied this compromise. It introduced the 'optional clause'
procedure by which a State could agree in advance to the jurisdiction of the court over
certain disputes, as well as the ability of a State to invoke a compromissory clause in a
treaty. *See* Rosenne, 'Permanent Court of International Justice', para. 30. Rosenne notes
that by the end of 1939, 40 States had made declarations accepting the jurisdiction of
the PCIJ.

[15] Rosenne, 'Permanent Court of International Justice', para. 26. *See for example*, PCIJ,
Mavrommatis Palestine Concessions, Series A, No 2, 30 August 1924; PCIJ, *Case*

The PCIJ was the first international court with jurisdiction to render advisory opinions.[16] The idea at the time was that the PCIJ would act as 'expert counsel' to the League of Nations.[17] However, the drafters of Article 14 of the Covenant of the League, in which the term 'advisory opinion' first appeared in connection with the Permanent Court, had not debated the use of this term at length, nor do they appear to have considered the practice of domestic courts that have the power to give such opinions.[18] At the time the PCIJ's Statute entered into force, there was no procedure provided for in relation to the rendering of opinions and in fact the original version of the PCIJ's Statute did not mention advisory proceedings at all.[19] A draft of the PCIJ Statute had mentioned the advisory function of the Court in Article 36, but ultimately this was not included, as the view was taken that Article 14 of the Covenant of the League was a sufficient basis for the advisory function of the Court.[20]

The lack of procedural provisions in relation to the advisory function was remedied by amendments which entered into force in 1936 and which set out a procedure for rendering advisory opinions.[21] In addition these

concerning *Certain German Interests in Polish Upper Silesia*, Series A No 7, 25 August 1925; PCIJ, *Pajzs, Csaky, Esterhazy*, Series A/B, 23 May 1936.

[16] M. Samson and D. Guilfoyle, 'The PCIJ and the "Invention" of International Advisory Jurisdiction' in M. Fitzmaurice and C. Tams (eds.), *Legacies of the Permanent Court of International Justice* (Brill, 2013), p. 41; J. Frowein and K. Oellers-Frahm, 'Advisory Opinions, Article 65', in Zimmermann and Tams, *Statute of the International Court of Justice*, para. 1. However, as Hudson noted, other international organisations had at the time been endowed with the power to render advisory opinions, such as the International Bureau of the Universal Postal Union: Hudson, *The Permanent Court of International Justice (1920–1942)*, 484.

[17] Samson and Guilfoyle, 'The PCIJ and the "Invention" of International Advisory Jurisdiction', p. 41; *See also, Report of the Informal Inter-Allied Committee on the Future of the Permanent Court of International Justice* (London: His Majesty's Stationery Office, 1944), 10 February 1944, p. 20.

[18] Hudson, *The Permanent Court of International Justice (1920–1942)*, 108.

[19] Ibid 210. However, Article 1 of the Permanent Court of Justice's Statute established the court 'in accordance with Article 14 of the Covenant'. This had the effect of incorporating into the Statute the advisory function as set out in Article 14 of the Covenant of the League: Hudson, *The Permanent Court of International Justice (1920–1942)*, 484. Until those amendments came into force, the legal basis of advisory proceedings was Article 14 of the Covenant: League of Nations, Committee of Jurists on the Statute of the Permanent Court of International Justice 1929, Ann. 5, p. 103.

[20] Frowein and Oellers-Frahm, 'Advisory Opinions, Article 65', para. 2.

[21] Hudson, *The Permanent Court of International Justice (1920–1942)*, 484.

amendments had the aim of preventing 'the surreptitious introduction of a form of compulsory judicial settlement through the advisory procedure',[22] following on from the PCIJ's refusal to render an opinion in *Eastern Carelia*.[23] In that matter the PCIJ found that the Council of the League was not competent to request an Opinion in relation to an actual dispute involving a State outside the League without that State's consent.[24] In the course of rendering a total of twenty-seven advisory opinions,[25] the PCIJ identified other circumstances in which the Court would refuse to provide an opinion.[26] The subject-matter of these opinions was varied, covering, inter alia, the application of the Covenant of the League to specific circumstances, the implementation of the 1919 peace settlement and the work of the International Labour Organization.[27]

B Establishment of the International Court of Justice

The ICJ is the successor to the PCIJ and its Statute is largely based on the Statute of the PCIJ.[28] As Rosenne remarked, following World War II there was no real demand to 'abandon the idea of a standing international judicial organ or to require any major change in its practices and procedures'.[29]

There was, however, discussion in relation to modifying the functions of the international court at the time of the ICJ's inception. The Inter-Allied

---

[22] Rosenne, 'Permanent Court of International Justice', para. 11.

[23] PCIJ, *Status of Eastern Carelia, Advisory opinion*, PCIJ Ser. B no 5.

[24] *Eastern Carelia*, p. 29. *See* Spiermann, 'Historical Introduction', para. 24.

[25] Rosenne, 'Permanent Court of International Justice', para. 36.

[26] For example, when the object of the opinion is moot: Hudson, *The Permanent Court of International Justice (1920–1942)*, 495–496.

[27] Frowein and Oellers-Frahm, 'Advisory Opinions, Article 65', para. 5.

[28] Charter of the United Nations, San Francisco, 26 June 1945, Art. 92; A Pellet, 'Judicial Settlement of International Disputes' (2013), in R. Wolfrum (ed.), *Max Planck Encyclopedia of Public International Law* (online ed., Oxford University Press), para. 66.

[29] Rosenne, 'Permanent Court of International Justice', para. 38. The 'broad outline' of the new international organization which resulted from the Proposals for the Establishment of a General International Organization (1944), commonly known as the Dumbarton Oaks Proposals, included, as one of the principal organs, an international court: Rosenne, 'Permanent Court of International Justice', para. 4. The Proposals included that the statute of the new international court be either a modified version of the Statute of the PCIJ or a new statute based on the Statute of the PCIJ: Documents of the United Nations Conference on International Organization, San Francisco, 1945, Vol. III, p. 11.

Committee, set up in 1943 to examine the establishment of a new international court,[30] was of the view that the 'very wide' competence of the PCIJ to determine all contentious cases was 'open to objection'.[31] Their proposal was to insert the word 'justiciable' into the statute of the new court to limit the contentious matters which could be determined by the court, such that the ICJ would not be 'used to deal with cases which are really political in their nature', as opposed to legal matters.[32] The Dumbarton Oaks Proposals included a similar recommendation that only 'justiciable disputes' be referred to the court.[33] These suggestions were not adopted. Article 38 of the Statute of the ICJ differs slightly from Article 38 of the PCIJ's Statute, as it added reference to the Court's 'function . . . to decide in accordance with international law such disputes as are submitted to it'. While the change is notable for its highlighting of the Court's function in contentious proceedings, the amendment simply expressly states what had been made evident by the practice of the PCIJ and did not substantively modify the function of the international court.[34]

There were also concerns raised by the Inter-Allied Committee about the risk of political matters being considered as part of the advisory function of the Court. Despite these concerns, the advisory function was maintained and broadened in the ICJ's Statute.[35] Only the Assembly and Council of the League had been able to seek advisory opinions from the PCIJ,[36] but the Inter-Allied Committee recommended expanding the list of entities able to make a request for an opinion.[37] In an attempt to avoid political matters

---

[30] Website of the International Court of Justice, *History*, available at www.icj-cij.org/en/history.

[31] *Report of the Informal Inter-Allied Committee on the Future of the Permanent Court of International Justice* (London: His Majesty's Stationery Office, 1944), 10 February 1944, p. 17.

[32] *Report of the Informal Inter-Allied Committee on the Future of the Permanent Court of International Justice* (London: His Majesty's Stationery Office, 1944), 10 February 1944, p. 17. Article 36 of the statute of the new international court would have read relevantly: 'The jurisdiction of the Court comprises all *justiciable* cases which the parties refer to it and all *justiciable* matters specially provided for in treaties and conventions in force'.

[33] Documents of the United Nations Conference on International Organization, San Francisco, 1945, Vol. III, p. 14.

[34] *See* Pellet, 'Competence of the Court, Article 38', para. 47.

[35] Frowein and Oellers-Frahm, 'Advisory Opinions, Article 65', para. 6.

[36] Statute of the Permanent Court of International Justice, Geneva, 1920, Art. 65.

[37] *Report of the Informal Inter-Allied Committee on the Future of the Permanent Court of International Justice* (London: His Majesty's Stationery Office, 1944), 10 February 1944, pp. 20–21; Frowein and Oellers-Frahm, 'Advisory Opinions, Article 65', para. 6.

being dealt with through the advisory function, the wording of the provision establishing the advisory function of the new court used the phrase 'legal question', instead of 'disputes' and 'questions'.[38] As Rosenne has stated, the competence of the ICJ to render advisory opinions 'is very different from what it was in the days of the League and the PCIJ'.[39] The modification of the provisions in relation to advisory opinions, replacing 'any dispute or question' with 'any legal question', was an important one.[40]

Overall, a 'bond of continuity' exists between the two international courts.[41] The core functions of the new international court remained largely the same as those of the PCIJ, save for an expanded advisory function. As the first yearbook of the ICJ states, the ICJ 'carries on the work and inherits the tradition of the Permanent Court of International Justice'.[42] This was facilitated by the retention at the ICJ of two judges of the PCIJ, including its President.

Composition of the ICJ

The ICJ first sat on 18 April 1946.[43] Fifteen judges sit on its bench, including the President and Vice-President.[44] The President exercises 'quasi-judicial' functions when required,[45] such as identifying States and international organisations eligible to provide statements in advisory proceedings,[46] as well as using her or his casting vote in the event of an equality of votes.[47] While the geographical composition of the Court's membership is continually changing,[48] it has generally been as follows in recent years: three judges from Africa, two from Latin America and the

---

[38] Frowein and Oellers-Frahm, 'Advisory Opinions, Article 65', para. 8.

[39] Rosenne, 'Permanent Court of International Justice', paras. 9, 13.

[40] Art. 14 of the Covenant of the League and Art. 65 of the ICJ Statute; *see* Oellers, para. 10.

[41] PCIJ, Sixteenth Annual Report, 15 June 1939–31 December 1945, (Sijthoff, 1945), p. 7.

[42] 'Historical Outline of the Constitution of the Court' (1946–1947) 1 *International Court of Justice Yearbook* 15, p. 15.

[43] International Court of Justice, *Handbook* (Maubeuge, France: Triangle Bleu, 2019), p. 17, available on the website of the International Court of Justice.

[44] The bench of the Permanent Court of International Justice was initially made up of eleven judges and four deputy judges. However, fifteen Judges sat on the PCIJ from 1930: *Report of the Informal Inter-Allied Committee on the Future of the Permanent Court of International Justice* (London: His Majesty's Stationery Office, 1944), 10 February 1944, p. 9.

[45] Rosenne, 'Permanent Court of International Justice', para. 48.

[46] Statute of the ICJ, Art. 66 (2).   [47] Statute of the ICJ, Art. 55 (2).

[48] Zimmermann and Tams, *Statute of the International Court of Justice*, 330.

Caribbean, three from Asia (including the Middle East), five from Western Europe and other States, and two from Eastern Europe.[49] Representation of the five permanent members of the Security Council is 'common practice, not a statutory obligation'.[50] When a litigating State in a contentious matter does not have a judge of its nationality on the Court, it may choose a judge ad hoc to sit on the bench for that case.[51] Litigating States usually do so.[52] When an Advisory Opinion is requested upon a legal question actually pending between two or more States, those States may also designate a judge ad hoc to sit in the proceedings.[53]

Since the inception of the Court, there have been concrete proposals from various sources for modifications to its functions.[54] Since 1975, UN Member States have been able to present their suggestions in relation to the amendment of the Court's Statute to the Special Committee on the Charter of the United Nations and on the Strengthening of the Role of the Organization.[55] In this forum, the most concrete proposal relating to

---

[49] International Court of Justice, *United Nations General Assembly and Security Council elect Ms Joan E. Donoghue as Member of the Court*, Press Release No. 2010/28, 10 September 2010; *see also* Zimmermann and Tams, *Statute of the International Court of Justice*, 330. The distribution of the membership of the Court roughly corresponds to that of the regional groupings in the Security Council: International Court of Justice, *Handbook* (fn 43) p. 17, available on the website of the International Court of Justice, p. 22. In relation to the nationalities of judges who sat on the PCIJ, *see Report of the Informal Inter-Allied Committee on the Future of the Permanent Court of International Justice* (London: His Majesty's Stationery Office, 1944), 10 February 1944, p. 12.

[50] *See* Max Sørensen, 'The International Court of Justice: Its Role in Contemporary International Relations' (1960) 14 *International Organization* 261, at 263.

[51] Statute of the International Court of Justice, Art. 31(3).

[52] In the year to end December 2019, there were thirty appointments of judges *ad hoc*. There were twenty-seven appointments of judges *ad hoc* in the year to end July 2019: *Report of the International Court of Justice, 1 August 2018-31 July 2019*, p. 17. An additional three appointments were made between end July and end December 2019, by Guatemala in *Guatemala's Territorial, Insular and Maritime Claim (Guatemala/Belize)*, and by both parties in *Application of the Convention on the Prevention and Punishment of the Crime of Genocide (The Gambia v. Myanmar)*.

[53] International Court of Justice, Rules of Court, Art. 102(3).

[54] For an overview of proposals from a variety of sources, *see* Wolfram Karl, 'Amendment' in Zimmermann and Tams, *Statute of the International Court of Justice*, 1485.

[55] An ad hoc Committee was created pursuant to GA Res 3349 (XXIX), 17 December 1974, in relation to the '[n]eed to consider suggestions regarding the review of the Charter of the United Nations'. In 1975, the ad hoc Committee was reconvened as the Special Committee on the Charter of the United Nations and on the Strengthening of the Role of the Organization pursuant to GA Res 3499 (XXX), 15 December 1975.

the Court's functions came from Guatemala and Costa Rica in 1997.[56] The proposal was that the UN and other international organisations be permitted to act as parties to contentious proceedings before the Court.[57] Under this proposal, the Court would have the additional function of determining disputes referred to it by public international organisations.[58] The proposal was not taken up and was later withdrawn.[59]

There have been no further concrete discussions in the Special Committee relating to the modification of the Court's functions. In fact for years the delegates to the Committee have been largely content to 'reaffirm[] the role of the [ICJ], as the principal judicial organ of the United Nations, in promoting the peaceful settlement of disputes' and discuss ways in which the existing functions of the Court might be accessed by States.[60] This cautious attitude[61] is representative of a general lack of momentum for modifying the functions of the ICJ. The two core functions of the ICJ are discussed below.

III Core Functions of the Court

A Deciding Such Disputes as Are Submitted to It

Article 38 of the ICJ Statute
According to Article 38 of the ICJ's Statute, the Court's 'function is to decide in accordance with international law such disputes as are submitted to it'. It is for the Court to determine whether a dispute has arisen between the parties, and the Court recently recalled the meaning of 'dispute' in

---

[56] Karl, 'Amendment', has opined that both proposals in reality came from Guatemala, with Costa Rica 'pretending to [provide] an alternative draft'.

[57] Working Paper Submitted by Guatemala, UN Doc. A/AC.182/L.95/Rev.1, 3 February 1997 and Working Paper Submitted by Costa Rica, UN Doc A/AC.182/L.97, 4 February 1997. *See* Shabtai Rosenne, *The Law and Practice of the International Court, 1920–2005*, (Leiden, Brill, 2006), p. 632.

[58] Karl, 'Amendment', pp. 1484–1485.   [59] Ibid., pp. 1486.

[60] Report of the Special Committee, UN Doc. A/75/33, 2020, para. 49. For example, since 2005 the Russian Federation has called for an Advisory Opinion in relation to the authorisation by the Security Council of the use of force: Report of the Special Committee, UN Doc. A/75/33, 2020, para. 12.

[61] When inviting States to present their comments and observations in relation to the ICJ in 1997, the Special Committee stressed that 'whatever action may be taken as a result of this invitation will have no implications for any changes in the Charter of the United Nations or the Statute of the International Court of Justice': GA Res 52/61, 15 December 1997, para. 4.

Marshall Islands.[62] In that case the Court stated that 'a dispute is "a disagreement on a point of law or fact, a conflict of legal views or of interests" between parties'[63] and that '[i]n order for a dispute to exist, "[i]t must be shown that the claim of one party is positively opposed by the other"'.[64]

Article 38 restricts the cases which may come before the Court to 'legal' disputes: that is, disputes which may be resolved by the application of international law. Moreover, pursuant to Article 36(2) of the Court's Statute, a State may only choose to recognise the jurisdiction of the Court in relation to 'legal disputes'. In this regard, the Court has often emphasised that disputes which may be resolved by proceedings before it must be of a legal character given its 'exclusively judicial nature'.[65] However, unsurprisingly in the context of inter-State litigation, disputes often possess a political, as well as a legal, character. The ICJ has recognised this and has repeatedly stated that applications initiating proceedings 'often present a particular dispute that arises in the context of a broader disagreement between the parties'.[66] To resolve this issue, the Court has found that the aspects of a dispute that fall outside the Court's jurisdiction (however political they may be) do not prevent those aspects which fall within the jurisdiction of the Court from being determined by the Court.[67] Most forcefully, the Court held in *United States Diplomatic*

---

[62] *Obligations concerning Negotiations relating to Cessation of the Nuclear Arms Race and to Nuclear Disarmament (Marshall Islands v. India),* Jurisdiction and Admissibility, Judgment, ICJ Reports 2016, p. 255.

[63] *Obligations concerning Negotiations relating to Cessation of the Nuclear Arms Race and to Nuclear Disarmament (Marshall Islands v. India),* Jurisdiction and Admissibility, Judgment, ICJ Reports 2016, p. 255, para. 34, quoting *Mavrommatis Palestine Concessions* (judgment) 19 No. 2, 1924, P.C.I.J., Series A, No. 2, p. 11.

[64] *Obligations concerning Negotiations relating to Cessation of the Nuclear Arms Race and to Nuclear Disarmament (Marshall Islands v. India),* Jurisdiction and Admissibility, Judgment, ICJ Reports 2016, p. 255, para. 34, quoting *South-West Africa (Ethiopia v. South Africa; Liberia v. South Africa),* Preliminary Objections, Judgment, ICJ Reports 1962, p. 328.

[65] Pellet, 'Competence of the Court, Article 38', para. 65.

[66] *See Certain Iranian Assets (Islamic Republic of Iran v. United States of America),* Preliminary Objections, 13 February 2019, para. 36, referring to other relevant cases of the International Court. *See also* R. Higgins, *Problems and Process: International Law and How We Use It* (Oxford University Press, 1994), p. 195.

[67] *See* Pellet, 'Judicial Settlement of International Disputes', para. 67, in which the author posits that '[t]here is no point in distinguishing legal disputes from political disputes'. *See also* Zimmermann and Tams, *Statute of the International Court of Justice,* 724–727.

and Consular Staff in Tehran that 'legal disputes between sovereign States by their very nature are likely to occur in political contexts'.[68] In that case, the Court decided that there was no basis in the UN Charter, nor in the Court's Statute, for the view that the Court should decline to resolve the legal questions at issue between the parties because the legal dispute submitted to the Court is only one aspect of a political dispute.[69]

In addition, in determining disputes, the Court will exercise functions to safeguard the proper functioning and fairness of its procedure. For example, in the event of non-appearance by a party, the Court must satisfy itself not only that it has jurisdiction in accordance with its Statute, but also that the claim is well founded.[70] Finally, the Court has further functions, in terms of the interpretation and revision of its judgments.[71]

Subject-Matter of Cases before the Court

As the Court is the only international court of general jurisdiction, the subject-matter of disputes submitted to the Court is broad. The settlement of land and maritime delimitation disputes has historically been one of the major functions of the ICJ.[72] These cases remain an important part of the Court's caseload, with cases involving more than the 'localised frontier revisions' which were once predominant before the Court, and increasingly 'the disposition of large stretches of territory with large populations whose human rights [are] a factor'.[73] Five cases finalised between 1980 and 1989 concerned land and maritime delimitation disputes, compared to ten cases between 2010 and 2019. There are currently five pending cases involving delimitation disputes.[74]

---

[68] *United States Diplomatic and Consular Staff in Tehran (United States of America* v. *Iran)*, Judgment, ICJ Reports 1980, p. 3, para. 37.

[69] *United States Diplomatic and Consular Staff in Tehran*, para. 37.

[70] Rosenne, 'Permanent Court of International Justice', para. 80.

[71] Statute of the ICJ, Art. 60; Rules of Court, Art. 98. Statute of the ICJ, Art. 61; Rules of Court, Art. 99.

[72] T. Ginsburg and R. McAdams, 'Adjudicating in Anarchy: An Expressive Theory of International Dispute Resolution' 45 *William and Mary Law Review* (2004) 1229, at 1317. See also M. G. Kohen and M. Hébié, Chapter 15, Territorial Disputes, in this volume.

[73] Rosenne, 'Permanent Court of International Justice', para. 110.

[74] The figures in this chapter are current as at December 2019. These pending cases are: *Question of the Delimitation of the Continental Shelf between Nicaragua and Colombia beyond 200 nautical miles from the Nicaraguan Coast (Nicaragua* v. *Colombia)*; *Alleged Violations of Sovereign Rights and Maritime Spaces in the Caribbean Sea (Nicaragua*

The number of cases involving allegations of the violation of human rights is growing.[75] Five of the nine 'core' human rights treaties (as designated by the UN High Commissioner for Human Rights) contain compromissory clauses allowing a dispute concerning that treaty to be brought to the Court.[76] Four cases have been brought on the basis of these treaties: one case, *Belgium* v. *Senegal*,[77] was brought in reliance on the Convention against Torture[78] (in 2009), and three cases[79] on the basis of the International Convention on the Elimination of All Forms of Racial Discrimination (in 2008, 2017 and 2018).[80] In other cases, both in contentious and advisory proceedings, the Court has been called upon to examine aspects of the core human rights treaties, without these treaties providing the basis of jurisdiction.[81]

Finally, in recent years the Court has seen a growing number of incidental proceedings.[82] In this regard, one of the functions of the Court has been to resolve preliminary objections to its jurisdiction. Pursuant to Article 36(6) disputes over the jurisdiction of the Court are a matter for the Court to determine. Another function has been to work swiftly to determine requests for provisional measures when a State has alleged that

v. *Colombia); Maritime Delimitation in the Indian Ocean (Somalia* v. *Kenya); Dispute over the Status and Use of the Waters of the Silala (Chile* v. *Bolivia); Guatemala's Territorial, Insular and Maritime Claim (Guatemala/Belize).*

[75] See also C. Espósito, Chapter 22, this volume.

[76] N. Rodley, 'The International Court of Justice and Human Rights Treaty Bodies' in J. Green and C. Waters (eds.), *Adjudicating International Human Rights* (Brill, 2014), p. 87.

[77] *Questions relating to the Obligation to Prosecute or Extradite (Belgium* v. *Senegal).*

[78] Convention against Torture and Other Cruel, Inhuman or Degrading Treatment or Punishment, New York, 10 December 1984, 1465 UNTS 85.

[79] *Application of the International Convention on the Elimination of All Forms of Racial Discrimination (Georgia* v. *Russian Federation); Application of the International Convention for the Suppression of the Financing of Terrorism and of the International Convention on the Elimination of All Forms of Racial Discrimination (Ukraine* v. *Russian Federation); Application of the International Convention on the Elimination of All Forms of Racial Discrimination (Qatar* v. *United Arab Emirates).*

[80] International Convention on the Elimination of All Forms of Racial Discrimination, New York, 4 January 1969, 660 UNTS 195.

[81] Examples of Advisory Opinions include: *Legal Consequences of the Construction of a Wall in the Occupied Palestinian Territory; Judgment No. 2867 of the Administrative Tribunal of the International Labour Organization upon a Complaint Filed against the International Fund for Agricultural Development.* An example of a contentious case is *Ahmadou Sadio Diallo (Republic of Guinea* v. *Democratic Republic of the Congo).* See Rodley, 'The International Court of Justice and Human Rights Treaty Bodies', p. 88.

[82] International Court of Justice, *Report of the International Court of Justice, 1 August 2017–31 July 2018*, UN Doc. A/73/4, para. 9.

their rights are at risk of irreparable harm.[83] In the period 2016 to 2018, five orders for the indication of provisional measures were made, compared with just two in the period 1996 to 1998, and just one in the period 1986 to 1988.[84]

Geographical Distribution of the Caseload of the Court

The geographical distribution of States participating in contentious proceedings and those involved in advisory proceedings has broadened and evolved since the establishment of the Court. The breadth of States litigating before the Court can be gleaned from the sixteen States that have been involved (as Applicant or Respondent) in five or more contentious cases at the Court. These States are: the United States of America (24 cases), Nicaragua (fifteen), the United Kingdom and France (fourteen each), Serbia/Serbia and Montenegro (ten),[85] Germany, Colombia and Belgium (seven each), Costa Rica, Democratic Republic of the Congo, Honduras, India, Libya and Iran (six each), and Australia and Pakistan (five each).[86] By early 2014, ninety-four States – or approximately half of all UN members – had participated in contentious proceedings.[87] Since then, a further twelve first-time litigants have become involved in cases before the Court, either as an Applicant or a Respondent.[88] None of these recent

---

[83] Ronny Abraham (then President of the International Court of Justice), Speech before the Sixth Committee of the General Assembly, 27 October 2017, p. 8. In relation to provisional measures, *see* R. Kolb, Chapter 7, Provisional Measures, in this volume.

[84] In addition, in 1988 there was one withdrawal of a request for provisional measures and a corresponding order by the Court: *Border and Transborder Armed Actions (Nicaragua v. Honduras)*, Provisional Measures, Order of 31 March 1988, ICJ Reports 1988, p. 9.

[85] The cases for both Serbia and Serbia and Montenegro are counted here. The number is somewhat inflated given that in 1999, Serbia and Montenegro brought eight cases against NATO States based on the same facts.

[86] Website of the International Court of Justice, *Contentious cases organized by State*, available at www.icj-cij.org/en/cases-by-country.

[87] A. Zimmermann, 'Between the Quest for Universality and Its Limited Jurisdiction: The Role of the International Court of Justice in Enhancing the International Rule of Law' in G. Gaja and J. Grote Stoutenburg, *Enhancing the Rule of Law Through the ICJ* (Brill, 2014), 33, at 36.

[88] These are: Belize (although the relevant Special Agreement was concluded prior to February 2014), Gabon, The Gambia, Guyana, Kenya, Marshall Islands, Myanmar, Palestine, Saudi Arabia, Somalia, the United Arab Emirates and Venezuela. In addition to these twelve litigants, Equatorial Guinea made its first Application to the Court in 2016, having previously only acted as an intervener in *Land and Maritime Boundary between Cameroon and Nigeria (Cameroon v. Nigeria: Equatorial Guinea intervening)*.

litigants is European. Rather, they are Central American, African, Asian, or from the Middle East and Oceania.

Historically, litigation before the Court was dominated by European States. Recently, however, the Court has seen increased litigation involving States from the Asia-Pacific region and from the Middle East, and especially from Central and South America.[89] Cases before the Court are characterised by a high level of intra-regional disputes. For example, of the ten cases involving at least one Asian State initiated since 1999,[90] seven have involved litigation with another State in Asia.[91] Asian and African States' involvement in litigation before the Court has accelerated. Since 1946, twenty-one cases have involved at least one litigant from Asia, of which almost half (ten) were initiated in 1999 or later. However, only one pending case involves an Asian State, namely *The Gambia* v. *Myanmar.*[92] Thirty cases have involved at least one litigant from Africa, of which fifteen have been initiated since 1999. Five pending cases involve at least one African State. By contrast litigation involving European States has slowed down, relative to litigation involving States from other regions.[93] The breadth of participation by States is an achievement, given that the Inter-Allied Committee was concerned, in 1944, that there might be 'a risk of non-European countries losing interest in the

---

[89] Yusuf, Speech before the Royal Academy of Belgium, *The strengths and challenges for supranational justice: the growing role of the International Court of Justice*, p. 4. Since the commencement of the Court, twenty-nine cases have involved at least one litigant from Central or South America, of which eighteen cases, or over 60 per cent were initiated in 1999 or later. Five pending cases involve at least one Central or South American State. By way of comparison, seventy-three cases have involved a European State but only twenty-seven of those cases, or about 36 per cent, were initiated in 1999 or later.

[90] Litigation involving Australia and New Zealand has been included in the figures relating to Asian States.

[91] As another example, all of the cases involving Costa Rica have involved litigation with its neighbour, Nicaragua, which exemplifies the high level of intra-regional litigation involving States of Central and South America before the Court.

[92] *Application of the Convention on the Prevention and Punishment of the Crime of Genocide (The Gambia* v. *Myanmar).*

[93] Belgium, France, Germany, and the United Kingdom have participated in a total of forty-two contentious cases since the commencement of the Court. Excluding litigation involving Serbia and Serbia and Montenegro, of these forty-two cases, only ten were initiated in the last twenty years. Just over half of these cases involving European States (twenty-four) were initiated in the 1950s, 1960s or 1970s. Only three pending cases involve at least one European State, and this figure includes one case which is essentially inactive (*Gabčíkovo-Nagymaros Project (Hungary/Slovakia)*).

Court and being tempted to set up separate judicial organisations'.[94] Although separate specialised regional institutions have emerged since the creation of the ICJ, the Court has continued to see an increase in cases involving non-European States.

B Exercising Its Advisory Functions

Article 65 of the ICJ Statute

The Statute of the Court, read in combination with the Charter of the United Nations, provides for the Court's power to deliver advisory opinions. Article 65(1) states that the Court 'may give an advisory opinion on any legal question at the request of whatever body may be authorised by or in accordance with the Charter of the United Nations to make such a request'.[95] All specialised agencies, except the Universal Postal Union, have been authorised to request advisory opinions within the scope of their activities.[96] Subsidiary organs of the Security Council and General Assembly may also be authorised to request an advisory opinion.[97] The Secretary-General of the United Nations may not request an advisory opinion, although there have been discussions in relation to empowering them to do so.[98] Some treaties mandate that a request be made by an authorised organ under certain circumstances.[99]

---

[94] *Report of the Informal Inter-Allied Committee*, p. 28. The Committee was so concerned with a lack of interest in the Court by non-European States that it included in its report a proposal to set up non-European outposts of the Court to ensure interest in the Court outside Europe: *Report of the Informal Inter-Allied Committee*, pp. 27–29.

[95] Statute of the ICJ, Art. 65; Charter of the United Nations, Art. 96. According to Article 68 of the ICJ's Statute, '[i]n the exercise of its advisory functions the Court shall further be guided by the provisions of the present Statute which apply in contentious cases to the extent to which it recognises them to be applicable'. The Rules of the Court also guide the procedure for the disposal of requests for advisory opinions.

[96] *See* website of the International Court of Justice, *Organs and agencies authorized to request advisory opinions*, available at www.icj-cij.org/en/organs-agencies-authorized; K. Oellers-Frahm, 'The International Court of Justice, Article 92' in B. Simma et al. (eds.), II *The Charter of the United Nations* (Oxford, Oxford Commentaries on International Law, 2012) para. 18.

[97] Oellers-Frahm, 'The International Court of Justice, Article 92', para. 19.

[98] Frowein and Oellers-Frahm, 'Advisory Opinions, Article 65' paras. 13, 71.

[99] UNGA, Convention on the privileges and immunities of the United Nations, New York, 13 February 1946, Art. VIII, section 30; UNGA, Convention on the privileges and immunities of the Specialized Agencies, New York, 21 November 1947, Art. IX, section 32. Pursuant to both these sections, any opinion given 'shall be accepted as decisive between the parties'.

In *Legality of the Use by a State of Nuclear Weapons in Armed Conflict* (in which an opinion was sought by the World Health Organization (WHO)),[100] the Court summarised the three conditions which must be satisfied to found the jurisdiction of the Court to provide an Opinion when so requested by a specialised agency. These are: 'the agency requesting the opinion must be duly authorised, under the Charter, to request opinions from the Court; the opinion requested must be on a legal question; and this question must be one arising within the scope of the activities of the requesting agency'.[101] The Court also clarified that it was incumbent on the Court to satisfy itself that 'the conditions governing its own competence to give the opinion requested' were met.[102] Specifically, the Court stated that '[t]he exercise of the functions entrusted to the Court under Article 65, paragraph 1, of its Statute require[d] it' to interpret the instrument which set out the activities of the WHO, its Constitution, to determine whether the opinion sought falls within the competence of the WHO.[103] While the WHO was clearly authorised to request the opinion,[104] and the requested opinion raised a legal question,[105] the Court held that the request did not relate to a question arising within the scope of the WHO's activities.[106] The Court concluded that 'an essential condition of founding its jurisdiction in the ... case [was] absent and that it [could not], accordingly, give the opinion requested'.[107]

The Court thus interpreted the Constitution of the WHO to determine the mandated activities of the Organization and decide whether the subject matter of the request fell within those activities.[108] The decision makes clear that the Court will prevent specialised agencies from using the advisory function to put 'issues of general policy' before it.[109]

The General Assembly has requested sixteen advisory opinions in the history of the International Court,[110] and the Security Council only one.[111]

---

[100] *Legality of the Use by a State of Nuclear Weapons in Armed Conflict*, Advisory Opinion, ICJ Reports 1996, p. 66.

[101] Ibid., para. 10. [102] Ibid., para. 29. [103] Ibid., para. 30. [104] Ibid., para. 12.

[105] Ibid., para. 12. [106] Ibid., paras. 21, 31. [107] Ibid., para. 31. [108] Ibid., para. 21.

[109] Oellers-Frahm, 'The International Court of Justice, Article 92', para. 30.

[110] Website of the International Court of Justice, *Organs and agencies authorized to request advisory opinions*, available at www.icj-cij.org/en/organs-agencies-authorized.

[111] *Legal Consequences for States of the Continued Presence of South Africa in Namibia (South-West Africa) notwithstanding Security Council Resolution 276 (1970)*; see C. Krari-Lahya, 'Cooperation and Competition between the International Court of Justice and the Security Council', in Gaja and Stoutenburg, 47.

The only other principal organ of the United Nations that has requested an opinion is the Economic and Social Council, which has requested two.[112] Relatively few specialised agencies have requested an Advisory Opinion.[113] Those agencies that have done so include the International Fund for Agricultural Development[114] and the WHO.[115] In its advisory proceedings, the ICJ has primarily dealt with legal questions unrelated to an actual dispute between States, although this may be changing.[116] For example, the bulk of early opinions comprised advice in relation to United Nations Law and procedure of international organisations.[117] However, more recent opinions have touched upon actual disputes, including the *Wall Opinion* (2004),[118] *Kosovo* (2010)[119] and *Chagos* (2019).[120]

Aim of the Advisory Function

The ICJ has identified the purpose of its advisory function as the provision of 'legal advice to the organs and institutions requesting the opinion',[121] or as providing guidance to United Nations organs so that they can fulfil their functions in accordance with the law.[122] Most recently the Court described its role in *Chagos* as assisting the General Assembly 'so that it may be guided in the discharge of its functions'.[123]

---

[112] *Difference Relating to Immunity from Legal Process of a Special Rapporteur of the Commission on Human Rights. See* Oellers-Frahm, 'The International Court of Justice, Article 92', para. 25.

[113] Higgins, *Problems and Process*, p. 198.

[114] *See Judgment No. 2867 of the Administrative Tribunal of the International Labour Organization upon a Complaint Filed against the International Fund for Agricultural Development.*

[115] *Interpretation of the Agreement of 25 March 1951 between the WHO and Egypt, Advisory Opinion*, ICJ Reports 1980, p. 73; *Legality of the Use by a State of Nuclear Weapons in Armed Conflict.*

[116] Oellers-Frahm, 'The International Court of Justice, Article 92', para. 10.

[117] Frowein and Oellers-Frahm, 'Advisory Opinions, Article 65'.

[118] *Legal Consequences of the Construction of a Wall in the Occupied Palestinian Territory*, Advisory Opinion, ICJ Reports 2004, p. 136.

[119] *Accordance with International Law of the Unilateral Declaration of Independence in Respect of Kosovo*, Advisory Opinion, ICJ Reports 2010, p. 403.

[120] *Legal Consequences of the Separation of the Chagos Archipelago from Mauritius in 1965*, Advisory Opinion, ICJ Reports 2019, p. 95.

[121] *Legality of the Threat or Use of Nuclear Weapons*, p. 14.

[122] Frowein and Oellers-Frahm, 'Advisory Opinions, Article 65', para. 29.

[123] *Legal Consequences of the Separation of the Chagos Archipelago from Mauritius in 1965*, para. 86.

The wider purpose of advisory opinions is discussed in the Court's reasoning in the *Legality of the Use by a State of Nuclear Weapons in Armed Conflict*. The Court stated that it must always interpret the enabling provisions relating to a specialised agency by taking account, inter alia, the 'logic of the overall system contemplated by the Charter'.[124] This system was 'designed to organise international co-operation in a coherent fashion by bringing the United Nations, invested with powers of general scope, into relationship with various autonomous and complementary organizations, invested with sectorial powers'.[125] The Court can thus be seen as a crucial part of this system, this 'constellation of specialized agencies established under Articles 57, 58 and 63 of the UN Charter' and agreements between the United Nations and these agencies.[126] It plays this role, inter alia, by providing advisory opinions, as explained above.

By contrast, at its origin the advisory function of the PCIJ was aimed at creating a 'flexible' way of resolving actual disputes between States, rather than answering abstract questions. Oellers-Frahm has opined that the advisory function of the ICJ has the potential to be an alternative to the lack of compulsory jurisdiction over disputes.[127]

The Court's Advisory Function Compared to Its Function in Contentious Proceedings

When the Court renders an advisory opinion, as with contentious proceedings, it exercises its judicial function.[128] The Court has also confirmed that in rendering advisory opinions it 'engage[s] its normal judicial function of ascertaining the existence or otherwise of legal principles and rules'.[129] The Court must apply international law as set out in Article 38 of the Statute, as it does in contentious proceedings.[130] As the Court has stated,

---

[124] *Legality of the Use by a State of Nuclear Weapons in Armed Conflict*, para. 26.

[125] Ibid.

[126] A. Lang, 'The Role of the International Court of Justice in the Context of Fragmentation', 62(4) *ICLQ* (2013) 777, at 791.

[127] Oellers-Frahm, 'The International Court of Justice, Article 92', para. 6.

[128] PCIJ, Series B, No. 13, p. 23. *Cf.* also *Conditions of Admission of a State to Membership in the United Nations (Article 4 of the Charter)* ICJ Reports (1947–1948), pp. 57, 61, quoted in Pellet, 'Competence of the Court, Article 38', para. 60; Oellers-Frahm, 'The International Court of Justice, Article 92' para. 3.

[129] Frowein and Oellers-Frahm, 'Advisory Opinions, Article 65', para. 23, quoting *Legality of the Threat or Use of Nuclear Weapons*.

[130] Oellers-Frahm, 'The International Court of Justice, Article 92', para. 3; Pellet, 'Competence of the Court, Article 38', 60.

its judicial function may result in it not being able to provide the full answer to a question posed.[131] For example, in the *Kosovo* opinion it was unable to engage in any political aspects of the questions put to it.[132]

However, advisory and contentious proceedings may be contrasted in a number of ways. Advisory opinions differ from the contentious function of the Court because opinions are not binding on any State or organisation.[133] It is the responsibility of the organisation that requested the opinion to implement it.[134] When an opinion has been given following a request of the General Assembly, a practice has developed whereby the General Assembly adopts a resolution in relation to the opinion.[135] This commenced in relation to the *Conditions for Admission* opinion.[136] Most recently, the General Assembly welcomed the *Chagos* opinion in a resolution of May 2019.[137] It also made certain demands in relation to the United Kingdom, with reference to the opinion provided.[138] Despite such action, an advisory opinion as such does not create a legal obligation for a State.[139]

Given the non-binding character of advisory opinions, the Court is able to answer questions posed by United Nations bodies, without the restriction of ensuring the consent of States that might have a vested interest in the answer. In its first advisory opinion, *Interpretation of Peace Treaties*, the Court dealt with the objection that by providing the opinion requested it would be 'violating the well-established principle of international law according to which no judicial proceedings relating to a legal question

---

[131] Frowein and Oellers-Frahm, 'Advisory Opinions, Article 65', para. 23.

[132] Ibid, para. 25.

[133] *Interpretation of Peace Treaties with Bulgaria, Hungary and Romania*, First Phase, Advisory Opinion, ICJ Reports 1950, p. 71.

[134] However, the binding character of an Advisory Opinion may emanate from the statute or other founding instrument of the requesting organ: Christopher Greenwood, 'Judicial Integrity and the Advisory Jurisdiction of the International Court of Justice' in Giorgio Gaja and Jenny Grote Stoutenburg (eds.), *Enhancing the Rule of Law through the International Court of Justice* (Leiden: Brill, 2014), p. 63. *See also* Frowein and Oellers-Frahm, 'Advisory Opinions, Article 65', para. 30. By operation of some instruments related to the organisation the opinion may become binding: Frowein and Oellers-Frahm, 'Advisory Opinions, Article 65', para. 47.

[135] Frowein and Oellers-Frahm, 'Advisory Opinions, Article 65', para. 43.

[136] Admission of a State to the United Nations (Charter, Art. 4), Advisory Opinion: ICJ Reports 1948, p. 57.

[137] UNGA Res. 73/295, 22 May 2019, para. 1.

[138] UNGA Res. 73/295, 22 May 2019, para. 3.

[139] Frowein and Oellers-Frahm, 'Advisory Opinions, Article 65', para. 55.

pending between States can take place without their consent'.[140] The Court
responded somewhat bluntly that the objection 'reveals a confusion
between the principles governing contentious procedure and those which
are applicable to advisory opinions'.[141] While the consent of States is the
basis of the Court's jurisdiction in contentious cases, 'no State ... can
prevent the giving of an Advisory Opinion which the United Nations
considers to be desirable in order to obtain enlightenment as to the course
of action it should take'.[142] This is because opinions are not binding and,
moreover, the opinion 'is given not to the States, but to the organ which is
entitled to request it'.[143] The Court – as in every other instance in which
that objection has been raised – determined that 'the legal position of the
parties to these disputes [underlying the substance of the advisory opinion]
cannot be in any way compromised by the answers that the Court may give
to the Questions put to it'.[144] In other words, the Court could provide the
opinion without impeding on the underlying dispute.[145]

The Court may provide an advisory opinion in relation to an abstract
question,[146] whereas in the past the Court has refused to deal with a
contentious case where the issue between the States was 'moot', or
abstract.[147] This is clear from Rule 102(3) of the Court's Rules, which
empowers States to choose a judge ad hoc pursuant to Article 31 of the
Statute when 'an advisory opinion is requested upon a legal question
actually pending between two or more States' (and, by implication, not
when it is an abstract question). An example of an abstract question,
unrelated to an actual dispute arose in *Reservations to the Convention on*

---

[140] *Interpretation of Peace Treaties*, Advisory Opinion, ICJ Reports 1950, p. 65, at p. 71.
[141] Ibid.   [142] Ibid.   [143] Ibid.   [144] Ibid., at p. 72.
[145] Lang, 'The Role of the International Court of Justice', at 799.
[146] Frowein and Oellers-Frahm, 'Advisory Opinions, Article 65' para. 21. But *see* Judge Oda
who, in a Separate Opinion to *Legality of the Use by a State of Nuclear Weapons in Armed
Conflict*, raised his concern that if greater use of the advisory function was encouraged,
the Court might be seised with 'unnecessary and over-simplistic' requests for opinions. In
his view, the Court:

> 'should primarily function as a judicial institution to provide solutions to inter-State
> disputes of a contentious nature and should neither be expected to act as a
> legislature ... nor to function as an organ giving legal advice ... in circumstances
> in which there is no conflict or dispute concerning legal questions between States or
> between States and international organizations'.

[147] *See for example, Case concerning the Northern Cameroons (Cameroon v. United Kingdom)*,
Preliminary Objections, Judgment of 2 December 1963, ICJ Reports 1963, p. 15.

Genocide.[148] In that case the Court noted that the 'questions [posed] are purely abstract in character [in that they] refer neither to the reservations which have, in fact, been made to the Convention ... nor to the objections which have been made to such reservations by other States'.[149] The Court has stated that all that is needed is a legal question, whether 'abstract or otherwise'.[150] Moreover, requests for advisory opinions need not be restricted to existing rights but may cover historical issues.[151]

The Court's power to provide an advisory opinion is of 'a permissive character': the Court may choose not to comply with a request.[152] This discretionary character was already evident in the language of Article 14 of the League Covenant, and is replicated in Article 65 of the Statute of the Court.[153] The ICJ has highlighted the discretionary character of providing an opinion in many decisions. At the same time, quoting its past jurisprudence, the Court has also recalled that 'its answer to a request for an advisory opinion "represents its participation in the activities of the Organization, and, in principle, should not be refused"'.[154] This is why only 'compelling reasons' will lead the Court to refuse to provide an opinion that has been sought within the jurisdiction of the Court.[155] Arguments as to compelling reasons have been raised by States in the course of written or

---

[148] *Reservations to the Convention on Genocide,* Advisory Opinion, ICJ Reports 19, p. 15, referred to in Oellers-Frahm, 'The International Court of Justice, Article 92', para. 26.

[149] *Reservations to the Convention on Genocide,* Advisory Opinion, ICJ Reports 19, p. 21.

[150] *Admission of a State to the United Nations (Charter, Art. 4),* Advisory Opinion, ICJ Reports 1948, p. 57, quoted in Frowein and Oellers-Frahm, 'Advisory Opinions, Article 65', para. 26.

[151] Frowein and Oellers-Frahm, 'Advisory Opinions, Article 65', para. 28, quoting *Western Sahara.*

[152] Frowein and Oellers-Frahm, 'Advisory Opinions, Article 65', para. 7; Interpretation of Peace Treaties, Advisory Opinion, ICJ Reports 1950, p. 65, p. 72. Oellers-Frahm, 'The International Court of Justice, Article 92', paras. 8–9.

[153] Art. 65 of the Statute reads 'The Court may give an advisory opinion on any legal question ...'

[154] *Legal Consequences of the Separation of the Chagos Archipelago from Mauritius in 1965,* para. 65, quoting inter alia, Interpretation of Peace Treaties with Bulgaria, Hungary and Romania, First Phase, Advisory Opinion, ICJ Reports 1950, p. 71.

[155] See A. Aust, 'Advisory Opinions', *Journal of International Dispute Settlement,* Vol. 1, No. 1 (2010), pp. 123–151, p. 140. *Legal Consequences of the Separation of the Chagos Archipelago from Mauritius in 1965,* para. 65; *Legal Consequences of the Construction of a Wall in the Occupied Palestinian Territory,* Advisory Opinion, ICJ Reports 2004 (I), p. 156, para. 44; *Accordance with International Law of the Unilateral Declaration of Independence in Respect of Kosovo,* Advisory Opinion, ICJ Reports 2010 (II), p. 416, para. 30.

oral statements, including in *The Wall* and *Chagos*, but have been unsuccessful.[156]

Whether there are 'compelling reasons' to refuse an opinion is linked to the enquiry as to whether the propriety of the exercise of its judicial function is imperilled.[157] For example, there would be a compelling reason for the Court to decline to give an advisory opinion when such a reply 'would have the effect of circumventing the principle that a State is not obliged to allow its disputes to be submitted to judicial settlement without its consent'.[158] In the *Chagos* opinion, the Court noted that this discretion to refuse to provide an opinion 'exists so as to protect the integrity of the Court's judicial function as the principal judicial organ of the United Nations'.[159] The concern, which has never eventuated in the view of the Court, is that a certain request might endanger or discredit its judicial role.[160] The Court held that providing an opinion in *Chagos* would not amount to circumvention.[161] It held that the fact that it might have to pronounce on legal issues on which divergent views have been expressed by the two States most involved, Mauritius and the United Kingdom, did not mean that, by replying to the request, the Court was dealing with a bilateral dispute and should decline to exercise jurisdiction to provide an opinion.[162] Therefore, there were no compelling reasons not to provide an opinion.[163]

Potential political implications do not hinder the provision of an advisory opinion which is within the jurisdiction of the Court.[164]

---

[156] *See for example*, Written Statement of the Government of Israel on Jurisdiction and Propriety, 30 January 2004, submitted in *The Wall* advisory proceedings and Written Statement of the Government of Australia, 27 February 2018, submitted in the *Chagos* advisory proceedings.

[157] *Legal Consequences of the Separation of the Chagos Archipelago from Mauritius in 1965*, para. 66.

[158] Ibid., para. 85, quoting Western Sahara, Advisory Opinion, ICJ Reports 1975, p. 25, para. 33; *see* Oellers-Frahm, 'The International Court of Justice, Article 92', para. 9.

[159] *Legal Consequences of the Separation of the Chagos Archipelago from Mauritius in 1965*, para. 64, with reference to past jurisprudence of the Court, including *Legal Consequences of the Construction of a Wall in the Occupied Palestinian Territory*, Advisory Opinion, ICJ Reports 2004 (I), pp. 156–157, paras. 44–45; *Accordance with International Law of the Unilateral Declaration of Independence in Respect of Kosovo*, Advisory Opinion, ICJ Reports 2010 (II), pp. 415–416, para. 29.

[160] Oellers-Frahm, 'The International Court of Justice, Article 92', para. 22.

[161] *Legal Consequences of the Separation of the Chagos Archipelago from Mauritius in 1965*, para. 90.

[162] Ibid., para. 89.   [163] Ibid., para. 90.

[164] Frowein and Oellers-Frahm, 'Advisory Opinions, Article 65', paras. 22–23.

In *Legality of the Use by a State of Nuclear Weapons in Armed Conflict*, the Court held that the question was a legal question because it was 'framed in terms of law and rais[ed] problems of international law [which] are by their very nature susceptible of a reply based on law [and] appear ... to be questions of a legal character'.[165] The fact that the question also possessed political aspects did not deprive it of its legal character.[166] The Court has taken the same approach in subsequent cases. This enables it to deal with particularly controversial issues through the lens of advisory opinions, when this might not be possible in the context of a contentious proceeding due to the absence of consent by one or more States involved.

In some respects, one might argue that the field of influence of advisory opinions has reduced over time: many questions relating to the United Nations have now been settled.[167] In addition, more specialised adjudicatory entities have been created to deal with specific issues, such as the WTO Panels for trade disputes. Lang points this out in the context of plain tobacco packaging: while the WHO might theoretically seek an advisory opinion on this topic from the ICJ, there would be a real concern that doing so would be seen as 'circumvent[ing] the WTO dispute settlement system or undermin[ing] its decisions'.[168]

Conversely, while the increase in compromissory clauses sending contentious matters to the International Court may have slowed down and some declarations accepting the compulsory jurisdiction of the Court have been withdrawn, the advisory function of the ICJ remains a means to address topical issues of international law. Examples of prospective requests for opinions include: a request from Pulau which has been lobbying for an opinion in relation to transboundary harm caused by greenhouse gas emissions;[169] certain African States potentially seeking an

---

[165] *Legality of the Use by a State of Nuclear Weapons in Armed Conflict*, para. 15, quoting *Western Sahara*, Advisory Opinion, ICJ Reports 1975, p. 18, para. 15.

[166] Ibid., para. 15, quoting *Application for Review of Judgement No. 158 of the United Nations Administrative Tribunal*, Advisory Opinion, ICJ Reports 1973, p. 172, para. 14.

[167] Oellers-Frahm, 'The International Court of Justice, Article 92', para. 39. Relevant opinions include *Conditions of Admission of a State to Membership in the United Nations (Article 4 of the Charter)* (1948), *Reparation for Injuries Suffered in the Service of the United Nations* (1949) and *Competence of the General Assembly for the Admission of a State to the United Nations* (1950).

[168] Lang, 'The Role of the International Court of Justice', at 793.

[169] *See* https://news.un.org/en/story/2011/09/388202.

opinion in relation to head of State immunities;[170] and Russia potentially seeking an opinion in relation to the use of force in the absence of Security Council authorisation.[171] There has even been academic discussion about requesting an opinion in relation to the COVID-19 pandemic.[172] There is therefore scope for reinvigorated use of the advisory functions of the Court, and it may evolve in different ways in the future.

IV Beyond the Court's Core Functions

A Finding and Developing the Law

Article 59 of the Court's Statute prescribes that a judgment of the Court has no binding force except between the parties and in respect of that particular case.[173] It follows that, on one view, the role of the Court should be limited to settling the dispute at issue in a particular case, rather than providing a more general statement of the law as it stands.[174] In fulfilling this role, the focus of the Court is exclusively on the law that will assist in the resolution of a dispute before it.

On another view, the Court may have a role to play in finding and developing international law.[175] In this regard, it is trite to remark that observations of the Court in relation to international law often become the

---

[170] UNGA, Letter dated 9 July 2018 from the Permanent Representative of Kenya to the United Nations addressed to the Secretary-General, 'Request for an advisory opinion of the International Court of Justice on the consequences of legal obligations of States under different sources of international law with respect to immunities of Heads of State and Government and other senior officials, UN Doc. A/73/144, 18 July 2018.

[171] UNGA, Report of the Special Committee on the Charter of the United Nations and on the Strengthening of the Role of the Organization, UN Doc. A/73/33, 2018, para. 11.

[172] *See* www.ejiltalk.org/a-reference-to-the-icj-for-an-advisory-opinion-over-covid-19-pandemic/; www.jurist.org/commentary/2020/04/atul-alexander-icj-covid/.

[173] Statute of the ICJ, Art. 59, although they are a subsidiary source of international law pursuant to Article 38(1)(d) of the Statute. *See* Higgins, *Problems and Process*, p. 203.

[174] A. Cançado Trindade, 'Reflections on a Century of International Justice and Prospects for the Future', p. 18. The Court is cognisant that its 'function, according to Article 38 of its Statute, is to "decide", that is, to bring to an end, "such disputes as are submitted to it"': *See for example, Application of the Convention on the Prevention and Punishment of the Crime of Genocide (Bosnia and Herzegovina v. Serbia and Montenegro)*, Judgment, ICJ Reports 2007, p. 43, para. 116.

[175] *Report of the International Court of Justice, 1 August 2018–31 July 2019*, p. 9. See also Dire Tladi, Chapter 3, this volume, The Role of the International Court of Justice in the Development of International Law.

interpretation generally followed by the international community.[176] As the only international court of general jurisdiction, the ICJ is well placed to make authoritative statements as to general international law,[177] and it has done so in relation to a broad spectrum of international legal topics. This has only increased with the complexity and volume of cases brought before it.[178] As a result, legal institutions respect findings on general international law by the ICJ, especially outside their own sphere of experience.[179] Both contentious and advisory proceedings play a role in the identification and development of the law, and at a minimum provide States and international organisations with legal certainty.[180]

There is arguably a tension between, on the one hand, the primary functions of the Court – the resolution of disputes brought before it and rendering advisory opinions – and its perceived role in the development of international law, whether conventional or custom. The Court held in *Legality of the Threat or Use of Nuclear Weapons* that it cannot legislate,[181] that 'its task is to engage in its normal judicial function of ascertaining the existence or otherwise of legal principles and rules applicable to [the subject-matter of the dispute]'.[182] However, the Court did venture in that same opinion that 'in stating and applying the law, the Court necessarily has to specify its scope and sometimes note its general trend'.[183] Contributing to the development of international law might be described as a 'by-product' of the Court's judicial activity.[184] Another good description of the Court's function in recognising new rules of international law is

---

[176] M. Kohen, 'The Court's Contribution to Determining the Content of Fundamental Principles of International Law', in G. Gaja and J. G. Stoutenburg (eds.), *Enhancing the Rule of Law through the International Court of Justice* (Brill, 2014), p. 150. Article 38 makes clear that, subject to Article 59 of the Court's Statute, the decisions of the Court itself are a subsidiary means for the determination of rules of law.

[177] *See* F. Messineo, 'The Functions of the International Court of Justice' in A. Kent, N. Skoutaris and J. Trinidad (eds.), *The Future of International Courts: Regional, Institutional and Procedural Challenges* (Routledge, 2019) 110.

[178] Ibid., p. 118.

[179] Lang, 'The Role of the International Court of Justice', at 795, in relation to the WHO Panels and Appellate Body.

[180] Ibid., at 788.

[181] *Legality of the Threat or Use of Nuclear Weapons*, ICJ Reports (1996), pp. 226, para. 15; *see* Frowein and Oellers-Frahm, 'Advisory Opinions, Article 65', para. 23.

[182] *Legality of the Threat or Use of Nuclear Weapons*, Advisory Opinion, I.C.J. Reports 1996, p. 226, para. 18.

[183] Ibid.   [184] Rosenne, 'Permanent Court of International Justice', para. 112.

that this is 'ancillary' to its function of settling disputes between States.[185] The Court's role in the development of international law is dealt with in more detail in Chapter 3.

B Maintenance of Peace and Security

The ICJ as a UN Organ

Just as the PCIJ was created as part of a plan to create a larger international organisation in the form of the League of Nations,[186] the ICJ was created in the framework of the United Nations. The ICJ has a stronger connection with the United Nations than the PCIJ had with the League:[187] it is the principal judicial organ of the United Nations,[188] on the same footing as the other principal organs such as the General Assembly and the Security Council.[189] States that become members of the United Nations automatically become parties to the Court's Statute, and Members of the United Nations General Assembly and Security Council elect the judges of the Court.

Perhaps the best example of the Court acting as the principal judicial organ of the United Nations is when it provides advisory opinions to other United Nations bodies.[190] By so doing, it acts as their legal adviser on questions of international law and seeks to assist UN organs in discharging their own functions according to law.[191] Those functions might be, for example, the peaceful resolution of disputes in Palestine[192] or decolonisation.[193] There is a certain overlap between the functions of the ICJ, in terms

---

[185] Messineo, 'The Functions of the International Court of Justice', at 119. Also: 'the Court was not designed primarily as a mechanism for achieving uniformity in international law, but as a dispute settlement mechanism': Ibid, p. 120.

[186] Hudson, *The Permanent Court of International Justice 1920–1942*, p. 93. See also p. 111 for a discussion about the connection between the Permanent Court and the League of Nations.

[187] Crawford, *Brownlie's Principles of Public International Law*, p. 696. For a description of the PCIJ's connection to the League, see Rosenne, 'Permanent Court of International Justice', para. 8.

[188] Charter of the United Nations, Art. 92 and Statute of the ICJ, Art. 1.

[189] *See* Max Sørensen, 'The International Court of Justice: Its Role in Contemporary International Relations' (1960) 14 *International Organization* 261, at 261.

[190] Oellers-Frahm, 'The International Court of Justice, Article 92', para. 4.

[191] *Legal Consequences of the Separation of the Chagos Archipelago from Mauritius in 1965*, para. 86; *Western Sahara*, Advisory Opinion, ICJ Reports 1975, pp. 26–27, para. 39.

[192] *Legal Consequences of the Construction of a Wall in the Occupied Palestinian Territory.*

[193] *Legal Consequences of the Separation of the Chagos Archipelago from Mauritius in 1965.*

of the promotion of peace and security, and those of other organs of the United Nations, especially the Security Council.[194] The Charter outlines the relationship between the Court and the Security Council and both organs are mentioned in the chapter devoted to peace and security.[195] However, the Security Council retains 'primary responsibility' for the maintenance of international peace and security.[196] It also has a role to play in recommending 'appropriate procedures or methods of adjustment' in case of a dispute, the continuance of which is likely to endanger the maintenance of international peace and security.[197] In this regard, the Security Council is mandated to take into consideration that legal disputes should, as a general rule, be referred to the ICJ.[198] However, this does not impose an obligation for the Security Council to recommend judicial settlement, nor to refer legal disputes to the ICJ.[199]

The Security Council has recommended that the parties to a dispute refer their matter to the ICJ in only one case, namely *Corfu Channel*.[200] However, the Court and the Security Council have simultaneously dealt with a number of cases, including *Aegean Sea Continental Shelf*,[201] *Lockerbie*,[202] and *Nicaragua*.[203] There have also been cases in which the Court has been called upon to review resolutions of the Security Council, or of other organs of the United Nations, such as the General Assembly.[204]

---

[194] Krari-Lahya, 'Cooperation and Competition', 51; G. Gaja, 'Preventing Conflicts between the Court's Orders on Provisional Measures and Security Council Resolutions', in G. Gaja and J. G. Stoutenburg (eds.), *Enhancing the Rule of Law through the International Court of Justice* (Brill, 2014), p. 87.

[195] Krari-Lahya, 'Cooperation and Competition', 51.

[196] Charter of the United Nations, Art. 24.   [197] Charter of the United Nations, Art. 36.

[198] Ibid.   [199] Krari-Lahya, 'Cooperation and Competition', 52.

[200] *Corfu Channel (United Kingdom of Great Britain and Northern Ireland v. Albania)*.

[201] *Aegean Sea Continental Shelf (Greece v. Turkey)*.

[202] *Questions of Interpretation and Application of the 1971 Montreal Convention arising from the Aerial Incident at Lockerbie (Libyan Arab Jamahiriya v. United Kingdom, and Libyan Arab Jamahiriya v. United States of America)*.

[203] *Military and Paramilitary Activities in and against Nicaragua (Nicaragua v. United States of America)*.

[204] *See for example, Certain expenses of the United Nations (Article 17, paragraph 2, of the Charter)*, Advisory Opinion of 20 July 1962, ICJ Reports 1962, p. 168. *See further*, R. Möhrlein, 'Act-dependent Judicial Review of Security Council and General Assembly Resolutions', in G. Gaja and J. Grote Stoutenburg (eds.), *Enhancing the Rule of Law through the International Court of Justice* (Brill, 2014), pp. 94–95.

On the other hand, a party may also rely on resolutions by other organs of the United Nations to support their case before the Court.[205]

The ICJ as One of Several Modes of Peaceful Dispute Settlement

Hudson opined that it was the PCIJ's assistance to the Council of the League of Nations through its advisory function that was its chief contribution to the maintenance of peace.[206] However, the delegates at the San Francisco Conference did not accept the Dumbarton Oaks Proposal for 'the integration of the advisory competence with the general structure for the pacific settlement of international disputes'.[207] Therefore, in the words of Rosenne, the ICJ 'was not given any special place in the general structure of the machinery for the maintenance of international peace and security established by the UN Charter'.[208]

Article 33 of the Charter sets out certain available modes of dispute settlement, including judicial settlement, without any hierarchy.[209] Parties to a dispute are free, pursuant to the Charter, to seek judicial settlement of their dispute in a tribunal or court other than the International Court,[210] or to make use of a different mode of dispute settlement. As to the latter, as the PCIJ recognised, the judicial settlement of international disputes is simply 'an alternative to the direct and friendly settlement of such disputes between the Parties'.[211]

---

[205] This occurred during the merits phase of *Armed Activities on the Territory of the Congo* (*Democratic Republic of the Congo* v. *Uganda*), during which the DRC relied on Security Council resolutions as proof of certain events and the Court cited this evidence in its merits judgment of 2005: *Armed Activities on the Territory of the Congo*, Judgment, ICJ Reports 2005, p. 168, para. 60.

[206] Hudson, *The Permanent Court of International Justice (1920-1942)*, 523. Similarly Rosenne expressed the view that the PCIJ, through its opinions, attempted to prop up the League of Nations to maintain international peace and security in the pre-World War II era: Rosenne, 'Permanent Court of International Justice', para. 37.

[207] Rosenne, 'Permanent Court of International Justice', para. 12.   [208] Ibid., para. 11.

[209] The purpose of the breadth of options for the settlement of international disputes contained therein is to 'counter-balance' the option of the use of force: Messineo, 'The Functions of the International Court of Justice', 113.

[210] Charter of the United Nations, Art. 95. *See* E. Wilmshurst, 'The International Court of Justice', in I. Roberts (ed.), *Satow's Diplomatic Practice*, 7th ed. (Oxford University Press, 2016), Book V, p. 530. *See also*, Messineo, 'The Functions of the International Court of Justice', 113.

[211] PCIJ, *Free Zones of Upper Savoy and the District of Gex, France* v. *Switzerland*, Order, (1930) PCIJ Series A No 24, at 13. *See also*, Messineo, 'The Functions of the International Court of Justice', 114.

Within the UN system, it is recognised that the Court contributes to the maintenance of international peace and security through both contentious proceedings and through its advisory function. For example, in 2018 a number of delegations to the Special Committee on the Charter of the United Nations and on the Strengthening of the Role of the Organization reaffirmed the ICJ's role in promoting the peaceful settlement of disputes, with particular emphasis on 'the usefulness of the Court's advisory opinions on legal questions'.[212] The Court itself has expressed its desire to 'lend its support to the purposes and principles laid down in the United Nations Charter, in particular the maintenance of international peace and security'.[213] As one illustration of this role of the Court in the context of contentious proceedings, when the Court deals with territorial disputes involving large populations (and therefore the human rights of these peoples), it is playing a crucial part in the maintenance of international peace and security.[214] This is all the more evident when the ICJ assumes this role alongside the Security Council, the UN Secretary-General and regional organisations with the mandate of preserving peace in the region.

In many cases before the Court, the parties simultaneously rely upon dispute settlement processes other than judicial settlement. This is in line with Article 33 of the Charter, which sets out a plethora of other peaceful means – both alternative and complementary[215] – for States to settle disputes. For example, in *Nicaragua,* a negotiation process involving Nicaragua and other Central American States, called the *Contadora* process, was taking place alongside the contentious proceedings before the Court. One of the arguments of the USA at the preliminary objections phase was that Nicaragua's Application was inadmissible because Nicaragua had failed to exhaust the *Contadora* process. The United States characterised the process as the 'appropriate method' for the resolution of issues concerning Central America.[216] The Court rejected this argument,

---

[212] UNGA, Report of the Special Committee on the Charter of the United Nations and on the Strengthening of the Role of the Organization, UN Doc. A/73/33, 2018, para. 50. The significance of the Manila Declaration on the Peaceful Settlement of International Disputes was also recalled.

[213] *Legal Consequences of the Construction of a Wall in the Occupied Palestinian Territory,* p. 161.

[214] Rosenne, 'Permanent Court of International Justice', para. 110.

[215] Messineo, 'The Functions of the International Court of Justice', 114.

[216] *Military and Paramilitary Activities in and against Nicaragua,* Jurisdiction and Admissibility, Judgment, ICJ Reports 1984, p. 392, para. 102.

holding that 'the existence of active negotiations in which both parties might be involved should not prevent both the Security Council and the Court from exercising their separate functions under the Charter and the Statute of the Court'.[217]

Even once a case has been brought before it, the Court retains the function of encouraging and facilitating ongoing negotiation, and other means of dispute settlement, between the parties,[218] with the ultimate aim of the maintenance of international peace and security. The ICJ has also supported negotiations between parties following its judgment on the merits of a case, in order for the parties to determine appropriate reparation[219] or to resolve any other matters still in dispute between them.[220] The Court often reminds parties of their obligation to settle a dispute peacefully, whether or not it has intervened in the dispute settlement process.[221]

Limits of the ICJ's Ability to Effectively Contribute to the Maintenance of Peace and Security

The Statute of the ICJ does not provide for the enforcement of the Court's judgments.[222] However, the Charter of the United Nations mandates that '[e]ach Member of the United Nations undertakes to comply with the decision of the International Court of Justice in any case to which it is a party'.[223] Member States have periodically reaffirmed this obligation.[224] Moreover, the Security Council has the power, pursuant to the Charter, to

---

[217] *Military and Paramilitary Activities in and against Nicaragua*, Jurisdiction and Admissibility, Judgment, para. 106.

[218] *See* PCIJ, *Free Zones of Upper Savoy and the District of Gex*, at 13.

[219] *See for example, Armed Activities on the Territory of the Congo (Democratic Republic of the Congo v. Uganda)*, Judgment, ICJ Reports 2005, p. 257, para. 261.

[220] *Arbitral Award of 31 July 1989 (Guinea-Buissau v. Senegal)*, Judgment, ICJ Reports 1991, p. 75, para. 68.

[221] Messineo, 'The Functions of the International Court of Justice', 114. *See for example, Obligation to Negotiate Access to the Pacific Ocean (Bolivia v. Chile)*, Judgment, ICJ Reports 2018, p. 507, para. 176.

[222] *See* Pellet, 'Judicial Settlement of International Disputes', para. 46. In this regard, the Inter-Allied Committee had recommended in 1946 that enforcement mechanisms be provided for in the Constitution of the future General International Organisation, not in the Court's Statute: *Report of the Informal Inter-Allied Committee*, p. 18.

[223] Charter of the United Nations, Art. 94(1).

[224] *See for example, Declaration of the High-level Meeting of the General Assembly on the Rule of Law at the National and International Levels*, A/RES/67/1, 2012, para. 31.

make recommendations, or decide upon measures to be taken, to give effect to a judgment when a party fails to perform their obligations pursuant to that judgment.[225] The aftermath of the *Nicaragua* case demonstrates the limitation of this power when a permanent member of the Security Council is involved. In that case, Nicaragua asked for an emergency meeting of the Security Council in October 1986 to consider the alleged non-compliance of the USA with the judgment of the Court. The United States vetoed all relevant resolutions and the Security Council was prevented from considering the matter.[226]

Provisional measures indicated by the Court are notified to the Security Council,[227] and in certain cases the Security Council has taken formal note of such measures, adding pressure to comply.[228] Finally, parties to cases before the Court have also relied on other organs of the United Nations for the implementation of the Court's judgments, but this is not provided for in the Court's Statute.[229]

V Conclusions

A 'bond of continuity' exists between the PCIJ and its successor, the ICJ, whose core functions remained largely the same, save for an expanded

---

[225] Charter of the United Nations, Art. 94(2).

[226] Wilmshurst, 'The International Court of Justice', 530; Pellet, 'Judicial Settlement of International Disputes', para. 46.

[227] Statute of the ICJ, Art 41(2).

[228] *See for example*, United Nations Security Council Resolution 819 (1993) of 16 April 1993: 'Taking note that the International Court of Justice in its Order of 8 April 1993 in ... Bosnia and Herzegovina v. Yugoslavia (Serbia and Montenegro) ... unanimously indicated as a provisional measure that the Government of the Federal Republic of Yugoslavia (Serbia and Montenegro) should immediately, in pursuance of its undertaking in the Convention on the Prevention and Punishment of the Crime of Genocide of 9 December 1948, take all measures within its power to prevent the commission of the crime of genocide ...'

[229] For example, Kofi Annan, then United Nations Secretary-General, was involved in the implementation of the Court's judgment in *Land and Maritime Boundary between Cameroon and Nigeria (Cameroon v. Nigeria: Equatorial Guinea intervening)*, the Court having determined that the sovereignty of the Bakassi Peninsula lay with Cameroon: Judgment, ICJ Reports 2002, p. 303, at p. 455; *see* President Abdulqawi Yusuf, Speech before the Royal Academy of Belgium, *The strengths and challenges for supranational justice: the growing role of the International Court of Justice*, Brussels, 12 November 2018, para. 20.

advisory function. Its first core 'function is to decide in accordance with international law such disputes as are submitted to it'. It is for the Court to determine whether a dispute has arisen between the parties, and if so, whether it is a dispute which may be resolved by the application of international law. As the Court is the only international court of general jurisdiction, the subject-matter of disputes submitted to the Court is broad, ranging from the settlement of land and maritime delimitation disputes to alleged violations of human rights law. The geographical distribution of States participating in contentious proceedings and those involved in advisory proceedings has broadened and evolved since the establishment of the Court. Where litigation before the Court used to be dominated by European States, the Court has recently seen increased litigation involving States from the Asia-Pacific region and from the Middle East, and especially from Central and South America.

As its second core function, the ICJ 'may give an advisory opinion on any legal question at the request of whatever body may be authorised by or in accordance with the Charter of the United Nations to make such a request'. When an authorised organ other than the Security Council or General Assembly requests an opinion, the Court may provide one as long as a legal question arises within the scope of the organ's activities. The Court has identified the purpose of its advisory function as the provision of 'legal advice to the organs and institutions requesting the opinion',[230] or as providing guidance to United Nations organs so that they can fulfil their functions in accordance with the law. Even though the Court exercises its judicial function when rendering an advisory opinion as well as when issuing a judgment in contentious proceedings, there are important differences between the two functions. For example, opinions are not binding on any State or organisation, so the Court does not require consent from any State which might be concerned by the question posed. The Court may provide an advisory opinion in relation to an abstract question, but will refrain from adjudicating 'moot' contentious cases. The Court's power to provide an advisory opinion is of 'a permissive character': the Court may choose not to comply with a request.

Beyond its two core functions, the Court has a role to play in finding and developing international law as its decisions are a subsidiary means for the

---

[230] *Legality of the Threat or Use of Nuclear Weapons*, p. 14.

determination of rules of law. Legal institutions respect findings on general international law by the ICJ, especially outside their own sphere of experience. Moreover, judicial settlement is one of the modes of dispute settlement set out in the UN Charter so, as a UN organ, the Court has a role to play in terms of maintaining peace and security. The Security Council is mandated to take into consideration that legal disputes should, as a general rule, be referred to the International Court but this does not amount to an obligation for the Security Council to recommend judicial settlement, nor to refer legal disputes to it. Even once a case has been brought before it, the Court retains the function of encouraging and facilitating ongoing negotiation, and other means of dispute settlement, between the parties. Although the ICJ Statute does not provide for the enforcement of the Court's judgments, the UN Charter mandates that each Member of the United Nations undertakes to comply with its decisions and the Security Council has the power to make recommendations, or decide upon measures to be taken to give effect to a judgment when a party fails to perform their obligations pursuant to it.

Further Reading

A. Pellet, 'Competence of the Court, Article 38', in A. Zimmermann and C. Tams (eds.), *The Statute of the International Court of Justice*, 3rd ed. (Oxford University Press, 2019)

J. Frowein and K. Oellers-Frahm, 'Advisory Opinions, Article 65', in A. Zimmermann and C. Tams (eds.), *The Statute of the International Court of Justice*, 3rd ed. (Oxford University Press, 2019)

G. I. Hernández, *The International Court of Justice and the Judicial Function* (Oxford University Press, 2014)

F. Messineo, 'The Functions of the International Court of Justice' in A. Kent, N. Skoutaris and J. Trinidad (eds.), *The Future of International Courts: Regional, Institutional and Procedural Challenges* (Routledge, 2019) 109

C. Brown, *A Common Law of International Adjudication* (Oxford University Press, 2017)

Y. Tanaka, *The Peaceful Settlement of International Disputes* (Cambridge University Press, 2018), pp. 175–226

W. Schabas, *The International Court of Justice* (Edward Elgar Publishing, 2020)

2 The Role of an ICJ Judge

Judge Sir Kenneth Keith

I Introduction

'La Cour' is the cry uttered by the huissier as the judges of the ICJ enter the Great Hall of Justice of the Peace Palace to hear the parties and to deliver judgments, advisory opinions and certain orders. They enter as members of the Court, a principal organ of the United Nations, indeed its principal judicial organ. They constitute a bench of magistrates, not an academy of jurists, let alone fifteen individual scholars, each marching to the measure of their own drum.

The chapters of the Statute of the Court regulating its jurisdiction and procedure consistently have 'the Court', and not the individual judges, at their centre. A principal exception, discussed later, appears in Article 57 which enables judges to deliver a separate opinion if the judgment of the Court does not represent in whole or part their opinion.

But the Statute does of course recognise the fact that the members of the Court are individuals with their different talents, backgrounds and experiences. That fact cannot be escaped. One of each judge's essential qualities in terms of Article 2 of the Statute is independence, particularly from the other judges among others, a quality emphasised by the solemn declaration each makes publicly at the outset of their terms that they will exercise their powers impartially and conscientiously. Other supports for their independence concern the method of their nomination and election, their secure tenure, their conditions and privileges and immunities and the provisions for recusal. The collective, worldwide character of all fifteen of them appears in the requirement in Article 9 of the Statute that the member States of the UN in electing judges are to bear in mind, not only the qualifications required by each individual member of the Court, but also

Thanks to Roger Clark, Marnie Lloydd, and Judge Peter Tomka for comments and corrections.

that the representation of the main forms of civilisation and of the principal legal systems of the world should be assured, 1920's language maintained in 1945.

In this chapter, I consider (II) the process of nomination and election of judges, their qualifications and the outcomes of that process; (III) the engagement by the Court as a judicial body with the parties, with some reference to the Court's exercise of its advisory jurisdiction; and (IV) the process of decision-making. I conclude with a word or two on the outcomes of that process, as seen in the judgments and opinions of the Court.

II How Are the Judges Chosen?

The procedure for the election of judges, like most other provisions of the Statute of the ICJ, is in essentially the same terms as in the 1920 Statute of the Permanent Court of International Justice (PCIJ). National groups appointed by each state party to the 1899 and 1907 Hague Conventions for the Peaceful Settlement of International Disputes or a similarly composed body, rather than governments, make the nominations. That step was intended to introduce a professional, independent element into the overall process. There is some evidence that that has happened, but very little is known generally about the work of those groups. The requirement also has the advantage that the groups can nominate nationals of other countries. The Institute of International Law in 2011 in its resolution on the position of the international judge expressed its concern that the groups did not always play the role accorded to them by the Statute.[1]

The qualifications, additional to independence and high moral character, are having the qualifications for appointment to their highest national judicial office or being 'jurisconsults of recognised competence in international law' (Article 2 of the Statute). The former was understandable when that provision was drafted in 1920 and several of the first bench, including the first President, qualified under it, but with two or three exceptions it appears not to have played any role recently. (Some who had had national judging experience may, as well, be seen as coming within the 'jurisconsult' qualification.) The Institute of International Law

---

[1] Institute of International Law, Rhodes Session (2011), The Position of the International Judge, Resolution, Article 1.2.

in 2011 declared that the quality of international courts and tribunals depends first of all on the intellectual and moral character of their judges; accordingly, the selection of judges must be carried out with the greatest care. States shall ensure that judges possess the required competence and that the court or tribunal is in a position effectively to deal with issues of general international law. The ability to exercise high judicial functions shall nonetheless remain the paramount criterion for the selection of judges.[2] That resolution and a similar one of 1954 had been anticipated by a recommendation of the Assembly of the League of Nations in 1929 that the 'candidates nominated should possess practical experience in international law'.[3]

The terms of Article 9 of the Statute may be seen as having been achieved from 1985 until 2017 by the overall composition of the Court matching that of the Security Council.

The Statute, the Court's Rules, its practice and especially the characteristics of the cases coming before it mean that the Court will, as a judicial body, have to resolve disputes of both fact and law. The factual complexity of cases and their number have been increasing in recent years, although that is not new, as appears from the *Corfu Channel* case, the first to be heard by the ICJ and the *Nicaragua* case in the 1980s. The claim by Ecuador that Colombia's aerial herbicide spraying had caused damage to its citizens, animals and plant life was supported by extensive evidence relating to the composition of the herbicide, the patterns and places of spraying, the winds at the time of spraying, the toxic effect of the herbicide, and the health status of humans, animals, and plants before and after. There were eyewitness accounts and expert reports of various kinds. Before the scheduled hearing date, the Court, basing itself on a detailed examination of the evidence, sent the parties a list of questions to be addressed at the hearing. It also made arrangements with the parties for some of the witnesses whose statements were in the pleadings to be called for questioning. When giving notice of discontinuance and agreeing to it, each party praised the Court for the time, resources, and energy it had devoted to the case; reaching a settlement would have been difficult, if not impossible, but for that involvement.[4]

---

[2] Ibid., Article 1.1.   [3] League of Nations Tenth Assembly.

[4] See *Aerial Herbicide Spraying (Ecuador v. Colombia)* Order of 13 September 2013, ICJ Reports 2013, p. 278, and the written pleadings on the ICJ website.

To date (2021) 109 judges have been elected, from only 46 of the 193 UN members. The nationals of just twelve States have occupied seats on the Court for about half of the years of the Court's existence, a proportion of fifteen, the number of judges, times seventy-five years. Seven of those States have never brought a case before the Court and seven (not exactly the same seven) do not recognise its compulsory jurisdiction, under Article 36(2) and its Statute.

Article 8 of the Charter requires the UN to place no restrictions on the eligibility of men and women to participate in any capacity and under conditions of equality in its organs. Notwithstanding that direction, only five women have been elected in the seventy-five years of the Court's existence. Three were nationals of the Permanent members of the Security Council, all being elected initially in uncontested casual elections and then re-elected, for total terms longer than the average judicial term of about ten years and with enhanced prospects of becoming President of the Court, as two of the women nationals of Permanent members have been. The fourth, not a national of a Permanent member, was initially elected by the narrowest of margins. And the fifth was elected to serve the remaining two years of a co-national who had died in office.

The lack of equal or better representation is not the fault of the UN as an institution but rather of the national groups who make the nominations and of the governments voting in the Assembly and Council. Only eight women candidates have been nominated, the first only in 1995 when the Court was approaching its fiftieth anniversary. Women have been appointed as ad hoc judges in six cases and more are appearing as counsel and have been contributing significantly to the written pleadings presented to the Court, as reflected in the parties' delegation's lists.[5]

A majority of the thirty-two judges elected in the last thirty-five years, including nationals of four of the five Permanent Members of the Security Council, have spent most of their working lives in their foreign services; thirteen have had international judging and arbitral experience; about half have had experience as counsel in international cases; six have had national judging experience; many have good records of published scholarship; fourteen had been members of the International Law Commission, many had participated in the work of UN legal bodies and in diplomatic

---

[5] For helpful data see S. Kumar and C. Rose, 'A Study of Lawyers Appearing before the International Court of Justice 1999–2012, *EJIL* Vol 25 (2014) 893.

conferences elaborating law-making conventions; seventeen are members of the Institute of International Law and three had been judges ad hoc at the ICJ. That is to say, many of the judges have long professional and personal relationships with their colleagues and the wider, now more visible, college of international lawyers.

Over the years, but also more recently, concern has been expressed about the predominance of those with extensive Foreign Service experience. On the other hand, that experience is of major value in the working of the Court, when it is accompanied by real independence and intellectual rigour. Another critical quality is that some of the judges must have leadership skills. In the national court systems I am familiar with, attention is given on a regular basis by those responsible for the appointment of judges to the issue of who is likely to become a good head of bench – one with the ability to deal with and lead colleagues and organise the work of the Court; and to deal with the parties (states in the case of the ICJ) and their lawyers, with the Registry, with the relevant public agencies (in the case of the ICJ this includes other UN bodies, especially in respect of its budget), with the profession, and with the wider public. In the case of the President of the ICJ, the responsibilities, particularly in chairing drafting committees which prepare draft judgments, opinions and some orders, and the lengthy, testing deliberations of members of the Court leading to those decisions call for the exercise of a wide range of skills. Is the availability of strong candidates for that position left too much to chance? I fear that it is.

That requirement provides for me a qualification to the proposition adopted by the Institute both in 1954 and 2011 that there should be no re-election – with a view, it said in 1954, to recognising the independence of the judges. In 2011 it declared that elections were not to be subject to prior bargaining, involving vote swaps.[6] But, as was recognised in the deliberations leading to the resolution, that proposition flies in the face of reality. Surely, excellent individual qualifications are necessary, but experience shows that in many cases they will not be sufficient. But I worry that that excellence has not always been seen as essential. Notwithstanding my emphasis on the collegial character of the Court, the intellectual and professional talents of each and every judge support that collegial character.

---

[6] The Position of the International Judge, Articles 2.1 and 1.6.

In 1920 the Advisory Committee of Jurists, charged with the preparation of the Statute of the Permanent Court of International Justice, recommended that judges of the nationality of a state party to a case before the Court be allowed to remain on the bench, unless, of course, they had been involved in the particular matter at some earlier stage[7] – a qualification which may well exclude judges who have had extensive practice, especially before the Court, as with one judge in respect of as many as ten cases (two of which were withdrawn and two heard together). The justification given in 1920 for the inclusion of that provision was put in terms of the confidence of the State party that its interests would be understood; the Court may also benefit from the specialised knowledge of the judge. That recommendation was matched by one allowing a judge ad hoc if the other state party to the proceeding did not have a judge of its nationality on the bench. These two provisions would also help overcome the traditional mistrust of states towards a permanent tribunal.[8] The Council and Assembly of the League of Nations accepted those proposals, as did the San Francisco Conference in 1945. Those provisions have continued to be controversial but there has been no serious attempt to remove them.

One judge ad hoc (not a national of the state appointing him) made an important observation about that role, an observation repeated by a number of others holding that role since.[9] The judge has the same obligation as the titular judges to exercise the powers impartially and conscientiously. There is nevertheless the distinction arising from the appointment that the judge is to ensure, so far as is reasonable, that every relevant argument is fully appreciated in the course of collegial consideration and is reflected, if not accepted, in any opinion that judge may write. Another judge ad hoc stated that a perspective from the region where the case arose could be added.[10]

One significant change which has occurred in recent years is the appointment of judges ad hoc who are not nationals of the state but are

---

[7] Statute, Art. 17(2).

[8] Proces-verbaux of the Proceedings of the Advisory Committee of Jurists (1920) 720–722.

[9] *Application of the Convention for the Prevention and Punishment of the Crime of Genocide,* Provisional Measures, ICJ Reports 1993, p. 325, separate opinion of Judge Lauterpacht, pp. 408–409, paras. 4–6.

[10] *Request for an Examination of the Situation in accordance with Paragraph 63 of the Court's Judgment of 20 December in the Nuclear Tests case (New Zealand v. France)* case, ICJ Reports 1995, p. 288, dissenting opinion of Judge Palmer, pp. 420–421, para. 118.

experts in the matter before the Court or are generally recognised as
international lawyers of real standing. There have been notable examples
of their agreeing fully with the decision of the Court, something also seen
in other tribunals.[11]

III How Are the Judges or Rather the Court to Engage with the Parties or Other Participants before Them?

The Court has frequently referred to the principle of the good or sound
(*bonne*) administration of justice. That principle may be seen as having
three components:

1. An independent and impartial court or tribunal;
2. Which follows a procedure which (a) gives the parties before it a full
   and equal opportunity to present their cases and to challenge those
   presented against them; and (b) provides the court or tribunal with
   sufficient material on which to decide the case; and
3. Which decides the dispute between the parties in a reasoned decision
   according to its findings on the facts as presented by the parties and the
   governing law.

This section of the chapter considers the second. Its coverage takes account
of the chapters in this volume concerned with procedural matters.[12]
I proceed on the basis that the principled application of the procedural
rules in the Statute of the PCIJ adopted in 1920 and 1929 (and in force in
1936) and carried over into the Statute of the ICJ, taken with the Rules of
Court prepared and amended by it from time to time on the basis of
developing practice, its Practice Directions and its practice, orders and
rulings in particular cases, may well, with other factors, help promote
greater confidence in the Court, wider acceptance of its jurisdiction and
greater use of it. Those consequences are evidenced by the increasing range
of countries and cases coming before the Court and more generally by the

---

[11] A. Zimmermann and C. Tams (eds.), *Statute of the International Court of Justice. A Commentary* 3rd ed., (Oxford University Press, 2018), Introduction, para. 40; see also para. 39 for a case where the parties decided not to appoint judges ad hoc, with consequent savings for the Court's budget.

[12] See C. Harris, Chapter 11, The Working Practices of the Court; K. Parlett and A. Sander, Chapter 12, Procedure in Contentious Cases: Evolution and Flexibility.

debates in the UN General Assembly which follow the presentation of the Court's Annual Report by its President. Their positive character is to be sharply contrasted with the debates in the late 1960s and early 1970s following the disaster of the 1966 South-West Africa cases and with the Court's empty or slight docket over that period.

In those 1966 cases, it may be recalled, the Court, on the casting vote of its President, decided that the cases would not proceed on a procedural ground which most involved, along with knowledgeable commentators, thought had been decided, with the force of *res judicata*, four years earlier.[13] The parties, assuming that the jurisdictional issues had been resolved, had argued the case fully on the merits with extensive evidence being called and it was a judgment on the merits they were expecting. After the judgment in the Barcelona Traction case,[14] just a few months later, in early 1967, again decided, to the surprise of the parties, on narrow procedural grounds, the Court had no cases before it, for the first time in its existence. These decisions, especially the first, led to strong criticism in the General Assembly and beyond and were seen by many as a factor in the setting up of a distinct tribunal, the International Tribunal on the Law of the Sea by the UN Convention on the Law of the Sea. The Court then faced a very difficult period in the 1970s in which respondent states refused to recognise its jurisdiction and to appear. There were also real tensions within the Court and it faced third world antipathy.[15]

The procedural provisions of the PCIJ Statute were not written on a blank page. Of the ten members of the Advisory Committee of Jurists which prepared it eight were civilians and two common lawyers. A Secretariat memorandum (prepared by Ake Hammarskjöld, later to be the first Registrar and all too briefly a Judge of the PCIJ) considers, along with the qualifications and method of election of judges and substantive matters, procedural issues including the Court's rule-making powers, the written and oral phases, agents and counsel, public and private hearings, evidence, reasons and dissent. They were able to draw on the thinking,

---

[13] *South-West Africa*, Second Phase, ICJ Reports 1966, p. 6.

[14] *Case Concerning the Barcelona Traction, Light and Power Company Limited*, Second Phase, ICJ Reports 1967, p. 3.

[15] *See for example*, A. Gros, 'La Cour International de Justice 1946–1986: reflexions d'un juge' in Y. Dinstein (ed.) *International Law in a Time of Perplexity: Essays in Honour of Shabtai Rosenne* (Nijhoff, 1989) 289.

practice and treaty making of the preceding decades, notably in the Institute of International Law in 1874 and 1875 and at the 1899 and 1907 Hague Peace Conferences.[16]

The Committee text, with amendments made by the League organs, became Part III, Procedure, of the Statute of the PCIJ which, with only limited changes, was carried into the Statute of the ICJ in 1945. That Statute also included Part IV, concerned with the advisory jurisdiction, which had been added to the earlier Statute in 1929 and came into force in 1936, after which no opinions were given by the PCIJ.

The changes made by the Council and Assembly of the League to Part III added English to the official languages of the Court, provided for dissenting opinions, provided for intervention by states which considered that they had an interest of a legal nature which might be affected by a decision in the case and, as a consequence, added what became Article 59, on *res judicata*, and which, contrary to a frequently expressed view, has nothing to do with *stare decisis*.

Foremost in the features of the procedural part of the Statute is their adversary character. The States parties to a contentious case are given full and equal opportunities to present their cases on the facts and the law. Those entitlements have been elaborated over the past almost 100 years by the Court in its rules, practice directions, orders, practice and rulings. Usually, the parties will have two written rounds, the first accompanied by extensive documentary evidence, sometimes supplemented in the second or very exceptionally third rounds. They also have two rounds of oral hearings which may include witnesses.

The Court has emphasised that the principle of the equality of the parties before it follows from the requirements of the good administration of justice. One particular area concerned the review power the Court exercised from 1973 to 2012 over the decisions of two international Administrative Tribunals. While it affirmed that the exercise of its advisory jurisdiction represents its participation in the activities of the Organization and, in principle, a request should not be refused, in its last case involving this power in 2012, it recalled this principle, using words written in 1923.

---

[16] Documents presented to the committee relating to existing plans for the establishment of a Permanent Court of International Justice (1920), pp. 90–108.

The Court, being a Court of Justice, cannot even in giving advisory opinions, depart from the essential rules guiding [its] activity as a Court. *(Status of Eastern Carelia (Advisory Opinion)* (1923) PCIJ series B No 5 at 29).

In that last case, it concluded that both the organisation and the former staff member had had adequate and in large measure equal opportunities to present their cases and to answer that made by the other; and, in essence, the principle of equality, required by its inherent judicial character and by the good administration of justice, had been met. In addition, the Court did have the information it required to decide the questions submitted.[17]

When the advisory jurisdiction was created, by a single sentence of Article 14 of the Covenant of the League of Nations, there were those on the advisory committee of jurists and among the initial judges of the PCIJ who declared that it was not a judicial function. But from the outset, in its rules, practice and the 1923 ruling, the Court has made it clear that it would adhere as closely as possible to the procedure it follows in contentious cases. The 1929 amendment to the PCIJ Statute captured that practice in Article 68:

In the exercise of its advisory functions the Court shall further be guided by the provisions of the present Statute which apply in contentious cases to the extent to which it recognizes them to be applicable.

The number of advisory opinions has fallen over the seventy-five years of the Court's existence – thirteen in the first twenty-five years, nine in the next twenty-five and seven (two on the same matter, nuclear weapons, and dealt with together by the Court) in the last.

Two of the requests are distinct – they involve disputes to which international organisations were parties.[18] Various international instruments avoid the restriction of Article 34 of the Statute – only States may be parties to contentious cases – by enabling such disputes to be resolved and with binding force by advisory opinions. Those matters have been resolved in all respects as if they were contentious cases, with only the disputing

---

[17] *Judgment No 2787 of the Administrative Tribunal of the International Labour Organisation upon a complaint against of the International Fund for Agricultural Development*, ICJ Reports 2012, p. 10 at p. 13, para. 48.

[18] *Documents* and *Difference relating to Immunity from Legal Process of a Special Rapporteur of the Commission of Human Rights*, ICJ Reports 1999, p. 62.

parties making submissions, as both the 1923 ruling and Article
68 indicate.

The remaining five cases (or four, treating the nuclear weapons cases as
one) do raise real issues about the current health of the advisory jurisdiction. In two of them, relating to the Wall in occupied Palestinian Territory
and the Chagos Island case, the matter referred to the Court, at least on one
view, concerned disputes between States where one of them had made it
very clear that it did not accept that the Court should have a role in
resolving the matter.[19] While the Court has made it clear over a lengthy
period that lack of consent is a factor that has to be given significant
weight in the exercise of its discretion not to give an opinion it is yet to
refuse to give an opinion on that basis.

In one of those cases, relating to the Chagos Islands and in another
relating to the Declaration of Independence of Kosovo, a further argument,
which again did not succeed, was that the requesting organ did not have a
real interest in the matter it had referred to the Court. In its response to the
opinion in the Kosovo case, the General Assembly did no more than
acknowledge the content of the opinion. It took no further action. That
opinion did not begin to assist the Assembly in its activities – the reason
the Court, as a principal organ of the UN, has regularly given in support of
what it sees as its duty to answer requests for opinions, with the qualification that it must do that consistently with its obligation to remain true to
its judicial character.[20]

The Nuclear Weapons opinion, given in response to the General
Assembly request, continues to play a part in the very large complex of
issues relating to general and complete disarmament, for instance in
debates about the obligations of the nuclear powers under the Non
Proliferation Treaty.[21] As appears from the array of dissenting and separate opinions and the President's casting vote on a critical element of the
ruling they provide a basis for extensive debate but were the requests a
wise use of the Court's jurisdiction? Consider the 1974 judgments in the
Nuclear Tests cases which did not even get to the issues of jurisdiction and

[19] *Legal Consequences of the Construction of the Wall in the Occupied Palestinian Territory,* ICJ Reports 2004, p. 136 and *Legal Consequences of the Separation of the Chagos Archipelago from Mauritius in 1986,* ICJ Reports 2019, p. 951.
[20] *Accordance with International Law of the Unilateral Declaration of Independence in Respect of Kosovo,* ICJ Reports 2010, p. 403 and GA Res 64/298.
[21] *Legality of the Threat or Use of Nuclear Weapons,* ICJ Reports 1996, p. 226.

admissibility which had been argued, let alone the merits, the 1995 order rejecting the attempt to reopen one of those cases and the failure of the Marshall Islands cases about the NPT, at the jurisdictional stage. A sense of the limits of adjudication?

Given the coverage of other chapters in this volume,[22] I emphasise three matters of procedure which are likely to continue to have value. The first concerns the early steps the Court or the judges, since it may be an individual judge who takes the initiative, may take to seek assistance. In its first contentious case, the *Corfu Channel* case, the Registrar, no doubt on the instructions of the President, following the filing by the UK of its reply, wrote to the Dutch, Norwegian and Swedish authorities indicating that the Court was considering the possibility of applying Article 50 of its Statute and Article 57 of its Rules to appoint experts on anchoring and mine clearage. Would the three named captains be available?[23] The Committee of Experts made two reports on particular matters which were the subject of comments by the parties and they were questioned by members of the Court.[24] Experts have also been called on the Court's initiative in two recent cases, one relating to geographical issues, the other to compensation.[25]

A related practice, again dating back to early days, is for the President to call the parties in before the hearing for a discussion of the issues to be argued. In the *Fisheries* case (*United Kingdom* v. *Norway*) in 1951 the object of the meeting was to suggest to the Agents that they should seek to reach agreement upon the points that each would wish particularly to deal with, while remaining free to complete the presentation of their case in conformity with the Statute and Rules. Counsel for the UK, in his opening, referring to that discussion and an earlier Court order, indicated

---

[22] See J. Devaney, Chapter 9, Fact-Finding and Expert Evidence; C. Harris, Chapter 11, The Working Practices of the Court; K. Parlett and A. Sander, Chapter 12, Procedure in Contentious Cases: Evolution and Flexibility; S. Wordsworth and K. Parlett, Chapter 13, Effective Advocacy at the ICJ.

[23] V Pleadings (correspondence) 208–209.

[24] V Pleadings 93–98 and 115–122; ICJ Reports 1949, p. 4 at pp. 142–150, 152, 162 and 163–169.

[25] *Maritime Delimitation in the Caribbean Sea and the Pacific Ocean (Costa Rica* v. *Nicaragua) Order,* ICJ Reports 2016, p. 235 at p. 240; Judgment, ICJ Reports 2018, p. 139 at pp.167–168, para. 71; and *Armed Activities on the Territory of the Congo (Democratic Republic of the Congo* v. *Uganda)* Orders of 8 September 2020 and 12 October 2020.

what they saw as the vital issues, the secondary issues, issues which must not be resolved and those which are irrelevant.[26]

More recently, the Court has made some use of the practice, provided for in Article 49 of the Statute, Article 62 of the Rules and Article 1 (i) of the Resolution on the Internal Judicial Practice of the Court (1976) (discussed further in the final part of this chapter), calling upon the parties to provide explanations (as well as evidence). Article 49 was the basis for a request to the employing agency in the final ILO Administrative Tribunal case (via Article 68) and to the UK in the *Corfu Channel* case, but it was not used in the *Bosnia* v. *Serbia Genocide* case, a failure criticised by some members of the Court.[27] The later *Genocide* case between Croatia and Serbia provides a sharp contrast; there were exchanges between the parties, facilitated by the Court, which led to a much fuller disclosure of evidence and not just by the Respondent.[28]

A second matter concerns the Court's negative response to the practice of experts appearing in effect as counsel, with the consequence of their not being subject to cross-examination. Both parties in the River Uruguay case were guilty of that action and the Court's strong words rejecting the practice have apparently had their effect; certainly no rule change nor a new Practice direction was seen as called for.[29]

Earlier practice was inconsistent. In *Bosnia* v. *Serbia* an 'expert counsel and advocate' speaking from the podium as an advocate gave what was in effect lengthy evidence for the Applicant about how Serbia 'financially dominated the ... governmental structures ... in what came to be called Republika Srpska' – the entity whose actions were to be attributed according to the Applicant, to the Respondent. He was answered, again from the bar, by counsel (not an expert) who, moreover, produced a bank note as 'evidence' of substantial hyperinflation. In the result, the Court did not have to rule on that matter.[30]

---

[26] Fisheries case IV Pleadings 24.

[27] *Application of the Convention on the Prevention and Punishment of the Crime of Genocide (Bosnia and Herzegovina* v. *Servia and Montenegro)* ICJ Reports 2007, p. 43 at pp. 254–255, para. 35 and p. 416, para. 57.

[28] *Application of the Convention of the Prevention and Punishment of the Crime of Genocide (Croatia* v. *Serbia)* ICJ Reports 2015, p. 3 at p. 16 (para 13) and pp. 73–74 (paras 170–176).

[29] *Pulp Mills on the River Uruguay (Argentina* v. *Uruguay)* ICJ Reports 2010, p. 14 at p. 72, para. 167.

[30] CR 2006/9 22–49 and CR 2006/38 31–40.

Third is the use by the Court and Judges of their right to ask the parties and witnesses questions. Do they make sufficient use of this right? The answers should be valuable not just for the Court and its members but also for the parties as possibly indicating the ways in which judges see some aspect of the case. Consider for instance a question in the *Genocide* case to counsel for Serbia in 2006 whether Serbia which had acceded to the 1948 Convention with a reservation to the provision giving the Court jurisdiction had acceded to any other treaties.[31] The answer was that it had – but the list provided was limited to treaties concluded under the auspices of the Council of Europe, treaties which can be accepted on their terms, only by members of the Council and to ICSID to which only members of the World Bank could become party. By contrast United Nations practice had long accepted declarations of succession by newly independent and seceding states and Serbia had declared its succession to other treaties to which the Federal Republic of Yugoslavia had become party, and of which the Secretary-General was depository; the sole exception was the Genocide Convention – a practice which counsel for Serbia did not confront. The *Whaling* case and another between Costa Rica and Nicaragua might also be seen as demonstrating the value of the questioning of experts by the parties and the judges.[32]

IV How Are the Judges to Come to Judgment?

The Statute requires that, following the completion of the hearing, the deliberations of the Court 'shall take place in private and remain secret' (Article 54 (3)). That prohibition does not, however, stand in the way of descriptions of the process of judgment making, descriptions assisted since 1931 by resolutions, amended from time to time most recently in 1976, with an addition being made in 2021, concerning the internal judicial

---

[31] CR 2006/40 62–63 and 2006/41 52–53.

[32] *Whaling in the Antarctic (Australia v. Japan; New Zealand intervening)* ICJ Reports 2010, p. 226 at p. 237, paras. 20 and 21, and e.g. pp. 270–271, paras. 138–144, and *Maritime Delimitation in the Caribbean Sea (Costa Rica v. Nicaragua) and the Pacific Ocean and Land Boundary in the Northern Part of Isla Portillo Islas (Costa Rica v. Nicaragua)*, ICJ Reports 2018, p. 139 at pp. 147–149, 150 and 151 and the written responses of the experts to questions put to them.

practice of the court.[33] In an early account, the Registrar of the PCIJ commented on the shock which took place between opinions based on different legal systems and different legal training. It was the source of a great completeness of consideration and a guarantee for the all-sided and impartial character of the final decision or opinion.[34] Three years later, Charles Evans Hughes, following his brief period on the PCIJ and on his return to the United States to become Chief Justice there, gave an address in which he declared:

> One cannot but have a feeling of exaltation in reading the preliminary opinions, and in realizing to what extent the minds of men drawn from many countries move along the same lines of careful reasoning. Whether one agreed or not with this or that opinion, one's respect was heightened by the exhibition of intelligent and conscientious application, of learning and mastery, of the power of analysis and cogent statement, which are the marks of judicial work of superior excellence.[35]

The current resolution, provides for six stages of deliberation by the judges – (1) following the completion of the written stage of the case, (2) during the oral phase particularly in relation to questions judges are proposing to put to the parties, (3) following the oral proceedings to consider and propose changes to a list of issues proposed by the President which will require discussion and decision, a stage at which judges may indicate their preliminary impressions on any issue, (4) following the preparation by each judge of a note expressing their tentative opinions, with reasons, on the questions which they think should be answered and a tentative conclusion on the correct solution, at the conclusion of which deliberation the President indicates what the likely resolution is and proposes names of members for election to a drafting committee, (5) following the preparation by the drafting committee of a draft judgment or opinion a deliberation on that draft, at which stage those judges who intend to dissent or write separately, indicate that and (6) following the preparation of a further draft of the judgment or opinion, at which stage each judge must vote yes or no, on each part of the *dispositif*, the decision.

---

[33] PCIJ D 2 2d add 300–301 (1931), E 12 196–197 (1935), 1967 ICJ YB 88 and 1975–1976 ICJYB 119.

[34] A. Hammarskjold 'Sidelights on the Permanent Court of International Justice' *Mich LR* Vol. 25 (1927) 327.

[35] C. E. Hughes 'The World Court as a Going Concern' *ABA JI* Vol. 16 (1930) 57.

Some aspects of that summary of a five-page resolution call for elaboration. Members of the Court have at times been reluctant to engage in any initial deliberation. But attitudes may be changing. For instance in the *Ecuador* v. *Colombia* case, the members of the Court engaged in extensive consideration and discussion of the 19 volumes, 12,294 pages and 90 scientific and technical reports, submitted by the parties, with the consequences mentioned earlier.

In another recent case concerning a maritime boundary dispute between Costa Rica and Nicaragua, the Court, of its own initiative, shortly after the parties agreed that the written stage was completed, advised them that it was considering arranging for an expert opinion about the state of the coast at the mouth of the San Juan River. An order to that effect was made and the experts prepared a report on which the parties could comment and about which a judge asked a question, a report which had a significant role in the judgment.[36]

The delay contemplated by the resolution between the end of the hearing and the third deliberation did not in my experience occur – the meeting is held immediately – nor was there any substantive discussion. The list of suggested issues is very helpfully supported by references to the written pleadings and oral submissions.

Over the years objections have been raised about the preparation by each judge of their notes at such an early stage in the process. Is there not a real danger that they will adhere doggedly to the positions that they have taken? I would note that the Resolution calls for the statement of tentative positions and conclusions. And certainly my experience is that some judges, having read their colleagues' notes and participated in at least three deliberations at which the two (or even more) draft judgments are discussed and reviewed, have changed their minds on critical matters.

The members of the drafting committee are to come from those supporting the conclusion reached at the fourth deliberation. The drafting committee prepares, first, a preliminary draft for written amendments and comments, then a draft for the first reading and finally a draft for the second reading. The first reading deliberation is the longest, lasting several days, sometimes more than a week. As the bench moves through the text, the deliberation involves amendments being accepted or rejected on the

---

[36] Costa Rica v Nicaragua at p. 178, para. 104.

spot or considered by the drafting committee over lunch or overnight, and generally the polishing of the text. All members of the Court, including those who intend to dissent, participate fully in the process. Those judges who intend to dissent or to write separately are to indicate that fact at the end of the first reading and to submit their drafts by a fixed date to enable the drafts to be taken into account by the drafting committee when it prepares its second draft.

That second reading draft, in particular the parts which have been substantively amended, is closely examined, in another lengthy series of meetings, and at the end of that process each member of the Court from the junior member to the President votes on the paragraphs of the dispositif, the decision. No abstention is allowed and since 1978 the votes of individual judges have been made public. The text of the judgment is then finalised as are the dissenting and separate opinions and declarations. The parties are advised of the date the judgment is to be delivered, and again the judges enter the Great Hall to the cry, 'La Cour'. The President reads the judgment, opinion or order of 'the Court', omitting the more formal sections, and the Registrar reads, in the other language, the operative part of the decision. That emphasis on the institution, as opposed to its members, comes through as well in the abandonment in 1950 of the reading by judges of their separate opinions; the Court records indicate that from 1958 the possibility of that happening had disappeared.

A judge and future President of the Court over thirty years ago, as the Cold War was ending, emphasised the link between the process of deliberation and the requirement in Article 9 of the Statute that in the body as a whole the representation of the main forms of civilisation and the principal legal systems of the world be assured. Its character as the world court was to be matched by its inclusive deliberative process, a process which also had to have a worldwide character. The practice, he concludes, 'lends to the Court's pronouncements a unique ecumenical authority in a world where a developing, general international law is most important – perhaps the most important – single vehicle of common action and understanding and where virtually any determination of a contentious point of international law must have a very considerable political, as well as legal, significance.'[37]

---

[37] R. Y. Jennings 'The Internal Practice of the International Court of Justice' *BYIL* Vol 59 (1988) 31–47, at 46.

The Court through its judgments may also be able to engage with the parties in terms of their ongoing relations. Unlike many litigants in other courts and tribunals, national and international, the parties, the States, will continue to live together on a single planet. The 1974 judgments in the Nuclear Testing cases provide one instance. The Court, having concluded that disputes no longer existed between the Applicants, on the one side, and the Respondent, on the other, saw no reason to allow the continuance of proceedings which it knows are bound to be fruitless – the needless continuance of litigation is an obstacle to international harmony when there is no longer a dispute.[38] And the Court may, if the circumstances allow, encourage the parties to take action in respect of matters associated with the dispute before it, even if outside its jurisdiction, as with its request to Croatia and Serbia in their *Genocide* case to continue with their cooperation in respect of the fate of missing persons.[39]

A final aspect of decision-making by the Court is the right of judges to deliver a separate opinion if the judgment does not represent their opinion. The 1920 Statute provided for dissenting opinions to judgments, practice allowed concurring opinions (recognised in the 1945 Statute) and both were attached to advisory opinions and orders. The right to dissent and to write separately may be seen as preferring the common law practice to the civilian, although one great early civilian member of the PCIJ, Max Huber, emphasised the value of dissents and separate opinions in this way:

... the possibility of publication [of dissenting opinions] was a guarantee against any subconscious intrusion of political considerations, and that judgments were more likely to be given in accordance with the real force of the arguments submitted.

The right of individual judges to publish their views was an essential condition, he declared, for the exercise of their liberty of conscience and their impartiality. That judge many years later underlined another, more personal, reason for allowing dissents. But for that freedom, he said, he would hardly have decided to accept office as a judge.[40] Another reason is

---

[38] *Nuclear Tests case (Australia v. France)*, ICJ Reports 1974, p. 253 at p. 257, para. 58; *Nuclear Tests case (New Zealand v. France)* ICJ Reports 1974, p. 457 at p. 477, para. 61.

[39] *Croatia v Serbia*, para. 523.

[40] See H. Lauterpacht, *The Development of International Law by the International Court (Stevens, London, 1958)* 64 and n 16, referred to with approval by Judge Jessup in the *South-West Africa* case, p. 325.

that a dissent may be, in the words of a great American judge, an appeal to the brooding spirit of the law, to the intelligence of a future day. And the assessment of a judge who had experienced both systems is that a single judgment must get the agreement of at least all in the majority so it tends to be no more than the highest common factor in their views.[41]

How is the right stated in Article 57 to be seen in practice? Does the practice comply with the requirements in Articles 7(ii) and (iv) of the Internal Judicial Practice Resolution? The answer to the second question is not available, given the secrecy of the deliberation, but, as has been remarked, the length and complexity of some opinions makes it unlikely that in their draft form they had any real impact on the preparation of the second reading draft.

My concern is about the scope of separate opinions and to some extent about their numbers and length. On numbers, the Court as of 17 March 2021 has given 327 decisions, a figure that includes substantive orders, to which Judges have appended 1439 opinions and declarations. Some opinions exceed by a large margin the length of the Court's decision: a matter which absorbed eight pages of the Court's unanimous decision in one case was the subject of a thirty-six-page discussion in a separate opinion which, in terms of the issue actually to be decided, did not depart from the Court's reasoning. I recall that Article 57 of the Statute permits a judge to write if the decision of the Court 'does not represent in whole or in part the opinion of that judge'. Thus judges may wish to indicate why they disagree with the decision or the reasoning or to provide additional or alternative reasons supporting the decision.

Who can disagree with these wise words, expressed jointly and succinctly by three former Presidents of the Court.

It could be desirable if those disagreeing with the Court would limit themselves to saying why rather than going on to explain at great length how they would themselves have decided the issues. Some opinions have been close to academic discourses rather than judicial pronouncements.[42]

Recall what King Solomon said 3,000 years ago – not everything that you think must you say; not everything you say must you write; and, most

---

[41] Lord Reid, 'The Judge as Law Maker' *JSPTL* Vol 12 (1972) 22, at 28–29 and see K. J. Keith, 'International Court of Justice: Primus inter Pares?' *Int Org L R* Vol 5 (2008) 16–17.
[42] Zimmermann and Tams, *Statute of the International Court of Justice*, para. 38.

important of all, not everything you write must you publish. A related and cautious word to the academic community is to recall that the dissenters have failed to persuade their colleagues, nine, ten, or even more of them. What the Court says and actually decides appears to me to be too often ignored in commentary, but recall that I was once a judge and not just of the ICJ!

V Conclusion

This chapter and the next are to consider in a more general way the relationship between the judges' or really the Court's role in settling the dispute before it and their and its role in stating and developing the law.[43] How too do they contribute to international peace and security? Article 38 of the Statute provides an important direction: the Court, whose function is to decide in accordance with international law such disputes as are submitted to it, shall apply .... That statement of function, one of the few substantive changes made to the Statute in 1945, is to be related to the preambular reference in the Charter to respect for the obligations arising from treaties and other sources of international law and to the purpose stated in Article 1(1) of the adjustment or settlement of international disputes and situations by peaceful means in conformity with the principles of justice and international law.

As paragraph (1)(d) of Article 38 recognises, the decisions of the Court, along with those of other courts, might have a part to play in the statement and development of the law, although as a 'subsidiary means'. That tag arose in part from the concern of the 1920 Committee of Jurists not to recognise that the rulings of a yet to be established Court had significant authority.[44]

Over their 100-year history, the two Courts have, in deciding the disputes submitted to them, clarified and developed international law. That may be seen, for instance, in the rulings of the PCIJ on treaty interpretation

---

[43] See D. Tladi, Chapter 3, 'The Role of the International Court of Justice in the Development of International Law.'

[44] *Proceedings of the Advisory Committee of Jurists*, pp. 332, 336, 344, 345, 584, 605, 620 and 635–636 (members of the committee demonstrating different views about the law-making power of courts and the role of publicists; the drafts at the time provided for the four 'sources' to be applied in sequence and, as in the present Statute, this reference to judicial decisions and scholarly opinion, as subsidiary sources, was the fourth and last in the list).

and state responsibility, rulings which have been adopted in the work of the International Law Commission and by States in the Vienna Convention on the Law of Treaties and in their practice and in rulings of the present Court. Early examples from decisions of the present Court appear in the Reparations, Reservations, Corfu Channel and Anglo-Norwegian Fisheries cases and more recently in the maritime delimitation cases, the *Bosnia v. Serbia Genocide* case and the *Pulp Mills* case. That list, incomplete as it is, recognises that, as in all legal systems, there will be unresolved issues of law which courts may have to resolve in deciding the dispute before them – did the United Nations have international personality; were reservations to multilateral human rights treaties allowed only if all the other parties consented; what was the extent of the right of innocent passage through territorial seas; how were territorial seas and fisheries zones to be set along a heavily serrated coast; given the failure of the UN conference on the law of the sea to state any standard, principle or rule for overlapping maritime zones (the 200 mile EEZ and the continental shelves), how was the Court to approach the task of delimitation; did the Convention on the Prevention and Prosecution of Genocide impose an obligation on States, and not just individuals, not to commit genocide; and were the parties to the Statute on the River Uruguay obliged, if there was a risk of significant transboundary harm from actions on their territory, to undertake an environmental impact assessment? Examples may also be given of the Court giving an evolutionary meaning to treaty language written in broad terms as in the Namibia opinion. But there are limits on the power of the Court to develop the law, as appear in the later substantive chapters. It made that clear in the case challenging Iceland's extension of its fisheries limits in 1972 to fifty miles. It could not, it said, anticipate the law before the legislature has laid it down.[45]

Further Reading

R. Higgins, 'A Comment on the Current Health of Advisory Opinions', in V. Lowe and M. Fitzmaurice (eds.), *Fifty Years of the International Court of Justice: Essays in Honour of Sir Robert Jennings* (Cambridge University Press, 1996), p. 567.

---

[45] *Fisheries Jurisdiction (United Kingdom v. Iceland)* Merits, ICJ Reports 1974, p. 3 at p. 25, para. 53 and *Fisheries Jurisdiction (Federal Republic of Germany v. Iceland)*, Merits, ICJ Reports 1974, p. 175 at p. 192 para. 45.

R. Jennings, 'The Internal Judicial Practice of the International Court of Justice' The *British Yearbook of International Law* Vol 59 (1988), pp. 31–47.

K. J. Keith, 'International Court of Justice: Reflections on the Electoral Process' The *Chinese Journal of International Law* Vol 9 (2010) pp. 49–80.

H. Lauterpacht, *The Development of International Law by the International Court* (Stevens & Sons, 1958).

R. McKenzie *et al.* (eds.), *Selecting International Judges: Principle, Process, and Politics* (Oxford University Press, 2010).

A. Sarvarian *et al.* (eds.), *Procedural Fairness in International Courts and Tribunals* (London: British Institute of International and Comparative Law, 2015).

O. Schachter, 'The Invisible College of International Lawyers' (1977) 72 *Northwestern University Law Review* 217–226.

3 The Role of the International Court of Justice in the Development of International Law

Dire Tladi

I Introduction

The International Court of Justice is unquestionably the pre-eminent international court in the international legal system – it is not for nothing that it is often referred to as the World Court.[1] Apex courts all over the world, even in legal systems where precedents do not formally constitute a source of law, have an immense impact on the development of the law.[2] This is certainly true of the International Court of Justice in international law.[3]

The function of the ICJ is to resolve disputes between parties.[4] It is not, at least not primarily, to develop rules of international law. Yet in practice, the Court has made 'a major contribution to the evolution of international law in the rapidly changing conditions' of modern times.[5] Many rules that international lawyers take for granted emerged or evolved from the jurisprudence of the Court. The idea that some obligations under international law are owed to the international community as a whole, *erga omnes*, the rule that States have a duty to prevent their territory from being used to cause harm to other States, the idea that unilateral acts of States can establish legal obligations, the notion that an international organisation

---

[1] See P.-M. Dupuy 'The Danger of Fragmentation or Unification of the International Legal System and the International Court of Justice', 31 *New York University Journal of International Law and Policy* (1999) 791, at 798, describing the ICJ as having a 'central role'.

[2] S. Rosenne 'International Court of Justice', *Max Planck Encyclopedia of Public International Law* (online 2006), para. 112 ('Contributing to the development of the law is the by-product of every "senior" court, and the ICJ is no exception.')

[3] L. Park 'The International Court and Rule-Making: Finding Effectiveness', 39 *University of Pennsylvania Journal of International Law* (2018) 1965, at 1074 *et seq*.

[4] See, Art. 38 of the Statute of the ICJ, describing the Court's function as being 'to decide in accordance with international law such disputes as are submitted to it'.

[5] Rosenne, 'International Court of Justice', at para. 112.

has legal personality distinct from that of the States that created it, as well as the rules of international law concerning the permissibility of reservations to multilateral treaties are just some examples of basic, uncontested rules of international law for whose existence the jurisprudence of the Court was a *sine qua non*.[6] The role of the Court in the development of international law has varied from laying the seeds for a new rule to refining the content and scope of existing rules. Perhaps even more significantly, the methodological rules on how substantive rules of international law, whether rules of customary international law or the peremptory status of existing rules of international law, are to be identified have developed mainly on the basis of the jurisprudence of the Court, or at least have been greatly influenced by it.

This chapter provides a brief description of the role of the Court in the development of international law. It begins in the next section by briefly outlining the doctrinal position concerning the Court's role in the development of international law. In the third section, the chapter juxtaposes the doctrine with the practice of the Court. Finally, some concluding remarks are offered.

II Doctrine

The function of the Court is primarily to resolve disputes between States. Making or developing international law is not a function, at least not a primary function, of the Court. Indeed, according to the Statute the 'decision of the Court has no binding force except as between the parties and in respect of that particular case.'[7] The effect of this provision is to exclude previous decisions as binding precedent – or put differently, to exclude

---

[6] The decisions from which these rules can be traced are *Case Concerning Barcelona Traction, Light and Power Company, Limited: New Application, Second Phase, ICJ Reports* 1970, p. 3 (some obligations are owed *erga omnes*); *The Corfu Channel case, ICJ Reports* 1949, p. 4 (States have a duty to prevent their territory from being used to cause harm to other States); *Nuclear Test Case (Australia v. France), ICJ Reports* 1974, p. 253; *Reparation for Injuries Suffered in the Service of the United Nations, Advisory Opinion, ICJ Reports* 1949, p. 174 (international legal personality of an international organisation); *Reservations to the Convention on the Prevention and Punishment of the Crime of Genocide, ICJ Reports* 1950, p. 15.

[7] Art 59 of the ICJ Statute.

stare decisis as a doctrine in international law.[8] Taken at face value, and on its own, this precludes the possibility of the Court 'making' or 'contributing to the development of' international law. Pierre Marie Dupuy observes, however, that in order for a court, any court, to settle a dispute between two or more parties – the principal function of the Court – it has to 'state the law' to be applied.[9] Yet 'stating the law' is not the same as developing or making the law. For Rosenne, the role of the Court in the making and development of international law is achieved 'in the nature of things, without any need for controversial theories of binding force of judicial precedents'.[10] The explanation that Rosenne puts forward is a rather practical one, namely 'the need for continuity and stability' in the Court's jurisprudence.[11] Yet, true though this is, even this only explains why the Court follows its own decisions; it does not explain the influence of those decisions on other actors, including States and other courts.

The ambiguity in the role of the Court in the development of international law – on the one hand the Statute excludes *stare decisis,* while, on the other hand, it is accepted that the Court has a central role in the development of international law – is reflected in Article 38 of the Statute which sets out the sources of law to be applied by the Court. Article 38(1)(a) – (c) identifies what might be referred to as the traditional sources of international law, i.e. treaties, customary international law and general principles. In Article 38(1)(d) is referenced, together with scholarly writings, 'judicial decisions' as 'subsidiary means for the determination of rules of law'. Needless to say, the term 'judicial decisions', includes decisions of the International Court of Justice, in addition to those of other courts, both national and international law. However, Article 38(1)(d) does not address the Article 59 preclusion of *stare decisis* and, for that reason, does not, without more, explain the significance of the Court's role in the development of international law. First, Article 38(1)(d) of the Statute, on its own terms, is subject to Article 59, thus leaving the proscription of *stare decisis* intact. Second, it includes two qualifiers that make it plain that decisions of the Court are not law or binding. The first qualifier is that Article 38(1)(d) refers to judicial decisions as 'subsidiary' – below the level

---

[8] See G. Acquaviva and F. Pocar, 'Stare decicis', in *Max Planck Encyclopedia of Public International Law* (2022).

[9] Dupuy, 'The Danger of Fragmentation', at 802.

[10] Rosenne, 'International Court of Justice', at para. 112.   [11] Ibid.

of law, and does not refer to them as sources of law. The second qualifier is that judicial decision are themselves not law but are merely 'means for the determination of rules of law'. Yet, even with Article 59 and the qualifiers in Article 38(1)(d), the Court's role in the development of international law can hardly be denied.

The tension – the explicit exclusion of *stare decisis*, on one hand, and on the other the reality of the Court's significant role in the development of international law – probably lies in the fact that law-making, and by extension the development of international law, is as a doctrinal matter, the purview of States. It is States that have the mandate to make law, whether through their practice and acceptance of that practice as law, or through the elaboration and adoption of treaties. Likewise, the development of law through the interpretation of treaties, or evolution of practice, remains the purview of States. Yet, at the same time, the Court is the principal judicial organ of the United Nations, empowered *to apply that law*. It would stand to reason that its determination of the content of the rules of law would be authoritative. If not, States would be free (as they sometimes do) after the adjudication of a dispute by the Court, to declare that the Court's decision was wrong in law and therefore refuse to comply. Since, under Article 59, States accept the binding force of judgments in disputes to which they are party, they must necessarily also accept the binding nature of the determination of the rules on which those judgments are based. In other words, it is difficult to separate the judicial function of settling disputes from the function of authoritatively stating the law.[12] The key issue is, thus, not merely that the Court states the law, but that it does so authoritatively.

In its recent work, the International Law Commission had acknowledged the special role of the Court in the identification of international law. In the Draft Conclusions on the Identification of Customary International Law adopted in 2018, the Commission identified the Court as a particularly important means for the identification of rules of customary international law.[13] The Commission explained singling out the Court on the basis, *inter alia*, of 'the significance of its case law and its particular position as the

---

[12] See, Dupuy, 'The Danger of Fragmentation', at 802 ('In other words, to settle a particular dispute, the judge must "state the law" to be applied ... this *jurisdictio* amounts, in some respect, to the exercise of a residual legislative function').

[13] Draft Conclusion 13 of the Draft Conclusions on the Identification of Customary International Law, *Report of the International Law Commission, Seventieth Session* (A/73/10) ('Decisions of international courts and tribunals, in particular of the International

only standing international court of general jurisdiction'.[14] The Commission adopts the same approach in its Draft Conclusions on Peremptory Norms of General International Law (*Jus Cogens*), adopted on first reading in 2019.[15] The explicit mention of the Court, according to the Commission, was because 'while the Court has been reluctant to pronounce on peremptory norms, its jurisprudence has left a mark on the development both of the general concept of peremptory norms and of particular peremptory norms'.[16] In both provisions, however, consisent with Article 38(1)(d) of the ICJ Statute, the Commission describes the Court's role as a subsidiary means for the determination of customary international law and the peremptory status of general norms of international law respectively. The decisions themselves, according to the Commission, are not law but are only means for the establishment of the law. The subsidiary nature of the decisions is reflected in how the Commission describes the relative weight to be accorded to the decisions:

The value of such decisions varies greatly, however, depending both on the quality of the reasoning (including primarily the extent to which it results from a thorough examination of evidence of an alleged general practice accepted as law) and on the reception of the decision, in particular by States ...[17]

This quoted extract serves to emphasise that, ultimately, international law is primarily made (and developed) by States. Thus, the extent to which decisions of the Court are to be taken as law falls to be determined by the extent to which they are based on State practice – that is the import of the description of the phrase 'quality of the reasoning' – and/or the extent to which such decisions are accepted subsequently by States – that is the import of the phrase 'the reception of the decision'. This doctrinal position would tend to reinforce the tension described above: while it is accepted

---

Court of Justice, concerning the existence and content of rules of customary international law are a subsidiary means for the determination of such rules').

[14] Ibid., para. 4 of commentary to Draft Conclusion 13.

[15] Draft Conclusion 9 of the Draft Conclusions on Peremptory Norms of General International Law (*Jus Cogens*), First Reading, *Report of the International Law Commission, Seventy-First Session* (A/74/10) ('Decisions of international courts and tribunals, in particular of the International Court of Justice, are a subsidiary means for determining the peremptory character of norms of general international law').

[16] Ibid., para. 4 of the commentary to Draft Conclusion 9.

[17] Para. 3 of commentary to Draft Conclusion 13 of the Draft Conclusions on Customary International Law.

that the Court has a significant role to play in the development of rules of international law, doctrinally it is States that make and develop the law, with Courts merely applying, and in the process stating, this State-made law.[18] This state of the doctrine applies both to decisions of the Court in contentious proceedings as well as to advisory opinions. If ultimately what matters is the reasoning in the decision and its reception by States, then it ought not to matter whether the reasoning was contained in a contentious or advisory proceeding.

The tension described has two elements. First, the general proposition that *stare decisis* is excluded under international law and that this significantly limits the role of the Court in the development of international law. The second element is that, notwithstanding this general proposition, the Court has played an important role in the development of international law. The discussion up to this point has focused on the first element, while the second element has merely been assumed based on some scholarly writing. It is to this second element that this chapter now turns.

III The Practice

The important role played by the Court in the development of international law is acknowledged in scholarly writings,[19] and whether one agrees that this *should* be so or not, it can hardly be denied as an empirical fact. In this section, three rules of law that illustrate the significant influence of the Court on the development of international law will be highlighted. The first rule concerns the place of *erga omnes* obligations in international law. The second area highlighted in this section concerns immunity *ratione personae*. Finally, this section will highlight the role of the Court in the development of the rules of international law concerning the use of force

---

[18] See also para. 1 of the commentary to Draft Conclusion 9 of the Draft Conclusions on Peremptory Norms of General International Law ('It is important to emphasize that the word "subsidiary" in this context is not meant to diminish the importance of such materials, but is rather aimed at expressing the idea that those materials facilitate the identification of "acceptance and recognition" but do not, themselves, constitute such acceptance and recognition. Draft conclusion 9 concerns such other materials').

[19] See, e.g., Park, 'The International Court and Rule-Making'; Rosenne, 'International Court of Justice'.

against non-State actors. There are, of course, other rules[20] and the rules addressed in this section were selected only for illustrative purposes.

Before addressing these more substantive areas of international law, it is useful to describe the immense influence of the Court in the more methodological aspects of the identification of rules of international law. In many ways, these more methodological aspects may perhaps be even more powerful than the examples pertaining to specific rules, since they are more broadly applicable to international law as a whole and are more systemic. The Court's immense influence on the methodological rules of international law can be illustrated by reference to the rules on the identification of customary international law.[21] The identification of customary international law has traditionally been said to require evidence of two elements, namely State practice and *opinio juris*. These requirements flow from the wording of Article 38(1)(b) of the Statute of the Court, which describes custom as 'evidence of State of general practice accepted as law'.

Yet, while this two-element approach has a strong pedigree in international law, in recent years it has come under pressure with arguments that it be abandoned.[22] While some have argued for emphasis on State practice at the expense of *opinio juris*, others have sought to emphasise *opinio juris* at the expense of State practice.[23] These arguments are certainly strengthened by the fact that courts, including the International Court of Justice itself, have not always been faithful to the two-element

---

[20] In addition to the examples cited in footnote 6, the notion that Articles 1 and 3 of the 1949 Geneva Conventions are reflective of customary international law was put forward by the Court in *Military and Paramilitary Activities in and against Nicaragua (Nicaragua v. United States of America), Merits, ICJ Reports* 1986, p. 14, at paras. 217 *et seq.* See for brief discussion, Park, 'The International Court and Rule-Making', at 1075; the customary international law status of the policy of *uti possidetis*, now generally accepted, was initially acknowledged in *Case Concerning the Frontier Dispute (Burkina Faso/Mali), ICJ Reports* 1986, p. 554, especially at para. 20; the rule that there is a duty to perform an impact assessment in respect of activities that could have an extraterritorial impact was laid down in *Pulp Mills on the River Uruguay (Argentina v. Uruguay), ICJ Reports* 2010, p. 14, at para. 204.

[21] See generally the Draft Conclusions on Customary International Law, especially the commentaries to Draft Conclusions 2 and 3, which are based almost entirely on the jurisprudence of the Court.

[22] See for discussion of these M. Wood 'The present position within the ILC on the topic "Identification of customary international law": in Partial Response to Sienho Yee, Report on the ILC Project on "Identification of Customary International Law"', 15 *Chinese Journal of International Law* (2016) 3, at 8.

[23] Ibid.

approach.[24] Here one can refer to the judicial decision-inspired, but much needed, rule that environmental impacts assessments are required under customary international law for acts that may have adverse transboundary impacts. In the first case, *Pulp Mills on the River Uruguay*, the Court decided without any assessment whatsoever of practice or *opinio juris*, that there was a rule of international law requiring environmental impact assessments for activities likely to have transboundary impact. The Court simply stated that environmental impact assessment is 'a practice, which in recent years has gained so much acceptance among States that it may now be considered a requirement under general international law'.[25] Yet no practice whatsoever, is offered for this conclusion. This view has been relied upon subsequently, including by the International Tribunal for the Law of the Sea.[26] Another example, discussed more below, in the Court's inapplication of the two-element approach is the *Arrest Warrant* case.[27] There the Court determines that Ministers for Foreign Affairs are entitled to the same type of immunities as heads of State without producing a single evidence of practice or *opinion juris*.[28] Even the *Military and Paramilitary Activities* case, which in some standard textbooks on international law, is put forward as an example of the two-requirement, does not apply the methodology.[29] The Court begins by reaffirming the two-element rule, stating that the Article 38(1)(b)'s reference to 'practice as accepted as a law', requires both a general practice and *opinio juris*.[30] Yet, in what follows, while the Court provides a lot of evidence in the form of several resolutions, it never makes clear what evidence is being advanced as practice and what is *opinio juris* – the essence of the two-element rule.[31]

Yet, even with this inconsistent application of the two-element approach, it has remained firmly entrenched as the methodology by which the rules of customary international law are to be determined. This is, in large part, because the International Court of Justice, even though

---

[24] See Tladi, ILC Summary Records A/CN.4/SR.3182. See also Murase, ILC Summary Records A/CN.4/SR.3181, para. 16, para. 31.

[25] *Pulp Mills on the River Uruguay*, at para. 204.

[26] *Responsibilities and Obligations of States Sponsoring Persons and Entities with Respect to Activities in the Area*, Advisory Opinion of 11 February 2011, at para. 147–148.

[27] *Case Concerning the Arrest Warrant of 11 April 2000 (Democratic Republic of Congo v. Belgium), ICJ Reports* 2000, p. 3.

[28] Ibid., at para. 51.   [29] See *Military and Paramilitary Activities* case.

[30] Ibid., at para. 184.   [31] See, ibid., at paras. 183 *et seq.*

inconsistent in its adherence to the two-element approach, has been consistent in the affirmation of that approach. It has thus been unsurprising that the International Law Commission, in its Draft Conclusions on the Identification of Customary International Law, has sought to emphasise the two-element approach to the identification of customary international law. Draft Conclusion 2 of the ILC Draft is titled 'Two Constituent Elements', and provides that to determine the existence of a rule of customary international law, it is necessary to show that 'there is a general practice that is accepted as law (*opinio juris*)'.[32] The general commentary introducing that part of the Draft Conclusions is even more explicit. It states that that 'determining a rule of customary international law requires establishing the existence of two constituent elements', namely 'a general practice, and acceptance of that practice as law (*opinio juris*)'.[33] It continues that this 'requires a careful analysis of the evidence for each element'.[34]

How, given the inconsistency in the application of the two-element rule, it is a fair question to ask on what basis the International Law Commission could be so bold as to emphatically reaffirm the two-element rule. The answer is because the Commission relied principally on the jurisprudence of the International Court of Justice. Members of the Commission generally supported the idea that priority should be given to the jurisprudence of the Court. Mr Caflisch, for example, noted that '[w]hile in principle there was no hierarchy among the various' international courts and tribunals 'that engaged in the identification of customary international law', it was clear to him 'that the judgments of the International Court of Justice enjoyed particular prestige as texts issued by the main judicial organ of the United Nations'.[35] Of course, as described above, the Court itself has not rigorously applied the two element approach. However, while not rigorously applying the two-element approach, it has consistently shown its commitment to the approach.[36]

The role of the Court in the emergence and entrenchment of the notion of *erga omnes* obligations cannot be overemphasised. In general terms,

---

[32] See Draft Conclusion 2 of the Draft Conclusions on Customary International Law.
[33] Ibid., General Commentary to Part II. See also para. 1 of the Commentary to Draft Conclusion 2.
[34] Ibid.   [35] See Caflisch, ILC Summary Records (A/CN.4/3182), at para. 40.
[36] It is unnecessary to repeat all the decisions of the Court in which the two-element approach is referred, but reference can be made to footnote 670 to 674.

under international law the responsibility of a State can be invoked only by a State whose rights are breached, and invoked only against the State responsible for the unlawful act.[37] Yet, in 1960, Ethiopia and Liberia, States not directly affected by South Africa's Apartheid policies, instituted proceedings against South Africa on the basis that its application of the policy of Apartheid in Namibia (then known as South-West Africa) was in violation of the sacred trust on which its mandate over the territory of South-West Africa was based.[38] It was submitted by Ethiopia and Liberia that the application of Apartheid to Namibia did not promote 'the material and moral well-being and the social progress of the inhabitants of the territory', and was therefore in violation of the sacred trust.[39] In its objections to the institution of proceedings, South Africa contended that there was no dispute between it, on the one hand, and Ethiopia and Liberia, on the other hand, since the disagreement in question 'did not affect any material interests of the Applicant States or their nationals'.[40] Without relying on *erga omnes*, the Court rejected South Africa's objection. Yet, in the merits phase in 1966, the Court returned to the traditional position, i.e. that a State can only invoke the responsibility of another State for an internationally wrongful act if its own rights have been breached. The Court noted, in 1966, that neither Ethiopia nor Liberia had 'established any legal right or interest appertaining to them in the subject-matter of the' claim against South Africa,[41] essentially reversing its decision in the preliminary phase of the proceedings.[42] While this decision has been

---

[37] *Phosphates in Morocco,* Judgment, 1938, P.C.I.J., Series A/B, No. 74, p. 10, at 28 ('This act being attributable to the State and described as contrary to the treaty right of another State, international responsibility would be established immediately as between the two States'). See also *Reparation for Injuries Suffered in the Service of the United Nations,* at 181–182 ('The first is that the defendant State has broken an obligation towards the national State in respect of its nationals. The second is that *only the party to whom an international obligation is due can bring a claim in respect of its breach*') (emphasis added).

[38] See *South-West Africa Cases (Ethiopia* v. *South Africa; Liberia* v. *South Africa),* Application Instituting Proceedings by the Government of Ethiopia (1966), *ICJ Pleadings, Oral Arguments, Documents,* Vol I 1966, at 4; and also Application Instituting Proceedings by the Government of Liberia, which, for the most part, reproduces the Ethiopia Application, with the word 'Liberia' inserted in the place of 'Ethiopia'.

[39] Ibid.   [40] Ibid.

[41] *South-West Africa cases (Ethiopia* v. *South Africa; Liberia* v. *South Africa), ICJ Reports* 1966, p. 6, at 51.

[42] *South-West Africa cases (Ethiopia* v. *South Africa; Liberia* v. *South Africa), ICJ Reports* 1962, p. 319.

criticised from a normative perspective,[43] it was probably justifiable from a purely positive law perspective, that is, State responsibility can only be invoked by a State whose rights were violated by the wrongful act.

More than a decade after the merits phase of the *South-West Africa* cases, and having suffered severe criticism for that decision, the Court in *Barcelona Traction,* came up with the famous distinction between obligations *inter partes* and obligations *erga omnes.*[44] It determined that some norms of international law, such as the right to self-determination and the prohibition of genocide, amongst others, had an obligations *erga omnes* character, permitting them to be enforced by States not directly harmed by them.[45] In this decision, the Court essentially makes amends for its normatively suspect decision in the 1966 *South-West Africa* cases.

While the Court's conclusion in *Barcelona Traction* is (normatively) justifiable, the Court offered not a single evidence of practice to support the distinction it put forward. This distinction, which when put forward by the Court, was not based on any identified evidence of State practice, is now generally accepted, unquestionably, as part of international law.[46] It has formed the basis of a line of jurisprudence that has had a significant effect on the development of international law.[47] The decision has been

[43] See L. Gross 'Conclusions' in L. Gross (ed.) *The Future of the International Court of Justice* (1976), at 747. See also J. Dugard and R. Elphick 'International Adjudication' in J. Dugard, M. du Plessis, T. Maluwa and D. Tladi (eds.) *Dugard's International Law: A South African Perspective* (2018), at 683–684, describing the judgment as 'unwarranted'. See further, J. Allain 'Decolonisation as the Source of Concepts of *Jus Cogens* and Obligations *Erga Omnes*', *Ethiopian Yearbook of International Law* (2016) 35, at 42. See also D. Tladi 'The International Court of Justice and South Africa' in Achilles Schodas *Handbook on the International Court of Justice* (forthcoming).

[44] *Barcelona Traction*, at para. 33-35.

[45] Ibid. See for discussion M. M. Bradley '*Jus Cogens*' Preferred Sister: Obligations *Erga Omnes* and the International Court of Justice: Fifty Years after the *Barcelona Traction* Case' in D. Tladi (ed.) *Peremptory Norms of General international Law* (Jus Cogens): *Disputations and Disquisitions* (Brill, 2021).

[46] See, e.g., Art. 48(1)(b) of the Articles on the Responsibility of States for Internationally Wrongful Acts, *Yearbook of the International Law Commission*, 2001, vol. II, Part Two; Draft Conclusion 17 of the Draft Conclusions on Peremptory Norms. See also generally *Legal Consequences of the Separation of the Chagos Archipelago from Mauritius in 1965*, Advisory Opinion, *ICJ Reports* 2019, p. 95. See also F. Martin, 'Delineating a Hierarchical Outline of International Law Sources and Norms', 65 *Saskatchewan Law Review* (2002) 335; S. Villalpando, *L'émergence de la communauté internationale dans de la Responsabilité des États* (2005), at 106.

[47] See for discussion Bradley, '*Jus Cogens*' Preferred Sister'.

followed in *East Timor*[48] and more recently in Gambia v Myanmar.[49] More importantly, these decisions have formed the bedrock for the emergence and subsequent entrenchment of the concept of *erga omnes* international law. In particular, the International Law Commission, in its Draft Articles on State Responsibility developed this notion further,[50] including not only the right of other States to invoke responsibility,[51] but also the duty to cooperate to bring to an end situations created by breaches of *jus cogens*, the duty to not recognise situations created by such breaches and the duty not to assist in the maintenance of such situations.[52] The latter obligations, flowing from the *erga omnes* nature of certain obligations were arrived at by the Commission on the basis, inter alia, of the Court's statement in *Namibia* opinion that 'the declaration of the illegality of South Africa's presence in Namibia [was] opposable to all States in the sense of barring *erga omnes* the legality of a situation which is maintained in violation of international law'.[53] At any rate, the notion that there are some obligations which are owed to the international community as a whole, *erga omnes*, is now well accepted in international law. The driver of the emergence and entrenchment of this concept has been the International Court of Justice.

Barcelona Traction, and the ensuing jurisprudence of the Court on obligations *erga omnes*, has had the effect of advancing more a humanitarian side of international law. In contrast, the *Arrest Warrant case*,[54] which has also had an immense impact on the development of international law, has had the effect of solidifying the more State-centric aspects of international law – those aspects emphasising the stability of international relations. In that case, the Court had to answer two interrelated questions. First, whether Ministers for Foreign Affairs were entitled to immunity *ratione personae*, and second, if so, whether there

---

[48] *Case Concerning East Timor (Portugal v. Australia), ICJ Reports* 1995, p. 90.

[49] *Legal Consequences of the Separation of the Gambia v Myanmar Archipelago from Mauritius in 1965,* Advisory Opinion, *ICJ Reports* 2019, p. 95.

[50] ILC 2001 Articles on the Responsibility of States for Internationally Wrong Acts, *Report of the UN International Law Commission,* Fifty-Third Session, General Assembly Official Records (A/56/10).

[51] Ibid. at Art. 48.   [52] Ibid. at Art. 41.

[53] *Legal Consequences for States of the Continued Presence of South Africa in Namibia (South-West Africa) notwithstanding Security Council Resolution 276 (1970), ICJ Reports* 1971, p. 16, at para. 126.

[54] *Case Concerning the Arrest Warrant.*

are exceptions to this type of immunity for serious crimes such as crimes against humanity and genocide. The Court answered the first question in the affirmative, i.e. Ministers for Foreign Affairs were entitled to immunity *ratione personae*, while determining that there were no exceptions to this rule. Yet, as was the case with the introduction of *erga omnes* obligation in *Barcelona Traction*, the Court did not provide any practice *whatsoever* in support of the conclusion that Ministers for Foreign Affairs are entitled to immunity *ratione personae*,[55] relying instead on deductions based on the functions of the Foreign Minister and comparisons with the Heads of State.[56] The Court states that 'to determine the extent of these immunities', it must 'consider the nature of the functions exercised by a Minister for Foreign Affairs'.[57] It noted that a Minister for Foreign Affairs 'is in charge of his or her Government's diplomatic activities and generally acts as its representative in international negotiations and intergovernmental meetings', noting that 'Ambassadors and other diplomatic agents carry out their duties under his or her authority' and that '[h]is or her acts may bind the State represented ... [and that] simply by virtue of that office, has full powers to act on behalf of the State'.[58] This was the basis of the rather far-reaching conclusion that Ministers for Foreign Affairs enjoy immunity *ratione personae*. In contrast, in response to the second question, that is, whether there were exceptions to the rule on immunity *ratione personae*, the Court does engage in a rigorous assessment of practice.[59] On the basis of that practice, the Court comes to the conclusion that there are no exceptions to the rules of international law on immunities.

The *Arrest Warrant* case thus stood for solidifying the respect for immunities by first, expanding the scope of immunity *ratione personae*, and second providing that there are no exceptions to that immunity. Moreover, subsequent cases in the Court's jurisprudence have been relatively consistent in the protection of the institution of immunities. In the *Jurisdictional Immunities of the State* case, the Court famously decided that there was no conflict between *jus cogens* and the rules on immunities,

---

[55] For its conclusion that there were no exceptions to immunity ratione personae, the Court did engage in a rather detailed analysis of State practice and *opinio juris*. *Case Concerning the Arrest Warrant*, at paras. 58 *et seq*.

[56] *Case Concerning the Arrest Warrant*, at para. 53.   [57] Ibid.   [58] Ibid.

[59] Ibid., at para. 56 *et seq*.

stating that they operate on different levels.[60] Even *Certain Questions of Mutual Assistance in Criminal Matters*,[61] in which the Court had found that there had not been a violation of immunities, the Court's decision serves to entrench the importance of immunity. There, the Court found that there had not been a violation of immunities because the head of State was not subjected to a 'constraining act of authority'.[62] Still, the Court recognised the absolute character of immunity *ratione personae*. This jurisprudence of the Court has been significant for the development of international law on immunities.[63] The International Law Commission's work on the Immunity of Officials from Foreign Criminal Jurisdiction has, at least in respect of immunity *ratione personae*, been based on the *Arrest Warrant* case findings concerning persons covered by immunity *ratione personae* and the rules on exceptions.[64]

It is true that the question of exceptions to immunity *ratione personae* has been contentious largely as a result of the now passé Al Bashir saga.[65]

---

[60] See, e.g., *Jurisdictional Immunities of the State (Germany v. Italy: Greece intervening)*, ICJ Reports 2012, p. 99.

[61] *Case Concerning Certain Questions of Mutual Assistance in Criminal Matters*, ICJ Reports 2008, p. 177.

[62] Ibid. at paras. 170 and 171.

[63] For more comprehensive discussion of this topic, see R O'Keefe, Chapter 19, Jurisdictional Immunities.

[64] On persons covered, see Draft Article 3 of the Draft Articles on Immunity of State Officials from Foreign Criminal Jurisdiction, *Report of the International Law Commission, Sixty-Ninth Session* (A/72/10) ('Heads of State, Heads of Government and Ministers for Foreign Affairs enjoy immunity ratione personae from the exercise of foreign criminal jurisdiction.') On exceptions, see Draft Article 7, which, while permitting exceptions to immunity *ratione materiae*, does not do the same for immunity *ratione personae*. See especially para. 2 of commentary to Draft Article 7 ('As Draft Article 7 refers solely to immunity from jurisdiction *ratione materiae*, it is included in Part Three of the draft articles and does not apply in respect of immunity from jurisdiction *ratione personae* . . .'). See also *Minister of Justice and Constitutional Development and Others* v. *Southern African Litigation Centre and Others* 2016 (4) BCLR 487 (SCA), where the South African Supreme Court of Appeal relied heavily on the *Arrest Warrant* case conclusion that there were, under customary international law, no exceptions to the rules on immunity from foreign criminal jurisdiction.

[65] See, e.g., *Case of the Prosecutor* v. *Omar Hassan Ahmad Al-Bashir, Judgment in the Jordan Referral re Al-Bashir Appeal*, ICC-02/05-01/09 OA2. See also D. Akande and S. Shah 'Immunities of State Officials, International Crimes and Foreign Domestic Courts', 21 *European Journal of International Law* (2010) 815; D. Akande 'The Legal Nature of the Security Council Referrals to the ICC and its Impact on Al Bashir's Immunity', 7 *Journal of International Criminal Justice* (2009) 333; D. Tladi 'Immunity in the Era of "Criminalisation": The African Union, the ICC and International Law', 58 *Japanese*

Yet even this aspect does not detract from the influence that the *Arrest Warrant* case has brought about. The debate over the duty to arrest and surrender Al Bashir when he was head of State had not centred on whether the *Arrest Warrant* case was correct in its statement that there were no exceptions to immunity. Put differently, those arguing that there was a duty to arrest and surrender Al Bashir did not question the consistency of *Arrest Warrant* with international law. Rather, they had sought to show that the *Arrest Warrant* case excluded from its scope cases concerning international courts, such as the case of Mr Al Bashir.[66] Thus, notwithstanding the doubts that may be expressed about whether the Court's decision, at the time it was handed down, was a correct reflection of law, its status as an accurate reflection of law today can hardly be questioned.

The Court's decisions in *Barcelona Traction* and *Arrest Warrant* were not based on existing rules – at best, the Court did not explain clearly, the basis of its conclusions in those decisions. The rules in the respective cases, however, are today accepted as customary international law *because* of the decisions of the Court. The decisions in *Barcelona Traction* and *Arrest Warrant* had, therefore, an immense impact on the development of international law. This has occurred not because of the existence, at the time of the decisions, of State practice and *opinio juris,* but rather because of the *ex post facto* acceptance of the decisions by the international community of States.[67] This is possible *only* because of the esteem in which the Court is held resulting in the authority of its decisions (even when the reasoning is somewhat suspect). States (and other actors, including other international courts) generally believe that decisions of the Court reflect rules of international law, and therefore act consistently with them – a self-fulfilling prophesy of sorts. The Court's influence on the development of international law is, for better or worse, even greater when its decisions are

---

Yearbook of International Law (2015) 17; D. Tladi, 'Of Heroes and Villains, Angels and Demons: The ICC-AU Tension Revisited', 60 *German Yearbook of International Law* (2017) 43, 55 *et seq.*

[66] See *Arrest Warrant* case, at para. 61, where the Court stated that a person with immunity ratione personae may be subject 'to criminal proceedings before certain international criminal courts, where they have jurisdiction'.

[67] As noted above, there have been other rules of international law that have developed in the same way. See for examples, footnotes 6, 20 and 37.

based on the work of some other entity that is also held in high esteem, such as the International Law Commission.[68]

While *Barcelona Traction* and *Arrest Warrant* are examples of judgments of the Court which galvanised State practice and thus contributed to the development of international law, the jurisprudence of the Court on the use of force against non-State actors has influenced the development of law in a slightly different way. In the *Military and Paramilitary Activities* case, the Court held that the right to use force in response to an attack from a non-State actor is permissible only if the non-State actors in question were sent by or acting on behalf of a State, that is, the State in whose territory the self-defence measures are to be taken must have exercised effective control over the non-State actors in question.[69] This view was confirmed by the Court in subsequent decisions.[70] Unlike *Barcelona Traction* and *Arrest Warrant*, this jurisprudence was based on State practice in the form of treaty practice and resolutions of General Assembly.[71] Furthermore, unlike the examples in *Barcelona Traction* and *Arrest Warrant*, the Court's jurisprudence concerning the use of force in self-defence against non-State actors has, at least in recent times, been

---

[68] See for discussion D. Tladi 'The Fate of the Draft Articles on State Responsibility: Act Soon or Face the Further Erosion of the Role of States in the International Law-Making Process', *Anuário Português de Direito Internacional* (2013) 87, at 89 to 90 in which the Court's determination that certain rules contained in the ILC's Articles on State Responsibility are customary international law is assessed. In the article, the following observation is made: 'The law-making process can be crudely described as follows: The Commission speaks through the Articles, the Court and academics endorse the work of the Commission and then *voila*, you have rules of customary international law. The role of the State in this process is invisible, if not non-existent' (at 91).

[69] *Military and Paramilitary Activities* case, at para. 195 ('There appears now to be general agreement on the nature of the acts which can be treated as constituting armed attacks. In particular, it may be considered to be agreed that an armed attack must be understood as including not merely action by regular armed forces across an international border, but also "the sending by or on behalf of a State of armed bands, groups, irregulars or mercenaries, which carry out acts of armed force against another State of such gravity as to amount to" (inter alia) an actual armed attack conducted by regular forces, "or its substantial involvement therein"').

[70] *Case Concerning Oil Platforms (Islamic Republic of Iran v. United States of America)*, ICJ *Reports* 2003, p. 161, at para. 51; *Case Concerning the Armed Activities in the Territory of the Congo (Democratic Republic of Congo v. Uganda)*, ICJ *Reports* 2005, p. 168, at para. 146; *Legal Consequences of the Construction of a Wall in the Occupied Palestinian Territory*, ICJ *Reports* 2004, p. 136, at para. 139.

[71] *Military and Paramilitary Activities* case, paras. 195–196.

questioned in some quarters.[72] The impact of the Court's jurisprudence on the development of international law has, therefore, not been in the form of putting forward a rule which was subsequently followed and solidified into a rule of customary international law. Rather, the Court's jurisprudence has been used to ward off attempts to amend the existing rule (some would say undermine) and put in place a system that is more permissive of the use of force.[73]

The focus in this section has been on the Court's contribution to the development of customary international law. There are, however, other ways through which decisions of the Court contribute to the development of international law which space did not permit to be considered. These include the direct influence on law-making in the sense that the conclusions reached by the Court are incorporated into treaties.[74] A more indirect way that the Court has had influence on the development of international law, not discussed in this chapter, is the influence of the Court on the work of the International Law Commission, which itself has a significant influence on the development of international law.

IV Conclusion

International law remains State-made and State-developed law. Courts, including the International Court of Justice, do not formally have a role in the development of international law. The role of the Court is to settle disputes between States and to do so on the basis of State-made and State-developed law. Yet, though without a formal mandate to develop international law, the Court has had an immense impact on the development of international law. Without the formal mandate to develop the law, the Court's contribution to the development of international law is dependent

---

[72] For an accessible account of the debate see M. E. O'Connell, C. Tams and D. Tladi *Max Planck Trialogues on the Law of War and Peace (Volume 1): Self-Defence against Non-State Actors* (2019). See also A Chehtman, Chapter 19, The Use of Force at the International Court of Justice.

[73] For the author's most recent views on this see D. Tladi 'The Extraterritorial Use of Force against Non-State Actors' 418 *Collected Courses of the Hague Academy of International law* (2021).

[74] See, e.g., *Reservations to the Genocide Convention* Advisory Opinion, on which Article 19 of the Vienna Convention on the Law of Treaties is based.

on the respect it attracts from States and the esteem with which it is held. The decisions analysed in the chapter, though not comprehensive, are representative of a general trend, namely that the determination by the Court of the existence of a rule, serves as the impetus of the generation of State practice consistent with the Court's decision, either confirming the existence of the rule or creating a new rule. What can hardly be denied, however, is that the Court has an important role to play in the development of international law.

Further Reading

Frulli, Michaela '"Time Will Tell Who Just Fell and Who's Been Left Behind": On the Clash between the International Court of Justice and the Italian Constitutional Court' 14 *Journal of International Criminal Justice* (2016) 587.

Hernandez, Gleider *The International Court of Justice and the Judicial Function* (Oxford, 2014).

Mistry, Hemi '"The Different Sets of Ideas at the Back of our Heads": Dissent and Authority at the International Court of Justice' 32 *Leiden Journal of International Law* (2019) 293.

Nouwen, Sarah M. H. 'Return to Sender: Let the International Court of Justice Justify or Qualify International-Criminal-Court Exceptionalism Regarding Personal Immunities' 78 *Cambridge Law Journal* (2019) 596.

Nucup, Neil B. 'Infallible or Final? Revisiting the Legitimacy of the International Court of Justice as the "Invisible" International Supreme Court' 18 *The Law and Practice of International Courts and Tribunals* (2019) 145.

Park, Leo 'The International Court and Rule-Making: Finding Effectiveness' 39 *University of Pennsylvania Journal of International Law* (2018) 1965.

Rosenne, Shabtai 'International Court of Justice' *Max Planck Encyclopedia of Public International Law* (online 2006).

Tams, Christian and James Sloan (eds.) *The Development of International Law by the International Court of Justice* (Oxford, 2013).

4 The Institutional Context of the International Court of Justice

Tom Ginsburg

I Introduction

Institutional analysis is an approach drawn from the social sciences that examines the ways in which an organisation's internal structures and external environment shape outcomes. There are many different kinds of institutionalism, but all have in common an emphasis on examining structures, as opposed to, say, the particular individuals who inhabit institutions, or the role of ideology at a macro level.[1] Institutional analysis has been productively applied to courts and invites two related inquiries: What is the court's institutional design, and what is its institutional environment?

Applying this approach to the International Court of Justice ('ICJ' or 'Court') requires identification of the relevant actors that shape the Court's operating environment, as well as the ways in which they interact with the ICJ. It also requires an examination of formal and informal rules, both inside and outside the ICJ, that frame these interactions. The attractiveness of any particular judicial institution, including the ICJ, will depend on the quality of the service it provides and the other options available. The former is in part a product of its institutional design, while the latter is part of the institutional environment.

Thanks to Marie Beudels and Arunima Bhattacharjee for research assistance.

[1] J. G. March and J. P. Olsen, *Rediscovering Institutions* (Free Press, 1989); P. J. Dimaggio and W. W. Powell (eds.), *The New Institutionalism in Organizational Analysis* (University of Chicago Press, 1991); C. W. Clayton and H. Gillman (eds.), *Supreme Court Decision-Making: New Institutionalist Approaches* (University of Chicago Press, 1999); D. C. North, *Institutions, Institutional Change and Economic Performance* (Cambridge University Press, 1990).

The formal institutional structures of the ICJ flow from the United Nations Charter ('Charter') and the Statute of the Court ('Statute').[2] These documents establish the Court and its relationships with other bodies. Neither has ever been amended, though there has been some informal evolution of the structures over time.

A good place to start is the statement in Article 94 of the Charter, repeated in Article 1 of the Statute, that the ICJ is the 'principal judicial organ of the United Nations'. This tells us, first of all, that the ICJ is a *court*. This point may seem so obvious as to not even bear mentioning, but courts have their own institutional characteristics and distinctive modes of operating. As a judicial organ, the Court's job is to adjudicate as well as to provide authoritative interpretations of law, including under Articles 65–68 of the Statute, which allow for advisory opinions.

Second, the ICJ is an *international* court. Its primary jurisdiction is over States and their disputes. This means that States will play an important role in determining the ICJ's workload and effectiveness.[3] States decide whether to file cases, whether to comply with decisions, and whether to act in accordance with the rules pronounced by the Court. In this sense, States are both a primary audience for the court and also its clients.

Third, the Court is an organ of the United Nations ('UN'). This tells us that the UN and its organs form a major part of the ICJ's institutional environment. The UN is not the only organisation with which the Court interacts, but it plays an important role in selecting judges, providing funding, bringing requests for advisory opinions, and, potentially, enforcing decisions. The relationship with the machinery of the UN conditions the performance and possibilities of the ICJ.

This chapter will examine each of these points in turn. One of the themes that emerges from the analysis in each area is the gap between the formal institutional structures and the actual operation of the Court. The formal rules matter a good deal, but they do not explain everything about the way the Court works. In this sense, the Court has had to adapt to its environment.

---

[2] United Nations, *Charter of the United Nations*, October 24, 1945, 1 UNTS XVI, available at www.refworld.org/docid/3ae6b3930.html [accessed March 17, 2020]; United Nations, *Statute of the International Court of Justice*, April 18, 1946, available at www.refworld .org/docid/3deb4b9c0.html [accessed March 17, 2020].

[3] Y. Shany, *Assessing the Effectiveness of International Courts* (Oxford University Press, 2014); J. E. Donoghue, 'The Effectiveness of the International Court of Justice', 108 *American Society of International Law Proceedings* (2014) 114–118.

II The ICJ as a Court: Adjudication, Consent, and Law-Making

As institutions, courts have distinctive features and qualities, driven by what Shapiro calls their 'social functions'.[4] These functions include, most obviously, the resolution of conflict, but also social control – the application of a set of norms to parties – and the making of law. Beyond these, Giladi and Shany identify other goals of the ICJ, including regime support for the UN, for example, through exercise of the advisory jurisdiction over internal matters; regime legitimation; and the compliance of States with primary international legal norms, in the shadow of dispute resolution.[5] One cannot, Shany emphasises, measure the effectiveness of a court simply by looking at the cases that come before it: One must also consider cases that do not arise because of the court's clarification of norms.[6]

We focus on dispute resolution and law-making as the core functions. It is worth noting that the former is squarely rooted in the Charter and Statute; the latter is not at all.

A Dispute Resolution

When two parties, be they individuals, companies, or States, have disputes, they will turn to a third party seeking help to resolve the problem. As Shapiro points out, a court is only one among many types of third parties that disputants might turn to. On the international plane, States have an array of options to fulfil their obligation under Article 33 of the Charter to seek peaceful resolution of disputes. These include arbitration (either ad hoc or through the Permanent Court of International Arbitration), mediation by regional organisations or individual leaders, use of good offices, and others. Any court, including the ICJ, thus 'competes' for business with other modes of dispute resolution. The fact that there are other options for

---

[4] M. Shapiro, *Courts* (University of Chicago Press, 1981).

[5] R. Giladi and Y. Shany, 'The International Court of Justice', in Y. Shany (ed.), *Assessing the Effectiveness of International Courts* (Oxford University Press, 2014). See also R. Giladi and Y. Shany, Chapter 5, this volume.

[6] Shany, *Assessing the Effectiveness of International Courts*, chapter 3; see also T. Squatrito, O. R. Young, A. Føllesdal, and G. Ulfstein (eds.), 'A Framework for Evaluating the Performance of International Courts and Tribunals', in *The Performance of International Courts and Tribunals* (Cambridge University Press, 2018).

dispute resolution means that only a subset of disputes will ever be brought before any court for formal resolution.[7]

A critical feature of the ICJ's institutional design is the importance of consent to jurisdiction. When parties consent to the jurisdiction of a court, they are more likely to find its actions legitimate and obey its orders. In contrast, when one of the parties does not want to be before the court (as occurs in, say, criminal law), compliance must be coerced. The distinctive feature of the international environment is that the ICJ has no direct means of coercing parties to participate in its proceedings or comply with its judgments. It is true that Article 33 of the Charter allows the Security Council to call upon parties to settle disputes by particular means, so that it could, as per Article 36(3) of the Charter, recommend that parties go before the Court. However, this tool has only been used once by the Security Council, in April 1947, when it recommended that Albania and the UK refer their dispute on the Corfu Channel to the Court.[8]

This means that most cases come before the ICJ as a result of State decisions taken under Article 36(1) of the Statute, which provides for contentious jurisdiction over cases for which the parties have agreed in a treaty or a special agreement to bring the dispute to the ICJ.[9] As of this writing, eighteen decided cases have come to the Court through special agreement/comprimis, fifteen of which have concerned disputes over territory or maritime delimitation. Such disputes are of the type in which the Court excels, in part because, once decided, the States have an incentive to comply rather than escalate the dispute.[10]

---

[7] W. Felstiner, R. Abel, and A. Sarat, 'The Emergence and Transformation of Disputes: Naming, Blaming, Claiming ...' 15 *Law and Society Review* (1981) 631–654.

[8] S.C. Res. 22 (April 9, 1947).

[9] Statute, Art. 36.1 ('The jurisdiction of the Court comprises all cases which the parties refer to it and all matters specially provided for in the Charter of the United Nations or in treaties and conventions in force').

[10] See T. Ginsburg and R. McAdams, 'Adjudicating in Anarchy: An Expressive Theory of International Dispute Resolution' 45 *William and Mary Law Review* (2004) 1229–1339. I can find only one such dispute in which compliance was not immediate, the case of *Sovereignty over Pedra Branca/Pulau Batu Puteh, Middle Rocks and South Ledge (Malaysia/Singapore) Judgment,* ICJ reports 2008, p. 12. The decision requested the creation of a joint technical committee to implement its decision. Malaysia claimed that the committee had reached an impasse in 2013 due to a problem interpreting the decision. It thus filed a request for interpretation on June 30, 2017, which the parties agreed to discontinue. See www.icj-cij.org/en/case/170 [accessed March 19, 2020].

The so-called Optional Clause of Article 36(2) of the Statute is another way in which contentious cases can come before the Court. Through this provision, States can agree to recognise the jurisdiction of the Court for, inter alia, 'any question of international law', which provides a kind of general jurisdiction among States. This sets up international adjudication as a sort of 'club good' among States that wish to be subject to general jurisdiction without specific consent through a treaty or special agreement, although, in practice, States often formulate reservations to Article 36(2) declarations so that jurisdiction may be somewhat limited. Seventy-four States have accepted this jurisdiction in some form as of this writing. Commentators claim that the Optional Clause is in decline, and cases brought under it tend to provoke preliminary objections to jurisdiction.[11]

Sometimes consent over jurisdiction may be fictive, taking the route of a long-dormant treaty clause that the current government wishes to resist. In such cases, the respondent State will file preliminary objections to jurisdiction, which has occurred in nearly half of the contentious cases outside of special agreements.[12] States might be less likely to comply when they lose a case in which they have filed preliminary objections.[13]

The centrality of consent for the exercise of its core institutional function of dispute resolution contrasts with the position of many courts in national systems and poses distinctive challenges to the ICJ. Some institutional features, such as the inclusion of judges ad hoc under Article 31 of the Statute, seem designed to soften the blow of being brought before the Court and are closer to the practice of arbitral institutions than a national court. The ICJ's 'courtness' is thus incomplete because it depends heavily on the consent of the parties to proceed, and the Court itself is not shy about reminding us of the importance of consent.[14]

This need to secure the parties' consent has implications for the Court's jurisprudence. All courts use mediatory techniques to maintain their

---

[11] On the alleged decline of the Optional Clause, see Eric A. Posner, 'The Decline of the International Court of Justice' in S. Voigt, D. Schmidtchen, and M. Albert (eds.), *International Conflict Resolution* (Mohr Siebeck, 2006); see also Shany, *Assessing the Effectiveness of International Courts*, at 170–171.

[12] Fifty-one out of 107 cases at this writing.

[13] Ginsburg and McAdams, 'Adjudicating in Anarchy'.

[14] *Armed Activities on the Territory of the Congo* 2002 DRC-Rwanda (Jurisdiction and Admissibility) [2006] ICJ Rep 6 para. 88.

legitimacy, but the ICJ eschews these in its procedure, and some scholars argue that it would be illegitimate for it to utilise them.[15] States have never asked the Court to use its power under Article 38(2) of the Statute to decide cases *ex aequo et bono*.[16] But, while the Court does not use mediatory *procedures*, it tends to issue *decisions* that are minimalist, cautious, and 'Solomonic' in nature.[17] This internal feature of the Court is arguably attributable to its weak institutional position.

B Law-Making

Besides resolving disputes, another major social function of courts is law-making.[18] Scholars of courts as institutions tend to assume that this is an inevitable part of the judicial function, as it is necessary in any case in which prior law runs out. This is especially true of international law, in which norms are produced in a decentralised process and not always perfectly clear. Ambiguity means there is a good deal of need for courts to interpret and fill in the gaps and thus make law.

The ICJ makes law in the course of both its contentious and advisory jurisdiction, though neither function is formally recognised. Article 59 of the Statute explicitly states that a 'decision of the Court has no binding force except between the parties and in respect of that particular case'. But many commentators accept that the Court's pronouncements about rules or principles are treated as authoritative statements of the law.[19] And judges, too, will sometimes admit that the Court has a role in developing

---

[15] N. Grossman, 'Solomonic Judgments and the Legitimacy of the International Court of Justice' in N. Grossman et al. (eds.), *Legitimacy and International Courts* (Cambridge University Press, 2014), 43.

[16] S. Dothan, '*Ex Aequeo et Bono*: The Uses of a Road Not Taken', in A. Skordas (ed.), *Research Handbook on the International Court of Justice* (Elgar, forthcoming).

[17] Grossman, 'Solomonic Judgments'.

[18] See also Dire Tladi, Chapter 3, this volume. A third major function is social control: helping to govern a population by imposing norms onto individuals on behalf of the society. Criminal law, administrative justice, and other fields are examples. See Shapiro, *Courts*. These have few analogies at the ICJ.

[19] James Crawford, *Brownlie's Principles of Public International Law*, 9th ed. (Oxford University Press, 2019), 40 ('In theory the Court applies the law and does not make it … Yet a decision, especially if unanimous or almost unanimous, may play a catalytic role in the development of the law'). For a critical view, see M. A. Weisburd, *Failings of the International Court of Justice* (Oxford University Press, 2016).

the law.[20] Thus, the ICJ plays a law-making role as a functional matter. Furthermore, by virtue of its status as the 'World Court', the ICJ has a certain authority in its pronouncements of law. As d'Aspremont writes in this volume, the ICJ is the 'master of the sources' with uncontested authority.[21]

Scholars have traced the ICJ's impact on many areas of law, and one theme is that the ICJ's impact varies with its caseload and the presence of other bodies that also contribute to the normative development of the law. In subject areas in which there is a profusion of specialised bodies and alternative adjudicative fora, such as human rights or international criminal law, the Court has had relatively little impact. In areas where there are few competitors, such as territorial boundaries, the Court's impact on the law is greater.[22] For example, one area in which the Court is competing for business with other tribunals is the law of the sea, in which the 1982 Convention on the Law of the Sea ('UNCLOS') allows States several options for dispute resolution, including the International Tribunal for the Law of the Sea ('ITLOS') as well as the ICJ.[23] The ITLOS, which has primary jurisdiction over cases of prompt release, has had more impact on the law in that area, while the ICJ has shaped the law of maritime delimitation as well as that of fisheries.

The Court also carries on implicit dialogues with the International Law Commission, the organ of the UN charged with the development of international law. As Crawford notes, the two have been quite complementary in the development of international law.[24]

The procedures of the ICJ facilitate its law-making role to some extent. Garoupa and Ginsburg argue that courts whose primary role is social control tend not to have separate opinions.[25] But courts that are engaged

---

[20] R. Y. Jennings, 'The Internal Judicial Practice of the International Court of Justice' 59 *British Yearbook of International Law* (1988) 31, at 34. (ICJ is 'crucially, intimately and inescapably concerned with the development and shaping of international law').

[21] J. d'Aspremont, Chapter 8, this volume.

[22] C. J. Tams, 'The ICJ as a 'Law-Formative Agency': Summary and Synthesis', in C. J. Tams and J. Sloan (eds.), *The Development of International Law by the International Court of Justice* (Oxford University Press, 2013), 377, 394–395.

[23] *United Nations Convention on the Law of the Sea*, Art. 287.

[24] J. Crawford, 'The International Court of Justice and the Law of State Responsibility', in Christian Tams and James Sloan (eds.), *The Development of International Law by the International Court of Justice* (Oxford University Press, 2014), 71, at 74.

[25] N. Garoupa and T. Ginsburg, *Judicial Reputation* (University of Chicago Press, 2015), 180–183.

in law-making do tend to allow separate opinions, because the content of law is something on which reasonable minds can and do disagree. The practice of the ICJ of having an unsigned opinion for the Court and signed separate opinions reflects this structure to some extent, and separate opinions are filed in virtually every contentious case.[26]

In summary, the ICJ is most decidedly a *court*. In its ritual structures and formality, the ICJ exudes 'courtness'. The judges wear robes and sit in a magnificent hall in the Peace Palace in The Hague.[27] They follow judicial rather than arbitral or mediatory procedures.[28] Yet, when compared with national courts, the ICJ lacks certain powers of coercion, and this has affected both the institutional structure and the jurisprudence of the Court. One might view the informal aspects of the institution – the grand procedures and the projection of authority – as compensating for the structural weakness of the Court.

III The International Court: Relations with States

States are a major part of the institutional environment of the Court, and the Statute provides that 'only states may be parties in cases before the Court'.[29] This means that the ICJ depends on States to bring it business; if States ignore it, the Court will have no role. State decisions to refer cases to the Court, in turn, depend on some perception of its effectiveness *from the perspective of States*. The literature on the effectiveness of international courts examines the overall ability of a court to achieve its goals.[30] But the goals of a court may be different from those of States. A court might seek to maximise its impact or reputation, and decisions provide a critical vehicle for doing so.[31] States, however, might sometimes refer cases to court without any genuine intention of resolving the dispute or complying with any judgment. For example, they might want to publicise their

---

[26] See Rules of the International Court of Justice, Art. 95.2 (allowing separate opinions).

[27] P. Tzeng, 'Judge Bhandari's Re-election to the International Court of Justice' 31 *National Law School of India Review* (2019) 98.

[28] *Handbook of the International Court of Justice*, available at www.icj-cij.org/files/publica tions/handbook-of-the-court-en.pdf.

[29] Art. 34.2.   [30] Shany, *Assessing the Effectiveness of International Courts*.

[31] S. Dothan, *Reputation and Judicial Tactics: A Theory of National and International Courts* (Cambridge University Press, 2015).

disputes internationally or shift blame to other parties to avoid domestic criticism.

Even setting aside such issues, States will have an interest in the quality of the judicial decision, as well as the probability of compliance with decisions. Compliance with international judicial decisions is a topic of major analysis by scholars. After reviewing various definitions, Huneeus says that 'compliance occurs when a State or other actor subject to the court carries out the actions required by a ruling of the court, or refrains from carrying out actions prohibited by said ruling'.[32] She argues that various factors will determine compliance, including those associated with the court regime, features of the State, and features of the dispute.

Existing studies of the ICJ tend to find relatively high levels of compliance with judgments, even though measurement issues make statistics tricky.[33] Data on file with this author suggests that out of sixty-three judgments and decisions that one can easily assess, some forty-nine (77 per cent) resulted in State behavior partly or wholly consistent with the operative part of the decision. Other scholars assert that there has been no case of full defiance of the ICJ since the *Nicaragua* decision.[34] Shany argues that compliance is not a particularly good metric in the ICJ context, and that his broader concept of effectiveness is a better one.[35] But, if the ICJ is viewed not as trying to maximise regime goals of peace and stability, but instead as trying to provide a service to States, compliance *is* relevant, and it seems to be fairly robust.

In summary, States are the primary clients of the Court. The Court has done relatively little to address the grand purposes of peaceful resolution of disputes outlined in the Charter. But it has provided a modest service to

[32] A. Huneeus, 'Compliance with Judgments and Decisions', in C. P. R. Romane, K. Alter, and Y. Shany (eds.), *The Oxford Handbook of International Adjudication* (Oxford University Press, 2013), 427; see also D. Kapiszewski and M. Taylor, 'Conceptualizing, Measuring, and Explaining Adherence to Judicial Rulings' 38 *Law and Social Inquiry* (2013) 803.

[33] C. Schulte, *Compliance with Decisions of the International Court of Justice* (Oxford University Press, 2004); C. Paulson, 'Compliance with Final Judgments of the International Court of Justice since 1987' 98 *American Journal of International Law* (2004) 434–461; A. P. Llamzon, 'Jurisdiction and Compliance in Recent Decisions of the International Court of Justice' 18 *European Journal of International Law* (2007) 815; H. L. Jones, 'Why Comply: An Analysis of Trends in Compliance with Judgments of the International Court of Justice since Nicaragua' 12 *Chicago-Kent Journal of International and Comparative Law* (2012) 57; Ginsburg and McAdams, 'Adjudicating in Anarchy'.

[34] Llamzon, 'Jurisdiction and Compliance'; Jones, 'Why Comply: An Analysis'.

[35] Shany, *Assessing the Effectiveness of International Courts*, at 134. See also Giladi and Y Shany, Chapter 5, this volume, [15–16].

States, particularly in resolving disputes regarding borders and diplomatic immunities. It has helped States to coordinate their behavior in relatively low-stakes matters. While it is difficult to tell in the abstract whether the usage of the Court has been high or low, it is worth noting that filings to the Court have increased in recent years. Twenty-six distinct contentious cases and requests for interpretation were filed in the 2010s, the most of any decade.[36] The Court seems to have found a place to operate within its institutional environment.

IV The United Nations and Its Organs

The Court must also interact with various UN organs as part of its institutional design. As a formal matter, the Court is composed by the General Assembly and the Security Council, which elects its judges in accordance with Article 10 of the Statute. The Secretary-General receives a list of nominations from national groups of the Permanent Court of Arbitration, ensures eligibility, and presents the list to the General Assembly and Security Council.[37] The electors, according to Article 9 of the Statute, are to consider the collective diversity of the Court, ensuring that 'the main forms of civilization and the principal legal systems of the world' are represented. The voting rule is an absolute majority in each body, proceeding independently, with no special privilege for the permanent members of the Security Council. There have been two informal norms that condition the selection of members: first, there has been by custom a certain distribution among the five regional groups in the UN system, and second, there was a norm that each permanent member would have a judge on the Court. Both norms were recently broken in 2017, when the Indian judge Dalveer Bhandari was elected over the British judge Sir Christopher Greenwood.[38]

---

[36] This statistic aggregates cases arising out of common fact patterns filed in the same year, but includes requests for interpretation opened later.

[37] Statute, Arts 5–7.

[38] The norm was also violated between 1967 and 1985 when there was no Chinese judge, due to the credentials contest between the People's Republic of China and the Republic of China. Tzeng, 'Judge Bhandari's Re-election to the International Court of Justice'. Tzeng notes that the mechanism designed to break deadlocks between the General Assembly and the Security Council, a joint conference laid out in Article 12 of the Statute, was not utilised and never has been. That clause allows judges who have been successfully elected to choose the remaining candidates to fill the vacancies.

This meant that the Asia-Pacific Group now had four judges on the Court, while the Western Europe and Others Group had four as well, an adjustment of the prior configuration.

In keeping with its special role under the Charter with regard to the United Nations budget, the General Assembly sets salaries for the members of the Court and registrar, along with the budget for the Court.[39] Similar to a rule found in many national constitutions, the Statute provides that salaries of judges may not be decreased during their terms of office.[40] This is designed to ensure independence of the members from political pressures.

Under the Charter, the Security Council has the role of ensuring the pacific settlement of disputes, and in doing so, is to 'take into consideration that legal disputes should as a general rule be referred by the parties' to the Court.[41] The Statute also provides for provisional measures, which are to be notified to the parties and to the Security Council.[42] Article 94 of the Charter provides that each member of the UN agrees to comply with decisions of the Court 'in any case to which it is a party'. Furthermore, Article 94 (2) of the Charter allows States to go to the Security Council in the event of non-compliance with judgements. The Security Council can then make recommendations or 'decide upon measures to be taken to give effect to the judgment'.[43] Since Security Council decisions are binding under Article 25 of the Charter, this is formidable power indeed. But despite occasional calls,[44] the Security Council has never employed its power under Article 94(2).[45] Again, we observe a gap between paper and practice.

The General Assembly or Security Council can by right seek advisory opinions from the Court, and to date 27 have been issued. Other UN organs are also welcome to seek such opinions in their areas of competence. While many of these are framed as internal questions of the organisation, they obviously have profound consequences for the operation of international law: admission to UN membership, for example, requires defining the characteristics of statehood, and decisions about the powers of UN bodies will have a general impact on the law of international organisations.

---

[39] Statute, Art 32.   [40] Ibid.   [41] Statute, Art 36.   [42] Statute, Art 41.
[43] Charter, Art 94.2.
[44] E.g., on 22 January 2002, Honduras sent a letter to the President of the Security Council, requesting its intervention to ensure the judgement of the ICJ of 11 September 1992 in the case concerning *Land, Island, and Maritime frontier dispute (Honduras, El Salvador)*.
[45] A. P. Llamzon, 'Jurisdiction and Compliance' at 847.

The scope of advisory opinions has arguably broadened in recent years in a more political direction, with opinions like the *Nuclear Weapons* Advisory Opinion, the *Wall* Advisory Opinion, and the *Kosovo* Advisory Opinion.[46] Many of these advisory opinions in fact concern bilateral conflict among States, and have distributive consequences among them. At least two of these recent decisions – those related to nuclear weapons and Kosovo – are notable for their caution and somewhat Solomonic character, but others involving great powers are bolder in their effect. In particular, the 2019 opinion on the *Legal Consequences of the Separation of the Chagos Islands from Mauritius* marked a frontal challenge to the legacies of colonialism and decolonisation, demanding that the British government give up its claim to Diego Garcia, a militarised atoll in the Indian Ocean.[47]

Another set of cases concerns the internal operations of the UN.[48] Sloan and Hernandez note that, as the principal judicial organ, the Court is implicitly and sometimes explicitly called on to deal with boundary disputes over authority within the organisation. Yet the Court has assumed a generally deferential attitude toward the other UN organs.[49] In the decision on *Conditions of Admission*, the Court held that member States could not add conditions to those listed in Article 4(1) of the Charter in voting for admission of a member State. This strengthened the General Assembly and Security Council relative to member States. The Court has also considered whether the General Assembly had the power to ignore awards made by an employment tribunal it establishes.[50]

The Court's famous decision in *Reparation for Injuries* adopted the view that the Court had an inherent power to interpret the Charter, and that the

---

[46] *Accordance with International Law of the Unilateral Declaration of Independence in Respect of Kosovo, Advisory Opinion,* ICJ Reports 2010, p. 403; *Legal Consequences of the Construction of a Wall in the Occupied Palestinian Territory,* Advisory Opinion, ICJ. Reports 2004, p. 136; *Legality of the Use by a State of Nuclear Weapons in Armed Conflict,* Advisory Opinion, ICJ Reports 1996, p. 66.

[47] *Legal Consequences of the Separation of the Chagos Islands from Mauritius,* Advisory Opinion, ICJ Reports *2019,* p. 95.

[48] J. Sloan and G. I. Hernandez, 'The Role of the International Court of Justice in the Development of the Institutional Law of the United Nations', in C. Tams and J. Sloan (eds.), *The Development of International Law by the International Court of Justice* (Oxford University Press, 2014) 198.

[49] Ibid at 199.

[50] *Effect of Awards of Compensation Made by the United Nations Administrative Tribunal,* Advisory Opinion, ICJ Reports.

Charter granted certain implied powers to the organisation, even if not explicitly set out in the text. Sought by the General Assembly, this Advisory Opinion gave the organisation international legal personality and the ability to pursue claims for damages to itself and its agents. Notably the Opinion found that the ability to pursue claims extended to claims against all States, not simply those that were signatories to the Charter. This was a formidable and important Opinion.

Relations between two political organs – the General Assembly and the Security Council – have been implicated in some advisory opinions. *Certain Expenses* provides one example.[51] *Certain Expenses* concerned two peacekeeping missions, one in the Suez and the other in the Congo. The first of these was established by the General Assembly, while the second had been the subject of a General Assembly resolution, seemingly infringing on the power of the Security Council over matters of peace and security. The Court found that the General Assembly's exercise of competence in this area did not infringe on that of the Security Council, reading the powers to be overlapping and mutually compatible.

Despite these cases, which in some sense examine whether powers are being exercised *ultra vires*, the Court has never claimed the power to review acts of the Security Council for conformity with the Charter. Yet at the same time, the Court has occasionally engaged out of necessity in interpretation of Security Council resolutions.[52] The Court has denied that this involves the practice of judicial review, or the ultimate and exclusive power to interpret the Charter.[53] In the *Kosovo* Advisory Opinion the Court had to look to the context of Security Council Resolution 1244 to examine whether it determined the final status of the territory. That Resolution had guaranteed the territorial integrity of the Federal Republic of Yugoslavia, but in a cautious opinion, the Court found sufficient ambiguity to decide that it could not declare that the Kosovo declaration of independence was illegal.[54]

In the *Lockerbie* case, Libya claimed that the request for extradition by the United States and the United Kingdom of the bombing suspects violated its rights under the Montreal Convention for the Suppression of

---

[51] *Certain Expenses of the United Nations (Article 17, paragraph 2, of the Charter)*, Advisory Opinion, ICJ Reports 1962, p. 151.
[52] *Kosovo.*   [53] *Certain Expenses*, at 168.   [54] *Kosovo.*

Unlawful Acts against Civil Aviation.[55] As the Court was preparing to decide on provisional measures, the two applicant States engineered the passage of a Security Council resolution under Chapter VII calling on Libya to give up the suspects. The Court then dismissed the request for provisional measures as moot. But as Sloan and Hernandez note, five years later the Court declined to find that the Security Council resolutions superseded the rights under the Montreal Convention, suggesting that this was an issue for the merits phase, which ultimately did not proceed.

In these matters, the ICJ has played its role as the principal judicial organ of the UN, but there has been some evolution in the types of cases brought before it. The organs have both shaped the composition and powers of the Court, and in the case of the General Assembly in particular also served as a client for the Court, bringing requests for advisory opinions.

V Conclusion

The ICJ has been deeply shaped by its institutional environment, both formal and informal, as it has sought to provide adjudicative services and contribute to the development of the law. Its performance has been subject to praise and criticism. But however much scholars criticise the Court's jurisprudence, it is helpful to understand that the ICJ is profoundly limited by its institutional design and the nature of the international system. Without coercive powers, and dependent on State consent for cases, the 'principal judicial organ of the United Nations' was destined to play a limited role from the outset, in a world in which States were not actively seeking to adjudicate disputes. It is noteworthy then, that its most important contributions have been in the development of the law, a task not formally assigned to the Court at all. This illustrates the utility of taking a broad institutional perspective to understand how courts operate.

---

[55] *Questions of Interpretation and Application of the 1971 Montreal Convention arising from the Aerial Incident at Lockerbie (Libyan Arab Jamahiriya v. United Kingdom)*, Preliminary Objections, Judgment, ICJ. Reports 1998, p. 9; *Questions of Interpretation and Application of the 1971 Montreal Convention arising from the Aerial Incident at Lockerbie (Libyan Arab Jamahiriya v. United States of America)*, Preliminary Objections, Judgment, ICJ Reports 1998, p. 115.

Further Reading

Dothan, Shai. 2014. *Reputation and Judicial Tactics: A Theory of National and International Courts.* New York: Cambridge University Press.

Giladi, Ronen and Yuval Shany. 2014 'The International Court of Justice', in Yuval Shany, *Assessing the Effectiveness of International Courts.* New York: Oxford University Press, 2014.

Kolb, Robert. 2014. *The International Court of Justice.* Oxford: Hart Publishing.

Schulte, Constanze. 2004. *Compliance with the Decisions of the International Court of Justice.* Oxford: Oxford University Press.

Tams, Christian and James Sloan, eds. 2014. *The Development of International Law by the International Court of Justice.* New York: Oxford University Press.

Assessing the Effectiveness of the   5
International Court of Justice

Rotem Giladi and Yuval Shany

I Introduction

Through continuity with its predecessor, the Permanent Court of
International Justice (PCIJ), the International Court of Justice (ICJ or
Court) is the oldest international court in existence. As the 'World Court',
it embodies a crucial link between the present-day reality of international
adjudication and its antecedent intellectual and ideological premises and
institutional incarnation. As such, the ICJ serves as the archetype of
international adjudication. Furthermore, as 'the principal judicial organ'
of the UN, it enjoys a special position among other international courts
and tribunals,[1] and forms part of a global organisation tasked with maintaining international peace and security. Among international courts and
tribunals, it alone can claim to exercise jurisdiction that is potentially both
general and universal, and its jurisdiction and jurisprudence may, and
often do, touch on high politics and global governance. These unique
features and the tensions they embody are crucial to the assessment of
the ICJ's effectiveness.

The ICJ's structure and process, quite deliberately, continue those of the
PCIJ, as the drafters of the Statute of the Court were of the view that the
PCIJ Statute had 'on the whole worked well',[2] notwithstanding the marginal role played by the PCIJ in international relations during the interwar
period and the League's evident failure to prevent a global war. Still, when
the ICJ took over the PCIJ's design (except that the Statute of the Court
'forms an integral part' of the UN Charter),[3] it also inherited much of its

---

[1] Charter of the United Nations, art. 92 (hereinafter – UNC); Statute of the International Court
of Justice, art.1 (hereinafter – ICJ Statute).

[2] United Nations, 'Report of the Informal Inter-Allied Committee on the Future of the
Permanent Court of International Justice' 39 AJIL Supp. (1945) 1, 2.

[3] UNC, art. 92.

late nineteenth-century outlook on international adjudication, law and the international society it governed.

The nature and magnitude of the challenges confronting the Court since 1945 are also crucial for assessing its effectiveness. It survived, without major structural adjustment, dramatic changes in the world and in the nature of its business. Its constituency radically transformed in numbers, identity and *outlook* shortly after its establishment. The new, decolonised membership of the UN shared old mistrust of the international order (of which the Court formed part) and new sensitivities about sovereignty and under-representation in seats of power; these directly challenged the Court's legitimacy. Cold War polarisation also was not conducive to the conduct of international relations through legal norms, process or institutions. Its end brought new challenges and expectations about the functioning of the UN and the Court in a new world order free of bipolar politics, yet still characterised by North-South tensions and deep skepticism of multilateralism. All of these twists and turns underscore the high degree of institutional resilience of the ICJ in the face of exogenous pressures; the Court's durability must also be accounted for when assessing its effectiveness.

The following chapter offers a 'broad brush' discussion of the effectiveness of the ICJ. In Section II we introduce the evaluative framework used throughout this chapter for assessing the Court's effectiveness – a goal-based analysis. Section III discusses the goals of the ICJ as they derive explicitly and implicitly from its core documents. Section IV introduces the structural features of the Court that facilitate, at times, and constrain, at other times, its potential for goal-attainment. Section V reviews the outcomes generated by the Court and juxtaposes them against its goals. Section VI concludes.

II Assessing the ICJ

Assessing the effectiveness of international courts involves an evaluation of judicial performance against objective standards or subjective expectations.[4] Assessing 'judicial effectiveness' should be distinguished

---

[4] Y. Shany, 'Effectiveness of International Adjudication', in *Max Planck Encyclopedia of International Procedural Law [MPEiPro]*, *online version* (Oxford University Press, 2019), at para. 1.

from assessing 'judicial efficiency' (evaluation of the positive and negative costs, benefits and externalities associated with judicial operations)[5] or 'judicial cost-effectiveness' (the relationship between judicial inputs and outputs).[6]

In a previous publication, we suggested that judicial effectiveness should be assessed on the basis of a goal-based (or 'rational system') approach, which focuses on the question of whether courts meet their official goals – their formally stated mission – and operative goals – the actual benchmarks set for evaluating the implementation of specific organisational policies that explicitly or implicitly capture stakeholder expectations.[7] Such an approach offers a method for assessing, at different points in time, the actual attainment of pre-defined goals formulated at different levels of abstraction. Some of the goals of international courts and tribunals are 'generic' in nature and are common to almost all international courts and tribunals. These 'generic' goals include conflict resolution, law interpretation and application (or norm-compliance), support for the operation of international regimes and legitimisation of international governance.[8] Such goals are highly relevant for the ICJ; in fact, they have been largely shaped out of its own historical experience.

Besides the goal-based approach, organisational sociology has developed other approaches for evaluating the effectiveness of organisations. According to the 'open system' approach, from which we draw a number of useful insights, the effectiveness of an organisation is measured by its ability to control in relevant ways its external environment and shape or modify the conduct of external actors through the outcomes it generates.[9] For the ICJ, this implies assessing its influence over the conduct of state and non-state actors and the dynamics of international relations.

---

[5] P. Druker, *Managing the Non-Profit Organization: Practices and Principles* (HarperCollins Publishers, 1992) 198.

[6] W. Van Dooren, G. Bouckaert and J. Halligan, *Performance Management in the Public Sector* (2nd ed., Routledge, 2015) 24.

[7] Y. Shany, *Assessing the Effectiveness of International Courts* (Oxford University Press, 2014) pp. 13–14. See also C. Perrow, 'The Analysis of Goals in Complex Organizations' 26 *American Sociological Review* (1961) 854–866.

[8] Shany, *Assessing the Effectiveness*, at 37–46; A. von Bogdandy and I. Venzke, *In Whose Name?: A Public Law Theory of International Adjudication* (Oxford University Press, 2014) 8–20.

[9] R. W. Scott and G. F. Davis, *Organizations and Organizing: Rational, Natural, and Open Systems Perspectives* (Routledge, 2007) 31.

Such judicial influence can manifest itself, for example, in the agreement of parties to volatile international conflicts to defuse the situation by resorting to peaceful resolution through ICJ adjudication, changes in state conduct in order to comply with ICJ judgments and internalisation of legal standards articulated by the Court in the practice of state and non-state actors.

Furthermore, according to the 'system resources' approach, an effective organisation is one that succeeds in attaining sufficient resources for its long-term survival.[10] Applied to the ICJ, this would suggest that the Court's longevity is indicative of a high degree of success in maintaining the support of strategic constituencies for the continued existence of the Court and therefore of a high degree of effectiveness. Still, the system resources approach is ill-suited for a normative evaluation of judicial effectiveness as it cannot be excluded that the provision of resources for the Court is made independently from the quality of its judicial performance, out of inertia, lack of better alternatives or out of a cynical interest in maintaining international courts as a form of 'window dressing' for the application of raw power in international relations.

Ascertaining whether the normative goals of the ICJ have been attained invites, therefore, an appreciation of the Court's judicial outputs – most importantly, its specific decisions and jurisprudence – and its judicial outcomes – for example, compliance with its judgments and change in the conduct of state and non-state actors due to the 'shadow effect' of the Court's judicial operations.[11] Such an appreciation involves a qualitative examination of the judicial outputs of the ICJ with a view to evaluating their actual, potential and perceived impact on goal attainment or the Court's environment, as well as studying relevant quantitative outcome indicators, which constitute useful (albeit imprecise) proxies of judicial effectiveness. Such indicators include data on judgment-compliance levels, citations of court decisions and diffused support.

Performance evaluation can also involve an assessment of the quality of the judicial process – its duration, affordability, transparency, inclusiveness, procedural fairness, and so on. Since judicial outputs derive from

---

[10] S. E. Seahore and E. Yuchtman, 'A System Resource Approach on Organizational Effectiveness' 32 *American Sociological Review* (1967) 891, at 898.

[11] Shany, *Assessing the Effectiveness*, at 53.

judicial processes, the effectiveness generated by the former is likely to be significantly influenced by the quality of the latter. In the same vein, judicial outputs and outcomes are influenced by structural features, such as the Court's budget and personnel, its reputation for judicial independence and the propensity of potential parties to resort to adjudication before it. The quality and quantity of such structural attributes can be evaluated through indicators, such as changes in the number of States parties to the Court's Statute and subject to its jurisdiction, fluctuation in its caseload and an assessment of the level of professionalism and independence of ICJ judges.

Finally, it is important to acknowledge that the ICJ, like other international courts and tribunals, operates through 'feedback loops', since judicial outputs influence subsequent inputs into the operations of the Court. For example, repetitive failure by parties to adjudication to comply with ICJ judgments may result in greater reluctance to refer new cases to the Court. In the same vein, a judgment which marks a significant departure from international law doctrine might result in the withdrawal of States from instruments conferring jurisdiction on the Court. At the same time, having a record of success in resolving difficult disputes can improve the perceived legitimacy of the ICJ raising, in turn, its international profile and potential for impact.

III Goals

Curiously, the UN Charter and the ICJ Statute contain no clear statement of the Court's goals, and the literature rarely discusses them. Instead, goals must be inferred from the constitutive instruments' text, context and their *telos*. Two 'generic' goals of all international courts – dispute settlement and norm-compliance – are implicit in the adjudicative function. According to Article 38 of the Statute, the ICJ is 'to decide in accordance with international law such disputes as are submitted to it.' Other provisions further confirm that *compliance with international law* and *dispute settlement* are among the ICJ's goals.[12] These goals also derive from the overarching goals of the United Nations, which the Court as a principal

---

[12] See e.g., UNC, preamble and arts.1, 2, and 36.

organ is expected to support.[13] Moreover, the manner in which conformity with international law and dispute settlement were articulated together suggests a shared understanding among drafters of the Charter about the potential for law-based adjudication to serve as a substitute, if not a cure, for war. Such beliefs remain embedded, implicitly, in the Statute and in academic scholarship. Interviews with ICJ Judges and diplomats posted to The Hague[14] – like judicial pronouncements[15] – confirm that the 'peaceful settlement of disputes' and promoting compliance with international law are still seen as central ICJ 'goals'.

The Court may thus be viewed as part of an overall international strategy aimed at maintaining peace through the application of international law.[16] Although observers of the Court tend to claim that it has played a marginal role in war-prevention and the restoration and maintenance of international peace and security,[17] the Court has nonetheless dealt over the years with a considerable number of violent or volatile conflicts and has provided important guidance relating to the applicable *jus ad bellum* norms.[18] Furthermore, even the mundane judicial settlement services provided by the Court that may facilitate resolution, often through transactional justice, of run-of-the-mill disputes, may resolve or de-escalate international conflicts which otherwise had the potential to

---

[13] UNC, art. 1(1)('to bring about by peaceful means, and in conformity with the principles of justice and international law, adjustment or settlement of international disputes or situations which might lead to a breach of the peace'); J. Pérez de Cuéllar, 'Forward', in N. Singh, *The Role and Record of the International Court of Justice* (Brill, 1989) at p. xi.

[14] R Giladi and Y Shany, 'International Court of Justice', in Shany, *Assessing the Effectiveness*, 161, at 165.

[15] See e.g., *Legality of the Threat or Use of Nuclear Weapons*, ICJ Reports 1996, p. 226, at 263; ibid., at 557 (dissenting opinion of Judge Koroma); *Legal Consequences of the Construction of a Wall in the Occupied Palestinian Territory*, ICJ Reports 2004, p. 136, at 159; *Oil Platforms (Iran v. USA)*, ICJ Reports 2003, p. 161, at 238 (separate opinion of Judge Simma).

[16] The Court's role in resolving dispute through the application of international law can be seen as an outgrowth of the late nineteenth and early twentieth century 'peace by law' movement. See generally M. Erpelding, B. Hess and H. Ruiz Fabri, *Peace Through Law: The Versailles Peace Treaty and Dispute Settlement After World War I* (Nomos Verlagsgesellschaft, 2019).

[17] See e.g., C. Kress, 'The International Court of Justice and the Law of Armed Conflicts', in C. J. Tams and J. Sloan (eds.), *The Development of International Law by the International Court of Justice* (Oxford University Press, 2013) 263, at 295.

[18] See e.g., *Military and Paramilitary Activities in and against Nicaragua (Nicaragua v. USA)*, ICJ Reports 1986, p. 14; *Oil Platforms (Iran v. USA)*, ICJ Reports 2003, p. 161.

jeopardise international peace and security.[19] Whether this positive yet modest contribution inheres in the Court's design or represents goal-shifting is further debated below.

Two additional, 'generic' goals of the Court may also be inferred from the constitutive instruments of the ICJ. *Regime-support* is implicit in the dispute settlement function, linked as it is with the UN's overall goals of maintaining international peace and security and settling international disputes in conformity with international law (and principles of justice);[20] the Court's advisory jurisdiction, and its own self-perception as part of the UN organisation,[21] further confirms this. Still, the Charter does not assign the ICJ a central role in UN decision-making or operations, and UN recourse to the Court remains haphazard. As a court of law, moreover, the ICJ inevitably confers legitimacy on the political system of which it forms part. More than the institutional aspect of *regime-legitimisation*, the existence of a court of *justice* applying international *law* to international disputes represents the *idea* of the rule of law and of justice in international relations. This constitutes the *symbolic goal* of the ICJ.

This symbolic goal links to another implicit goal of the ICJ found outside the Charter and Article 38 of the Statute. As the principal judicial organ of the world institution, the Court is expected to *develop* international law, not merely engage in law-application. This reflects a core belief of the international legal profession, expressed in the title of Hersch Lauterpacht's 1958 work.[22] Constructivists are prone to cite the Court's norm-generating function as a redeeming feature compensating for the lack of a central international legislature and balancing realist critiques concerning enforcement avenues and compliance records.[23] This goal draws, evidently, on ideological persuasions of the nineteenth century in which 'gentle civilisers' had shared beliefs in the progressive, civilising

---

[19] A. Spain, Examining the International Judicial Function: International Courts as Dispute Resolvers 34 *Loyola of Los Angeles International and Comparative Law Review* (2011–2012) 5, 10.

[20] UNC, art. 1(1), 36(3).

[21] See e.g., *Legal Consequences of the Separation of the Chagos Archipelago from Mauritius in 1965, Advisory Opinion,* ICJ Reports 2019, p. 95, at 113.

[22] H. Lauterpacht, *The Development of International Law by the International Court* (1958) 3–7.

[23] L. R. Helfer and A.-M. Slaughter, 'Why States Create International Tribunals: A Response to Professors Posner and Yoo' 93 *California Law Review* (2005) 1.

power of international law and judicial institutions.[24] This *law-development* goal continues to mark the role of the Court, in the expectations of professional constituencies, as a symbol of the aspiration of present and past generations for an international rule-based political system.[25]

IV Factors Controlling Judicial Outcomes

A Jurisdictional Powers and Usage Rates

The effectiveness of the Court is facilitated and limited by its structures and procedures, and the scope of its jurisdictional powers and their actual utilisation are principal factors controlling the Court's capacity to attain its goals. Theoretically, the Court's contentious jurisdiction is very broad. It is universal in nature and unlimited in terms of its subject-matter. State consent, however, remains the controlling feature of jurisdiction – and, therefore, of effectiveness – notwithstanding the Court's power to determine its own competence. The ICJ's jurisdictional design makes it resemble, therefore, more an arbitral body – dispensing transactional justice – than a domestic court of law with plenary jurisdiction. The need for consent constrains the ICJ's capacity to meet its normative, dispute settlement and institutional goals, rendering the Court 'a service institute' that offers States a readily available dispute settlement mechanism – should they elect to use it.

It can be argued that the limited acceptance of the Court's jurisdiction in practice has meant that it has not been allowed to fully discharge its role:[26] the 'compromissory clause network' suffers from significant gaps, and new clauses come into being at decreasing rates.[27] The *relative* portion of UN membership accepting compulsory jurisdiction has also remained quite low over time. As of 8 May 2021, Article 36(2) declarations were made by 66 (of 193) members (approximately 34 per cent);[28] only one of which

---

[24] M. Koskenniemi, *The Gentle Civilizer of Nations: The Rise and Fall of International Law 1870–1960* (Cambridge University Press, 2001).

[25] T. Ginsburg and R. H. McAdams, 'Adjudicating in Anarchy: An Expressive Theory of International Dispute Resolution' 45 *William & Mary Law Review* (2005) 1229–1339.

[26] S. Oda, 'The Compulsory Jurisdiction of the ICJ: A Myth?' 49 *International and Comparative Law Quarterly* (1999) 251–277.

[27] C. Tomuschat, 'Article 36', in A. Zimmermann, C. J. Tams, K. Oellers-Frahm and C. Tomuschat (eds.), *The Statute of the International Court of Justice: A Commentary* (3rd ed., Oxford University Press, 2019) 712, at 752.

[28] See Giladi and Shany, 'International Court of Justice', at n. 14.

(the UK) is a permanent Security Council member. That declarations are attended by broad reservations suggests that, effectively, acceptance is much lower.

Time has not eroded the jurisdictional limits on the Court's capacity to meet its goals. Its ability to apply international norms to serious disputes in ways that advance UN goals remains modest, as does the actual propensity of States to refer disputes to ICJ adjudication, which often stands in inverse relation to the gravity of the underlying cause and the case's potential for law-application and law-development. The stable, low rate of Advisory Opinion requests – since the mid-1950s, two to three per decade, on average – also suggests that jurisdictional design enables member states to constrain, through limiting the engagement of UN organs with the ICJ, the Court's ability to meet its institutional-support goals.[29]

In fact, when constituency size – UN membership – is factored in, the data demonstrate an overall *decrease* in recourse by States and the UN to the ICJ, starting immediately after the ICJ's first decade of operations, when rates of both contentious and advisory cases dropped radically.[30] Since the mid-1980s, some recovery in the number of contentious cases has occurred; nonetheless, ICJ usage in each of the last three decades comes to about one third of the usage in its first decade and does not show signs of increase (twenty-eight cases were submitted to the Court between 2011–2020, as opposed to twenty-nine between 2001–2010 and thirty-eight between 1991–2000). The overall trend of under-utilisation is reinforced by the exponential growth in the number of competing judicial institutions, which can be seen as a form of acknowledgment of the institutional limits of the ICJ. The usage-aversion of the P5 and other powerful States may reflect a broader aversion on their part to the international rule of law, which further complicates the Court's mission.[31] And while the 'profile' of ICJ cases appears to have risen somewhat since the 1980s (*Chagos* being a recent example), the sustainability of this trend is still open to question. Whether the Court continues to exercise judicial restraint and avoidance, as it sometimes has in the recent past,[32] may also have a

[29] Ibid.   [30] Ibid.

[31] See e.g., S. Chesterman, 'An International Rule of Law?' 56 *American Journal of Comparative Law* (2008) 331, at 360.

[32] See e.g., *Accordance with International Law of the Unilateral Declaration of Independence in Respect of Kosovo*, ICJ Reports 2010, p. 403; *Legality of Use of Force (Serbia and Montenegro* v. *Belgium*), ICJ Reports 2004, p. 279.

significant impact on the nature of its future docket. The upshot is that limits on jurisdiction and, even more so, the limited propensity of States to utilise the Court, remains a major bar to the ICJ's effectiveness.

B Judicial Independence and Impartiality

Judicial independence and impartiality also play an important role in affecting the confidence of ICJ disputants in the adjudicative process, sustaining the legitimacy of the process, and thereby, its potential for goal attainment – that is, its effectiveness. Notwithstanding statutory provisions intended to ensure judicial independence,[33] nomination and election to the Court are 'designed to reflect political considerations'.[34] Judges are elected by the UN's two political bodies – the Security Council and the General Assembly; and regional group politics dominate the process.[35] For many years, the Court's composition tended to reflect that of the Security Council, with seats reserved for each of the P5. The loss in a run-off of a UK candidate to an Indian candidate in 2017 does not appear to signify any detachment of the election process from political considerations; rather it reveals a change in the political equilibrium at the UN.[36]

The fact that judges may and do seek re-election after a nine-year term has been critiqued as diminishing judicial independence.[37] States may not actively exert *control* over judges, but evidently try to control, through appointment, judicial perspectives, and the growing presence of lawyer-diplomats on the bench only reinforces the perception of the Court as composed of judges deferential to States' interests and sovereignty. In the same vein, the involvement of ICJ judges in inter-State arbitrations and other professional activities has also been regarded as incompatible with their independence, a concern which recently led to a partial ban on such

---

[33] ICJ Statute, arts. 2, 16–20.

[34] M. Shaw, *Rosenne's Law and Practice of the International Court of Justice 1920–2015* (5th ed., 2016) p. 354. Regarding the election, and the independence and impartiality, of Judges, see also Kenneth Keith, Chapter 2, The Role of an ICJ Judge.

[35] Ibid at p. 382.

[36] See e.g., J. Landale, How UK Lost International Court of Justice Place to India, BBC News, 21.11.2017, www.bbc.com/news/uk-politics-42063664.

[37] Resolutions adopted by the Institute of International Law at its Session at Aix-en-Provence, 22 April–1 May 1954, 45-II *Annuaire IDI* (1954) 296, 297.

practice.[38] Formally, then, ICJ judges are independent; the extent to which they are constrained by re-election prospects, education, experience, professional commitments and legal worldview warrants further study. The recent comments offered by former Judge Bruno Simma, proposing to eliminate re-election by limiting judicial appointments to a single term of twelve years suggest, perhaps, that more than a study is required.[39]

Similarly, it seems that judicial perspectives constrain the Court's perceived impartiality, inasmuch as judges appear to tend to vote 'for states that are similar to their home states'.[40] Today the Court may not appear as blatantly pro-Western as it did in 1966 (*South-West Africa*); yet, many States still hesitate to bring cases to the Court out of concern that the bench and the law it applies might run contrary to their interests. Here, too, formal structures ensuring professionalism, independence and impartiality tend to cohere with general expectations from *judicial* bodies, while informal selection processes and actual judicial conduct suggest a degree of judicial responsiveness to 'client preferences'. The Court thus appears as a professional, independent, yet politically sensitive body. Managing such conflicting expectations is likely to continue and influence the Court's ability to maintain legitimacy and remain effective.

C Judicial Legitimacy

Position and pedigree combine to invest the ICJ with legitimacy reinforced by its structure and process: universality, embodied in a geographically diverse composition, implies representative legitimacy, bolstered by the involvement of the UN political bodies in judicial elections, which seek to ensure that the composition represents global power-distribution. Judicial independence, 'moral character' and competence affect the professional-ethical dimensions of legitimacy. On the other

---

[38] N. Bernasconi-Osterwalder and M. Dietrich Brauch, 'Is "Moonlighting" a Problem? The Role of ICJ judges', in *ISDS – IISD Commentary* (2017); C. Musto, New Restrictions on Arbitral Appointments for Sitting ICJ Judges, *EJIL: Talk!*, 5.11.2018.

[39] J. Kaiser and R. Oidtmann, 'The ICJ Then and Now', Interview with Professor Bruno Simma and Professor Georg Nolte, Völkerrechtsblog, 18.03.2021, doi: 10.17176/20210318-153724-0, https://voelkerrechtsblog.org/the-icj-then-and-now-interview-with-professor-bruno-simma-and-professor-georg-nolte/.

[40] E. A. Posner and M. del Figueiredo, 'Is the International Court of Justice Biased?' 34 *The Journal of Legal Studies* (2005) 599.

hand, the Court's legitimacy is inevitably linked to that of its parent organisation, the UN, particularly when required to deal with problems stemming from historical UN failures.[41]

Managing legitimacy is therefore a major challenge for the Court: handling disparate expectations in order to translate formal and symbolic acceptance of authority into long-term acceptance of jurisdiction, compliance with decisions and political and financial support for the Court. It may have overcome legitimacy crises brought by the Cold War, decolonisation and the exercise of jurisdiction over recalcitrant superpowers; yet the aforementioned data on consent to jurisdiction and usage rates belie assertions of growing acceptance by States. The Court, notably, remains invested in legitimacy associated with offering a fair judicial process and producing high quality output. Whether these earn it sufficient long-term legitimacy in the eyes of all relevant constituencies remains unclear, especially in light of the growing role of non-state actors in influencing international relations and the Court's general lack of accessibility to such actors.

D Compliance

How to assess compliance with ICJ rulings, and the degree to which such rulings attract primary norm- or judgment-compliance, are hotly contested questions.[42] The Court generally enjoys high judgment-compliance rates despite the structural weakness of the formal, 'transactional' and political enforcement design in Article 94 of the UN Charter, which the Security Council has never used. To the extent that norm- and judgment-compliance take place, the explanation must be found in the authority of the Court, the political environment of its operation, the type of disputes it adjudicates or the remedies it prescribes.

It is instructive to note in this regard that politically charged advisory opinions relating to the *Wall in the Palestinian Territory* and *Chagos* have not been implemented to date. While the non-formally binding nature of the opinions may partly explain their non-implementation, their dramatic

---

[41] See e.g., *Wall*, ICJ Reports 2004, at p. 159.
[42] C. Schulte, *Compliance with Decisions of the International Court of Justice* (Oxford University Press, 2004) 39.

political ramifications appear to have been at the root of non-compliance. This underscores the point that state interests and the existence of genuine consent to jurisdiction are likely to influence the motivation to comply and constrain ICJ effectiveness. The actual record of compliance with the Court's decisions is furthered discussed in Section IV below.

E Resources

The Court has been subject to criticism for the inefficiency of the adjudicative procedure before it and, in particular, the length of its proceedings.[43] Furthermore, whereas the legal quality of ICJ decisions has been generally well-appreciated, concerns have been raised about the capacity of the Court and its registry to evaluate factually and technically complex cases.[44] Some of these problems reflect design flaws over which the Court has little control; others stem from policy choices adopted by the Court in its Rules of Procedure, which arguably reflect a conservative ethos prioritising judicial demeanor and symbolic authority at the expense of efficiency.

Yet, another source of the Court's difficulties in handling its backlog and other case-management challenges is its unsatisfactory budgetary situation. Despite some improvement in recent years (for example, the employment of more support staff), the Court remains under-resourced,[45] and it operates on less than one per cent of the overall UN regular budget, with the UN General Assembly keeping 'a tight rein' on its expenditure.[46] The worsening budgetary situation of the UN has further complicated the Court's position in this regard. The limited budget adversely affects the capacity of the Court to attain its goals, particularly in connection with time-sensitive and factually or technically complex international disputes or requests for advisory opinions.

---

[43] S. Yee, 'Article 45', in *ICJ Statute Commentary*, 1314, at 1328; C. Rose, 'Questioning the Silence of the Bench: Reflections on Oral Proceedings at the International Court of Justice' 18 *Journal of Transnational Law & Policy* (2008) 47–64.

[44] See e.g., J. G. Sandoval Coustasse and E. Sweeney-Samuelson, 'Adjudicating Conflicts Over Resources: The ICJ's Treatment of Technical Evidence in the Pulp Mills Case' 3 *Göttingen Journal of International Law* (2011) 447, at 460–461. See also James Devaney, Chapter 8, Fact-finding and Expert Evidence, pp. [15–16].

[45] Report of the International Court of Justice to the UN General Assembly, 1 August 2018–31 July 2019, UN Doc. A/74/4 (2019) 10–11.

[46] Shaw, *Rosenne's Law and Practice*, at 103.

V Outcomes

Whether the ICJ, over nearly eight decades, has been effective depends on how broadly, or narrowly, one reads its goals. A broad reading of dispute settlement and regime-support involves expectations that the World Court play a role in the transformation of international relations to rule-based relations abhorrent of the use of force. It is difficult to assess the Court's contribution to political transformation from this very broad perspective, in particular because of the ambiguous nature of the transformation itself: while real progress has been made with regard to the renunciation of force in international relations, the goal of the international rule of law remains elusive. In all events, the jurisdictional constraints placed on the Court, by design, appear to limit its capacity to meet such ambitious goals. A more modest reading of the Court's long-term goals portrays it as a service institution where States, *if* willing, may resolve their disputes – something like a *really* permanent court of arbitration. Under this reading, the ICJ has had some success in meeting its goals, especially in specific areas of the law, in relation to which it has developed particular expertise, such as with respect to land and maritime border delimitation.

Some of the nearly 170 cases which the ICJ has disposed of to date have concerned volatile territorial disputes and, increasingly, in recent decades, the use of force, humanitarian law or human rights.[47] Many more, however, involved technical disputes of the type far less likely to propel States to war. On numerous occasions, the Court elected to decline jurisdiction or used other avoidance techniques, arguably in order to manage State expectations and preserve its legitimacy in their eyes.[48] Some rulings emphasised the letter of the law; in others, the Court offered litigants transactional justice, where the Court's effect on the long-term relations between the disputing parties is hard to measure. Alongside success stories

---

[47] See also M. G. Kohen and M. Hébié, Chapter 15, The International Court of Justice and Territorial Disputes; A. Chehtman, Chapter 20, The Use of Force at the International Court of Justice; C. Espósito, Chapter 22, The International Court of Justice and Human Rights, all in this volume.

[48] See e.g., *Nuclear Tests (Australia v. France)*, ICJ Reports 1974, p. 253; *Request for an Examination of the Situation in Accordance with Paragraph 63 of the Court's Judgment of 20 December 1974 (New Zealand v. France)*, 1995 ICJ 288; *Use of Force*, ICJ Reports 2004, p. 279.

(*Fisheries Jurisdiction, North Sea Continental Shelf*)[49] and outright failures (*Hostages*),[50] there have been cases where, despite compliance by the parties, the impact of the ICJ on the underlying dispute between the parties appears to have been modest. That some issues (consular notification)[51] or concrete disputes (*Preah Vihear*)[52] return to the docket suggests the limits of crafting both principled and pragmatic solutions. The tendency of States to negotiate implementation of rulings underscores both the ICJ's contribution to dispute settlement and its limits. Notably, disputants rarely resort to force during or following ICJ proceedings (Aouzou Strip);[53] yet, whether this is the cause or effect of its involvement is open to debate.

The ICJ's ability to make a significant contribution to international dispute settlement has been further limited by the emergence of new, specialised judicial institutions. The Court did streamline some of its procedures and practices in response; jurisdictional limits, nonetheless, have allowed it to offer its services only in a fraction of unresolved disputes amenable to judicial resolution. Other factors reinforce the ICJ's relative marginality: praxis confirms the fringe role the Charter gives the Court in the maintenance of international peace and security. The UN may occasionally encourage States to accept jurisdiction or submit disputes, but such encouragement remains infrequent and largely hortatory in nature.

Since 1945, the Court has provided the organisation with just over two dozen Advisory Opinions, rarely declining to exercise this jurisdiction. Some addressed technical aspects of the UN's operation; others concerned specific disputes. On occasion, the Court clarified the legal situation underlying an international dispute (*Western Sahara*;[54] *Chagos*); on others, it largely avoided the issue at hand (*Kosovo, Nuclear Weapons*). The Security Council avoids turning to the Court or exercising its Article 94 powers to enforce its decisions in contentious cases and rarely refers disputing parties to the Court under Article 36(3). Hence, although the ICJ

---

[49] *Fisheries Jurisdiction* (*Iceland* v. *UK*), ICJ Reports 1974, p. 3; *North Sea Continental Shelf* (*FRG* v. *Denmark*), ICJ Reports 1969, p. 3.

[50] *United States Diplomatic and Consular Staff in Tehran*, ICJ Reports 1980, p. 3.

[51] *Vienna Convention on Consular Relations* (*Paraguay* v. *USA*), ICJ Reports 1998, p. 248; *LaGrand* (*Germany* v. *USA*), 2001 ICJ 466; *Avena* (*Mexico* v. *USA*), ICJ Reports 2004, p. 12.

[52] *Temple of Preah Vihear* (*Cambodia* v. *Thailand*), ICJ Reports 1961, p. 17; *Request for Interpretation of the Judgment of 15 June 1962* (*Cambodia* v. *Thailand*), ICJ Reports 2013, p. 281.

[53] *Territorial Dispute* (*Libya* v. *Chad*), ICJ Reports 1994, p. 6.

[54] *Western Sahara*, ICJ Reports 1975, p. 12.

may help resolve some of the disputes actually brought before it, it was given precious little opportunity to contribute to the management of international peace and security. It remains unclear whether this relative marginality stems from under-utilisation of the Court or from a realistic appreciation by potential parties and referring bodies and agencies of its limited conflict resolution potential, and of its relative advantages and disadvantages when compared to other dispute settlement venues and avenues.

The Court's overall record with regard to promoting primary-norm compliance is equally hard to assess. Compliance remains an imperfect proxy for goal-based effectiveness: on top of the methodological difficulties of measuring judgment-compliance, or demonstrating causation between specific rulings and State conduct, one cannot evaluate the goal-attaining value of compliance in detachment from the goal-attaining value of the decision with which compliance is sought.[55] As a result, it is difficult to assess the significance of the relatively high judgment-compliance rate which ICJ decisions enjoy (with a few notable instances of open defiance).[56] When the Court produces norm-rich outputs, these may generate and reinforce rule-of-law expectations, but also introduce a higher standard of compliant behavior. When engaging in transactional justice, however, the Court lowers this standard, increases the appearance of judgment-compliance, but with little contribution to norm-compliance.[57] Remedy design may also distort the compliance picture: for example, the *dispositif* in *Gabčíkovo-Nagymaros*[58] invites a finding of compliance as long as 'good faith negotiations' took place, yet such a finding tells very little regarding how the ruling affected the actual dispute (and the case remains on the Court's docket of open cases, more than twenty years after the judgment).

It must also be borne in mind that the total of cases *referred* to the Court represents a very small portion of norm-violations in international relations.

---

[55] Y. Shany, 'Compliance with Decisions of International Courts as Indicative of their Effectiveness: A Goal-based Analysis', James Crawford and Sarah Nouwen (eds.), *Select Proceedings of the European Society of International Law 2010* (Hart, 2012) 229.

[56] C. Paulson, 'Compliance with Final Judgments of the ICJ Since 1987' 98 *AJIL* (2004) 434; Schulte, *Compliance with Decisions.*

[57] G. Plant, 'Case Report: Maritime Delimitation and Territorial Questions Between Qatar and Bahrain (Qatar v. Bahrain)' 96 *AJIL* (2002) 198.

[58] *Gabčíkovo-Nagymaros Project (Hungary/Slovakia)*, ICJ Reports 1997, p. 7.

Fluctuations in ICJ usage notwithstanding, what remains clear – and underscored when compared to the business of regional courts – is that it is infrequently utilised. Whatever its achievement in concrete cases, the combination of jurisdictional design, usage rate, limited resources and politically constrained enforcement regime adversely affects the Court's capacity to affect norm-compliance across the board of international relations.

Still, the Court's legitimacy in the eyes of its constituencies helps its rulings transcend the specific aspects of particular cases, so as to offer States a rich body of normative guidance. The Court's decisions appear to have been successful in occupying pride of place among the sources of international law precisely because they are lengthy, highly deliberated, well-scrutinised – and relatively few in number. Anecdotal evidence suggests that ICJ rulings sometimes induce change in the future behaviour of parties,[59] create an impetus to negotiate settlement and invite external pressure on disputants to abide with the specific interpretations of international law articulated by the Court. They also generate or feed professional discourses on national or global decision-making and governance. This resulting shadow effect on the international rule of law, however, remains largely uncharted.

Furthermore, the deference ICJ judgments generally enjoy does seem to suggest that States have internalised the Court's symbolic, rule-of-law function. This implies that the Court might have been more effective with regard to regime-legitimisation than it has been with regard to promoting dispute resolution and norm-compliance: it remains, limitations notwithstanding, a symbol of a principle of legality in international relations. And since the Court has emphasised often its organic affiliation with the UN organisation, its jurisprudence has fortified the UN's institutional capacity and demonstrated respect for the powers and responsibilities of the UN's political organs (*Reparations, Lockerbie*).[60] Nonetheless, the UN only rarely actively taps on the Court's formal and symbolic legitimacy to legitimise its own action.

---

[59] A. Nollkaemper, 'The Role of Domestic Courts in the Case Law of the International Court of Justice' 5 *Chinese JIL* (2006) 301; L. R. Helfer and A.-M. Slaughter, 'Towards a Theory of Effective Supranational Adjudication' 107 *Yale Law Journal* (1997) 273, at 285.

[60] *Reparation for Injuries Suffered in the Service of the United Nations*, ICJ Reports 1949, p. 174; *Questions of Interpretation and Application of the 1971 Montreal Convention arising from the Aerial Incident at Lockerbie (Libya v. USA)*, ICJ Reports 1998, p. 115.

The ICJ has also succeeded in enhancing the legitimacy of the broader system of international law. Notwithstanding occasional lapses to transactional justice or normative equivocation, the Court has made a significant contribution to the development of international law as a coherent legal system responsive to changing social and political conditions. Its primary achievement may have been the rendering of a growing collection of rules and practices constituting a single normative system. Producing extensive, exhaustive, pluri-vocal and formal judicial outputs has served the Court's symbolic goals well. The Court's conservative leanings – reinforcing judicial aversion to international law-making – appear to have facilitated its success in this respect, allowing it to combine 'restraint and positive contribution'.[61] Indeed, with a few notable exceptions, its contribution to the development of specific legal fields appears to reflect more a validation of trends in scholarship or geopolitical agendas (for example, self-determination) than leaps of innovative doctrine. The principal normative outcome of the ICJ has been to legitimise, as much as generate, international law.

In practice, a combination of broad and narrow readings underpins the perception of the ICJ's goals by mandate providers, judges and academics who display a surprisingly uniform view of its goals. In interviews, ICJ judges and Hague-based diplomats have offered an expansive view of the role of the UN Court as an institution promoting peace through the international rule of law and, at the same time, have spoken of a voluntary service institution of limited capacity and design. That few saw the need to account for the tension between these two outlooks points to the prevalence and power of a deeply entrenched set of sensibilities about the Court's role in international life.[62] These shape both perceptions of the Court's goals *and* of its actual record; they help reconcile ideologically driven high aspirations regarding the Court with the reality of limited means, capacity and usage. They entrench the assumption that by producing judicial outputs, the Court generates positive outcomes that go in the direction of goal attainment: settling disputes, contributing to the maintenance of international peace and security, and generally promoting the

---

[61] Lauterpacht, *The Development of International Law*, at 84.

[62] M. Koskenniemi, 'The Ideology of International Adjudication and the 1907 Hague Conference', in Y. Daudet (ed.), *Topicality of the 1907 Hague Conference, the Second Peace Conference* (Brill, 2008) 127.

goals of the UN. In this mindset, expectations, outputs and outcomes are merged and acquire an axiomatic nature. What the Court in fact does turns into what it ought to be doing. Its very existence and resilience become the best evidence of its achievement.[63] The prevalence of such sensibilities suggests, perhaps, that the principal goal of the ICJ remains symbolic – a living embodiment of the promise of a rule-based international order.

VI Conclusions

A goal-based assessment of the ICJ's record of achievement produces mixed results. The Court has made some, albeit modest, contribution to international peace and security by lending its dispute settlement facilities to interested States and its advisory service to international organisations enmeshed in international disputes. Its jurisdictional limits, resource constraints and never-utilised enforcement capacities suggest, however, that the potential impact of the Court on its international environment is likely to remain modest. The limited effectiveness of the ICJ as a dispute settlement forum appears to be matched in its record as promoter of international law norms. Here too, under-utilisation of the Court seems to overshadow the important contribution it has made to the development and elucidation of many areas of international law.

Understanding the ICJ and its goals as symbolic in essence yields, however, a different assessment of its record. The constituent documents suggest that a predominant goal of the Court is to legitimise, through representation of the idea of legality, the operations of the UN and, more generally, the role of law in international relations. It captures thereby the aspirations of the international legal profession as to the transformative effects of international adjudication for law-enforcement, law-development, and legitimating laws and institutions. If so, the record of the Court's resilience and durability, together with the fact that judges, States, and scholars continue to subscribe to and express shared beliefs as to its goals and actual functioning, attest to a success in projecting the continuing promise of international adjudication. Whether effectiveness in preserving perceptions is a good enough reason for placing so much hope in a World Court remains, however, an open question.

---

[63] Lauterpacht, *The Development of International Law*, at 3–4.

Further Reading

A. von Bogdandy and I. Venzke, *In Whose Name? A Public Law Theory of International Adjudication* (Oxford University Press, 2014).

Philip Couvreur, *The International Court of Justice and the Effectiveness of International Law* (Brill, 2017).

Laurence Helfer, The Effectiveness of International Adjudicators, in *The Oxford Handbook on International Adjudication*, in C. P. R. Romano, K. J. Alter and Y. Shany (eds.), Oxford University Press, 2013) 464.

Gleider Hernandez, *The International Court of Justice and the Judicial Function* (Oxford University Press, 2014).

Yuval Shany, *Assessing the Effectiveness of International Courts* (Oxford University Press, 2014).

Part II

The ICJ and International Dispute Settlement

The Jurisdiction of the Court 6

Jean-Marc Thouvenin

I Introduction

Edvard Hambro, who served as the first Registrar of the International Court of Justice, wrote that the jurisdiction of the Court is 'of capital importance'.[1] He was referring to the importance of knowing the requirements for the Court to be entitled to exercise its jurisdiction. He was of course right, and it is precisely the ambit of this chapter to present the key elements useful to know on the Court's jurisdiction. What Hambro did not mean is that the Court is important because of the scope of its jurisdiction. In fact, the Court would be far more important, in the sense of its usefulness to resolve disputes, if the question of its jurisdiction was approached differently.

Certainly, the more the Court is entitled to exercise its jurisdiction over international disputes, the better it can contribute to their peaceful settlement. And there has always been a strong support since the Court's inception after the First World War for the attractive view that its jurisdiction should be compulsory. In 1920, prominent international lawyers, including the majority of the members of the Committee of Jurists mandated by the League of Nations to elaborate the Statute of the Permanent Court of International Justice, supported the idea that this Court should have a mandatory jurisdiction vis-à-vis States adhering to its statute.[2] But the Council of the League of Nations rejected it in 1920.[3] The same proposal was put forward after the Second World War during the preparatory works of the Statute of the International Court of Justice which succeeded to the PCIJ. It was then optimistically thought that since the

---

[1] E. Hambro, 'The Jurisdiction of the International Court of Justice' 76 *Collected Courses of the Hague Academy of International Law* (1950) 134.

[2] C. Tomuschat, 'Article 36', in A. Zimmermann, C. Tams, K. Oellers-Frahm and C. Tomuschat (eds.), *The Statute of the International Court of Justice: A Commentary* (Oxford University Press, 2019), 717–718, para. 3.

[3] Ibid.

experience of the PCIJ had been successful, States were likely to be more open to the idea that world court should have a compulsory jurisdiction. It is fair to say that if this principle had prevailed, the world of international justice would be far different from what it is today, and indeed the Court would be far more used. But it did not. Neither the First, nor the Second World Wars dissipated the resistance of reluctant States that wanted to maintain, and still maintain today, what they see as a core element of their sovereignty, namely their right to choose if, when, and on what subject-matter they can accept to defend the lawfulness of their acts before an international court. Thus, the jurisdiction of the International Court of Justice, like the one of its predecessor, is not 'compulsory' for States for the sole reason that they are parties to the Statute of the Court. In each case this jurisdiction must be based on the parties' consent. And since they do not consent so often, the Court generally keeps being at the periphery of their concern.

However, in addition to their poorly utilised contentious function, both the PCIJ and the ICJ have been entitled to deliver 'advisory opinions'. Some prominent – but not well inspired in this case – lawyers like Nicola Politis and Elihu Root claimed that in principle a Court of law should not be called to deliver 'advices';[4] yet, and quite fortunately, Article 14 of the Covenant of the League of Nations enabled both the Council and the Assembly to refer to the PCIJ any dispute between members of the League of Nations for obtaining an advisory opinion. This proved to be very successful, with twenty-seven advisory opinions delivered between 1922 and 1940. The measure of this success is also illustrated by the fact that in 1923 the PCIJ delivered no less than five advisory opinions. Likewise, the ICJ can be seized of a request for advisory opinion, even if not with respect to any 'dispute', but rather to any 'legal question'.[5] The success of this mechanism is less apparent, with only twenty-seven advisory opinions delivered between 1945 and 2001, but some of the legal questions addressed at these occasions are of particular importance.

The ICJ can therefore exercise both a contentious and an advisory jurisdiction. In both circumstances it can be said that the Court exercise

---

[4] See M. O. Hudson, 'Les avis consultatifs de la Cour permanente de Justice internationale' 8 *Collected Courses of the Hague Academy of International Law* (1925) 347–348, 406–407.

[5] Statute of the International Court of Justice, 18th April 1946, UKTS 67 (1946); Cmd 7015; 3 Bevans 1153; Article 62, para. 1.

its 'jurisdiction' in so far as it bases its decision or opinion on the law. But the former is based on individual State's consent, and leads to a binding judgment, while the latter is based on the provisions of the UN Charter and leads to non-binding opinions. It is therefore opportune to address them in turn.

II Contentious Jurisdiction

Since it is not compulsory, not even with respect to the most dangerous or dramatic unresolved disputes,[6] the contentious jurisdiction of the ICJ is the exception rather than the rule, and in fact a small number of inter-State cases are submitted to it. One could sustain the view that this is mainly because States prefer to have recourse to the other means of settlement of disputes listed at Article 33 of the UN Charter, and that, finally, cases really needing a judicial settlement are relatively rare. It is probably true that the non-compulsory jurisdiction of the Court is a strong incentive for States to settle their disputes by other means, beginning with good faith negotiation. However, the massive caseload of the Dispute Settlement Body of the World Trade Organisation, the jurisdiction of which is compulsory, reflects another reality, namely that when a judicial avenue is offered to States, they do rely on the rule of law for the settlement of their disputes and do not hesitate to go to courts.[7] The same phenomenon of explosion of cases from the moment adjudicative bodies are accessible is visible with respect to investor-States disputes – but of course the applicants in these cases are investors, not States. This suggests that in the absence of judicial

---

[6] There is no automatic jurisdiction with respect to disputes 'the continuance of which is likely to endanger the maintenance of international peace and security' (Article 33 of the UN Charter), nor with respect to violations of the most fundamental norms (jus cogens); *Armed Activities on the Territory of the Congo (New Application: 2002) (Democratic Republic of the Congo* v. *Rwanda), Jurisdiction and Admissibility,* ICJ Reports 2006, p. 6, at p. 32, para. 64, and p. 52, para. 125; and see e.g. J.-M. Thouvenin, 'La saisine de la Cour internatioanle de Justice en cas de violation des règles fondamentales de l'ordre juridique international', in C. Tomuschat and J.-M. Thouvenin (eds.), *The Fundamental Rules of the International Legal Order* (Brill 2006), 331–334

[7] Of course, the WTO DSB is not a proper court, but it renders the same sort of service in stating the law. It is arguable that the extraordinarily heavy caseload of the WTO DSB is a symptom of the inadequacy of the WTO law. But it remains that States do not hesitate to choose to have recourse to the WTO DSB to resolve their disputes, rather than having recourse to other mechanisms.

possibility, plenty of legal disputes are simply unresolved according to the law or otherwise. Problems will stay as they are, without resolution, however frustrating or dangerous it can be.

Yet, even if underexploited, there *is* a Court, and it can exercise its jurisdiction when the required conditions are met. The rules in this respect are to be found in Articles 93 of the UN Charter and chapter II of the Statute of the Court which is titled 'Competence of the Court'. The five articles of this chapter address three different questions: 'access' to the Court (*locus standi*), States' 'consent' to the Court hearing their cases, and, finally, the 'sources' of the law applicable by the Court. Since the 'sources' as enumerated in Article 38 are discussed in Chapter 10 of this book, it will not be addressed in this chapter. The focus will rather be on 'access' and 'consent', both being key requirements for the exercise of the Court's jurisdiction.

A Access to the Court (*locus standi*[8])

Only States (Article 34(1) of the Statute)

Article 34(1) of the Statute provides that '[o]nly States may be parties in cases before the Court'. The French text reads '[s]euls les Etats ont qualité pour se presenter devant la Cour', which clearly refers to the so-called 'qualité pour agir', a requirement different from the 'intérêt pour agir' in French, or 'standing' in English.[9] There is no provision defining 'States' for the purpose of the Statute, suggesting that there could be difficulties with respect to entities the statehood of which is disputed.[10] It does not follow from Article 34(1) that all States may appear before the Court since some conditions are set out in Article 35, discussed below. But it clearly means

---

[8] On the notion of *locus standi*, see *Legality of Use of Force (Serbia and Montenegro v. France), Preliminary Objections, Judgment*, ICJ Reports 2004, p. 575, Separate opinion of Judge Kreća, pp. 663–665.

[9] On the difference between 'access' to the Court and 'standing', see J. J. Quintana, *Litigation at the International Court of Justice, Practice and Procedure*, (Brill: Nijhoff, 2015),14–24.

[10] See the pending *Relocation of the United States Embassy to Jerusalem (Palestine v. United States of America)* case which raises this question; it may be noted that on the ICJ's website Palestine does not appear in the list of 'States entitled to appear before the Court'. See also, with respect to Liechtenstein's request to be accepted as State party to the UN in 1949, W. Kohn, 'The Sovereignty of Liechtenstein' 61 *AJIL* (1967) 547, and, on Hyderabad's request in 1948, C. Eagleton, 'The Case of Hyderabad Before the Security Council' 44 *American Journal of International Law* (1950) 277.

that subjects of international law which are not States, in particular international organisations, cannot appear before the Court in contentious cases.[11] Of course, if such a limitation was unquestionable when the Statute of the PCIJ was drafted, it is no surprise that since then it has often been commented as outdated.[12] By contrast, the recently created ITLOS is open to international organisations like the European Union[13] which the UNCLOS assimilates to a State party.[14] One could surely argue that the Statute of the ICJ should be revised according to the current characteristics of the international community, but it is an uneasy task. Assuming that a consistent project can be elaborated,[15] not only amending the Statute would be a complicated undertaking,[16] but, in addition to the current 'revival' of 'sovereignism',[17] illustrated for example by the spectacular 'Brexit', or by the tendency of respondent States to refuse to appear before the Court or to abide by court's decisions, some cases are likely to

---

[11] It has also been noted that the Registrar receives quite a lot of letters every year referring to disputes between individual persons and their own State; see H. Xue, 'Jurisdiction of the International Court of Justice' 10 *Collected Courses of the Xiamen Academy of International Law* (2017) 133.

[12] See e.g., Henri Rolin's proposal to amend Article 34 of the Statute of the Court during the travaux préparatoires of the Institut de droit international, 'Etude des amendements au Statut de la CIJ' (1954) 45 *Annuaire de l'Institut de droit international* 408–553 at 486–487 ; see also e.g. M. Bedjaoui, 'L'humanité en quête de paix et de développement, Cours général de droit international public' 325 *Collected Courses of The Hague Academy of International Law* (2006) 40, 46 ; P. M. Dupuy, C. Hoss, 'Article 34', in Zimmermann et al. *The Statute of the International Court of Justice*, 562–563; Quintana, *Litigation at the International Court*, 6–7.

[13] See *Case concerning the Conservation and Sustainable Exploitation of Swordfish Stocks in the South-Eastern Pacific Ocean (Chile/European Union)* before the ITLOS, Case No 7 (2000); E. Paasivirta, 'The European Union and the United Nations Convention on the Law of the Sea' 38 *Fordham International Law Journal* (2015) 1054–1061.

[14] United Nations Convention on the Law of the Sea, Montego Bay, 10 December 1982, 1833 U.N.T.S. 397; 21 ILM 1261 (1982); Article 1, para. 2(2).

[15] On the numerous questions that have to be addressed, see H. Lauterpacht, 'The Revision of the Statute of the International Court of Justice', 1 *The Law & Practice of International Courts and Tribunals* (2002) 104–108.

[16] Under Article 69 of the Statute, the amendments follow the same procedure as the one of the UN Charter. The Court itself endeavoured in 1969 to amend its Statutes insofar as it relates to its seat (Article 22) but with no success; see G. Guyomar, *Commentaire du Règlement de la Cour internationale de Justice*, (Pedone, 1983), vol. 2, 358; M Bedjaoui, 'L'humanité en quête de paix et de développement', 58–60.

[17] See e.g., on this 'revival', A. Pellet, 'Values and Power Relations – The "Disillusionment" of International Law?', *KFG Working Paper Series*, No. 34, Berlin Potsdam Research Group 'The International Rule of Law: Rise or Decline?', Berlin, May 2019.

deepen State's resistance with regard to any proposal to enlarge the competence of the Court by allowing cases involving international organisations as parties. The one brought a bit surprisingly against Myanmar by The Gambia, which has been accused of acting in 'lieu et place' or as a 'proxy' of the Organisation of Islamic Conference,[18] could be an example.

Conditions (Article 35 of the Statute)

Article 35 of the Statute specifies that the Court is 'open' to two categories of States, those which are parties to the Statute, and those which are not.

First, it is open to States parties to the Statute (Article 35(1) of the Statute). This group contains nearly all States since Article 93(1) of the UN Charter provides that all Members of the United Nations are *ipso facto* parties to the Statute. With respect to States which are not Members of the United Nations,[19] Article 93(2) of the Charter provides that they may become parties to the Statute if they so wish, based on conditions decided in each case by the UNGA upon recommendation of the UNSC. In all logic, because there is no reason for discriminating between different candidates, the first set of conditions decided by UNGA Resolution 91(I) of 11 December 1946 related to Switzerland became the standard.[20] Moreover, the conditions to be fulfilled are mere formalities. In substance, the applicant must formally accept the provisions of the Statute as well as the obligations set out in Article 94 of the UN Charter, and must undertake to contribute to the expenses of the Court upon request of the UNGA.

Second, Article 35(2) of the Statute lays down access conditions for States which are not Members of the UN and do not intend to – or cannot, or did not yet – become parties to the Statute. It provides that 'subject to the special provisions contained in treaties in force', the Security Council shall lay down the conditions under which the Court is also open to these States.

---

[18] See *Application of the Convention on the Prevention and Punishment of the Crime of Genocide (The Gambia* v. *Myanmar)*, Order on Provisional Measures, 23 January 2020, para 23.

[19] Article 35(3) of the Statute states that when a State which is not a Member of the United Nations is a party to a case, the Court shall fix the amount which that party is to contribute towards the expenses of the Court, unless such State is bearing a share of the expenses of the Court.

[20] Resolutions 92 (I), 11 December 1946 (Switzerland), 363 (IV), 1 December 1949 (Liechtenstein), 805 (VIII), 9 December 1953 (Japan), 806 (VIII), 9 December 1953 (San Marino), 42/21, 18 November 1987 (Nauru).

In the *Legality of the Use of Force* case, the Court interpreted the reference to 'the special provisions contained in treaties in force' as to only apply 'to treaties in force at the date of the entry into force of the Statute, and not to any treaties concluded since that date', although it recognised that 'no such prior treaties, referring to the jurisdiction of the present Court, have been brought to the attention of the Court, and it may be that none existed'.[21] In this case, it concluded that 'even assuming that Serbia and Montenegro was a party to the Genocide Convention at the relevant date, Article 35, paragraph 2, of the Statute does not provide it with a basis to have access to the Court, under Article IX of that Convention, since the Convention only entered into force on 12 January 1951, after the entry into force of the Statute'.[22]

As required by the Statute, the Security Council adopted Resolution 9 (1946) of 15 October 1946, stating that for the Court to be open to a State that is not party to the Statute, this State must declare that it accepts, in general or for (a) particular dispute(s), the jurisdiction of the Court, in accordance with the Charter and with the Statute and Rules of the Court, and undertake to comply in good faith with the decision or decisions of the Court and to accept all the obligations of a Member of the United Nations under Article 94 of the Charter.[23] A number of such declarations are mentioned on the Court's website, and some cases were brought to the Court on this ground by States which subsequently became Members of the United Nations. For example, in the *Monetary Gold* case, Italy submitted a declaration before seizing the Court.[24] Of course, the validity of a unilateral declaration made under Resolution 9 (1946) can be challenged before the Court if the statehood of the declaring entity is contested. In such a

---

[21] *Legality of Use of Force (Serbia and Montenegro v. France), Preliminary Objections, Judgment*, p. 618, para. 112.

[22] *Ibid.*, pp. 618–619, para. 113.

[23] It may appear difficult to understand why under Article 93(2) of the UN Charter access to the Court through becoming party to the Statute needs a decision of the UNGA upon recommendation of the UNSC, while under article 35(2) of the Statute access to the Court necessitates only to fulfill the conditions laid down by the UNSC. But as has been explained, this is a 'relic of the League of Nations'; Malcolm N. Shaw, 'Access to the Court of States Not Parties to the Statute', in *M.N. Shaw (ed.), Rosenne's Law and Practice of the International Court: 1920–2015*, Brill, 5th edn. (2016), Vol. 2, Chap. 10, para 168.

[24] *Monetary gold removed from Rome in 1943 (Italy v. France, United Kingdom of Great Britain and Northern Ireland and United States of America), Preliminary Question, Judgment*, ICJ Reports 1954, p. 19, at pp. 22–23.

case, para. 5 of Resolution 9 (1946) provides that '[a]ll questions as to the validity or the effect of a declaration made under the terms of this resolution shall be decided by the Court'. It may be noted that Palestine, recognised by the UNGA as a UN non-member observer State,[25] made such a declaration before submitting its Application in the *Relocation of the United States Embassy to Jerusalem (Palestine* v. *United States of America)* case.

Three further points can be made.

First, it is legitimate to ask whether the conditions for having access to the Court as set out in Article 35(2) should only apply to the applicant – in particular in case of a unilateral application – or to both the applicant and the respondent. Even if the text, which makes no distinction between the applicant and the respondent, seems to support the latter position, arguments can be put forward in favour of the former.[26] This question seems now resolved by the Court in favour of applying the requirements to both the applicant and the respondent.[27] However, on the basis that 'rules of procedure must be approached in a common-sense and flexible manner',[28] it may be suggested that if consent to the jurisdiction is granted by the respondent, the interpretation favouring the competence of the Court is the more convincing.

Second, the question can arise as to the date at which the conditions set out in Article 35(2) must be fulfilled. The situation is normally assessed as it was at the date of the application instituting proceedings,[29] but the Court has admitted that the defect of a party in this respect at this date can be 'cured by a subsequent event in the course of the proceedings, for example

[25] UN General Assembly, Resolution 67/19: Status of Palestine in the United Nations, 29 November 2012, UN doc. A/RES/67/19.

[26] In favor of the first position in case of a unilateral application, see *Application of the Convention on the Prevention and Punishment of the Crime of Genocide (Croatia* v. *Serbia), Preliminary Objections, Judgment,* ICJ Reports 2008, p. 412, Individual opinion of Judge Abraham, at pp. 524–538, paras. 1–44; in favor of the second position, see the Declaration of Judge Owada in the same case, pp. 513–514, paras. 28–32; see also Zimmerman, 'Article 35', in Zimmermann et al., *The Statute of the International Court of Justice,* 699–701, paras. 54–61.

[27] *Application of the Convention on the Prevention and Punishment of the Crime of Genocide (Croatia* v. *Serbia), Preliminary Objections,* pp. 432–444, paras. 60–92.

[28] Sir Elihu Lauterpacht, 'Principles of Procedure in International Litigation' 345 *Collected Courses of the Hague Academy of International Law* (2011) 430.

[29] *Application of the Convention on the Prevention and Punishment of the Crime of Genocide (Croatia* v. *Serbia), Preliminary Objections, Judgment,* p. 437, para. 79.

when that party acquires the status of party to the Statute of the Court which it initially lacked'.[30]

Third, even if, as we have seen, Article 35(2) provides for mere formalities, it remains that 'where the conditions of Article 35 are not met, the Court is without jurisdiction to adjudicate the dispute on the merit',[31] because, '[o]nly those States which have access to the Court can confer jurisdiction upon it'.[32] This jurisprudence is of course exaggeratedly formalistic, and one could support the view that consent to the jurisdiction is the most important aspect to secure, and should be sufficient both to have access to the Court and to confer jurisdiction to it. Some judges have apparently been attracted by such a position, itself espoused by the Court in an order on provisional measures.[33] However, the 'formalistic' view seems currently well in place.

B Consent to the Court's jurisdiction

As the ICJ has noted, it can 'exercise jurisdiction only between States parties to a dispute who not only have access to the Court but also have accepted the jurisdiction of the Court, either in general form or for the individual dispute concerned'.[34] It is indeed a 'well-established principle of international law' that the Court 'may not exercise jurisdiction over a State except with the consent of that State'.[35] As a consequence, the Court's jurisdiction is wholly dependent of the disputing parties' consent, as ascertained at the date of the application instituting proceedings,[36] or later

---

[30] Ibid., p. 442, para. 87.

[31] Ibid., p. 432, para. 66.

[32] *Legality of Use of Force (Serbia and Montenegro* v. *Canada), Preliminary Objections, Judgment,* ICJ Reports 2004, p. 429, at p. 448, para. 45.

[33] See ibid., Joint Declaration of Judges Ranjeva, Guillaume, Higgins, Koojmans, Al-Khasawneh, Buergenthal and Elaraby, p. 769, para. 11, quoting with apparent approval *Application of the Convention on the Prevention and Punishment of the Crime of Genocide (Bosnia and Herzegovina* v. *Yugoslavia (Serbia and Montenegro)), Provisional Measures,* ICJ Reports 1993, p. 3, at p. 14, para. 19.

[34] *Legality of Use of Force (Serbia and Montenegro* v. *Germany), Provisional Measures,* ICJ Reports 1999, p. 422, at 429, para. 19.

[35] *Monetary Gold Case taken in Rome in 1943, Preliminary Issue, Judgment, ICJ Reports 1954,* p. 19, at p. 32.

[36] If consent to the jurisdiction does exist at the date of the application, a subsequent withdrawal of such consent has no effect on the jurisdiction already established;

in case of a *forum prorogatum*.[37] But this may not be sufficient. Indeed, under the 'monetary gold' or 'indispensable third party' principle, if, in a case between two parties accepting the Court's jurisdiction, 'the essential question to be decided relates to the international responsibility of a third State' or where the interests of a third State would constitute 'the very subject-matter' of the dispute, [the Court] cannot assume jurisdiction over the dispute without the consent of that State'.[38]

It follows quite logically from the basic requirement of parties' consent that an application instituting proceedings must specify 'as far as possible the legal grounds upon which the jurisdiction of the Court is said to be based'.[39] Where the respondent immediately opposes that there is a manifest lack of jurisdiction, as did France in the *Request for an examination* case, the Court is likely to organise hearings and decide by way of an order, not a judgement, to pursue the proceedings or to dismiss the request.[40] In any event, it should not take such a position without giving to the parties the possibility to present their views. Also, if there is an application for provisional measures, the Court 'can remove the case from the List at the provisional measures stage',[41] again by way of an order adopted after hearings.

Nottebohm (Liechtenstein v. Guatemala), Preliminary Objection, Judgment, ICJ Reports 1953, p. 111, at 123.

[37] See below.

[38] *M/V Norstar (Panama v. Italy), Preliminary Objections Judgment of 4 November 2016*, p. 45, para. 172, providing its own assessment of the ICJ's case law regarding the 'Monetary Gold Principle', which includes *Continental Shelf (Libyan Arab Jamahiriya/ Malta), Application for Intervention, Judgment*, ICJ Reports 1984, p. 25, para. 40; *Military and Paramilitary Activities in and against Nicaragua (Nicaragua v. United States of America), Jurisdiction and Admissibility, Judgment*, ICJ Reports 1984, p. 431, para. 88; *Frontier Dispute (Burkina Faso/Republic of Mali), Judgment, ICJ Reports 1986, p. 579*, para. 49; *Land, Island and Maritime Boundary Dispute (El Salvador/Honduras), Application for Intervention, Judgment*, ICJ Reports 1990, pp. 114–116, paras. 54–56, and p. 122, para. 73, *Certain Phosphate Lands* in *Nauru (Nauru v. Australia), Preliminary Objections, Judgment, ICJ Reports 1992*, pp. 259–262, paras. 50–55, and *East Timor (Portugal v. Australia), Judgment*, ICJ Reports 1995, p. 90, at 105, para. 34.

[39] Article 38(2) of the Rules of Court.

[40] *Request for an Examination of the Situation in Accordance with Paragraph 63 of the Court's Judgment of 20 December 1974 in the Nuclear Tests (New Zealand v. France)*, ICJ Reports 1995, p. 288.

[41] *Legality of Use of Force (Yugoslavia v. Spain), Provisional Measures, Order of 2 June 1999*, ICJ Reports 1999 (II), p. 761, at p. 773, para. 35; *Legality of Use of Force (Yugoslavia v. United States of America), Provisional Measures, Order of 2 June 1999*, ICJ Reports 1999 (II), p. 916, at p. 925, para. 29; *Immunities and Criminal Proceedings (Equatorial Guinea v. France), Provisional Measures*, ICJ Reports 2016, p. 1148, at p. 1165, para. 70.

There are basically two means of acceptance of the Court's jurisdiction: by agreement between the parties,[42] or through the mechanism of the 'optional clause'.[43] Although the optional clause was one of the most promising innovation when the PCIJ was created,[44] it did not become the prominent way for consenting to the Court's jurisdiction, and in contemporary practice 'compromissory clauses play a significantly more important role in establishing the jurisdiction of the Court'.[45]

Of course, the question of the scope of State's consent is crucial. It will depend on each case, but in any event the contentious jurisdiction of the Court extends only to 'disputes'. It is true that Article 36(1) provides that the Court can be seized of 'cases' ('affaires' in French) or 'matters' ('cas' in French), while Article 36(2) speaks of 'disputes' ('différends' in French), but as stated in Article 38 of the Statute, the 'function' of the Court 'is to decide in accordance with international law such disputes as are submitted to it'.[46] Unsurprisingly, the jurisprudence testifies to the fact that the notion of 'dispute' is a frequent source of contention notably in regards to what it is, how to define the true subject matter of a particular dispute, or as to the moment it was born.

Consent by Agreement

With respect to consent by agreement, three situations are contemplated by Article 36(1) of the Statute, which reads: '[t]he jurisdiction of the Court comprises all cases which the parties refer to it and all matters specially provided for in the Charter of the United Nations or in treaties and conventions in force'.

First, a 'case', that is, an existing dispute, can be referred to the Court by a special agreement concluded between the parties for this specific purpose. It could appear like a quite simple situation characterised by the fact that States agree in good faith to bring their case to the Court, and it

---

[42] Article 36(1) of the Statute.
[43] Article 36(2) of the Statute.
[44] Cesare P. R. Romano, 'The Shift from the Consensual to the Compulsory Paradigm in International Adjudication: Elements for a Theory of Consent' (2007) 39 (4) *NYU Journal of International Law and Politics*, 791–872 at 808.
[45] A. A. Yusuf, 'Compulsory Jurisdiction of the Court under the Optional Clause' in S. van Hoogstraten (eds.), *New Challenges to International Law* (Brill: Nijhoff, 2018), 9.
[46] Quintana, *Litigation at the International Court*, 54; Tomuschat, 'Article 36', 721, para. 8.

happens frequently.[47] However, the process leading a dispute to be brought to the Court by special agreement can be very long. For example, the *Pedra Branca* case[48] took sixteen years from the beginning of the negotiation of a special agreement to a judgment.[49] A more recent example is the *Guatemala/Belize* case.[50] The two States decided by special agreement signed in 2008 upon recommendation of the Secretary-General of the Organisation of American States to refer Guatemala's territorial, insular and maritime claim to the International Court of Justice, after approval of their respective population. The case has actually been brought to the Court eleven years later. A special agreement has also been concluded between Gabon and Equatorial Guinea to refer to the Court a dispute regarding their boundaries and the sovereignty over certain islands, after having exhausted other non-judicial means of dispute settlement. In these two cases, the four States concerned decided to bring their disputes to the Court after lengthy unsuccessful discussion, including under the auspices of international organisations. They illustrate to a certain extent Sir Elihu Lauterpacht's view that litigation is considered positively by a State when it is convinced that it has 'nothing to lose if it loses, or unless political factors oblige it to involve itself in the process'.[51] Of course, a special agreement must be carefully drafted in order to confer jurisdiction to the Court on the exact point of contention. But even once agreed, the scope of a special agreement can be challenged, in particular insofar as it defines the dispute for which the jurisdiction of the Court has been accepted. In such a case, the Court decides.

The question was raised in the *Corfu Channel* case as to whether, despite not being seized by both parties on the basis of a special agreement, the Court could nevertheless be lawfully seized under Article 36(1) by a unilateral application followed by a later declaration or conduct by the respondent showing acceptance of the jurisdiction of the Court. The Court's answer was positive, thus rejecting the assumption that

---

[47] The list provided on the ICJ's website references eighteen cases submitted to the Court by special agreement.

[48] *Sovereignty over Pedra Branca/Pulau Batu Puteh, Middle Rocks and South Ledge (Malaysia/Singapore), Judgment,* ICJ Reports 2008, p. 12.

[49] Xue, 'Jurisdiction of the International Court', 59–60; see also S. Jayakumar and T. Koh, *Pedra Branca: The Road to the World Court,* NUS Press, 2009.

[50] *Guatemala's Territorial, Insular and Maritime Claim (Guatemala/Belize),* pending.

[51] Lauterpacht, 'Principles of Procedure', 485.

proceedings can only be instituted by a formal special agreement in cases where compulsory jurisdiction under Article 36(2), discussed below, does not exist.[52] To the contrary, the Court considered that Article 36(1) covers a situation where a unilateral application gives the opportunity to the respondent to accept the jurisdiction of the Court. This is the so-called *forum prorogatum*. As recalled by the Court in the *Djibouti* v. *France* case, under the *forum prorogatum* doctrine, the acceptance of jurisdiction of the respondent State can be deduced from its 'conduct before the Court or in relation to the applicant party', in so far as it 'acted in such a way as to have consented to the jurisdiction of the Court'.[53] The 'element of consent must be either explicit or clearly to be deduced from the relevant conduct of a State'.[54] *Forum prorogatum* 'can be founded . . . in a variety of ways',[55] but one specific modality of establishing it is provided for in Article 38(5) of the Rules of Court, as amended in 1978.[56] Needless to say that the scope of the dispute referred to the Court by consent given through *forum prorogatum* can be disputed.[57]

Second, according to Article 36(1) of the Statute, the Court can exercise its jurisdiction upon 'all matters specially provided for in the Charter of the United Nations'. However, in reality there is no such thing in the UN Charter. As confirmed by the Court in the *Aerial Incident* case: 'the United Nations Charter contains no specific provision of itself conferring compulsory jurisdiction on the Court'.[58] It has been argued that the UN Security Council could decide under Chapter VII of the UN Charter to refer a case to the Court.[59] It seems somewhat unlikely given the reluctance of some permanent Members of the UNSC vis-à-vis the jurisdiction of the Court, but not impossible. It may be reminded that the UNSC decided in a binding resolution to establish the United Nations Compensation

---

[52] *Corfu Channel (UK* v. *Albania), Preliminary Objections,* ICJ Reports 1948, p. 15, at p. 27.

[53] *Certain Questions of Mutual Assistance in Criminal Matters (Djibouti* v. *France), Judgment,* ICJ Reports 2008, p. 177 at pp. 203–204, para. 61.

[54] Ibid., p. 204, para. 62.

[55] Ibid., p. 205, para. 64.

[56] Ibid., p. 205, paras. 63–64.

[57] As was the case, for example, in the *Djibouti* v. *France* case; see Ibid., pp. 206–213, paras. 65– 95.

[58] *Aerial Incident of 10 August 1999 (Pakistan* v. *India), Jurisdiction of the Court, Judgment,* ICJ Reports 2000, p. 12 at p. 32, para. 48.

[59] Tomuschat, 'Article 36', 665, para. 47; *contra,* Quintana, *Litigation at the International Court,* 47.

Commission to address damage claims against Iraq, without requesting any special consent from Iraq.[60]

Third, the jurisdiction of the Court comprises all matters provided for 'in treaties and conventions in force'.[61] There are in fact quite a number of treaties, both bilateral and multilateral, containing a compromissory clause, as illustrated by the list provided for on the Court's website, and most of the pending cases are grounded on such a clause. The wording of the compromissory clauses varies and can raises different sort of interpretive difficulties.[62]

Consent under the 'Optional Clause' (Article 36(2))

As recalled above, the contentious jurisdiction of the ICJ is not automatically compulsory for States members of the UN or parties to its Statute. Yet, Article 36(2) of the Statute sets out an 'option' for States to unilaterally accept as obligatory the jurisdiction of the Court, by depositing a declaration to this effect. Under this mechanism, said the 'optional clause', a State consenting to the Court's jurisdiction in this way can seize the Court by unilateral application against another State accepting the same obligation. Article 36(2) reads: '[t]he states parties to the present Statute may at any time declare that they recognise as compulsory ipso facto and without special agreement, in relation to any other state accepting the same obligation, the jurisdiction of the Court in all legal disputes concerning: a. the interpretation of a treaty; b. any question of international law; c. the existence of any fact which, if established, would constitute a breach of an international obligation; d. the nature or extent of the reparation to be made for the breach of an international obligation.'

The number and content of such declarations is both encouraging and disappointing. On the one hand, seventy-four of them appear on the

---

[60] UN Security Council, Resolution 692 (1991) [Iraq-Kuwait], 20 May 1991, UN doc. S_RES_692(1991) referring to Resolution 687 (1991), 8 April 1991, UN doc. S/RES/687 (1991). See Lauterpacht, 'Principles of Procedure', 445.

[61] In addition, Article 37 of the Statute provides that '[w]henever a treaty or convention in force provides for reference of a matter to a tribunal to have been instituted by the League of Nations, or to the Permanent Court of International Justice, the matter shall, as between the parties to the present Statute, be referred to the International Court of Justice'. On this provision and the practice of the Court, see B. Simma, D. Richemond-Barack, 'Article 37', in Zimmermann et al., *The Statute of the International Court of Justice*, 799–813.

[62] Tomuschat, 'Article 36', in Zimmermann et al., *The Statute of the International Court of Justice*, 747–758, paras. 48–67.

Court's website, which is a substantial number.[63] They include States from all continents, such as 'small' States, like Malta or Lesotho, as well as States like Australia, Canada, Japan, Germany, Italy, the Netherlands, Mexico, India, Pakistan, the UK. Some have been deposited a long time ago, even before the entry into force of the current Statute, under the PCIJ's optional clause mechanism.[64] Since they are still in force they are deemed to have been made under the ICJ's optional clause, as stated by Article 36(5) of the Statute.

On the other hand, less than half of the 193 States Members of the UN are enrolled in the optional clause mechanism. Moreover, a closer look to the text of the declarations shows that most States limit substantially the scope of their acceptance of the compulsory jurisdiction of the Court. Regarding the validity of these reservations, Article 36(3) can be misleading since it seems to limit their extent to certain aspects only,[65] but the Statute has always been interpreted liberally.[66] Reservations which exclude certain categories of disputes are unchallenged, and States are even 'free to limit the scope *ratione personae* which they wish to give to their acceptance of the compulsory jurisdiction of the Court'.[67] Australia, for example, excludes 'any dispute concerning or relating to the delimitation of maritime zones'; India provides for a long list of reservation covering disputes 'with the government of any State which is or has been a Member of the Commonwealth of Nations', and 'relating to or connected

---

[63] This number of 74 can be compared to the 35 declarations under the optional clause discussed in 1958 by Herbert W Briggs, 'Reservations to the Acceptance of Compulsory Jurisdiction of the International Court of Justice' 93 *Collected Courses of the Hague Academy of International Law* (1958) 231, and to the fifty-six declarations in force in 1993 in contrast with the sixty-seven observed in 2009 by J. G. Merrils, 'Does the Optional Clause still matters ?', in K. H. Kaikobad and M. Bohlander (eds.), *International Law and Power: Perspectives on Legal Order and Justice. Essays in Honour of Colin Warbrick* (Brill: Nijhoff, 2009), 431–454, 432.

[64] See the declarations of Haiti (1921); Panama (1921); Uruguay (1921); the Dominican Republic (1924); Luxembourg (1930).

[65] Article 36(3) provides that declarations 'may be made unconditionally or on condition of reciprocity on the part of several or certain states, or for a certain time'.

[66] Briggs, 'Reservations to the Acceptance of Compulsory Jurisdiction', 232–233; as acknowledged by the Court: '[i]t is for each State, in formulating its declaration, to decide upon the limits it places upon its acceptance of the *jurisdiction* of the Court'; *Fisheries Jurisdiction (Spain v. Canada), Jurisdiction of the Court, Judgment,* ICJ Reports 1998, p. 432, at p. 452, para. 44.

[67] *Aerial Incident of 10 August 1999 (Pakistan v. India), Jurisdiction of the Court, Judgment,* ICJ Reports 2000, p. 12, at p. 30, para. 40.

with facts or situations of hostilities, armed conflicts, individual or collective actions taken in self-defence, resistance to aggression, fulfilment of obligations imposed by international bodies, and other similar or related acts, measures or situations in which India is, has been or may in future be involved, including the measures taken for protection of national security and ensuring national defence'; likewise, UK's declaration excludes disputes with a member or former member of the Commonwealth, and, among others, 'any claim or dispute that arises from or is connected with or related to nuclear disarmament and/or nuclear weapon'. Perhaps the most remarkable reservation is the one of Pakistan, dated 2017. It excludes from its scope, among others, disputes 'arising under a multilateral treaty or any other international obligation that the Islamic Republic of Pakistan has specifically undertaken unless: i) all the parties to the treaty affected by the decision are also parties to the case before the Court, or ii) the Government of the Islamic Republic of Pakistan specifically agrees to jurisdiction'. Beyond the fact that this sentence raises rather difficult interpretive questions, the requirement of a 'specific' agreement to jurisdiction seems inconsistent with the optional clause mechanism since Article 36(2) provides that declarations are made for recognising 'as compulsory ipso facto and without special agreement' the jurisdiction of the Court.[68]

An important aspect of the optional clause is reciprocity, which is 'inherent' to this mechanism.[69] It means that the declaration of one State under this mechanism will operate only vis-a-vis other States which themselves adopt such declaration. The *rationale* here is that through the optional clause a State exposes itself to be sued by another State only if and to the extent this other State accepts itself to be sued before the Court in the same manner. As a consequence, 'jurisdiction is conferred on the Court [by declarations under the optional clause mechanism] only to the extent to which the two Declarations coincide in conferring it'.[70] Of course, the interpretation of the more restrictive declaration can be disputed, in

---

[68] On a broader perspective, scholars generally mention or support the view that purely self-judging (or Connally) reservation are arguably invalid (Lauterpacht 'Principles of Procedure', 442) or that the reservations are valid only if they are not inconsistent with the Statute (Briggs, 'Reservations to the Acceptance of Compulsory Jurisdiction', 233).
[69] Xue, 'Jurisdiction of the International Court, 63.
[70] *Anglo-Iranian Oil Co. (United Kingdom v. Iran)*, preliminary objections, ICJ Reports 1952, p. 93, at p. 103.

particular when the respondent tries to escape the Court's jurisdiction on the basis of the applicant's reservation,[71] but it is the task of the Court to provide the correct interpretation.

One problem with the optional clause mechanism is that it can be 'abused of', because nothing prevents a State used to shielding itself from complaints from other States from depositing a declaration for the sole purpose of lodging an application against a State accepting the compulsory jurisdiction. The ICJ's jurisprudence is of no protection since it establishes that a declaration has immediate legal effect. In the *Land and Maritime Boundary* case, the Court held, consistent with its previous case law,[72] that: '[a]ny State party to the Statute, in adhering to the jurisdiction of the Court in accordance with Article 36, paragraph 2, accepts jurisdiction in its relations with States previously having adhered to that clause. At the same time, it makes a standing offer to the other States party to the Statute which have not yet deposited a declaration of acceptance. The day one of those States accepts that offer by depositing in its turn its declaration of acceptance, the consensual bond is established and no further condition needs to be fulfilled.'[73] In a somewhat surprising contrast, the Court is of the view that the notification of withdrawal of a declaration under the optional clause has effect only after a 'reasonable period of notice'.[74] In reaction, States' declarations are now often drafted so as to

---

[71] In the *Whaling* case, the Court recalled that it 'must seek the interpretation which is in harmony with a natural and reasonable way of reading the text, having due regard to the intention' of the declaring State (*Anglo-Iranian Oil Co.*,p. 104), noted that in the *Fisheries Jurisdiction* case it had 'not hesitated to place a certain emphasis on the intention of the depositing State' (*Fisheries Jurisdiction*, p. 454, para. 48) and observed that '[t]he intention of a reserving State may be deduced not only from the text of the relevant clause, but also from the context in which the clause is to be read, and an examination of evidence regarding the circumstances of its preparation and the purposes intended to be served' (Ibid., p. 454, para. 49). See *Whaling in the Antarctic (Australia* v. *Japan: New Zealand intervening), Judgment*, ICJ Reports 2014, p. 226, at p. 244, para. 36.

[72] *Right of Passage over Indian Territory, Preliminary Objections, Judgment*, ICJ Reports 1957, p. 125, at 146–147; *Temple of Preah Vihear, Preliminary Objections*, ICJ Reports 1961, p. 17, at 31–32; *Military and Paramilitary Activities in and against Nicaragua (Nicaragua* v. *United States of America), Jurisdiction and Admissibility, Judgment*, ICJ Reports 1984, p. 392, at 412, para. 45.

[73] *Land and Maritime Boundary between Cameroon and Nigeria, Preliminary Objections, Judgment*, ICJ Reports 1998, p. 275, at 291, para. 25.

[74] *Military and Paramilitary Activities in and against Nicaragua*, p. 420, para. 63; *Land and Maritime Boundary between Cameroon and Nigeria, Preliminary Objections, Judgment*, ICJ Reports 1998, p. 275, at 295, para. 33.

openly contradict the Court's case law. For example, Germany, Cyprus, or Nigeria's declarations provide expressly that the withdrawal of their consent under the optional clause will have effect immediately upon notification. In the same vein, Australia and Italy's declarations, for example, exclude the Court's jurisdiction 'where the acceptance of the Court's compulsory jurisdiction on behalf of any other party to the dispute was deposited less than twelve months prior to the filing of the application bringing the dispute before the Court'. And it is common ground for declarations to exclude the Court's jurisdiction where the other party 'has accepted the compulsory jurisdiction of the International Court of Justice only in relation to or for the purpose of the dispute' (see e.g., Australia and Italy's declarations). One may say that the current situation is not glorious since, as a consequence of these reservations, there is not much left of the *rationale* of the optional clause mechanism.

III Advisory Jurisdiction

The advisory jurisdiction of the Court is governed by Article 65(1) of the Statute, which provides that '[t]he Court may give an advisory opinion on any legal question at the request of whatever body may be authorised by or in accordance with the Charter of the United Nations to make such a request.' Article 96 of the UN Charter adds that only two UN bodies are authorised to request advisory opinions on any legal question, the General Assembly and the Security Council (para. 1), while other bodies may be authorised at any time by the UNGA to request advisory opinions on legal questions arising within the scope of their activities (para 2).

This suggests three questions to be addressed in turn: the jurisdictional requirement, the margin of discretion that the Court reserves to itself to possibly decline the exercise of its contentious jurisdiction, and finally the effect of an advisory opinion.

A Jurisdiction

Two elements trigger the Court's advisory jurisdiction, meaning its legal entitlement to deliver an advisory opinion: the subject-matter of the request, which must be a 'legal question', or a question 'legal in character',[75] and the author of the question, which must be an author-ised body, namely the UNGA, the UNSC, or other bodies authorised by the UNGA.

Legal Question

The subject-matter of a request is clarified in the question put to the Court. Of course, questions put by an organ like the UNGA are the outcome of political discussions, but it is sufficient that they are formulated in such a manner as to have a legal character and raise questions of international law for the Court to have jurisdiction to examine them. When ensuring that this requirement is fulfilled, the Court applies a formalistic standard, considering that 'questions "framed in terms of law and rais[ing] problems of international law ... are by their very nature susceptible of a reply based on law"'.[76] The Court is thus 'not concerned with the political nature of the motives which may have inspired the request or the political implications which its opinion might have',[77] and it frequently adds that in any event, 'in situations in which political considerations are prominent it may be particularly necessary for an international organization to obtain an advisory opinion from the Court as to the legal principles applicable with respect to the matter under debate'.[78] It may of course happen that the manner the question is drafted is inadequate, unclear, or subject to discus-sions, but these difficulties are generally addressed by the Court when it considers whether, in the exercise of its discretion, it should decline to answer the request.

[75] *Legal Consequences of the Separation of the Chagos Archipelago from Mauritius in 1965, Advisory Opinion*, ICJ Reports 2019, p. 95, at 112, para. 59.

[76] *Accordance with International Law of the Unilateral Declaration of Independence in Respect of Kosovo, Advisory Opinion*, ICJ Reports 2010, p. 403, at 415, para. 25, quoting *Western Sahara, Advisory Opinion*, ICJ Reports 1975, p. 18, para. 15. See also *Legality of the Threat or Use of Nuclear Weapons, Advisory Opinion*, ICJ Reports 1996, p. 226, at 233–234, para. 13.

[77] *Accordance with International Law of the Unilateral Declaration of Independence in Respect of Kosovo*, p. 415, para. 27, referring to *Conditions of Admission of a State to Membership in the United Nations (Article 4 of the Charter), Advisory Opinion, 1948*, ICJ Reports 1947–1948, p. 61, and *Legality of the Threat or Use of Nuclear Weapons, Advisory Opinion*, ICJ Reports 1996 (I), p. 234, para. 13.

[78] *Interpretation of the Agreement of 25 March 1951 between the WHO and Egypt, Advisory Opinion*, ICJ Reports 1980, p. 73, at p. 87, para. 33.

In so far as bodies other that the UNGA and the UNSC, namely special-ised agencies or related organisations, are concerned,[79] another require-ment is at point since the question must not only be 'legal in character', but should also arise within the scope of their activities or areas of competence. This assessment requires the Court to interpret, in case of specialised agencies or related organisations, 'the relevant rules of the organization and, in the first place, [..] its constitution'.[80] Where it is a UN organ authorised by the UNGA,[81] the Court analyses the scope of its activities in taking account of its 'function and programme'.[82] It should be men-tioned that the authorisations granted by the UNGA to specialised agencies and related organisations systematically contain a reservation, the validity of which has never been disputed. This reservation appears for example in Article X of the Agreement between the UN and the WHO,[83] which provides that the latter is authorised to put questions to the Court except where they concern 'the mutual relationships of the Organization and the United Nations or other specialized agencies'.[84]

Discretion

Even if the Court is satisfied that it has jurisdiction to entertain a request for advisory opinion, it may exercise its discretion to decline to answer 'so as to protect the integrity of the Court's judicial function as the principal judicial organ of the United Nations'.[85]

It is at this stage that the Court proceeds to the interpretation of the question. The PCIJ considered in 1926 that when the question does 'not exactly state the question upon which its opinion is sought', it can proceed

---

[79] The list of the related agencies (15, including e.g., the WHO, the IFAD, the UNESCO, the ICAO, the IMF, the IMO, and the ILO), and related organisations (only one, the AIEA) is given by the Court on its website.

[80] *Legality of the Use by a State of Nuclear Weapons in Armed Conflict, Advisory Opinion,* ICJ Reports 1996, p. 66, at 79, para. 19.

[81] The list mentioned by the ICJ on its website includes three organs, the Economic and Social Council, the Trusteeship Council, and the Interim Committee of the General Assembly.

[82] *Applicability of Article VI, Section 22, of the Convention on the Privileges and Immunities of the United Nations, Advisory Opinion,* ICJ Reports 1989, p. 177, at 187, para. 28.

[83] This agreement has been approved by the UNGA resolution 124(II) of 15 November 1947.

[84] This provision is standard in the Agreements between the UN and specialised agencies. See e.g., Article X of the Agreement between the UN and the UNESCO. See also Article X of the Agreements between the UN and the IAEA.

[85] See e.g., *Legal Consequences of the Separation of the Chagos Archipelago from Mauritius in 1965,* p. 113, para. 54.

to its interpretation. But it added that it was possible for the Court to do this 'owing to the relatively simple nature of the case; this, however, may not always be so'.[86] However, it never happened that a question put was so complicated and inappropriate that the Court could not understand what it meant. The ICJ also proceeds with no reluctance to the interpretation of a vague or unclear question.[87] It also stated repeatedly that it may depart from the language of the question put to it where the question does not reflect the 'legal questions really in issue'.[88] However, it may be argued that the Court refused to acknowledge what was the real issue in the *Kosovo* case in sticking to a narrow reading of the question, when it affirmed that 'the question posed by the General Assembly is clearly formulated. The question is narrow and specific; it asks for the Court's opinion on whether or not the declaration of independence is in accordance with international law. It does not ask about the legal consequences of that declaration. In particular, it does not ask whether or not Kosovo has achieved statehood. Nor does it ask about the validity or legal effects of the recognition of Kosovo by those States which have recognized it as an independent State.'[89]

The Court's consistent position is that it would exercise its discretion to decline its advisory jurisdiction only for 'compelling reasons'.[90] But it never happened up to now.[91] However, what has been acknowledged as a potential compelling reason by the Court is where a reply to the question put 'would have the effect of circumventing the principle that a State is not obliged to allow its disputes to be submitted to judicial settlement without its consent'.[92] To date, the existence of an inter-State dispute, even very

---

[86] *Interpretation of the Greco-Turkish Agreement of 1 December 1926 (Final Protocol, Article IV), Advisory Opinion, 1928, P.C.I.J.,* Series B, No. 16, p.14.

[87] *Legal Consequences of the Separation of the Chagos Archipelago from Mauritius in 1965,* p. 112, para. 61.

[88] Ibid., p. 129, para. 135.

[89] *Accordance with International Law of the Unilateral Declaration of Independence in Respect of Kosovo, Advisory opinion,* p. 423, para. 51. For critics, see e.g., appended to this judgment, the Declaration of Judge Simma, pp. 478–481, and the Separate Opinions of Judges Sepulveda-Amor, pp. 498–499, and Yusuf, pp. 619–625.

[90] *Legal Consequences of the Separation of the Chagos Archipelago from Mauritius in 1965,* p. 113, para. 65.

[91] The list of potential 'compelling reasons' that the Court might take into account is given by Pierre D'Argent, 'Article 65', in Zimmermann et al., *The Statute of the International Court of Justice,* 1804–1808, paras. 44–47.

[92] *Western Sahara, Advisory Opinion,* ICJ Reports 1975, p. 25, para. 33.

closely related to the legal question put, never convinced the Court to refrain from entertaining the request,[93] including in a case involving a permanent member of the UNSC.[94]

In the same vein, the Court will not decline to exercise its jurisdiction when it is not in a position to answer completely to the question put. In the *Legality of the Threat or Use of Nuclear Weapons* case, the Court stated that '[a]n entirely different question is whether the Court, under the constraints placed upon it as a judicial organ, will be able to give a complete answer to the question asked of it. However, that is a different matter from a refusal to answer at all'.[95] The Court was referring to the fact that it 'cannot legislate' and can only take account of positive international law as it stands.[96] On this basis, in this case, while it did not refuse to respond in the absence of 'compelling reasons' for doing so, it concluded that it was not in a position to 'reach a definitive conclusion as to the legality or illegality of the use of nuclear weapons by a State in an extreme circumstance of self-defence, in which its very survival would be at stake'.[97]

Non-binding Character

An advisory opinion 'is given not to States, but to the organ which is entitled to request it'.[98] By contrast compared to a judgment, such opinion is only 'advisory' and therefore non-binding, even for the requesting organ[99] which is sole competent to determine the usefulness of the response.[100] Of course, the latter may oblige itself to consider the advisory

---

[93] See e.g., J.-M. Thouvenin, 'La saisine de la Cour internatioanle de Justice en cas de violation des règles fondamentales de l'ordre juridique international', 331–332. On this point, Judge Oda curiously affirmed that '[t]he settlement of disputes between States is without doubt a principal object of the contentious function of the ICJ'; S. Oda, 'The International Court of Justice Viewed from the Bench (1976–1993)' 244 *Collected Courses of the Hague Academy of International Law* (1993) 102, para. 150.

[94] See *Legal Consequences of the Separation of the Chagos Archipelago from Mauritius in 1965*.

[95] *Legality of the Threat or Use of Nuclear Weapons*, p. 238, para. 19.

[96] Ibid., p. 237, para. 18.

[97] Ibid., p. 263, para. 97.

[98] *Interpretation of Peace Treaties with Bulgaria, Hungary and Romania, First Phase, Advisory Opinion*, ICJ Reports 1950, p. 71.

[99] Ibid.

[100] *Legal Consequences of the Separation of the Chagos Archipelago from Mauritius in 1965*, p. 115, para. 76.

opinion as binding, but this does not change the fact that, as such, the advisory opinion is not binding.[101]

Yet, advisory opinions are authoritative pronouncement of the law as it is, by the most respected international judicial organ, and are therefore very influential in the international community. Since the Court seems eager to exercise its advisory jurisdiction even in the most sensible political situation, as illustrated by the *Western Sahara*, *Wall in Palestine*, and *Chagos* cases, it is not impossible that the advisory function of the Court, still a 'sleeping beauty', will emerge in the future as a more frequently used tool by an international community claiming its dedication to the rule of law.

IV Conclusion

Many voices have advocated that triggering the contentious jurisdiction of the Court to the Parties consent is now wholly outdated. This is notably the case of Judge Cançado Trindade, who consistently denounces the anachronism of reliance upon the will of States and on their consent as a precondition of access to justice.[102] His Dissenting Opinion in *Georgia v. Russia* is a brilliant and convincing plea for compulsory jurisdiction. Even if he lucidly acknowledges that 'there is still a long way to go to attain the idealism of compulsory jurisdiction in the inter-State *contentieux*', the author keeps confident because 'there is nothing more invincible than an ideal that has not been attained', and is convinced that time will come when 'the conjunction of stars' will allow it.[103]

Such plea could well have already provided some effects. Indeed, State's consent has at least once been overcome via the advisory jurisdiction of the Court. Indeed, a Special Chamber of the ITLOS has adopted the

---

[101] *Judgments of the Administrative Tribunal of the ILO upon complaints made against the UNESCO, Advisory Opinion of October 23rd, 1956,* ICJ Reports 1956, p. 77, at p. 84.

[102] A. Cançado Trindade, 'Reflections on the Realization of Justice in the Era of Contemporary International Tribunals' 408 *Collected Courses of the Hague Academy of International Law* (2020) 33.

[103] *Application of the International Convention on the Elimination of All Forms of Racial Discrimination (Georgia v. Russian Federation),* Preliminary Objections, Judgment, ICJ Reports 2011, p. 70, Dissenting opinion of Judge Cançado Trindade, p. 239, at 263, para. 60.

groundbreaking view in a recent judgement that the Advisory opinion of the ICJ in *Chagos* did not only 'advise' the UNGA as to what the law is, but actually put an end to the longstanding bilateral sovereignty dispute between the UK and Mauritius, despite the uncontested fact the UK has never consented to have this dispute resolved by the ICJ or the ITLOS, and continues to claim sovereignty over the Chagos.[104] According to the Special Chamber of the ITLOS, as a result of the ICJ's advisory opinion, UK's legal claim to sovereignty has vanished into a 'mere assertion'.[105] Time will tell whether this creative approach, seemingly assimilating contentious and advisory jurisdiction of the ICJ, will gain support and usefully promote the 'conjunction of stars' anticipated by Judge Cançado Trindade, or be criticised as fundamentally flawed and dangerous for the ICJ's credibility, and finally be ignored as quickly as a falling star fades away.

Further Reading

Roberto Ago, 'Binding Advisory Opinions of the International Court of Justice', 85 *American Journal of International Law* (1985) 439.

Robert Kolb, *The International Court of Justice* (Hart, 2013).

Shigeru Oda, 'The Compulsory Jurisdiction of the International Court of Justice: A Myth? A Statistical Analysis of Contentious Cases', 49 *The International and Comparative Law Quarterly* (2000) 251.

Swiss Federal Department of Foreign Affairs FDFA, Directorate of International Law, *Handbook on accepting the jurisdiction of the International Court of Justice; Model clauses and templates* (2014).

Peter Tomka, 'The Special Agreement', *in* A. Nisuke, E. McWhinney, W. Rüdiger (eds), *Liber Amicorum, Judge Shigeru Oda*, Vol. 1 (Brill, 2002) 553.

---

[104] *Dispute concerning delimitation of the maritime boundary between Mauritius and Maldives in the Indian Ocean (Mauritius/Maldives)*, Preliminary Objections, ITLOS, 28 January 2021.

[105] Ibid., para. 243.

Robert Kolb

I Introduction

Article 41(1) of the ICJ Statute provides that: 'The Court shall have the power to indicate, if it considers that circumstances so require, any provisional measures which ought to be taken to preserve the respective rights of either party.'[1] This text leaves open some crucial legal questions. First, it does not state under what conditions the Court can adopt interim measures of protection. Under a modified *Lotus* principle – in which the issue is not that conduct not prohibited is allowed, but that a measure for which restrictive conditions are not stated can be freely taken under any conditions the adopting organ may wish – the Court would seem to have a sort of initial discretionary power which it can progressively bind by restrictive conditions in its jurisprudence. The words 'if it considers that circumstances so require' buttresses this point. Second, the text leaves open the effects of the measures indicated. The terms 'indicate' and 'ought to be taken' give rise to interpretative quibbles. Words such as 'impose' and 'shall be taken' would have settled the point. Third, it is not clear whether the phrase 'to preserve the respective rights of either party' is an exhaustive description of the object of such measures. It could be that 'rights-preservation measures' are but one type of provisional measures the Court can indicate. It is therefore through practice that a series of questions relating to provisional measures have been clarified. This practice has been evolving up to the most recent times, as the requirement of 'plausibility of rights'

---

[1] On the drafting of this provision, see C. Miles, *Provisional Measures Before International Courts and Tribunals*, (Cambridge, 2017) 51; K. Oellers-Frahm and A. Zimmermann, 'Article 41', in: A. Zimmermann and C. J. Tams (eds), *The Statute of the International Court of Justice, A Commentary* (3rd ed., Oxford, 2019) 1139–1140. I will try here not to restate what has been amply written, but to search into new ground. My own standard treatment of the question of provisional measures at the ICJ can be found in R. Kolb, *The International Court of Justice* (Hart, 2013) 611.

shows. In short terms, provisional measures at the ICJ have been shaped not so much by a statutory text as by the Court's practice. The statutory provision stopped short, stating only what was considered to be a general principle of law.[2]

II Phases of Evolution

There are roughly speaking three phases in the evolution of the Court's practice on provisional measures. As a whole, the practice shows a shift from discretion to law, from a vague textual cloth hardly constraining the provisional measures function to an increasingly tighter legal straightjacket.

A PCIJ Times: Charting a Way

The first stage was set in the times of the PCIJ.[3] The case law of this Court was based on a broad judicial discretion.[4] At the same time, this discretion was already constrained by certain jurisprudential statements.

The main clarification related to the object and type of provisional measures. On the one hand, the Court followed the text of its Statute by indicating measures protecting the rights forming the subject matter of the disputes submitted to it.[5] On the other hand, it innovated by indicating interim measures having the aim of preventing aggravation of disputes. This latter type of measure was suggested to the Court by the applicant in the *South-Eastern Greenland* case. But the Court found it unnecessary to rule on this question, since both parties reassured the Court.[6] However, in the *Electricity Company* case, the Court stated that Article 41 of the Statute 'applies the principle universally accepted by international tribunals ... that the parties to a case must abstain from any measure capable of

---

[2] There were some forerunner provisions on provisional measures at the international judicial plane, notably Article XVIII of the Convention for the Establishment of a Central American Court of Justice (1907): *AJIL*, vol. 2 (Supplement, 1908), 238.

[3] On its jurisprudence, see Miles, *Provisional Measures*, 60.

[4] See M. O. Hudson, *The Permanent Court of International Justice, 1920–1942, A Treatise* (The Macmillan Company, 1943) 428.

[5] See e.g., the *Polish Agrarian Reform* Case, PCIJ, ser A/B, no. 58, p. 177.

[6] PCIJ, ser. A/B, no. 48, p. 288.

exercising a prejudicial effect in regard to the execution of the decision to be given and, in general, not to allow any step of any kind to be taken which might aggravate or extend the dispute'.[7] This is particularly bold language: 'any measure capable of' embraces a broad range of behaviours, since potentially innumerable acts and omissions could extend or aggravate a dispute. The reach of the statement is enhanced by the objective standard of judgement: no subjective intention to extend or aggravate the dispute is required. The Court linked this power to Article 41, which does not itself contain any rule on 'non-aggravation'. Instead, it is inferred from the underlying rationale of the provision, in reasoning which resembles that used for implied powers in the law of international organisations. The rationale of the rule is to ensure that the final decision taken (if there is one) can be executed and that its object is not irremediably destroyed. This can occur in two ways: objectively, because the object of the rights of the parties is irremediably frustrated (rights-protection measures); and subjectively because the relations between the parties are so much worsened that execution of the decision appears improbable (non-aggravation measures). In view of this rationale, an argument can be made that if the Court may indicate measures to protect rights, it must also have an implied power to take measures to protect the dispute settlement process as a whole against premature and irreparable damage.

The case law of the PCIJ provides some other clarifications. The Court clarified that measures may be taken at the request of one party (usually the applicant), but that they may also be indicated by the Court *proprio motu*.[8] As a consequence, the Court may proceed independently of any request made by the parties and also may prescribe measures which go beyond any requests made by them. Thus, the Court may indicate its own measures, according to what it considers to be necessary in the circumstances. This enhances and widens the discretion of the Court.

The Court was also sometimes confronted with difficult substantive questions. Thus, in the *Polish Agrarian Reform* case, the measures request was framed to cover future events, but the substantive claims of the applicant related to past events. This temporal dissonance raised the question whether provisional measures should be indicated; that is,

---

[7] PCIJ, ser. A/B, no. 79, p. 199.
[8] See the *Southeastern Greenland* case, PCIJ, ser. A/B, no. 48, 287–289. See also the 1936 Rules of Court, Article 61, paras. 4 and 6.

whether rights to be protected still existed.[9] In that case, the Court ultimately declined to indicate any measures.

Finally, it is remarkable that the issue of jurisdiction was not addressed. Perhaps the Court implicitly considered that its measures were not binding and that it consequently had an inherent power to indicate them without addressing any question of jurisdiction. International tribunals prefer not to take a position on issues of jurisdiction at an early stage of a dispute, as doing so can lead to apparent contradictions with later findings. However, in some cases the jurisdictional point was at least indirectly hinted at. Thus, in the *Sino-Belgian Treaty* case, the President of the Court indicated that both parties had deposited an optional clause and that the terms of the dispute fell within its scope.[10] There was no further development of this important point.

The PCIJ was restrictive in issuing provisional measures. Out of six requests to indicate measures, the Court granted measures only in two cases.[11] This might suggest that the PCIJ privileged the sovereign freedom of States (not to be limited by provisional indications) over preservation of the effectiveness of the dispute settlement mechanism.

B First Phase at the ICJ: Times of Diarchy

The first phase at the ICJ spans from the 1952 order in the *Anglo-Iranian Oil Company* case to the landmark *LaGrand* decision of 2001.[12] During this phase, the Court applied two criteria for the indication of measures: that the Court have *prima facie* jurisdiction over the case; and that there be a risk of irreparable harm to the objects underlying the claimed rights.

On the issue of jurisdiction, the Court moved from a negative test to a positive one, thus tightening the conditions for the indication of provisional measures. In the *Anglo-Iranian Oil Company* case, the question of

[9] PCIJ, ser. A/B, no. 58, p. 201–203.

[10] PCIJ, ser. A, no. 8, p. 7. Possibly, this statement can be taken as an implicit ruling on the point of jurisdiction: J. Sztucki, *Interim Measures in the Hague Court* (Deventer, 1983) 226; B. Cheng, *General Principles of Law as Applied by International Courts and Tribunals* (Stevens & Sons, 1953) 272. Greater doubts are expressed by L. Daniele, *Le misure cautelari nel processo dinanzi alla Corte internazionale di giustizia* (Giuffrè, 1993) 23.

[11] Hudson, *The Permanent Court of International Justice*, 428.

[12] On the orders issued in that phase, see Oellers-Frahm and Zimmermann, 'Article 41', 1198–1199.

the competence of the Court was squarely an issue as Iran claimed that the Court lacked competence on the merits; Iran inferred from this that the Court ought also to decline to indicate provisional measures.[13] The Court ruled that in view of the object of the dispute, 'it cannot be accepted a priori that a claim based on such a complaint falls completely outside the scope of international jurisdiction'.[14] The criterion was set out in negative terms: 'not manifestly incompetent'.[15] The Court later reverted to a positive formulation in its orders in the *Nuclear Test* cases.[16] The standard formula is now prima facie jurisdiction.

The issue of 'irreparable harm' was completely marginal in the *Anglo-Iranian Oil Company* case,[17] but featured prominently in the *Fisheries Jurisdiction* orders in 1973.[18] Overall, in this phase the Court started to set out the main conditions for the indication of provisional measures. These jurisprudential developments began to operate as restrictions on an initially almost unfettered discretion to order measures.

C Second Phase at the ICJ: A Four-Pronged Fork

In the *LaGrand* judgment issued in 2001, the Court decided that provisional measures indicated under Article 41 of the Statute are binding upon the parties.[19] The issue arose because, at the merits phase, Germany claimed reparation for violations of interim measures previously indicated by the Court. This judgment profoundly changed the stakes of the law on provisional measures. Since it was made clear that such measures are binding, the risk of abuse by States has been heightened: a claim could be brought with little legal basis in order to lure the Court into the indication of binding measures, constraining the opponent State for a potentially long period of time. The path was thus set for a progressive

---

[13] ICJ, *Reports*, 1951, p. 92.
[14] Ibid., p. 93. See also Ind. Op. H Lauterpacht, *Interhandel* case, ICJ, *Reports*, 1957, p. 117.
[15] This was still the approach of the Court in the Fisheries Jurisdiction order: ICJ, *Reports*, 1972, p. 15, para. 15.
[16] ICJ, *Reports*, 1973, p. 101, para. 13 and p. 137, para. 14.
[17] ICJ, *Reports*, 1951, p. 93, where the issue is only the preservation of the rights of the parties, a formula which reproduces the text of Article 41.
[18] ICJ, *Reports*, 1972, p. 16, par.a 21: '. . . presupposes that irreparable prejudice should not be caused to the rights which are the subject of dispute'. See also ibid., p. 34, para. 22.
[19] ICJ, *Reports*, 2001, p. 501, paras. 98 et seq.

tightening of the conditions under which provisional measures should be indicated. Consequently, the Court expanded the list of conditions in the law of provisional measures to four items, some of them multifaceted (see below, Section IV). All four elements have to be established before the Court proceeds to indicate the measures requested. The relevant case law is now to be found in a series of orders.[20] The newer case law shows how much legal elaboration of these new criteria is still needed; for example, regarding the 'plausibility of rights' criterion.

III Functions and Types of Provisional Measures

There is one function of provisional measures, and there are two types of measures.

A Function

The function of provisional measures is to ensure the *effet utile* of the judicial proceedings. The aim is to guarantee, to the extent feasible, that the judgment on the merits, if rendered, will be capable of being meaningfully executed. A judgment will be unable to be executed if the respondent uses the time in which the case is pending to destroy the underlying object of the dispute; for example, to impair some physical item for which the applicant seeks restitution or to cause irreparable damage.

[20] *Obligation to Prosecute or Extradite* (Belgium v. Senegal), ICJ, *Reports*, 2009, p. 139; *Certain Activities Carried Out by Nicaragua in the Border Area* (*Costa Rica v. Nicaragua*), ICJ, *Reports*, 2011-I, p. 6, and the new request in the same case, ICJ, Reports, 2013, p. 354; *Request for Interpretation of the Judgment of 15 June 1962 in the Case Concerning the Temple of Preah Vihear* (*Cambodia v. Thailand*), ICJ, *Reports*, 2011-II, p. 537; *Construction of a Road in Costa Rica Along the San Juan River* (*Nicaragua v. Costa Rica*), ICJ, Reports, 2013, p. 398; *Seizure and Detention of certain Documents and Data* (*Timor Leste v. Australia*), ICJ, *Reports*, 2014, p. 147; *Immunities and Criminal Proceedings* (*Equatorial Guinea v. France*), ICJ, *Reports*, 2016-II, p. 1148; *Application of the ICSFT and of the CERD* (*Ukraine v. Russia*), ICJ, *Reports*, 2017, p. 105; *Jadhav* (*Pakistan v. India*), ICJ, *Reports*, 2017, p. 232; *Application of the CERD* (*Qatar v. UAE*), ICJ, *Reports*, 2018-II, p. 407; *Alleged Violations of the 1955 Treaty of Amity* (*Iran v. USA*), ICJ, *Reports*, 2018-II, p. 624; *Application of the CERD* (new measures, *Qatar v. UAE*), Judgment 2019, see the website of the Court; and finally *Application of the Convention on the Prevention and Punishment of the Crime of Genocide* (*Gambia v. Myanmar*), Judgment 2020, see the website of the Court.

The wording of the Statute may in this regard not be entirely satisfactory. It speaks of measures 'to preserve the respective rights of either party'. In a certain sense, rights as abstract legal positions cannot be impaired by any unilateral conduct or breach.[21] A right violated or stymied remains a right; it can be vindicated; thus, the law of responsibility remains viable, because the rights and obligations continue to exist even where they are breached. In this sense, a right need not be preserved for it cannot be impaired. In this light, only the *object underlying the right* must be preserved. That object belongs to the physical world; consequently, it may be impaired to such an extent that the final judgment is in jeopardy. However, in a larger sense, a right can also be impaired if the factual circumstances in which it is exercised are taken to be part and parcel of it. This seems to be the understanding of the drafters of Article 41 of the Statute. In any event, it is not simply the 'rights' which are to be preserved. It is moreover the usefulness of the proceedings themselves, which require that a final judgment be able to be meaningfully executed.

B Types

The two types of provisional measures which have been adopted in the Court's jurisprudence flow from the function identified above. Type I is 'subjective' in the sense that it is related to the 'preservation of the rights' of the applicant and the corresponding obligations of the respondent.[22] The aim of such measures is to prevent irreparable harm to the particular setting of rights or obligations of the parties. The subject matter of these

---

[21] See PCIJ, *Legal Status of the South-Eastern Territory of Greenland*, ser. A / B, no. 48, p. 287: '... no act on the part of the said Governments in the territory in question can have any effect whatever as regards the legal situation which the Court is called upon to define'. See Oellers-Frahm and Zimmermann, , 'Article 41', p. 1145; H. Thirlway, 1 *The Law and Procedure of the International Court of Justice* (Oxford University Press, 2013) 940. It is therefore rather the factual use of the right which must be protected; and eventually also the protection of evidence related to these 'rights'. This can amount to a duty 'not to change the situation' prevailing at the time the case was brought to the Court with regard to its factual and legal elements: cf. M. S. Gemalmaz, *Provisional Measures of Protection in International Law: 1907-2010* (Legal Kitapevi, 2011) 149.

[22] See Miles, *Provisional Measures*, 175. The words applicant and respondent relate in this context to the request of provisional measures and not to the main claim on the merits, neither also to the question whether there is a general applicant and respondent (which may not be the case when a proceeding is brought to the Court by a compromise under Article 36(1) of the Statute).

legal positions – to the extent it is indispensable to the performance of a possible judgment granting relief to the applicant on the merits – has to be maintained as far as feasible until the final judgment is rendered. Type II is 'objective' in the sense that it is related to the 'preservation of the proceedings' in such a way that they are not aggrieved by a successive poisoning of the relations between the parties and that the final judgment's ability to be executed is not jeopardised by constantly deteriorating relations. These are measures geared at the 'non-aggravation' of the dispute.[23] Type I goes to the interests of the parties. Type II covers these interests but extends to a public interest: the proper administration of justice.

The power to indicate Type II measures is now accepted in a constant line of jurisprudence[24] and is implied in Article 75 of the Rules of Court (1978). The ordinary conditions for indicating provisional measures may apply only in part to non-aggravation measures.[25] The Court verifies that it has prima facie jurisdiction, but it does not venture into analysis of irreparable harm to the rights of the parties. However, the Court's case law shows that non-aggravation measures have heretofore been indicated only when rights-protecting measures were also adopted and have not been adopted in isolation.[26] It is only to the extent that rights are in jeopardy that a judgment's final execution is protected additionally by non-aggravation measures. This approach is not mandated by Article 75 of the Rules. The protection of the proceedings could be viewed by the Court as a consideration deserving attention in itself. The principle of good faith would reinforce such a position.[27] The extent to which the newer conditions of provisional measures (such as plausibility of rights) apply to non-aggravation measures is not yet clear. The Court may refrain from ordering a non-aggravation measure and limit itself to recommending a certain course to the parties or recalling their obligations under general international law.[28] This is not a 'measure' under Article 41 of the Statute and is therefore not limited by the conditions of provisional measures.

---

[23] For the most recent account, see Miles, *Provisional Measures*, 208.

[24] See e.g., the *Land and Maritime Boundary* case, ICJ, *Reports*, 1996-I, p. 22–23, para. 41.

[25] On this issue, cf. P. Palchetti, 'The Power of the ICJ to Indicate Provisional Measures to Prevent the Aggravation of a Dispute' 21 *Leiden JIL* (2008) 630.

[26] Cf. Oellers-Frahm and Zimmermann, 'Article 41', p. 1147; Palchetti, 'The Power of the ICJ', 634.

[27] On this principle, R. Kolb, *Good Faith in International Law* (Hart, 2017).

[28] Oellers-Frahm and Zimmermann, 'Article 41', p. 1147.

Since non-aggravation is objective in outlook, it may occur that the Court is tempted to impose such measures on the applicant and the respondent.[29] The question may also arise as to what extent a non-aggravation measure is useful outside the contentious context of Article 36 of the Statute. If the dispute before the Court turns on the interpretation of a previous judgment under Article 60 of the Statute, to what extent could conduct of the parties interfere with this function of the Court, which is geared towards clarification of judgments given in the past? The underlying dispute may flare up during the proceedings and need to be addressed. Therefore, autonomous measures while such a dispute is pending are not ruled out. The *Preah Vihear (Interpretation)* case[30] shows that the Court will not refrain from indicating provisional measures in this context, even if the measures there related to the revival of the underlying territorial dispute. The Court could act similarly in other types of proceedings, such as proceedings concerning revision under Article 61 or intervention as a non-party under Articles 62–63.

The most difficult point is to determine what falls under 'aggravation' of a dispute. It cannot be that parties are stalemated from taking any action during all the time that judicial proceedings are pending: a very broad array of acts or omissions can have an aggravating effect, directly or indirectly. The Court has not yet found an answer to this question, apart from the fact that the general formula prohibiting 'aggravation' is sometimes accompanied by specific measures, such as ceasefires or withdrawal of armed forces.

IV Conditions for Indication

According to the newer case law, four conditions have to be met for the indication of provisional measures:

(i) prima facie jurisdiction and prima facie admissibility;
(ii) a link between the measures requested and the rights underlying the main claim;

---

[29] See the *Preah Vihear (Request for Interpretation)* case, ICJ, *Reports*, 2011-II, pp. 555–556, para. 69.
[30] See the previous footnote.

(iii) plausibility of the rights that are the basis of the measures requested; and

(iv) the risk of irreparable prejudice to the legal position of the applicant (which also implies urgency) and a prejudice capable of materialising prior to the final determination of the dispute.

A Jurisdiction[31]

The Court has shifted from its earlier jurisprudence requiring the absence of a 'manifest lack of jurisdiction' to a positive test of prima facie jurisdiction.[32] The indication of provisional measures is thus linked to the merits: Article 41 does not confer a free-standing jurisdiction to the Court; the Court must ascertain whether it has jurisdiction over the merits (albeit on a low threshold test). What is the relevant test? At the early stage of proceedings at which provisional measures are normally demanded, the Court does not have all the arguments and time to examine its jurisdiction over the merits. It must content itself with some summary examination. The best view on the standard is that the probability of jurisdiction must be greater than the probability of lack of jurisdiction (somewhat akin to voting processes, 50 per cent plus one vote). If the basis of jurisdiction is burdened with reservations, the Court must, albeit on a prima facie basis, examine a whole lot of complex questions, relating to temporal aspects, to other means of settlement of disputes, to material limitations and so on. Issues of prima facie admissibility may also arise.[33]

B Link[34]

There must be a link between the measures requested and the rights underlying the main claim. The relief sought must be such that it protects the rights claimed: it is these rights and their objects that the provisional measures seek to protect. If the measures were not taken, the right underlying the main claim would be jeopardised (causality). If the rights claimed

[31] Oellers-Frahm and Zimmermann, 'Article 41', 1150; Miles, *Provisional Measures*, 147.
[32] See above II B.   [33] Miles, *Provisional Measures*, 162.
[34] Oellers-Frahm and Zimmermann, 'Article 41', 1159–1160; Miles, *Provisional Measures*, 179.

are insufficiently related to the measures demanded, the Court will not indicate provisional measures. Thus, as noted above, in the *Polish Agrarian Reform* case, the request for measures was framed in regard to future events, but the claims of the applicant related only to liquidations conducted in the past.[35] There was no causal link. Difficult issues arise in proceedings which are not brought under Article 36. When the Court is seised of a case for the interpretation of a judgment, how do the claims of the parties as to interpretation relate to possible provisional measures for protecting related rights whose infringement will not jeopardise the interpretation decision of the Court?[36] One possibility is that the Court could prescribe free-standing non-aggravation measures, rather than rights-preserving measures.

C Plausibility[37]

This criterion gives rise to complex issues, the main thrust of which is that the Court should not limit the freedom of a State while proceedings are pending unless the rights invoked by the applicant are sufficiently established (*fumus boni juris*, or *non mali juris*). The problem here is that this requires the Court to examine matters closely linked to the merits and makes it difficult to take swift action. Plausibility does not only depend on the credibility of the rights claimed, but also on the evidence presented and claims made. If the rights contain subjective requirements (such as genocide: special intent), the plausibility test extends to them. It has also been

---

[35] PCIJ, ser A/B, no. 58, p. 177.

[36] See *Preah Vihear (Request for Interpretation)* case, ICJ, *Reports*, 2011-II, p. 537.

[37] Oellers-Frahm and Zimmermann, 'Article 41', pp. 1156–1159; Miles, *Provisional Measures*, p. 193. See also H. Thirlway, *The Law and Procedure of the International Court of Justice*, (vol. I, 2013), pp. 937; vol. II, pp. 1783; C. Miles, 'Provisional Measures and the "New" Plausibility in the Jurisprudence of the International Court of Justice', 89 *BYIL* (2018) 1 (online version); M. Lando, 'Plausibility in the Provisional Measures Jurisprudence of the ICJ' 31 *Leiden Journal of International Law* (2018) 641; Y. Saab, 'The Requirement of "Plausibility of Rights" in Provisional Measures', in: *Liber Amicorum G. Eiriksson* (Gurgaon / San José / Sonipat, 2017) 195; and L. Marotti, '"Plausibilità" dei diritti e autonomia del regime di responsabilità nella recente giurisprudenza della CIG in Tema di misure cautelari' 109 *Rivista di diritto internazionale* (2014) 761; and R. Kolb, 'Digging Deeper into the "Plausibility of Rights"- Criterion in the Provisional Measures Jurisprudence of the ICJ' 19 *The Law & Practice of International Courts and Tribunals* (2020) 365.

suggested that the graver the breach claimed, the more plausible it must be. What is plausible? The best view is that the claims must show an 'arguable possibility of existence of rights, high or low',[38] or that 'the rights invoked are not manifestly unfounded'.[39] What is required must be related to the object of the condition of 'plausibility': if the aim of the latter is to prevent the Court being used for abusive purposes to the detriment of the respondent, then this approach seems the most appropriate. The practice is now very dense on this difficult requirement.[40]

D Irreparable Prejudice and Urgency[41]

What is irreparable prejudice to 'rights'? As we have already seen, in a strict sense, a right cannot be rendered nugatory by unilateral action; it remains in force and can form the basis of claims for responsibility. Further, 'prejudice to a right' (if this formula is accepted) can in a strict sense never be irreparable. If the right is impaired, the aggrieved party may claim reparation[42] – at least if there is an internationally wrongful

---

[38] Sep. Op. Owada, *Ukraine* v. *Russia* case, ICJ, *Reports*, 2017, p. 144, para. 10.

[39] Sep. Op. Bhandari, *Ukraine* v. *Russia* case, ICJ, *Reports*, 2017, pp. 195–196, para. 16.

[40] *Obligation to Prosecute or Extradite* Order (*Belgium* v. *Senegal*), ICJ, *Reports*, 2009, pp. 151–152, para. 57; *Certain Activities Carried Out by Nicaragua in the Border Area (Costa Rica* v. *Nicaragua*), ICJ, *Reports*, 2011-I, pp. 18–20 ; Sep. Op. Koroma, ibid., pp. 29–34; Sep. Op. Sepulveda-Amor, ibid., pp. 36–38; Declaration Greenwood, ibid., pp. 47–48; Sep. Op. Dugard (ad hoc), ibid., pp. 61–65; *Request for Interpretation of the Judgment of 15 June 1962 in the Case Concerning the Temple of Preah Vihear* (*Cambodia* v. *Thailand*), ICJ, *Reports*, 2011-II, pp. 545–546; *Seizure and Detention of certain Documents and Data* (*Timor Leste* v. *Australia*), ICJ, *Reports*, 2014, pp. 152–153; *Immunities and Criminal Proceedings (Equatorial Guinea* v. *France*), ICJ, *Reports*, 2016-II, pp. 1165–1167; Sep. Op. Kateka (ad hoc), ibid., pp. 1185–1186; *Application of the ICSFT and of the CERD (Ukraine* v. *Russia*), ICJ, *Reports*, 2017, pp. 126–135; Sep. Op. Owada, ibid., pp. 144–148; Sep. Op. Cançado Trindade, ibid., pp. 169–171; Sep. Op. Bhandari, ibid., pp. 195–206; Sep. Op. Pocar (ad hoc), ibid., pp. 217–220; *Jadhav (Pakistan* v. *India)*, ICJ, *Reports*, 2017, pp. 240–243; Sep. Op. Cançado Trindade, ibid., pp. 254–256; Declaration Bhandari, ibid., pp. 271–272; *Application of the CERD (Qatar* v. *UAE*), ICJ, *Reports*, 2018, pp. 421–427; *Alleged Violations of the 1955 Treaty of Amity (Iran* v. *USA*), ICJ, *Reports*, 2018, pp. 638–643; Sep. Op. Cançado Trindade, ibid., p. 676; *Application of the CERD* (new measures, *Qatar* v. *UAE*), Judgment 2019, para. 17; Sep. Op. Cançado Trindade, ibid., para. 40; *Application of the Convention on the Prevention and Punishment of the Crime of Genocide (Gambia* v. *Myanmar*), Judgment 2020, para. 43; and Sep. Op. Cançado Trindade, ibid., para. 75; Declaration Kress, ibid., paras. 2–5; Sep. Op. Xue, ibid., paras. 2–3).

[41] Oellers-Frahm and Zimmermann, 'Article 41', p. 1160; Miles, *Provisional Measures*, p. 225.

[42] See Articles 34–37 ARSIWA (2001).

act.[43] The binding nature of provisional measures puts the last point beyond doubt. However, it seems clear that the *objects* of rights can be significantly impaired during proceedings by some unilateral action of the other party. It is this 'significant impairment' – that is, the significant worsening of the position of the applicant – that is to be avoided or equally flagrant violations of rights, which cannot be tolerated.[44] Sometimes, a public interest can be added: to prevent the continuation or the spread of the use of force or to prevent the continuation of a genocide. The case law shows that the Court has adopted provisional measures in a wide range of cases: to prevent the complete deprivation of access to fishing resources in certain areas;[45] to prevent nuclear fallout;[46] to prevent the capital punishment of a person;[47] to prevent the continuation of acts which may amount to genocide.[48] Purely financial damage is not normally irreparable. There is no risk of prejudice if the parties are on good terms and the respondent has made statements or taken measures to reassure the applicant.[49]

Provisional measures are urgent measures of relief. The danger of irreparable prejudice must seem sufficiently probable and threatening. A mere possibility that rights may be impaired is not enough. Thus, if the parties engage in some negotiation parallel to the seizing of the Court, it may be appropriate not to indicate provisional measures for lack of urgency.[50] Overall, the urgency criterion depends on the importance of the rights claimed, on the predictability of the conduct of the parties and on the imminence of prejudicial action. It may also depend on external circumstances: if a minister of foreign affairs is not any more in office, the probability that he will have to travel abroad under the coverage of immunity is reduced and so is the urgency to indicate measures on this point.[51]

---

[43] But then provisional measures would never be necessary and Article 41 deprived of any *effet utile*. Thus, the Court stated that reparation does not rule out irreparable prejudice: PCIJ, *Sino-Belgian Treaty* case, ser. A, no. 8, p. 7.

[44] Oellers-Frahm and Zimmermann, 'Article 41', 1163.

[45] *Fisheries Jurisdiction* order, ICJ, *Reports*, 1972, p. 16, paras. 21–22.

[46] *Nuclear Tests* order, ICJ, *Reports*, 1973, p. 105, para. 30.

[47] *LaGrand* order, ICJ, *Reports*, 1999-I, p. 15, para. 24.

[48] *Application of the Convention on the Prevention and Punishment of the Crime of Genocide* (*Gambia* v. *Myanmar*, 2020).

[49] PCIJ, *Southeastern Greenland* case, ser. A/B, no. 48, p. 288.

[50] *Pakistani Prisoners of War* case, ICJ, *Reports*, 1973, p. 330, para. 13.

[51] *Arrest Warrant* case, ICJ, *Reports*, 2000, p. 201, para. 72.

V Effects

For a long period, from 1920 to 2001, the issue whether the provisional measures indicated by the Court were binding upon the parties or were mere recommendations (garnished possibly with some good faith duties) was extremely controversial.[52] With the *LaGrand* judgment of 2001, the ICJ clarified the point: based on a teleological interpretation, it affirmed the binding nature of such measures.[53] The underlying reasons for this finding were the fact that many international tribunals had affirmed their power to indicate binding measures[54] and that some even had a statutory power to indicate binding measures.[55] The ICJ did not want to remain aloof from these developments and to possibly lose some appeal for applicants. The binding force of an order on provisional measures continues to the final decision, be it jurisdictional or on the merits.[56] If the Court wants to uphold some aspects of its provisional measures beyond that date, it has to incorporate the contents of the provisional measures order into the final judgment. At this stage, the parties have to execute the judgment. No *provisional* measures are necessary to secure this future execution: the obligation not to frustrate the execution of the judgment now flows from *pacta sunt servanda* and the principle of good faith.[57] The order incorporating the measures lapses automatically with the final judgment; the Court does not need formally to repeal it.

On 21 December 2020, the Court went one step further. It adopted a new Article 11 of the Resolution concerning the Internal Judicial Practice of the Court.[58] According to the Press Release: 'The article provides for the establishment of an ad hoc committee, composed of three judges, which will assist the Court in monitoring the implementation of the provisional

---

[52] Several constructions attempted to give the measures some enhanced status with regard to mere recommendations or to imply their binding force: see Kolb, *The International Court of Justice*, 638.

[53] ICJ, *Reports*, 2001, p. 501, para. 98. On the effects of provisional measures, see Miles, *Provisional Measures*, 275; Oellers-Frahm and Zimmermann, 'Article 41', 1182.

[54] See R. Kolb, 'Note on New International Case-Law Concerning the Binding Character of Provisional Measures', 74 *Nordic JIL* (2005) 117.

[55] This is the case of ITLOS under Article 290(6) of the Montego Bay Convention of the Law of the Sea (1982) and Article 25 of the Statute of ITLOS in Annex VI of the quoted Convention.

[56] See e.g., the *Fisheries Jurisdiction* order, ICJ, *Reports*, 1973, p. 302.

[57] Article 26 of the VCLT, 1969.   [58] See ICJ, Press Release no. 2020/38.

measures that it indicates. The committee will examine the information supplied by the parties in this regard, report periodically to the Court, and recommend potential options for it. Any decision, if required, will be taken by the Court.'[59] It is too early to state how this procedure will function and to what extent it will impact upon State practice. What is certain is that the Court wants to strengthen the pressure on parties to comply. For too long a time, a habit of taking provisional measures indicated by the Court with some lukewarm detachment has prevailed. Apparently, the Court would prefer to see this attitude as belonging to bygone times. The findings of the committee could give rise to some form of 'sanction' by the full Court, perhaps even absent any formal demand by the aggrieved State. A certain degree of 'contempt of Court' findings could creep into the procedural law of the ICJ, but it also seems that the Court will steer a prudent course in such matters.

The Court is not obliged to adopt binding provisional measures. It could opt merely to recommend some action or express a desire that certain action be taken.[60] However, there is a presumption in favour of the binding force of any measures ordered. This could of course be overcome by the specific wording of the order (for example, 'parties are invited', 'should') or by a general statement to indicate that the measures are not binding.[61] ITLOS took this approach in the *M/V Saiga (No. 2)* case of 1998.[62]

In the case of a breach of provisional measures, the other party may ask for reparation (directly from the State or through the Court's judgment on the merits). Whether it can also take countermeasures is controversial. In principle, countermeasures are ruled out if a court of justice is seised of a dispute – unless the court cannot itself redress the breach by taking decisions.[63] Unilateral measures could moreover aggravate the dispute

---

[59] Here is the full text of the new provision:
   '(i) Where the Court indicates provisional measures, it shall elect three judges to form an ad hoc committee which will assist the Court in monitoring the implementation of provisional measures. This committee shall include neither a Member of the Court of the nationality of one of the parties nor any judges ad hoc. (ii) The ad hoc committee shall examine the information supplied by the parties in relation to the implementation of provisional measures. It shall report periodically to the Court, recommending potential options for the Court. (iii) Any decision in this respect shall be taken by the Court.'

[60] The situation is analogous for the Security Council of the UN: Article 39 of the Charter allows it to decide or recommend in the context of Chapter VII.

[61] Oellers-Frahm and Zimmermann, 'Article 41' 1187.   [62] ITLOS, *Reports*, 1998, p. 24.

[63] Article 52(3)(b) and 52(4) ARSIWA (2001).

and therefore be contrary to non-aggravation measures or obligations (which are commonly expressed in general terms, applying to both parties to a proceeding).[64] A certain restraint is recommended here. Perhaps the aggrieved party could ask the Court to issue an order allowing it to take certain specified countermeasures.

The Security Council of the UN can decide on the execution of judgments – and only judgments – under Article 94(2) of the UN Charter.[65] As the Court has decided that orders on provisional measures are binding, the question has arisen as to whether the Security Council may enforce them. On the one side, there is a formalistic argument according to which an order is not a 'judgment' as required by the Charter. On the other hand, there is a teleological argument which looks at the binding force of the legal act and not at its formal status. This question has not been resolved.[66]

VI Procedure

Five short points may be made on the procedure relating to provisional measures.[67]

(1) Interim measures are indicated at the request of one party to the proceedings and can be indicated at any time while the case is pending.[68] More than one request can be made.[69] The modification of previous measures may also be requested repeatedly.[70] This is the reason why provisional measures are incorporated in an order and not in a judgment. A judgment is *res judicata*; an order is not. The order is merely an act directing the flow of the proceedings.

(2) The Court can indicate provisional measures *proprio motu*[71] and it can therefore also indicate measures other than the ones requested by the parties.[72]

---

[64] See the *Electricity Company* case of 1939, PCIJ, ser. A/B, no. 79, p. 199.

[65] On enforcement of provisional measures, see generally Miles, *Provisional Measures*, 319.

[66] See Oellers-Frahm and Zimmermann, 'Article 41', 1191–1192.

[67] See also K. Parlett and A. Sander, Chapter 12, Procedure in Contentious Cases: Evolution and Flexibility.

[68] Article 75(1) Rules of Court of 1978. For a detailed commentary of these Rules, see G. Guyomar, *Commentaire du Règlement de la Cour internationale de Justice* (Pedone, 1983).

[69] Article 75(3) Rules.   [70] Article 76(1) Rules.   [71] Article 75(1) Rules.

[72] Article 75(2) Rules.

(3) Requests for provisional measures are urgent and have priority over other proceedings at the Court.[73] It may become necessary to act very swiftly, as the *LaGrand* case showed.[74] That request referred to a capital execution which was about to take place the next day.

(4) In extremely urgent cases, it may be necessary to invite the parties to refrain from some activities even before the provisional measures order is adopted. In such cases, the President of the Court may call upon the parties to act in such a way as will enable any order the Court may take on provisional measures to have its appropriate effects, although such a request would not be binding.[75]

(5) Provisional measures are notified to the UN Security Council.[76] The reason is that the Court may take measures on issues pending before the Security Council (such as ceasefires) and the Security Council ought therefore to be informed. Moreover, as noted above, the Security Council has functions regarding the execution of judgments of the ICJ.[77]

VII Conclusion

From this survey of the Court's approach to provisional measures, three conclusions may be drawn.

The first conclusion is that provisional measures at the ICJ have and continue to evolve significantly. Since its beginnings, the PCIJ fleshed out the conditions encapsulating the power of the Court. A number of further conditions were developed and applied after the *LaGrand* decision, but they are in broad terms and there is a continuing search to understand what they mean and how they apply in practice. The Court still has much work to do on this issue.

The second conclusion is that the law on provisional measures has now been fleshed out and is relatively complex. There is therefore a risk that the Court is enmeshed at the early stages of the proceedings in delicate issues, more or less linked with the merits, and that its examination proves time-consuming (which is at odds with the celerity required) and also requires

---

[73] Article 74(1) Rules.   [74] ICJ, *Reports*, 1999-I, p. 9.

[75] Article 74(4) Rules. This has been done for the first time in the *Anglo-Iranian Oil Cy.* case: see G. Guyomar, *Commentaire du Règlement*, 484.

[76] Article 42(2) Statute, 77 Rules.   [77] Article 94(2) Charter of the UN.

consideration of issues of the merits (which is at odds with the efforts of the Court to keep the provisional and merits stages separate). In this respect, there is a delicate balance to be struck in steering the right course between the protection of the sovereignty of States and the requirements of the proper administration of justice.

The third conclusion is that the jurisprudence of the Court has been influential on other international courts and tribunals. Both international investment tribunals[78] and ITLOS[79] have referred to the conditions set out by the ICJ to interpret their own provisions on provisional measures. The ICJ is to some extent the leading international tribunal on procedural issues: it has existed since 1920 (including in the guise of its predecessor, the PCIJ) and has had the longest time to develop its jurisprudence.

Further Reading

L. Daniele, *Le misure cautelari nel processo dinanzi alla Corte internazionale di giustizia* (Giuffrè, 1993).

M. S. Gemalmaz, *Provisional Measures of Protection in International Law: 1907–2010* (Legal Kitapevi, 2011).

C. Miles, *Provisional Measures Before International Courts and Tribunals* (Cambridge University Press, 2017).

S. Rosenne, *Provisional Measures in International Law: The International Court of Justice and the International Tribunal for the Law of the Sea* (Oxford University Press, 2005).

J. Sztucki, *Interim Measures in the Hague Court* (Deventer, 1983).

---

[78] See R. Kolb and T. Gazzini, 'Provisional Measures in ICSID Arbitration. From "Wonderland's Jurisprudence" to Informal Modification of Treaties' 16 *LPICT* (2017) 159.

[79] See T. Treves, 'Article 290', in A. Proelss (ed.), *United Nations Convention on the Law of the Sea, A Commentary* (Nomos, 2017) 1866.

The International Court of Justice as the Master of the Sources 8

Jean d'Aspremont

The International Court of Justice shall apply the sources of international law. This is the very command addressed to the Court by Article 38 of its Statute. Article 38 provides nothing more and nothing less than a command that Court applies the sources of international law. Subject to decision ex *aequo et bono* if the parties agree thereto, Article 38 thus represses other modes of decision by the Court. And yet, as is argued in this chapter, Article 38's repressive command as to the modes of decision of the Court has made the latter the uncontested master of the sources of international law, that is of the very modes of decision imposed upon it by Article 38.

That the International Court of Justice is the master of the sources of international law is nowadays a very unspectacular thing to say. Indeed, most international lawyers naturally turn to the Court's judgments and advisory opinions to find authoritative guidance as to the content of the main law-ascertainment criteria found in the sources of international law. The mastery of the Court in terms of sources of international law is unrivalled. Few other institutions could claim a similar influence on the design of law-ascertainment criteria. This chapter shows that the uncontested and unrivalled mastery of the International Courts of Justice in terms of sources of international law originates in Article 38 which is a provision originally meant to subdue the Court and repress its modes of decision. In doing so, this chapter offers a new story about the International Court of Justice and the sources of international law. It is a story where repression is what it takes to be a master.

This chapter starts by formulating some preliminary remarks on the widely recognised mastery of the sources of international law recognised to the Court (Section I). In Section II, it then sheds light on the repressive dimension of Article 38 and particularly demonstrates how such repression was, in 1920, meant to justify the very power conferred upon the Court. Section III then elaborates on the concrete uses by the Court of its recognised mastery of the sources of international law, especially with respect to customary international law, treaties,[1] and general principles. Finally, Section IV offers some concluding remarks on why repression and mastery often work together in international legal thought.

Before developing this argument, an important theoretical observation is in order with a view to precisely delineating the contours of the following discussion. The story offered in this chapter is not yet another story of heroic emancipation. In particular, it is not a story about a repressed legal actor breaking the chains of its repressive constitutive instrument and securing powers that were not anticipated and that can now be exercised for a good cause. Instead, the story that unfolds in the following paragraphs is a story about how repressive legal constructions constitute the very powers of those that they are meant to subdue. In other words, the ensuing discussion tells a story where repression and mastery function as a structure where exceptions are the foundations of what they exclude.[2]

I An Uncontested Master

Most international lawyers look at the International Court of Justice's judgments and advisory opinions to find authoritative guidance as to how international law ought to be ascertained.[3] Said differently, there seems to be no resistance towards the Court being the principle

---

[1] See also A. Remiro Brotóns, Chapter 14, The Law of Treaties in the Jurisprudence of the International Court of Justice.

[2] The relationship between repression and mastery that is construed here as the work of self-difference corresponds to a structure of discourses that has often been acknowledged in the literature. See gen. J. Derrida, *L'écriture et la différence* (Editions du Seuil, 1967) 12; M. Foucault, *L'archéologie du savoir* (Gallimard 1969) 205; B. Latour, *Nous n'avons jamais été modernes. Essai d'anthropologie symétrique* (La Découverte 1997) 77. On the idea that slavery and power work together, see R. Barthes, *Leçon* (Seuil 1978) 15. On the idea that the paradox between universality and particularism cannot be solved because one cannot exist without one another, see E. Laclau, *Emancipation(s)* (Verso 2007) 34. On the idea that life and death are distinct but work together, see J. Derrida, *La vie la mort (séminaire 1975–1976)* (Le Seuil 2019).

[3] See H. Thirlway, *The Sources of International Law* (Oxford University Press, 2014), 1–30. See the remarks of J. d'Aspremont, Book review of H. Thirlway, *The Sources of International Law*, 57 *German Yearbook of International Law* (2014).

meta-law-maker, that is the maker of the modes of law-making.[4] This means, in the terms of analytical jurisprudence, that, for international lawyers, the social practice feeding into the legal forms is primarily produced by the Court.[5] As a result, whenever they are pressed to justify the functioning of the sources of international law or the foundations thereof, international lawyers look at the Court.

The Court's mastery of the sources of international law is unrivalled. No other international institution has ventured to claim any authoritative say on this matter. Even the International Law Commission has explicitly relinquished its own authority to the Court when it comes to define (or refine) the criteria to ascertain international law.[6] What is more, few would dare to explicitly claim that this defining law-ascertainment criteria should be primarily bestowed upon scholars.[7] This unrivalled mastery of the Court is obviously not limited to the sources of international law. Albeit, to a lesser extent, the same can be witnessed in terms of the law on state responsibility,[8]

---

[4] It must be acknowledged that such assertion of power of the sources is sometimes contested. For instance, the Court is sometimes stigmatised for the liberty it has taken with the doctrine of sources and its adoption of 'new rules of recognition' at convenience (A. Sofaer, 'Adjudication in the International Court of Justice: Progress through Realism' 44 Rec. A. B. City N. Y. (1989) 462, at 477). For an overview of the criticisms of the International Court of Justice, see A. Mark Weisburd, *Failings of the International Court of Justice* (Oxford University Press, 2016).

[5] See gen. J d'Aspremont, *Formalism and the Sources of International Law* (Oxford University Press, 2011), especially 195–220.

[6] See the 1st Report of the Special Rapporteur on the identification of customary international law, A/CN.4/663, 17 May 2013, p. 21, para. 54. See e.g., Third report on identification of customary international law, A/CN.4/682, 27 March 2015, para. 4. It is also interesting to note that the International Court of Justice is mentioned forty-five times in the International Law Commission's 2018 conclusions on identification of customary international law (A/73/10), *Yearbook of the International Law Commission*, 2018, vol. II, Part Two.

[7] Sometimes international lawyers recognise that the design of the structures of international legal argumentation and of their main doctrines is bound to be a scholarly enterprise. This is well illustrated by the candidness of Roberto Ago in his famous course on 'the international delict' at the Hague Academy in 1938 – which paved the way for the subsequent codification of the subject after the Second World War – and where he recognises that the making of the main patterns of argumentative structure is a matter of scholarly choices. See e.g., R. Ago, *Le délit international*, 68 *Collected Courses of the Academy of International Law* (1938) 420–421. See also C. de Visscher, *Théories et Réalités en Droit International Public* (4th ed., Pedone, 1970) 171.

[8] See also F. Paddeu, Chapter 18, The Law of State Responsibility. The modes of legal reasoning on the allocation of the burden of compensation and the possibility to take countermeasures that have been codified by the International Law Commission are often

jus cogens,[9] and interpretation. But this chapter is focused on the Court's uncontested mastery of the sources of international law.

The social support which the mastery of the Court enjoys originates in compound and sometimes impenetrable assumptions and constructions. Only a few can be mentioned here. For instance, the mastery of the Court in terms of sources is supported by the functioning of Article 38 of the Statute as a semi-constitutional mechanism in international legal thought and practice.[10] The social support for the Court's mastery of the sources is also possibly informed by the more general role recognised to the Court in terms of system-design.[11] It can also be surmised that the recognition of such mastery is reinforced by the more general veneration of the Court in international law circles,[12] and especially the celebration of its alleged role for resolving disputes in a principled manner.[13]

seen as a 'synthesis' of what is essentially judicial practice. See e.g., J. Crawford, State Responsibility: *The General Part* (Cambridge University Press, 2013) 45–93. With respect to responsibility, Koskenniemi, has written that this is a pragmatism that sometimes 'involves an illegitimate naturalization of practitioner frameworks'. See M. Koskenniemi, 'Doctrines of State Responsibility', in J. Crawford, A. Pellet and S. Olleson (eds.), *The Law of International Responsibility* (Oxford University Press, 2010) 45 (citing S Marks, *The Riddle of All Constitutions*, 2000, pp. 66–67). On the making of secondary rules with an emphasis on the law of international responsibility, see F. Lusa Bordin, 'Reflections of Customary International Law: The Authority of Codification Conventions and ILC Draft Articles in International Law', 63 *International and Comparative Law Quarterly* (2014) 535.

[9] I have discussed the refuge in judicial validation in relation to jus cogens in greater depth elsewhere. See J. d'Aspremont, 'Jus Cogens as a Social Construct without Pedigree' 46 *Netherlands Yearbook of International Law* (2015) 85.

[10] On the constitutional value of Article 38 in international legal thought and practice, see the critical remarks of H. Charlesworth, 'Law-making and Sources' in J. Crawford and M. Koskenniemi (eds.), *Cambridge Companion to International Law* (Cambridge University Press 2012) 187. See also J. Klabbers, 'Law-making and Constitutionalism' in J. Klabbers, A. Peters and G. Ulfstein (eds.), *The Constitutionalization of International Law* (Oxford University Press 2009) 89; See generally A. Pellet, 'Article 38', in A. Zimmermann, C. Tomuschat, K. Oellers-Frahm (eds.), *The Statute of the International Court of Justice* (Oxford University Press, 2002) 677, 731–870; D. Bederman, *Globalization and International Law* (Palgrave Macmillan) 47.

[11] I have looked at this phenomenon elsewhere. See J. d'Aspremont, 'The International Court of Justice and the Irony of System-Design' 8 *Journal of International Dispute Settlement* (2017) 366.

[12] For some general remarks on the reverence of the Court see gen. J. d'Aspremont, 'International Lawyers and the International Court of Justice: Between Cult and Contempt' in Crawford, Koroma, Mahmoudi and Pellet (eds.), *The International Legal Order: Current Needs and Possible Responses: Essays in Honour of Djamchid Momtaz* (Brill, 2017), 117–139. See also A. Mark Weisburd, *Failings of the International Court of Justice* (Oxford University Press, 2016), 1–4; A D'Amato, 80 ASIL Proccedings (1986) 204, at 214.

[13] T. Franck, *Fairness in International Law and Institutions* (Clarendon Press, 1995) at 346.

Whatever the reason for the wide support for the Court's mastery of the sources of international law, it must be acknowledged that such mastery is not without contradictions. Indeed, in their modern acceptation,[14] sources are meant to have no master. Sources are supposed to be fixed and out there, and mechanically deployable by law-applying authorities to ascertain the rules of international law. From such modern perspective, the Court's role should be limited to translating the existing law-ascertaining criteria in operable evaluative delimitations between law and non-law to decide the situations that are brought in before it and which it is meant to adjudicate. For this reason, the Court's mastery of the sources, and its meta-law-making power can be seen to be at odds with the traditional and modern understanding of the sources. This contradiction has, however, not been deemed a compelling obstacle to the recognition of the Court as a master of sources. It may be that such encroachment to one of the modern paradigms is offset by the empiricism that the mastery of the Court confers upon international law-ascertainment as a whole. Indeed, for international lawyers, having the modes of law-ascertainment mastered by the Court is the expression of a modern empirical attitude as it allows the sources of international law to be considered a product of 'practice'. The mastery of the Court in terms of sources thus makes the making of the sources look like an empirical process governed by inductive methods.[15] In that sense, it can be said that the Court's mastery of the sources is solidly entrenched in modern thinking and it is no surprise that it has remained uncontested.

II A Repressed Master

In international legal discourse, the Court's mastery of the sources of international law has never been presented as a mere ontology or as a

---

[14] On the idea of sources being the expression of modernity, see Jean d'Aspremont, *International Law as a Belief System* (Cambridge University Press, 2017). More generally on the idea that the question of production of human artefacts and human discourses is very modern, see M. de Certeau, *L'écriture de l'histoire* (Gallimard, 1975) at 27–28.

[15] Elsewhere, I have questioned such unanimous recognition of the mastery of the Court and inquired whether it constitutes a form of fetishism towards judicial institutions, entailing 'judicialisation' of international legal thought. See J. d'Aspremont, If International Judges Say So, It Must Be True: Empiricism or Fetishism? (November 23, 2015). ESIL Reflections, November 2015, Vol 4, Issue 9. Pierre Schlag prefers to speak about the 'juridification' of legal thought. See P. Schlag, *Laying Down the Law* (New York University Press, 1996), p. 139 and pp. 141–142.

compelling actuality, calling for no other justification. In fact, such mastery has always been nested in a formal legal instrument to make it look as the product of the sources of international law.[16] In particular, the mastery of the sources of international law has been construed as a stipulation of the Statute of the Court and, in particular, of Article 38. The grounding of the Court's mastery of the sources in Article 38 is key to the argument made here and thus warrants some observations. It must, however, be made clear that this chapter is not the place for yet another inquiry into the world signified by Article 38, and especially the semi-constitutional function performed by that provision. What matters here is only what Article 38 means for the Court and its mastery of the sources of international law.

As was said above, Article 38 of the Statute of the International Court of Justice contains a single but strict command: the International Court of Justice shall apply the sources of international law. It must be added here that this command to apply the sources of international law is rather exclusive. Indeed, this is a command addressed to the Court and to the Court only. Article 38 compels no one else to apply the sources of international law.[17] This command is also exclusive because Article 38 contains no instruction for the Court other than this command to apply the sources of international law. Thus, Article 38 provides that the Court – and the Court only – shall apply – and shall do nothing else than applying – the sources of international law. The command of Article 38 is very demanding as well.[18] In fact, Article 38 requires the application of some

---

[16] On the self-referential foundations of modern international law, see Jean d'Aspremont, *International Law as a Belief System* (Cambridge University Press, 2017).

[17] On the idea that Article 38 creates an internal rule for the Court, see A. Pellet, Article 38, 759; P.-M. Dupuy, 'La pratique de l'article 38 du Statut de la Cour internationale de Justice dans le cadre des plaidoiries écrites et orales' in *Collection of Essays by Legal Advisers of States, Legal Advisers of International Organizations and Practitioners in the Field of International Law* (United Nations, 1999) 377, 379; P. Weil, 'Le droit international en quête de son identité' 237 *Collected Courses of the Academy of International Law* (1992-VI) 139. The idea that Article 38 creates a rule binding the Court has been confirmed by the Court itself on several occasions. See *Continental Shelf* (Tunisia/Libya), ICJ Rep 1982, para. 23; *Nicaragua*, ICJ Rep 1986, para. 187; *Frontier Dispute* (Burkina Faso/Mali), ICJ Rep 1986, para. 42; *Gulf of Maine*, ICJ Rep 1999, para. 93; *Maritime Delimitation in the Area Between Greenland and Jan Mayen*, ICJ Rep 1993, para. 52; *Jurisdictional Immunities*, ICJ Reports 2012, para. 55.

[18] This has sometimes been challenged. See Joe Verhoeven who argues that Article 38 only gives 'indications' to the Court. See J. Verhoeven, 'Considérations sur ce qui est commun.

specific legal materials rather than others. Accordingly, the Court cannot decide by applying domestic law, roman law, canon law, FIFA law or the law of the international space station. It must apply the sources of international law. More importantly, Article 38 simultaneously compels the Court to a specific action, that is, an application. The Court must *apply* the sources of international law. Its decisions must thus be produced by the action of applying the sources.[19] In other words, by virtue of Article 38, there are only so many actions that the Court can perform: to decide the Court must apply the sources.

The foregoing should suffice to show that Article 38 is a fundamentally repressive construction. By providing that the International Court of Justice shall apply the sources of international law, Article 38 restricts the modes of decision available to the Court as well as the legal materials the Court can rely on. The Court is thus subdued into some specific modes of decision, themselves articulate around certain legal materials.[20]

The repressive character of Article 38 is confirmed by the *travaux préparatoires* of the Statute of the Permanent Court of International Justice. In this respect, it is relevant to recall the discussions within the Advisory Committee of Jurists on Thursday 1st of July 1920 after the presentation by Baron Descamps of his proposition for a provision about the rules to be applied by the Court.[21] Indeed, as soon as Descamps finished introducing his proposition of what was to become Article 38, members of the Advisory Committee of Jurists stressed how important it is to define the rules applied by the Court to induce States

---

Cours général de droit international public' 334 *Collected Courses of the Academy of International Law* (2002) 109.

[19] This is also emphasised by Article 38's reference to the role of the Court ('whose function is to decide in accordance with international law such disputes as are submitted to it').

[20] It must be acknowledged that Article 38 does not have the monopoly on the repression of the power of the Court and thus the alienation of law-making. For instance, Article 59 of the Statute could also be read in this way. Yet, the repression – and thus the alienation of law-making – by Article 38 is most notable given the extent to which Article 38 is the referent for anything related to the sources of international law. See gen. C. Brown, 'Article 59', in A. Zimmermann and C. J. Tams, *The Statute of the International Court of Justice. A Commentary* (3rd ed., Oxford University Press, 2019) 1561.

[21] Advisory Committee of Jurists, Procès-Verbaux of the Proceedings of the Committee, p. 293. The project of Baron Descamps is reproduced in Advisory Committee of Jurists, Procès-Verbaux of the Proceedings of the Committee, 16 June–24 July 1920, with Annexes, The Hague, Van Langenhuysen Brothers, 1920, Annex No. 3 to the meeting of 1 July 1920, p. 306.

to accept the – then envisaged compulsory – jurisdiction of the Court.[22] For the Advisory Committee of Jurists, Article 38 was primarily a marketing measure to enhance the acceptability of the new Court in the eyes of the major powers represented in the League of Nations by presenting the Court as a very benign body whose modes of decision are very constrained. In this context, it is no surprise that the sources of international law mentioned in Article 38 were themselves never discussed by the Advisory Committee of Jurists,[23] the attention of the members of the Committee being almost exclusively drawn to the bold construction meant to address the much dreaded hypothesis of the Court declaring itself incompetent because of lack of applicable rules (*non liquet*).[24] Interestingly, the passionate debates on general principles of law confirmed that Article 38 was all about repressing the modes of decision of Court in situations where it is faced with a lack of applicable legal materials.[25] The *travaux* thus show that Article 38 was conceived by its authors as a repressive construction whose function is to legitimise and justify the very object of what it represses, that is, the Court's power to decide. It is in the repression of the Court's power to decide and the restriction placed on the Court's modes of decision with a view to making the Court look more benign to States that the *raison d'être* of Article 38 lies. It could even be said that, if not to repress the Court's power to decide, there would have been no Article 38.[26]

It is argued here that the repression of the Court's modes of decision – by Article 38's command that the Court applies the sources of international law – is what enables the Court to be a master of the sources of international law. This can be explained as follows. It is first contended here

---

[22] Advisory Committee of Jurists, Procès-Verbaux of the Proceedings of the Committee, p. 293.

[23] Loder made the point that the sources themselves did not call for any discussion right after Baron Descamps' presentation of its project about the rules to be applied by the Court. See Advisory Committee of Jurists, Procès-Verbaux of the Proceedings of the Committee, p. 294.

[24] Advisory Committee of Jurists, Procès-Verbaux of the Proceedings of the Committee, p. 296.

[25] Advisory Committee of Jurists, Procès-Verbaux of the Proceedings of the Committee, 16 June–24 July 1920, pp. 322–325.

[26] Although the power that Article 38 was meant to justify was not made automatically opposable to all parties to the statute as the compulsory jurisdiction of the Court was scraped from the Statute, Article 38 notably survived the scaling down of the power it was meant to support.

that Article 38, by repressing the modes of decision, presupposes that there is such a thing as a power to decide conferred upon the Court. Indeed, there cannot be any repression on the modes of decision if there is no power to decide vested in the Court in the first place. Said differently, to operate as a repressive mechanism, Article 38 is dependent on there being a power to decide. But enabling by Article 38 of the mastery of the Court is not only a matter of necessitarian presupposition. More importantly, the repression conducted by Article 38 on the Court's modes of decision, because it does not define the very mode of decision it allows, makes it necessary for the Court to define the scope of the repression and thus what it means to decide by applying the sources of international law. Indeed, to allow Article 38 to perform its repressive function, the Court is bound to define the sources of international law, that is the scope of what Article 38 allows and prohibits. Even the very little Article 38 says about customary international law has left the Court with a wide interpretive space to define customary international law and the way it is ascertained. In that sense, the Court's mastery of the sources can be understood as the condition of the repression of Article 38. It is only once the Court has defined what deciding through the application of the sources of international law is that Article 38 can perform its repressive function. It is in defining what it is to decide by applying the sources of international law and thus in defining the scope of repression of Article 38's command that the Court asserts its mastery on the sources.

III A Tireless Master

It is argued in this section that the Court, endowed with an uncontested mastery of the sources of international law by virtue of the repression by Article 38, has proved remarkably active as a master of the sources. This section provides a snapshot of the extent of the considerable use by the Court of its recognised mastery of the sources and the way in which it came to decisively design the modes of law-ascertainment prescribed by Article 38. Attention is paid to the mastery of the Court with respect to customary international law, treaties and general principles of law. As will be shown in the following paragraphs, the Court has asserted its mastery on each of these three distinct sources in a very different manner.

A Customary International Law: An Assertive Master

It is probably as far as customary international law is concerned that the
Court has asserted its mastery the most strikingly. The ascertainment of
customary international law commonly requires the establishment of two
elements, namely the practice of States (and possibly that of other actors)
as well as the so-called *opinio juris*, understood as the requirement that the
practice in question is undertaken with a sense of legal right or obligation
by the actors concerned. These two requirements correspond to the so-
called two constitutive elements of customary international law. They are
said to be prescribed by Article 38 of the Statute of the International Court
of Justice. The following shows how the Court came to write and rewrite
these two elements as they are allegedly provided by Article 38. It will be
argued here that it is in reinventing the approach to custom-ascertainment
found in Article 38 that the Court came to assert its mastery of custom.

A preliminary remark is in order to capture the breadth of the Court's
asserting of its mastery of customary international law. As has been widely
documented and demonstrated,[27] Article 38 of the Statute of the Permanent
Court of International Justice, as it had been drafted in 1920, did not support
an ascertainment of customary international law through the establishment
of two elements. That provision, instead, reflected a monolithic understanding of custom-ascertainment. This reading of Article 38 is supported by the
travaux of the Advisory Committee of Jurists.[28]

---

[27] See P. Haggenmacher, '*La doctrine des deux éléments en droit coutumier dans la pratique
de la Cour international*', 90 RGDIP (1986) 5 at 30–31; C. Tams, '*Meta-Custom and the
Court: A Study in Judicial Law-Making*', 14 *The Law and Practice of International Courts
and Tribunals* (2015) 51, at 59–60; M. Fitzmaurice, The History of Article 38 of the Statute
of the International Court of Justice: The Journey From the Past to the Present in S. Besson
and J. d'Aspremont, *Oxford Handbook on the Sources of International Law* (Oxford
University Press, 2017) 179; Pellet, 'Article 38', at 813; J. d'Aspremont, 'The Four Lives
of Customary International Law' 21 *International Community Law Review* (2019) 229.

[28] See the mention of a 'rule established by the continual and general usage of nations, which
has consequently obtained the force of law' (see Advisory Committee of Jurists, Procès-
Verbaux of the Proceedings of the Committee p. 307 and 322) or the claim that custom
'results entirely from the constant expression of the legal convictions and of the needs of
the nations in their mutual intercourse' (see Advisory Committee of Jurists, Procès-
Verbaux of the Proceedings of the Committee, p. 322). This is also supported by the
commentary of provision on the rules to be applied by the Court in the final report of
the Advisory Committee of Jurist which refers to 'international custom in so far as its
continuity process a common usage'. The French text reads: 'la coutume international dont
la continuité atteste une pratique commune'), Advisory Committee of Jurists, Procès-
Verbaux of the Proceedings of the Committee, p. 729.

Albeit deemed a reliable source by the Advisory Committee of Jurists,[29] the monolithic approach to custom-ascertainment found in Article 38 at the time may not have proved sufficiently 'reliable' for the new Permanent Court of International Justice in need of modes of law-ascertainment that look mechanical and hence more conducive to the Court's emerging authority. This is why, as early as 1927, the Permanent Court of International Justice, in its *Lotus* decision, came to require a distinct subjective element, namely the 'conscience of having a duty'. The departure from the 1920 monolithic understanding of custom-ascertainment consists of the requirement that such subjective element is not inferred from the practice but is established independently.[30]

Although the judgment in the *Lotus* is often read as an authoritative vindication of the two-element doctrine of customary international law,[31] it must be emphasised that the Court was dealing with the difficult question of establishing customary international law in relation to a duty of abstention and thus faced the challenge of extracting a customary rule from the absence of action. To distinguish between absence of action that qualifies as practice for the sake of customary international law and absence of practice that is irrelevant in terms of custom-ascertainment, the Court invented a requirement of 'conscience of having a duty'. Yet, it is far from evident that the Court meant to generalise that requirement of 'conscience of having a duty' to any custom-ascertainment exercise. The *Lotus* judgment is better read as reserving the subjective element only for situations where the customary character of a duty of abstention arises. So interpreted, the *Lotus* judgment only amounts to a limited departure from the monolithic understanding of custom-ascertainment as it limits the

---

[29] See the Speech of Baron Descamps on the Rule of Law to be applied, Advisory Committee of Jurists, Procès-Verbaux of the Proceedings of the Committee, p. 322.

[30] Case of the S.S. 'Lotus' (France/Turkey), Judgment, PCIJ Series A, No. 10 (1927), p. 28.

[31] See e.g., M. Fitzmaurice, 'The History of Article 38 of the Statute of the International Court of Justice: The Journey From the Past to the Present' in S. Besson and J. d'Aspremont, *Oxford Handbook on the Sources of International Law* (Oxford University Press, 2017) 179; see also P. Tomka, 'Custom and the International Court of Justice', *The Law and Practice of International Courts and Tribunals*, vol. 12, No. 2 (2013), p. 195, at 202. I have myself contended that the two-element doctrine originates in the Lotus. See J. d'Aspremont, 'The Decay of Modern Customary International Law in Spite of Scholarly Heroism' in G. Ziccardi Capaldo (ed.), *The Global Community Yearbook of International Law and Jurisprudence* (2015) 9.

distinction between practice and 'the conscience of having a duty' to the ascertainment of customary duties of abstention.

More than the judgment in the *Lotus*, it is the judgment of the International Court of Justice in the *Asylum* case that came to break away from the monolithic understanding of custom-ascertainment by generalising the requirement of a subjective element distinct from the practice and tested separately. Indeed, in the *Asylum* case, and in contrast to the *Lotus*, the requirement of a subjective element no longer is limited to the situation where the customary character of a duty of abstention is at stake. Responding to an argument of the Colombian Government drawing on an alleged regional or local customary international law peculiar to Latin-American States, the Court indicated that 'The Colombian Government must prove that the rule invoked by it is in accordance with a constant and uniform usage practiced by the States in question, and that this usage is the expression of a right appertaining to the State granting asylum and a duty incumbent on the territorial State'.[32] It is submitted here that, with the *Asylum* case, the rupture with the monolithic understanding of custom-ascertainment was consumed: practice and what corresponds to a sense of duty ought to be ascertained separately.

For the sake of the argument made in this chapter, it is important to highlight that, in the *Asylum* case, the Court, not only generalised the distinction between practice and a subjective element, but also traced back this distinction to Article 38 itself and the definition of customary international law 'as evidence of a general practice accepted as law'. In that sense, the *Asylum* case entailed a rewriting of the monolithic understanding of custom-ascertainment and of Article 38 itself in favour of a dualist approach to custom-ascertainment still to be located in Article 38.

The hammering of the monolithic understanding of custom-ascertainment originally found in Article 38 and its generalisation pushed forward by the *Asylum* judgment were soon confirmed by the Court in the *North Sea Continental Shelf* which is often cited to support the

---

[32] *Asylum case (Colombia/Peru)*, Judgment, Judgment of 20 November 1950, ICJ Reports 1950, p. 266, 276–277. It is interesting to add that the Court added: 'This follows from Article 38 of the Statute of the Court, which refers to international custom "as evidence of a general practice accepted as law".'

two-element doctrine.[33] Despite some signs of conceptual fatigue[34] in the *Gulf of Maine*[35] and *Nicaragua*[36] judgments, the International Court of Justice has continued until today to draw on this axiomatic two-element doctrine initiated in the *Lotus* and generalised by the judgment in the *Asylum* case.[37] It is noteworthy that the rewriting of Article 38 by the Court and its vindication of dualist approach to custom-ascertainment has also been widely perpetuated by a very obedient and admiring legal scholarship[38] and explicitly upheld by the International Law Commission in its 2018 conclusions on the identification of customary international law,[39] thereby confirming the uncontested mastery of the Court on customary international law.

B Treaties: An Undecided Master

By contrast with customary international law, Article 38 does not define the notion of treaty. This is why, as far as treaty-identification is concerned, the Court, in asserting its mastery over treaty-identification, did not come to rewrite Article 38 but took advantage of its silence on treaty identification. As is well-known, not only Article 38 but also the Vienna Convention on the Law of Treaties is silent on the matter. Indeed, the latter's reference, in its definition of a treaty in Article 2, to an agreement

---

[33] North Sea Continental Shelf (Federal Republic of Germany/Denmark; Federal Republic of Germany/Netherlands), Judgment, ICJ Reports 1969, p. 3, 44 (para. 77).

[34] See the discussion in J. d'Aspremont, 'The Four Lives of Customary International Law'.

[35] *Delimitation of the Marine Boundary in the Gulf of Maine Area (Canada v. United States of America)* (Judgment) [1984] ICJ Rep 246, 269, para. 111.

[36] Military and Paramilitary Activities in and against Nicaragua (*Nicaragua v. United States of America*), Merits, Judgment, ICJ Reports 1986, pp. 14, 98, para. 186.

[37] See e.g., ICJ, *Legality of the Threat or Use of Nuclear Weapons*, pp. 254–255, para. 70; see also ICJ, Jurisdictional Immunities of the State (*Germany v. Italy*, Greece intervening), ICJ Reports 2012, p. 99, 122 (para. 55); *Case Concerning Pulp Mills on the River Uruguay (Argentina v. Uruguay)* (Judgment) [2010] ICJ Rep 14, 83, para. 204.

[38] See e.g., H. Thirlway, *International Customary Law and Codification: An Examination of the Continuing Role of Custom in the Present Period of Codification of International Law* (Brill, 1972). For a rare exception, see A. D'Amato, *The Concept of Custom in International Law* (Cornell University Press, 1971).

[39] I have argued elsewhere that the International Law Commission, on the contrary, did resuscitate the monolithic understanding informing Article 38. See J. d'Aspremont, 'The Four Lives of Customary International Law', 21 *International Community Law Review* (2019) 229.

'governed by international law' does not provide for any indications in terms of treaty-identification, for such reference only points to the consequence of an agreement being identified as a legal agreement rather than its ascertainment as a legal agreement.[40] Article 38 and the Vienna Convention on the Law of Treaties thus leave a significant space for the Court to design the criteria of treaty-identification.

It must be acknowledged that such space is not entirely unfettered. Although both Article 38 and the Vienna Convention are silent as to the decisive treaty-ascertainment criterion, the International Law Commission, when preparing the draft of what would become the Vienna Convention on the Law of Treaties, was of the view that the legal nature of an act hinges on the intent of the parties. Apart from Fitzmaurice who sought to make it an explicit criterion,[41] the International Law Commission and its Special Rapporteurs took it for granted that legal nature of a treaty is determined on the basis of intent of the parties[42] and did not deem it necessary to specify it in their definition of a treaty.[43]

That intent is held to be the decisive criterion to identify a treaty[44] does, however, not carry much guidance as to how a treaty ought to be identified. Indeed, by saying that the identification of a treaty hinges on the intent of the parties!!!!, one says very little, for such an intent is itself in

---

[40] Fitzmaurice had explicitly made a distinction between the law-ascertainment criterion and the consequence of an agreement being ascertained as a treaty. See ILC Report, A/3159 (F) (A/11/9), 1956, chp. III(I), para 34 et seq.

[41] ILC Report, A/3159 (F) (A/11/9), 1956, ch. III(I), para 34 et seq.

[42] See e.g,. A. Orakhelashvili, *The Interpretation of Acts and Rules in Public International Law* (Oxford University Press, 2008) 59–60.

[43] ILC Report, A/6309/Rev.1 (F) (A/21/9), 1966, part I(E), paras.11–12, and part II, chp. II, paras. 9–38.

[44] This position is shared by most international legal scholars. Among others, see A. Aust, *Modern Treaty Law and Practice* (2nd ed., Oxford University Press, 2007) at 20; Oppenhein (Jennings & Watts eds.) *International Law*, Vol. I (Oxford University Press, 1992) at 1202. J. Klabbers, *The Concept of Treaty in International Law* (Kluwer, 1996) at 68; M. Fitzmaurice, 'The Identification and Character of Treaties and Treaty Obligations between States in International Law' 73 *British Yearbook of International Law* (2003) 141, 145 and 165–166; A. Orakhelashvili, *The Interpretation of Acts and Rules in Public International Law* (Oxford University Press, 2008) at 59. See also the general remarks of I. Seidl-Hohenveldern, 'Hierarchy of Treaties', in J. Klabbers and R. Lefeber, *Essays on the Law of Treaties: A Collection of Essays in Honour of Bert Vierdag* (Martinus Nijhoff, 1998) at 7. See J.-P. Jacqué, *Elements pour une théorie de l'acte juridique en Droit international public* (LDGJ, 1972) at 121; See C. Chinkin, 'A Mirage in the Sand? Distinguishing Binding and Non-Binding Relations between States' 10 *Leiden Journal of International Law* (1997) 223.

need of criteria and guidance to be established.[45] By virtue of the role conferred upon intent of the parties, the identification of international treaties is made dependent on a fickle and indiscernible psychological element and reduced to a deeply speculative operation.[46] This is why the space left for the Court to define the criteria for treaty-identification has not been restricted by the consensus around the role of the intent of the parties.

It is against the backdrop of such an inconsequential approach to treaty-identification that the Court came to assert its mastery on treaty. Indeed, confronted with the speculative nature of the establishment of the intent of the parties, the Court came to design more precise and formal tools to organise treaty-identification,[47] and in particular, to devise a method to ascertain the intent of the parties. Although taking its role very seriously, the Court has however not shown as much resolution as it did in relation to customary international law. In fact, it has regularly been contested that the criteria designed by the Court to determine the legal nature of an agreement, as well as lacking consistency, have failed to provide much guidance in the establishment of the intent of the parties.[48] It is noteworthy that following the criticisms of its earlier fluctuating positions as expressed in its *Aegean Sea Continental Shelf* (where the Court expressly rejected the form of the agreement to be determinative of its legal status and gave relevance to the actual terms of the agreement, the context and the circumstances of its making, and the subsequent behaviour of the actors concerned) and in *Maritime Delimitation and Territorial Questions between Qatar and Bahrain* (where the Court looked at the content of the agreement but played down the subsequent behaviour of the actors

---

[45] In the same vein see Klabbers, *Essays on the Law of Treaties*, at 11 et seq. See also the remarks of G. M. Danilenko, *Law-Making in the International Community* (Martinus Nijhoff Publishers, 1993) at 57 (who pleads for the necessity of a formal act of acceptance).

[46] High Court of Justice, Queen's Bench Division, 5 December 2007, The Czech Republic and European Media Ventures SA, 2007 EWHC 2851 (Comm), para. 17.

[47] See e.g., K. Widdows 'On the Form and Distinctive Nature of International Agreements' 7 *Australian Yearbook of International Law* (1976–1977) 114. On this point, see the remarks of M. Fitzmaurice, 'The Identification and Character of Treaties and Treaty Obligations Between States in International Law' 73 *British Yearbook of International Law* (2003) 141, 145.

[48] See Klabbers, *Essays on the Law of Treaties*, esp. 245–250.

involved),[49] the Court ceased to offer much guidance as to the establishment of the intent of the parties. This came to a head in its decisions in the case of the *Land and Maritime Boundary between Cameroon and Nigeria*[50] and *Pulp Mills on the River Uruguay*.[51] In the more recent case pertaining to the *Maritime Delimitation in the Indian Ocean*, the Court nonetheless ventured to indicate that the inclusion of a provision addressing the entry into force of the memorandum of understanding whose legal bindingness is being tested is indicative of the instrument's binding character.[52]

It is fair to say that the mastery asserted by the Court with respect to treaty-identification has not been asserted with the same self-confidence and determination as the one witnessed in relation to custom-ascertainment. The Court seems to have been dithering between various treaty-identification criteria. And yet, such irresolution of the Court – and the criticisms thereof in the literature – have confirmed the Court's recognised mastery of treaty-identification.

C General Principles of Law: A Reluctant Master

The way in which the Court has asserted its mastery of general principles of law is yet very different. In fact, it is argued that the Court has ironically shown mastery over general principles by refraining from resort to such a source of international law. Notwithstanding a few authors mechanically identifying a possible resort by the Court to general principles of law every

---

[49] As regards the identification of international treaties, see ICJ, *Aegean Sea Continental Shelf* (*Greece* v. *Turkey*), Judgment of 19 December 1978, para. 95–107: emphasis is put on the actual terms and circumstances. Compare *Maritime Delimitation and Territorial Questions between Qatar and Bahrain (Qatar* v. *Bahrain)*, Judgment of 1 July 1994. Regarding the identification of unilateral promise, see ICJ, *Nuclear Tests (Australia* v. *France)*, 20 December 1974, para. 43. *Military and Paramilitary Activities in and against Nicaragua (Nicaragua* v. *United States of America)*, Merits, ICJ Rep. (1986). See ICJ, Burkina-Faso Mali. See the remarks of Christine Chinkin, 'A Mirage in the Sand?', 223. See also J. Klabbers, 'Qatar v. Bahrain: The Concept of "Treaty" in International Law', 33 *ARV* (1995) 361.

[50] See the laconic consideration of the Court regarding the nature of the Maroua Declaration adopted by Cameroon and Nigeria in Land and Maritime Boundary between Cameroon and Nigeria (*Cameroon* v. *Nigeria*: Equatorial Guinea intervening), 10 October 2002, para. 263.

[51] ICJ, Pulp Mills on the River Uruguay (*Argentina* v. *Uruguay*), Judgment of 20 April 2010, ICJ Rep 2010, para. 138.

[52] ICJ, *Maritime Delimitation in the Indian Ocean (Somalia* v. *Kenya)*, Judgement of 2 February 2017, ICJ Rep 2017, para. 42.

time it mentions the very words 'general principles',[53] it is commonly contended by commentators that general principles have played a very marginal role in the case law and advisory opinions of the Court.[54] As far as the International Court of Justice is concerned, mention of general principles of law as a source of international law in accordance with Article 38 of its Statute can be found in the *South-West Africa case*,[55] the *Case on the Passage over Indian Territory*, in the *Advisory Opinion on the Reservations to the Genocide Convention*,[56] and – possibly albeit with some ambiguity – in the *North Sea Continental Shelf case*,[57] the *Barcelona Traction case*,[58] and *Avena and other Mexican Nationals*.[59] In all these cases, the reference to general principles has been brief and

---

[53] C. Bassiouni, 'A Functional Approach to "General Principles of International Law"' 11 *Michigan Journal of International Law* (1990) 768, at 787–801; A. Blondel, 'Les Principles Généraux de Droit devant la Cour Permanente de Justice Internationale et la Cour Internationale de Justice', in *Recueil d'Etudes de Droit International en Hommage à Paul Guggenheim* (Institut Universitaire de Hautes Études Internationales, 1968) 201, at 204–234.

[54] A. Pellet, 'Article 38' in A. Zimmermann, C. Tomuschat, K. Oellers-Frahm, C. Tams (eds.), *The Statute of the International Court of Justice: A Commentary* (2nd ed., Oxford University Press 2012), p. 767; G. Hernandez, *The International Court of Justice and the Judicial Function* (Oxford University Press, 2014), p. 261; S. Besson, 'General Principles in International Law: Whose Principles?' in S. Besson and P. Pichomaz (eds.), *Les principes en droit européen/Principles in European law* (Schulthess, 2011) 19, at 36 and 39; V. Degan, *Sources of International Law* (Kluwer, 1997) 58; J. Ellis, 'General Principles and Comparative Law' 22 *European Journal of International Law* (2011) 949, at 950; G. Gaja, 'General Principles of Law', *Max Planck Encyclopedia of Public International law (MPEPIL)*, paras. 9–16; J. Verhoeven, *Droit International Public* (Larcier, 2000) at 348. With respect to the absence of general principles of law in the case-law of the PCIJ, see C. Rousseau, *Principes généraux du droit international public* (Pedone, 1944), 898; M. Koskenniemi, *From Apology to Utopia* (Cambridge University Press, 2005) 49.

[55] ICJ, *South-West Africa Case (Ethiopia* v. *South Africa)* Judgment of 18 July 196, ICJ Reports 1966, para.88.

[56] ICJ, *Reservations to the Convention on the Prevention and Punishment of the Crime of Genocide*, Advisory Opinion of 28 May 1951, ICJ Reports 1951, p. 23: 'the principles underlying the Convention which are recognized by civilized nations as binding on States, even without any convention obligation'.

[57] ICJ, *North Sea Continental Shelf (Federal Republic of Germany v Denmark; Federal Republic of Germany v Netherlands)*, Judgment of 20 February 1969, ICJ Reports 1969, para.17.

[58] In Barcelona Traction, the Court referred to 'rules generally accepted by municipal legal system'. ICJ, *Barcelona Traction, Light and Power Company Limited (Belgium* v. *Spain)*, Judgment of 5 February 1970, ICJ Reports 1970, para. 50.

[59] ICJ, *Avena and Other Mexican Nationals (Mexico* v. *United States of America)* (Admissibility) Judgment of 31 March 2004 ICJ Reports (2004), para.127.

inconsequential. It is only in separate and dissenting opinions that general principles of law have been made a linchpin of legal arguments.[60] Occasional mentions thereof are also made in the pleadings of parties.[61] It is true that the Court has regularly referred to a wide range of denominations containing the very wording 'general principles'.[62] Yet, it can be argued that references to general principles by the Court often manifest a reliance of the Court on customary international law.[63] Given the absence

---

[60] For instance, see PCIJ, *Lighthouses in Crete and Samos (France v. Greece)*, Judgment of 8 October 1937, PCIJ, Series A/B, No. 71, Separate Opinion by Judge Séfériadès, pp. 137–138; ICJ, *International Status of South-West Africa*, Advisory Opinion of 11 July 1950, ICJ Reports 1950, Separate Opinion by Sir Arnold McNair, p. 148; ICJ, *Anglo-Iranian Oil Co. (United Kingdom v. Iran)*, Preliminary Objection, Judgment of 22 July 1952, ICJ Reports 1952, Dissenting Opinion of Judge Levi Carneiro, p. 161; ICJ, *Application of the Convention of 1902 Governing the Guardianship of Infants (Netherlands v. Sweden)*, Judgment of 28 November 1958, ICJ Reports 1958, Separate Opinion of Judge Moreno Quintana, p. 107; ICJ *Right of Passage over Indian Territory (Portugal v. India)*, Merits, Judgment of 12 April 1960, ICJ Reports 1960, Separate Opinion of Judge Wellington Koo, pp. 66–67; ICJ, *Temple of Preah Vihear (Cambodia v. Thailand)*, Merits, Judgment of 15 June 1962, ICJ Reports 1962, Dissenting Opinion of Judge Alfaro, pp. 42–43; ICJ, *Legality of the Threat or Use of Nuclear Weapons*, Advisory Opinion of 8 July 1996, ICJ Reports 1996, Declaration of Judge Fleischhauer, pp. 308–309; ICJ, *Case Concerning Oil Platforms (Islamic Republic of Iran v. United States of America)*, Judgment of 6 November 2003, Merits, ICJ Reports 2003, Separate Opinion of Judge Simma, paras.66–74; ICJ, *Questions relating to the Seizure and Detention of Certain Documents and Data (Timor-Leste v. Austria)*, Provisional Measures, Order of 3 March 2014, ICJ Reports 2014, Dissenting Opinion of Judge Greenwood, para.12.

[61] Ibid., majority opinion, p. 152, para. 24; on this point, see the remarks of S. Yee, 'Article 38 of the ICJ Statute and Applicable Law: Selected Issues in Recent Cases' 7 *Journal of International Dispute Settlement* (2016) 472, at 487–488; More impressive is the pleadings of Portugal in The Right of Passage over Indian Territory where Portugal produced a comparative law study covering 64 different national laws with a view to establishing the existence of a general principle concerning the right of access to enclaved pieces of land – ICJ, *Right of Passage over Indian Territory (Portugal v. India)*, Pleadings, vol. I, ICJ Reports 1960, p. 714, 858; see also the remarks by Pellet (2012) p. 770.

[62] See e.g., 'traditional principle' – PCIJ, *Question of Jaworzina (Polish-Czechoslovakian Frontier)*, Advisory Opinion of December 6th 1923, Series B, No. 8, p. 37; 'principle[s] generally accepted' – PCIJ, *Case Concerning the Factory at Chorzow*, Jurisdiction, Judgment of 26 July 1927, Series A, No.9, para.87; 'well-known rule [in reference to a general principle]' – PCIJ, *Interpretation of Article 3, paragraph 2 of the Treaty of Lausanne*, Advisory Opinion of 21 November 1925, Series B, No.12, para.95; 'well-established and general recognized principle of law' – ICJ, *Effect of awards of compensation made by the UN Administrative Tribunal*, Advisory Opinion of 13 July 1954, ICJ Reports 1954, p. 53.

[63] In many decisions, they can hardly be distinguished from customary international law, see PCIJ, *Mavrommatis Palestine Concessions*, Judgment of 26 March 1925, Series A, No.5, p. 30; PCIJ, *Case Concerning the Factory at Chorzow*, Merits, Judgment of 13 September 1928,

of any significant use of general principles of law by the Court, it seems no coincidence that the *Handbook of the International Court of Justice*, which refers to the use of the sources of international law, does not mention general principles.[64]

The reasons for the limited relevance of general principles as a source of international law are well-known.[65] For instance, this tepidity of the Court has been explained by virtue of the growing body of conventional and customary rules which the Court can rely on,[66] the alleged absence of a consent-based foundation of general principles,[67] the uncertainty affecting their very nature,[68] their systematic exclusion by virtue of the *lex specialis* mechanism,[69] their overly explicit functioning as a law-making tool,[70] the formulation of Article 38 and its reference to civilised nations,[71] the difficulty to select those legal systems that will undergo a comparative scrutiny,[72] the challenges of the comparative law analysis which their

---

Series A No.17, p. 29; ICJ, *Corfu Channel (United Kingdom v. Albania)*, Merits, Judgment of 9 April 1949, ICJ Reports 1949, p. 22; ICJ, *Application for Review of Judgment No. 158 of the UN Administrative Tribunal*, Advisory Opinion of 12 July 1973, ICJ Reports 1973, p. 177; ICJ, *La Grand (Germany v. United States)*, Merits, Judgment of 27 June 2001, ICJ Rep 2001, p. 503; for some comments, see Danilenko, *Law-Making in the International Community*,182.

[64] See The International Court of Justice (2013) *Handbook*. 6th ed.

[65] J. d'Aspremont, 'What Was Not Meant to Be: General Principles of Law As a Source of International Law' in R. Pisillo Mazzeschi and P. De Sena (eds.), *Global Justice, Human Rights, and the Modernization of International Law* (Brill, 2018) 163.

[66] Degan, *Sources of International Law*, 67; Yee, 'Article 38 of the ICJ Statute and Applicable Law', 489.

[67] The question of whether general principles of law emanate from consent has been the object of diverging views in the literature. For some authors, they constitute an expression of consent. See C. Bassiouni, 'A Functional Approach to "General Principles of International Law"' 11 *Michigan Journal of International Law* (1990) 768, at 786; Rousseau, *Principes généraux du droit international public*, 890. For others, general principles of law as introduced in Article 38 constitute an innovative departure from state consent. See e.g., Dissenting Opinion Tanaka, p. 298. General principles is a source that is alien to consent; Brierly, The Law of Nations, 6th edition, p. 63); H. Lauterpacht, *Private Law Sources and Analogies of International Law* (Longmans, 1927), 298–299.

[68] Danilenko, *Law-Making in the International Community*, 184.

[69] Degan, *Sources of International Law*, 67.

[70] Ellis, 'General Principles and Comparative Law', at 950. See also R. Jennings, *What Is International Law and How Do We Tell It When We See It* (Kluwer, 1983) 39–40.

[71] Gaja, 'General Principles of Law', para. 2; Yee, 'Article 38 of the ICJ Statute and Applicable Law', 489.

[72] Gaja, 'General Principles of Law', para. 16.

ascertainment possibly requires,[73] their transitional nature,[74] the possible contradictions with the internationalist spirit of the profession,[75] etc.

This chapter is not the place to give yet a new explanatory narrative for the miserable fate encountered by general principles of law as a source of international law in the case law and advisory opinions of the PCIJ and the ICJ. Yet, for the sake of the argument made in this section, another reason for the reluctance of the Court to assert its mastery about general principles of law must be mentioned. Contrary to the dominant idea that the inclusion of general principles of law in Article 38 of the Statute boils down to a codification of earlier judicial and arbitral practice,[76] it is argued here that the elevation of general principles of law into one of the sources of the rules applicable by the Court can be construed as a radical invention by the Advisory Committee of Jurists which the Court may feel uncomfortable with.[77] Indeed, it should be noted that general principles of law did not generally appear as a source of international law in classical treatises of the late nineteenth century and beginning of the twentieth century.[78] Also, the earlier arbitral practice denotes a use of general principles of law in a way alien to the idea of sources.[79] In fact, in arbitral practice prior to Article 38, general principles of law were relied on as an interpretive principle,[80] as an

---

[73] Ibid.   [74] Yee, 'Article 38 of the ICJ Statute and Applicable Law', 489.

[75] M. Koskenniemi, 'The Case for Comparative International Law', 20 *Finnish Yearbook of International Law* (2009) 1, at 3.

[76] Gaja, 'General Principles of Law', para. 1; A. Verdross, 'Les principes généraux du droit dans la jurisprudence internationale' 52 *Collected Courses* (1935) 191, at 207; A. Pellet, 'Article 38', in A. Zimmermann, C. Tomuschat, K. Oellers-Frahm (eds.), *The Statute of the International Court of Justice*, Oxford University Press, 2002, p. 763; L. Brierly, *The Law of Nations: An Introduction to the International Law of Peace* (Clarendon Press, 1949) 64; T. Gazzini, 'General Principles of Law in the Field of Foreign Investment', 10 *Journal of World Investment and Trade* (2009) 103.

[77] I have articulated this claim further elsewhere. See J. d'Aspremont, 'What Was Not Meant to Be'.

[78] See e.g., J. Lorimer, *Principes de Droit International* (trad. Ernest Nys), (Muquardt, 1884), 19–64; T. Woolsey, *Introduction to the Study of International Law* (Scribner and Armstrong, 1877); T. J. Lawrence, *The Principles of International Law* (McMillan, 1923) 95–114.

[79] Degan, *Sources of International Law*, 34–41; Lauterpacht, *Private Law Sources*, 203–296; A. Verdross, 'Les principes généraux du droit dans la jurisprudence internationale', 52 *Collected Courses of the Academy of International Law* (1935) 207–219.

[80] See, e.g., *Affaire des réclamations des sujets italiens résidant au Pérou (Italie, Pérou)* Award of 30 September 1901 RIAA Vol XV p. 389–453 (where general principles were applied to interpret a conventional rule of international law).

expression of equity,[81] or more generally as a 'spontaneous argumentative move'.[82] Even when general principles of law were used, in the practice of arbitral tribunals, as mechanism playing a law-ascertainment function – that is as a source of law – they were derived from Roman Law.[83] This is why it is rather simplistic to consider the inclusion of general principles of law in Article 38 of the Statute as a codification of the pre-1920 scholarship and practice. This should thus be seen as a major innovation, one that the Court may feel uncomfortable with. In that sense, the conscious choice to avoid making decisions on the basis of general principle of law can be interpreted as a way for the Court to indicate its unease towards the idea of general principles of law as a source. Should the Court's reluctance to resort to general principles of law as one of the sources it is entitled to apply by virtue of Article 38 manifest the Court's discomfort with such construction, the Court can be seen as asserting its role of master of the sources. Tepidity and reluctance are also the privileges of masters.

IV Concluding Remarks

The International Court of Justice shall apply the sources of international law. This is the very command formulated by Article 38 towards the Court. It has been shown in this chapter that this command is very repressive of the Court's modes of decision. And yet, as was discussed in this chapter, this repressive construction has simultaneously been constitutive of an uncontested and unrivalled mastery of the sources of international law being conferred upon the Court.

The claim developed in this chapter should certainly not be deemed idiosyncratic. After all, it is no coincidence that the word 'command' in English can mean either order or mastery. The relationship between repression and mastery corresponds to a common structure of discourses,[84]

---

[81] Degan, *Sources of International Law*, 40.   [82] Lauterpacht, *Private Law Sources*, 67–68.

[83] See e.g., Affaire Yuille, Shortridge and Cie, arbitrage de la Commission désignée par le Sénat de la Ville libre de Hambourg, sentence du 21 octobre 1861. See also The Russian Indemnity Case, Russia and Turkey, PCA, Award of 11 November 1912 (cited by Lauterpacht, *Private Law Sources*, 257). In the same vein, K. Strupp, 'Les règles générales du droit de la paix', 47 *Collected Courses of the Academy of International Law* (1934-I), pp. 335–336; Lauterpacht, *Private Law Sources*, 257; Degan, *Sources of International Law*, 40.

[84] See references cited in fn 2.

including international discourses.[85] Unsurprisingly, this is a structure that can be observed elsewhere in international legal discourse. This is the case, for instance, in international criminal law where the principle of legality introduced at Nuremberg, originally designed to curtail the expansion of international criminal law, came to justify the very expansion it was meant to curtail.[86] A similar discursive structure can be observed in the law of international responsibility where, for instance, the subjection of international organisations to a regime of responsibility entails an empowerment of such actors, as well as a recognition of these actors as having the power to breach international law.[87] The structure of the discourse on the sources of international law, and especially its empowering prescription that the Court shall apply the sources of international law, is thus no discursive oddity.

Further Reading

J. d'Aspremont, 'What Was Not Meant to Be: General Principles of Law As a Source of International Law', in R. Pisillo Mazzeschi and P. De Sena (eds.), *Global Justice, Human Rights, and the Modernization of International Law* (Springer, 2018) 163.

J. d'Aspremont, 'The Four Lives of Customary International Law', 21 *International Community Law Review* (2019) 229.

M. Fitzmaurice, 'The History of Article 38 of the Statute of the International Court of Justice: The Journey from the Past to the Present', in S. Besson and J. d'Aspremont, *Oxford Handbook on the Sources of International Law* (Oxford University Press, 2017), p. 179.

C. Tams, 'Meta-Custom and the Court: A Study in Judicial Law-Making' 14 *The Law and Practice of International Courts and Tribunals* (2015) 51.

P. Tomka, 'Custom and the International Court of Justice', 12(2) *The Law and Practice of International Courts and Tribunals* (2013) 195.

---

[85] On the general idea that law structures and constitutes politics and powers, see. C. Reus Smit, 'The Politics of International Law', in C. Reus-Smit, *The Politics of International Law* (Cambridge University Press, 2004) 14–44. See also C. Reus Smit, 'Politics and International Legal Obligation', 9 *European Journal of International Law* (2003) 591.

[86] See J. d'Aspremont, 'The Two Cultures of International Criminal Law' in K. Heller, F. Mégret, S. Nouwen, J. D. Ohlin, Robinson (eds.), *Oxford Handbook of International Criminal Law* (Oxford University Press, 2020) 400.

[87] See J. d'Aspremont, 'International Responsibility and the Constitution of Power: International Organizations Bolstered', 12 *International Organizations Law Review* (2015) 382. In the same vein, see also P. Allott, 'State Responsibility and the Unmaking of International Law', 29 *Harvard International Law Journal* (1988) 1.

Fact-Finding and Expert Evidence 9

James Devaney

Parties dedicate significant time and effort to the establishment of the facts in proceedings before the International Court of Justice ('the Court', or 'ICJ'). The handling of evidence, including expert evidence, proffered by parties in support of their factual assertions is an important and unavoidable part of what the Court is asked to do. How exactly the Court treats competing evidentiary claims, and how it eventually establishes legal facts for the purpose of the proceedings before it, commonly termed the fact-finding process, is the focus of Section I of the present contribution. Section II examines recent significant criticisms of this fact-finding process. Finally, Section III shows that the Court has already begun to address these criticisms and briefly sets out how it can continue to ameliorate its fact-finding process.

I The Court's Approach to Fact-Finding: Rudimentary Fact-Finding Provisions and Party Autonomy

The Court's judgments are the product of real disputes between states, based on legal facts established through a (more or less) adversarial process.[1] A fundamental, if not entirely unproblematic,[2] distinction between the law and the facts lies at the heart of this process. While the Court is presumed to know the law,[3] the facts must be established in each

---

[1] M. Mbengue, 'International Courts and Tribunals as Fact-Finders: The Case of Scientific Fact-Finding in International Adjudication' 34 *Loy.L.A.Int'l & Comp.L.Rev* (2012) 53–80 at 53–54.

[2] Ibid.; W. Twining, *Rethinking Evidence* (Cambridge University Press, 2006) p. 41.

[3] *Fisheries Jurisdiction (Federal Republic of Germany v. Iceland), Merits, Judgment,* ICJ Reports 1974, p. 175; *Military and Paramilitary Activities in and against Nicaragua (Nicaragua v. United States of America) Merits, Judgment:* ICJ Reports 1986, p. 14, at para. 18; J. Verhoeven, 'Jura novit curia et le juge international' in P.-M. Dupuy et al. (eds.),

and every case that comes before it.[4] Certain provisions of the Court's constitutive instruments ensure that issues of evidence and fact-finding are a regular feature of every case, whether contentious or advisory,[5] the Court is tasked with handling.[6]

The Court's approach to fact-finding in practice has been defined by two factors: (i) the rudimentary nature of the fact-finding provisions in its constitutive instruments, and (ii) a prioritising of the wishes of the parties in accordance with the principle of party autonomy. The latter is facilitated by the former, and as a preliminary matter it is helpful to comment on both factors.

First, in contrast to practice before domestic courts (whether in common or civil law jurisdictions) where detailed and well-developed rules of evidence and procedure are the norm, 'the typical evidentiary regime in international proceedings can be characterised by the generality, liberality and scarcity of its provisions'.[7] Proceedings before the ICJ are no different in this regard. The Court's Statute and its Rules have been described as rudimentary with regard to issues of procedure,[8] creating 'neither a strict adversarial nor an inquisitorial model and can best be described as a modified adversarial procedure firmly based on party autonomy and initiative in matters of evidence'.[9] In the absence of clear and detailed procedural provisions, the Court has been left to develop its own practice over time.

Common Values in International Law, Essays in Honour of Christian Tomuschat (N. P. Engel Verlag 2006) at pp. 635–653. Note that this principle does not apply to domestic law, see *Certain German Interests in Polish Upper Silesia (Germany v. Poland) (Merits)*, 1926, PCIJ, Series A, No. 7, p. 19.

[4] Mbengue, 'International Courts and Tribunals as Fact-Finders', at 54.
[5] This applies mutatis mutandis to advisory opinions, *see Legal Consequences for States of the Continued Presence of South Africa in Namibia (South-West Africa) notwithstanding Security Council Resolution 276 (1970), Advisory Opinion*: ICJ Reports 1971, p. 16, para. 40.
[6] E.g., Articles 49(1) and (2) Rules of Court, stipulating that Memorials must include 'a statement of the relevant facts' and Counter-Memorials must include an admission or denial of these facts. Article 38(2) Rules of Court, similarly provides that cases brought on the basis of a unilateral application much also include a statement of the facts.
[7] A. Riddell and B. Plant, *Evidence before the International Court of Justice* (British Institute of International and Comparative Law 2009) p. 2; J. G. Devaney, *Fact-Finding before the International Court of Justice* (Cambridge University Press, 2016) 12.
[8] C. J. Tams, 'Article 51' in A. Zimmermann et al. (ed.) *The Statute of the International Court of Justice: A Commentary* (3rd ed., Oxford University Press, 2019) 1303.
[9] M. Benzing, 'Evidentiary Issues' in A. Zimmermann et al. (ed.) *The Statute of the International Court of Justice: A Commentary* (Oxford University Press, 2019) 1377; R. Kolb, *The International Court of Justice* (Hart, 2014) 941–942.

Second, in relation to issues of fact-finding, the Court has largely prioritised the wishes of the parties by interpreting those (limited) procedural provisions in a manner consistent with the principle of party autonomy.[10] For instance, the Court has typically not scrutinised the credentials of witnesses and experts that parties wish to put forward in support of their factual assertions,[11] nor has it drawn adverse inferences from any refusal by a party to comply with its requests for information, despite the existence of a rule explicitly empowering it to do so.[12]

Of course, we must recognise the constraints that the Court operates under. Its financial resources are limited, and fact-finding expensive. Further, its jurisdiction is consensual which no doubt limits how demanding it feels it can be of states party to cases before it. Relatedly, the Court is wary of being seen to favour one (sovereign equal) party over another by intervening in procedural matters, and fiercely seeks to protect its impartiality by deferring to the wishes of the parties.[13] Consequently, perhaps it is unsurprising that deference to the wishes of the parties and related flexibility in the application of its procedural rules is one of the central features of proceedings before the Court, especially in relation to the fact-finding process.[14]

Nevertheless, the criticisms of the Court's fact-finding process, considered in Section II, are merited, and the Court has and should take steps to address these criticisms accordingly. Before turning to such criticisms, it is necessary to describe how the Court has conducted fact-finding in cases that have come before it to date. In doing so, its practice in relation to issues such as the admissibility of evidence, proof and the use of its fact-finding powers will be examined.

A Admissibility and the Liberty of Proof

The Court's constitutive instruments make no mention of the admissibility of evidence whatsoever. In practice, the Court has never operated or

---

[10] Benzing, 'Evidentiary Issues'.

[11] B. Plant, 'Expert Evidence and the Challenge of Procedural Reform in International Dispute Settlement', 9 *JIDS* (2018) 3 at 465.

[12] Devaney, *Fact-Finding before the International Court*, 27.

[13] Plant, 'Expert Evidence', at 465.

[14] Ibid; see also H. Lauterpacht, *The Development of International Law by the International Court* (Stevens & Sons 1958), p. 366.

developed strict rules on admissibility of the kind typically seen in domestic courts or international criminal tribunals.[15] Rather, the Court operates in accordance with the principle of the free admissibility of evidence.[16] In effect, this means that the Court admits almost any evidence proffered by a party in support of its claims.[17]

The few exceptions to this general approach, which are advocated from time to time, are so closely circumscribed as to be essentially meaningless. For instance, while the PCIJ stated that evidence that emerged as a result of negotiations between the parties could be excluded,[18] the Court in subsequent cases significantly limited this exception.[19] Similarly, while the Court suggested in *Corfu Channel* and *Tehran Hostages* that information obtained illegally could be excluded, the Court has never actually gone as far as doing so.[20] Today, given the Court's previous practice, what is most likely to happen is that the information in question would be admitted and then subsequently given appropriate weight at the fact-assessment stage.[21] The upshot of the operation of the principle of the free admissibility of

---

[15] G. Boas, 'Admissibility of Evidence under the Rules of Procedure and Evidence of the ICTY: Development of the "Flexibility Principle"' in R. May et al. (eds.), *Essays on ICTY Procedure and Evidence in Honour of Gabrielle Kirk McDonald* (Martinus Nijhoff, 2001) 265, P. V. Sellers, 'Rule 89 (C) and (D): At Odds or Overlapping with Rule 96 and Rule 95?' in R. May et al. (eds.), *Essays on ICTY Procedure and Evidence in Honour of Gabrielle Kirk McDonald* (Martinus Nijhoff, 2001).

[16] *Mavrommatis Palestine Concessions*, PCIJ, Series A No. 2, 34 (1924); C. Brown, *A Common Law of International Adjudication* (Oxford University Press, 2007) p. 91, Speech by H. E. Judge Rosalyn Higgins, President of the International Court of Justice to the General Assembly of the United Nations, 1 November 2007, www.icj-cij.org/press com/files/3/141113.pdf.

[17] D. Sandifer, *Evidence Before International Tribunals* (University Press of Virginia, 1975) 176; C. Brower, 'Evidence Before International Tribunals: The Need for Some Standard Rules' 28 *The International Lawyer* (1994) 47, at 48.

[18] *Case Concerning the Factory at Chorzów (Claim for Indemnity) (Merits)*, 1927 Series A No. 17, 19; the PCIJ stated it would not take into account 'declarations, admissions or proposals which the Parties may have made during direct negotiations between themselves, when such negotiations have not led to complete agreement'.

[19] See subsequent limitations in *Frontier Dispute (Burkina Faso: Mali)* Judgment: ICJ Reports 1986, p. 554, para. 147.

[20] *Corfu Channel Case, Judgment*, 1949: ICJ Reports 1949, p. 4, *United States Diplomatic and Consular Staff in Tehran (United States of America* v. *Iran)*, Judgment: ICJ Reports 1980, p. 10,

H. Thirlway, 'Dilemma or Chimera: Admissibility of Illegally Obtained Information in International Adjudication' 78 *AJIL* (1984) 622, 633.

[21] *South-West Africa Cases, Ethiopia* v. *South Africa; Liberia* v. *South Africa*, ICJ Pleadings, 1966, vol X, 123.

evidence is that the Court has spent significantly less time dealing with issues of admissibility which are the bread and butter of (especially common law) domestic courts. Rather, the Court's energies have been directed towards accommodating the wishes of the parties, and subsequently assessing the probative weight of the evidence submitted at the next stage of the fact-finding process.

B Burden and Standard of Proof

Likewise, despite being central parts of the fact-finding process, neither the Court's constitutive instruments nor any subsequent Practice Directions provide any guidance to the parties as to the burden or standard of proof applicable in proceedings before the Court. In practice, the ICJ does not operate a strict burden or standard of proof. Like most international courts and tribunals,[22] the Court generally has been said to allocate the burden of proof in accordance with the maxim of *actori incumbit probatio,* that the burden generally lies with the party seeking to establish a certain legal fact.[23] Accordingly, the burden is not allocated according to which party has instituted proceedings, for instance, but rather on the party trying to assert a certain proposition.[24]

In the same vein the Court has not articulated a single, strict standard of proof, such as might be found in domestic law.[25] Del Mar has shown that the Court has even applied different standards of proof within the same case.[26] The *Whaling in the Antarctic* case is a good example in this regard, with the Court applying a 'double standard of review' – a different standard with regard to the two legal issues at the heart of the dispute.[27]

---

[22] G. Fitzmaurice, *The Law and Procedure of the International Court of Justice* (Grotius 1986), p. 576.

[23] *Application of the Convention on the Prevention and Punishment of the Crime of Genocide (Bosnia and Herzegovina v. Serbia and Montenegro), Judgement:* ICJ Reports 2007, p. 43, para. 204.

[24] *Case Concerning Ahmadou Sadio Diallo (Republic of Guinea v, Democratic Republic of the Congo), Judgment,* 30 November 2010, para. 56.

[25] K. Del Mar, 'The International Court of Justice and Standards of Proof', in Bannelier et al. (eds.), *The ICJ and the Evolution of International Law* (Routledge, 2012), p. 99.

[26] Ibid., p. 101.

[27] *Whaling in the Antarctic (Australia v. Japan: New Zealand intervening),* ICJ Judgment of 31 March 2014, at 67, E. Cannizzaro, 'Proportionality and Margin of Appreciation in the Whaling Case: Reconciling Antithetical Doctrines?', 27(4) *EJIL* (2016) 1061.

Some flexibility with regard to the standard of proof may be sensible, as opposed to the imposition of a 'one size fits all' approach which would not take into account the vastly different roles that the Court is asked to play from one case to another. That said, for the purposes of this chapter, it is important only to note the approach of Court, in the absence of a prescribed burden and standard of proof in its own constitutive instruments, valuing flexibility and deference to the wishes of the parties. These same factors can again be seen in relation to the presentation of evidence by the parties.

C Presentation of Evidence by the Parties

With regard to the presentation of evidence by the parties,[28] and documentary evidence more specifically,[29] the Court's constitutive instruments provide limited guidance. For example, they state that such evidence must be submitted within the time limits for the Memorial, Counter-Memorial (and Reply and Rejoinder if applicable).[30] In the absence of the consent of the other party, or the Court itself, any factual assertion relying solely on a document submitted outwith these time limits, the Court may consider unproven.[31]

However, with regard to testimonial evidence of witnesses and experts, neither the Court's Statute nor Rules set out the procedure to be followed.[32]

---

[28] The presentation of evidence before the ICJ are governed by Articles 48–54 ICJ Statute, Articles 56–70 Rules of Court, and Practice Directions IX, IXbis, IXter, and IXquater. See also S. Wordsworth and K. Parlett, Chapter 13, Effective Advocacy at the ICJ.

[29] Although no specific definition is provided in the Court's constitutive instruments, documentary evidence has been given a broad interpretation and includes maps, photographs, judgments of domestic courts etc; see E. Valencia-Ospina, 'Evidence before the International Court of Justice'1 (1999) *International Law Forum du droit international* 202, 204.

[30] Articles 50 (1) and (2) Rules of Court.

[31] Articles 56 (1) and (2) ICJ Rules provide that additional documentary evidence can only be subsequently submitted with the consent of the other party or the Court itself. On this point, Practice Direction IX sets out states that documents should not be submitted after the end of the oral proceedings, although the Court may authorise late submission in exceptional circumstances if good reasons are given, see *Land, Island and Maritime Frontier Dispute (El Salvador/Honduras: Nicaragua intervening), Judgment of 11 September 1992:* ICJ Reports 1992, p. 455, para. 360.

[32] K. Mačák, 'Article 43' in A. Zimmermann et al. (eds.), *The Statute of the International Court of Justice: A Commentary* (3rd ed., Oxford University Press, 2019) 1280; see Article 58(2) Rules of Court.

Even those limited provisions which do exist, 'fail to address many of the more intricate problems connected with the examination of [witnesses and] experts'.[33] As such, aside from stipulating that parties 'shall be represented by agents'[34] and 'may have the assistance of counsel or advocates before the Court', or that 'the oral proceedings shall consist of the hearing by the Court of witnesses, experts, agents, counsel and advocates',[35] the Court has again been left to develop a practice for the hearing of such testimonial evidence.[36] The Court's approach has been typically flexible, seemingly happy to accept that an individual put forward as either a witness or an expert by a party does in fact appear as such, without probing further into their credentials.

Taken together, then, in relation to evidence put forward by the parties, we can see that the Court has not played an active role as an evidentiary gatekeeper in any real sense. Rather, the Court seeks to accommodate the wishes of the parties, allowing both documentary and testimonial evidence to come before it. This suggests that the Court is a passenger in the fact-finding process. But what can the Court do when the evidence presented to it by parties is either insufficient or contested, in order to elucidate the facts and make the determinations that it is tasked with making? The following section illustrates that the Court is endowed by its constitutive instruments with a significant range of powers which constitute its fact-finding arsenal, although in practice it has not made extensive use of them.

D The Court's Fact-Finding Powers

A full enumeration of the Court's fact-finding powers is not necessary here, but suffice it to note that the Court has the power to request information from parties and draw inferences from any refusal to comply,[37] to intervene in proceedings and ask questions,[38] to appoint its own experts and commissions of inquiry,[39] to request information from international organisations,[40] and even to visit the site in question should that be

[33] Tams, 'Article 51', 1447, para. 12.   [34] Article 42 (2) ICJ Statute.
[35] Article 43 (5) ICJ Statute.   [36] *Corfu Channel Case*, 244.
[37] Article 49 ICJ Statute, Article 62 Rules of Court.   [38] Article 61 Rules of Court.
[39] Article 50 ICJ Statute.   [40] Article 34(2) ICJ Statute.

considered necessary.[41] That said, the Court has not made regular use of those fact-finding powers that it possesses.

The traditional starting point for any analysis of how the ICJ has used its fact-finding powers is Thomas Franck's famous allegation that the Court utilises a number of 'avoidance techniques' to minimise the need to make use of its fact-finding powers and engage with scientific or other factually complex questions.[42] Franck's argument was that, faced with complex or technical factual issues, the Court would seek to shift the focus to legal issues instead, in relation to which it was on firmer ground. In Franck's words, 'in different questions of fact, the Court tends to make a complicated task of fact-finding unimportant or unnecessary by devising a rule which downgrades the importance of the elusive facts'.[43]

However, the accusation that the Court has over the years demonstrated an active desire to avoid conducting its own fact-finding in order to place greater emphasis on legal issues is hard to maintain. The Court has in the past stated that it was simply addressing 'the issues arising in all their aspects by applying the legal rules relevant to the situation'.[44] And indeed, without having been in the Court's position in these cases, it is hard to dispute its assertions that it was not necessary to conduct further fact-finding. Who is to say that it was not in fact the case that the Court had sound reasons for not conducting its own fact-finding such as considerations of judicial economy or the fact that resolution of those factual issues was not material to the resolution of the dispute at hand?[45] It is for this reason that speaking in terms of avoidance techniques is not particularly helpful.

Rather, it is more accurate to say that the Court's practice has been, until relatively recently, remarkably consistent in displaying a number of tendencies which taken together demonstrate a reactive, rather than

---

[41] Article 44(2) ICJ Statute, Article 66 Rules of Court.

[42] T. Franck, 'Fact-finding in the I.C.J.' in R. B. Lillich (ed.), *Fact-Finding before International Tribunals: Eleventh Sokol Colloquium* (Transnational Publishers 1992) 21; J. D'Aspremont and M. Mbengue, 'Strategies of Engagement with Scientific Fact-Finding in International Adjudication', 5 *JIDS* (2014) 240.

[43] Franck, 'Fact-finding in the I.C.J.'; see also S. Rosenne, 'Fact-Finding before the International Court of Justice' in *Essays on International Law and Practice* (T.M.C. Asser Press, 1999), p. 237.

[44] *Legality of the Use by a State of Nuclear Weapons in Armed Conflict, Advisory Opinion: ICJ Reports* 1996, p. 66, para. 15.

[45] Devaney, *Fact-Finding before the International Court*, 29.

proactive, approach to the use of its fact-finding powers and fact-finding in general.[46] This reactive approach, encapsulated by the Court's attitude towards admissibility and infrequent use of its own fact-finding powers, has meant that the Court has focused its energies not on conducting its own fact-finding, but rather on assessing the facts put before it by the parties.

E Fact-Assessment

The evaluation of the probative weight of evidence placed before it by the parties, the fact-assessment process, is crucially important for the Court. The Court has described its role in assessing the facts put before it by the parties as being to 'identify the documents relied on and make its own clear assessment of their weight, reliability and value'[47] or 'identify the documents relied on and make its own clear assessment of their weight, reliability and value'.[48] Similarly, in *Pulp Mills* the Court stated that:

it is the responsibility of the Court, after having given careful consideration to all the evidence placed before it by the Parties, to determine which facts must be considered relevant, to assess their probative value, and to draw conclusions from them as appropriate ... the Court will make its own determination of the facts, on the basis of the evidence presented to it, and then it will apply the relevant rules of international law to those facts which it has found to have existed.[49]

Here too, it should be noted, the Court's constitutive instruments do not provide any guidance for the Court and it has been left to the Court itself to provide some guidance regarding which evidence it finds more or less persuasive. For example, the Court has stated that certain forms of testimony such as that of a disinterested witness or evidence of a party against its own interest would be of 'prima facie superior credibility'.[50]

---

[46] M. O. Hudson, *The Permanent Court of International Justice 1920–1942* (MacMillan, 1943) 565.

[47] *Armed Activities on the Territory of the Congo (Democratic Republic of the Congo v. Uganda)*, Judgment: ICJ Reports 2005, p. 168, paras. 58–59.

[48] *Land and Maritime Boundary between Cameroon and Nigeria (Cameroon v. Nigeria: Equatorial Guinea intervening)* Judgment: ICJ Reports 2002, p. 303 para. 8.

[49] *Pulp Mills on the River Uruguay (Argentina v. Uruguay)*, Judgment, para. 168; *Armed Activities*, para. 57.

[50] *Military and Paramilitary Activities in and against Nicaragua (Nicaragua v. United States of America)*, Merits, Judgment, 27 June 1986, ICJ Reports 1986, 14, paras. 59–60.

The Court has had occasion to consider evidence that has already been treated by other courts. Factual determinations reached by the International Criminal Tribunal for the Former Yugoslavia (ICTY) were subject to contestation before the ICJ in the *Bosnian* and *Croatian Genocide* cases. In these cases the Court indicated that it would accord significant weight to such factual determinations, considering them highly persuasive.[51] In contrast, the Court has stated that it will accord less probative weight to evidence prepared specifically for the case before it as well as any evidence 'emanating from a single source'.[52]

In short, rather than focusing on the admissibility of evidence, or conducting its own fact-finding, the Court has focused its attention on assessing the probative weight of evidence put before it by the parties. In doing so, through its jurisprudence, the Court has indicated (albeit hardly in a systematic manner) the kinds of evidence to which it will attach greater weight. Such indications may be helpful to parties in introducing an element of predictability not otherwise provided by the Court's own constitutive instruments. However, a number of significant and factually complex cases in the last couple of decades have focused attention on how the Court handles facts in proceedings before it. The criticisms levelled at the Court's approach to fact-finding are the topic of the following section.

II Criticisms of the Court's Fact-Finding Process

Much of the recent attention paid to the Court's fact-finding process, it is fair to say, has been critical.[53] The following sections consider a selection

---

[51] *Application of the Convention on the Prevention and Punishment of the Crime of Genocide (Bosnia and Herzegovina v. Serbia and Montenegro),* Judgement: ICJ Reports 2007, p. 43, paras. 223, 248, 254, 261, 264, 266, 268, 272–274, 278–281, 283–318.

[52] *Armed Activities,* para. 61. Perhaps a useful shorthand for the kinds of factors that the Court takes into account when considering issues of probative weight are the comments of Judge Simma who stated that the Court generally considers seven factors: its source, interest, relation to events, method, verification, contemporaneity and its procedure: Judge Simma in *Application of the International Convention on the Elimination of all Forms of Racial Discrimination (Georgia v. Russian Federation) (Preliminary Objections)* ICJ Reports 2011, p. 70 Separate Opinion of Judge Simma, para. 20.

[53] E.g., Riddell and Plant, *Evidence before the International Court*; Devaney, *Fact-Finding before the International Court*'; Plant, 'Expert Evidence',; K. Parlett, 'Parties' Engagement with Experts in International Litigation' 9 *JIDS* (2018) 440; L. Boisson de Chazournes et al., 'One Size Does Not Fit All: Uses of Experts before International Courts and Tribunals: An Insight into Practice' 9 *JIDS* (2018) 477.

of criticisms which can be said to be broadly illustrative of the recent criticism that the Court has faced. These range from blatant factual errors to more general criticisms of how the Court deals with expert evidence and fact-finding.

First of all, and perhaps most straightforwardly, a number of the Court's judgments have contained demonstrable errors.[54] In the *Qatar* v. *Bahrain* case, for instance, in which the Court was tasked with determining whether there had been a channel navigable between two islands central to the maritime delimitation, the Court declined to conduct its own fact-finding, despite the fact the evidence put forward by the parties was inconclusive as to this issue.[55] The Court drew the maritime boundary over dry land belonging to both parties – an error, it has been suggested, which could 'have been avoided if experts had been recruited to help with the task'.[56]

Similarly, in *Cameroon* v. *Nigeria* the Court drew a land and maritime boundary that the parties have been unable to implement due to a number of factual discrepancies in the Court's judgment .[57] The parties subsequently asked the United Nations Secretary-General to establish a Mixed Commission to assist in the implementation of the Court's judgment.[58] Some mistakes are perhaps inevitable in conducting such complicated fact-finding. However, simple factual errors that are not the result of a lack of evidence and could have been prevented by greater reliance on experts are more problematic.[59] Leaving aside these rather clear-cut factual errors, perhaps the most significant contemporary criticism of the Court's fact-finding processes came in the context of the *Pulp Mills* case. This is a case which in retrospect has turned out to be a watershed moment for the way the Court conducts fact-finding.

In this particular case the Court's fact-finding was criticised both from international legal scholarship and, perhaps more interestingly, from

---

[54] A. Riddell, 'Scientific Evidence in the International Court of Justice: Problems and Possibilities' 20 *FYBIL* (2009) 229, at 243.

[55] *Maritime Delimitation and Territorial Questions between Qatar and Bahrain, Merits, Judgment*, ICJ Reports 2001 40, 98 para. 189.

[56] Riddell, 'Scientific Evidence', 243; see also T. Daniel, 'Expert Evidence before the ICJ', Paper presented at the Third Bi-Annual Conference of ABLOS (2003) 5.

[57] *Cameroon* v. *Nigeria*, 303; Riddell, 'Scientific Evidence', at 243.

[58] See www.unowa.unmissions.org/Default.aspx?tabid=804 and www.un.org/apps/news/story.asp?NewsID=43779&Cr=cameroon&Cr1=nigeria#.Uja9kxaZbww.

[59] Riddell, 'Scientific Evidence', at 243; see also Daniel 'Expert Evidence before the ICJ'.

within the Court itself. This dispute concerned Argentina's claims that the construction of two pulp mills by Uruguay were or would be damaging to the quality of the waters of the River Uruguay and cause significant transboundary harm. Ultimately the Court found 'no conclusive evidence in the record to show that Uruguay has not acted with the required degree of due diligence' and that Argentina had not proven that the pulp mills in question had had a 'deleterious effect or caused harm to living resources or to the quality of the water or the ecological balance of the river . . .'[60]

Judges Al-Khasawneh and Simma were the most fervent critics of the ICJ's approach to the complex factual issues that were disputed in this case, branding the Court's approach 'flawed methodologically'.[61] The main subject of the judges' criticism was that the Court 'omitted to resort to possibilities provided by its Statute' to test the evidentiary claims made by both parties regarding the (potential) harm of the pulp mills to the environment. This failure, the judges argued, hamstrung the Court and prevented it from doing what was 'necessary in order to arrive at a basis for the application of the law to the facts as scientifically certain as possible in a judicial proceeding'.[62] Further, Judges Al-Khasawneh and Simma criticised the Court for 'clinging to the habits it has traditionally followed in assessing and evaluating evidence',[63] namely by being reluctant to conduct its own fact-finding, and simply relying on evidence submitted by the parties. This, the judges suggested, had the potential to 'increase doubts in the international legal community whether it, as an institution, is well-placed to tackle complex scientific questions'.[64]

It is important to emphasise that criticisms of the Court's approach to fact-finding are not limited to the *Pulp Mills* case. For instance, the Court's handling of expert evidence over the course of several decades has been a particularly thorny issue. Concerns have been voiced in relation to two separate but related aspects of expert evidence, namely the Court's

---

[60] *Pulp Mills Case,* para. 265.

[61] *Pulp Mills Case,* Dissenting Opinion of Judges Al-Khasawneh and Simma, para. 2.

[62] *Pulp Mills Case,* B. Simma, 'The International Court of Justice and Scientific Expertise' 106 (2012) *Proceedings of the Annual Meeting (ASIL)* 230, 232.

[63] *Pulp Mills Case,* Dissenting Opinion of Judges Al-Khasawneh and Simma, para. 2.

[64] Ibid., para. 3. Similarly, Judge Ad Hoc Vinuesa openly questioned 'the Court's ability to make appropriate determinations of fact . . . based on sound scientific findings' without utilising its own fact-finding powers since the Court, as it was constituted, lacked the necessary 'specialised expert knowledge', *Pulp Mills Case,* Dissenting Opinion of Judge Ad Hoc Vinuesa, para. 71.

handling of party-appointed experts, and its use of so-called *experts fantômes*. It is worth considering each aspect in turn.

Until the *Pulp Mills* case, the standard practice of parties was to include experts as part of their teams as counsel, and to have expert evidence presented to the Court in that capacity.[65] For instance, parties have typically included experts as 'scientific advisors and experts' as part of their team, having them then present *ex parte* evidence to the Court on an area of their expertise.[66] This, in essence, meant that due to their status as counsel rather than experts, parties were able to avoid having their experts cross-examined in open court by the opposing party.[67] This deprived the Court of the benefits of cross-examination, namely intense scrutiny both of the subject of the expert opinion offered as well as the credentials and prejudices of the expert themselves.[68] Consequently, the Court was left to reckon with equally well-qualified party-appointed experts presenting completely contradictory expert evidence, ultimately leaving the Court none the wiser.[69]

A related strand of criticism related to its use of so-called *experts fantômes*. As stated above, the Court has the power to appoint its own experts to assist it in the fact-finding process.[70] However, it has traditionally been reluctant to use it since the *Corfu Channel* case, save from a select number of situations where it was explicitly asked to do so by the parties

---

[65] Devaney, *Fact-Finding before the International Court*, 78.

[66] *Kasikili/Sedudu Island (Botswana/Namibia)*, Judgment: ICJ Reports 1999, p. 1045, *Gabčikovo-Nagymaros Project (Hungary/Slovakia)*, Judgment: ICJ Reports 1997, p. 7, *Pulp Mills* Case,
Oral Proceedings, 2009.

[67] *Continental Shelf (Libyan Arab Jamahiriya/Malta)*, Judgement, 3 June 1985, Correspondence, at 518–519; Tams, 'Article 51', 1442, para. 5; A Watts, 'Burden of Proof and Evidence before the ICJ', in F. Weiss (ed.) *Improving WTO Dispute Settlement Procedures: Issues and Lessons from the Practice of Other International Courts and Tribunals* (Cameron May, 2000) 289, at 299.

[68] On this, see further: A. J. Van den Berg, *Arbitration Advocacy in Changing Times* (Kluwer, 2011), D. Bishop and E. G. Kehoe (eds.), *The Art of Advocacy in International Arbitration* (Second Edition, Juris, 2010), and K. Hobér and H. S. Sussman, *Cross-Examination in International Arbitration* (Oxford University Press, 2014).

[69] Only experts appearing on behalf of the parties under Article 43 (5) ICJ Statute come within the scope of Articles 57, 58, 63, and 64 ICJ Rules and are subject to cross-examination The same does not apply to counsel.

[70] Article 50 of the Court's Statute, and the related Articles 62(2), 67 and 68 of its Rules; see B. Simma, 'The International Court of Justice and Scientific Expertise', 106 *Proceedings of the Annual Meeting (American Society of International Law)* (2012) 230, at 231.

themselves.[71] Rather, the Court developed a practice of utilising so-called *experts fantômes,* or informally consulting experts temporarily contracted by the Registry to assist the Court in technical matters. The Court's informal use of experts in this way raised obvious due process concerns. For instance, it circumvented the procedure laid down in the Court's constitutive instruments and raised a number of serious issues, including the fact that the parties were not aware that the judges are receiving expert assistance, and did not know the identity of the experts being consulted.[72]

Fundamentally, this practice gives rise to very serious questions with respect to fairness of the judicial process. The parties in such circumstances are unable to have any say in, or to challenge, the substance of the assistance given to the Court by these experts.[73] Parties have no input on what issues experts are being consulted on, no input on the substance of their advice, as well as no information on the identity of the expert being consulted (and their attending biases which are not capable of being tested, for instance, through cross-examination). All of these factors have meant that the use of *experts fantômes* has been vociferously criticised.[74]

In summary, this section has highlighted a select number of recent criticisms of the manner in which the Court conducts fact-finding in cases which come before it. Such criticisms are both specific and general, pertaining to particular procedural issues as well as the Court's generally

---

[71] E.g. Article II (3) of the Special Agreement in ICJ, *Delimitation of the Maritime Boundary in the Gulf of Maine Area,* Judgement, 20 January 1982, ICJ Reports 1984, 246, at 253. Technical Report annexed to the Judgment, at 347 para. 3; see also: *Delimitation of the Maritime Boundary in the Gulf of Maine Area,* Order, 20 January 1982, ICJ Reports 1984, 246; finally, see the request made of the Chamber in Art IV (3) Special Agreement in *Frontier Dispute (Burkina Faso/Republic of Mali),* Judgement, 22 December 1986, ICJ Reports 1986, 554, at 558.

[72] *Pulp Mills* Case, 14, Joint Dissenting Opinion of Judges Al-Khasawneh and Simma, para. 14; C. J. Tams and J. G. Devaney, 'Article 50', in A. Zimmermann et al. (eds.), *The Statute of the International Court of Justice: A Commentary* (Oxford: Oxford University Press, 3rd ed., 2019) 1427, para. 26.

[73] A right which would otherwise be available to the parties under Article 67(2) of the Court's Rules in accordance with the procedure envisaged for Court-appointed experts.

[74] Tams and Devaney, 'Article 50', 1427, para. 26; Parlett, 'Parties' Engagement with Experts', 441; L. Malintoppi, 'Fact Finding and Evidence before the International Court of Justice (Notably in Scientific-Related Disputes)' 7 *JIDS* (2016) 421, at 436–438; D. Peat, 'The Use of Court: Appointed Experts by the International Court of Justice' 84 *BYBIL* (2014) 271, 300; J. G. Sandoval Coutasse and E. Sweeney-Samuelson, 'Adjudicating Conflicts Over Resources: The ICJ's Treatment of Technical Evidence in the Pulp Mills Case' 3 *Go. J.I.L.* (2011) 447.

reactive approach to fact-finding as a whole. It has been shown that there is merit in such criticisms, and as such it is worth taking a moment to reflect on why the Court's fact-finding process falls short in the way that it does and what can be done to improve it.

III Taking Facts Seriously: Party Autonomy vs. Proper Administration of Justice

Section I showed that the Court's approach to fact-finding is characterised by two factors, the rudimentary nature of the fact-finding provisions in its constitutive instruments, and deference to the wishes of the parties in accordance with the principle of party autonomy. Both of these factors have contributed to the merited criticisms of the Court's fact-finding process in recent times, set out in Section II.

Such criticisms are by now well known. However, what has hardly been considered in international legal scholarship to date is that, since the *Pulp Mills* case, the Court has taken significant steps towards addressing those criticisms levelled at it, and, just as importantly, has the ability to address the remaining criticisms. While the Court does not (realistically) have the ability to address the rudimentary nature of the fact-finding provisions in its constitutive instruments, it has been able to take steps towards addressing problematic aspects of the way in which it conducts fact-finding by recognising that it cannot prioritise the wishes of the parties above all else. In other words, when faced with the interpretation of relevant provisions of its constitutive instruments, the Court has recognised that the principle of party autonomy is not the only principle which is relevant to the judicial process. The remainder of this contribution will focus on one of these principles in particular, which is crucially important due to its potential to counteract some of the more problematic consequences of party autonomy.

The principle in question is that of the proper administration of justice.[75] It is important for ICJ judges to recognise that party autonomy is not the

---

[75] *Nicaragua* Case, 14, para. 31; see also: *Territorial and Maritime Dispute (Nicaragua v. Colombia), Application for Permission to Intervene*, Judgement, 4 May 2011, ICJ Reports 2011, 420, para. 36; *Barcelona Traction, Light and Power Company, Limited, Preliminary Objections*, Judgment, 24 July 1964, ICJ Reports 1964, 6, at 42. Although it

only principle at play.[76] Rather, when faced with the task of interpreting a particular procedural provision, for example, the judge must consider the relative weight of the principles of party autonomy and the proper administration of justice in the context of the particular case.[77]

Party autonomy cannot, for example, mean that maritime boundaries are drawn over dry land because errors in the establishment of the facts cannot be considered a legitimate interest of anyone involved. In such circumstances, where reliance on the principle of party autonomy alone would lead to unsound factual determinations, the Court can (and should) consider the relative weight of the principle of the proper administration of justice, and intervene in the fact-finding process in a way which is not completely deferential to the parties.

Take the example of the 'merry contradiction' of party-appointed experts appearing as counsel in cases before it.[78] Here, as we have seen, in deferring to the wishes of the parties, the Court may struggle to ensure that it delivers a judgment which is well-founded in fact and law in a procedurally fair manner. Consequently, it may decide that parties should not pursue such strategies in the future but rather put forward experts for cross-examination, in the interests of the proper administration of justice.[79]

In this context, there are certain areas in which we have seen procedural reform in recent times. For instance, since the Court spoke disapprovingly the practice of experts appearing as counsel in *Pulp Mills*, experts have

---

should be noted the Court has also referred to this principle as the 'good' or 'better' administration of justice, see *Territorial and Maritime Dispute (Nicaragua* v. *Colombia), Preliminary Objections*, Judgement, 13 December 2007, ICJ Reports 2007, 832, paras. 50–51; *Application of the Convention on the Prevention and Punishment of the Crime of Genocide, Counter Claims*, Order, 17 December 1997, ICJ Reports 1997, 243, para. 30. See also Callista Harris, Chapter 11, The Working Practices of the Court.

[76] R. Kolb, 'General Principles of Procedural Law', in A. Zimmermann et al. (ed.) *The Statute of the International Court of Justice: A Commentary* (Oxford University Press, 2019) 977.

[77] For an elaborated version of this argument see J. Devaney 'Reappraising the Role of Experts in Recent Cases before the International Court of Justice' 62 *Germ Yearbook Intl L* (2019) 337. Principles provide a reason for making a legal determination in a certain way, without requiring it, see R. Dworkin, 'The Model of Rules' 35, *U.Chi.L.Rev*, (1967) 26, see also J. Raz 'Legal Principles and the Limits of Law' 81 *Yale L. J.* (1972) 838 stating that '[r]ules prescribe relatively specific acts; principles prescribe highly unspecific actions'.

[78] B. Simma, 'The International Court of Justice and Scientific Expertise' at 232.

[79] See further J. G. Devaney, 'Reappraising the Role of Experts in Recent Cases before the International Court of Justice', 62 *Germ Yearbook Intl L* (2019) 337.

generally been put forward by the parties as such, to be cross-examined. In particular, in the *Whaling in the Antarctic* case the President of the Court clearly set out how he envisaged examination of party-appointed experts should proceed in cases before it.[80] Judges then had the opportunity to, and did in fact, put their own questions to the experts.[81]

In subsequent cases, such as in the joined *Certain Activities* and *Construction of a Road* proceedings experts were again put forward as such and cross-examined by opposing counsel.[82] In the course of proceedings the Court in fact made a small but significant alteration to this procedure, actively becoming involved in the proceedings to inform parties that it 'would find it useful if, during the course of the hearings in the two cases, they could call the experts whose reports were annexed to the written pleadings ...'[83] The Court also asked the parties to both inform it of the experts that they wished to present in the oral hearings and to provide a summary of the testimony of such experts in advance.[84]

In relation to the Court's consultation of *experts fantômes,* too, there have been developments. Despite the fact certain judges and former judges have spoken in favour of the continued informal consultation of such experts,[85] even if only in limited circumstances,[86] the Court recently took the noteworthy step of appointing its own experts in the *Maritime Delimitation* case.[87] In doing so, the Court demonstrated a willingness to

---

[80] *Whaling in the Antarctic* Case, Verbatim Record 2013/9, para. 38.

[81] *Whaling in the Antarctic* Case, para. 21; Questions were asked of Australia's expert Professor Mangel by Judges Bennouna, Cançado Trindade, Greenwood, Donohue, Keith, and Owada, Verbatim Record 2013/9, at paras. 63, 64, 67, 69, and 70 respectively. Judges Greenwood, Cançado Trindade, Yusuf, Bennouna, Keith and Charlesworth asked questions of Japan's expert, Verbatim Record 2013/14, at paras. 49–50, 50–53, 53–55, 55–57, and 57–59 respectively.

[82] *Certain Activities Carried Out by Nicaragua in the Border Area (Costa Rica v. Nicaragua) and Construction of a Road in Costa Rica along the San Juan River (Nicaragua v. Costa Rica), Judgment, ICJ Reports 2015, p.* 665. Verbatim Record 2015/2, para. 18.

[83] *Certain Activities/Construction of a Road* case, ibid., para. 31.

[84] Ibid., 134, J. Quintana, *Cuestiones de procedimento en los casos* Costa Rica c. Nicaragua y Nicaragua c. Costa Rica *ante la Corte Internacional de Justicia, ACDI – Anuario Colombiano de Derecho Internacional,* vol. 10 (2017), 146.

[85] Bennouna, 'Experts before the International Court of Justice: What For?', 4.

[86] *Pulp Mills* Case, Dissenting Opinion of Judges Al-Khasawneh and Simma, para. 14; see also Simma, 'The International Court of Justice and Scientific Expertise', 231.

[87] *Maritime Delimitation in the Caribbean Sea and the Pacific Ocean (Costa Rica v. Nicaragua),* Orders of 31 May 2016 and 16 June 2016.

utilise its fact-finding powers to go beyond the facts placed before it by the parties.

The Court's experts conducted two site visits to undertake specific investigations,[88] ultimately producing a detailed ninety-two-page report.[89] This report played a significant role in oral proceedings, with both parties making repeated references to it to support their factual assertions,[90] as well featuring heavily in that part of the Judgment itself that addressed the disputed factual issue.[91] Overall, the Court's experience in this case has generally been seen as a positive one, by the parties, international legal scholarship, and the Court itself.[92] For the avoidance of doubt, the Court need not appoint its own experts in each and every case that comes before it.[93] However, where the facts submitted by the parties are either insufficient or conflicting, the Court must take into account the proper administration of justice and do what it considers necessary to make sound factual determinations. That may include, in an appropriate case, the Court appointing its own expert(s).

Consideration of these developments is intended to demonstrate that the Court's recent willingness to act in a more prescriptive manner in the interests of ensuring the proper administration of justice has led to positive procedural reform. Today, the Court is able to observe the reputation and credibility of party-appointed experts being tested through cross-examination in proceedings before it, and is not subject to the wishes of

---

[88] See for example correspondence of 19 January 2017 and 24 January 2017, correspondence related to the organisation of the expertise ordered by the Court, available at www.icj-cij.org/en/.

[89] *Maritime Delimitation* case. Written Proceedings, Report of the Court-appointed experts, 30 April 2017.

[90] Ibid., paras. 19, 26.

[91] Ibid., para. 71; see further Separate Opinion of Judge Xue, paras. 6, 12, and 14, and Declaration of Judge Gevorgian, para. 4; see also at paras. 77, 86, and 104.

[92] *Maritime Delimitation* case, Verbatim Record 2017/10, at para. 10.

[93] There are advantages and disadvantages to the Court appointing its own experts under Article 50 of its Statute, including that the Court must pay for its own experts out of its own budget, and that these experts rely on the consent of the parties in order to, for instance, gain access to any location they are investigating. In the context of the *Maritime Delimitation* case, the expense of the services of the Court's experts was submitted to the UN General Assembly (GA) for approval, see: UNGA Res. 71/272, 23 December 2016, at VIII. See also recent reference to funds for such experts in requesting an increase in budget to the UNGA: UNGA, Proposed programme budget for the biennium 2018–2019, Part III, International justice and law, Section 7, International Court of Justice, UN Doc. A/72/6 (Sect. 7), at para. 7.17.

the parties presenting experts as counsel. In addition, in utilising those fact-finding powers that it possesses, the Court has been able to gain assistance of experts in comprehending complex factual issues which arise in the course of proceedings, or which the parties' experts are examined on.[94] Of course, while the Court has taken a number of significant steps in recent cases, certain issues remain. For instance, the Court may wish to consider providing settled guidance to parties on how it wishes the presentation of testimonial evidence to proceed, and it may seek to allow parties to question Court-appointed experts in future cases.[95]

IV Conclusion

The ICJ is a court of first and last instance, and as such, the establishment of the facts is a fundamental part of the judicial function.[96] And one need look no further than the amount of time and effort that parties put into contesting the facts to understand that the parties feel similarly.[97] Whatever one considers the role of the Court to be, whether simply the settlement of the dispute before it,[98] or the achievement of some objective notion of justice (or anything in between), the establishment of the facts matters. Any failure to establish the facts could lead to the application of the wrong rule, or of the right rule in the wrong manner. Alternatively, such failure could lead to a judgment which is not capable of being implemented. Without the establishment of facts in a way that coheres with the dispute before it, the Court's judgments would be a 'mere abstraction' which 'would address facts that are either moot or disconnected from

---

[94] P. Couvreur, 'Le Règlement Juridictionel', in Institut du droit économique de la mer (ed.), *Le Processus de delimitation maritime étude d'un cas fictive: colloque international Monoco 17–29 mars 2003* (2004) 349, 382.

[95] For detailed proposals in this regard, see Devaney, 'Reappraising the Role of Experts'.

[96] See *Armed Activities Case*, para. 57; *Pulp Mills Case*, paras. 162, 163 and 168; Devaney, *Fact-Finding before the International Court*, p. 8, 9; K. Highet, 'Evidence and Proof of Facts' in L. F. Damrosch (ed.), *The International Court of Justice at a Crossroads* (Transnational, 1987), p. 355; Franck, 'Fact-finding in the I.C.J.', 21.

[97] Kolb, 'The International Court of Justice', 928.

[98] C. Romano, 'The Role of Experts in International Adjudication' (2009) *Société Française Pour le droit International*, 'it can be argued that the ultimate purpose of international adjudication is not establishing the facts, or truths, even, The Truth, but rather to settle the dispute.'

a legal dispute', ultimately undermining its function as a judicial body.[99] Accordingly, where the prioritising of the wishes of the parties results in factual determinations which so threaten the Court's function, it is incumbent upon it to consider the relative weight of other principles, such as the principle of the proper administration of justice. A number of factually complex cases are currently on the Court's docket,[100] and other issues on the horizon not explored in this contribution, such as the difficulties that non-appearance creates for the Court in terms of fact-finding, strongly suggest the Court will continue to be confronted with issues of fact-finding and expert evidence for years to come.

Further Reading

M. Benzing, 'Evidentiary Issues' in A. Zimmermann et al. (eds.) *The Statute of the International Court of Justice: A Commentary* (Oxford University Press, 2019) 1377.

J. G. Devaney, *Fact-Finding before the International Court of Justice* (Cambridge University Press 2016).

J. G. Devaney 'Reappraising the Role of Experts in Recent Cases before the International Court of Justice', *Germ Yearrbook Intl L* 62 (2019) 337.

K. Del Mar, 'The International Court of Justice and Standards of Proof', in Bannelier et al. (eds.), *The ICJ and the Evolution of International Law* (Routledge, 2012) 99.

R. Kolb, 'General Principles of Procedural Law', in A. Zimmermann et al. (ed.) *The Statute of the International Court of Justice: A Commentary* (3rd ed., Oxford University Press, 2019) 977.

L. Malintoppi, 'Fact Finding and Evidence before the International Court of Justice (Notably in Scientific-Related Disputes)' 9 *JIDS* (2018) 421.

M. Mbengue, 'International Courts and Tribunals as Fact-Finders: The Case of Scientific Fact-Finding in International Adjudication' 34 *Loy. L. A. Int'l & Comp. L. Rev* (2012) 53–80 at 53–54.

K. Parlett, 'Parties' Engagement with Experts in International Litigation' 9 *JIDS* (2018) 440.

---

[99] Mbengue, 'International Courts and Tribunals as Fact-Finders' 53–54.

[100] *Maritime Delimitation in the Indian Ocean (Somalia v. Kenya)*, available at www.icj-cij .org/en/case/161, *Alleged Violations of Sovereign Rights and Maritime Spaces in the Caribbean Sea (Nicaragua v. Colombia)*, see: www.icj-cij.org/en/case/155, *Dispute Over the Status and Use of the Waters of the Silala (Chile v. Bolivia)*, available at www.icj-cij .org/en/case/162; *Application of the Convention on the Prevention and Punishment of Genocide (The Gambia v. Myanmar)*; available at www.icj-cij.org/en/case/178; *Guatemala's Territorial, Insular and Maritime Claim* (Guatemala/Belize), available at www.icj-cij.org/en/case/177/.

D. Peat, 'The Use of Court: Appointed Experts by the International Court of Justice' 84 *BYBIL* (2014) 271.

B. Plant, 'Expert Evidence and the Challenge of Procedural Reform in International Dispute Settlement' 9 *JIDS* (2018) 464.

A. Riddell and B. Plant, *Evidence before the International Court of Justice* (British Institute of International and Comparative Law 2009).

10 The ICJ and Other Courts and Tribunals: Integration and Fragmentation

Philippa Webb

I Introduction[1]

The International Court of Justice (ICJ) possesses special authority due its status as the only court of general jurisdiction and the United Nations' principal judicial organ. It is permanent and has the ability to deal with a wide variety of topics involving both treaty and custom. The ICJ has well-established, collegial procedures and strong judicial control over the drafting process.

In this chapter, I examine the degree of integration or fragmentation among the ICJ and other courts and tribunals. Integration 'does not equate to total uniformity' but rather 'requires that similar factual scenarios and similar legal issues are treated in a consistent manner, and that any disparity in treatment is explained and justified.'[2] Fragmentation is used in the sense of 'decisional fragmentation': 'when two courts seised of the same issue (legal or factual) render contradictory decisions, or a single court contradicts a finding in an earlier case, without explaining the reasons for the divergence.'[3]

I contend that three factors influence the degree of integration or not of fragmentation: the identity of the court, the substance of the law, and the procedures employed.[4] Identity encompasses the type of court, including its temporal nature, its function, and the institutional regime it is embedded within (whether the UN system or something else) appears to be an important factor in the degree to which judges seek to integrate their

I am grateful to Giulia Bernabei and Drishti Suri for research assistance and to the editors and Judge Keith for their comments on earlier drafts.

[1] This chapter draws on my monograph, P. Webb, *International Judicial Integration and Fragmentation* (Oxford University Press, 2013).

[2] Ibid., p. 5.   [3] Ibid., p. 6.

[4] Cf. the twelve factors identified in C. Brown, *A Common Law of International Adjudication* (Oxford University Press, 2007), ch. 7.

decisions with existing jurisprudence. The area of law involved in the case and whether it is governed by treaty or custom, is regularly subject to judicial settlement, or is controversial, has an impact of the degree of flexibility judges have in interpreting and developing the law. Finally, the procedural rules and practices of a court relating to evidence, judgment drafting, and the use of existing case law also affect the degree of fragmentation or convergence.

For illustrative purposes, this chapter addresses three legal issues that have been the subject of consideration by the ICJ and other courts and tribunals in recent years. These issues are necessarily specific in nature and proceed from process to substance: jurisdiction over issues of immunity involving treaties that do not expressly refer to immunity; inferring specific intent for genocide; and the nature of consular assistance as a treaty obligation, individual right or human right. Although narrow in content, these issues provide a gateway into the way that identity, area of law and procedure influence integration or fragmentation among international courts.

II Immunity: Jurisdictional Aspects

Unlike the law on genocide or consular assistance, the law on immunities has no overarching treaty. The 2004 United Nations Convention on Jurisdictional Immunities of States and Their Property (UNCSI) has not entered into force, having only twenty-three of the required thirty ratifications. There are specific treaties on the immunities of diplomas, consular officials, members on special mission, and representatives of States to international organisations, but they form a 'patchwork of rules'[5] not a comprehensive text. International courts are therefore often deciding questions relating to immunity on the basis of customary international law.[6]

In recent years, a question that has arisen before the ICJ and an inter-State arbitral tribunal is: does a court or tribunal have jurisdiction over a dispute concerning immunity when no provision of relevant treaty expressly refers to immunity?

---

[5] Ibid., 173.
[6] See R O'Keefe, Chapter 18, Jurisdictional Immunities in this book for an analysis on the ICJ's case law on jurisdictional immunities in cases that proceeded to the merits.

In *Equatorial Guinea* v. *France*, Equatorial Guinea sought to bring a dispute concerning, inter alia, the alleged violation of the immunity of the Vice-President caused by criminal proceedings in France. In this regard, it invoked the compromissory clause in the UN Convention against Transnational Organized Crime (the Palermo Convention). Equatorial Guinea relied on Article 4 of the Palermo Convention, which provides that 'States Parties shall carry out their obligations under this Convention in a manner consistent with the principles of sovereign equality and territorial integrity of States and that of non-intervention in the domestic affairs of other States'.[7] Specifically, it argued that 'the rules relating to the immunity *ratione personae* of certain holders of high-ranking office and the immunity from execution of State property flow directly from the principles of sovereign equality and non-intervention referred to in Article 4'.[8] France, for its part, contended that Article 4 'does not incorporate the rules of customary international law, in particular those concerning immunities of States and State officials'.[9] The Court found that even though the rules of state immunity 'derive from the principle of sovereign equality', Article 4 'does not refer to the customary international rules ... [and] does not impose, through its reference to sovereign equality, an obligation on States parties to act in a manner consistent with the many rules of international law which protect sovereignty in general, as well as all the qualifications to those rules'.[10] Consequently, the aspect of the dispute relating to the 'asserted immunity of the Vice-President' did not concern the interpretation or application of the Palermo Convention and therefore did not fall within the Court's jurisdiction.[11]

The questions of jurisdiction over claims regarding immunity was raised again in a case between Iran and the United States concerning, inter alia, the alleged breach of the immunity of Iran through the attachment and seizure of the assets of its central bank. Iran relied on several provisions of the 1955 Treaty of Amity, Economic Relations, and Consular Rights (Treaty of Amity) that did not contain the word 'immunity' but incorporated by

---

[7] *Immunities and Criminal Proceedings (Equatorial Guinea* v. *France)* (Judgment on Preliminary Objections) [2018] ICJ Rep 292, para. 78.
[8] Ibid., para. 81.   [9] Ibid., para. 79.   [10] Ibid., para. 93.
[11] Ibid., para. 102. The Court found that it did have jurisdiction on the basis of the Optional Protocol to the Vienna Convention on Diplomatic Relations to entertain the claims relating to the status of a building in Paris as diplomatic premises, including claims relating to the seizure of furnishings and movable property from the premises.

reference to rules of customary international law on immunities through, for example, reference to 'the require[ments of] international law' (Article IV(2) of the Treaty of Amity),[12] 'freedom of access to the courts of justice and administrative agencies ... both in defense and pursuit of their rights' (Article III(2)),[13] 'fair and equitable treatment' and restraint on 'unreasonable or discriminatory measures' (Article IV(1)),[14] and 'freedom of commerce' (Article X(1)).[15] Iran also argued that the reference to an exception to immunity for enterprises that are 'publicly owned or controlled' and engage in 'commercial [or] industrial' activities in Article XI(4) 'confirms by strong implication the existence of a Treaty obligation that such immunity must be upheld' when state entities engage in activities in the exercise of sovereign authority.[16] The Court rejected all of these arguments, finding none of the provisions were 'capable of bringing within the jurisdiction of the Court the question of the United States' respect for the immunities to which certain Iranian State entities are said to be entitled, is of such a nature as to justify such a finding.'[17]

The ICJ's textual approach was followed by the arbitral tribunal in the inter-State dispute between Italy and India concerning the 'Enrica Lexie' Incident, but more creative reasoning led to a different outcome on jurisdiction. Italy asserted, inter alia, that India had violated the immunity *ratione materiae* of two Italian Marines by exercising criminal jurisdiction over them. It argued that the tribunal, constituted under Annex VII of the UN Convention on the Law of the Sea (UNCLOS), had jurisdiction regarding the issue of the immunity of the Marines under Articles 2(3), 56(2) and 58(2) of UNCLOS which refer to 'other rules of international law', the rights and duties of other States' and 'other pertinent rules of international law'.[18] India contended that following the jurisprudence of the ICJ, including in *Equatorial Guinea* v. *France*, such references to international law 'cannot be a basis for jurisdiction of the court in the matter of the immunity of the marines, which is simply alien to the provision[s]'.[19] Italy maintained that the ICJ's decisions 'do not stand for any general

---

[12] *Certain Iranian Assets (Islamic Republic of Iran* v. *United States of America)* (Judgment on Preliminary Objections) [2019] ICJ Reports 7, para. 54.

[13] Ibid., para. 67.   [14] Ibid.   [15] Ibid., para. 76.   [16] Ibid., para. 60.

[17] Ibid., para. 80.

[18] *The 'Enrica Lexie' Incident* (Award) PCA Case No. 2015–28 (21 May 2020), para. 797.

[19] Ibid., para. 746.

proposition that rules on immunity cannot be read into a treaty that does not expressly provide for them'.[20]

The tribunal initially took a textual approach in finding that the provisions of UNCLOS invoked by Italy were 'not pertinent and applicable' to the case because, for example, they applied to the exercise of rights and duties in maritime zones that were not relevant to the facts of the case.[21] However, it then considered the argument that 'it would make no sense whatsoever for the Tribunal to determine that a State has jurisdiction under [UNCLOS] without, at the same time, deciding whether the exercise of such jurisdiction would be lawful under international law. This necessarily requires a decision on immunity'.[22] The tribunal considered that while UNCLOS 'may not provide a basis for entertaining an independent immunity claim under general international law', the tribunal's 'competence extends to the determination of the issue of immunity of the Marines that necessarily arises as an incidental question in the application of the Convention'.[23] Interestingly, ICJ Judge Robinson, sitting as an arbitrator, dissented from this conclusion on jurisdiction, although he had taken the position in the *Certain Iranian Assets* and *Equatorial Guinea* v. *France* that the ICJ did have jurisdiction over the claims relating to immunity by the Applicant states.[24] In his dissenting opinion in the *Enrica Lexie* case, Judge Robinson praised the ICJ Judgments for which he had been in the minority:[25]

This approach [in *Certain Iranian Assets* and *Equatorial Guinea* v. *France*] to determining the Court's jurisdiction is deferential to, and protective of, the limits of a State party's consent to jurisdiction in a compromissory clause conferring on the Court jurisdiction over a dispute concerning the interpretation or application of a treaty. In this case, the Majority has not been deferential to and protective of the limits of India's consent to the Arbitral Tribunal's jurisdiction over the dispute.

Judge Robinson's critique goes to the heart of the difference in *identity* between the ICJ and an Annex VII tribunal. In his view, the ad hoc arbitral tribunal should have been just as deferential and cautious regarding State consent as the ICJ. But the majority appear to have taken a more creative

---

[20] Ibid., para. 771.   [21] Ibid., para. 798.

[22] Ibid., para. 807, citing Italy's counsel Sir Michael Wood.

[23] Ibid., para. 809, see also para. 811.

[24] Ibid., Dissenting Opinion of Judge Patrick Robinson, para. 36.

[25] Ibid., Dissenting Opinion of Judge Patrick Robinson, para. 37.

approach based on a concept of a 'necessary incidental question'.[26] Commentators have speculated that the tribunal's approach 'was likely motivated by a desire to offer a meaningful response to an important question argued by the parties' leading it to 'open the gates' of jurisdiction under UNCLOS 'at least a bit, so that immunity ... could sneak in'.[27]

An observation I made in an earlier work provides an explanation based on identity:[28]

Arbitral tribunals usually exist only for the purposes of the specific dispute; the tribunal disbands once the case is over and the award rendered. The registries, arbitrators, and applicable rules vary from case to case. There is inconsistent publication of pleadings and reporting of awards, which hinders the accumulation of a body of jurisprudence that may be referred to by parties and arbitrators. All these factors contribute to a sense of deciding in a vacuum rather than as part of an international legal system.

The *procedure* of an arbitral tribunal, with sporadic meetings in varied locations scheduled in between the 'day jobs' of arbitrators who are full-time judges or academics, is also more conducive towards reasoning tailored to resolving a particular dispute rather than integration into the corpus of existing jurisprudence.

III Genocide: Inferring Specific Intent

The specific intent (*dolus specialis*) of genocide is its 'essential character-istic, which distinguishes it from other serious crimes'.[29] Courts with jurisdiction over individual or State responsibility for genocide have had to engage with the question of intent in every case in which the crime is alleged. Article II of the Genocide Convention provides:

---

[26] Ibid., para. 811. See also C. Harris, 'Incidental Determinations in Proceedings under Compromissory Clauses' 70 ICLQ (2021) 417 for a discussion of practice before the ICJ and tribunals under UNCLOS. She observes that the ICJ in *Certain Iranian Assets* 'appears to have accepted, in principle, it can make incidental determinations' (at 438).

[27] E. Methymaki and C. Tams, 'Immunities and Compromissory Clauses: Making Sence of Enrica Lexia (Part II)', (*EJIL:Talk!*, 27 August 2020) <www.ejiltalk.org/immunities-and-compromissory-clauses-making-sense-of-enrica-lexie-part-ii/> accessed 22 December 2020.

[28] Webb, *International Judicial Integration and Fragmentation*, p. 152.

[29] *Application of the Convention on the Prevention and Punishment of the Crime of Genocide (Croatia v. Serbia)* (Merits) [2015] ICJ Rep 3 (hereafter *Croatia v. Serbia*), para. 132.

In the present Convention, genocide means any of the following acts committed
with intent to destroy, in whole or in part, a national, ethnical, racial or religious
group, as such:

(a) Killing members of the group;
(b) Causing serious bodily or mental harm to members of the group;
(c) Deliberately inflicting on the group conditions of life calculated to bring about
   its physical destruction in whole or in part;
(d) Imposing measures intended to prevent births within the group;
(e) Forcibly transferring children of the group to another group.

The question of intent arises in two ways in Article II. First, the *chapeau* refers
to the specific 'intent to destroy, in whole or in part, a national, ethnical,
racial or religious group, as such'. Second, sections (a) through (e) list acts that
each contain their own mental element. At least four aspects of specific intent
have generated various lines of reasoning in the different courts: whether the
specific intent can be inferred from a pattern of acts, whether the intent is
purpose-based or knowledge-based, whether the existence of a plan or policy
is an essential element, and how different modes of liability may affect the
requirement of specific intent.[30] This chapter addresses the first aspect:
whether genocidal intent can be inferred from a pattern of conduct as the
only reasonable inference or as one of several reasonable conclusions.

In its cases on state responsibility for genocide in the Balkans conflict,
the ICJ has taken a clear position that specific intent must be the only
reasonable inference. In the *Bosnian Genocide* case, Bosnia and
Herzegovina had relied on the existence of an overall plan to commit
genocide, indicated by the pattern of acts of genocide committed throughout the territory against persons identified on the basis of their belonging
to a specified group.[31] It argued that the specific intent could be inferred
from the pattern of atrocities. The Court rejected this argument:

The *dolus specialis*, the specific intent to destroy the group in whole or in part, has
to be convincingly shown by reference to particular circumstances, unless a general
plan to that end can be convincingly demonstrated to exist; and for a pattern of
conduct to be accepted as evidence of its existence, it would have to be such *that it
could only point* to the existence of such intent.[32]

---

[30] Webb, *International Integration and Fragmentation*, 25.
[31] *Application of the Convention on the Prevention and Punishment of the Crime of Genocide
(Bosnia v. Serbia)* (Merits) [2007] ICJ Rep 43, para. 370.
[32] Ibid., para. 373 (emphasis added).

In the *Croatian Genocide* case, the ICJ confirmed and implied an element of reasonableness into its high standard for drawing inferences of specific intent:

The Court recalls that, in the passage in question in its 2007 Judgment, it accepted the possibility of genocidal intent being established indirectly by inference. The notion of 'reasonableness' must necessarily be regarded as implicit in the reasoning of the Court. Thus, . . . in order to infer the existence of *dolus specialis* from a pattern of conduct, it is necessary and sufficient that this is the only inference that could reasonably be drawn from the acts in question. To interpret paragraph 373 of the 2007 Judgment in any other way would make it impossible to reach conclusions by way of inference.[33]

The ad hoc ICTY and ICTR were, for a period of years, unclear in their case law as to whether the existence of specific intent has to be the only reasonable inference from the facts.[34] In *Brdjanin*, for example, the ICTY Trial Chamber noted it was 'generally accepted' in the jurisprudence of the ICTY and of the ICTR that, in the absence of direct evidence, the specific intent can be inferred from 'the facts, the concrete circumstances, or a "pattern of purposeful action"'.[35] However, in the 2012 *Tolimir* Judgment, the ICTY clarified that it took the 'only reasonable inference' approach:

Indications of such intent are rarely overt, however, and thus it is permissible to infer the existence of genocidal intent based on 'all of the evidence taken together', as long as this inference is 'the only reasonable [one] available on the evidence'.[36]

In the 2001 *Kayishema* Judgment, the ICTR Appeals Chamber spoke broadly of inference 'from relevant facts and circumstances'.[37] However, by 2007, it had clarified that that genocidal intent must be 'the only reasonable inference from the totality of the evidence'.[38]

---

[33] *Croatia v. Serbia*, para. 148.   [34] Webb, *International Integration and Fragmentation*.

[35] *Prosecutor v. Brdjanin* (Judgment) IT-99-36-T, T Ch II (1 September 2004), para. 704, referring also inter alia to *Prosecutor v. Stakić* (Judgment) IT-97-24-T, T Ch II (31 July 2003), para. 526.

[36] *Prosecutor v. Tolimir* (Judgment) IT-05-88/2-T, T Ch II (12 December 2012), para. 745. This was upheld on appeal in *Prosecutor v. Tolimir* (Judgment) IT-05-88/2-A, A Ch (8 April 2015), paras. 495, 499.

[37] *Prosecutor v. Kayishema/Ruzindana* (Judgment) ICTR-95-1-A, A Ch (1 June 2001), para. 159.

[38] *Nahimana, Barayagwiza, Ngeze v. Prosecutor* (Judgment) ICTR-99-52-A, A Ch (28 November 2007), para. 524.

The ICC had the opportunity to address the question of inference of specific intent in the context of the decision to issue an arrest warrant for Sudanese President Al-Bashir in 2010. It concluded that the Pre-Trial Chamber would err if it denies a warrant on the basis that 'the *existence* of ... genocidal intent is only one of several reasonable conclusions available on the materials provided by the Prosecution'.[39] The ICC Appeals Chamber noted that the evidentiary threshold for issuing an arrest warrant ('reasonable grounds to believe') differs from the thresholds for confirmation of charges ('substantial grounds to believe') and conviction ('beyond reasonable doubt').[40] In this context, it explained how inference interacts with the standard of proof:

> In the view of the Appeals Chamber, requiring that the existence of genocidal intent must be the *only* reasonable conclusion amounts to requiring the Prosecutor to disprove any other reasonable conclusions and to eliminate any reasonable doubt. If the only reasonable conclusion based on the evidence is the existence of genocidal intent, then it cannot be said that such a finding establishes merely 'reasonable grounds to believe'. Rather, it establishes genocidal intent 'beyond reasonable doubt'.[41]

Although this was a decision taken at an interlocutory stage, it confirmed that the ICC intends to take the 'only reasonable inference' approach in determining responsibility for genocide.

Several factors may explain the consistency on this question among the ICJ and the international criminal courts, after a brief period of uncertainty in the case law of the ad hoc tribunals. First, in terms of identity, the temporary nature of the ad hoc tribunals gives them a greater propensity towards experimentation compared with the permanent ICJ and ICC. 'The incentives to take a long-term view and embed themselves in existing legal frameworks are weaker for ad hoc courts.'[42] Interestingly, the ad hoc tribunals began to share some of the features of permanent courts over time. As the institutions aged, 'the pull of internal integration [became] stronger; a certain inertia may set in that pushes against creative legal reasoning and solutions'.[43] Moreover, the identity of the international criminal courts as respecting a defendant's right to the presumption of innocence pushed them towards the strict approach to inference adopted

---

[39] *Prosecutor* v. *Al Bashir* (Decision) ICC-02/05-01/09-OA, A Ch (3 February 2010), para. 1.
[40] Ibid., para. 30.   [41] Ibid., para. 33.
[42] Webb, *International Integration and Fragmentation*, 152.   [43] Ibid.

by the ICJ: 'In the absence of direct evidence of genocidal intent, the special intent of the accused may be circumstantially inferred from his actions and words. However, because of the presumption of innocence, an inference based on circumstantial evidence must be the only reasonable inference that can be drawn from the evidence.'[44] Accordingly, the ICTY and ICTR came to align themselves with the 'only reasonable inference' standard over time. Second, in terms of the substance of the law, the Genocide Convention (and its verbatim reproduction in the statutes of the international criminal tribunals) is comprehensive in coverage. Working from a common text enhances integration among courts. Third, the lack of a common approach to drafting judgments within and among the international criminal courts heightens the risk of fragmentation as courts may employ diverse techniques for assessing evidence, studying case law from other courts, and expressing legal reasoning.[45] However, this risk appears to have been mitigated by the first two factors.

IV Consular Assistance: State Obligation, Individual Right or Human Right?

Article 36(1) of the Vienna Convention on Consular Relations (the VCCR) codifies a right to consular assistance. It provides that when an individual is arrested or detained by the authorities of a foreign state, the consular post is to be informed 'without delay' upon the request of the individual. Any communication by the individual 'shall also be forwarded by the said authorities without delay' and they shall also inform the individual concerned of his rights in this regard.[46] Consular officers shall have the right to visit the individual in detention, communicate with him and arrange legal representation.[47]

This right was at the centre of a series of ICJ cases brought by Paraguay, Germany, Mexico and India concerning foreign nationals detained and facing the prospect of the death penalty in the United States and

[44] G. Mettraux, *International Crimes Law and Practice Volume I: Genocide* (Oxford University Press, 2019), pp. 224–225.
[45] Webb, *International Integration and Fragmentation*, 24–25.
[46] Vienna Convention on Consular Relations (adopted 24 April 1963, entered into force on 19 March 1967) 596 UNTS 261, Art. 36(1)(b).
[47] Vienna Convention on Consular Relations Art. 36(1)(c).

Pakistan.[48] It has also been the subject of an advisory opinion issued by the Inter-American Court of Human Rights.

There are three possible visions of Article 36 of the VCCR. First, there is the traditional, State-centric vision whereby the right belongs to the state of nationality of the arrested/detained individual and is to be asserted or exercised at its discretion.[49] Second, there is the view that consular assistance is an *individual right* to be asserted by the individual in custody. Third, and most progressively, consular assistance may be conceived of as a *human right* associated with due process and fair treatment, and as an aspect of the right to a fair trial.[50]

In its case law, the ICJ has opted for the second view of consular assistance as an individual right.[51] According to the Court, 'Article 36, paragraph 1, creates individual rights, which, by virtue of Article 1 of the Optional Protocol, may be invoked in this Court by the national State of the detained person.'[52] It rejected the argument of the United States in the *LaGrand* and *Avena* cases that the consular assistance was a right of states and not of individuals.[53] It also did not find it necessary to address Germany's argument that the consular assistance had 'assumed the

[48] *Vienna Convention on Consular Relations (Paraguay v. United States of America)*, Application of 3 April 1998; *LaGrand (Germany v. United States of America)* (Judgment) [2001] ICJ Rep 466 (hereafter *Germany v. United States of America*); *Avena and Other Mexican Nationals (Mexico v. United States of America)* (Judgment) [2004] ICJ Rep 12 (hereafter *Mexico v. United States of America*); *Jadhav (India v. Pakistan)* (Judgment) [2019] ICJ Rep 418 (hereafter *India v. Pakistan*).

[49] D. P. Stewart, 'The Emergent Right to Consular Notification, Access and Assistance' in A. Von Arnauld, K. Von der Decken, and M. Susi (eds.), *The Cambridge Handbook of New Human Rights: Recognition, Novelty, Rhetoric* (Cambridge University Press, 2020) 440.

[50] C. Cerna, 'The Right to Consular Notification as a Human Right' 31 *Suffolk Transnational Law Review* (2008) 419; Stewart, 'The Emergent Right to Consular Notification, Access and Assistance', 440.

[51] In its provisional measures order in the *Breard* case, the Court did not address the nature of consular assistance but called on the United States to take all measures at its disposal to prevent the execution of Breard pending its decision on the merits: *Vienna Convention on Consular Relations (Paraguay v. United States of America (Paraguay v. United States of America)*, Provisional Measures, Order of 9 April 1998, [1998] ICJ Rep 248.

[52] *Germany v. United States of America*, para. 77.

[53] Ibid., paras. 75–76. *Mexico v. United States of America*. Note that the United States had argued in the *United States Diplomatic and Consular Staff in Iran* case that Art. 36 of the VCCR 'establishes rights not only for the consular officers but, perhaps even more importantly, for the nationals of the sending State who are assured access to consular officers and through them to others': Memorial of the United States, 12 January 1980, p. 174, cited in D. P. Stewart, 'The Emergent Right to Consular Notification, Access and Assistance', p. 444.

character of a human right'.[54] Similarly, in the *Avena* case, the ICJ did not find it necessary to decide on Mexico's argument that consular assistance was a 'due process' right and 'human right'.[55] It did however observe that 'neither the text nor the object and purpose of the Convention, nor any indication in the *travaux préparatoires*, support the conclusion that Mexico draws from its contention in this regard'.[56]

In the *Jadhav* case before the ICJ, India argued that Pakistan's alleged breach of the right to consular assistance also breached Article 14 of the International Covenant on Civil and Political Rights (ICCPR) because denial of consular access affected Mr Jadhav's right to a fair trial.[57] India based its claim primarily on the jurisprudence of the Inter-American Court of Human Rights, which has held that consular rights form part of the 'due process' guarantees under the ICCPR.[58] The ICJ responded that its jurisdiction in the case did 'not extend to the determination of breaches of international law obligations other than those under the Vienna Convention'.[59] But it considered the 'principles of a fair trial [to be] of cardinal importance in any review and reconsideration' of Mr Jadhav's conviction and sentence by the Pakistani courts to ensure 'full weight is given to the effect of the violation' of his consular rights.[60]

In *Jadhav*, two judges found that the right to consular assistance was inextricably tied to the right to a fair trial.[61] It is noteworthy that these two judges, Judge Cançado Trindade and Judge Robinson, had previously served as Judge and President of IACtHR (1995–2006) and as Commissioner of the Inter-American Commission on Human Rights (1988–1995), respectively. Unlike the ICJ, the Inter-American bodies have taken the third view of consular assistance – considering it to be a human right. In an advisory opinion, over which Judge Cançado Trindade presided, the Inter-American Court concluded that Article 36 of the VCCR 'concerns the protection of the rights of a national of the sending State and

---

[54] *Germany* v. *United States of America*, para. 78.
[55] *Mexico* v. *United States of America*, paras. 40, 124.
[56] Ibid. Regarding the Court's jurisprudence relating to human rights, see C Espósito, Chapter 22, The ICH and Human Rights.
[57] *India* v. *Pakistan*, para. 36.
[58] *Jadhav (India* v. *Pakistan)* (Memorial of the Republic of India) 13 September 2017, paras. 151–163.
[59] *India* v. *Pakistan*, para. 36.   [60] Ibid., paras. 139, 145.
[61] Ibid., Separate opinion of Judge Cançado Trindade and Declaration of Judge Robinson.

is part of the body of international human rights law'.[62] It reasoned that the right 'must be recognized and counted among the minimum guarantees essential to providing foreign nationals the opportunity to adequately prepare their defense and receive a fair trial', noting the shared understanding of the drafters that the right 'is a means for the defense of the accused that has repercussions – sometimes decisive repercussions – on enforcement of the accused' other procedural rights.'[63]

The Inter-American Commission has similarly taken the third approach, finding that consular assistance is 'a fundamental component of the due process standard'.[64] It has highlighted the importance of the right in capital punishment cases in which States are 'bound by international law to comply with the strictest standards of due process ... including and the right to consular notification and assistance for foreign nationals'.[65] The African Commission has analysed the right alongside the right to access a lawyer, treating it as an aspect of due process.[66] The Human Rights Committee has only considered consular assistance in the context of the prohibition on torture, noting that 'The diplomatic and consular authorities of the State party were not given due notice of the complainant's extradition and not informed of the need to stay in close and continuous contact with him from the moment he was handed over. In this case the diplomatic assurances and the foreseen consular visits failed to anticipate the likelihood that the complainant had the highest risk of being tortured during the initial days of his detention.'[67] The Human Rights Council has firmly pronounced that consular assistance is a human right and fair trial guarantee.[68]

---

[62] 'The Right to Information on Consular Assistance in the Framework of The Guarantees of the Due Process of Law,' Advisory Opinion OC-16/99, Inter-American Court of Human Rights Series A No 16 (1 October 1999), para. 141(operative paragraph).

[63] Ibid., paras. 122–123.

[64] See, e.g., Rocha Diaz v. United States (Merits) Inter-American Commission of Human Rights Case 12.833 (23 March 2015), para. 69.

[65] The Death Penalty in the Inter-American Human Rights System: From Restrictions to Abolition, Inter-American Commission of Human Rights OEA/Ser.L/V/II. Doc. 68 (31 December 2011), para. 141.

[66] Elgak, Hummeida and Suliman v. Sudan (Merits) ACmHPR Comm No 379/09 (10 March 2015), para. 106. See also International Commission of Jurists, 'Pre-Trial Rights in Africa. A Guide to International Human Rights Standard' (September 2016).

[67] Régent Boily v. Canada, HRC Comm. no. 327/2007 (14 November 2011), para. 14.5.

[68] Human Rights Council, 'Set universal standards for effective consular assistance, UN expert urges States' (25 October 2019) <www.ohchr.org/EN/HRBodies/HRC/Pages/NewsDetail.aspx?NewsID=25213&LangID=E>.

The divergent treatment of consular assistance by the ICJ and other courts may be principally explained by their *identity*: the ICJ as a forum for resolving inter-State disputes and the other courts as human rights bodies holding states accountable for violations vis-à-vis individuals. The identity of the court also helps explain why counsel before the ICJ made human rights arguments as a supplement to cases grounded in classic arguments on treaty obligations. As Stewart has observed, for advocates before the ICJ, '[c]asting the argument in terms of treaty obligations ... offered a rhetorical advantage by permitting [them] to overcome the fact that the domestic courts had reviewed the cases and found no violation of applicable domestic law'.[69]

In practice, the adoption of the second (individual rights) or third (human rights) approach does not make a significant difference in individual cases. The ICJ still found a violation in international law in every case concerning consular assistance, and ordered it to be remedied. In the *Jadhav* case, moreover, the Court linked fair trial principles with the review and reconsideration required by the breach of consular assistance.[70] The adoption of the third approach in the same way as the Inter-American Court would detach the entitlement to consular assistance from a largely technical treaty and apply it to all individuals 'by virtue of their humanity regardless of nationality', making it an indispensable aspect of their right to fair trial.[71] In other words, it would on this view 'perfect its own restrained case law on the matter'.[72]

V Conclusion

The three factors identified here – the identity of the court, the substance of the law, and the procedures employed – do not automatically determine whether a particular court will promote the integration or fragmentation of international law. Instead, they suggest tendencies in a certain direction.[73] The permanent nature of a court and its prominent place in an institutional

---

[69] Stewart, 'The Emergent Right to Consular Notification, Access and Assistance', 445–446.
[70] *India* v. *Pakistan*, paras. 139, 145.
[71] Stewart, 'The Emergent Right to Consular Notification, Access and Assistance', 451–452.
[72] *India* v. *Pakistan*, Separate opinion of Judge Cançado Trindade, para. 33. See also *India* v. *Pakistan*, Declaration of Judge Robinson, para. 2(xi).
[73] Webb, *International Integration and Fragmentation*, 202.

system encourages stability and convergence, as epitomised by the ICJ. The fact that an area of law is governed by a treaty will facilitate convergence through the simple fact that courts are interpreting a common text. Multi-stage, collective decision-making processes and engagement in judicial dialogue also promote coherence in the development of international law. On the other hand, the ad hoc nature of a court or tribunal increases the risk that it may decide in a vacuum. If an area of law is governed by customary international law, this may also result in diverging decisions in different courts. Variations in fact-finding and the assessment of evidence, lack of attention to existing case law, and decentralised and delegated judgment-drafting processes increase the tendency towards fragmentation.[74]

This brief survey of three legal issues considered by the ICJ and other international courts and tribunals indicates that fragmentation remains a small but real risk in the international legal system. It also suggests that the restrained approach of the ICJ is not always preferable, as seen by its refusal to date to recognise consular assistance as a human right. While the ICJ rightly remains the touchstone for the development and application of general international law, it would also benefit from increased and transparent participation in judicial dialogue with other courts and tribunals.

Further Reading

G. Hernández, *The International Court of Justice and the Judicial Function* (Oxford University Press, 2014)

G. Mettraux, *International Crimes: Law and Practice Volume I: Genocide* (Oxford University Press, 2019)

D. Pulkowski, *The Law and Politics of International Regime Conflict* (Oxford University Press, 2014)

D. P. Stewart, 'The Emergent Right to Consular Notification, Access and Assistance' in A. Von Arnauld, K. Von der Decken, and M. Susi (eds.), *The Cambridge Handbook of New Human Rights: Recognition, Novelty, Rhetoric* (Cambridge University Press, 2020), p. 439

P. Webb, *International Integration and Fragmentation* (Oxford University Press 2013, paperback 2015)

---

[74] Ibid.

The Working Practices of the Court 11

Callista Harris[*]

I Introduction

One can think of the International Court of Justice (the 'ICJ' or 'Court') as a machine which produces judgments and advisory opinions. This chapter is not concerned with the judgments and advisory opinions that come out of the machine, but with what goes on *inside* of the machine. It is concerned with the way in which the Court works; that is, with the Court's working practices. The first part of this chapter sets out the framework within which the Court does its work. The second part then provides an overview of how this framework operates in practice, as proceedings make their way through the machine of the Court.

II The Framework for the Working Practices of the Court

The framework within which the Court works is made up of a number of components. There are various instruments that govern the Court's working practices and principles that inform those practices.[1] Before looking at these instruments and principles, it is helpful to consider the context within which the Court exists, as this also informs the Court's working practices.

A Context

The ICJ is one of the six principal organs of the United Nations and the principal judicial organ. The connection between the Court and the UN has

---

[*] The author would like to thank Professor Mathias Forteau for his suggestions regarding issues to be discussed in this chapter.
[1] The instruments are available at www.icj-cij.org/en/basic-documents.

a number of consequences for how the Court works. As one example, the budget of the Court forms part of the regular budget of the UN.[2] At times, financial issues within the UN have impacted the Court's finances and, consequently, its work.[3]

While the ICJ was established as a new court in 1945, the creation of the Court did 'not break the chain of continuity with the past'.[4] The Statute of the ICJ is based on the Statute of the Court's predecessor from the League of Nations era, the Permanent Court of International Justice ('PCIJ'). Similarly, the first Rules of Court adopted by the ICJ in 1946 were based on the Rules of the PCIJ. Consequently, the working practices of the ICJ, which are primarily governed by the Court's Statute and its Rules, are based on and have evolved from the working practices of the PCIJ.

B The Key Instruments: The Statute and the Rules

During the drafting of both the Statute of the PCIJ and the Statute of the ICJ, it was recognised that, apart from fundamental points of principle, which would be dealt with in the Statute, questions of procedure should be left to be regulated by the Court itself.[5] Consequently, under Article 30(1) of the Statute of the ICJ, the Court has the power to 'lay down rules of procedure', which it has done in the Rules of Court. The Rules 'set forth the detailed means of application of the Statute'.[6]

The Statute of the ICJ is part of the UN Charter. For this reason, it is politically difficult to amend the Statute. Amendment requires the support of two-thirds of UN Member States, including the five permanent members of the UN Security Council.[7] The Statute has not been amended to date.

In contrast to the Statute, the Rules have evolved over time and continue to do so. In 1967, the Court established a Committee for the Revision of the

---

[2] Statute, Art. 33; UN Charter, Art. 17(1)–(2).

[3] See, e.g., footnote 17 and the accompanying text.

[4] 'Report of the Rapporteur of Committee IV/1', 12 June 1945, in *Documents of the United Nations Conference on International Organization*, 22 vols. (1945), vol. XIII, p. 381 at p. 384.

[5] M. O. Hudson, *The Permanent Court of International Justice 1920–1942* (Macmillan, 1943), p. 270; 'Report of the Informal Inter-Allied Committee on the Future of the Permanent Court of International Justice' 39 *AJIL Supplement* (1945) 1 at 23, para. 76.

[6] 'Report of the International Court of Justice: 1 August 1967–31 July 1968', UN Doc A/7217, 1 August 1968, p. 3, para. 29.

[7] UN Charter, Art. 108; Statute, Art. 69; UN General Assembly Resolution 2520 (XXIV), UN Doc A/RES/2520(XXIV), 4 December 1969.

Rules of Court, which was made a standing body in 1979 and still exists today. The principal stimulus for the work commenced in 1967 was criticism of the Court's handling of the *South-West Africa* cases: in 1966, the Court declined to rule on the merits of those cases after 'exceptionally long and costly' proceedings.[8] The work of the Committee led to a series of amendments to the Rules in 1972 and to a complete revision of the Rules in 1978.[9] One of the principal purposes of these revisions was to reduce the length and cost of proceedings before the Court.[10]

The Court was able to undertake the work necessary for the complete revision of 1978 because there was a 'relative famine of cases in the 1970s'.[11] Since 1978, the Court has only amended a few specific provisions of the Rules, in 2000, 2005, 2019 and 2020. Most recently, in June 2020 during the COVID-19 pandemic, the Court amended Article 94 of the Rules with immediate effect to give itself the power to hold hearings by video link. These amendments were implemented swiftly and 'have brought the working methods of the Court squarely into the twenty-first century'.[12]

As the Statute is part of a treaty, the UN Charter, States that are parties to the UN Charter (UN Member States) are bound by the provisions of the Statute. States are similarly bound by the Rules, either by virtue of their agreement to the Court's rule-making power in Article 30(1) of the Statute,[13] or by virtue of the principle that parties having recourse to a constituted judicial body are held to have accepted its rules of procedure.[14]

---

[8] M. Shaw, *Rosenne's Law and Practice of the International Court: 1920–2015*, 4 vols. (5th ed., Brill Nijhoff, 2016), vol. II, p. 834, and vol. III, p. 1059, footnote 26.

[9] Between 1970 and 1974, the UN General Assembly also conducted a review of the International Court of Justice, in which States voiced concerns regarding the Court's working practices.

[10] *ICJ Yearbook 1977–1978*, 111, 112–113.

[11] R. Jennings, R. Higgins and P. Tomka, 'General Introduction', in A. Zimmermann *et al.* (eds.), *The Statute of the International Court of Justice: A Commentary* (3rd ed., Oxford University Press, 2019) (*Zimmermann Commentary*), p. 3 at p. 27, para. 78, p. 29, para. 83, p. 34, para. 103. See also K. J. Keith, 'Challenges to the Independence of the International Judiciary: Reflections on the International Court of Justice' 30(1) *LJIL* (2017) 137 at 137–139.

[12] Speech by President Yusuf to the UN General Assembly, 2 November 2020, in 'Note by the President of the General Assembly', UN Doc A/75/613, 25 January 2021, p. 2 at pp. 2, 6. See generally G. Pinzauti and P. Webb, 'Litigation before the International Court of Justice during the Pandemic' 34(4) *LJIL* (2021) 787.

[13] H. Thirlway, 'Article 30', in *Zimmermann Commentary*, p. 589 at p. 591, para. 4.

[14] Shaw, *Rosenne's Law*, vol. III, pp. 1055–1056; *Interpretation of Article 3, Paragraph 2, of the Treaty of Lausanne, Opinion No. 12, 1925*, PCIJ, Series B, No. 12, p. 31.

The Court cannot depart from the provisions of its Statute, but it can depart from the Rules. Article 101 of the Rules provides that parties to a case can jointly propose modifications or additions to the Rules, which the Court can apply, if it considers appropriate.[15]

C Other Instruments Governing the Working Practices of the Court

Beyond the Statute and the Rules, a number of other instruments govern the working practices of the Court. The most important of these are the Practice Directions.

By the mid-1990s, the Court had successfully overcome the 'period of mistrust and of little use' that followed the *South-West Africa* cases, and there had been a major increase in the Court's activity.[16] However, the Court's working practices in the mid-1990s were not appropriate for a court with a significant number of cases and the Court also faced budgetary constraints due to the broader financial issues within the UN at the time.[17] This led to a backlog of cases and, in particular, to a long wait between the time when a case was ready for hearing and when a case was actually heard, at least in most cases.[18] Consequently, in 1997, the Court tasked the Rules Committee with developing proposals that would maximise the Court's efficiency, short of amending the Rules (amendment of the Rules being seen as a longer-term project).[19]

The Court announced a collection of reforms in 1998. It would begin conducting hearings in preliminary proceedings back-to-back, so that work on different cases could proceed concurrently,[20] and the Judges would dispense with their practice of preparing (and translating) written notes after

---

[15] Parties can only propose modifications and additions to Part III of the Rules, excluding Arts. 93–97.

[16] Jennings, Higgins and Tomka, 'General Introduction', p. 42, para. 138; Press Release 98/14, 6 April 1998, p. 1.

[17] 'Process, Practice and Procedure of the International Court of Justice' 92 *ASIL Proceedings* (1998) 278 at 279 (Gardner); Press Release 98/14, 6 April 1998, p. 1. The budgetary constraints created particular difficulties for translation work. See 'Process, Practice and Procedure', 283 (Higgins).

[18] 'Speech by Stephen M. 'Schwebel on the Report of the International Court of Justice' 92(3) *AJIL* (1998) 612 at 616; 'Process, Practice and Procedure', 280 (Crawford).

[19] Schwebel, 'Schwebel on the Report', 616; 'Process, Practice and Procedure', 283 (Higgins).

[20] Prior to this, the Court only dealt with one case at a time. See 'Process, Practice and Procedure', 280 (Crawford).

hearings in preliminary proceedings, prior to meeting for deliberations.[21] As part of the reforms, the Court also began providing a 'Note containing recommendations to the parties to new cases'.[22] Shortly after this, in 2001, the Court converted these recommendations into 'Practice Directions'.[23] Since 2001, the Court has continued to adopt new Practice Directions and amend existing ones, taking such action in 2002, 2004, 2006, 2009, 2013, 2019 and 2020. With the collection of reforms in the late 1990s and early 2000s, the Court was able to clear its backlog of cases by 2010.[24]

The precise source of the Court's power to make Practice Directions is unclear. Some suggest that Practice Directions derive their force from Article 30(1) of the Statute.[25] Others suggest that no provision in the Statute or Rules in terms authorises the issuing of Practice Directions, but that Practice Directions can be made in exercise of the Court's inherent power to regulate its own procedure.[26] In either case, Practice Directions are only 'exhortatory' or 'non-compulsory'.[27] The Practice Directions tend to be followed by parties,[28] although there is some variation in practice depending on the particular Practice Direction.[29]

In addition to the Practice Directions, the other instruments that govern the working practices of the Court are the following:

1. *Resolution concerning the Internal Judicial Practice of the Court*: This Resolution sets out the procedure followed by the Court in its deliberations in contentious and advisory proceedings, although the Court remains 'entirely free' to depart from the Resolution.[30]

---

[21] Press Release 98/14, 6 April 1998. See also 'Process, Practice and Procedure', 283–284 (Higgins); Press Release 2002/12, 4 April 2002, pp. 2–3.

[22] Amended in 2000. See Press Release 2001/1, 12 January 2001, p. 3.

[23] Press Release 2001/32, 31 October 2001.

[24] 'Report of the International Court of Justice: 1 August 2009–31 July 2010', UN Doc A/65/4, 1 August 2010, p. 6, para. 22.

[25] Thirlway, 'Article 30', p. 593, para. 11.

[26] A. Watts, 'New Practice Directions of the International Court of Justice' 1(2) *LPICT* (2002) 247 at 255.

[27] A. Keene (ed.), 'Outcome Paper for the Seminar on the International Court of Justice at 70: In Retrospect and in Prospect' 7(2) *JIDS* (2016) 238 at 252 (Pellet); International Law Association Committee on the Procedure of International Courts and Tribunals, 'Preliminary Report', 17 January 2017, p. 14.

[28] The ILA Report concludes that parties generally treat the Practice Directions as if they were binding. See ILA Report, p. 15.

[29] See, e.g., the text at footnotes 92–95.

[30] See also K. Keith, Chapter 2, The Role of an ICJ Judge.

2. *Compilation of decisions adopted by the Court concerning the external activities of its Members*: The Court made this Compilation of decisions available in December 2020. The first decision, on 'Arbitration activities of Members of the Court', was adopted in 2018 and sets out 'clearly defined rules' regulating the circumstances in which the members of the Court may serve as arbitrator.[31] The decision was adopted after concerns were expressed about Judges accepting appointments as arbitrator, in particular in investor-State proceedings.[32] On its face, the decision clearly prevents Judges from accepting such appointments.[33] President Yusuf explained the decision as being 'essential to place beyond reproach the impartiality and independence of Judges in the exercise of their judicial functions'.[34]

3. *Instructions for the Registry*: These Instructions elaborate upon the duties assigned to the Registrar under the Statute and Rules.[35]

4. *Note for the Parties concerning the Preparation of Pleadings*: This Note sets out the formal requirements for written pleadings filed in the Registry. The Note goes beyond the Rules, setting out details such as the number of pleadings that must be filed (125 copies, at least 75 in paper form) and the page size to be used (19 cm by 25 cm).

5. *Guidelines for the parties on the organization of hearings by video link*: Shortly after the 2020 amendment to the Rules permitting the holding of hearings by video link, the Court adopted these Guidelines, which deal with various procedural matters associated with the holding of hearings by video link.

D Principles Informing the Working Practices of the Court

Beyond the instruments described above, there are also principles that inform the working practices of the Court, including the principles of the

---

[31] Speech by President Yusuf to the UN General Assembly, 25 October 2018, in UN Doc A/73/PV.24, 25 October 2018, p. 2 at p. 10.

[32] See, e.g., P. Sands, 'Reflections on International Judicialization' 27(4) *EJIL* (2016) 885 at 895; N. Bernasconi-Osterwalder and M. D. Brauch, 'Is "Moonlighting" a Problem? The role of ICJ judges in ISDS', International Institute for Sustainable Development, November 2017.

[33] But see A. Ross, 'Tomka resigns from China case as third ICJ term starts', *Global Arbitration Review*, 16 February 2021.

[34] 2018 Yusuf speech, p. 11.

[35] Available at www.icj-cij.org/en/texts-governing-registry.

proper administration of justice and the equality of the parties. These principles are given concrete expression in the Statute and the Rules. For example, as the Court explained in the *Nicaragua* proceedings, the 'provisions of the Statute and Rules of Court concerning the presentation of pleadings and evidence are designed to secure a proper administration of justice, and a fair and equal opportunity for each party to comment on its opponent's contentions'.[36]

These principles also inform the working practices of the Court more generally. When the Court is faced with situations not provided for in its Statute and Rules, it is guided by what is required by the proper administration of justice. As stated by the PCIJ in the *Mavrommatis* proceedings, in such circumstances it is 'at liberty to adopt the principle which it considers best calculated to ensure the administration of justice most suited to procedure before an international tribunal'.[37]

The 'proper administration of justice' is a nebulous concept, but in general terms the principle 'connotes the idea of good and fair procedure'.[38] As the Court identified in *Croatia* v. *Serbia*, one component of the proper administration of justice is 'concern for judicial economy'.[39] The principle of the equality of the parties also follows from the proper administration of justice.[40] This principle requires that parties be given an equal opportunity to present their case.[41]

III How Proceedings before the Court Work

How the above framework works in practice can conveniently be considered in three parts: first, proceedings are commenced; next, the bench is composed; and then the proceedings progress through their various phases.

---

[36] *Military and Paramilitary Activities in and against Nicaragua (Nicaragua* v. *USA), Merits, Judgment,* ICJ Reports 1986, p. 14 at p. 26, para. 31.

[37] *Mavrommatis Palestine Concessions, Judgment No. 2, 1924, PCIJ, Series A, No. 2,* p. 16.

[38] R. Kolb, *The International Court of Justice* (Hart, 2014), p. 1242.

[39] *Application of the Convention on the Prevention and Punishment of the Crime of Genocide (Croatia* v. *Serbia), Preliminary Objections, Judgment,* ICJ Reports 2008, p. 412 at p. 441, para. 85, p. 443, para. 89.

[40] *Judgments of the Administrative Tribunal of the ILO upon complaints made against the UNESCO, Advisory Opinion,* ICJ Reports 1956, p. 77 at p. 86.

[41] See R. Kolb, 'General Principles of Procedural Law', in *Zimmermann Commentary,* p. 963 at p. 969, para. 9; Shaw, *Rosenne's Law,* vol. III, pp. 1079–1080.

A Commencement of Proceedings

Seisin of the Court

There are two methods by which contentious proceedings can be instituted and the Court can become seised of a dispute.[42] Where States have agreed to refer a dispute to the Court under a special agreement between them, proceedings are instituted by notification of that agreement to the Registrar. Where an applicant State seeks to base the Court's jurisdiction on something other than a special agreement, such as on optional clause declarations, the applicant State institutes proceedings by unilateral written application to the Registrar. The commencement of proceedings by unilateral application was a 'revolution in international thinking' when it was introduced in the Statute of the PCIJ.[43] It is also possible to file an application against a State that has not yet consented to the Court's jurisdiction. Such an application gives the proposed respondent State the 'opportunity of accepting the jurisdiction of the Court'.[44] In such situations, the Court is not seised of the dispute, and takes no action beyond transmitting the application to the proposed respondent State, unless and until that State consents to the Court's jurisdiction.[45]

A notification or application is made in one of the two official languages of the Court, French and English. Proceedings are considered to have been instituted once the original document instituting proceedings is received by the Registry, and this is normally delivered to the Registry in the Hague by hand.[46] The Statute and Rules set out a number of requirements regarding the content of documents instituting proceedings. If a document instituting proceedings does not comply with these requirements, this will be 'brought ... to the notice' of the State concerned by the Registrar.[47] It appears that the Registrar has only once rejected an application on this basis – an application made by Yugoslavia in February 1994.[48] Where

---

[42] Statute, Art. 40(1). Regarding the contentious jurisdiction of the Court, see J.-M. Thouvenin, Chapter 6, The Jurisdiction of the Court.

[43] Shaw, *Rosenne's Law*, vol. III, pp. 1209–1210.

[44] *Corfu Channel case, Judgment on Preliminary Objection*, ICJ Reports 1948, p. 15 at p. 28.

[45] Rules, Art. 38(5). A press release is also issued. See, e.g., Press Release 2014/25, 7 August 2014.

[46] S. Yee, 'Article 40', in *Zimmermann Commentary*, p. 1021 at p. 1063, para. 8.

[47] Instructions for the Registry, Art. 12.

[48] Shaw, *Rosenne's Law*, vol. III, pp. 1213–1214. It appears the application was refiled. See Press Release 94/11, 21 March 1994.

issues arise regarding whether a person purporting to commence proceedings on behalf of a State has the necessary authorisation, they are dealt with by the Court.[49]

In contrast to contentious proceedings, advisory proceedings are instituted by the UN Secretary-General transmitting to the Court the relevant question on which the Court's opinion is sought, together with all documents likely to throw light upon the question.[50]

Notification of Proceedings

In contentious cases, as soon as proceedings are instituted, the Registrar transmits the notification or application, in its original language, to the other parties to the case.[51] In addition, various other actors are informed of the proceedings:

- As soon as proceedings are instituted, the Registrar notifies the UN Secretary-General.
- The notification or application is translated into the other official language of the Court and is printed as a bilingual text by the Registry. This text is then communicated, through the UN Secretary-General, to all UN Member States.
- Additionally: (i) if the construction of a treaty is in question, the Registrar will notify the States and public international organisations that are parties to the treaty; and (ii) if the constituent instrument of a public international organisation (or a treaty adopted under it) is in question, the Registrar will notify the organisation concerned.[52]

When advisory proceedings are instituted, the Registrar gives notice of the request for an advisory opinion to all States entitled to appear before the Court, as well as to certain international organisations.[53]

---

[49] See, e.g., Press Release 2017/12, 9 March 2017. Issues regarding the authority to represent a State may arise in the pending proceedings involving Myanmar and Venezuela.

[50] Statute, Art. 65(2); Rules, Art. 104. Regarding the advisory jurisdiction of the Court, see J.-M. Thouvenin, Chapter 6, The Jurisdiction of the Court.

[51] Statute, Art. 40(2); Rules, Arts. 38(4), 39(1).

[52] Statute, Arts. 34(3), 40(3), 63(1); Rules, Arts. 42, 43(2). See, e.g., *Appeal relating to the Jurisdiction of the ICAO Council under Article 84 of the Convention on International Civil Aviation (Bahrain, Egypt, Saudi Arabia and United Arab Emirates v. Qatar), Judgment,* ICJ Reports 2020, p. 81 at pp. 88–89, paras. 4–6.

[53] Statute, Art. 66(1)–(2). Regarding the meaning of 'public international organisation' and 'international organisation', see P.-M. Dupuy and C. Hoss, 'Article 34', in *Zimmermann Commentary,* p. 661 at pp. 665–666, paras. 3–4.

These various notifications serve two purposes. Generally, they provide States and other actors with the information necessary for the conduct of international affairs. More specifically, the notifications provide them with information they will need when deciding whether to become involved in the proceedings.[54] When contentious and advisory proceedings are instituted, the notification, application or request for an advisory opinion is also published on the website of the Court and a press release is issued informing the public about the institution of proceedings.

The Naming of Proceedings and Entry in the General List

Once the Court is seised of a dispute, even if 'it is evident that the basis for jurisdiction invoked is not serious', the Registrar is under a duty to enter the proceedings in the Court's General List.[55] This is a list of all contentious and advisory proceedings before the Court, which is kept by the Registrar.[56]

While in domestic legal systems cases are often named '*Party 1* v. *Party 2*', contentious and advisory proceedings before the ICJ are given a name that reflects the subject of the proceedings. Proceeding names are chosen by the Court, on the recommendation of the Registrar.[57] The Court endeavours to choose neutral names.[58] On occasion, however, States have considered a name chosen by the Court to be prejudicial to them.[59]

In a number of cases, a respondent State has asked for proceedings to be removed from the General List at an early stage, on the basis that the Court manifestly lacks jurisdiction. At present, there is no provision in the Rules empowering the Court to remove proceedings in such circumstances. However, the Court has held that it can remove a case from the General List during a provisional measures stage of proceedings if it

[54] Shaw, *Rosenne's Law*, vol. III, p. 1216; Yee, 'Article 40', p. 1072, para. 87, p. 1074, para. 90.

[55] J. J. Quintana, *Litigation at the International Court of Justice: Practice and Procedure* (Brill Nijhoff, 2015), p. 293 (quoting Couvreur).

[56] Rules, Art. 26(1)(b). See also Instructions for the Registry, Art. 5(1).

[57] Quintana, *Litigation at the International Court of Justice*, p. 279.

[58] See *Questions of Interpretation and Application of the 1971 Montreal Convention arising from the Aerial Incident at Lockerbie (Libya v. United Kingdom), Provisional Measures, Order of 14 April 1992*, ICJ Reports 1992, p. 3, Dissenting Opinion of Judge Bedjaoui, p. 33, para. 1.

[59] See, e.g., *Nicaragua*, Dissenting Opinion of Judge Schwebel, pp. 320–321, paras. 128–131. See further H. Jamil, 'Does the Name of a Case Matter?' 20(3) *LPICT* (2021) 469.

manifestly lacks jurisdiction.[60] The Court has explained that 'within a system of consensual jurisdiction, to maintain on the General List a case upon which it appears certain that the Court will not be able to adjudicate on the merits would most assuredly not contribute to the sound administration of justice'.[61] Recently, in *Relocation of the United States Embassy to Jerusalem*, the USA claimed at an early stage that the Court manifestly lacks jurisdiction and asked for the case to be removed from the General List, in circumstances where Palestine was not seeking any provisional measures. In response, the Court ordered that there be a preliminary stage of proceedings, dealing with issues of jurisdiction and admissibility.[62]

Agents

In proceedings before the Court, parties are assisted by counsel, but they are represented by agents. While agents can play a number of roles in proceedings, the agent's role is essentially of a political and diplomatic character.[63] The agent is the representative of the State before the Court, and agents are commonly senior government lawyers.[64]

Once proceedings have been instituted, all steps on behalf of a party are taken by its agent and all communications are sent to the agent.[65] The various instruments relating to the Court's working practices refer to a number of specific steps that are to be taken by the agent. These range from relatively minor procedural steps – such as certifying the accuracy of translations – to more important procedural steps – such as meeting with the President to discuss procedural matters. As soon as possible after agents are appointed in proceedings, the President 'summon[s] the agents

---

[60] *Immunities and Criminal Proceedings (Equatorial Guinea v. France), Provisional Measures, Order of 7 December 2016*, ICJ Reports 2016, p. 1148 at p. 1165, para. 70.

[61] *Legality of Use of Force (Yugoslavia v. Spain), Provisional Measures, Order of 2 June 1999*, ICJ Reports 1999, p. 761 at p. 773, para. 35.

[62] *Relocation of the United States Embassy to Jerusalem (Palestine v. USA), Order of 15 November 2018*, ICJ Reports 2018, p. 708. See also *Arbitral Award of 3 October 1899 (Guyana v. Venezuela)*, Judgment on Jurisdiction, 18 December 2020, paras. 5, 138(1).

[63] Shaw, *Rosenne's Law*, vol. III, p. 1156.

[64] F. Berman and G. Hernández, 'Article 42', in *Zimmermann Commentary*, p. 1203 at p. 1207, para. 10. See also S. Ugalde and J. J. Quintana, 'Managing Litigation before the International Court of Justice' 9 *JIDS* (2018) 691 at 695, 697.

[65] Rules, Art. 40(1).

of the parties to meet him', to discuss questions of procedure.[66] In proceedings commenced during the COVID-19 pandemic, the President had his initial meeting with the agents by video link.[67]

A State may decline to appoint an agent or to otherwise participate in proceedings. The USA, Venezuela and Kenya have each recently declined to participate in at least part of the proceedings brought against them.[68] Such non-participation by a respondent State does not affect the Court's power to decide a case in favour of the applicant State, but the Court must satisfy itself that it has jurisdiction over the applicant State's claims and that the claims are well-founded.[69] As is common in cases of non-participation, in these recent examples, while not *formally* participating in proceedings, each respondent State has nonetheless submitted letters, a 'memorandum' or a 'position paper' to the Court. In determining what weight to attribute to such documents, the Court is concerned to maintain the equality of the parties and to ensure that the party that declines to appear does not profit from its absence.[70]

B The Composition of the Bench

While the Court is composed of fifteen members, particular proceedings may be heard by fewer judges or by more. This can occur for a number of reasons. First, contentious proceedings can be heard by a chamber of the Court, composed of fewer judges. The Statute provides for three types of chambers, which can be utilised at the request of the parties:

1. *The Chamber of Summary Procedure*: This chamber of five judges may hear and determine cases by summary procedure. To date, the chamber has not been used by the ICJ, but two related proceedings were determined by the equivalent chamber of the PCIJ.[71]

---

[66] Note for the Parties concerning the Preparation of Pleadings; Rules, Art. 31. See also Practice Directions X, XIII.

[67] *Land and Maritime Delimitation and Sovereignty over Islands (Gabon/Equatorial Guinea)*, Order, 7 April 2021.

[68] *Relocation of the United States Embassy*, p. 709; *Arbitral Award of 3 October 1899 (Guyana v. Venezuela)*, Order, 8 March 2021; *Maritime Delimitation in the Indian Ocean (Somalia v. Kenya)*, Judgment, 12 October 2021, paras. 19–20.

[69] Statute, Art. 53.   [70] *Nicaragua*, pp. 25–26, para. 31.

[71] See Statute, Art. 29; *Treaty of Neuilly, Article 179, Annex, Paragraph 4 (Interpretation)*, Judgment No. 3, 1924, PCIJ, Series A, No. 3; *Interpretation of Judgment No. 3, Judgment No. 4, 1925*, PCIJ, Series A, No. 4.

2. *Special chambers*: The Court may establish chambers of three or more judges to deal with particular categories of case. Currently, no such chambers exist. A seven-member Chamber for Environmental Matters existed between 1993 and 2006, but was never used.[72]
3. *Ad hoc chambers*: Under Article 26 of the Statute, chambers may also be formed to deal with individual cases. This has happened on six occasions, between 1981 and 2002.[73] While the number of judges constituting an ad hoc chamber is flexible – it is to be determined by the Court with the approval of the parties – on all six occasions when ad hoc chambers have been used, the chamber has consisted of five judges. The main attraction of proceedings before a chamber is that the parties have a say in the composition of the chamber.[74] This feature of ad hoc chambers was introduced in the Rules in 1972 'to try to bring work back to the Court'.[75]

There are both calls for, and opposition to, greater use of chambers. Speaking in 2016, Judge Tomka stated that if States want chambers, the Court will establish them, but that that is not the current wish of parties to disputes before the Court.[76]

Second, judges ad hoc may be appointed. If a party in contentious proceedings does not have a judge of its nationality on the bench, it may choose a person to sit as judge for the case (a 'judge ad hoc'), who need not have its nationality.[77] Judges ad hoc may also be appointed in advisory proceedings when an opinion is requested on a legal question 'actually pending between two or more States'.[78] The institution of judges ad hoc is not found in domestic legal systems,[79] but during the drafting of the Statute of the PCIJ, it was thought that providing for the possibility of judges ad hoc could be instrumental in overcoming the traditional reluctance of States to accept a permanent judicial body.[80]

---

[72] See Statute, Art. 26(1), (3); *ICJ Yearbook 2017–2018*, 48.

[73] *ICJ Yearbook 2017–2018*, 112–114.   [74] Rules, Art. 17(2).

[75] Jennings, Higgins and Tomka, 'General Introduction', p. 36, para. 111.

[76] Keene, 'Outcome Paper for the Seminar on the International Court of Justice at 70', 244 (Tomka). Regarding the composition of the Court, see further J. Crawford, F. Baetens and R. Cameron, Chapter 1, Functions of the International Court of Justice; K. Keith, Chapter 2, The Role of an ICJ Judge.

[77] Statute, Art. 31(2)–(3); Rules, Arts. 1(2), 35(1).   [78] Rules, Art. 102(3).

[79] I. Scobbie, '*Une hérésie en matière judiciaire*'? The Role of the Judge *ad hoc* in the International Court' 4(3) *LPICT* (2005) 421 at 422.

[80] P. H. Kooijmans and F. Lusa Bordin, 'Article 31', in *Zimmermann Commentary*, p. 604 at p. 606, para. 2.

In 2002, the Court adopted a Practice Direction which states that, when choosing a judge ad hoc, parties 'should refrain' from nominating persons who have appeared before the Court as counsel in the preceding three years.[81] The purpose of the Practice Direction was to put an end to a practice that had developed since the 1980s, where persons had acted simultaneously as judge ad hoc in one case before the Court and as counsel in another.[82] As the Court explains in the Practice Direction, 'it is not in the interest of the sound administration of justice that a person sit as judge ad hoc in one case who is also acting or has recently acted as agent, counsel or advocate in another case before the Court'.

Third, judges may be recused from particular proceedings. Members of the Court cannot participate in proceedings in which they have previously taken part as agent or counsel, or in which they have taken part in 'any other capacity'. Additionally, a member of the Court may not take part in particular proceedings for 'some special reason'.[83] Recusals are not uncommon.[84] Since 1978, Article 34(2) of the Rules has provided that, if a party wants to bring facts that are possibly relevant for recusal to the attention of the Court, the party 'shall communicate confidentially such facts to the President in writing'. This addition was prompted by the Court's experience in proceedings including the *Namibia* advisory opinion. In those proceedings, South Africa publicly raised the question of disqualification in its written pleadings.[85] It appears that since the 1970 *Namibia* advisory opinion, a communication under Article 34(2) has only been made on one occasion – by Israel in the *Wall* advisory proceedings – and it did not result in a recusal.[86]

---

[81] Practice Direction VII. See also Practice Direction VIII.

[82] P. Couvreur, 'Article 17', in *Zimmermann Commentary*, p. 444 at pp. 453–454, para. 17.

[83] See Statute, Arts. 17(2), 24(1)–(2).

[84] C. Giorgetti, 'The Challenge and Recusal of Judges at the International Court of Justice', in C. Giorgetti (ed.), *Challenges and Recusals of Judges and Arbitrators in International Courts and Tribunals* (Brill, 2015), p. 3 at pp. 18–25.

[85] *Legal Consequences for States of the Continued Presence of South Africa in Namibia (South-West Africa) notwithstanding Security Council Resolution 276 (1970), Advisory Opinion*, ICJ Reports 1971, p. 16 at pp. 18–19, para. 9; R. Jennings and P. Couvreur, 'Article 24', in *Zimmermann Commentary*, p. 526 at pp. 534–535, paras. 25, 28–29.

[86] *Legal Consequences of the Construction of a Wall in the Occupied Palestinian Territory, Order of 30 January 2004*, ICJ Reports 2004, p. 3. Although see also *Maritime Delimitation in the Indian Ocean (Somalia v. Kenya)*, Application requesting the Court to authorise Kenya to file new documentation and evidence, 22 February 2021, paras. 12–13.

C The Phases of Proceedings

The Written Phase

Both contentious and advisory proceedings have two phases: (i) a written phase; and (ii) an oral phase. This procedure 'represents something of a blend of, on the one hand, the Continental system of extensive written pleadings, and on the other the Anglo-American common law system in which ... the hearing, the "day in court", is the essential element'.[87]

After the President's meeting with the agents, the Court issues an order setting out the order of the initial written pleadings (a memorial and counter-memorial) and the time-limits within which they are to be filed. These time-limits may be extended and often are.[88] Since 1972, any subsequent written pleadings have required the authorisation of the President and the general practice is for a second round of written pleadings to be authorised.[89] To ensure the equality of the parties, parties will be given the opportunity to submit the same number of written pleadings and the same amount of time in which to prepare them.[90]

Written pleadings deal with both matters of fact and matters of law. Additionally, certified copies of the documents relied on in a pleading must be annexed to it. Written pleadings and the documents annexed to them must be submitted in one of the official languages of the Court (either as their original language or a certified translation).[91]

The Court has made various attempts to limit the volume of written pleadings. Already in its 1998 'Note containing recommendations to the parties to new cases', the Court referred to the 'excessive tendency towards the proliferation and protraction of annexes' and 'strongly urge[d]' parties

---

[87] H. Thirlway, *The International Court of Justice* (Oxford University Press, 2016), p. 92. See also J. Crawford, A. Pellet and C. Redgwell, 'Anglo-American and Continental Traditions in Advocacy before International Courts and Tribunals' 2(4) *CJICL* (2013) 715 at 725–726 (Crawford).

[88] See Rules, Art. 44(1), (3).

[89] Rules, Arts. 45(2), 46(2). In 2002, the Court stated that a single round of written pleadings 'is to be considered as the norm'. See Press Release 2002/12, 4 April 2002. Nonetheless, it appears that the Court has decided not to authorise a second round in circumstances where a party wanted one on only one occasion. See *Whaling in the Antarctic (Australia v. Japan: New Zealand intervening), Judgment,* ICJ Reports 2014, p. 226 at p. 235, para. 6. See further Separate Opinion of Judge Greenwood, pp. 418–419, paras. 32–38.

[90] Kolb, 'General Principles of Procedural Law', p. 970, para. 12.

[91] See Statute, Art. 39(2)–(3); Rules, Arts. 49(1)–(2), 50(1), 51(1)–(3).

to annex 'only strictly selected documents'.[92] In 2009, the Court amended Practice Direction III and 'strongly urged' parties to keep their written pleadings 'as concise as possible'.[93] Nonetheless, little progress has been made on this front.[94] Recently, in January 2021, the Court further amended Practice Direction III to state that the 'number of pages of annexes attached by a party to its written pleadings shall not exceed 750 in total, unless the Court decides, upon request of a party, that a number in excess of that limit is warranted, in the particular circumstances of the case'.[95]

The written pleadings remain confidential until the start of the oral phase. At that point, and after 'ascertaining the views of the parties', the Court makes the pleadings available to the public on its website. The requirement to ascertain the views of the parties is a 'mere formality' and in practice parties do not object.[96]

The Oral Phase

Article 1(i) of the 'Resolution concerning the Internal Judicial Practice of the Court' provides that, prior to an oral hearing, a 'deliberation is held at which the judges exchange views concerning the case, and bring to the notice of the Court any point in regard to which they consider it may be necessary to call for explanations during the course of the oral proceedings'. Historically, the Court has not made much use of such deliberations.[97] However, speaking in 2016, Judge Owada stated that deliberations are beginning to be used,[98] and there are a number of recent cases in which such deliberations are said to have occurred.[99]

---

[92] Press Release 98/14, 6 April 1998.   [93] Press Release 2009/8, 30 January 2009.

[94] A. Miron, 'Working Methods of the Court' 7(2) *JIDS* (2016) 371 at 373; A. Sarvarian, 'Procedural Economy at the International Court of Justice' 18(1) *LPICT* (2019) 74 at 88. For example, Iran's memorial in *Alleged Violations of the 1955 Treaty*, filed in May 2019, contained over 3,000 pages of annexes.

[95] Press Release 2021/2, 20 January 2021.

[96] See Rules, Arts. 53(2), 106; Quintana, *Litigation at the International Court of Justice*, p. 343.

[97] Keene, 'Outcome Paper for the Seminar on the International Court of Justice at 70', 252 (Owada); Keith, 'Challenges to the Independence of the International Judiciary', 149. See also 'Process, Practice and Procedure', 287 (Higgins) (stating that this Resolution is 'ignored').

[98] Keene, 'Outcome Paper for the Seminar on the International Court of Justice at 70', 252 (Owada).

[99] Namely, *Aerial Herbicide Spraying*, *Whaling* and the *Maritime Delimitation* proceedings between Costa Rica and Nicaragua. See Speech by President Tomka to the UN General

During the oral phase, agents and counsel deliver oral pleadings, and witnesses and experts are examined.[100] Agents and counsel typically plead in one of the official languages of the Court, and there is simultaneous translation of their pleadings into the other official language. Parties can plead in another language, but this is rare in practice.[101]

Pursuant to Article 46 of the Statute, hearings of the Court are public unless the Court decides otherwise. During the drafting of the Statute of the PCIJ, public hearings were chosen as the default because the 'principle of the publicity of judicial discussion was of capital importance in winning for the Court and its judges the confidence of the public'.[102] Proceedings in closed session are rare and in recent years have only occurred in connection with the giving of witness testimony.[103] The Court's public hearings are announced in advance by press release and are also live streamed.

Proceedings before the Court are adversarial; the parties 'are responsible for the presentation of their cases, and the Court takes no active part in that aspect of the proceedings, beyond an occasional question for purposes of clarification'.[104] At the same time, the Court has various powers pursuant to which it could take a more active role in proceedings. The Court can, for example, conduct site visits and appoint its own experts (which has implications for the Court's budget).[105] Since 1972, Article 61(1) of the Rules has provided that the Court may indicate to parties issues that the Court would like them to address at the hearing. In 2002, the Court stated

---

Assembly, 30 October 2014, in A/69/PV.33, 30 October 2014, p. 5 at p. 10; Keith, 'Challenges to the Independence of the International Judiciary', 149. See also *Armed Activities on the Territory of the Congo (DRC v. Uganda), Order of 8 September 2020*, ICJ Reports 2020, p. 264 at p. 264 ('[a]fter deliberation').

[100] Statute, Art. 43(5). Regarding experts and witnesses, see J Devaney, Chapter 9, Fact-finding and Expert Evidence; S. Wordsworth and K Parlett, Chapter 13, Effective Advocacy at the ICJ.

[101] See Rules, Arts. 70(1), 71(2); International Court of Justice, *Handbook* (2018), p. 54.

[102] 'Report and draft scheme presented to the Assembly by the Third Committee', in *Documents concerning the action taken by the Council of the League of Nations under Article 14 of the Covenant* (1921), p. 206 at p. 212.

[103] S. von Schorlemer and A. Tzanakopoulos, 'Article 46', in *Zimmermann Commentary*, p. 1330 at pp. 1337–1339, paras. 24–31.

[104] Shaw, *Rosenne's Law*, vol. III, p. 1062.

[105] See Statute, Art. 50; Rules, Arts. 66, 67; *Gabčíkovo-Nagymaros Project (Hungary/Slovakia), Order of 5 February 1997*, ICJ Reports 1997, p. 3; *DRC v. Uganda, Order of 8 September 2020*, ICJ Reports 2020, p. 264; *Armed Activities on the Territory of the Congo (DRC v. Uganda), Order of 12 October 2020*, ICJ Reports 2020, p. 295; 2020 Yusuf speech, p. 4.

that it intended to make greater use of this power.[106] However, the Court has made very limited use of the power to date, notwithstanding calls for it to do so (in connection with pre-hearing deliberations), so as to increase the utility of hearings.[107]

Incidental Proceedings

In contentious proceedings, in addition to the mainline proceedings concerning the merits of the parties' dispute, certain types of 'incidental' proceedings can be initiated. There are five main types of incidental proceeding:

1. *Provisional measures*: At any time, a party may request the Court to indicate provisional measures (interim measures of protection).[108] In December 2020, the Court adopted a new article in the 'Resolution concerning the Internal Judicial Practice of the Court', which provides for the establishment of ad hoc committees to assist the Court in monitoring the implementation of provisional measures that it orders.[109]

2. *Joinder*: The Court may direct that proceedings be joined.[110] The Court does so where joinder is consonant with the sound administration of justice and the need for judicial economy.[111]

3. *Preliminary questions and preliminary objections*: The Rules provide two procedures by which the Court's jurisdiction over a particular case, or the admissibility of a particular application, can be considered as a preliminary matter.[112] Under the current Rules, the Court itself may decide that questions concerning jurisdiction or admissibility are to be

---

[106] Press Release 2002/12, 4 April 2002, p. 2, para. 4.

[107] See Press Release 2002/12, 4 April 2002, p. 2, para. 4; K. Keith, Chapter 2, The Role of an ICJ Judge, discussing the *Aerial Herbicide Spraying* proceedings; J. Crawford and A. Keene, 'Editorial' 7(2) *JIDS* (2016) 225 at 228; Miron, 'Working Methods of the Court', 387–388; Keene, 'Outcome Paper for the Seminar on the International Court of Justice at 70', 249 (Sands), 251 (Sands, Pellet).

[108] Rules, Art. 73(1). See further R. Kolb, Chapter 7, Provisional Measures.

[109] Press Release 2020/38, 21 December 2020.

[110] Rules, Art. 47. The Court may also 'direct common action' in two or more sets of proceedings without formally joining them.

[111] *Maritime Delimitation in the Caribbean Sea and the Pacific Ocean (Costa Rica v. Nicaragua); Land Boundary in the Northern Part of Isla Portillos (Costa Rica v. Nicaragua), Order of 2 February 2017*, ICJ Reports 2017, p. 91 at p. 94, para. 16.

[112] See Rules, Arts. 79, 79*bis*, 79*ter*.

determined separately, before proceedings on the merits (preliminary questions). If the Court does not make such a decision, the respondent State can nonetheless make a preliminary objection to jurisdiction or admissibility.[113] On receipt of a preliminary objection, the proceedings on the merits are suspended; that is, proceedings are automatically bifurcated. Under either procedure, there is then a separate, preliminary stage of the proceedings devoted specifically to jurisdiction and admissibility. After an oral hearing, the Court may decide a preliminary question, may uphold or reject a preliminary objection, or may declare that the preliminary question or objection 'does not possess an exclusively preliminary character', meaning that it will not be decided until the subsequent merits stage of the case.

The original Rules of the PCIJ did not provide for any such procedure. The practice on these matters developed through case law, before being embodied in the Rules and subsequently revised on a number of occasions.[114] One of the particular concerns behind the 1972 revisions to the Rules was to change the Court's handling of preliminary objections.[115] As amended in 1972, the Rules give the Court less latitude to defer the resolution of objections to the merits stage of a case.[116] In 1972, the Court did not feel that it should require preliminary objections to be made by a respondent State within a short period of time after the delivery of the applicant State's memorial.[117] This had changed by 2000. In 2000, the Court amended its Rules to require preliminary objections to be brought within three months and also adopted a Practice Direction stipulating that the applicant would in turn have four months to present its written observations on the objection.[118]

---

[113] Objections to jurisdiction and admissibility can be made after the three-month deadline, but they will be dealt with together with the merits of the dispute.

[114] See Shaw, *Rosenne's Law*, vol. II, pp. 859–880.

[115] See E. Jiménez de Aréchaga, 'The Amendments to the Rules of Procedure of the International Court of Justice' 67(1) *AJIL* (1973) 1 at 1, 11; S. Rosenne, *Procedure in the International Court: A Commentary on the 1978 Rules of the International Court of Justice* (Martinus Nijhoff, 1983), pp. 159–160.

[116] See *Certain Iranian Assets (Iran v. USA), Preliminary Objections, Judgment,* ICJ Reports 2019, p. 7, Joint Separate Opinion of Judges Tomka and Crawford, pp. 46–48, paras. 3–7; Jiménez de Aréchaga, 'The Amendments to the Rules', 12–19.

[117] Jiménez de Aréchaga, 'The Amendments to the Rules', 19.

[118] Press Release 2001/1, 12 January 2001.

4. *Intervention*: When the construction of a treaty is in question in a case, third States that are parties to the treaty have a right to intervene and may make a declaration of intervention. Additionally, if a State considers that it has an interest of a legal nature which may be affected by the decision in a case, it may apply to the Court for permission to intervene.[119]

5. *Counter-claims*: A respondent State may also make counter-claims in its counter-memorial.[120]

Incidental proceedings regarding provisional measures and preliminary questions or objections occur relatively frequently, but the three other types of incidental proceedings – joinder, intervention and counter-claims – are less common.[121]

The Post-adjudication Phase

After the Court has deliberated, it reads its judgment or advisory opinion in open Court.[122] On average, it takes the Court between three to four years from the commencement of proceedings to render a judgment on the merits, a comparable period to the time taken in inter-State arbitration proceedings.[123]

After the Court has rendered a judgment on the merits of a contentious case, it may remain involved in proceedings, or may be called upon to become involved once again, sometimes a long time after it rendered its judgment. First, there may be a further stage of proceedings dealing with reparation. In some proceedings, the Court has not determined the quantum of compensation due in its judgment on the merits, but has instead ruled that the matter will be settled by the Court failing agreement between the parties. In earlier cases, the Court did not specify how long parties were to have to reach such an agreement. Thus, in one set of proceedings the applicant State requested the Court to determine the quantum of compensation due ten years after the Court's judgment on the merits.[124] In more recent proceedings, the Court has given parties six or twelve months to

---

[119] Statute, Arts. 62, 63; Rules, Arts. 81, 82.   [120] Rules, Art. 80(2).

[121] See *ICJ Yearbook 2017–2018*, 136–153.   [122] Statute, Arts. 58, 67.

[123] Miron, 'Working Methods of the Court', 372; Sarvarian, 'Procedural Economy', 86.

[124] *Armed Activities on the Territory of the Congo (DRC v. Uganda), Order of 1 July 2015*, ICJ Reports 2015, p. 580.

reach an agreement and, when an agreement has not eventuated, has determined the compensation due.[125]

Second, in special agreements, the parties sometimes request the Court to perform tasks which the Court may perform after its judgment on the merits. For example, the Court may subsequently nominate experts to assist in demarking a boundary determined by the Court.[126]

Third, under Article 60 of the Statute, any party may request interpretation of a judgment when there is a dispute regarding its meaning or scope. In 2011, a State requested, and obtained, an interpretation of a judgment forty-nine years after it was rendered.[127]

Fourth, within ten years of a judgment, a party may apply for revision of the judgment based on the discovery of some fact that was unknown at the time of judgment and which is 'of such a nature as to be a decisive factor'.[128] When a State applies for revision of a judgment, the Court may require compliance with the terms of the judgment before it admits the proceedings. Beyond this, the Court has no explicit power under the Statute to assess or enforce compliance with its judgments; 'both compliance with a decision and the enforcement of a decision is in each case a political operation'.[129] Recent proceedings have raised the question of whether the Court has an inherent jurisdiction over disputes regarding non-compliance with its judgments. But as yet the Court has not commented on this matter.[130]

IV Conclusion

Historically, the machine of the Court worked slowly. In the late 1960s and early 1970s, proceedings before the Court were seen as taking an excessive

---

[125] *Ahmadou Sadio Diallo (Guinea v. DRC), Compensation, Judgment,* ICJ Reports 2012, p. 324; *Certain Activities Carried Out by Nicaragua in the Border Area (Costa Rica v. Nicaragua), Compensation, Judgment,* ICJ Reports 2018, p. 15.

[126] *Frontier Dispute (Burkina Faso/Niger), Order, Nomination of Experts,* ICJ Reports 2013, p. 226.

[127] *Request for Interpretation of the Judgment of 15 June 1962 in the Case concerning the* Temple of Preah Vihear (Cambodia v. Thailand) *(Cambodia v. Thailand), Judgment,* ICJ Reports 2013, p. 281.

[128] Statute, Art. 61.

[129] Shaw, *Rosenne's Law,* vol. I, p. 197. See also UN Charter, Art. 94(2).

[130] *Alleged Violations of Sovereign Rights and Maritime Spaces in the Caribbean Sea (Nicaragua v. Colombia), Preliminary Objections, Judgment,* ICJ Reports 2016, p. 3 at p. 13, para. 16, pp. 39–42, paras. 102–110.

amount of time. The Court responded, effecting key changes to its Rules in 1972 and a wholesale revision of its Rules in 1978. In the late 1990s, a particular part of the work of the Court was seen as taking too long: the period between the close of the written phase and the time when a case was heard. In 1998, the Court again responded, this time by changing its practices – commencing a practice of conducting hearings on preliminary proceedings back-to-back and dispensing with judicial notes for hearings in preliminary proceedings – and by adopting its initial Practice Directions (then labelled 'recommendations'). These efforts were successful and cleared the Court's backlog of cases by 2010. In the last decade, the Court has been operating at a good speed.

Since the reforms of 1998, work on the machine of the Court has been more in the nature of fine tuning. In the early 2000s, further changes to the Court's working practices were certainly still made with a view to making the machine work faster.[131] But in the period since 1998, and particularly more recently, the focus seems to have been on making the machine work *better*. The Court has changed practices in the interest of the sound administration of justice – including by adopting Practice Directions in 2002 addressing who may serve as a judge ad hoc and a decision in 2018 regulating the circumstances in which the members of the Court may serve as an arbitrator. The Court has also made changes to respond to developments in technology and how litigation is practiced – adopting, for example, amendments to the Rules in 2020 to allow hearings to occur by video link.[132]

The 2020 amendments to the Rules demonstrate that the Court can quickly adapt its working practices and overcome obstacles when necessary. At the same time, the Court has not succeeded in overcoming other, long-standing obstacles. Concerns to increase the utility of oral hearings are not new.[133] Similarly, concerns to reduce the length of parties' written pleadings and annexes are not new.[134]

---

[131] Such as the establishment of the three-month time limit for the brining of preliminary objections. See Press Release 2001/1, 12 January 2001.

[132] Another change that could be noted in this respect is the adoption of a Practice Direction in 2006 regarding Judges' folders. See Practice Direction IX*ter*.

[133] See, e.g., Jiménez de Aréchaga, 'The Amendments to the Rules', 6.

[134] See R. Higgins, 'Respecting Sovereign States and Running a Tight Courtroom' 50(1) *ICLQ* (2001) 121 at 124 (referring to the 'Court's desire for less prolix annexes').

Is there reason to think that the Court will be able to overcome these and other obstacles in the future? There are at least two reasons for a positive outlook. First, at least in part, the Court has not overcome these obstacles to date because of a tendency to defer to the wishes of litigating States in procedural matters.[135] In 2001, Judge Higgins stated that it was 'time to move away ... from undue deference to the litigants by virtue of their rank as sovereign States',[136] and there certainly has been a change over time regarding the degree to which the Court defers to the wishes of States in procedural matters.[137] Recent developments – such as the establishment of a page limit for annexes to written pleadings and provision for the establishment of ad hoc committees to monitor the implementation of provisional measures – tend to suggest that the Court may become more assertive.[138]

Second, the Judges appear receptive to continuing to work to improve the machine of the Court. Speaking before the UN General Assembly in 2019, then-President Yusuf stated that, despite a heavy case load, the Court 'remains committed to the review of its rules and methods of work'.[139] Current-President Donoghue has expressed interest in learning from the working practices of other courts and tribunals.[140] As Judge Crawford noted following the 2016 seminar held at the ICJ at which the Court's working practices were discussed, '[p]articipants agreed that the Court needs to demonstrate to governments and to the world as a whole

---

[135] See, e.g., Jiménez de Aréchaga, 'The Amendments to the Rules', 5–6 (McNair referring, in the early 1970s, to the 'tendency for the Court to reflect the diplomatic origin of international justice and to be somewhat subservient to the wishes of litigants by granting long periods for the filing of their pleadings'); 'Process, Practice and Procedure', 288 (Brower).

[136] Higgins, 'Respecting Sovereign States', 124.

[137] See, e.g., the text at footnotes 117–118. See also Miron, 'Working Methods of the Court', 373.

[138] Unsurprisingly, there is variation in the Court's practice. For example, the Court appears to have been quite assertive in the initial time limits it set for the first round of written pleadings in *Application of the Convention on the Prevention and Punishment of the Crime of Genocide (The Gambia v. Myanmar), Order of 23 January 2020*, ICJ Reports 2020, p. 69. In contrast, in *Maritime Delimitation in the Indian Ocean*, the Court postponed the hearing on the merits two times at the request of Kenya (and subsequently postponed the hearing a third time due to the COVID-19 pandemic, also at the request of Kenya). See *Maritime Delimitation in the Indian Ocean*, paras. 13–16.

[139] Speech by President Yusuf to the UN General Assembly, 30 October 2019, in UN Doc A/74/PV.20, 30 October 2019, p. 1 at p. 6.

[140] Keene, 'Outcome Paper for the Seminar on the International Court of Justice at 70', 243.

that it is willing to innovate to meet changing needs, and to deal adequately with the cases that come before it'.[141] There are positive signs that the Court is taking on this challenge.

Further Reading

International Law Association Committee on the Procedure of International Courts and Tribunals, 'Preliminary Report', 17 January 2017, Section II.

A. Miron, 'Working Methods of the Court' 7(2) *JIDS* (2016) 371.

G. Pinzauti and P. Webb, 'Litigation before the International Court of Justice during the Pandemic' 34(4) *LJIL* (2021) 787.

J. J. Quintana, *Litigation at the International Court of Justice: Practice and Procedure* (Brill Nijhoff, 2015).

S. Ugalde and J. J. Quintana, 'Managing Litigation before the International Court of Justice' 9(4) *JIDS* (2018) 691.

---

[141] Crawford and Keene, 'Editorial', 225.

Procedure in Contentious Cases: 12
Evolution and Flexibility

Kate Parlett and Amy Sander

I Introduction

The rules of procedure are essential to any method of dispute resolution, and the Court is no exception. For the Court's users (i.e. States) to have confidence in its ability to reach a just outcome, it is necessary that there be a clear and level playing field when it comes to the way in which a case is presented, answered, and decided. Transparent and coherent rules of procedure enable the efficient and effective resolution of disputes, whilst according the parties a fair and equal opportunity to present their case.

There are four potential sources of rules governing the Court's procedure.[1] The first is the Court's Statute. Chapter III of the Court's Statute (Articles 39-64) is devoted to procedure, and Article 30 empowers the Court to lay down rules of procedure. These are the second source of rules governing its procedure: Rules of Court were adopted in 1946, then completely revised in 1978, with subsequent amendments made, most recently in 2020 to allow for video link to be used for hearings and delivery of judgments. Since 2001, the Court has also adopted Practice Directions, which are the third source of rules governing its procedure. The Practice Directions address a range of practical issues, and they enable the Court to issue encouragement to the parties as to various aspects of procedure.[2] The final source of rules governing the Court's procedure are its practices, which will be well known to those who have been involved with cases, but may not be so apparent to those who have not. More generally, regard should also be had to the body of case law which has progressively established a series of rules and general propositions about the judicial

---

[1] See also C. Harris, Chapter 11, this volume, The Working Practices of the Court.

[2] In addition, the Court has issued a Resolution concerning the Internal Judicial Practice of the Court (first adopted in 1968, revised in 1976, with the most recent amendment in 2020), available at www.icj-cij.org/en/other-texts/resolution-concerning-judicial-practice.

handling of disputes, including equality of the parties, the principle of the proper administration of justice, res judicata and the prohibition of abuse of procedure.[3]

As Sir Elihu Lauterpacht explained, rules of procedure are servants, not masters: they should not unduly constrain the parties from presenting their cases, nor prevent the Court from reaching a just and fair outcome. The Court is a court of general jurisdiction: given the range of disputes that come before it, in both subject matter, complexity and type, it is clear that for some aspects of procedure, one size does not fit all. It follows that procedure should not be overly prescriptive and be approached in a common sense and flexible manner.[4] At the same time, if the parties contravene the agreed procedural rules, the Court risks undermining confidence in its processes. There is therefore a delicate balance to be struck between flexibility and certainty, to ensure the overall goals of fairness in the process and fairness in the result.

The Court has evidenced a willingness to adapt its procedure over time, and keeps its procedure under constant review. In 2019, President Yusuf reported to the General Assembly on 'the ongoing initiative of the Court to ensure that its Rules and methods of work correspond to its changing requirements'.[5] The Court's adaptations are evidenced by amendments to its Rules, internal practices, and Practice Directions; specific examples of these are discussed further below.

This chapter is focused on the key features of procedure in contentious cases (which form the vast majority of the cases to go before the Court). These are the institution of proceedings (Section II); provisional measures (Section III); preliminary objections (Section IV); intervention (Section V); and non-appearance (Section VI).[6] For each of these aspects of procedure,

---

[3] R. Kolb, 'General Principles of Procedural Law' in A. Zimmerman et al. (eds.), *The Statute of the International Court of Justice: A Commentary* (3rd ed., Oxford University Press, 2019), paras. 1 and 8.

[4] E. Lauterpacht, 'Principles of Procedure in International Litigation' 345 *Collected Courses of the Academy of International Law* (2009) 387, at 430–431.

[5] See Speech by HE Abdulqawi A. Yusuf, President of the ICJ on the occasion of the 74th Session of the United Nations General Assembly, 30 October 2019, available at www.icj-cij .org/public/files/press-releases/0/000-20191030-STA-01-00-EN.pdf, p. 7.

[6] The procedural rules governing written and oral proceedings are covered in Chapter 13 (S. Wordsworth and K. Parlett, 'Effective Advocacy') Further, procedural rules governing fact and expert evidence are addressed in Chapter 10 (J. Devaney, 'Fact Finding and Expert Evidence').

the chapter sets out the current rules, commenting on the way in which they have evolved, and making some suggestions for further innovation by the Court.

II Institution of Proceedings and Consultations with the Parties

Contentious cases are instituted in one of two ways: either by the notification of a special agreement (or *compromis*), or by a written application addressed to the Registrar.[7] Where proceedings are instituted by notification of a special agreement, the notification may be made by the parties jointly or by any one of them.[8] Where proceedings are instituted by application, the application is to indicate the party making it; the State against which the claim is brought, and the subject of the dispute.[9] The application is also required to specify the legal grounds upon which the jurisdiction of the Court is based, and the precise nature of the claim, together with a succinct statement of the facts and grounds upon which the claim is based.[10]

An application may also be made with a request for the respondent State to consent to jurisdiction, a so-called *forum proragatum* application. Before 1978, when the Court revised its Rules, the Court was obliged to enter such applications on its General List and then it had to issue orders to remove them if the respondent State did not consent. But since 1978, the Rules provide that the Court will not take any action on such applications unless and until the respondent State consents to the Court's jurisdiction for the purposes of the case.[11] This amendment preserves the fundamental principle of State consent and also promotes efficiency. The Court records the filing of any *forum prorogatum* applications via its press releases, so a record of them remains publicly available.[12] In cases where the applicant's intention is to raise the public profile of a dispute, the press release may

---

[7] Statute, Article 40(1).   [8] ICJ Rules, Article 39(1).   [9] ICJ Rules, Article 38(1).
[10] ICJ Rules, Article 38(2).   [11] ICJ Rules, Article 38(5).
[12] See e.g., Press Release No 2014/18, The Republic of the Marshall Islands files Applications against nine States for their alleged failure to fulfil their obligations with respect to the cessation of the nuclear arms race at an early date and to nuclear disarmament, available at www.icj-cij.org/public/files/press-releases/0/18300.pdf.

serve that purpose, without requiring the Court to take any further procedural steps.

The Court's Statute provides that the parties are to be represented by agents.[13] All steps on behalf of the parties are taken by the agents, and all communications from the Court to the parties are addressed to the agents.[14] In proceedings commenced by application, the agent for the applicant must be named in the application; the respondent should inform the Court of the name of its agent upon receipt of the application, or as soon as possible thereafter.[15] In proceedings commenced by special agreement, the agent's name should be provided with the notification, and any other party should provide the name of its agent upon receipt of the notification or as soon as possible thereafter.[16]

In its communications with agents, the Court's practice is to facilitate correspondence between the parties and to communicate with each of them through personalised letters. This approach appears to be linked to the tradition of diplomatic correspondence, and avoids 'copying in' agents without directly addressing them. The Court's letters go separately to each party and use a formulation along the lines of: 'a similar letter has been sent to the other Party' to indicate that the same message has been conveyed to the other side. It is not clear why the corresponding letter is not described as 'identical' (at least in material respects, leaving aside the addressee). But in any event, a shift in the Court's approach, so that each of the parties is copied on all relevant correspondence with the Court, would promote transparency and efficiency, which in turn promotes confidence that the parties are being treated on equal footing. It would also safeguard against the possibility of a letter to one party being overlooked, especially in the heavy traffic of correspondence that may take place in advance of an oral hearing.

Pursuant to Article 31 of the Rules, the President is to ascertain the views of the parties with regard to questions of procedure, and for this purpose, the President is to meet with the agents of the parties as soon as possible after their appointment, and whenever necessary thereafter.[17] Practice Direction XIII, adopted in 2009, specifies that the reference in Article 31 to ascertaining the views of the parties is to be understood as follows:

---

[13] ICJ Statute, Article 42(1).   [14] ICJ Rules, Article 40(1).   [15] ICJ Rules, Article 40(2).
[16] ICJ Rules, Article 40(3).   [17] ICJ Rules, Article 31.

After the initial meeting with the President, and in the context of any further ascertainment of the parties' views relating to questions of procedure, the parties may, should they agree on the procedure to be followed, inform the President by letter accordingly.

The views of the parties as to the future procedure may also, should they agree, be ascertained by means of a video or telephone conference.

By Practice Direction X, adopted in 2004, the Court indicated that, whenever a decision on a procedural issue needs to be made and the President considers it necessary to call a meeting of the agents under Article 31 of the Rules, 'agents are expected to attend that meeting as early as possible.'

These Practice Directions expressly and implicitly affirm, consistently with the practice, that the Court will be guided by the parties in determining matters of procedure. In practice, the President meets with the agents soon after proceedings are instituted, with a focus on discussing the schedule for the written pleadings. Where a case is commenced by special agreement, the parties may be agreed as to the schedule and number of pleadings, or in any case the parties may reach an agreement in advance of or during the meeting with the President. In light of the information obtained by the President, the Court then makes orders to determine the number and order of written pleadings and the time limits within which they are to be filed.[18] In making such orders, 'an agreement between the parties which does not cause unjustified delay shall be taken into account';[19] in practice, although in the past the Court generally accepted extended periods for the filing of written pleadings if the parties were agreed, in a number of recent cases the Court has ordered filings within a shorter timeframe than that requested by the parties,[20] suggesting that the

---

[18] ICJ Rules, Article 44(1).   [19] ICJ Rules, Article 44(2).

[20] See, for example, *Application of the International Convention for the Suppression of the Financing of Terrorism and of the International Convention on the Elimination of All Forms of Racial Discrimination (Ukraine v. Russian Federation), Order of 12 May 2017, ICJ Reports 2017*, p. 228; *Jadhav (India v. Pakistan), Order of 13 June 2017, ICJ Reports 2017*, p. 279; *Question of the Delimitation of the Continental Shelf between Nicaragua and Colombia beyond 200 Nautical Miles from the Nicaraguan Coast (Nicaragua v. Colombia), Order of 8 December 2017, ICJ Reports 2017*, p. 361; *Maritime Delimitation in the Indian Ocean (Somalia v. Kenya), Order of 2 February 2018, ICJ Reports 2018*, p. 11; *Appeal relating to the Jurisdiction of the ICAO Council under Article 84 of the Convention on International Civil Aviation (Bahrain, Egypt, Saudi Arabia and United Arab Emirates v. Qatar), Order of 27 March 2019, ICJ Reports 2019*, p. 344; and *Application of the Convention on the Prevention and Punishment of the Crime of Genocide (The Gambia v. Myanmar), Order of 23 January 2020, ICJ Reports 2020*, p. 69.

Court will impose time limits 'on the basis of what seems to be reasonable in all the circumstances'.[21] This is a welcome development and demonstrates the Court's intention to manage the cases on its docket, while providing the parties with a fair opportunity to present their case.

The ILA has recently proposed that the Court amend Article 44(1) of its Rules to provide for a range of standardised time limits: four to six months for jurisdiction and admissibility and six to nine months for the merits pleadings.[22] These are suggested to be appropriate based on practice, although the ILA's own survey of the practice indicated longer time frames, at least for merits pleadings (with a mean of eleven months).[23] While it is useful to identify the usual practice, given the range of cases that come before the Court and the variance between them in terms of the time needed to prepare or respond to a claim, in our view this is an area where flexibility is to be preferred, especially as the Court has demonstrated in its more recent practice that it will take a reasonable approach and will not defer to parties' requests for excessively long time limits.

There is provision in the Court's rules for a party to request an extension of the fixed time limits, following consultation with the other party.[24] Since 2020, the Court has granted several extensions of time requested with reference to the Covid-19 pandemic.[25]

On the number of pleadings, in 2002 the Court adopted a measure to the effect that 'a single round of written pleadings is to be considered as the norm in cases begun by means of an application'.[26] However, in

---

[21] R. Higgins, 'Respective Sovereign States and Running a Tight Courtroom' 50 *ICLQ* (2001) 121, at 127. See also A. Miron, 'The Working Methods of the Court' 7 *JIDS* (2016) 371, at 381–382.

[22] ILA, Procedure of International Courts and Tribunals, Final Report, 1 May 2020, p. 29.

[23] ILA, Procedure of International Courts and Tribunals, Final Report, 1 May 2020, p. 29.

[24] ICJ Rules, Article 44(3).

[25] See *Guatemala's Territorial, Insular and Maritime Claim (Guatemala/Belize)*, Order of 22 April 2020, ICJ Reports 2020, p. 72; *Application of the Convention on the Prevention and Punishment of the Crime of Genocide (The Gambia v. Myanmar)*, Order of 18 May 2020, ICJ Reports 2020, p. 75; *Application of the International Convention for the Suppression of the Financing of Terrorism and of the International Convention on the Elimination of All Forms of Racial Discrimination (Ukraine v. Russian Federation)*, Order of 13 July 2020, ICJ Reports 2020, p. 78; and *Application of the International Convention for the Suppression of the Financing of Terrorism and of the International Convention on the Elimination of All Forms of Racial Discrimination (Ukraine v. Russian Federation)*, Order of 20 January 2021.

[26] ICJ, Press Release 2002/12, 4 April 2002, para. 1.

practice, the Court generally defers to the parties if a second round is requested, and in practice two rounds of written pleadings remains the norm in contentious cases.[27] In *Whaling in the Antarctic*, the parties disagreed as to whether a second round of written pleadings should be filed and the Court agreed with the applicant, Japan, that a second round was not necessary.[28] The decision not to order a second round was addressed by Judge Greenwood in his separate opinion. He set out three considerations which he considered to be important in the Court's discretion to decide whether to order a second round. First, it must be open to the Court to order a second round if it considers it necessary, for example, because it does not have sufficient information on a particular matter. Second, the Court has an obligation to ensure that proceedings do not become unnecessarily protracted. The applicant should set out its entire case in its Memorial and the respondent in its Counter-Memorial: '[a] State should never hold part of its case – whether argument or evidence – in reserve for a second round.' Third, he noted that there is a distinction between the applicant and respondent which followed from the fact that the respondent files second: if the applicant is denied the opportunity to respond to evidence or argument contained in the Counter-Memorial, a serious injustice may follow; while the respondent cannot claim to need a second round, since its Counter-Memorial would constitute the last word.[29]

The Court's approach has been the subject of some criticism, on the grounds that the parties do not usually reveal their respective claims in the written pleadings (or perhaps not fully in the first round); and that respondents may need extra time to assemble factual evidence.[30] But there is flexibility in other aspects of the Rules to take account of a need for an extension of time for the filing of the Counter-Memorial, or for the submission of relevant evidence after the closure of the written proceedings. Moreover, the practice – if it exists – of holding back evidence and argument for the second round of written pleadings is arguably not

---

[27] K. Mačák, 'Article 43' in A. Zimmerman et al. (eds.), *The Statute of the International Court of Justice: A Commentary*,(3rd ed., Oxford University Press, 2019), para. 51.

[28] *Whaling in the Antarctic (Australia v. Japan; New Zealand intervening), Judgment, ICJ Reports 2014*, p. 235, para. 6.

[29] *Whaling in the Antarctic (Australia v. Japan; New Zealand intervening), Separate Opinion of Judge Greenwood, ICJ Reports 2014*, pp. 418–419, paras. 32–36.

[30] Miron, 'The Working Methods of the Court', at 385–386.

conducive to the effective and timely administration of justice: a respondent holding material back to include in its rejoinder may deprive the applicant of a fair opportunity to respond to that material in writing. The Court will likely not be assisted in its role in case-managing disputes by written pleadings that are partial or incomplete by deliberate strategic choice of the respondent.

The Court has discouraged the practice of simultaneous exchange of pleadings which developed in cases instituted by special agreement.[31] In Practice Direction I, adopted in 2001, the Court stated that it expected in future cases that special agreements would provide for the number and order of pleadings, and if not, that the parties would reach agreement to that effect. While several special agreements concluded after the adoption of Practice Direction I provided for simultaneous exchange of pleadings,[32] in the two most recent cases submitted to the Court by special agreement, the agreements provided for consecutive pleadings:[33] the special agreement in *Guatemala/Belize* also specified that the Memorial would be filed by Guatemala;[34] and in *Gabon/Equatorial Guinea*, the parties agreed in the meeting with the President of the Court that Equatorial Guinea would file the first pleading.[35] This most recent practice indicates a welcome trend for compliance with Practice Direction I, without the Court needing to incorporate this into its Rules.[36] It also demonstrates the utility of the Practice

---

[31] The uniform practice of simultaneous exchange of pleadings (at least since 1978) is noted in P. Tomka, 'The Special Agreement' in N. Ando et al. (eds.), *Liber Amicorum Judge Shigeru Oda* (Brill, 2002), 553, p. 562.

[32] See Article 3 of the Special Agreement in *Frontier Dispute (Benin/Niger)*, Order of 27 November 2002, ICJ Reports 2002, p. 613; Article 3 of the Special Agreement in *Frontier Dispute (Burkina Faso/Niger)*, Order of 14 September 2010, ICJ Reports 2010, p. 631; Article 4 of the Special Agreement in *Pedra Branca (Malaysia/Singapore)*, Order of 1 September 2003, ICJ Reports 2003, p. 146.

[33] Article 3(2) of the Special Agreement between Belize and Guatemala to submit Guatemala's Territorial, Insular and Maritime Claim to the International Court of Justice, 8 December 2008; and Article 3 of the Special Agreement in *Land and Maritime Delimitation and Sovereignty over Islands (Gabon/Equatorial Guinea)*, 15 November 2016.

[34] Article 3(2) of the Special Agreement between Belize and Guatemala to submit Guatemala's Territorial, Insular and Maritime Claim to the International Court of Justice, 8 December 2008.

[35] See *Land and Maritime Delimitation and Sovereignty over Islands (Gabon/Equatorial Guinea)*, Order of 7 April 2021, p. 2.

[36] Cf. K. Mačàk, 'Article 43' in A. Zimmerman et al. (eds.), *The Statute of the International Court of Justice: A Commentary* (3rd ed., Oxford University Press, 2019), para. 49. The ILA has urged the Court to amend its Rules to abolish the practice of simultaneous pleadings,

Directions as a means by which the Court can encourage parties to take a particular approach to procedure, without constraining them by imposing a requirement though the Court's Rules.

Upon receipt of an application, a respondent may wish to consider the possibility of bringing a counter-claim.[37] The Court's Statute makes no provision for counter-claims but they are dealt with in Article 80 of the Court's Rules. Pursuant to Article 80, a counter-claim may be brought provided it is within the jurisdiction of the Court and is directly connected with the subject-matter of the principal claim.[38] Thus, there are two requirements for a counter-claim to be admissible: it must 'come within the jurisdiction of the Court' and be 'directly connected with the subject matter of the claim of the other party'.[39]

Any counter-claim should be made in the Counter-Memorial.[40] In the usual course, the applicant would respond to the counter-claim in its reply, but the rules also preserve the possibility of an additional pleading if a second round of written pleadings is not ordered.[41]

III Provisional Measures

The Court has the power, under Article 41 of its Statute, to 'indicate, if it considers that circumstances so require, any provisional measures which

---

and to provide that in the absence of agreement between the parties, the order will be determined by lot: see ILA, Procedure of International Courts and Tribunals, Final Report, 1 May 2020, p. 30. Given that the recent practice is consistent with Practice Direction I, it appears to be having its desired effect and a further amendment to the rules is not, in our view, necessary.

[37] See generally, S. D. Murphy 'Counter-Claims, Article 80 of the Rules' in A. Zimmerman et al. (eds.), *The Statute of the International Court of Justice: A Commentary* (3rd ed., Oxford University Press, 2019), 1104.

[38] ICJ Rules, Article 80(1).

[39] See *Oil Platforms, Counter-claim, order of 10 March 1998, ICJ Reports 1998*, p. 203, para. 33; *Armed Activities (DRC v. Uganda), Counter-claims, Order of 29 November 2001, ICJ Reports 2001*, p. 678, para. 35; *Jurisdictional Immunities of the State, Counter-claim, Order of 6 July 2010, ICJ Reports 2010*, pp. 315–316, para. 14; *Certain Activities Carried out by Nicaragua in the Border Area* and *Construction of a Road in Costa Rica along the San Juan River, Counter-claims, Order of 18 April 2013, ICJ Reports 2013*, p. 208, para. 20; *Alleged Violations of Sovereign Rights and Maritime Spaces in the Caribbean Sea (Nicaragua v. Colombia), Counter-Claims, Order of 15 November 2017, ICJ Reports*, pp. 285–286, para. 19.

[40] ICJ Rules, Article 80(2).   [41] ICJ Rules, Articles 80(2); and 45(2).

ought to be taken to preserve the respective rights of either party'.[42] The
Statute provides no more detailed guidance.[43] The Court's Rules elaborate
on the procedure: initially, the Court replicated Article 61 of the PCIJ's
1936 Rules (save for the paragraph permitting the attendance of judges ad
hoc in provisional measures hearings 'if their presence can be assured at
the date fixed for hearing', which was considered unnecessary given the
possibility of international air travel). In the 1978 revision, the Court
adopted Articles 73–78 on provisional measures, which largely codified
the practices that had been developed in the requests heard by the ICJ over
the preceding three decades.

Article 73(1) provides that a written request for the indication of provisional measures may be made at any time during the course of the
proceedings.[44] While there are no formal time limits for making a request,
there may be practical limits: one of the substantive criteria that has
developed in the jurisprudence of the Court is urgency, and a party may
be prejudiced if it does not bring a provisional measures request in a
manner which supports its case on urgency.[45]

Article 73(2) indicates that the request should specify 'the reasons
therefor, the possible consequences if it is not granted, and the measures
requested'. Article 74 emphasises that provisional measures requests take
priority over all other cases, and the Court will convene to proceed to a
decision as a matter of urgency, and will fix a hearing. Under Article 74(4),
pending a meeting of the Court, the President may call upon the parties to

---

[42] ICJ Statute, Article 41(1). Notice of the measures is to be given to the parties and to the
Security Council: Article 41(2). As this chapter is focused on contentious cases, the question whether provisional measures may be requested in advisory opinions, which has never
been explicitly considered by the Court, is not addressed. For views on that subject, see K.
Oelllers-Frahm, A. Zimmerman, 'Article 41' in A. Zimmerman et al. (eds.), *The Statute of
the International Court of Justice: A Commentary*, 3rd ed. (Oxford University Press, 2019),
paras. 90–92; C. Miles, *Provisional Measures before International Courts and Tribunals*
(Cambridge University Press, 2017), pp. 397–405. On the subject of provisional measures
more generally, see R. Kolb, Chapter 8, 'Provisional Measures'.
[43] S. Rosenne, *Provisional Measures in International Law: The International Court of Justice
and the International Tribunal for the Law of the Sea* (2004) 62: he described the Statute
as 'sparse'.
[44] As noted in R. Kolb, Chapter 8, 'Provisional Measures,' more than one request can be made,
and modification of measures may also be requested repeatedly.
[45] See also in *LaGrand*, the Court stated that 'the sound administration of justice requires that
a request for the indication of provisional measures ... be submitted in good time':
*LaGrand (Germany v. United States of America), Provisional Measures, Order of 3 March
1999, ICJ Reports 1999*, p. 14, para. 19.

act in such a way as to enable any order the Court may make on the request to have its appropriate effect.

Article 75(1) reserves the power of the Court to decide to examine *proprio motu* whether provisional measures should be indicated. The Court has used this power sparingly, and has indicated such measures only once, in the *LaGrand* case, to indicate measures without an oral hearing.[46] In *Construction of a Road Along the San Juan River*, in a letter accompanying its Memorial, Nicaragua expressly requested the Court to consider, *proprio motu*, whether the circumstances of the case required the indication of measures. By letters to the parties, the Court stated that 'the circumstances of the case, as they presented themselves to it at that time, were not such as to require the exercise' of the Court's power to indicate provisional measures *proprio motu*.[47]

Article 75(2) provides that the Court may indicate measures that are different, in whole or in part, from those requested by a party. The Court frequently makes use of this power, to grant measures that are more general or limited than those requested.[48] The Court may and has granted measures in addition to those requested; frequently to restrain both parties from any action which may aggravate the dispute.[49]

Article 76 provides that a party may request revocation or modification of a provisional measures order at any time before final judgment, specifying the change in circumstances to justify the request, and the parties are entitled to present observations on any such request. A request for modification will only be granted if the underlying conditions are met with

---

[46] *LaGrand (Germany v. United States of America), Provisional Measures, Order of 3 March 1999, ICJ Reports 1999*, p. 9. In his separate opinion, Judge Schwebel disagreed that Article 75(1) applied in circumstances where a request has been made by a party: *LaGrand (Germany v. United States of America), Provisional Measures, Order of 3 March 1999, ICJ Reports 1999, Separate Opinion of Judge Schwebel*, p. 21ff.

[47] *Construction of a Road in Costa Rica along the San Juan River and Certain Activities Carried Out by Nicaragua in the Border Area, Provisional Measures, ICJ Reports 2015*, paras. 17–18.

[48] See K. Oellers-Frahm, A. Zimmerman, 'Article 41' in A. Zimmerman et al. (eds.), *The Statute of the International Court of Justice: A Commentary*, 3rd ed. (Oxford University Press, 2019), para. 83.

[49] See, for example, *Certain Activities Carried Out by Nicaragua in the Border Area (Costa Rica v. Nicaragua), Provisional Measures, Order of 8 March 2011, ICJ Reports 2011*, para. 86(3); *Georgia v. Russia, Provisional Measures, ICJ Reports 2009*, para. 149(C). On the duty of non-aggravation generally, see S. R. Ratner, 'The Aggravating Duty of Non-Aggravation' 31(4) (2020) *EJIL* 1307–1342.

regard to the new situation and if the modified measures meet the conditions for the grant of provisional measures, including a risk of irreparable harm and urgency. A request for modification does not require an oral hearing: the Court fixes a time limit for the responding party to file observations and permits the applying party to file written observations in response. Such requests can therefore be dealt with in a short period of time, although the time between the request for modification and the order has not in practice been much shorter than for a fresh request, with an oral hearing.[50] In July 2013, the Court found that the conditions for modification of its 2011 provisional measures order were not met in the joined cases *Certain Activities* and *Construction of a Road*, and rejected Costa Rica's request for modification, although it affirmed its 2011 order in the operative part of the judgment.[51] Three months later, Costa Rica filed a fresh request for provisional measures, based on new facts discovered since July 2013; the Court dealt with that request in the usual way, and ordered further provisional measures after an oral hearing.[52]

Under Article 77, any measures indicated by the Court are communicated to the Secretary-General of the United Nations, for transmission to the Security Council.[53] Article 78 empowers the Court to request information from the parties on implementation of any measures it has indicated. In this regard, the Court has commonly required the parties to submit reports on the measures taken to give effect to the provisional measures order at timely intervals (for example, every three months), until a final judgment is rendered.[54] Depending on the measures to be reported

---

[50] In *Construction of a Road in Costa Rica along the San Juan River and Certain Activities Carried Out by Nicaragua in the Border Area, Order of 16 July 2013, Provisional Measures, ICJ Reports 2013*, the request was made on 23 May 2013 and the order was made on 16 July 2013. Costa Rica then presented a fresh request on 24 September 2013 and the Court made orders on 22 November 2013, after an oral hearing: see *Construction of a Road in Costa Rica along the San Juan River and Certain Activities Carried Out by Nicaragua in the Border Area, Provisional Measures, Order of 22 November 2013, ICJ Reports 2013*.

[51] See *Construction of a Road in Costa Rica along the San Juan River and Certain Activities Carried Out by Nicaragua in the Border Area, Order of 16 July 2013, Provisional Measures, ICJ Reports 2013*, paras. 35–40.

[52] *Construction of a Road in Costa Rica along the San Juan River and Certain Activities Carried Out by Nicaragua in the Border Area, Provisional Measures, Order of 22 November 2013, ICJ Reports 2013*, para. 59.

[53] See also R. Kolb, Chapter 8, 'Provisional Measures.'

[54] See, for example, *Application of the Convention on the Prevention and Punishment of the Crime of Genocide (The Gambia v. Myanmar), Provisional Measures, Order of 23 January*

upon, the parties may therefore be submitting detailed and complex reports, and then commenting on each others' reports, resulting in a significant amount of material for the Court to take into consideration and potentially respond to. In these circumstances, it is not surprising that the Court has developed a mechanism to assist it in monitoring the implementation of provisional measures. In December 2020, the Court adopted a new Article 11 of the Resolution concerning the Internal Judicial Practice of the Court, which provided for the establishment of an ad hoc committee of three judges. This was the first time that the present version of the Resolution had been amended since it was adopted in 1976. The committee 'shall examine the information supplied by the parties in relation to the implementation of provisional measures' and 'report periodically to the Court, recommending potential options for the Court'.[55] It remains to be seen how the committee operates in practice, but it has the potential to ensure that implementation is carefully monitored. In the past, failures by the parties to submit information as required by provisional measures orders were not always picked up by the Court in the final judgment,[56] suggesting that they may not have been noted or followed up. The Court's new approach should ensure careful and comprehensive monitoring of compliance with provisional measures orders, in a procedurally efficient way.

As noted above, provisional measures requests are usually dealt with at an oral hearing, as provided for in Article 74 of the Rules. The Court has issued guidance to the parties on the content of their submissions at hearings through Practice Direction XI, adopted in 2004 and amended in

---

2020, *ICJ Reports 2020*, para. 86(4); *Jadhav Case (India v. Pakistan), Provisional Measures, order of 18 May 2017, ICJ Reports 2017*, para. 61; *Construction of a Road in Costa Rica along the San Juan River and Certain Activities Carried Out by Nicaragua in the Border Area, Provisional Measures, Order of 22 November 2013, ICJ Reports 2013*, para. 59 (3); *Request for Interpretation of the Judgment of 15 June 1962 in the Case concerning the Temple of Preah Vihear (Cambodia v. Thailand), Provisional Measures, Order of 18 July 2011, ICJ Reports 2011*, para. 69(C); and *Certain Activities Carried Out by Nicaragua in the Border Area (Costa Rica v. Nicaragua), Provisional Measures, Order of 8 March 2011, ICJ Reports 2011*, para. 86(4).

[55] Resolution concerning the Internal Judicial Practice of the Court, available at www.icj-cij .org/en/other-texts/resolution-concerning-judicial-practice, Article 11.

[56] See K. Oelllers-Frahm, A. Zimmerman, 'Article 41' in A. Zimmerman et al. (eds.), *The Statute of the International Court of Justice: A Commentary* (3rd ed., Oxford University Press, 2019) para. 84.

2006. It states that in the oral pleadings on request for provisional measures:

> parties should limit themselves to what is relevant to the criteria for the indication of provisional measures as stipulated in the Statute, Rules and jurisprudence of the Court. They should not enter into the merits of the case beyond what is strictly necessary for that purpose.

This guidance is consistent with the Rules (Article 60(1)) and Practice Direction VI, on hearings generally, both of which indicate that the parties should deliver focused oral submissions that are directed to the issues that divide the parties.[57]

Given that the basis of a provisional measures request is the risk of imminent irreparable harm and urgency, it has been questioned whether the Court deals with provisional measures requests in a timely manner. In this respect, it is fair to say that the practice of the Court is mixed: unless there is a very urgent need (for example, in the *Jadhav Case*, where there was an issue as to the potential application of the death penalty, measures were ordered within ten days of the request, after a one-day hearing), recent orders tend to have been made around two months after the request is filed.[58] Considering that the Court usually provides for written observations of the respondent and then must convene a hearing, this does not seem overly long, and the Court clearly gives priority to provisional measures requests, consistently with its Rules.

IV Preliminary Objections

The Court's procedure for addressing preliminary objections continues to evolve.[59] The initial set of rules of its predecessor, the PCIJ, made no provision in this regard,[60] but the rules have since developed, with the latest set of amendments made in October 2019.

---

[57] See discussion in S. Wordsworth and K. Parlett, Chapter 13, Effective Advocacy.

[58] The first provisional-measures request in *Certain Activities* is something of an outlier: it took nearly four months from request to order: *Certain Activities Carried Out by Nicaragua in the Border Area (Costa Rica* v. *Nicaragua), Provisional Measures, Order of 8 March 2011, ICJ Reports 2011*.

[59] On the Court's jurisdiction, see J.-M. Thouvenin, Chapter 6, Jurisdiction.

[60] See Rules of the PCIJ dated 1922 available at www.icj-cij.org/files/permanent-court-of-international-justice/serie_D/D_01.pdf. For a historical overview, see the Separate Opinion

Pursuant to those most recent changes, Article 79 is now reorganised into three separate Articles: Article 79, Article 79*bis* and Article 79*ter*. The purpose of this reorganisation is to distinguish between on the one hand where the Court has raised *proprio motu* a 'preliminary question' concerning its jurisdiction or the admissibility of the application, and on the other hand where a 'preliminary objection' is raised by a party to the case.[61] More generally, it can be inferred that these amendments reflect the Court's concern to be a modern institution that promotes the efficiency of proceedings[62] and responds to the requirements of its users (who continue to invoke preliminary objections frequently).[63] Clearly a streamlined process to address bona fide[64] jurisdictional objections (with the potential that the proceedings are then terminated at an early stage of proceedings) is desirable, ensuring the burden of full proceedings is not imposed on a party that has a valid objection to the court hearing the matter in the first place.[65]

---

of Judge Shahabuddeen dated 13 December 1989 at p. 146 following in *Aerial Incident of 3 July 1988 (Islamic Republic of Iran v. United States of America)*.

[61] See press release issued by the Court on 21 October 2019, available at www.icj-cij.org/files/press-releases/0/000-20191021-PRE-01-00-EN.pdf and see also President Yusuf's speech at the 74th session of the UNGA dated 30 October 2019 at p. 7, available at www.icj-cij.org/files/press-releases/0/000-20191030-STA-01-00-EN.pdf .

[62] See Practice Direction V referred to below.

[63] As noted in the ICJ Handbook at p. 62, available at www.icj-cij.org/files/publications/handbook-of-the-court-en.pdf. For recent examples see *Maritime Delimitation in the Indian Ocean (Somalia v. Kenya), Application of the International Convention for the Suppression of the Financing of Terrorism and of the International Convention on the Elimination of All Forms of Racial Discrimination (Ukraine v. Russian Federation)* and *Certain Iranian Assets (Islamic Republic of Iran v. United States of America)* (the objecting parties being Kenya, Russia and USA respectively). It has been observed that out of the 132 contentious cases filed as at December 2018 by application in the docket of the Court, parties have raised preliminary objections in no less than forty-seven of those cases (P d'Argent, 'Preliminary Objections: International Court of Justice (ICJ)', MPEPIL (2019)).

[64] If the preliminary objections are not upheld, the proceedings may end up being longer and more costly. See in the context of international arbitral proceedings, L. Greenwood, 'Revisiting Bifurcation and Efficiency in International Arbitration Proceedings' (2019) 36 *Journal of International Arbitration* 421 at p. 426. In respect of increased costs and delays caused by incidental proceedings at the ICJ, see Miron, 'The Working Methods of the Court', p. 388; and A. Miron, 'La coût la justice internationale. Enquête sur les aspects financiers du contentious interétatique' LX *Annuaire français du droit international* (2014) 18.

[65] *Appeal Relating to the Jurisdiction of the ICAO Council, Judgment, ICJ Reports 1972*, p. 46 para. 18 noting a State 'should not have to give an account of itself on issues of merits

Accordingly, Article 79 deals exclusively with preliminary questions identified by the Court, providing that following the submission of the application the Court may decide that questions concerning its jurisdiction or the admissibility of the application shall be determined separately (Article 79(1)) and that the 'parties shall submit pleadings concerning jurisdiction or admissibility within the time-limits fixed, and in the order determined, by the Court' (Article 79(2)). A recent example is *Arbitral Award of 3 October 1899 (Guyana v. Venezuela)* where, at the meeting with the Parties, the Vice-President of Venezuela made clear Venezuela's position that the Court manifestly lacks jurisdiction and that it would not take part in the proceedings. The Court accordingly decided that pursuant to Article 79(2) 'it must resolve first of all the question of the Court's jurisdiction, and that this question should accordingly be separately determined before any proceedings on the merits'.[66]

Article 79*bis* addresses preliminary objections, that is, where the Court has not exercised its case management powers to make a decision under Article 79 and there is an objection by a party to the jurisdiction of the Court or to the admissibility of the application, or other objection on which a decision is requested before any further proceedings on the merits. If the objection is raised by 'a party other than the respondent',[67] the objection(s) must be filed within the time-limit fixed for the delivery of that party's first pleading. If the party making the objection(s) is the respondent (which is obviously much more likely and common) it 'shall be made in writing as soon as possible, and not later than three months after the delivery of the Memorial', reflecting an amendment to the time limit made in 2001.[68] The previous 1978 Rules had provided that such objections should be made within the time limit fixed for the delivery of the Counter-Memorial, which led to undue delay and a perceived 'free ride' for the Respondent.[69]

---

before a tribunal which lacks jurisdiction in the matter, or whose jurisdiction has not yet been established'.

[66] *Arbitral Award of 3 October 1899 (Guyana v. Venezuela)*, Order of 19 June 2018, ICJ *Reports 2018*, p. 402.

[67] See e.g., *Case of the monetary gold removed from Rome in 1943 (Preliminary Question)*, *Judgment of June 15th 1954: ICJ Reports 1954*, at p. 22 where Italy (the applicant) raised the preliminary question.

[68] Adopted by the Court on 5 December 2000 and entered into force on 1 February 2001.

[69] See further the ILA, Procedure of International Courts and Tribunals, Interim Report, 1 May 2018 (corrected 12 August 2018), p. 25 and noting a moderate shortening of the duration

The timetable set out in Article 79*bis* can be contrasted with the approach adopted in the ITLOS Rules (Article 97) where objections must be filed within ninety days of the institution of proceedings. The obvious downside to this alternative process is that objections must be filed *before* the non-objecting party has developed its case in a Memorial. Such an approach is arguably feasible given that preliminary objections are necessarily focused on legal rather than factual grounds, and the application must 'specify as far as possible the legal grounds upon which the jurisdiction of the Court is said to be based … the precise nature of the claim, together with a succinct statement of the facts and grounds on which the claim is based'.[70] Further, as in the ITLOS Rules, express provision can be made for further sets of written observations.[71] In practice, however, the application may not provide sufficient detail,[72] objections may have fact-specific elements, and there is a risk that further preliminary objections are raised after receipt of the Memorial.

Returning to the timetable set out in Article 79*bis*, there will be practical and strategic considerations in determining when to make an objection, specifically whether to submit prior to the ultimate deadline of three months after the delivery of the Memorial.[73]

In favour of an earlier filing, there may be a clean dispositive objection that can be launched shortly after the application instituting proceedings is submitted with a view to minimising expenditure of resources and

---

of written phases in preliminary objections cases as a result of the amendment (available at www.ila-hq.org/images/ILA/DraftReports/DraftReport_InternationalCourts.pdf).

[70] ICJ Rules, Article 38.

[71] See recently, *Dispute concerning delimitation of the maritime boundary between Mauritius and Maldives in the Indian Ocean (Mauritius/Maldives)* Case No. 28.

[72] S. Rosenne, *Procedure in the International Court: A Commentary on the 1978 Rules of the International Court of Justice* (Martinus Nijhoff, 1983), p. 161: 'As is well known, and as is maintained in this paragraph, the Court's practice is only to take formal preliminary objections by the respondent after the merits have been laid before it in a pleading, normally the memorial, and it will be rare that the application alone will be sufficient to elucidate questions of jurisdiction or admissibility'.

[73] The approach taken in recent cases is to wait until the last possible moment: see *Maritime Delimitation in the Indian Ocean (Somalia v. Kenya), Application of the International Convention for the Suppression of the Financing of Terrorism and of the International Convention on the Elimination of All Forms of Racial Discrimination (Ukraine v. Russian Federation) – Preliminary objections, Certain Iranian Assets (Islamic Republic of Iran v. United States of America)* where the objecting parties (Kenya, Russia and USA respectively) filed preliminary objections three months after receipt of the applicant's Memorial.

shutting down the case as efficiently as possible, and, as noted above, crafting objections based only on the application is sometimes feasible in practice.

On the other hand awaiting the delivery of the Memorial provides the objecting party: (1) with a more detailed understanding of the applicant's case (including a more precise formulation of its claim and the supporting documents upon which they rely)[74] ensuring that its preliminary objections are as comprehensive and targeted as possible; (2) with additional time to prepare the anticipated objections; and (3) with the potential tactical advantage of being able to prepare its Counter-Memorial on the merits while litigating the preliminary objections.[75]

Once the preliminary objection has been received by the Registry, the proceedings on the merits shall be suspended (Article 79*bis*(3)). If a party fails to avail itself of the Article 79 procedure it forfeits the right to bring about a suspension of the proceedings on the merits, but it can still raise the objection(s) in its Counter-Memorial and argue the objection(s) along with the merits.[76] Reflecting the foundational principle of party consent, the Court is mandated to give effect to any agreement between the parties that an objection submitted under

---

[74] It is well-established in the Court's jurisprudence that the parties to a case cannot in the course of proceedings 'transform the dispute brought before the Court into a dispute that would be of a different nature' (see e.g., *Oil Platforms (Islamic Republic of Iran v. United States of America), Judgment, IC J Reports 2003*, para. 117; *Ahmadou Sadio Diallo (Republic of Guinea v. Democratic Republic of the Congo), Merits, Judgment, ICJ Reports 2010*, p. 639 at para. 44), but clearly the Memorial will provide a more particularised statement of the applicant's case. See further Eduardo Jiménez de Aréchaga (then President of the Court), 'The Amendments to the Rules of Procedure of the International Court of Justice', 67 (1973) *AJIL* 19 commenting that 'it was felt that a Respondent had a right to wait for the full development of the Applicant's case in the Memorial before being obliged to file its objection'.

[75] On this latter point see the ILA, Procedure of International Courts and Tribunals, Interim Report, 1 May 2018 (corrected 12 August 2018), p. 25 (link provided above). The point does not appear to be referred to in the 2020 Final Report.

[76] *Avena and Other Mexican Nationals (Mexico v. United States of America), Judgment, ICJ Reports 2004*, p. 28, para. 24. See *Whaling in the Antarctic (Australia v. Japan: New Zealand intervening), Judgment, ICJ Reports 2014*, p. 226 at paras. 30–41 where the Court first considered its jurisdiction, before addressing the merits. If the respondent fails to raise the objections in its counter-memorial, it may be deemed to have acquiesced in the jurisdiction of the Court (see *Appeal Relating to the Jurisdiction of the ICAO Council, Judgment, ICJ Reports 1972*, p. 46 para. 13).

Article 79(1) be heard and determined within the framework of the merits (Article 79*bis*(4)).[77]

The Court then fixes a time-limit fixed for the presentation by the other party of a written statement of its observations and submissions (Article 79*bis*(3)). Practice Direction V provides that this time limit 'shall generally not exceed four months from the date of the filing of the preliminary objections', expressly acknowledging the Court's newly invigorated objective of 'accelerating proceedings on preliminary objections'.

Article 79*ter* concerns general procedural issues applicable to both Article 77 and 79*bis*, noting that (1) following the written phases outlined above, unless otherwise decided by the Court, the further proceedings shall be oral (Article 79*ter*(2)), and (2) the Court, whenever necessary, may request the parties to argue all questions of law and fact, and to adduce all evidence, which bear on the preliminary questions or objections (Article 79*ter*(3)).

The options open to the Court are to then (1) uphold the preliminary objection (2) reject the preliminary objection or (3) decide that the question or objection does not possess an exclusively preliminary character (Article 79*ter*(4)).[78] Of course, where more than one preliminary objection is raised, the options are not mutually exclusive; in the recent case of *Certain Iranian Assets (Islamic Republic of Iran* v. *United States of America)*, the Court rejected three of the five preliminary objections raised by the United States, upheld one and found that one did not possess an exclusively preliminary character, resulting in the case proceeding to the merits, at least in part.[79]

---

[77] For an example of such an agreement following the submission of the Counter-Memorial see *East Timor (Portugal* v. *Australia), Judgment, ICJ Reports 1995*, p. 90 para. 4.

[78] See further the 'Resolution concerning the Internal Judicial Practice of the Court' 1976 available at www.icj-cij.org/en/other-texts/resolution-concerning-judicial-practice.

[79] *Certain Iranian Assets (Islamic Republic of Iran* v. *United States of America), Preliminary Objections, Judgment, ICJ Reports 2019*, p. 7. See also *Application of the International Convention on the Elimination of all Forms of Racial Discrimination (Qatar* v. *UAE), Preliminary Objections, Judgment, ICJ Reports* 2021, p. 109, para. 114 concluding that the first preliminary objection raised by the UAE must be upheld and that it was not therefore necessary to examine the second preliminary objection raised by the UAE.

V Intervention

The mechanism by which a third State may elect[80] to intervene in contentious proceedings is two-fold.[81] First, where a State considers it has an interest of a legal nature which may be affected by the decision in the case, it may submit a *request* to be allowed to intervene and the Court shall decide whether or not the State can intervene (Statute, Article 62), with Article 81 of the Court's Rules setting out the formalities that must[82] be complied with. Second, where the construction of a convention is in question, and States other than the parties to the case are parties to the convention, the Registrar notifies all such States and every State so notified has the *right* to intervene in the proceedings (Statute, Article 63), with Article 43 of the Court's Rules addressing the notification process and Article 82 providing details[83] as to the

---

[80] There is no system of compulsory intervention (*Continental Shelf (Libyan Arab Jamahiriya/ Malta), Application to Intervene, Judgment, ICJ Reports 1984*, p. 3.at para. 40), although the Court can encourage an intervention (see *Land and Maritime Boundary between Cameroon and Nigeria, Preliminary Objections, Judgment, ICJ Reports 1998*, p. 275 para. 116).

[81] There are other mechanisms for engagement of third parties in a contentious case, notably: (1) the Court may 'take note of' the information supplied by the unsuccessful intervenor (see *Territorial and Maritime Dispute (Nicaragua v. Colombia), Application of Costa Rica for Permission to Intervene), ICJ Reports 2011*, p. 363, para. 51); (2) a State may ask to be furnished with copies of pleadings and documents annexed (Rules, Article 53); (3) a public international organisation may be requested to provide information and, where the construction of the constituent instrument of a public international organisation or of an international convention adopted thereunder is in question in a case before the Court, it shall be notified (Statute, Article 34); (4) the Court may entrust any individual, body, bureau, commission, or other organisation that it may select, with the task of carrying out an enquiry or giving an expert opinion (Statute, Article 50); (5) States may informally convey information (see non-appearance section below). The position of the third States is further protected by (a) the scope of Article 59 (*Land and Maritime Boundary between Cameroon and Nigeria (Cameroon v. Nigeria: Equatorial Guinea intervening), Judgment, ICJ Reports 2002*, p. 303, para. 238; Dissenting Opinion of Judge Jennings at para. 34 in *Continental Shelf, Malta/Libya Italy's Request to Intervene, 1984*); (b) application of the 'Monetary Gold principle'; and (c) the Court ensuring that its decision does not affect their interests (*Land and Maritime Boundary between Cameroon and Nigeria (Cameroon v. Nigeria: Equatorial Guinea intervening), Judgment, ICJ Reports 2002*, p. 303, para. 238). As to *amicus curiae*, see below.

[82] *Territorial and Maritime Dispute (Nicaragua v. Colombia), Application for Permission to Intervene, Judgment, ICJ Reports 2011*, p. 348 at para. 25.

[83] Notably, (a) particulars of the basis on which the declarant State considers itself a party to the convention; (b) identification of the particular provisions of the convention the construction of which it considers to be in question; (c) a statement of the construction

declaration that must[84] be filed by the party exercising its right to intervene.

Despite previous high hopes,[85] neither Article 62[86] nor Article 63[87] have been successfully invoked much in practice; and there are currently two competing trends which make predictions as to whether that will change difficult.

On the one hand, there is the busy docket of the Court[88] (including relatively recent examples of intervention)[89] arguably reflecting a 'growing complexity of issues in contemporary international disputes'[90] and a broader engagement with matters such as environmental protection (see for example, New Zealand's intervention in the *Whaling* case to which there was no formal objection).

---

of those provisions for which it contends; (d) a list of the documents in support, which documents shall be attached.

[84] *Whaling in the Antarctic (Australia v. Japan), Declaration of Intervention of New Zealand, Order of 6 February 2013, ICJ Reports 2013*, p. 3, para. 8.

[85] For a historical overview of the development of the relevant provisions on intervention, see A. Miron and C. Chinkin, 'Article 62' in A. Zimmerman et al. (eds.), *The Statute of the International Court of Justice: A Commentary* (3rd ed., 2019), paras. 4–10 and 25–37; and A. Miron and C. Chinkin, 'Article 63' in A. Zimmerman et al. (eds.), *The Statute of the International Court of Justice: A Commentary* (3rd ed., 2019), paras. 3–7; M. Papadaki, 'Intervention: ICJ' (MPEPIL, 2018), paras. 4–8; M. N. Shaw, *Rosenne's Law and Practice of the International Court: 1920–2015* (2016), pp. 1491–1496.

[86] See Nicaragua's request in *Land, Island and Maritime Frontier Dispute* case, Equatorial Guinea in *Land and Maritime Boundary* case, and Greece in the *Jurisdictional Immunities of the State* case).

[87] See Poland in the *Case of SS Wimbledon*; Cuba in *Haya de la Torre*; and New Zealand in *Whaling in the Antarctic*.

[88] '[T]he confidence of States in the work of the Court has been steadily increasing in the last decade. Today, we have sixteen cases pending before the Court. These cases involve twenty-six nations from all parts of the world': President Yusuf, Statement dated October 2019 at the London Law Conference 2019 available at www.icj-cij.org/files/press-releases/0/000-20191003-STA-01-00-EN.pdf.

[89] See Separate Opinion of Judge Cançado Trindade in *Whaling in the Antarctic (Australia v. Japan: New Zealand intervening)*, para. 64: 'The ICJ's decision contained in the present Order in the case concerning Whaling in the Antarctic is significant: looking back in time, we may well be witnessing lately the resurrection of intervention in contemporary judicial proceedings before the ICJ'.

[90] *Territorial and Maritime Dispute (Nicaragua v. Colombia), Application for Permission to Intervene, Judgment, ICJ Reports 2011*, p. 348, Joint Dissenting Opinion of Judges Cançado Trindade and Yusuf at para. 27.

On the other hand, there is the 'disquieting return to unilateralism in world affairs'.[91] Coupled with the practical reality that as long as the relevant Articles of the Statute remain riddled with ambiguities resulting in uncertainty,[92] the Court is perceived as taking a restrictive approach on the topic,[93] and States consider that their interests are best served by keeping their 'powder dry',[94] the prospects of any significant increased use seem slim. It can also be queried whether such increased use would necessarily be a good thing, noting the potential for political posturing. One commentator has noted that the greater likelihood of third States intervening 'might further discourage states from litigating because of the uncertainty [the proposal] could introduce into the proceedings'.[95]

Despite the limited opportunities offered to the Court to develop its jurisprudence, there are examples where welcome clarification has been provided.

With respect to Article 62, for example, it has clarified (1) the requirements with respect to establishing a jurisdictional link[96] (although its comments in this regard have arguably created yet further scope for

---

[91] President Yusuf, Statement dated October 2019 at the London Law Conference 2019 (link provided above). See also J. Crawford, *Brownlie's Principles of Public International Law* (Oxford University Press, 2019), p. 716 referring to a growing rejection of international adjudication.

[92] *Continental Shelf (Tunisia/Libyan), Application to Intervene, Judgment, ICJ Reports 1981*, p. 3 para. 23; Separate Opinion of Judge Weeramantry at para. 2 in *Sovereignty over Pulau Ligitan und Pulau Sipudan (Indonesia/Malaysia, Application for Permission to Intervene, Judgment, ICJ Reports 2001*, p. 575; M. N. Shaw, *Rosenne's Law and Practice of the International Court: 1920–2015* (2016), p. 1497 noting Article 62 features an 'imposing array of obscurities, ambiguities and lack of concordance between the two language versions of the Statute' and at p. 1500 noting 'the difficulties of Article 63 are no less complex'.

[93] See e.g., M. N. Shaw, *International Law* (8th ed., Oxford University Press, 2017), p. 836; Miron and Chinkin, 'Article 62', para. 143.

[94] Cf *Whaling in the Antarctic (Australia* v. *Japan), Declaration of Intervention of New Zealand, Order of 6 February 2013, ICJ Reports 2013*, p. 3 para. 20 noting that by exercising its right to intervention, New Zealand became bound by the construction of the convention given in its judgment.

[95] I. Scobbie, '"All right, Mr DeMille, I'm ready for my close-up": Some Critical Reflections on Professor Cassese's "The International Court of Justice: It is High Time to Restyle the Respected Old Lady"' 23 *EJIL* (2012) 1071, p. 1078. Miron and Chinkin, 'Article 62', para. 145.

[96] See Judge Abraham (then President of the Court) speech before the sixth committee of the UNGA: www.icj-cij.org/files/press-releases/0/000-20171027-PRE-01-00-EN.pdf; M Papadaki, 'Intervention: ICJ' (MPEPIL, 2018), paras. 26–27 and 41–42.

confusion)[97] (2) the object of an intervention, namely as 'preventive' to protect a State's interest of a legal nature and not to 'tack on a new case'[98] (3) the meaning of an 'interest of a legal nature which may be affected by the decision in the case'.[99]

An example with respect to Article 63 is confirmation as to the limited scope of the intervention and that the intervenor does not become a party to the proceedings: in the *Whaling* case, Japan's judge raised concerns regarding the equality of the parties given that, in addition to Australia's judge ad hoc, there was already a New Zealand judge on the court,[100] but the Court rejected these concerns, noting New Zealand was not a party.[101]

However, there remain many areas ripe for innovation.[102] Five examples are as follows.

First, the timing for make an application under Article 62 (currently 'not later than the closure of the written proceedings'[103]) and Article 63 (currently 'not later than the date fixed for the opening of the oral proceedings'[104]), both with the possibility in 'exceptional circumstances' to be submitted at an even later date, pose potential practical difficulties

---

[97] See e.g., Miron and Chinkin, 'Article 62', para. 144.

[98] *Land, Island and Maritime Frontier Dispute (El Salvador/Honduras), Application to Intervene, Judgment, ICJ Reports 1990*, p. 92 para. 97; *Sovereignty over Pulau Ligitan und Pulau Sipadan (Indonesia/Malaysia), Application for Permission to Intervene, Judgment, ICJ Reports 2001*, p. 575 para. 53; *Territorial and Maritime Dispute (Nicaragua v. Colombia), Application for Permission to Intervene, Judgment, ICJ Reports 2011*, p. 348 at para. 27; *Territorial and Maritime Dispute (Nicaragua v. Colombia); Application for Permission to Intervene, Judgment, ICJ Reports 2011*, p. 420 at para. 47; *Jurisdictional Immunities of the State (Germany v. Italy), Application for Permission to Intervene, Order of 4 July 2011, ICJ Reports 2011*, p. 494 paras. 28–29.

[99] *Territorial and Maritime Dispute, Nicaragua v. Colombia, Honduras's Application 2011*, at para. 37; *Jurisdictional Immunities, Germany v. Italy*, Greece's Application, 2011, at para. 24; *Pulau Ligitan and Pulau Sipadan, Indonesia/Malaysia*, Philippine's Application, 2001 at para. 83. See further M. Papadaki, 'Intervention: ICJ' (MPEPIL, 2018) paras. 37–38; Zimmermann et al., *The Statute of the International Court of Justice: A Commentary* (3rd ed., 2019), Ch III, Article 62 at paras. 45–71.

[100] Referring to Article 31(5) of the Statute and Article 36(1) of the Rules.

[101] *Whaling in the Antarctic (Australia v. Japan), Declaration of Intervention of New Zealand, Order of 6 February 2013, ICJ Reports 2013*, p. 3 para. 21. C.f., Declaration of Judge Owada at paras. 3–5.

[102] See Judge Donoghue's comments in her dissenting opinion (paras. 35 and 59) in *Territorial and Maritime Dispute (Nicaragua v. Colombia), Application for Permission to Intervene, Judgment, ICJ Reports 2011*; ILA, Procedure of International Courts and Tribunals, Final Report, 1 May 2020, pp. 18–22.

[103] Rules, Article 81.   [104] Rules, Article 82.

for the intervener (notably its ability to know when written proceedings are indeed closed) and the parties (notably their ability to take a third party's submissions into account and respond effectively).[105] A possible solution would be to amend the Rules to provide for an earlier deadline, for example, after the submission of the first round of pleadings.[106]

Second, clarification could be provided as to the relationship between the provisions on intervention and that of joinder of a State as a new party (which is addressed in the Rules at Article 47, but which is treated as a form of intervention under Article 62 of the Statute).[107]

Third, the Court could confirm that the right to intervene can be exercised in incidental proceedings.[108]

Fourth, consideration should be given as to whether the intervenor should have a right to access to the pleadings *prior* to its application being determined. Article 53 of the Rules states that pleadings and documents annexed shall be made available to a State 'entitled to appear before it'. But to be of any utility in formulating the application to intervene, the State requires access *prior* to a determination of its entitlement to intervene,[109] and it is unsatisfactory that early sight of papers appears to depend on the parties' consent.[110] Clearly a tension arises here in light of the parties' competing right to confidentiality.

Finally, and more generally, there is no provision for third States (or non-State actors) to participate as *amicus curiae*, that is, to provide information with respect to issues of general interest.[111] Rather than seek to

---

[105] *Sovereignty over Pulau Ligitan und Pulau Sipadan (Indonesia/Malaysia), Application for Permission to Intervene, Judgment, ICJ Reports 2001*, p. 575 at paras. 21–25.

[106] See further ILA, Procedure of International Courts and Tribunals, Final Report, 1 May 2020, p. 18.

[107] See further ILA, Procedure of International Courts and Tribunals, Final Report, 1 May 2020, pp. 17–18.

[108] See Miron and Chinkin, 'Article 62', paras. 19–24; see M. N. Shaw, *Rosenne's Law and Practice of the International Court: 1920–2015* (2016) 1534.

[109] See the comments of Judge Schwebel at p. 35 of his Separate Opinion in *Continental Shelf (Tunisia/ Libyan Arab Jamahiriya), Application to Intervene, Judgment, ICJ Reports 1981*, p. 3. See also *Sovereignty over Pulau Ligitan und Pulau Sipadan (Indonesia/Malaysia), Application for Permission to Intervene, Judgment, ICJ Reports 2001*, p. 575 at para. 22.

[110] *Continental Shelf (Libyan Arab Jamahiriya /Malta), Application to Intervene, Judgment, ICJ Reports 1984*, p. 3, para. 4.

[111] C.f. above referring to the power of the Court to request information of public international organisations pursuant to Article 34 of the Court's statute. See generally, P. Sands and R. Mackenzie 'International Courts and Tribunals, Amicus Curiae' MPEPIL (2008).

lower the threshold of the 'legal interest' under Article 62, or tinker with Article 34 of the Rules, it might be preferable to create a separate procedural mechanism, for example for the submission of written briefs.[112]

VI Non-appearance

The scenario of a non-appearing party before the Court is no mere remote theoretical problem; there are many instances where this occurred prior to 1995 (either throughout proceedings or at certain phases of proceedings),[113] and there are indicators that it may be back on the rise, noting the recent non-appearances in inter-State litigation: Kenya,[114] Venezuela[115] and Pakistan[116] before the ICJ, Russia before ITLOS,[117] and Croatia[118] and China[119] in separate

---

[112] See further ILA, Procedure of International Courts and Tribunals, Final Report, 1 May 2020, p. 20.

[113] In chronological ascending order: *Corfu Channel (United Kingdom of Great Britain and Northern Ireland* v. *Albania) Judgment of December 15th,1949 ICJ Reports 1949* at p. 247; *Anglo-Iranian Oil Co. Case (United Kingdom/Iran), Order of July 5th, 1951: ICJ Reports 1951*, at p. 92; *Nottebohm case (Preliminary Objections), Judgment of November 18th, 1953: ICJ Reports 1953*, p. 117; *Trial of Pakistani Prisoners of War* (Pakistan/ India), Order of 13 July 1973 ICJ Reports 1973 paras. 7–9; *Fisheries Jurisdiction (UK* v. *Iceland), ICJ Reports 1974*; *Nuclear Tests Cases, Judgment, ICJ Reports 1974*; *Aegean Sea Continental Shelf, Judgment, ICJ Reports 1978*; *United States Diplomatic and Consular Staff in Tehran Judgment, ICJ Reports 1980*; *Case concerning Military and Paramilitary Activities in and against Nicaragua* (Nicaragua/United States of America) *Merits Judgment. ICJ Reports 1986* para. 26; *Maritime Delimitation and Territorial Questions case* (Qatar/Bahrain) *Jurisdiction and Admissibility, Judgment, ICJ Reports 1995* at pp.10–11; *Arbitral Award of 3 October 1899 (Guyana* v. *Venezuela).*

[114] *Maritime Delimitation in the Indian Ocean (Somalia* v. *Kenya)* (at the oral proceedings held in March 2021). For a helpful overview of the various twists and turns on this case, see A. Zimmermann, 'To Appear or Not to Appear This Was the Question', EJIL: Talk!, 29 March 2021.

[115] *Arbitral Award of 3 October 1899 (Guyana* v. *Venezuela).*

[116] *Obligations concerning Negotiations relating to Cessation of the Nuclear Arms Race and to Nuclear Disarmament (Marshall Islands* v. *Pakistan), Jurisdiction and Admissibility, Judgment, ICJ Reports 2016* para. 28. This was on the basis that its participation in the oral proceedings would not 'add anything to what has already been submitted through its Counter-Memorial'.

[117] *Case concerning the detention of three Ukrainian naval vessels (Ukraine* v. *Russian Federation)*, Provisional Measures ITLOS Case No. 26.

[118] *Arbitration between the Republic of Croatia and the Republic of Sloven*ia PCA Case No. 2012-04, Final Award dated 29 June 2017 at para. 196.

[119] *The South China Sea Arbitration (The Republic of Philippines* v. *The People's Republic of China)* PCA Case No. 2013-19, Award dated 12 July 2016 at para. 116.

PCA arbitral proceedings, perhaps reflecting a more general trend towards rejection of international adjudication.[120]

In terms of the Court's governing instruments, only Article 53 of the ICJ Statute provides express guidance in the event of a non-appearing party,[121] be it the applicant or the respondent,[122] and be it at any phase[123] of contentious[124] proceedings. Article 53 provides that where 'one of the parties does not appear before the Court, or fails to defend its case, the other party may call upon the Court to decide in favour of its claim'. In those circumstances the Court must first satisfy itself that it has jurisdiction[125] in accordance with Articles 36 and 37, and second that the claim is 'well founded in fact and law'.

As to whether the claim is well-founded in *law*, the Court has commented it must 'attain the same degree of certainty as in any other case that the claim of the party appearing is sound in law ... the principle *jura novit curia* signifies that the Court is not solely dependent on the argument of the parties before it with respect to the applicable law, so that the absence of one party has less impact ...'.[126]

---

[120] The position of the USA in *Case concerning Relocation of the United States Embassy to Jerusalem (Palestine v. United States of America)*, is yet to be formally confirmed: see Order of 15 November 2018, ICJ Reports 2018, p. 709 (noting the USA had not appointed an agent and considered the case ought to be removed from the List).

[121] Once an application has been filed pursuant to Art. 40 of the Rules of Court, the named State is a 'party' to a case. The exception would be if the applicant State proposes to found the jurisdiction of the Court upon a consent thereto yet to be given or manifested by the State against which such application is made (see Art. 38(5) of the Rules of Court).

[122] Whilst it is clearly more likely that the Respondent would not appear, Article 53 addresses either party's non-appearance. See further Zimmermann, 'Article 53' in 'The Statute of the International Court of Justice: A Commentary' (2nd ed.), Chapter III, para. 5 (p. 1327).

[123] Whilst there has been some debate about the scope of Article 53 *ratione materiae*, it is clear from the underlying rationale of Article 53 and the Court's practice that, in addition to the merits phase of proceedings, Article 53 applies to non-appearance in incidental proceedings (preliminary objections, and interpretation and revision proceedings). See further Zimmermann, 'The Statute of the International Court of Justice: A Commentary' (2nd ed.), Chapter III, para. 6 and 32–48; M. Goldmann, 'International Courts and Tribunals, Non-Appearance', MPEPIL (2006) at paras. 9–10.

[124] Article 53 does not apply to advisory opinions, as to which see *Legal Consequences of the Construction of a Wall in the Occupied Palestinian Territory, Advisory Opinion, ICJ Reports 2004* paras. 55–56. See further, the Declaration of Judge Buergenthal at para. 10 and the Separate Opinion of Judge Owada, at paras. 20–21.

[125] In provisional measures it is prima facie jurisdiction that must be established. A finding on jurisdiction would include a determination of admissibility: see e.g., the *Nuclear Tests cases*.

[126] *Military and Paramilitary Activities in and against Nicaragua (Nicaragua v. United States of America). Merits, Judgment. ICJ Reports 1986*, p. 14 para. 29. See also *Fisheries Jurisdiction (UK v. Iceland), ICJ Reports 1974*, para. 17.

The *facts* are more problematic. Whilst the Court has stated it is 'especially incumbent upon the Court to satisfy itself that it is in possession of all the available facts',[127] the question arises as to how it is to achieve that, and what is implied by the caveat of 'available'. A key issue in practice is that the non-appearing party does not have the opportunity to present its full factual evidence on the case through – depending on which phase(s) it is absent – written and/or oral submissions, with the consequential risk that the Court may make its decision without having before it all the relevant and material documents.

This potential hole in the factual landscape is compounded by two additional factors.[128] First, the lack of any clear rules governing the disclosure obligations of the parties. Second, the fact individuals appearing before the Court are not subject under international law to any compulsory code of conduct which would guide them in navigating issues of professional ethics including with respect to disclosure of evidence.

Whilst one might adopt the somewhat resigned tone of the Court in the *Nicaragua* case that non-appearance 'obviously has a negative impact on the sound administration of justice' and the 'Court cannot by its own enquiries entirely make up for the absence of one of the Parties ... [it] must necessarily limit the extent to which the Court is informed of the facts',[129] the challenge is clearly to develop mechanisms to address this potential evidential deficiency.

The Court has already used some tools at its disposal, notably the use of independent experts[130] and information in the public domain.[131] There are

---

[127] *Military and Paramilitary Activities in and against Nicaragua (Nicaragua* v. *United States of America), Merits, Judgment. ICJ Reports 1986*, p. 14 para. 30.

[128] See further K. Parlett and A. Sander 'Into the Void: A Counsel Perspective on the Need to Articulate Rules Concerning Disclosure before the ICJ', 113 *AJIL Unbound* (2019) 302.

[129] *Military and Paramilitary Activities in and against Nicaragua (Nicaragua* v. *United States of America). Merits, Judgment. ICJ Reports 1986*, paras. 27 and 30. See also *Arbitral Award of 3 October 1899 (Guyana* v. *Venezuela)*, para. 25. See also Simma et al., 'The Charter of the United Nations: A Commentary', Volume II (3rd ed.) Ch XIV para. 116: 'the non-appearing State bears the risk of a judgment delivered on the basis of incomplete evidence'.

[130] The Court's Statute, Article 50; see *Military and Paramilitary Activities in and against Nicaragua (Nicaragua* v. *United States of America). Merits, Judgment. ICJ Reports 1986*, p. 14 para. 61; *Corfu Channel Case, Judgment of December 15th 1949, ICJ Reports 1949* p. 244 at 248.

[131] *United States Diplomatic and Consular Staff in Tehran, Judgment, ICJ Reports 1980*, para. 12; *Military and Paramilitary Activities in and against Nicaragua (Nicaragua* v. *United States of America). Merits, Judgment. ICJ Reports 1986*, p. 14 para. 63.

also examples where the non-appearing party has indirectly or informally provided its position on relevant issues;[132] recent examples in inter-State litigation include the Memorandum submitted by Venezuela in *Arbitral Award of 3 October 1899 (Guyana v. Venezuela)*,[133] the Memorandum submitted by Russia in *Case concerning the detention of three Ukrainian naval vessels (Ukraine v. Russian Federation)*[134] and the statements including a Position Paper submitted by China in the *South China Sea Arbitration*.[135] In terms of the utility of information provided in this way,[136] it can cut both ways, both from the perspective of assisting the Court and the appearing party, as well as protecting the position of the non-appearing party. For example, it may be characterised as a partial presentation of the case by a party not abiding by the same rules of procedure as the appearing party, or as serving as a helpful engagement of the non-appearing party recording what it considers to be the key issues and supporting documents. It is clearly essential that the appearing party be given a full and fair opportunity to comment on any information which the Court takes into account, and an opportunity to present rebuttal evidence.

In addition to setting out clear rules governing the disclosure obligations of the parties and the professional obligations of those appearing before it, another way that the Court could address the potential inadequacies in the evidence before it, is to make greater use of the ability to ask for further information from the parties[137] and to pose specific questions at each stage

---

[132] E.g., *Aegean Sea Continental Shelf, Judgment, ICJ Reports 1978* para. 14; *Case concerning Military and Paramilitary Activities in and against Nicaragua (Nicaragua/United States of America) Merits Judgment. ICJ Reports 1986* para. 31.

[133] *Arbitral Award of 3 October 1899 (Guyana v. Venezuela)*, para. 28. Memorandum available at: www.icj-cij.org/public/files/case-related/171/171-20191128-WRI-01-00-EN.pdf.

[134] Provisional Measures ITLOS Case No. 26, Memorandum available at www.itlos.org/filead min/itlos/documents/cases/case_no_26/Memorandum.pdf.

[135] Award on Jurisdiction and Admissibility, 29 October 2015, para. 10. In *Maritime Delimitation in the Indian Ocean (Somalia v. Kenya)*, Kenya's request to submit a Position Paper was rejected by the Court, with the Court noting the pleadings and volumes of materials already on the case file (CR 2021/2, p. 11).

[136] See e.g., Sir G. Fitzmaurice, 'The Problem of the "Non-appearing" Defendant Government' 51 *BYIL* (1980), pp. 116–18.

[137] See Article 62 of the Rules: 'The Court may at any time call upon the parties to produce such evidence or to give such explanations as the Court may consider to be necessary for the elucidation of any aspect of the matters in issue, or may itself seek other information for this purpose'.

of the proceedings. Establishing this dialogue assists both the parties' understanding of the issues concerning the Court, ensuring the appearing party is not engaging in 'shadow boxing' and that the non-appearing party continues to be given every opportunity to present its position. Such a strategy was foreshadowed some thirty years ago in the 1991 Basle Resolution of the Institut de Droit International on non-appearing States in proceedings before the ICJ (which stated the Court should 'invite argument from the appearing party on specific issues which the Court considers have not been canvassed or have been inadequately canvassed in the written or oral pleadings'),[138] and was an approach adopted by the arbitral tribunal in the *South China Sea* proceedings.[139] It would also align with the Court's evident increasing appetite generally to make use of the facility of posing questions to the parties.

VII Concluding Remarks

With the broad range of cases that come before the Court, the danger of the process becoming overly prescriptive – with rules 'the (uncompromising) master' – cannot be overlooked. Some urge the Court to codify aspects of its practice on procedural issues into generally applicable rules. While this might at first blush appear attractive, given that it gives the parties certainty as to the approach that will be followed, it also has the potential to unduly restrict the way in which the Court addresses cases – each of which may have its own particular procedural needs. On balance, looking back at the way the Court has developed its procedure, particularly through amendments to its rules, adoption and revision of its Practice Directions, the Court has demonstrated an appetite to evolve its procedure to ensure it adapts in a flexible and pragmatic manner to the needs of its users and the objective of ensuring a fair and just outcome, as reflected in the various

[138] At para. 3. Full text available at www.idi-iil.org/app/uploads/2017/06/1991_bal_01_en.pdf.
[139] See its Final Award of 12 July 2016 at paras. 124–125, noting it issued a 'Request for Further Written Argument' containing twenty-six questions pertaining to jurisdiction and the Merits, in advance of the Hearing on Jurisdiction and on the Merits, the Tribunal sent to the Parties lists of specific issues which it wished to be addressed, and during both hearings, the Tribunal circulated lists of questions to be addressed during the second round.

developments outlined above. This is a positive trajectory that it is hoped will continue.

Further Reading

R. Higgins, 'Respecting Sovereign States and Running a Tight Courtroom' 50 *ICLQ* (2001) 121.

C. Miles, *Provisional Measures before International Courts and Tribunals* (Oxford University Press, 2017).

A. Miron, 'The Working Methods of the Court' 7 *JIDS* (2016) 371.

K. Parlett and A. Sander 'Into the void: a counsel perspective on the need to articulate rules concerning disclosure before the ICJ', 113 *AJIL Unbound* (2019) 302.

Effective Advocacy at the ICJ 13

Samuel Wordsworth KC and Kate Parlett

I Introduction

The task of the advocate is to persuade. That task is difficult enough in any setting, but the ICJ presents its own particular and additional challenges given that the bench is comprised of fifteen or more judges with different legal backgrounds and experience. It follows that the advocate will have limited indications as to what the specific concerns of individual judges are likely to be. However, the advocate is not reduced to shooting in the dark, and there are some indications from the Court and its judges as to what does and does not work.

When it comes to written advocacy, the ICJ has been sending out signals for years that it considers the pleadings it receives as overlong and unwieldy while, as to oral advocacy, Sir Christopher Greenwood said in a recent interview: 'I don't think the ICJ is where you see the best of advocacy in international law'.[1] So there is plainly much for all practitioners before the ICJ to work on, although Sir Christopher did also say that, when sitting as a judge, his mind had been changed 180 degrees by oral submissions before the ICJ; so all is not lost.

In this chapter, we focus first on the written and then oral advocacy before the Court, but there are three points which it is useful to identify up front.

This chapter draws up and develops ideas published in the authors' article on 'Advocacy' in the *Max Planck Encyclopedia of International Procedural Law*, 2019. The authors are indebted to Professor Carlos Espósito, Ms Amy Sander and Sir Michael Wood for their helpful comments on an earlier draft. The views expressed herein are the views of the authors alone and are not an expression of the views of other members of the authors' Chambers, nor any of the authors' clients.

[1] Sir Christopher Greenwood KC (former Judge at the ICJ), 18 January 2021, at https://essexcourt.com/sir-christopher-greenwood-qc-interviewed-as-part-of-camarb-series/. His focus here was on the fact that oral advocacy at the ICJ is through a pre-prepared speech.

First, given that the advocate's task is one of persuasion, it is critical to consider the case from the perspective of the judges' side of the bench: to ask what they need to know, to seek to identify what aspects of the case they are going to be most troubled by and to consider how best to address those aspects. As the Court has sought to indicate to practitioners time and again, they neither need nor want undue length and repetition, and the same must apply to lack of clarity and the over-stating of a case.[2]

Second, a leading practitioner (speaking from the perspective of an international arbitrator) has recently referred to 'the invaluable currency of counsel's credibility'.[3] Of course, regardless of the advocate's background, counsel will need to observe high standards of honesty and professional integrity in order to engender the trust of the Court.[4] This point applies regardless of the fact that counsel appearing before the ICJ are not subject to any common set of professional standards or common regulatory procedures.[5] The absence of such common standards and regulations can give rise to different practices and it has been suggested that this threatens the legitimacy of and public confidence in international adjudication.[6] Ultimately individuals acting as counsel will need to

---

[2] For a list of further common flaws, see T. Landau, 'Dysfunctional Deliberations and Effective Advocacy', in A. Menaker (ed.), *International Arbitration and the Rule of Law: Contribution and Conformity, ICCA Congress Series, Volume 19* (Kluwer Law International, 2017) 285, pp. 297–301.

[3] Sir Daniel Bethlehem KC, BIICL ITF Public Conference, Keynote Address, 29 April 2021, www.biicl.org/documents/10698_bethlehem_-_evidence_in_investor-state_arbitration_final.pdf.

[4] A. Watts, 'Enhancing the Effectiveness of Procedures of International Dispute Settlement' 5 (2001) *Max Planck Yearbook of United Nations Law* 21, p. 27; J. Crawford, 'Advocacy before International Tribunals in State-to-State Cases', in D. Bishop and E. G. Kehoe (eds.), *The Art of Advocacy in International Arbitration* (2nd ed., Juris, 2010) 303, p. 330; I. Brownlie, 'The Perspective of International Law from the Bar', in M. Evans, *International Law* (2nd ed., 2003) p. 11, at pp. 13–14; J.-P. Cot, 'Appearing "for" and "on behalf of" a State: The Role of Private Counsel Before International Tribunals', in *Liber Amicorum Judge Shigeru Oda, Volume 2* (Kluwer Law International, 2002) 835, p. 839; M. Longobardo, 'States' Mouthpieces or Independent Practitioners? The Role of Counsel before the ICJ from the Perspective of the Legal Value of Their Oral Pleadings' 20 *The Law and Practice of International Courts and Tribunals* (2021) 54.

[5] See discussion in K. Parlett and A. Sander, 'Into the Void: A Counsel Perspective on the Need to Articulate Rules Concerning Disclosure Before the ICJ' 113 *AJIL Unbound* (2019) 302.

[6] There have thus been initiatives to set out general ethical standards that could apply to counsel appearing before international courts and tribunals, but these have had little direct impact to date. See M. Wood and E. Sthoeger, *'The International Bar'* in C. P. R. Romano,

observe their own personal professional obligations and of course, as noted above, basic standards of honesty and professional integrity.[7]

But the point on counsel's credibility goes further. Given the importance of obtaining the trust and respect of the Court, in particular at the oral phase, the advocate is best advised to be filtering out all the bad or peripheral points – so that the judges know that their time is not being wasted and that they are being directed to the real and difficult issues in the case. Thus the point has been made (in the context of investment treaty arbitration) that

> there is often an inclination on the part of counsel to throw everything they can find against the wall, regardless of the provenance, reliability and weight of the evidence, in the hope that the tribunal will be persuaded by the momentum, volume and patchwork of the materials to adopt the position advanced. While this 'everything into the air' approach – an approach that afflicts both evidence and argument – is perhaps understandable, it is less than ideal, and it is less than persuasive, as poor evidence and argument has the unnerving capacity to infect good evidence and argument.[8]

Third, before turning to written and oral pleadings, it is useful to recall that effective advocacy before the ICJ will encompass the role to be played by counsel in the pre-litigation stage and in early procedural exchanges. Before a case can be commenced before the Court, a claimant State will need to be advised on the jurisdictional basis and the strengths and weaknesses of any claim, as well as the fundamental question whether

---

K. J. Alter and Y. Shany (eds.), *The Oxford Handbook of International Adjudication* (Oxford University Press, 2014), 639, pp. 641–647; A. Sarvarian, *Professional Ethics at the International Bar* (Oxford University Press, 2013); and Working Session of the Study Group on the Practice and Procedure of International Tribunals, 'The Hague Principles on Ethical Standards for Counsel Appearing Before International Courts and Tribunals' in *ILA Report of the Seventy-Fourth Conference (The Hague 2010)* (International Law Association, 2010) pp. 952–960; and J. Crawford, 'The International Law Bar: Essence before Existence?' in J. d'Aspremont et al., *International Law as a Profession* (Cambridge University Press, 2017) 338, pp. 354; A. R. Ziegler and K. R. Jonathan, 'The Legitimacy of Private Lawyers Representing States before International Tribunals' in F. Baetens (ed.), *Legitimacy of Unseen Actors in International Adjudication* (Cambridge University Press, 2019), 544, pp. 560–564.

[7] See J. Crawford, 'The International Law Bar: Essence before Existence?' in J. d'Aspremont et al., *International Law as a Profession* (Cambridge University Press, 2017) 338, pp. 348–350.

[8] Sir Daniel Bethlehem KC, BIICL ITF Public Conference, Keynote Address, 29 April 2021, www.biicl.org/documents/10698_bethlehem_-_evidence_in_investor-state_arbitration_final.pdf.

there is a dispute of a legal character, capable of resolution by the Court (or by another international court or tribunal). If proceedings are to be commenced (including on the basis that there is no reasonable prospect of agreed settlement), consideration will often need to be given to the appointment of a judge ad hoc, and to settlement of the schedule of proceedings, on which the President meets with the parties to discuss their views. Throughout the proceedings, the advocate will continue to advise and to discuss the best way of presenting the client's case with the client, and particularly with the Agent. In this way, the advocate is 'not merely a mouthpiece but rather an active intermediary',[9] and has a dual function of presenting the best case for the client to the Court, whilst also persuading the client as to the most effective way in which to do that.[10]

II Written Pleadings

Before the ICJ, effective advocacy through written pleadings is of ever-increasing importance. This is partly because of pressure to shorten oral hearings.[11] The trend is towards shorter oral hearings: in 1964, in the Second Phase of the *Barcelona Traction* case, the Court devoted sixty-four half days to the merits hearing; whereas since about 2009, it has generally allocated some ten to fifteen half days (usually over the course of two weeks) to a full merits hearing. While it remains essential for counsel to use the oral hearings to present the most important aspects of their argument in full, a large amount of the detail will be included in the written pleadings, which will of course be available to the Court to re-read and digest during deliberations (along with the transcript of the oral hearings).

[9] J. Crawford, 'Advocacy before International Tribunals in State-to-State cases', in D. Bishop and E. G. Kehoe (eds.), *The Art of Advocacy in International Arbitration* (2nd ed., Juris, 2010) 303, p. 330.

[10] This envisages that the client will keep its counsel informed of all relevant political developments and any communications with the other party to a dispute. Generally, this is not an issue; but competing voices and priorities within a State or other factors may mean that counsel is not always kept well-informed. Such a situation is very unlikely to be in the best interests of the State concerned.

[11] See discussion in K. Mačák, 'Article 43' in A. Zimmerman et al. (eds.), *The Statute of the International Court of Justice: A Commentary* (3rd ed., Oxford University Press, 2019) para. 95.

A The Court's Procedure and Practice

The written pleadings are addressed in the ICJ Statute, Rules, Practice Directions and the Court's Note for the Parties Concerning the Preparation of Pleadings.

In summary, Article 43(2) of the ICJ Statute provides that the written proceedings consist of the 'memorials, counter-memorials and, if necessary, replies; also all the papers and documents in support.' Article 45 of the Rules provides that the pleadings in a case begun by way of application will consist of a Memorial, and a Counter-Memorial; and that the Court may authorise or direct a second round of written pleadings (Reply and Rejoinder) if the parties are so agreed, or if the Court decides that these are necessary (either *proprio motu* or at the request of one of the parties). On the number of rounds, Court is guided by the parties: where the applicant does not request a second round, the Court will ordinarily proceed to a hearing after the first round of written pleadings, while if one of the parties requests a second round, it will usually be granted. In the latter case, the Court does not appear to apply a stringent test for a second round being considered 'necessary'. Thus, despite the Court's measure adopted in 2002 to the effect that 'a single round of written pleadings is to be considered as the norm in cases begun by means of an application',[12] in practice two rounds of written pleadings remains the usual procedure.[13]

The Rules contain little guidance for the content of the pleadings: Article 49 provides that the Memorial shall contain 'a statement of the relevant facts, a statement of the law, and the submissions'; and the Counter-Memorial is to contain 'an admission or denial of the facts' stated in the Memorial; additional facts, if necessary; observations on the statement of law in the Memorial and a statement of law in answer thereto. The second round is to be 'directed to the issues that still divide' the parties.

Each pleading must contain the party's 'submissions', that is, a concise statement of precisely what the party is asking the Court to adjudge and

---

[12] ICJ, Press Release 2002/12, 4 April 2002, para. 1.

[13] Mačák, 'Article 43', para. 51. The ILA Committee on Procedure of International Courts and Tribunals has recently recommended that the Court amend Article 45(2) of its Rules to abolish multiple rounds of pleadings, although it indicates that the Court's usual practice is to allow for two rounds of written pleadings: see ILA, Procedure of International Courts and Tribunals, Final Report, 1 May 2020 (available at https://ila.vettoreweb.com/Storage/Download.aspx?DbStorageId=24643&StorageFileGuid=e323b72c-968a-431b-9c49-ea9424c40bfa), pp 30–31.

declare. The submissions should reflect what the party desires for the Court to include in the operative part of its judgment. (For those with a background in common law, the submissions are similar to a draft order.)[14]

Where a case is commenced by special agreement, in the past it was common to have a simultaneous exchange of written pleadings, but by Practice Direction I (adopted in 2001), the Court has called upon the parties to ensure that pleadings are not simultaneous; instead, the parties usually agree as to who should file first and will ordinarily agree on two rounds of written pleadings.[15]

The Court has issued several further Practice Directions dealing with written submissions. Practice Direction II (adopted in 2001) urges the parties to make their pleadings responsive and clear, asking them to:

... bear in mind the fact that these pleadings are intended not only to reply to the submissions and arguments of the other party, but also, and above all, to present clearly the submissions and arguments of the party which is filing the proceedings.

In the light of this, at the conclusion of the written pleadings of each party, there is to appear a short summary of its reasoning.

In Practice Direction III, promulgated in 2009, 'parties are strongly urged to keep the written pleadings as concise as possible, in a matter compatible with the full presentation of their positions'.

As noted above, the documents relied upon by the parties, including any witness statements or expert reports, are to be annexed to every pleading. In January 2021, the Court amended Practice Direction III to impose a page limit on annexes. In addition to the paragraph quoted above, it now also provides:

---

[14] See Mačák, 'Article 43', para. 27. The submissions set out in the written pleadings are not final and may be modified up to the end of the oral proceedings, when the parties' final submissions must be read out, and a copy of them signed and provided to the Court by the Agents of the Parties: ICJ Rules, Article 60(2).

[15] For example, in *Land and Maritime Delimitation and Sovereignty Over Islands (Gabon/Equatorial Guinea)*, the two States agreed to the number (four) and order of pleadings in their Special Agreement, and agreed in a meeting with the President that Equatorial Guinea would file the first pleading, and Gabon would file the second pleading: see *Land and Maritime Delimitation and Sovereignty Over Islands (Gabon/Equatorial Guinea)*, Order, 7 April 2021, p 2. As noted in Chapter 11, K. Parlett and A. Sander, 'Procedure in Contentious Cases', while several special agreements concluded after the adoption of Practice Direction I provided for simultaneous exchange, in the two most recent cases submitted to the Court by special agreement, the parties provided for consecutive pleadings, consistently with Practice Direction I.

In view of an excessive tendency towards the proliferation and protraction of annexes to written pleadings, the parties are also urged to append to their pleadings only strictly selected documents. The number of pages of annexes attached by a party to its written pleadings shall not exceed 750 in total, unless the Court decides, upon request of a party, that a number in excess of that limit is warranted, in the particular circumstances of the case.

This new Practice Direction is likely to require parties to make significant adjustments to the practice that has developed of filing extensive annexes. The Court's indication is clear, and it is consistent with statements that have been made by individual judges to the effect that the Court is not assisted by voluminous pleadings and lengthy annexes on often tangential issues.

The written pleadings provide the materials from which counsel present the case, and they likewise constrain a party in the case presented at the hearing, but the ICJ Rules and practice provide some welcome flexibility in this regard. First, pursuant to Article 56 of the Court's Rules, documents may be submitted to the Court after the closure of the written proceedings, with the consent of the other party or if the Court decides, after hearing the parties, that the document is necessary.[16] Second, the Court permits reference to any other document, not in the record, provided that it is 'part of a publication readily available'.[17] The Court has provided further guidance to the parties on such documents in Practice Direction IX*bis*. It reinforces the general rule that all documents relied upon should be annexed to the pleadings or produced in accordance with the post-hearing procedure identified in Article 56 of the Rules.[18] It also sets out two criteria for documents to be considered 'part of a publication readily available': first, that it should be available in the public domain; and second, that its availability should be assessed by reference to its accessibility to the Court as well as to the other party.[19] These two practices – permitting a party to make an application to admit relevant evidence after the closure of written proceedings, and to refer to publicly available documents – provides significant assistance both to the advocate and to the Court, and minimises the risk of the Court having to ignore relevant evidence because it becomes available at a late stage, or because its relevance was not foreseen at the time of the written pleadings.

---

[16] ICJ Rules, Articles 56(1) and (2).   [17] ICJ Rules, Article 56(4).
[18] ICJ Practice Direction IX*bis*, para. 1.   [19] ICJ Practice Direction IX*bis*, para. 2.

B The Essentials of Written Pleadings

The function of the written pleadings is to present a party's case, together with all relevant evidence.[20] The written pleadings are the first opportunity to communicate a party's position to the Court,[21] and for the parties to engage with the substance of each other's positions. A judge may well form (at least) a preliminary view based on the written pleadings, and on the evidence submitted with those pleadings. It follows that the impression given in the written pleadings is at least as important as the case that is put orally. For example, there is an obvious forensic advantage in going into a hearing on the back of written pleadings where it is plain that the advocate has already made the decision to jettison weak lines of argument, or has elected to confront in a first pleading the difficult documents on the facts, instead of waiting for orders on disclosure and having to fight a rear-guard action to explain a given document in a reply or rejoinder.

There is a tendency for written pleadings to be very lengthy, commonly running to several hundred pages. This has been the subject of negative remarks, including from ICJ judges,[22] and, as noted above, the ICJ has urged parties through Practice Direction II to 'keep the written pleadings as concise as possible'. This requires the advocate to strike a difficult balance. In a domestic case, it may be possible to have much shorter written pleadings because the oral hearing will be lengthy. Before the ICJ, hearings rarely exceed two weeks, so the case may well have to be set out in some detail in writing – although the longer the written pleadings, the more likely it is that key points will get lost and the less likely that the judge will be fully read in. Ultimately it is the bench that has to be persuaded, and if the prevalent view of the bench is that written pleadings are often over-long, repetitive, with the key points of the case being obscured by

---

[20] For a perspective on the process of drafting, particularly where there is a team of counsel involved, see A. Pellet, 'The Role of the International Lawyer in International Litigation' in C. Wickremasinghe (ed.), *The International Lawyer as Practitioner* (BIICL, 2000), 147, pp. 158–159. Typically, the advocates in the team divide up issues in the case, but there is of course a need for good communication and coordination in order to present a consistent case overall.

[21] Of course, in a case commenced by application, the Applicant will have communicated the basic case to the Court in its application, but the Memorial will be a much fuller presentation of its case, and the Counter-Memorial will be the Respondent's first opportunity to present its case.

[22] See, e.g., M. McIlwrath and J. Savage, *International Arbitration and Mediation: A Practical Guide* (Kluwer, 2010) 288.

extraneous legal and factual material, then the advocate must draft with that view firmly in mind. The Court has given a strong indication that counsel should strive for a pleading which is clear, to the point, and as succinct as possible.

So far as concerns the legal arguments, a written pleading is likely to aggravate, rather than persuade, if these are presented in an academic style or it reads like a textbook. An easy to follow and logical structure is vital, within which the case on the law can be set out succinctly, with reference to relevant authorities, with detailed attention where it is required, notably for decisive issues. Careful thought should be given to the possible views and pre-existing depth of knowledge of the readers, and the argument tailored accordingly. Written pleadings that address the heart of the disputed issues in a case are likely to be more useful and to have more impact than those which leave issues blurred.[23] Moreover, a party is unlikely to be disadvantaged by a clear presentation of its case at an early stage, and particularly so if that case remains unchanged throughout the proceedings.

The tone of a pleading will be a matter of style of the author, and there are inevitably differences in taste. But the most effective written pleadings are likely to strike a moderate tone and not be overwritten. They set out a party's case in short sentences that will be easy to follow even for a judge whose mother tongue is not that of the pleading, without using language which is overstated or unsustainable, or which takes an excessively argumentative or theoretical approach.[24] It should also be kept in mind that the Registry will produce translations of pleadings for those judges who wish to read them in the other language of the Court: shorter and simpler sentences are more likely to be translated accurately, avoiding misunderstandings or confusion. It may be useful to approach adverbs with caution: if the opponent's argument is said to be 'clearly untenable' or some similar formulation, it is doubtful that the adverb adds anything – other than to raise a question in the reader's mind as to whether it is there to disguise a perception of weakness. A written pleading will ideally be engaging,

---

[23] See M. A. Clodfelter, 'Written Proceedings in International Investment Arbitration' in C. Giorgetti (ed.), *Litigating International Investment Disputes: A Practitioner's Guide* (Brill Nijhoff, 2014) 206, pp. 230–233.

[24] G. A. Alvarez, 'Effective Written Advocacy', in D. Bishop and E. G. Kehoe (eds.), *The Art of Advocacy in International Arbitration* (2nd ed., Juris, 2010), 195, pp. 205–208.

logical, and maintain momentum and pace, even when addressing technical, detailed, or complex issues.[25] As is obvious, the use of headings and signposting of points and arguments will assist in both the structuring and comprehension of a pleading. A well-constructed table of contents can help to explain a complex case.

It will be a matter of judgement in the particular case whether to anticipate in advance the other party's likely case/responsive points. The primary function of a statement of claim/memorial is to set out a claimant's positive case. There may be an advantage in answering obvious points or those that have already been raised in correspondence between the disputing parties. On the other hand, it may be preferable to wait until it is known precisely how the opposing party has elected to make its points and there may be a concern about appearing overly defensive – all will depend on the individual case.[26]

Unlike the situation which applies to proceedings before many domestic courts, there is little scope for compelling a party to disclose documents which are adverse to its case.[27] There may nevertheless be ways of formulating a pleading in order to provoke the other party to disclose relevant documents, or at least to make a failure to disclose appear inexplicable, such that the Court might be prepared to draw an inference, or otherwise come to a view, as to the likely content of the non-disclosed documents.[28] To similar effect, a pleading may be formulated so as to require the opposing party to address particularly difficult issues, including through asking direct questions which, whether answered or not, will provide a useful platform for oral submissions.[29]

[25] M. Friedman, 'Pleadings, Memorials and Post-Hearing Briefs' in D. Bishop and E. G. Kehoe (eds.), *The Art of Advocacy in International Arbitration* (2nd ed., Juris, 2010), 209, pp. 226–230.

[26] J. Crawford, 'Advocacy before International Tribunals in State-to-State cases', in D. Bishop and E. G. Kehoe (eds.), *The Art of Advocacy in International Arbitration* (2nd ed., Juris, 2010), 303, p. 322.

[27] On the rules concerning disclosure, see K. Parlett and A. Sander, 'Into the Void: A Counsel Perspective on the Need to Articulate Rules Concerning Disclosure before the ICJ', (2019) 113 *AJIL Unbound* 302, esp pp. 303–306.

[28] Cf. *Corfu Channel Case, Judgment of April 9th, 1949, ICJ Reports 1949*, p. 32, where the Court refused to draft an inference from the refusal of the UK to produce documents for the use of the Court.

[29] See e.g., *Obligation to Negotiate Access to the Pacific Ocean (Bolivia v. Chile)*, Reply of Bolivia, paras. 47, 388–399.

C Issues of Evidence, Including Fact Witnesses and Expert Opinions

An important aspect of advocacy is using relevant evidence to support a party's position. Many cases are won or lost on the facts. This will include documentary evidence, which might comprise correspondence between the parties; relevant documents made or published by a party; records of meetings or discussions; and media releases or press reports. As noted above, the documentary evidence must generally be annexed to the written pleadings. An effective submission will reference and highlight important aspects of that evidence.

In addition to documentary evidence, statements of witnesses of fact and reports setting out the opinions of party-appointed experts may also be annexed to the written pleadings. So far as concerns witnesses of fact, written statements are the primary way in which witness evidence is put forward, with the potential for fact witnesses to be examined by the parties and the Court during a hearing. Counsel will generally have limited involvement in the preparation of witness statements, since these are the account given by the fact witness and should therefore reflect his or her own words and perspective. But counsel can provide crucial assistance to the witness in structuring their statements and in ensuring that all relevant issues are addressed, with references to supporting documentary evidence, if appropriate.[30]

A party may also solicit the opinion of an expert in support of scientific or technical issues. In recent years, there has been increased attention on expert evidence in international disputes, including before the ICJ. This attention has followed from a rise in the number of fact-intensive technical or scientific disputes.

Once a party has identified a need for independent expertise, the general practice is to engage an expert at an early stage. In the past, there were some cases in which experts were engaged to act as advocates in cases before the ICJ, but this was discouraged by the Court and the rule which is now uniformly followed is that expert evidence is tendered in the traditional way, that is, through the submission of an expert report (consistent with professional ethics rules applicable in many domestic jurisdictions). The usual practice is as follows:

---

[30] K. Parlett, 'Parties' Engagement with Experts in International Litigation' 9(3) *Journal of International Dispute Settlement* (2018) pp. 448–451.

(a) experts are identified by a party or its counsel and are contacted to indicate their availability for a case, subject to identifying and addressing any potential conflicts;

(b) there is a preliminary discussion with the expert about the scope of the opinion;

(c) counsel work with the expert to formulate questions to be answered (sometimes referred to as the 'terms of reference'), which usually forms the basis of an outline for the expert's report (and is commonly included in the report); and

(d) the expert produces a draft report, reflecting his or her honest opinion. The expert may then refine the report to address any queries that have been raised by counsel, with counsel keeping in mind that the report must reflect the expert's true opinion. In this process, it is important to ensure that the expert's evidence can be easily understood by a non-expert (i.e. the Court).[31]

An effective written submission will of course refer to and highlight relevant aspects of the expert and witness evidence, quoting where necessary. It will also draw together the legal consequences of that evidence. So far as concern expert evidence, counsel may also find it necessary and useful to 'translate' the expert opinion into plain language, which can be easily understood by the Court, and in the context of the dispute.

III Hearings

An appropriate starting point will always be to reflect on how the judges will likely be viewing matters at the start of the hearing. It is a reality, however, that the time that judges have spent reading in will vary greatly, and it cannot be presumed that all of them have gone beyond a reading of the main pleadings and a look at certain key documents. There will generally be a long list of issues that the Court has to determine, and a bewildering amount of paper that the Court is being asked to master. The task for the advocate is to identify and distil the important issues, with clarity, and provide a set of succinct and coherent answers that will (ideally) resonate with the Court, and that the Court can latch on to in

---

[31] Ibid., p. 447.

subsequent reading and deliberations. This process can be seen as one of establishing beacons that will light the way for the Court seeking to navigate through an overwhelming mass of paper.[32] Also, in the words of Sir Christopher Greenwood:

> Another [important thing] is to be clear, to be able to show a clear pattern of how the case unfolds, and that is very difficult in a large courtroom because if you've got 15 judges there will be some who have read everything and have very clear views about what the case is about even if they haven't made up their minds . . . But you will have others who have read next to nothing and really need to be taken by the hand and shown what the case is all about. The art there is to present the case in such a way that you don't just duplicate what has been said in your written arguments, but you do provide a way, a path through the forest of the pleadings.[33]

There are three further points worth emphasising at the outset. First, as a practical matter, most, if not all, of the hearing will be taken up by oral submissions, with reference to jurisprudence[34] and supporting evidence, whether documentary or witness evidence.[35] Although there is increasing reliance on expert evidence and questioning of experts is becoming more frequent, most hearings still do not involve examination of experts, and witnesses of fact remain a rarity. Second, whatever time limits are set (and these may not appear generous), the advocate must work within these.[36]

---

[32] T. Landau, 'Dysfunctional Deliberations and Effective Advocacy', in A. Menaker (ed.), *International Arbitration and the Rule of Law: Contribution and Conformity, ICCA Congress Series, Volume 19* (Kluwer, 2017) 285, pp. 289-294.

[33] Sir Christopher Greenwood QC, 18 January 2021, at https://essexcourt.com/sir-christopher-greenwood-qc-interviewed-as-part-of-camarb-series/. The first point made was by reference to advice given to Sir Christopher when a student: "The most important thing in advocacy is keeping a septuagenarian awake at 3 o'clock on a Friday afternoon.' That's good advice. I think one of the things that is important is to be able to stimulate your audience.'

[34] While in the past, there was a tendency for the ICJ to rely predominantly on its own previous judgments for authoritative and persuasive statements of the law, more recently, it has become increasingly common for parties to cite a wide range of decisions of international courts and tribunals, as well as national courts, and for these to be taken into account by the Court: T. Buergenthal, 'Lawmaking by the ICJ and Other International Courts', 103 *American Society of International Law Proceedings* (2009) 397, p. 405.

[35] J. Crawford and A. Pellet, 'Anglo-Saxon and Continental Approaches to Pleading before the ICJ; Aspects des modes continentaux et Anglos-Saxons de plaidoiries devant la C.I.J.' in I. Buffard et al. (eds.), *International Law between Universalism and Fragmentation, Festschrift in Honour of Gerhard Hafner* (Martinus Nijhoff, 2008), 831.

[36] A further factor to bear in mind is that the pace of oral submissions must take account of the fact that there is simultaneous translation into the other official language (English or

Third, preparation is everything. Although the ICJ does not interrupt the advocate with difficult (or generally any) questions, it is essential that the advocate has thought through in advance what the questions would be and address them although unasked.

A The Court's Procedure and Practice

The Court's Rules provide for an oral hearing in all cases. Article 54(2) of the Court's Rules provides that after the closure of the written proceedings, the case is ready for hearing, and the dates for hearing will be fixed by the Court. Article 59(1) provides that hearings shall be in public 'unless the Court shall decide otherwise, or unless the parties demand that the public be not admitted. Such a decision or demand may concern either the whole or part of the hearing, and may be made at any time.' The general practice is that hearings are held in public and the Court also provides a live webstream of the hearings. In 2020, in light of the Covid-19 pandemic, the Court's Rules were amended to add a second paragraph to Article 54, allowing for the Court 'to decide, for health, security or other compelling reasons, to hold a hearing entirely or in part by video link. The parties shall be consulted on the organization of such a hearing.' At the same time, Article 94 of the Rules was amended to allow for the reading of the Court's judgments to take place via video-link. Since June 2020, the Court has held several hearings by video-link, or held hybrid hearings, with an in-person element and a video-link element. Despite the obvious limitations, these appear to have worked well, although clarity and succinctness may be seen as all the more important.

The Court settles the procedure for the oral hearing, including the order in which the parties will be heard, the method for handling of evidence including from witnesses and/or experts, and the number of counsel to be heard on behalf of the parties, in accordance with Article 52(2) of the Rules.

French), and the President will intervene to ask an advocate to slow their pace if the interpreters are finding it difficult to keep up. Given that there is simultaneous translation, the advocate should also give consideration to the language used, and avoid words that may not be easily understood by non-native speakers.

Concerning the number of counsel, in practice, the arguments are almost always made by a number of different advocates,[37] and there is no record of any case before the ICJ where the Court has limited the number of persons allowed to speak.[38] Each of the parties provides the Court with a list of advocates for each session and with estimates of time for their oral argument and the language in which they will address the Court.

A practice has developed by which parties provide the Court with judges' folders for each round of argument. These usually contain outlines of each of the advocates' arguments, copies of any presentation which is projected onto the screen during oral argument, and key documents. The Court effectively endorsed this practice, by Practice Direction IX*ter*, promulgated in 2006, but urged the parties to 'exercise restraint' and clarified that all documents contained in the judges' folder should be taken from the annexes or form part of a publication readily available in accordance with the conditions set out in Practice Direction IX*bis*. The judges' folders can be a very useful tool to the advocate in highlighting the key documents to the Court, together with key maps (if relevant), which will usually also have been projected onto the screens during the hearing.

In terms of oral submissions, Article 60(1) of the Court's Rules urges the parties to make oral submissions which are succinct and directed to the issues in dispute. It provides:

The oral statements made on behalf of each party shall be as succinct as possible within the limits of what is requisite for the adequate presentation of that party's contentions at the hearing. Accordingly, they shall be directed to the issues that still divide the parties, and shall not go over the whole ground covered by the pleadings, or merely repeat the facts and arguments these contain.

Practice Direction VI, amended in 2009, stresses that the parties should comply with Article 60(1) and deliver focused submissions. It provides:

The Court requires full compliance with Article 60, paragraph 1, of the Rules of Court and observation of the requisite degree of brevity in oral pleadings. In that context, the Court will find it very helpful if the parties focus in the first round of the oral proceedings on those points which have been raised by one party at the

---

[37] Agents and counsel for the parties are traditionally dressed in accordance with the practice of the court in their own jurisdiction: see *ICJ Handbook* (2019), p 54. Thus, many advocates appear in suits; English and/or Australian barristers appear in wigs and gowns; academics often appear in their academic attire.

[38] Mačàk, 'Article 43', para. 111.

stage of written proceedings but which have not so far been adequately addressed by the other, as well as on those which each party wishes to emphasize by way of winding up its arguments. Where objections of lack of jurisdiction or of inadmissibility are being considered, oral proceedings are to be limited to statements on the objections.

Article 61(1) provides that, before or during the hearing, the Court may indicate any points or issues which it would like the parties specifically to address, or on which it considers that there has been sufficient argument. In 2002, the Court indicated that it intended to make greater use of this provision 'in the future to give specific indications to the parties of areas of focus in the oral proceedings, and particularly in any second round of oral arguments'.[39] However, in practice, directions are rarely, if ever, given,[40] and instead the Court generally accords the parties a large degree of discretion as to which issues they address in oral hearings. Both counsel and judges of the Court have urged use of these provisions, and it would likely greatly assist both advocates and the Court if they were utilised.[41]

Article 61(2) provides that the Court 'may, during the hearing, put questions to the agents, counsel and advocates, and may ask them for explanations'. Article 61(3) provides for a similar right for judges, although they are required to make their intentions known to the President in advance. Article 61(4) provides that agents, counsel and advocates may 'answer either immediately or within a time-limit fixed by the President'.

As has been frequently observed by commentators, questions from the bench during oral proceedings are the exception rather than the rule. As a

---

[39] ICJ, Press Release 2002/12, 4 April 2002, para. 4.

[40] Mačák, 'Article 43', para. 118. One example from 2008 is the Court's request that the parties address an issue which had not been addressed in the written pleadings, during the hearings: see *Application of the Convention on the Prevention and Punishment of the Crime of Genocide (Croatia v. Serbia), Preliminary Objections, Judgment, ICJ Reports 2008*, 412, p. 417, para. 16: for the answers, see p. 424, para. 36 and p. 434, para. 69.

[41] See, e.g., discussion in C. Brown, 'Mock Debate: Is the Primacy of the International Court of Justice in International Dispute Settlement under Threat?' 110 *ASIL Proceedings* (2016) 191, pp. 198–199: 'Another suggestion was that the ICJ might make better use of hearings by "sharpening the issues" in advance. Thus, after the written proceedings are closed, the ICJ could be prepared for what the key questions should be for the hearing. Oral hearings are unlikely to be of value to the ICJ if the parties are simply reciting their memorials. It was suggested that the ICJ could issue a note to the parties after the close of the written proceedings that identifies the matters on which it would be interested in hearing oral submissions. This is something that is achievable for the Court and would change the dynamic of the oral proceedings.'

general rule, the Court will not interrupt advocates to ask questions, and will almost never expect an immediate answer, but instead ask the parties to prepare an oral answer for a future sitting, or to submit an answer in writing at a later date.[42] While many have suggested that a greater dialogue between the bench and the bar would assist the Court to focus on the important issues,[43] and to render judgments within reasonable timeframes,[44] a significant obstacle to change is the Court's long-standing deference to sovereign States,[45] alongside the practical difficulty of managing questions from a bench of up to seventeen judges.[46] In practice, it

---

[42] C. Rose, 'Questioning the Silence of the Bench: Reflections on Oral Proceedings at the International Court of Justice', 18 *Journal of Transnational Law and Policy* (2008) 47, pp. 49–51; Mačàk, 'Article 43', para. 132.

[43] Including judges of the Court: see the comments of Judge (now President) Donoghue, 'Plenary Discussion: A Conversation with International Court of Justice Judges Joan Donoghue, Julia Sebutinde, and Xue Hanqin' 108 *ASIL Proceedings* (2014) 383, pp. 393–394: 'Many people are surprised to know that it is very rare that ICJ judges ask questions from the bench. We have started more recently to ask questions in which we ask in the first round of oral proceedings for the party to respond to our questions in the second round, and I find that very useful. I imagine that it's helpful to the states as well, because they feel like they have a chance to answer questions that are bothering a judge, that we don't just go away and feel unhappy that we never got an answer.'

[44] R. Higgins, 'Respecting Sovereign States and Running a Tight Courtroom' 50 *ICLQ* (2001) 121, p. 128; cf M. Bedjaoui, 'The "Manufacture" of Judgments at the International Court of Justice' 3 *Pace YB Int'l Law* (1991) 26, p. 42. See comments of Judge Xue in 'Plenary Discussion: A Conversation with International Court of Justice Judges Joan Donoghue, Julia Sebutinde, and Xue Hanqin' 108 (2014) *ASIL Proceedings* 383, p 394: '... in the oral proceedings whether to raise question or not is something that members have to be very careful about, because such questions are directed at the State parties. They could concern very nuanced factual issues, which may be decisive for the outcome. When it comes to national interests of a sovereign State, the matter has to be handled with great caution.'

[45] Rose, 'Questioning the Silence of the Bench', at 57–58.

[46] Higgins, 'Respecting Sovereign States', at 127–128. The constraints on interaction between the bench and advocates was discussed in a debate at ASIL in 2016 (with Judge Greenwood in the chair), a record of which appears in C. Brown, 'Mock Debate: Is the Primacy of the International Court of Justice in International Dispute Settlement under Threat?' at 198: 'As for greater interaction between the bench and the advocates, it was accepted that it could be a source of frustration for judges on the ICJ not to be able to intervene and ask questions. But at the same time, it had to be recognised that in a court where there are fifteen or more judges who work in two different languages, permitting spontaneous interventions would give rise to difficulties. In recent years, the ICJ has adopted the practice of asking questions at the end of the opening round of oral submissions, and asking the parties to provide answers on the final day of the hearing, rather than what had been done in the past, which was to obtain the answers in writing some weeks later. This enabled the ICJ to test the arguments that were being made, and also seemed to address the perceived difficulty that if questions were asked from the bench during an advocate's oral

appears that the relatively static procedure which forms part of the Court's tradition is unlikely to change in the near future. The challenge for an advocate, in these circumstances, and as mentioned at the outset, is to think through in advance the difficult points and to answer the questions that a judge is likely to have in his or her principal submissions.

B Legal Argument and Presentation of Evidence

Effective advocacy is likely to require that the case be presented in a simple way, without rhetorical flourishes, aimed at the anticipated level of legal or factual knowledge of the members of the Court. This requires focus on the key issues, at the expense of addressing every minor and tangential point. Certain points may be politically important to a client, but legally irrelevant or unpersuasive, and part of the advocate's job will be to agree with the client beforehand which points should be emphasised and which dealt with lightly.[47] The client may reach the conclusion that some points which are not essential for the Court may need to be made in order to meet the expectations of the client's domestic audience. Commonly such points will be made by the Agent in his or her opening submissions.

However legally or factually complex the case may be, it is essential for an advocate to distil and set out the key issues, and then address each of them in turn. The key issues are likely to include both positive and responsive/defensive points. A skeleton argument (outline) may help, even if it just serves as an aide to the advocate in structuring their presentation, and is not handed to the Court. This takes the key issues in turn and references the evidence and authorities relevant to each point.

There are a number of ways to organise submissions. They might usefully be structured by issues to be addressed, propositions to be established, or by themes. The most effective structure will depend on the case, and the particular issue to be addressed. One question will be how to present the relevant facts (if any). It has been said that the 'facts of the case are more than just a collection of discrete or disconnected pieces of evidence. Properly conceived, the facts form a mosaic pattern that fits

submissions, the advocate's replies to those questions would be on the record publicly for all time, and would henceforth constitute part of that state's practice.'

[47] See e.g., Sir Daniel Bethlehem above with respect to the chuck 'everything into the air' approach.

together neatly into a narrative story.'[48] That may be over-hopeful, but the advocate will generally seek to arrange the evidence into a story line, giving the adjudicator a way of organising and remembering the facts. Needless to say, the story must be built upon the evidence, and an effective narrative will explain and therefore be consistent with the evidence, taking into account discrepant evidence and making logical sense in the particular circumstances.

It will of course be necessary to draw the crucial evidence to the attention of the Court, explaining its significance to the case. Although it might be assumed that, by the time of the oral hearing, the judges will be familiar to some extent with the written pleadings and the basic outline of the case, it cannot be assumed that they are familiar with much if any of the evidence, and it will generally be necessary for the advocate to guide the bench through the evidence.[49] Here, an important part of the advocacy will have to have been done beforehand, in the sense that the key documents should be identified and capable of ready presentation to the Court – in the judges' folder, and/or on the screen. It is not unusual to have the documents that the advocate wishes to take to the Court in paper or electronic form that can be marked up on a screen. Power point presentations of extracts from documents may be helpful, but generally the judge will wish to see the context for a given extract, so it is questionable whether such a presentation can be a sufficient substitute for showing the actual document and aiming to encourage the use of an actual or electronic highlighter pen.

Overly broad assertions, sound-bites, and unsupported propositions are unlikely to be persuasive, and will give grounds for criticism from the other side in their responsive submissions. Likewise gratuitous remarks directed at the opposing counsel or party will not have any useful impact on the judges, and will most likely be off-putting. An advocate's time is better spent on making sharply focused points which are both relevant to the key points in dispute, and which rely on and draw the Court's attention to evidence in the record. If criticism of the other side's argument is over-emphasised, it risks losing the focus on the real issues at hand. At the same

---

[48] T. Landau and D. Bishop, 'Opening Statements', in D. Bishop and E. G. Kehoe (eds.), *The Art of Advocacy in International Arbitration* (2nd ed., Juris, 2010), 359, p. 373.

[49] See comments of Sir Christopher Greenwood KC (former Judge of the ICJ), in 'Desert Islands Law Reports', especially around 59.30.

time, it may on occasion be useful to seek to put the opposing party on the spot by asking a direct question that they will then have either to address in the next round or – which may be very telling – ignore.[50] In general, a good point does not get any better, and may well start to lose its impact, through over-emphasis or repetition.[51]

It is highly unusual for a party's case to be without any weakness. An effective advocate will be ready to address the weaknesses of the case, whether or not those have already been raised by the other party in written or oral submissions.

C Witness Examination

Witness evidence is increasingly used in inter-State litigation. The Court may hear evidence from fact witnesses and opinion from expert witnesses. Usually such witnesses are involved in the proceedings at the election or appointment of the parties, although the ICJ's Rules empower it to arrange for an expert opinion. The Court has used this power in two recent cases: soliciting an expert opinion (from two experts) in 2016 in *Delimitation in the Caribbean Sea and the Pacific Ocean (Costa Rica v. Nicaragua)* relating to the state of a portion of the Caribbean Coast near the border between the two States; and soliciting an expert opinion (from four experts) in 2020 in *Armed Activities on the Territory of the Congo (Democratic Republic of Congo v. Uganda)* relating to some heads of damage claimed by the applicant State. Any Court-appointed expert should be made available to the parties for questioning, to which the usual approach of

---

[50] See e.g., *Alleged Violations of the 1955 Treaty of Amity (Iran v. USA)*, provisional measures phase, 16 September 2020, at CR 2020/11, p. 21 para. 16 and p. 24, paras. 30–31 (Lowe); *Obligation to Negotiate Access to the Pacific Ocean (Bolivia v. Chile)*, merits phase, 26 March 2018, at CR 2018/10 p. 34, para. 5 (Sander).

[51] J. Crawford, 'Advocacy before International Tribunals in State-to-State cases', in D. Bishop and E. G. Kehoe (eds.), *The Art of Advocacy in International Arbitration* (2nd ed., Juris, 2010), 303, p. 328. Cf the remarks of Professor Pellet to the effect that one might make a pleading 'where, if a were a judge, I would have voted against myself' but also 'pleading something which is untenable, I would never do that': UNTV, 'Interview with Alain Pellet, Counsel before the ICJ', 28 July 2011 (available at http://webtv.un.org/ news-features/audiovisual-library-of-international-law-avl/lecture-series/states/watch/ interview-with-alain-pellet-counsel-before-the-icj/2621182919001/?term=&sort=popu lar&page=1) at 10:00 minutes.

cross-examination would apply (otherwise their evidence could be accorded great weight despite being untested).[52]

As noted above, fact and expert witnesses provide a written statement or opinion which is submitted with the written pleadings. This serves as the evidence-in-chief of the witness and the purpose of their appearance at a hearing is two-fold. First, it permits the opposing party an opportunity to test the evidence through questions, most commonly through cross-examination. Second, it affords the bench an opportunity to pose questions to the witness, with a view to clarifying, elaborating, or testing their evidence. In recent cases where experts have given oral evidence, there have been a number of detailed and focused questions asked by members of the Court, demonstrating a high level of engagement with the evidence, which is to be welcomed.

The process of testing witness evidence through questioning from counsel is more familiar for common-law trained lawyers than those with civil law backgrounds. Nevertheless, litigation before the ICJ differs in significant ways from litigation before a common-law domestic court, and advocates need to take account of both cultural and evidentiary differences in approaching witness evidence.

The usual approach to witness evidence in a hearing is as follows. Counsel presenting a witness usually conducts a very short examination in chief, asking the witness to confirm that their statement represents their honest belief or opinion, and whether there are any corrections or additions to be made. The witness is then offered for cross-examination by the opposing party.

At a minimum, the purpose of cross-examination is to reduce the adverse impact of the witness's evidence on one's case. The questions asked might be aimed at undermining the credibility of the witness, including by showing that some part of his or her testimony is not to be believed or that an expert is not nearly so expert as he or she has professed to be on paper. The witness may be taken to documentary evidence that does not support his or her version of events, or which is contrary to his or her opinion evidence.

---

[52] See, e.g., *Pulp Mills on the River Uruguay (Argentina* v. *Uruguay), Judgment, ICJ Reports 2010* (I), declaration of Judge Yusuf, para. 14, and dissenting opinion of Judges Al-Khawsaneh and Simma, para. 14. See also L. Malintoppi, 'Fact Finding and Evidence before the International Court of Justice (Notably in Scientific-Related Disputes)' 7 *JIDS* (2016) 421, pp. 436–438; D. Peat, 'The Use of Court-Appointed Experts by the International Court of Justice' 84 *BYBIL* (2014) 271.

It is of course important to keep control of the witness during cross-examination. This is achieved through the way in which questions are asked. The advocate will almost always wish to use closed questions: short and unambiguous statements which seek to confine the witness to addressing a single fact or issue and to elicit the answer yes or no. An advocate will generally wish to avoid open questions which allow a witness to give expansive evidence that is much more difficult to predict or indeed confine.[53] It is also a risk – generally to be avoided – to ask a question as to which the advocate does not know the answer. There can, however, be lines of questioning where the advocate is more intent on challenging credibility, or using the witness as a means of showing certain documents to the Court, such that the actual answer given by the witness is of less importance.

The key to an effective cross-examination is once again preparation. This includes understanding how the witness's testimony fits within the broader context of the factual and legal issues in dispute in the case. The next step will be to identify, as to each witness, what you want and can reasonably expect to achieve through cross-examination. There will be a question as to whether it is useful or necessary to call a witness for cross-examination. The answer to that will depend on two issues. First, if the witness's testimony is contrary to the opposing party's case, it will in principle be necessary to challenge that evidence. If the witness is not cross-examined, his or her evidence will stand unchallenged and therefore undermine the case. However, there may in reality be little to challenge, and the best approach may be to get the witness in and out of the witness box as rapidly as possible. Second, even if it is not strictly necessary to challenge a witness's evidence, it can be useful: that will depend on whether the advocate can reasonably expect to obtain useful evidence through cross-examination.

Further Reading

J. Crawford, 'Advocacy before International Tribunals in State-to-State cases', in D. Bishop and E. G. Kehoe (eds), *The Art of Advocacy in International Arbitration* (2nd edn, Juris, 2010) 303.

[53] K. Hobér and H. S. Sussman, *Cross-Examination in International Arbitration* (Oxford University Press 2014), pp. 32–45.

J. Crawford and A. Pellet, 'Anglo Saxon and Continental Approaches to Pleading Before the ICJ; Aspects des modes continentaux et Anglo-Saxons de plaidoiries devant la C.I.J.' in I. Buffard et al. (eds.), *International Law between Universalism and Fragmentation, Festschrift in Honour of Gerhard Hafner* (Martinus Nijhoff, 2008) 831.

T. Landau, 'Dysfunctional Deliberations and Effective Advocacy', in A. Menaker (ed.), *International Arbitration and the Rule of Law: Contribution and Conformity*, ICCA Congress Series, Volume 19 (Kluwer, 2017) 285.

M. Wood and E. Sthoeger, 'The International Bar' in C. P. R. Romano, K. J. Alter and Y. Shany (eds.), *The Oxford Handbook of International Adjudication* (Oxford University Press, 2014) 639.

Part III

The Impact of the ICJ's Jurisprudence

The Law of Treaties 14

Antonio Remiro Brotóns

I Introduction

According to Article 38.1 of its Statute, treaties are the first source of law that the International Court of Justice applies to a dispute submitted to it. Likewise, in accordance with Articles 35.1, 35.2, 36.1 and 37, treaties are the basis of – and, sometimes, potential obstacle to[1] – its jurisdiction. The interpretation of treaties is also the first type of dispute that Article 36.2 includes among the disputes that States parties can submit to the Court under the *optional clause*. Unsurprisingly, treaties in general, and their application and interpretation in particular, permeate the jurisprudence of the Court; they are its 'bread and butter'.[2] What is proposed in the pages that follow is a review of the position of the Court on key selected issues of treaty interpretation (II), and systemic integration, hierarchy and concurrence of rules (III) as they emerge from its jurisprudence over the last thirty years.

II Treaty Interpretation: General Rule and Supplementary Means

The *general rule of interpretation* is laid down in Article 31 of the Vienna Convention on the Law of Treaties (the *1969 VCLT*), while Article 32 provides the *supplementary means* assisting it. According to Article 31, treaties must be interpreted 'in good faith in accordance with the ordinary

---

[1] This may be the case when the object is governed by a treaty (*pacta sunt servanda*) and this is considered a cause of inadmissibility of the Application (see, for instance, Article II of the Pact of Bogotá), or when a reservation to the declaration of acceptance of its jurisdiction (*optional clause*) excludes the interpretation of specific treaties.

[2] V. Gowlland-Debbas, 'The Role of the ICJ in the Development of the Contemporary Law of Treaties', in C. J. Tams and J. Sloan (eds.), *The Development of International Law by the ICJ* (Oxford University Press, 2013) 29.

meaning to be given to the terms of the treaty in their context and in the light of its object and purpose.'[3] The context of the treaty is defined as including

(a) any agreement relating to the treaty which was made between all the parties in connection with the conclusion of the treaty; (b) any instrument which was made by one or more parties in connection with the conclusion of the treaty and accepted by the other parties as an instrument related to the treaty.[4]

And together with the context,

(a) any subsequent agreement between the parties regarding the interpretation of the treaty or the application of its provisions; (b) any subsequent practice in the application of the treaty which establishes the agreement of the parties regarding its interpretation; (c) any relevant rules of international law applicable in the relations between the parties.[5]

Finally, the *general rule* ensures that

A special meaning shall be given to a term if it is established that the parties so intended.[6]

As for the *supplementary means*, these include the *travaux préparatoires* of the treaty and the circumstances surrounding its conclusion, and can be used to confirm the meaning resulting from the application of the general rule or to determine this meaning when the general rule '(a) leaves the meaning ambiguous or obscure; or (b) leads to a result which is manifestly absurd or unreasonable.'[7]

The declaratory character of the rules of interpretation, codifying customary international law, has been a constant and undisputed principle in the jurisprudence of the Court. No party to a dispute has ever invoked its non-party status to the VCLT to elude its application, even to treaties predating its entry into force; nor has the Court ever hesitated to apply it. In general, the Court takes into account the unitary and combined character of the elements of the *general rule*.[8] When the text shows

---

[3] Article 31(1).   [4] Article 31(2).   [5] Article 31(3).   [6] Article 31 (4).   [7] Article 32.

[8] It even recreates itself with them. See, for instance, Application of the Convention on the Prevention and Punishment of the Crime of Genocide (*Bosnia and Herzegovina v. Serbia and Montenegro*), Judgment, ICJ Reports 2007, para. 160; Application of the Interim Accord of 13 September 1995 (*the former Yugoslav Republic of Macedonia v. Greece*), Judgment of 5 December 2011, ICJ Reports 2011, para. 91 ff.; Maritime Dispute (*Peru v. Chile*), Judgment, ICJ Reports 2014, para. 58 ff.; Alleged Violations of Sovereign Rights

unequivocally the agreement of the parties, it is natural that the logical, systematic and teleological criteria play a more limited role.[9] Sometimes, context, object and purpose of the treaty have a greater role to play where there is ambiguous text.[10] When the *general rule* provides a clear conclusion, the Court is not required to look at the supplementary means,[11] though its jurisprudence shows a frequent confirmatory reliance on them.[12] This is only more logical when ambiguities in a literal expression persist or remain open to multiple interpretations; a situation that the

and Maritime Spaces in the Caribbean Sea (*Nicaragua* v. *Colombia*), Preliminary Objections, Judgment, ICJ Reports 2016, para. 40 ff.; Question of the Delimitation of the Continental Shelf between Nicaragua and Colombia beyond 200 nautical miles from the Nicaraguan Coast (*Nicaragua* v. *Colombia*), Preliminary Objections, Judgment, ICJ Reports 2016, paras. 38-39; Maritime Delimitation in the Indian Ocean (*Somalia* v. *Kenya*), Preliminary Objections, Judgment, ICJ Reports 2017, paras. 63-64, 89, 126; Immunities and Criminal Proceedings (*Equatorial Guinea* v. *France*), Preliminary Objections, Judgment, ICJ Reports 2018, para. 91 ff.; Application of the International Convention for the Suppression of the Financing of Terrorism and the International Convention on the Elimination of All Forms of Racial Discrimination (*Ukraine* v. *Russian Federation*), Preliminary Objections, Judgment, ICJ Reports, 2019, par. 107 ff.; Application of the International Convention on the Elimination of All Forms of Racial Discrimination (*Qatar* v. *United Arab Emirates*), Judgment, 4 February 2021, paras. 78-88.

[9] In Territorial Dispute (Libyan Arab Jamahiriya/Chad) in 1994, the Court looked at the context and object and purpose of the treaty only to confirm its interpretation. In Sovereignty over Pulau Ligitan and Pulau Sipadan (Indonesia/Malaysia) in 2002, the Court stated, quoting previous jurisprudence, that the interpretation had to be based 'above all' on the text of the treaty. See also Application of the International Convention on the Elimination of All Forms of Racial Discrimination (*Qatar* v. *United Arab Emirates*), Judgment, 4 February 2021, para. 81.

[10] See a recent example in Immunities Criminal Proceedings (*Equatorial Guinea* v. *France*), Judgment, 11 December 2020, para. 62 ff.

[11] Application of the Interim Accord of 13 September 1995 (the former *Yugoslav Republic of Macedonia* v. *Greece*), Judgment of 5 December 2011, ICJ Reports 2011, para. 102; Application of the International Convention for the Suppression of the Financing of Terrorism and of the International Convention on the Elimination of All Forms of Racial Discrimination (*Ukraine* v. *Russian Federation*), Preliminary Objections, Judgment, ICJ Reports 2019, paras. 61, 107-112.

[12] Territorial Dispute (Libyan Arab Jamahiriya/Chad), Judgment, ICJ Reports 1994, para. 55; Maritime Delimitation and Territorial Questions between Qatar and Bahrain (*Qatar* v. *Bahrain*), Jurisdiction and Admissibility, Judgment, ICJ Reports 1995, paras. 40-42; Land and Maritime Boundary between Cameroon and Nigeria (*Cameroon* v. *Nigeria*: Equatorial Guinea intervening), Preliminary Objections, Judgment, ICJ Reports 1998, para. 31; LaGrand (*Germany* v. *United States of America*), Judgment, ICJ Reports 2001, paras. 104-107; Sovereignty over Pulau Ligitan and Pulau Sipadan (Indonesia/Malaysia), Judgment, ICJ Reports 2002, para. 53; Legal Consequences of the Construction of a Wall in the Occupied Palestinian Territory, Advisory Opinion, ICJ Reports 2004, paras. 95, 109; Avena and Other Mexican Nationals (*Mexico* v. *United States of America*), Judgment, ICJ

Court may face even when dealing with its own Statute (i.e. Article 35.2).[13] *A contrario* interpretation is also used where consistent with the general rule and the conditions for its exercise.[14] Nevertheless, it is worth noting that neither the *travaux préparatoires* of a treaty nor the circumstances surrounding its conclusion can be invoked to elude, alter or modify an interpretation resulting from the application of the *general rule*.

Be that as it may be, it should be kept in perspective that treaties are more often than not the result of negotiation processes where the pursuit of agreement may encourage the use of unclear, generic, or blurred wording and expressions. It is not uncommon that in these cases the interpreter has to embark on a careful examination using every interpretative and confirmatory tool available to find proper light and guidance. When it comes to the Court, it is possible to identify a series of ingredients

Reports 2004, paras. 86–87; Application of the Convention on the Prevention and Punishment of the Crime of Genocide (*Bosnia and Herzegovina* v. *Serbia and Montenegro*), Judgment, ICJ Reports 2007, para. 163 ff., 194; Application of the International Convention on the Elimination of All Forms of Racial Discrimination (*Georgia* v. *Russian Federation*), Preliminary Objections, Judgment, ICJ Reports 2011, para. 142 ff.; Maritime Dispute (*Peru* v. *Chile*), Judgment, ICJ Reports 2014, para. 66; Alleged Violations of Sovereign Rights and Maritime Spaces in the Caribbean Sea (*Nicaragua* v. *Colombia*), Preliminary Objections, Judgment, ICJ Reports 2016, para. 47; Question of the Delimitation of the Continental Shelf between Nicaragua and Colombia beyond 200 nautical miles from the Nicaraguan Coast (*Nicaragua* v. *Colombia*), Preliminary Objections, Judgment, ICJ Reports 2016, para. 45; Maritime Delimitation in the Indian Ocean (*Somalia* v. *Kenya*), Preliminary Objections, Judgment, ICJ Reports 2017, para. 99 ff, 127; Immunities and Criminal Proceedings (*Equatorial Guinea* v. *France*), Preliminary Objections, Judgment, ICJ Reports 2018, para. 96; Jadhav (*India* v. *Pakistan*), Judgment, ICJ Reports 2019, para. 76 ff.; Application of the International Convention on the Elimination of All Forms of Racial Discrimination (*Qatar* v. *United Arab Emirates*), Judgment, 4 February 2021, para. 89.

[13] Legality of Use of Force (*Serbia and Montenegro* v. *Belgium*), Preliminary Objections, Judgment, ICJ Reports 2004, paras. 100–114.

[14] Territorial and Maritime Dispute (*Nicaragua* v. *Colombia*), Application for Permission to Intervene of Honduras, Judgment, ICJ Reports 2011, para. 29. The inferred outcome in these cases must be deduced safely from every relevant provision, in its context, and in conformity with the object and purpose and, even in this case, it is still required to determine its exact content, see Alleged Violations of Sovereign Rights and Maritime Spaces in the Caribbean Sea (*Nicaragua* v. *Colombia*), Preliminary Objections, Judgment, ICJ Reports 2016, paras. 36–37; Question of the Delimitation of the Continental Shelf between Nicaragua and Colombia beyond 200 Nautical Miles from the Nicaraguan Coast (*Nicaragua* v. *Colombia*), Preliminary Objections, Judgment, ICJ Reports 2016, para. 35; Certain Iranian Assets (*Islamic Republic of Iran* v. *United States of America*), Preliminary Objections, Judgment, ICJ Reports 2019, para. 64; Immunities Criminal Proceedings (*Equatorial Guinea* v. *France*), Judgment, 11 December 2020, para. 68.

adding extra layers of complexity to the endeavor which are worth ana-
lysing in closer detail, namely the use of different languages and translations (A), the passage of time and the role of presumptions (B) or the
presence of ulterior motivations tainting the interpretation with *policy*
undertones (C).

A The Languages of the Treaty

Treaties that are authenticated in more than one language may give rise to
difficulties. This is particularly the case when discrepancies between the
authentic texts arise, and the parties to the instrument have not established – or are unable to agree on – a hierarchy.[15] After all, for sovereign
equality reasons, which frequently translate into a legal prohibition, States
are usually willing to accept the prevalence of other languages over their
own.[16] In the event that the *general rule* and the *travaux préparatoires* fail
to remove the discrepancies, Article 33.4 of the 1969 VCLT provides for a
conciliatory solution based on the adoption of 'the meaning which best
reconciles the texts, having regard to the object and purpose of the treaty'.
In *LaGrand* the Court put major emphasis on the potential of this provision.
After identifying the differences between the French and English texts of
Article 41 of the Court's Statute, it concluded on the *binding* character of its
provisional measures. The exercise leading to this finding built on the
object and purpose of the rule in the broader context of its Statute, and
the *travaux préparatoires* for confirmation; finally, the Court verified that
its interpretation was consistent with Article 94 of the UN Charter.[17]

Considering that it is the authentic text that is authoritative and the
one that must be interpreted, a slightly more challenging situation arises
when the treaty that the Court is called to interpret and apply[18] is not

---

[15] Article 33 of the 1969 VCLT.

[16] In the 1955 Franco-Libyan Treaty of Friendship and Good Neighbourliness the preference
was given to the French text over the Arabic text. Thirty years later, Libya regretted its lack
of negotiation experience. The territorial rights of Chad (successor State) were based on this
treaty, see Territorial Dispute (Libyan Arab Jamahiriya/Chad), Judgment, ICJ Reports 1994,
paras. 36–38.

[17] LaGrand (*Germany* v. *United States of America*), Judgment, ICJ Reports 2001, paras.
98–108.

[18] Dispute regarding Navigational and Related Rights (*Costa Rica* v. *Nicaragua*), Judgment,
ICJ Reports 2009, paras. 37, 43, 56.

authenticated in any of the official languages of the Court, English and French, and the translations provided by the parties becomes key part of the dispute at its jurisdictional level. A case that comes to mind is *Maritime Delimitation and Territorial Questions between Qatar and Bahrain*, and the interpretation of the Arab expression *al tarafan* used in the *procés verbal* of Doha of 1990, which was relied upon as an expression of the agreement of the parties to submit their differences to the Court. The diverging translations provided by Qatar (*the parties*) and Bahrain (*the two parties*) did little to dispel the doubt as to whether the instrument provided for the possibility to proceed unilaterally (as claimed by Qatar) or instead it bound the parties to proceed jointly (as argued by Bahrain). The Court proceeded to apply the *general rule* and thoroughly examined each sentence of the paragraph containing this expression.[19] Ultimately, it agreed with Qatar. It considered this conclusion, confirmed by the *travaux préparatoires*, as the only logical and useful interpretation, according to the object and purpose of the agreement.[20]

In *Pulp Mills*, Argentina and Uruguay provided the Court with English and French translations of the minutes *(procès-verbal)* of a meeting during which they have worked an *entendimiento* or *compromiso* on how to proceed in the matter, however the Court finally opted for using its own translation.[21] When the analysis turned to the differing translations of a rule in the Statute of River Uruguay, the discussion was settled in favour of the French version ,due to its closer alignment with the Spanish original.[22] The Court was a little luckier in *Dispute regarding Navigational and Related Rights*. In this case, the expression at issue between the Parties was 'con objetos de comercio' as used in Article VI of the 1858 Treaty. While for Costa Rica it meant 'for the purposes of commerce', Nicaragua's translation was 'with articles of commerce'. While the Court strived to base its interpretation on the literal analysis of the sentence containing the

---

[19] Maritime Delimitation and Territorial Questions between Qatar and Bahrain (*Qatar* v. *Bahrain*), Jurisdiction and Admissibility, Judgment, ICJ Reports 1995, para. 34 ff.

[20] Maritime Delimitation and Territorial Questions between Qatar and Bahrain (*Qatar* v. *Bahrain*), Jurisdiction and Admissibility, Judgment, ICJ Reports 1995, para. 40. Some judges voiced their criticism concerning the (lack of) consideration of the *travaux préparatoires*, left out of the exam because they challenged its interpretation. See Dissenting opinion of Vice-President Schwebel.

[21] Pulp Mills on the River Uruguay (*Argentina* v. *Uruguay*), Judgment, ICJ Reports 2010, paras. 125, 131.

[22] *Ib.*, para. 81.

expression, it found itself a lifeline or 'significant indication' of the understanding of the Parties in form of a previous arbitration between the same parties where both had consented to an English translation of the expression as 'purposes of commerce'.[23]

B Time and Treaty Interpretation

In addition to the intricacies of language, *time* ranks high in the list of factors which tend to add controversy in the object under consideration. A recurrent difficulty concerns the adequate interpretation of treaties with long or unlimited duration, and the identification of the relevant time: when the treaty was concluded *versus* when its interpretation is disputed. The intention of the Parties when they agreed to the text is instrumentally decisive. Yet, translating it into practice is not as easy as theory suggests. Sometimes that intention is not clearly expressed or cannot be easily deduced from ulterior agreements between the parties or the subsequent practice.

These difficulties are a breeding ground for *presumptions* which, based on the nature and object and purpose of the treaty, can lead to different approaches and solutions, namely static or dynamic/evolving interpretations. For instance, it has been presumed that the intention of the parties to a treaty on protection of human rights or international humanitarian law is to liberalise its terms, adjusting them to change. The opposite occurs when the treaties under consideration deal with territory-related issues, especially when limitations to sovereignty are prescribed.[24] Notwithstanding this, for the Court, there is no reason to automatically support an a priori restrictive or static interpretation of these clauses. The *general rule* has to be applied in those cases[25] and the solution depends on

---

[23] Dispute regarding Navigational and Related Rights (*Costa Rica* v. *Nicaragua*), Judgment, ICJ Reports 2009, para. 50 ff. In *Obligation to Negotiate Access to the Pacific Ocean*, the Court observed discrepancies between the English translations provided by the Parties, which do not alter its position. Obligation to Negotiate Access to the Pacific Ocean (*Bolivia* v. *Chile*), Judgment, ICJ Reports 2018, paras. 108, 118.

[24] Kasikili/Sedudu Island (Botswana/Namibia), Judgment, ICJ Reports 1999, para. 25; Land and Maritime Boundary between Cameroon and Nigeria (*Cameroon* v. *Nigeria*: Equatorial Guinea intervening), Judgment, ICJ Reports 2002, paras. 59, 205. See also Marcelo Kohen & Mamadou Hébié, Chapter 16, The ICJ and Territorial Disputes.

[25] Dispute regarding Navigational and Related Rights (*Costa Rica* v. *Nicaragua*), Judgment, ICJ Reports 2009, para. 48.

the circumstances; put differently, a restriction of sovereignty can still require the application of an evolving interpretation.[26]

In *Dispute regarding Navigational and Related Rights (Costa Rica v. Nicaragua)*, the Court stated that the intention of the Parties to confer an evolving meaning must be presumed in case of generic terms used in treaties concluded for long or unlimited duration, whose capacity to evolve cannot be ignored. In this case, this applied to the term 'commerce', which had evolved since 1858, date of the Treaty of Limits between Costa Rica and Nicaragua.[27]

Arguably, it is in the very nature and object and purpose of treaties aimed at the protection of the environment to opt for evolving interpretations sensitive to technical developments and new threats. A clear distinction must, however, be drawn and kept in perspective in these cases. One thing is an *evolving interpretation* and quite another, the incorporation of mechanisms allowing the *evolution of the provisions* of the treaty in question.[28]

C Policies

The jurisprudence of the Court reveals cases in which a pre-determined *policy* has led the interpretation through unorthodox roads.

A treaty is a written agreement between international subjects governed by international law.[29] Verbal agreements, even the tacit ones, can also be the source of rights and obligations should the Parties wish so, but this

---

[26] Aegean Sea Continental Shelf, Judgment, ICJ Reports 1978, para. 77.

[27] Dispute regarding Navigational and Related Rights (*Costa Rica* v. *Nicaragua*), Judgment, ICJ Reports 2009, paras. 63–71. It is worth recalling the lengthy considerations of the Court on commerce and freedom of commerce in the context of the 1955 Treaty of Amity, Economic Relations and Consular Rights between United States and Iran to base its jurisdiction in Oil Platforms (*Islamic Republic of Iran* v. *United States of America*), Preliminary Objection, Judgment, ICJ Reports 1996, para. 45 ff.).

[28] Gabčíkovo-Nagymaros Project (Hungary/Slovakia), Judgment, ICJ Reports 1997, paras. 112, 140; Pulp Mills on the River Uruguay (*Argentina* v. *Uruguay*), Judgment, ICJ Reports 2010, para. 204.

[29] Article 2.*1, a*, of the 1969 VCLT. Land and Maritime Boundary between Cameroon and Nigeria (*Cameroon* v. *Nigeria*: Equatorial Guinea intervening), Judgment, ICJ Reports 2002, para. 263; Maritime Delimitation in the Indian Ocean (*Somalia* v. *Kenya*), Preliminary Objections, Judgment, ICJ Reports 2017, para. 42.

does not turn them into treaties.[30] In *Maritime Dispute* the Court attached great relevance to a tacit agreement which, it was said, was presupposed and then crystallised in a written agreement, that is, a treaty. Nevertheless, determining the scope or extent of the tacit agreement required an assessment of an extensive practice that left the impression (justified or not) that the Court had conjured up the idea of the tacit agreement only to manufacture a result that was palatable for both Parties. This approach might be laudable in cases involving maritime delimitations governed by equitable criteria but, in others, it can turn the interpretation into a branch of engineering.[31]

It is well-known that, in order to identify a written agreement between international subjects as a treaty, the common intention of the parties to be bound under international law is decisive no matter the form of the agreement or the vague character of an obligation conceived in terms of aspirations or objectives.[32] In principle, the title or denomination of the instrument can be a useful indication but it is neither important nor final. As the 1969 VCLT provides (Article 2.1, a), and the jurisprudence of the Court has confirmed, most treaties do not introduce themselves as such in their title;[33] and even when they do, this does not automatically indicate that they are a *treaty*.

An illustrative example of the above can be found in the *protection treaties* with tribal chiefs, a technique extensively used by the colonial powers to consolidate, under legal terms, the occupation of territories in

---

[30] Territorial and Maritime Dispute between Nicaragua and Honduras in the Caribbean Sea (*Nicaragua* v. *Honduras*), Judgment, ICJ Reports 2007, para. 253; Sovereignty over Pedra Branca/Pulau Batu Puteh, Middle Rocks and South Ledge (Malaysia/Singapore), Judgment, ICJ Reports 2008, para. 120; Dispute regarding Navigational and Related Rights (*Costa Rica* v. *Nicaragua*), Judgment, ICJ Reports 2009, para. 64; Obligation to Negotiate Access to the Pacific Ocean (*Bolivia* v. *Chile*), Judgment, ICJ Reports 2018, para. 97.

[31] Maritime Dispute (*Peru* v. *Chile*), Judgment, ICJ Reports 2014, paras. 91, 102 ff.

[32] Certain Questions of Mutual Assistance in Criminal Matters (*Djibouti* v. *France*), Judgment, ICJ Reports 2008, para. 104.

[33] Aegean Sea Continental Shelf, Judgment, ICJ Reports 1978, para. 96; Maritime Delimitation and Territorial Questions between Qatar and Bahrain (*Qatar* v. *Bahrain*), Jurisdiction and Admissibility, Judgment, ICJ Reports 1994, paras. 21 ff., 41; Pulp Mills on the River Uruguay (*Argentina* v. *Uruguay*), Judgment, ICJ Reports 2010, paras. 125–131; Land and Maritime Boundary between Cameroon and Nigeria (*Cameroon* v. *Nigeria*: Equatorial Guinea intervening), Judgment, ICJ Reports 2002, para. 263 ff.; Maritime Dispute (*Peru* v. *Chile*), Judgment, ICJ Reports 2014, para. 45 ff.; Maritime Delimitation in the Indian Ocean (*Somalia* v. *Kenya*), Judgment, Prel. Obj., ICJ Reports, 2017, para. 41 ff.

Africa. The Court has not attached relevance to these *treaties* in territorial disputes concerning the boundaries between the new States born out of the decolonisation. Instead, it has given a sort of sacred value to the treaties of limits between the colonial powers.[34]

The right to self-determination has provided a more generous perspective when the agreements between the colony and the administering power) was not considered a treaty. In *Legal Consequences of the Separation of the Chagos Archipelago from Mauritius in 1965,* the Court denied that the Lancaster Agreement (1965) between United Kingdom and representatives of Mauritius was a treaty, considering that all the powers of the colony were in the hands of the administering power.[35] Fifteen years earlier, this same right to self-determination led the Court to treat the Interim Agreement of 28 September 1995 between Israel and the Palestine Liberalization Organization (PLO), then a national liberation movement, as a treaty.[36]

It is also well-established that a treaty can be constituted by two or more related instruments (Article 2.1 and Article 13 of the 1969 VCLT). This is

---

[34] The *continuity* of treaties creating *objective territorial regimes* in cases of succession is a well-established customary rule, confirmed by the jurisprudence (see, for example, Territorial Dispute (Libyun Aruh Jamuhiriyu/Chad), Judgment, ICJ Reports 1994, paras. 72–73; Gabčíkovo-Nagymaros Project (Hungary/Slovakia), Judgment, ICJ Reports 1997, para. 26; Land and Maritime Boundary between Cameroon and Nigeria (*Cameroon* v. *Nigeria*: Equatorial Guinea intervening), Judgment, ICJ Reports 2002, para. 194 ff.). It is also codified in Articles 11 and 12 of the 1978 Vienna Convention on succession of States in respect of treaties. This *continuity* was reflected on the principle of *intangibility* of the borders agreed in the treaties concluded by the colonial powers – often confused with the principle of *uti possidetis iuris* – which has governed the settlement of disputes between the new States born after the decolonisation, whose title has been based on the succession of rights and obligations of former colonial powers (Land and Maritime Boundary between Cameroon and Nigeria (*Cameroon* v. *Nigeria*: Equatorial Guinea intervening), Judgment, ICJ Reports 2002, paras. 31–38, 194 ff.). In some cases, the ambiguity of these treaties has caused lengthy discussions leading the Court to leave the treaties aside and look for a solution in the *effectivités* (Sovereignty over Pulau Ligitan and Pulau Sipadan (Indonesia/Malaysia), Judgment, ICJ Reports 2002, paras. 32 ff., 41 ff., 94 ff., 137 ff.; Sovereignty over Pedra Branca/Pulau Batu Puteh, Middle Rocks and South Ledge (Malaysia/Singapore), Judgment, ICJ Reports 2008, paras. 52, 59, 68–69, 96, 98). For a reference work on the topic, see Mamadou Hébié, *Souveraineté territoriale par traité. Une étude des accords entre puissances coloniales et entités politiques locales* (PUF, 2015).

[35] Legal Consequences of the Separation of the Chagos Archipelago from Mauritius in 1965, Advisory Opinion, ICJ Reports 2019, paras. 171–172.

[36] Legal Consequences of the Construction of a Wall in the Occupied Palestinian Territory, Advisory Opinion, ICJ Reports 2004, para. 118.

the paradigmatic case of the *exchange of letters*. In *Obligation to Negotiate Access to the Pacific Ocean,* the Applicant relied on an exchange of letters – followed by other agreement expressions – as the backbone of the impugned obligation. The Court, arguably cornered by the *policy* to ensure the broadest freedom of states in their diplomatic relations, in an extremely formalistic approach, held that none of the instruments before it manifested any intention of Respondent to be bound. In the Court's view, the fact of negotiating does not suffice to give rise to an obligation to negotiate. For the latter to materialise, it is necessary that the terms used, the object and the negotiation conditions show the *intention* of the Parties to be legally bound. This *intention*, in absence of express terms, can be established by an objective assessment of the evidence. In this case, the Court considered that Bolivia had not proved the existence of any obligation.[37] In reaching this conclusion, it can be argued that the Court did not see or go beyond the literal text, and ignored all the rest, the context included. It arguably elevated the threshold to prove the intention to be bound to heights that turns the latter into an ethereal, divine creature. The Court decontextualised and isolated each of the instruments relied on by the Applicant, and declined to find an obligation based on the principle of good faith.[38]

---

[37] Obligation to Negotiate Access to the Pacific Ocean (*Bolivia* v. *Chile*), Judgment, ICJ Reports 2018, paras. 91, 116–118, 126, 131–132.

[38] The negotiation must be conducted in accordance with the principle of *good faith,* which is essential in the process of creation and execution of international obligations (Article 26 of the 1969 VCLT) and implicit in any clause creating an obligation to negotiate (for a good number of examples, see Application of the Interim Accord of 13 September 1995 (the former *Yugoslav Republic of Macedonia* v. *Greece*), Judgment of 5 December 2011, ICJ Reports 2011, para. 131). However, the principle of good faith does not constitute a source of obligations when the latter do not have any other basis (Border and Transborder Armed Actions (*Nicaragua* v. *Honduras*), Jurisdiction and Admissibility, Judgment, ICJ Reports 1988, para. 94; Land and Maritime Boundary between Cameroon and Nigeria (*Cameroon* v. *Nigeria*: Equatorial Guinea intervening), Preliminary Objections, Judgment, ICJ Reports 1998, paras. 38–39. The obligation to cooperate in order to reach an agreement can be derived from a *pactum de negotiando* or *de contrahendo.* If this is the case, the Parties have to ensure that the negotiation is meaningful, which excludes conducts or actions aimed at insisting on or merely repeating their own positions without considering modifications or concessions or other interests, or seeking to unilaterally alter the procedures and time frames or to break off the talks without justification. In Application of the Interim Accord of 13 September 1995 (the former *Yugoslav Republic of Macedonia* v. *Greece*), Judgment of 5 December 2011, ICJ Reports 2011, paras. 132–138), the Court referred extensively to its previous jurisprudence to outline the characteristics of the obligation and apply them to the case. This also includes *compromissory clauses* that, as pre-condition before resorting

It might be suggested that the Court's desire to reach a determined outcome has inspired extremely formalistic decisions in other areas. In *Armed Activities on the Territory of the Congo,* the Court found that the reservations made by Rwanda to Article IX of the Genocide Convention (1948) and to Article 22 of the Convention on Racial Discrimination (1965) had not been withdrawn in absence of a written note to the Depositary, in accordance with Articles 22.3a) and 22.4 of the Convention, a disposition which materialised an international law rule derived from the principle of legal security and well-established in practice.[39] This rigorous formalism contrasted with the Court's flexibility when Croatia, in order to prove that the then Federal Republic of Yugoslavia (FRY) was party to the 1948 Convention, invoked as equivalent to a notification of succession the generic declaration adopted on 27 April 1992 in joint session of the Assembly of the former Socialist Federal Republic of Yugoslavia (SFRY), the National Assembly of the Republic of Serbia, and of the Assembly of the Republic of Montenegro. This document had been transmitted through a note to the UN Secretary General requiring its distribution as an official document of the Organisation. The Court ignored the formal requirements under Articles 2.1, *g,* 17 and 22 of the Vienna Convention on Succession of States in respect of Treaties (1978) and, considering the circumstances of the case, it essentially concluded that while this declaration was not *per se* a notification, it could still produce its effects.[40]

Clearly, this approach can only be explained by a desire to reach a specific outcome. The series of cases involving the FRY – then Serbia and Montenegro and finally Serbia – following the disintegration of what it will be called *Former Yugoslavia,* provides a complex picture that only becomes intelligible when its bottom-line is kept in perspective, namely that, before the Court, the FRY was welcomed as *Defendant* but rejected as

to arbitration or judicial settlement, bind the parties to negotiate. In conducting comparative analysis of texts and jurisprudence, the Court has pointed out the positive function of these clauses, indicating how and when the condition to negotiate has been satisfied (Application of the International Convention on the Elimination of All Forms of Racial Discrimination (*Georgia* v. *Russian Federation*), Preliminary Objections, Judgment, ICJ Reports 2011, paras. 131 ff., 156 ff.).

[39] Armed Activities on the Territory of the Congo (New Application: 2002) (*Democratic Republic of the Congo* v. *Rwanda*), Jurisdiction and Admissibility, Judgment, ICJ Reports 2006, paras. 29 ff., 41 ff.

[40] Application of the Convention on the Prevention and Punishment of the Crime of Genocide (*Croatia* v. *Serbia*), Preliminary Objections, Judgment, ICJ Reports 2008, paras. 108–111.

Applicant.[41] Given its negative reputation, it may be suspected that the *clean hands* doctrine, rejected by the Court every time it has been invoked without having to take a position on the principle,[42] still had an influence through the back door.

The resort to the *subsequent practice* as element of treaty interpretation (Article 31.3.b of the 1969 VCLT) provides the opportunity to unveil other cases where *policies* predetermine an interpretation.[43] While the Court takes into account frequently the *subsequent practice* in the application of a treaty to support its interpretation following the *general rule*, to determine the adequate interpretation of an expression or to assess its evolving sense or identify the object and purpose of the treaty,[44] there

---

[41] See Application of the Convention on the Prevention and Punishment of the Crime of Genocide (*Bosnia and Herzegovina* v. *Serbia and Montenegro*), Preliminary Objections, Judgment, ICJ Reports 1996, paras. 21–26; Application for revision of the Judgment of 11 July 1996 … (*Yugoslavia* v. *Bosnia and Herzegovina*, Judgment, ICJ Reports, 2003, paras. 69, 72; Legality of Use of Force (for instance, *Serbia and Montenegro* v. *Belgium*), Preliminary Objections, Judgment, ICJ Reports 2004, para. 100 ff.; Application of the Convention on the Prevention and Punishment of the Crime of Genocide (*Bosnia and Herzegovina* v. *Serbia and Montenegro*), Judgment, ICJ Reports 2007, paras. 80–140; Application of the Convention on the Prevention and Punishment of the Crime of Genocide (*Croatia* v. *Serbia*), Preliminary Objections, Judgment, ICJ Reports 2008, para. 101 ff.

[42] Avena and Other Mexican Nationals (*Mexico* v. *United States of America*), Judgment, ICJ Reports, 2004 (I), para. 47; Maritime Delimitation in the Indian Ocean (*Somalia* v. *Kenia*) Prel. Obj., Judgment, ICJ Reports, 2017, para. 142; Certain Iranian Assets (*Islamic Republic of Iran* v. *United States of America*), Prel. Obj., Judgment, ICJ Reports, 2019, paras. 105, 116–123. Israel also refers to it (*nullus commodum capere potest de sua iniuria propria*) in the context of the advisory proceedings concerning Legal Consequences of the Construction of a Wall in the Occupied Palestinian Territory, ICJ Reports, 2004, paras. 63–64.

[43] In 2018 the ILC adopted on second Reading thirteen conclusions on treaties and subsequent practice in relation of the interpretation of treaties. See George Nolte, *Treaties and their practice. Symptoms of their rise and decline*, Pocketbooks of the Hague Academy of International Law, 2018, pp. 173–216. The UNGA took note and reproduced the text of the conclusions in its resolution 73/202, 20 December 2018.

[44] Maritime Delimitation in the Area between Greenland and Jan Mayen (*Denmark* v. *Norway*), Judgment, ICJ Reports 1993, paras. 28–29; Territorial Dispute (Libyun Aruh Jamuhiriyu/Chad), Judgment, ICJ Reports 1994, para. 66 ff.; Legality of the Threat or Use of Nuclear Weapons, Advisory Opinion, ICJ Reports 1996, para. 19; Oil Platforms (*Islamic Republic of Iran* v. *United States of America*), Preliminary Objection, Judgment, ICJ Reports 1996, para. 30; Kasikili/Sedudu Island (Botswana/Namibia), Judgment, ICJ Reports 1999, para. 48; Sovereignty over Pulau Ligitan and Pulau Sipadan (Indonesia/Malaysia), Judgment, ICJ Reports 2002, para. 59 ff., 92; Legal Consequences of the Construction of a Wall in the Occupied Palestinian Territory, Advisory Opinion, ICJ Reports 2004, para. 96 ff.; Application of the Interim Accord of 13 September 1995 (The former *Yugoslav Republic*

seems to be a tendency to present *modifying* practices as *interpretative* exercises. In *Legal Consequences of the Construction of a Wall in the Occupied Palestinian Territory*, the Court found that the recommendatory practice of the General Assembly on matters that are being addressed by the Security Council is compatible with Article 12.1 of the UN Charter.[45] Tacit agreements or the institution of *acquiescence* could offer an alternative explanation.[46]

III Systemic Integration, Hierarchy and Concurrence

A Systemic Integration

Article 31.3.c) extends the basis of the interpretive exercise, adding to the materials to take into account 'any relevant rules of international law applicable in the relations between the parties'. This refers to other treaties that the Parties have concluded and the international law norms applicable to them.[47] This creates a normative context, a 'systemic integration' of the

of Macedonia v. *Greece*), Judgment, ICJ Reports 2011, paras. 99–101; Alleged Violations of Sovereign Rights and Maritime Spaces in the Caribbean Sea (*Nicaragua* v. *Colombia*), Preliminary Objections, Judgment, ICJ Reports 2016, para. 46; Immunities Criminal Proceedings (*Equatorial Guinea* v. *France*), Judgment, 11 December 2020, para. 69. In Whaling in the Antarctic (*Australia* v. *Japan*: New Zealand intervening), Judgment, ICJ Reports 2014 (para. 83) the Court considered that the IWC resolutions were mere recommendations that, without the support of all States parties, could not be regarded as subsequent agreement or subsequent practice within the meaning of subparagraphs (a) and (b), respectively, of paragraph (3) of Article 31 in relation of the interpretation of Article VIII of the 1946 International Convention for the Regulation of Whaling.

[45] Legal Consequences of the Construction of a Wall in the Occupied Palestinian Territory, Advisory Opinion, ICJ Reports 2004, para. 25 ff. Article 12.1 of the Charter disposes that: 'While the Security Council is exercising in respect of any dispute or situation the functions assigned to it in the present Charter, the General Assembly shall not make any recommendation with regard to that dispute or situation unless the Security Council so requests'.

[46] Land and Maritime Boundary between Cameroon and Nigeria (*Cameroon* v. *Nigeria*: Equatorial Guinea intervening), Judgment, ICJ Reports 2002, paras. 62–70, 223–224; Sovereignty over Pedra Branca/Pulau Batu Puteh, Middle Rocks and South Ledge (Malaysia/Singapore), Judgment, ICJ Reports 2008, para. 121. In Dispute regarding Navigational and Related Rights (*Costa Rica* v. *Nicaragua*), Judgment, ICJ Reports 2009, para. 64, the Court speculates with the idea that the subsequent practice can result in a departure from the original intention on the basis of a tacit agreement.

[47] Application of the Convention on the Prevention and Punishment of the Crime of Genocide (*Bosnia and Herzegovina* v. *Serbia and Montenegro*), Judgment, ICJ Reports 2007, para. 149; Application of the Convention on the Prevention and Punishment of the

treaty where it no longer applies hermetically sealed. The Court had the occasion to apply this principle in *Oil Platforms* (2003), assessing 'in the light of international law on the use of the force' the actions of United Sates against Iranian oil platforms. To justify them, United States had invoked Article XX.1, *d* of the 1955 Treaty of Amity, Economic Relations and Consular Rights between the United States of America and Iran, which allowed to the parties the application of measures necessary to protect their essential security interests.[48] In this case, the necessity to accommodate the subject-matter of the dispute to the basis of the Court's jurisdiction determined the peculiar form of the judgment's *dispositif.* The judges composing the majority were not satisfied with declaring only that, in the circumstances of the case, the freedom of commerce had not been perturbed, therefore adding that the actions of the United States could not be justified as necessary measures under Article XX.1, *d,* of the Treaty.

Article 31.3, *c,* has turned into a tabernacle of the unity of the system against its fragmentation.[49] However, handling it properly remains a delicate matter, especially considering that the consolidation of the *ius cogens* as cause of nullity and termination of treaties incompatible with peremptory norms (Article 53 and 64 of the 1969 VCLT) and the *constitutional* character recognised to the UN Charter in enshrining the primacy of its obligations (Article 30.1 in relation to Article 103 of the Charter), have given rise to a hierarchy with consequences that have not always been assessed thoroughly. The task is not easy. In addition to the *technique,* some sensitivity to and awareness of *values* is equally required, and the interpreter is not always immune to politically charged considerations.

The collision between the prosecution of international crimes by national judges and the immunities traditionally recognised to certain agents of the foreign State is a paradigmatic example. The rights of the individuals and the desire of justice (sometimes obligation to prosecute/ extradite) compete with the right of the foreign State to not have its agents

---

Crime of Genocide (*Croatia v. Serbia*), Judgment, ICJ Reports 2015, para. 125; Maritime Delimitation in the Indian Ocean (*Somalia v. Kenya*), Preliminary Objections, Judgment, ICJ Reports 2017, paras. 89–91.

[48] Oil Platforms (*Islamic Republic of Iran v. United States of America*), Judgment, ICJ Reports 2003, paras. 43–78.

[49] See the Report of the Study Work of the ILC on the Fragmentation of International Law: Difficulties arising from the diversification and expansion of International Law, A/CV.4/ L.682.

judicially prosecuted as consequence of the respect of their sovereign equality and the stability of international relations. To date, as far as the Court is concerned, in *Arrest Warrant of 11 April 2000,* the immunity has prevailed with dissenting votes, and doctrinal criticism.

The same holds when obligations arising from the UN Charter, such as those under the Chapter VII, apparently collide with those that underpin the *rule of law* and guarantee fundamental rights of the individual in democratic States.

Again, *time* intervenes with its own inquires when it comes to the determination of the rules that form the normative context of the treaty: are those that were born when the instrument was concluded or those existing when the dispute arose?

B Ius Cogens

To what extent and with what consequences has the *ius cogens* appeared in the jurisprudence of the Court? The ink of the 1969 VCLT was barely dry when the Judgment of 5 February 1970 in *Barcelona Traction* included an *obiter dictum* prompting a wave of doctrinal analysis: there were *erga omnes* obligations and their respect was a *legal interest,* a common interest shared by all States.[50] In reality, the underlying idea was already present and can be traced back to the advisory opinion of 1951 concerning *Reservations to the Convention on the Prevention and Punishment of the Crime of Genocide,* then evoked in *Questions relating to the Obligation to Prosecute or Extradite* in 2012. In this case, the Court admitted the Application filed by Belgium against Senegal for its mere condition of Party to the Convention against Torture and Other Cruel, Inhuman or Degrading Treatment or Punishment (1984), which contains obligations *erga omnes partes.*[51] The *erga omnes partes* character of the treaties that protect public common goods give States a basis to require compliance in defense of a general interest. However, when it comes to conventional obligations, its compliance could be required only with respect to facts

---

[50] Barcelona Traction, Light and Power Company, Limited (*Belgium* v. *Spain*), Judgment, ICJ Reports 1970, para. 33.
[51] Questions relating to the Obligation to Prosecute or Extradite (*Belgium* v. *Senegal*), Judgment, ICJ Reports 2012, para. 69.

occurring after the entry into force of the Convention for the Defendant. Therefore, the Court applied Article 28 of the 1969 VCLT.[52]

As *Barcelona Traction* showed, the fact that instances of peremptory norms have often been identified as *erga omnes* obligations,[53] when there existed still some reluctance to openly use that qualification, have led to some confusion between these two distinct concepts. While every peremptory norm has this *erga omnes* effect, not every *erga omnes* obligation qualifies as peremptory norm. It was only in 2006, after years tiptoeing around the question,[54] that the Court expressly mentioned for the first time that the 1948 Genocide Convention contained *erga omnes* obligations, and that its prohibition had the character of a *peremptory norm* (*ius cogens*).[55]

The next year, in 2007, the Court dealt with peremptory norms and obligations *erga omnes* in the context of the protection of essential humanitarian values.[56] In *Ahmadou Sadio Diallo* , the Court found that the prohibition of inhumane or degrading treatments is part of a rule of general international law that States have to respect in all circumstances, with independence of any conventional obligation.[57] In the advisory opinion concerning the *Accordance with International Law of the Unilateral Declaration of Independence in Respect of Kosovo*, the Court noted that the Security Council had condemned in the past some similar declarations (resolutions concerning South Rhodesia, northern Cyprus, and Republic of Srpska) for being connected with the unlawful use of force or other serious violations of norms general international law 'in particular

---

[52] *Ib.*, para. 100 ff.

[53] East Timor (*Portugal* v. *Australia*), Judgment, ICJ Reports 1995, para. 29.

[54] Application of the Convention on the Prevention and Punishment of the Crime of Genocide (*Bosnia and Herzegovina* v. *Serbia and Montenegro*), Preliminary Objections, Judgment, ICJ Reports 1996, para. 31; Legal Consequences of the Construction of a Wall in the Occupied Palestinian Territory, Advisory Opinion, ICJ Reports 2004, para. 155 ff..

[55] Armed Activities on the Territory of the Congo (New Application: 2002) (*Democratic Republic of the Congo* v. *Rwanda*), Jurisdiction and Admissibility, Judgment, ICJ Reports 2006, para. 64.

[56] Application of the Convention on the Prevention and Punishment of the Crime of Genocide (*Bosnia and Herzegovina* v. *Serbia and Montenegro*), Judgment, ICJ Reports 2007, paras. 147, 161; see also Application of the Convention on the Prevention and Punishment of the Crime of Genocide (*Croatia* v. *Serbia*), Judgment, ICJ Reports 2015, paras. 87–88.

[57] Ahmadou Sadio Diallo (*Republic of Guinea* v. *Democratic Republic of the Congo*), Merits, Judgment, ICJ Reports 2010, para. 87.

those of a peremptory character (*ius cogens*)'.[58] In *Questions relating to the Obligation to Prosecute or Extradite*, the Court referred to the prohibition of torture as a consuetudinary norm that has acquired the character of peremptory norm.[59] In its advisory opinion concerning the *Legal Consequences of the Separation of the Chagos Archipelago from Mauritius in 1965*, it emphasised that the respect for the right self-determination is an obligation *erga omnes*, and all States have a legal interest in protecting that right.[60]

It is notorious the impact of peremptory norms and, more generally, *erga omnes partes* treaty obligations in the field of human rights, humanitarian law, environment or protection of other public common goods, on the affirmation of their extraterritoriality. These treaties apply wherever the jurisdiction is exercised, territory or not of the concerned State. A treaty can be binding on a State regardless the status of the territory where it exercises its competences, by reason of its object. The advisory opinion concerning the *Legal Consequences of the Construction of a Wall in the Occupied Palestinian Territory* shed light on this.[61] The Court also delineated how States must conduct themselves with respect to the situation created by Israel in violation of the right to self-determination of Palestinian people and international humanitarian law, in particular Geneva Convention IV relative to the protection of civil population, all unconditional obligations *erga omnes*: non-recognition of the situation, no assistance to Israel, the duty to monitor that obstacles to the exercise of the Palestinian right to self-determination end, and observance of Geneva Convention IV by Israel.[62]

This boldness against crime has not been replicated, at least so far, in the context of contentious cases. The doctrine of the *indispensable party*, the

---

[58] Accordance with International Law of the Unilateral Declaration of Independence in Respect of Kosovo, Advisory Opinion, ICJ Reports 2010, para. 81.

[59] Questions relating to the Obligation to Prosecute or Extradite (Belgium v. Senegal), Judgment, ICJ Reports 2012, para. 99.

[60] Legal Consequences of the Separation of the Chagos Archipelago from Mauritius in 1965, Advisory Opinion, ICJ Reports 2019, para. 180.

[61] Legal Consequences for States of the Continued Presence of South Africa in Namibia (South-West Africa) notwithstanding Security Council Resolution 276 (1970), Advisory Opinion, ICJ Reports 1971, para. 118; Legal Consequences of the Construction of a Wall in the Occupied Palestinian Territory, Advisory Opinion, ICJ Reports 2004, 109 ff.

[62] Legal Consequences of the Construction of a Wall in the Occupied Palestinian Territory, Advisory Opinion, ICJ Reports 2004, paras. 159, 163.3.D).

strict standards to assess the basis of jurisdiction, and the absolute scope of the immunity of the foreign State and its agents constitute unsurmountable obstacles to the exercise by the Court of its natural function. In *East Timor*, the violation of obligations *erga omnes* did not cause the Court to depart from its strict requirement to link its jurisdiction to the consent of the third party with interests in the case that could be affected. Certainly, the Court faithfully recited the theory that the self-determination of peoples is 'one of the essential principles of contemporary international law',[63] but the *erga omnes* character of a norm is one thing and the consent to jurisdiction is another. In other words, the doctrine of the *indispensable party* buries the judicial pronouncement on the legal consequences of the peremptory norm.

In *Armed Activities on the Territory of the Congo (New Application: 2002)* and *Application of the Convention on the Prevention and Punishment of the Crime of Genocide (2007)*, the Court reiterated the separation between the issue of jurisdiction (consent requirement) and issues affecting the merits (the compatibility or not of state acts with international law), which can only be assessed once its jurisdiction has been asserted; a process that is not altered by the involvement of *erga omnes* obligations or the breach of an obligation of peremptory character.[64] In the former case, the Applicant relied on Article 66*a* of the 1969 VCLT as basis of jurisdiction. However, the Court went off on a tangent and stated that the jurisdiction provided by this provision to address causes of nullity and termination concerning *ius cogens* did not have (Article 4 of the 1969 VCLT) retroactive effect. They were applicable only to treaties concluded after the entry into force of the Convention for the Parties concerned; besides, Article 66 was not declaratory of a customary rule.[65]

On the other hand, it is worth noting that in this case the Applicant, in order to establish the jurisdiction of the Court, challenged the reservations

---

[63] East Timor (*Portugal* v. *Australia*), Judgment, ICJ Reports 1995, para. 29.

[64] Armed Activities on the Territory of the Congo (New Application: 2002) (*Democratic Republic of the Congo* v. *Rwanda*), Jurisdiction and Admissibility, Judgment, ICJ Reports 2006, paras. 64, 125; Application of the Convention on the Prevention and Punishment of the Crime of Genocide (*Bosnia and Herzegovina* v. *Serbia and Montenegro*), Judgment, ICJ Reports 2007, paras. 147–148.

[65] Armed Activities on the Territory of the Congo (New Application: 2002) (*Democratic Republic of the Congo* v. *Rwanda*), Jurisdiction and Admissibility, Judgment, ICJ Reports 2006, paras.120 ff., 125.

made by Rwanda to Article IX of the 1948 Convention on the Prevention and Punishment of the Crime of Genocide and to Article 22 of 1965 International Convention on the Elimination of All Forms of Racial Discrimination. It argued that they hinder the protection of peremptory norms and, in consequence, they should be considered without effect. According to the Court, the fact that a dispute involves rights and obligations *erga omnes* or peremptory norms (*ius cogens*) does not suffice to make an exception to the principle that its jurisdiction is based on consent.[66]

While in *Arrest Warrant of 11 April 2000*, the Court confirmed the immunity of a Foreign Affairs Minister accused of international crimes,[67] in *Jurisdictional Immunities of the State*, it affirmed that the commission of an international crime does not affect the immunity of the State concerned. In its view, there is no conflict between the latter, of procedural nature, and the legality of the conduct according to international humanitarian law (*ius cogens*) and the obligation of reparation, of substantive nature, only assessable once established the jurisdiction. Therefore, the Court does not wish to subject the stability of international relations to the turbulences originated by a decentralised prosecution of crimes, no matter how heinous they can be. It attempted to mitigate the criticism affirming that the immunity does not entail impunity, for the prosecution is still possible before international tribunals (when they exist) or before national tribunals of the nationality of the agent(s) in question or by tribunals of third States (when the immunity is lifted). The Court also appeared to be interested in pointing out how national courts adopted a similar approach.[68]

In short, the Court seems particularly sensitive to the maintenance of the rights of the State and, of course, the State itself over any other value. It is worth recalling its advisory opinion in *Legality of the Threat or Use of Nuclear Weapons*, and how it finally chose the agonic prevalence of the survival of the State over humanitarian principles.[69]

---

[66] *Ib.*, paras. 66–79, 125.

[67] Arrest Warrant of 11 April 2000 (*Democratic Republic of the Congo* v. *Belgium*), Judgment, ICJ Reports 2002, paras. 58, 78).

[68] Jurisdictional Immunities of the State (*Germany* v. *Italy*: Greece intervening), Judgment, ICJ Reports 2012, paras. 58, 92–97.

[69] 'In view of the current state of international law the Court cannot conclude definitively whether the threat or use of nuclear weapons would be lawful or unlawful in an extreme circumstance of self-defence, in which the very survival of a State would be at stake'. Legality of the Threat or Use of Nuclear Weapons, Advisory Opinion of 8 July 1996, para. 105, E. It was the casting vote of President Bedjaoui that allowed the approval of

C The Constitutional Character of the UN Charter

Turning now to the *constitutional* character of the UN Charter, based on its virtually universal scope, the Court had already confirmed its *erga omnes* effects in its second advisory opinion.[70] Although the Court has not been conceived as a constitutional court, invested with powers to decide on the validity or nullity of the resolutions adopted by the UN organs, its character as principal judicial organ of the UN (Article 92 of the UN Charter) has allowed it to tackle its interpretation and application when necessary.[71]

In the advisory opinion concerning the *Accordance with International Law of the Unilateral Declaration of Independence in Respect of Kosovo*, it was noted that, while the responsibility to interpret and apply a decision by one of the political UN organs concerns first the organ in question, the Court has been often called, as principal judicial organ of the Organisation, to interpret and assess its legal effects.[72]

As far as its contentious jurisdiction is concerned, the resort of the Security Council to its coercive discretionary powers in the context of the maintenance of international peace and security has given rise to claims accusing the UN organ of acting *ultra vires*, placing the focus on the issue of the judicial control of its resolutions. The *Lockerbie* cases were a first significant test. The Court had to deny *prima facie* the provisional measures requested by the Applicant for their collision with the resolutions of the Security Council, which prevailed as a result of the combined effect of Article 25 and Article 103 of the UN Charter.[73] However, in the

---

this paragraph (tied vote 7 to 7). The defeated half was a diverse combination of views divided between judges strongly condemning the weapons and others considering their use as a last resort.

[70] Reparation for Injuries Suffered in the Service of the United Nations, Advisory Opinion, ICJ Reports 1949, p. 185.

[71] Certain Expenses of the United Nations (Article 17, paragraph 2, of the Charter), Advisory Opinion, ICJ Reports 1962, pp. 175–177; Legal Consequences for States of the Continued Presence of South Africa in Namibia (South-West Africa) notwithstanding Security Council Resolution 276 (1970), Advisory Opinion, ICJ Reports 1971, paras. 56, 107–116.

[72] Accordance with International Law of the Unilateral Declaration of Independence in Respect of Kosovo, Advisory Opinion, ICJ Reports 2010, para. 46.

[73] Questions of Interpretation and Application of the 1971 Montreal Convention arising from the Aerial Incident at Lockerbie (*Libyan Arab Jamahiriya* v. *United Kingdom*), Provisional Measures, Order of 14 April 1992, ICJ Reports 1992, paras. 39–41. Questions of Interpretation and Application of the 1971 Montreal Convention arising from the Aerial Incident at Lockerbie (*Libyan Arab Jamahiriya* v. *United States of America*), Provisional Measures, Order of 14 April 1992, ICJ Reports 1992, paras. 42–44.

Judgment of 1998 on preliminary objections, the Court asserted its jurisdiction and declared the claims admissible on the ground that the resolutions had been adopted *after* the Application, reserving for the merits its
decision on whether the claims had lost their object as result of the
resolutions. For the Court, this objection did not have an exclusively
preliminary character as it required a decision on: 1) the compatibility
between the rights of Libya according to the Montreal Convention and
its obligations arising from the SC resolutions; and, 2) the prevalence of
the latter according to Article 25 and Article 103 of the UN Charter.[74] These
questions were left unaddressed as a result of the decision of the Parties to
discontinue the proceedings and the removal of the cases from the List.[75]

In *Application of the Convention on the Prevention and Punishment of
the Crime of Genocide,* Bosnia and Herzegovina asked the Court to lift the
embargo of arms imposed by the Security Council to all parties to the
conflict, claiming that it violated its right to legitimate defense according
to the UN Charter. The Court summarily dismissed the request pointing out
that, since its jurisdiction was based on the Genocide Convention, it could
only decide on issues related to it. Following this first attempt, Bosnia and
Herzegovina claimed that it has the right to protect itself including by
means of obtaining military equipment and armament. Again, the Court
rejected the argument noting that, in accordance with Article 41 of its
Statute, it could decide provisional measures only *inter partes.*[76]

In short, while decisions concerning the nullity of a SC resolution that is
incompatible with the UN Charter or with peremptory norms of international law fall outside the jurisdictional limits of the Court, it seems
possible that the Court can decide on its *applicability* to properly exercise

---

[74] Questions of Interpretation and Application of the 1971 Montreal Convention arising from
the Aerial Incident at Lockerbie (*Libyan Arab Jamahiriya* v. *United Kingdom*), Preliminary
Objections, Judgment, ICJ Reports 1998, para. 46 ff.; Questions of Interpretation and
Application of the 1971 Montreal Convention arising from the Aerial Incident at
Lockerbie (*Libyan Arab Jamahiriya* v. *United States of America*), Preliminary Objections,
Judgment, ICJ Reports 1998, para. 45 ff.

[75] Questions of Interpretation and Application of the 1971 Montreal Convention arising from
the Aerial Incident at Lockerbie (*Libyan Arab Jamahiriya* v. *United Kingdom*), Order of
10 September 2003; Questions of Interpretation and Application of the 1971 Montreal
Convention arising from the Aerial Incident at Lockerbie (*Libyan Arab Jamahiriya*
v. *United States of America*), Order of 10 September 2003.

[76] Application of the Convention on the Prevention and Punishment of the Crime of
Genocide, Provisional Measures, Order of 13 September 1993, ICJ Reports 1993, para. 41.

its function. This is not an exercise alien to the 'systemic integration' principle, and the obligation of the judge to decide 'in conformity with international law'. How the Security Council approaches fundamental human rights in the fight against terrorism creates tensions, in particular when its resolutions come into contact with treaties protecting human rights and peremptory norms that the Court cannot sacrifice in the name of Article 25 and Article 103 of the UN Charter. The Security Council is not *legibus solutus*; its prevalence is predicated on a presumption of respect for the purposes and principles of the Charter.

D Particular Regimes or Subsystems

The so-called *particular regimes* or *subsystems* are not *self-contained*. Their validity and continuity still require the application of general rules of international law.[77] International regimes have specific rules to address and resolve their own conflicts applying express rules or finding guidance in principles such as the principle of hierarchy, *lex specialis, lex posterior, more favorable provision*, principle of harmonisation and evolving inter-pretation, which would be applicable under the circumstances. These are rules that also apply to conflicts between – or with – treaties concluded by the same parties outside the international regimes (Article 30 and Article 41 of the 1969 VCLT). A more difficult issue arises from situations of concurrence and conflict between norms of different regimes. In these cases, the friction is further qualified by the fact that the organs of each subsystem will tend to give *constitutional* character to the treaties that found their own

---

[77] A *particular international regime* or *subsystem* is based on a multilateral treaty of universal or regional scope, normally concluded by the primary subjects of the system in accordance with the general norms governing the conclusion of treaties. For a *regime* to be created, the treaty in question has to include primary and secondary rules. It will be 'more' regime, 'more subsystem' if it has its own organs: a) to formulate new rights and obligations through the modification of the treaties, the conclusion of other treaties for its execution and development or the articulation of subordinate regulation methods; b) to monitor and control the observance of the agreed obligations; c) to facilitate the binding settlement of disputes concerning the interpretation and application of the treaties and subordinate rules; and d) to regulate and decide the consequences of their breach. See A. Remiro Brotons, 'La noción de regímenes internacionales en el Derecho Internacional Público', in A. J. Rodrigo Hernández and C. García Segura (eds.), *Unidad y Pluralismo en el Derecho Internacional Público y en la Comunidad Internacional*, Coloquio en Homenaje a Oriol Casanovas (Tecnos, 2011) pp. 167–176.

powers. As the Report on Fragmentation of International Law of the Study Group of the International Law Commission, described it: 'The whole complex of inter-regime relations is presently a legal blackhole'.[78]

For a principle to become general it must transcend the regime of origin so that it can prevail when invoked in the context of any other regime. However, in order to properly verify this evolution it is necessary to resort to an external organ (outside the regimes concerned) and/or to establish general norms to resolve conflicts between regimes. In the context of international judicial policy discussions, there have been proposals to turn the Court into a supreme court or a court of cassation of sorts. It would become a guardian of the unity of doctrine issuing preliminary rulings that other tribunals harbouring doubts concerning the existence, content and applicability of a general rule of international law could use for guidance. That is institutional science fiction. In actuality, there is no doubt that the Court, on one hand, *takes note of* the approaches of other courts and tribunals[79] suggesting, on the other hand, that these courts and tribunals avoid pronouncements on general norms of international law when it is not necessary for the case under their jurisdiction.[80]

E Together but Distinct

According to the Court, the interaction between conventional norms and general or customary norms does not prevent them from retaining their own individuality, independence, and distinct binding force, including when their content is identical. It was in *Military and Paramilitary Activities in and against Nicaragua* that this independence of the sources and its practical consequences were more clearly expressed. The Respondent had challenged jurisdiction, invoking the reservation concerning the interpretation of multilateral treaties incorporated to the declaration of acceptance under the *optional clause* (Article 36.2 of the Statute). In its view, the Court lacked, in procedural terms, norms applicable to the

---

[78] *Fragmentation of International Law*, p. 253.

[79] See, for instance, Ahmadou Sadio Diallo (*Republic of Guinea* v. *Democratic Republic of the Congo*), Merits, Judgment, ICJ Reports 2010, paras. 66–68. See also Philippa Webb, Chapter 11, The ICJ and other Courts and Tribunals: Integration and Fragmentation.

[80] Application of the Convention on the Prevention and Punishment of the Crime of Genocide (*Bosnia and Herzegovina* v. *Serbia and Montenegro*), Judgment, ICJ Reports 2007, paras. 399–407.

merits and therefore could not pass a judgment because its reservation excluded the application of customary norms which content could only be spell out looking at the UN and OAS Charters invoked by Nicaragua. The Court rejected the challenge to jurisdiction.[81]

Subsequent judgments seemed to confirm the position of the Court. In *Armed Activities on the Territory of the Congo*, the Court, reiterating its approach in *Application of the Convention on the Prevention and Punishment of the Crime of Genocide* (1996) held that 'the principles underlying the [Genocide] Convention are principles which are recognised by civilised nations as binding on States, even without any conventional obligation'[82]. However, in the Genocide cases, this distinction between the general or customary norm and the conventional one, examined in terms of a jurisdiction founded on the 1948 Convention, carried as a consequence the impossibility to rely on consuetudinary norms to assess the facts submitted to the jurisdiction of the Court.[83] Nevertheless, international humanitarian rules could still be relevant to the question whether they constituted genocide under Article II of the Convention.[84]

F The Role of Municipal Law

Every treaty in force has to be respected in good faith (Article 26 of the 1969 VCLT). The Court has recalled this on multiple occasions.[85] According to Article 27 of the 1969 VCLT, a State cannot invoke its national law as justification for its failure to perform a treaty. The provision is supported

---

[81] Military and Paramilitary Activities in and against Nicaragua (*Nicaragua* v. *United States of America*), Jurisdiction and Admissibility, Judgment, ICJ Reports 1984, para. 69 ff. and Military and Paramilitary Activities in and against Nicaragua (*Nicaragua* v. *United States of America*), Merits, Judgment. ICJ Reports 1986, para172 ff.

[82] Armed Activities on the Territory of the Congo (New Application: 2002) (*Democratic Republic of the Congo* v. *Rwanda*), Jurisdiction and Admissibility, Judgment, ICJ Reports 2006, para. 64.

[83] Application of the Convention on the Prevention and Punishment of the Crime of Genocide (*Croatia* v. *Serbia*), Judgment, ICJ Reports 2015, paras. 85–88, 124.

[84] *Ib.,* para. 153.

[85] Nuclear Tests (*Australia* v. *France*), Judgment, ICJ Reports 1974, para. 46, Nuclear Tests (*New Zealand* v. *France*), Judgment, ICJ Reports 1974, para. 49; Border and Transborder Armed Actions (*Nicaragua* v. *Honduras*), Jurisdiction and Admissibility, Judgment, ICJ Reports 1988, para. 94; Certain Questions of Mutual Assistance in Criminal Matters (*Djibouti* v. *France*), Judgment, ICJ Reports 2008, para. 145; Pulp Mills on the River Uruguay (*Argentina* v. *Uruguay*), Judgment, ICJ Reports 2010, para. 145.

by a well-established jurisprudence.[86] In Article 46, the Convention includes as an exception *the manifest violation of an internal law provision regarding competence to conclude treaties,* as cause of nullity, or better yet, annulation of a treaty. However, considering the restrictive interpretation applied by the Court, finding an example of this is like looking for a needle in a haystack.

In *Application of the Convention on the Prevention and Punishment of the Crime of Genocide* (1996), the Court did not considere it necessary to look at the legality of the nomination of a Head of State under municipal law, once it is recognised as such by United Nations and international law presumes that it could act, in that capacity, on behalf of the State in international relations.[87] In *Land and Maritime Boundary between Cameroon and Nigeria,* the Court affirmed that States are not bound to be informed of constitutional or legislative norms of other States that could be important for international relations. It concluded that limitations prescribed by fundamental norms of national law to the capacity of a Head of State who is, according to the function, representing the State (Article 7.2 of the 1969 VCLT), cannot be considered *manifest* under Article 46.2 unless adequately publicised.[88]

It is well-known that, in general, national law and its application at domestic level are considered as mere facts vis-a-vis international law and its agents. Nevertheless, the Court has been interested to determine whether a State has breached its international obligations through domestic law;[89] to establish an interpretation of some terms used in a

---

[86] See Questions relating to the Obligation to Prosecute or Extradite (*Belgium* v. *Senegal*), Judgment, ICJ Reports 2012, para. 113.

[87] Application of the Convention on the Prevention and Punishment of the Crime of Genocide (*Bosnia and Herzegovina* v. *Serbia and Montenegro*), Preliminary Objections, Judgment, ICJ Reports 1996, para. 44.

[88] Land and Maritime Boundary between Cameroon and Nigeria (*Cameroon* v. *Nigeria*: Equatorial Guinea intervening), Judgment, ICJ Reports 2002, paras. 265–266. The Court reiterated it in Maritime Delimitation in the Indian Ocean (*Somalia* v. *Kenya*), Preliminary Objections, Judgment, ICJ Reports 2017, para. 48 ff. See also Armed Activities on the Territory of the Congo (New Application: 2002) (*Democratic Republic of the Congo* v. *Rwanda*), Jurisdiction and Admissibility, Judgment, ICJ Reports 2006, para. 46.

[89] Application of the Convention of 1902 Governing the Guardianship of Infants (*Netherlands* v. *Sweden*), Judgment, ICJ Reports 1958, para. 62 ff.; LaGrand (*Germany* v. *United States of America*), Judgment, ICJ Reports 2001, paras. 50, 79 ff., 90–91, 125; Avena and Other Mexican Nationals (*Mexico* v. *United States of America*), Judgment, ICJ Reports 2004, paras. 27–28; Certain Questions of Mutual Assistance in Criminal Matters

treaty;[90] to prove the content of a consuetudinary norm, namely the principle of *uti possidetis,* which depends on constitutional and administrative law (*Indian* or colonial law);[91] to assess the *effectivités* supporting a territorial title;[92] to verify the immunities of a foreign State,[93] Head of State, Government, and Ministers of Foreign Affairs;[94] to examine the conditions to exercise diplomatic protection;[95] to determine whether and how the Parties approach the delimitation of a future maritime border;[96] to decide the remedies following the establishment of responsibility for the commission of an international illicit;[97] or, exceptionally, to *correct* an interpretation of national law when the concerned State provides one that is manifestly incorrect.[98]

(*Djibouti* v. *France*), Judgment, ICJ Reports 2008, para. 123 ff., 145 ff.; Ahmadou Sadio Diallo (*Republic of Guinea* v. *Democratic Republic of the Congo*), Merits, Judgment, ICJ Reports 2010, para. 63 ff.; Questions relating to the Obligation to Prosecute or Extradite (*Belgium* v. *Senegal*), Judgment, ICJ Reports 2012, para. 85 ff.; Immunities and Criminal Proceedings (*Equatorial Guinea* v. *France*), Preliminary Objections, Judgment, ICJ Reports 2018, paras. 113–114.

[90] Certain Iranian Assets (*Islamic Republic of Iran* v. *United States of America*), Preliminary Objections, Judgment, ICJ Reports 2019, para. 81 ff.

[91] Frontier Dispute (Burkina Faso/Republic of Mali), Judgment, ICJ Reports 1986, para. 63; Land, Island and Maritime Frontier Dispute (El Salvador/Honduras: Nicaragua intervening), Judgment, ICJ Reports 1992, para. 333; Frontier Dispute (Benin/Niger), Judgment, ICJ Reports 2005, paras. 24 ff, 37 ff.; Territorial and Maritime Dispute between Nicaragua and Honduras in the Caribbean Sea (*Nicaragua* v. *Honduras*), Judgment, ICJ Reports 2007, para. 159 ff.

[92] Frontier Dispute (Burkina Faso/Republic of Mali), Judgment, ICJ Reports 1986, para. 63; Sovereignty over Pulau Ligitan and Pulau Sipadan (Indonesia/Malaysia), Judgment, ICJ Reports 2002, para. 137 ff.; Frontier Dispute (Benin/Niger), Judgment, ICJ Reports 2005, paras. 27, 75 ff.; Territorial and Maritime Dispute between Nicaragua and Honduras in the Caribbean Sea (*Nicaragua* v. *Honduras*), Judgment, ICJ Reports 2007, para. 165 ff.; Sovereignty over Pedra Branca/Pulau Batu Puteh, Middle Rocks and South Ledge (Malaysia/Singapore), Judgment, ICJ Reports 2008, para. 164 ff.; Territorial and Maritime Dispute (*Nicaragua* v. *Colombia*), Judgment, ICJ Reports 2012, para. .82 ff.

[93] Jurisdictional Immunities of the State (*Germany* v. *Italy*: Greece intervening), Judgment, ICJ Reports 2012, para. 70 ff.

[94] Arrest Warrant of 11 April 2000 (*Democratic Republic of the Congo* v. *Belgium*), Judgment, ICJ Reports 2002, para. 58.

[95] Ahmadou Sadio Diallo (*Republic of Guinea* v. *Democratic Republic of the Congo*), Preliminary Objections, Judgment, ICJ Reports 2007, paras. 36, 43, 48, 68, 74.

[96] Maritime Dispute (*Peru* v. *Chile*), Judgment, ICJ Reports 2014, para. 39.

[97] Avena and Other Mexican Nationals (*Mexico* v. *United States of America*), Judgment, ICJ Reports 2004, para. 128 ff.

[98] Ahmadou Sadio Diallo (*Republic of Guinea* v. *Democratic Republic of the Congo*), Merits, Judgment, ICJ Reports 2010, para. 70.

IV Conclusion

In interpreting treaties, the Court has relied constantly on Articles 31 and 32 VCLT as general norms of international law. The problems stemming from generic texts, willfully ambiguous or obscure in order to facilitate the agreement of the parties, have called for the full operation of all the rules of interpretation, particularly when the intrinsic difficulties of the exegetic exercise have been accompanied with the complications created by the uses of languages other than the Court's official languages or the passing of time. Deciphering the intention of the parties through translations of an authentic text or recurring to presumptions to support its evolutive meaning are controversial exercises.

The role of the *policies* of the Court must be further discussed. Those policies, not always explicit, may be contentious. The biggest risk is that their pursuit in specific cases could require the adoption of interpretations adapted to the goals of the majority of the judges, which may result in an incongruent jurisprudence taken as a whole. For instance, in relation to the consent of States to be bound by treaties, the Court has oscillated from the most rigid formalism in certain cases to laxness in others. The step from policy to prejudice is as tenuous as dangerous. The conclusion of a judicial reasoning cannot become its premise. Judges must not behave as advocates.

The application of the systemic integration principle, as established in article 31.1.c VCLT, has numerous practical problems when applied according to the hierarchy of legal sources, due to the prevalence of the *jus cogens* and the obligations arising from the Charter of the United Nations, and to the relative autonomy of the different particular regimes or subsystems. Sensibility towards the values, technical skills and political considerations abound in the solutions, which are variable according to the percentage of these elements in the mix. Until now the Court has been the guardian of the interests of the sovereign state and has reclaimed that any other judicial institution abides by its view of general international law when deciding within their own ambits of competence.

Lastly, domestic law is considered pure fact by international law and the possibility of invalidating a treaty due to the manifest breach of any of its fundamental provisions regarding the competence to conclude treaties is more theoretical than real. However, in practice, domestic law has played and continues to have a very relevant role in the correct application of treaties and, more generally, in the due exercise of the judicial function by the Court.

Further Reading

E. Bjorge, *The Evolutionary Interpretation of Treaties* (Oxford University Press, 2014).

Irina Buga, *Modification of Treaties by Subsequent Practice*, Oxford University Press, 2018.

Ch Djeffal, *Static and Evolutive Treaty Interpretation: A Functional Reconstructio* (Cambridge University Press, 2016).

Chang Fa Lo, *Treaty Interpretation under the Vienna Convention on the Law of Treaties: A New Round of Codification* (Springer, 2018).

Richard Gardiner, *Treaty Interpretation* (Oxford University Press, 2015).

Vera Gowlland-Debbas, 'The Role of the ICJ in the Development of the Contemporary Law of Treaties', in Christian J. Tams and James Sloan (eds.), *The Development of International Law by the ICJ* (Oxford University Press, 2013) 29.

Mamadou Hébié, *Souveraineté territoriale par traité. Une étude des accords entre puissances coloniales et entités politiques locales* (Presses Universitaires de France, 2015).

Report of the Study Work of the ILC, finalised by Martti Koskenniemi, Fragmentation of International Law: Difficulties arising from the diversification and expansion of International Law, A/CV.4/L.682, 13 April 2006.

Robert Kolb, 'L'Article 103 de la Charte des Nations Unies', *Recueil des Cours de l'Académie de Droit International de la Haye*, v. 367, 2013, pp. 9–252 (edited also in the series of the Pocketbooks of the Academy, 2014).

Georg Nolte, 'Treaties and their Practice: Symptoms on Their Rise and Decline', *Recueil des Cours de l'Académie de Droit International de La Haye*, v. 392, 2017, pp. 205–397 (edited also in the series of the Pocketbooks of the Academy, 2018).

Antonio Remiro Brotóns, 'La noción de regímenes internacionales en el Derecho Internacional Público', in Ángel J. Rodrigo Hernández y Caterina García Segura (eds.), *Unidad y Pluralismo en el Derecho Internacional Público y en la Comunidad Internacional*, Coloquio en Homenaje a Oriol Casanovas (Tecnos, 2011) 167.

J. Wyatt, *Intertemporal Linguistics in International Law: Beyond Contemporaneous and Evolutionary Treaty Interpretation*, Hart Publishing, 2021.

15 Territorial Disputes

Marcelo Kohen and Mamadou Hébié

I Introduction

This chapter deals with the contribution of the jurisprudence of the International Court of Justice (the ICJ, or the Court) to the development of the 'law of territory'. As a term of art within the meaning of international law, the notion of 'territory' refers not only to the emerged land, but also to the airspace, the territorial sea, and the internal waters.[1] However, by referring to 'territorial disputes', this chapter concerns itself only with disputes relating to the sovereignty over emerged land. There are no specific rules of international law governing the acquisition of sovereignty over the airspace and the internal waters that are only land appurtenances. Accordingly, sovereignty over the airspace and the internal waters derives from sovereignty over the emerged land.[2] As far as the 'territorial sea' is concerned, disputes relating to the delimitation of the territorial sea are governed by the law of the sea. They are settled according to rules that are neatly distinguishable from those applicable to land disputes.[3] Nonetheless, some maritime features form part of state territory and can therefore be appropriated under international law. The case law of the Court clarified that, unlike low-tide elevations, islands and rocks can be appropriated.[4]

---

[1] *Military and Paramilitary Activities in and against Nicaragua (Nicaragua v. United States of America), Merits*, ICJ Reports 1986, p. 14 at 111, para. 212.

[2] In the *Croatia/Slovenia* case, the arbitral tribunal considered that the rules applicable to the delimitation of international waters were those applicable to the delimitation of land. Consequently, it applied *uti possidetis iuris* and the rules governing the relationship between titles and *effectivités* as those rules are applied in territorial disputes (Croatia/ Slovenia Arbitration, Award, 2017, para. 886 (Perm. Ct. Arb, 27 June).

[3] See Articles 3 and 15 of the UN Convention on the Law of the Sea.

[4] *Territorial and Maritime Dispute (Nicaragua v. Colombia), Judgment*, ICJ Reports 2012, p. 624 at 641, para. 26.

They can therefore be characterised as 'territory' within the meaning of international law.[5]

The law applicable to the settlement of territorial disputes is not codified. The large majority of the rules in this field are to be found in customary international law, as derived from century-long state practice and *opinio iuris*, echoed by their arbitral and judicial application since the beginning of the nineteenth century. In addition, the international law rules applicable to the settlement of territorial disputes have evolved over time and have been influenced by the changes that the fundamental principles contained in the Charter of the United Nations brought to the contemporary international legal order. The task of conceptualising and systematising the international legal framework deriving from these heterogeneous sources fell on the Court, which is nowadays the leading forum for the settlement of territorial disputes (II). As a result, understanding the jurisprudence of the Court is a fundamental prerequisite for any meaningful engagement with territorial disputes. The contribution of the Court is omnipresent in this field and can be regrouped in the following three categories: first, the reconceptualisation of the rules of international law governing the acquisition of territorial sovereignty (III); the clarification of the territorial implications of the fundamental principles of international law (IV); and finally, the elaboration of a clear and coherent method for the legal settlement of territorial disputes, the core of which rests on respect for the principle of legality (V).

II The Court as the Leading Forum for the Settlement of Territorial Disputes

The Court is the only permanent judicial organ with a general jurisdiction encompassing the settlement of territorial disputes (A). This permanence has laid the ground for the Court to establish a competitive edge over arbitral tribunals for their settlement (B).

A The Unique Jurisdiction of the Court

The jurisdiction of the Court is both large and limited. Under Article 34 of the Statute of the Court, only States have access to the Court. This limited

---

[5] This chapter does not deal with disputes relating to other territorial rights, such as navigational rights, rights of transit, servitudes, etc.

jurisdiction *ratione personae* excludes other entities that may have rights or interests in territorial disputes, especially peoples and secessionist movements. Yet, the Court had the opportunity to deal with claims by peoples or secessionist movements thanks to its advisory function. Under Article 65(1) of its Statute, the Court may deliver an advisory opinion on 'any legal question' upon the request of the General Assembly, the Security Council or any other UN organ or specialised agency authorised by the General Assembly to request such opinion. As a result, the Court delivered advisory opinions involving the territorial rights of the peoples of South-West Africa (currently Namibia), Western Sahara, Palestine, and Mauritius. The Court also delivered an advisory opinion on the conformity with international law of the declaration of independence of Kosovo.

Ratione materiae, the jurisdiction of the Court extends to all disputes under international law, including therefore territorial disputes. No other permanent international tribunal has a comparable jurisdiction *ratione materiae*. The jurisdiction of the International Tribunal for the Law of the Sea, the other permanent tribunal that is universal in design and possesses jurisdiction over States, is limited to disputes relating to the interpretation and application of the 1982 United Nations Convention on the Law of the Sea (hereinafter UNCLOS), and conventions related to the purposes of UNCLOS.[6] Tribunals exercising jurisdiction under UNCLOS may deal with 'in some instances a minor issue of territorial sovereignty' that are 'ancillary' to a dispute concerning the interpretation and application of the Convention. However, when the very subject-matter of a dispute relates to territorial sovereignty, such a dispute cannot be brought before tribunals established under UNCLOS.[7]

B Possible Reasons Justifying the Court's Attractiveness

Since its first sitting on 18 April 1946, the Court has been seized of twenty-four territorial disputes by States. Six advisory opinions involving

---

[6] Article 288, paras. 1 and 2 UNCLOS.

[7] *Award in the Arbitration regarding the Chagos Marine Protected Area between Mauritius and the United Kingdom of Great Britain and Northern Ireland*, XXI UNRIAA 359 at p. 460, paras. 220–221 (2015); See also, *The South China Sea Arbitration (The Republic of Philippines* v. *The People's Republic of China)*, Judgment on preliminary objections, 29 October 2015 (PCA), pp. 59–60, paras. 152–153 (2015).

territorial matters, out of twenty-nine in total, have been requested from the Court by the General Assembly and the Security Council.[8] During the same period, only eight territorial disputes have been submitted to arbitration.[9] Some of the territorial disputes that were submitted to arbitration could not be submitted to the Court due either to its limited jurisdiction *ratione personae*[10] or the specific needs of the parties to the disputes.[11]

Thanks to this significant number of cases, the Court had exposure to all key territorial issues and was able to develop a coherent and comprehensive jurisprudence on their settlement, securing therefore a competitive advantage over arbitration. At the outset, recourse to the Court has both

---

[8] These are: *Legal Consequences of the Separation of the Chagos Archipelago from Mauritius in 1965, Advisory Opinion*, ICJ Reports 2019, p. 95; *Accordance with International Law of the Unilateral Declaration of Independence in Respect of Kosovo, Advisory Opinion*, ICJ Reports 2010, p. 403; *Legal Consequences of the Construction of a Wall in the Occupied Palestinian Territory, Advisory Opinion*, ICJ Reports 2004, p. 136; *Western Sahara, Advisory Opinion*, ICJ Reports 1975, p. 12; *Legal Consequences for States of the Continued Presence of South Africa in Namibia (South-West Africa) notwithstanding Security Council Resolution 276 (1970), Advisory Opinion*, ICJ Reports 1971, p. 16; *International status of South-West Africa, Advisory Opinion*, ICJ Reports 1950, p. 128.

[9] See, *The Indo-Pakistan Western Boundary (Rann of Kutch) between India and Pakistan (India, Pakistan)*, XVII UNRIAA 1–576 (1968); *Dispute between Argentina and Chile concerning the Beagle Channel*, XXI UNRIAA 53–264 (1977); *In the Matter of an Arbitration concerning the Border between the Emirates of Dubai and Sharjah* (1981) 91 ILR 543 (1981); *Case concerning the location of boundary markers in Taba between Egypt and Israel*, XX UNRIAA 1–118 (1988); *Boundary dispute between Argentina and Chile concerning the frontier line between boundary post 62 and Mount Fitzroy*, XXII UNRIAA 3–149 (1994); *Territorial Sovereignty and Scope of the Dispute (Eritrea/Yemen)*, XXII UNRIAA 209–332 (1998); *Award in the Arbitration regarding the delimitation of the Abyei Area between the Government of Sudan and the Sudan People's Liberation Movement/Army*, XXX UNRIAA 14 (2009); *In the Matter of an Arbitration under the Arbitration between the Government of the Republic of Croatia and the Government of the Republic of Slovenia*, signed on 4 November 2009, PCA (2017).

[10] See for instance, *Award in the Arbitration regarding the delimitation of the Abyei Area between the Government of Sudan and the Sudan People's Liberation Movement/Army*, XXX UNRIAA 145 (2009). See also, *In the Matter of an Arbitration concerning the Border between the Emirates of Dubai and Sharjah*, 91 ILR 543 (1981).

[11] See, Article 4, paragraphs 2 and 12 of the Agreement between the Government of the State of Eritrea and the Government of the Federal Republic of Ethiopia, Annex to the Identical Letters dated 12 December from the Permanent Representative of Algeria to the United Nations addressed to the Secretary-General and the President of the Council (A/55/686 – S/2000/1183). The mandate of the Commission encompassed both the delimitation and the demarcation of the boundary. The arbitral award was to be delivered within six months after the first meeting of the arbitral tribunal.

procedural and financial advantages compared to arbitration. Litigants do not pay the administrative costs inherent to proceedings before the Court whose budget is part of the 'expenses of the Organization' within the meaning of Article 17 of the Charter. In addition, litigants facing difficulties may request the financial assistance of the *Secretary General's Trust Fund to assist States in the Settlement of Disputes through the International Court of Justice* 'to cover only the expenses incurred in connection with proceedings on the merits, as well as the implementation of the judgement of the Court'.[12] This Trust Fund was established in light of the difficulties that Burkina Faso and Mali faced for the settlement of their border dispute through the Court in 1986.

Procedurally, as a permanent organ, the Court is already established and the parties to a dispute do not need to constitute a tribunal, as it occurs with arbitration. The possibility of requesting immediately provisional measures upon seizing the Court, pursuant to Article 41 of its Statute, may also be attractive to some litigants. Territorial disputes may degenerate into armed conflicts capable of causing irreparable prejudice to the rights of the parties even before the constitution of an arbitral tribunal. Permanence allows the Court to be able to address such requests without delay.[13] Another comparative advantage deriving from the Court's permanence is its jurisdiction to entertain requests by the parties for the interpretation of its judgments pursuant to Article 60 of its Statute. Despite a few requests, the Court never revised its judgments concerning territorial disputes pursuant to Article 61 of the Statute.[14] In general, arbitral tribunals cease to function after the delivery of the award or the

---

[12] See the Revised Terms of Reference, Guidelines and Rules of the Secretary-General's Trust Fund to Assist States in the Settlement of Disputes through the International Court of Justice, Annex to the 2004 Report of the Secretary-General (A/59/372), para. 6.

[13] See for instance, *Request for Interpretation of the Judgment of 15 June 1962 in the Case concerning the Temple of Preah Vihear (Cambodia v. Thailand), Provisional Measures*, ICJ Reports 2011, p. 537 at 551, para. 55.

[14] See among others, the Request by El Salvador in *El Salvador/Honduras (Nicaragua intervening)* case (see *Application for Revision of the Judgment of 11 September 1992 in the Case concerning the* Land, Island and Maritime Frontier Dispute (El Salvador/ Honduras: Nicaragua intervening) *(El Salvador v. Honduras), Judgment*, ICJ Reports 2003, p. 392); the Request by Malaysia in *Malaysia/Singapore* case from which Malaysia desisted at a later stage: *Request for Interpretation of the Judgment of 23 May 2008 in the Case concerning* Sovereignty over Pedra Branca/Pulau Batu Puteh, Middle Rocks and South Ledge (Malaysia/Singapore) *(Malaysia v. Singapore), Order*, ICJ Reports 2018, p. 288).

boundary demarcation, depending on the terms of the arbitration agreement. They do not have jurisdiction to decide on allegations of nullity of their own decisions. Hence, the Court was seized by parties to a concluded arbitration to decide allegations of inexistence or nullity of their arbitral awards or to interpret them.[15] Finally, in the event that the parties wish to have some influence on the composition of the Court in a given case, they may request from it to establish a Chamber to decide their dispute. This would allow the parties to combine in one single forum some of the advantages attaching arbitration with those pertaining to judicial settlement. It is noteworthy that chambers of the Court have been established primarily in territorial and maritime boundary disputes.[16]

III The Court's Reframing of How Sovereignty Is Established over Territory

The field of territorial disputes is replete with doctrinal constructions purporting to explain how states establish sovereignty over a territory. Some of these doctrines were relied upon by states in disputes before the Court. This gave to the Court the opportunity to clarify which doctrinal theories deserves credence, and which ones should be rejected. The Court departed, although not entirely, from the 'modes of acquisition' doctrine (A) to reconstruct the acquisition of territorial sovereignty around the concept of 'title' (B).

A Reassessing the Legal Significance of the Traditional 'Modes of Acquisition' of Sovereignty

Scholars have traditionally explained the acquisition of territorial sovereignty through what is referred to as the 'modes of acquisition of territorial

---

[15] See *Arbitral Award made by the King of Spain on 23 December 1906 (Honduras v. Nicaragua)*, Judgment, ICJ Reports 1960, p. 192; *Arbitral Award of 31 July 1989 (Guinea Bissau v. Senegal)*, Judgment, ICJ Reports 1991, p. 53 (a case concerning maritime delimitation and state succession); *Arbitral Award of 3 October 1899 (Guyana v. Venezuela)* (pending, see the judgment on jurisdiction of 18 December 2020).

[16] The first Chamber formed was in the *Gulf of Maine (Canada/United States of America)* case and concerned a maritime delimitation. The second one was in the *Frontier dispute (Burkina Faso/Mali)* and then followed in territorial matters by the Chambers formed in the *Land, Maritime and Island Dispute (El Salvador/Honduras: Nicaragua intervening)* and *Frontier Dispute (Benin/Niger)* cases.

sovereignty', namely occupation, cession, discovery, conquest and acquisitive prescription. However, the establishment of sovereignty over a territory is a more complex process than the 'modes of acquisition' may appear to suggest. It may involve other factors such as the conduct of the parties to the dispute. In this respect, it is crucial to determine, at the outset, whether the territory concerned was already placed under the sovereignty of another state before its alleged acquisition. Acquisition of territorial sovereignty may also be affected by the fundamental principles of international law mentioned below, namely the right of peoples to self-determination and the prohibition on the use of force. It can also be influenced by some technical rules of international law of special relevance in territorial disputes such as the critical date and the principle of intertemporal law. Instead of the 'modes of acquisition' doctrine, the Court adopted this comprehensive approach. As a result of this approach, the traditional modes of acquisition of territorial sovereignty play only a minor role in the case law of the Court.

It is the Court's approach to the doctrine of *terra nullius* and acquisitive prescription that has seriously challenged the contemporary relevance of the 'modes of acquisition' doctrine. Traditionally, scholars considered that European colonial expansion took place primarily through the occupation of the territories of non-European political entities that they characterised as '*terrae nullius*'. In the *Western Sahara* advisory opinion, the Court looked at this question in light of the nineteenth-century state practice. The Court noted that:

Whatever differences of opinion there may have been among jurists, the State practice of the relevant period indicates that territories inhabited by tribes or peoples having a social and political organization were not regarded as *terrae nullius*.[17]

Subsequent decisions of the Court confirmed that local political entities enjoyed sovereignty over their territory. Thus, in the case concerning the *Sovereignty over Pedra Branca/Pulau Batu Puteh, Middle Rocks and South Ledge (Malaysia/Singapore)*, the Court observed that 'it is not disputed that the Sultanate of Johor, since it came into existence in 1512, established itself as a sovereign State with a certain territorial domain under its

---

[17] *Western Sahara* at 39, para. 80.

sovereignty in this part of southeast Asia'.[18] The acknowledgement by the Court that territories inhabited by non-European political entities were not *terrae nullius* reduced to a large extent the role of discovery and effective occupation as titles of territorial sovereignty.

Acquisitive prescription is rarely invoked by parties to territorial disputes before the Court since such an allegation would have the counter-effect of conceding that the title of sovereignty belonged to the other party. In the *Kasikili/Sedudu* case, both Bostwana and Namibia acknowledged that acquisitive prescription was a title of territorial sovereignty under international law. They further agreed on the conditions under which a title of territorial sovereignty could be acquired through acquisitive prescription. Nonetheless, the Court considered that it did not need to 'concern itself with the status of acquisitive prescription in international law or with the conditions for acquiring title to territory by prescription'. For the Court, the conditions which were cited by Namibia itself were not satisfied.[19] By raising *proprio motu* the question of the 'status of acquisitive prescription in international law', and by characterising it as a 'doctrine',[20] the Court seems to cast a doubt on its status as a title of territorial sovereignty under customary international law.

To overcome the difficulties faced by the traditional modes of acquisition, some scholars argued that a State may acquire sovereignty over a territory belonging to another State when the former demonstrates a special interest in the territory, and the general tolerance or recognition by other States of its claim.[21] This process, which is referred to as the 'historic consolidation of title', was invoked by Nigeria in the *Cameroon* v. *Nigeria* case. The Court acknowledged that it referred to this doctrine in the *Fisheries (United Kingdom* v. *Norway)* case.[22] Nevertheless, the Court

---

[18] *Sovereignty over Pedra Branca/Pulau Batu Puteh, Middle Rocks and South Ledge (Malaysia/Singapore), Judgment,* ICJ Reports 2008, p. 12 at 33, para. 52.

[19] *Kasikili/Sedudu Island (Botswana/Namibia), Judgment,* ICJ Reports 1999, p. 1045 at 1105, para. 97.

[20] Ibid. at 1059, para. 19.

[21] C. de Visscher, *Théories et réalités en droit international public* (Pedone, 1970) 226 ; See also, C. de Visscher, *Les effectivités en droit international public* (Pedone, 1967) 106; G. Schwarzenberger, 'Title to Territory : Response to a Challenge' 51 *AJIL* (1957) 310–311; Y. Z. Blum, *Historical Titles in International Law* (Nijhoff, 1965) 335–337 ; D. H. N. Johnson, 'Consolidation as a Root of Title in International Law' 13 (2) *Cambridge Law Journal* (1995) 215–225.

[22] See, *Fisheries (United Kingdom* v. *Norway), Judgment,* ICJ Reports 1951, p. 116 at 130.

observed that 'the notion of historical consolidation has never been used as a basis of title in other territorial disputes, whether in its own or in other case law'.[23] For the Court, 'the theory of historical consolidation is highly controversial and cannot replace the established modes of acquisition of title under international law, which take into account many other important variables of fact and law. It further observed that nothing in the *Fisheries* Judgment suggested that the "historical consolidation" referred to, in connection with the external boundaries of the territorial sea, allows land occupation to prevail over an established treaty title.[24]

The current jurisprudence of the Court focuses on the concept of 'title' instead of the traditional modes of acquisition of territorial sovereignty. In *Burkina Faso/Mali*, the Court noted that the parties used the word 'title' to refer to 'documentary evidence alone'. For the Court, however, 'the concept of title may also, and more generally, comprehend both any evidence which may establish the existence of a right, and the actual source of that right.'[25] In this respect, the concept of 'title' can refer to various legal relations that a state may have with respect to a territory, including sovereignty. Some titles to a territory may only grant to a state the power to exercise some minor territorial competencies, which do not include the right to dispose of it. Only titles of sovereignty give to a state the power to alienate a territory. Thus, it is possible to distinguish between titles of administration of a territory and titles of territorial sovereignty.[26] The overwhelming majority of disputes that are submitted to the Court concern titles of territorial sovereignty, and not titles of administration.[27]

In the *Pedra Branca/Pulau Batu Puteh, Middle Rocks and South Ledge (Malaysia* v. *Singapore)*, the Court noted that '[i]n international litigation "ownership" over territory has sometimes been used as equivalent to "sovereignty"'.[28] Yet, the Court stressed that 'in law "ownership" is distinct from "sovereignty"',[29] having referred in a previous paragraph to the 'long

[23] *Land and Maritime Boundary between Cameroon and Nigeria* at 352, para. 65.

[24] Ibid. at 352, para. 65.

[25] *Frontier Dispute (Burkina Faso/Mali), Judgment,* ICJ Reports 1986, p. 554 at 564, para. 18.

[26] For a comprehensive list of titles of administration, see M. G. Kohen, *Possession contestée et souveraineté territoriale* (Pedone, 1997) at 501.

[27] For this type of dispute, see *Rights of nationals of the United States of America in Morocco (France* v. *United States of America), Judgment,* ICJ Reports 1952, p. 176.

[28] *Sovereignty over Pedra Branca/Pulau Batu Puteh, Middle Rocks and South Ledge* at 80, para. 222.

[29] Ibid.

established distinction between sovereignty and property rights'.[30] Indeed, the latter are essentially governed by domestic law. The Chamber of the Court applied this distinction between ownership and sovereignty when it indicated, in the *Frontier Dispute (Benin/Niger)* case, 'that the question of the course of the boundary on the bridges is totally independent of that of the ownership of those structures, which belong to the Parties jointly'.[31] Some titles of sovereignty are created from the expression of the will of subjects of international law. They include treaties, acquiescence, unilateral declarations, and attribution through papal bulls during the relevant times and judicial decisions attributing territory *ex aequo et bono*. Other titles arise from facts to which law attaches consequences. They include *debellatio*, which was valid until the prohibition of the use of force in international law, accretion, discovery at the relevant times, occupation of *terra nullius* and independence, which triggers *uti possidetis* and state succession.[32]

B Detailing the Legal Regime Governing Key Titles of Territorial Sovereignty

The Court's engagement with titles of territorial sovereignty depends on the circumstances of each case and the arguments pleaded by the parties. Concerning legal facts, the Court has not dealt with discovery, effective occupation of *terrae nullius*, *debellatio*, or accretion. However, it referred to the absence of *terrae nullius* in a number of cases, such as the advisory opinion on *Western Sahara* and the judgments in *El Salvador/Honduras*, *Nicaragua v. Honduras* and *Malaysia/Singapore*.[33] In the majority of its case law, the Court did not have the opportunity to settle territorial disputes based on attribution and unilateral declarations. In practice, the

---

[30] Ibid., p. 57, para. 139.

[31] *Frontier Dispute (Benin/Niger), Judgment,* ICJ Reports 2005, p. 90 at 141–142, para. 124.

[32] See a list of titles of territorial sovereignty in M. G. Kohen, 'Titles and *effectivités* in Territorial Disputes', in M. Kohen and M. Hébié (eds.), *Research Handbook on Territorial Disputes in International Law* (Elgar, 2018) 145 at 151.

[33] *Western Sahara, Advisory Opinion,* ICJ Reports 1975, p. 39, para. 79; *Land, Island and Maritime Frontier Dispute (El Salvador/Honduras: Nicaragua intervening), Judgment,* ICJ Reports 1992, p. 387, para. 42; *Territorial and Maritime Dispute between Nicaragua and Honduras in the Caribbean Sea (Nicaragua v. Honduras), Judgment,* ICJ Reports 2007, p. 707, para. 158; *Sovereignty over Pedra Branca/Pulau Batu Puteh, Middle Rocks and South Ledge (Malaysia/Singapore), Judgment,* ICJ Reports 2008, pp. 31–35, paras. 46–59.

large majority of the decisions of the Court are based on treaties, *uti possidetis* and acquiescence.

Treaties

Treaties may serve to create legal situations, especially to delimit territories and to transfer territorial sovereignty from a state to another state. Maps are often annexed to treaties or other legal instruments dealing with territorial sovereignty. In such a case, the map forms part of the treaty and 'fall[s] into the category of physical expressions of the will of the State or States concerned'.[34] Except for that scenario, maps serve as evidence, the legal weight of which may vary in accordance with their technical reliability as well as the neutrality of their sources towards the dispute in question or the parties to that dispute.[35]

In addition to treaties among states, the Court has considered that the agreements concluded between local political entities and colonial powers could establish a title of territorial sovereignty. In the *Western Sahara* advisory opinion, the Court explained that on territories inhabited by tribes or peoples having a social and political organisation:

> the acquisition of sovereignty was not generally considered as effected unilaterally through 'occupation' of *terra nullius* by original title but through agreements concluded with local rulers. ... [S]uch agreements with local rulers, whether or not considered as an actual 'cession' of the territory, were regarded as derivative roots of title, and not original titles obtained by occupation of *terrae nullius*.[36]

In the *Chagos* advisory opinion, the Court examined the legal significance of the undertakings in the Lancaster House agreement, a document concluded between the United Kingdom and the local organ of Mauritius, its colony (at the time). In the view of the Court, the Lancaster House agreement could not be characterised as an 'international agreement when one of the parties to it, Mauritius, which is said to have ceded the territory to the United Kingdom, was under the authority of the latter'. The Court stressed that 'heightened scrutiny should be given to the issue of consent in a situation where a part of a non-self-governing territory is separated to create a new colony'.[37] For the Court, such agreements could not effect a valid cession of territorial

---

[34] *Frontier Dispute (Burkina Faso/Mali)* at 582, para. 54.
[35] Ibid. at 582–583, paras. 55–56.   [36] *Western Sahara* at 39, para. 80.
[37] *Legal Consequences of the Separation of the Chagos Archipelago from Mauritius in 1965* at p. 163, para. 172.

sovereignty, in a consistent manner with the principle of self-determination, unless in circumstances where they are 'based on the free and genuine expression of the will of the people concerned'.[38] In light of the circumstances of the case, the Court concluded that the Lancaster House agreement did not satisfy this condition of free and genuine consent.

Interpreting treaties is a key issue that often arises in territorial disputes.[39] When parties to a dispute invoke treaties, the Court interprets the relevant clauses to determine whether 'these treaties contain anything which might throw light' or help 'elucidate' the status of the disputed territory or the course of the boundary.[40] In practice, the Court seems to construe strictly treaties when determining their territorial significance based on the customary rules of treaty interpretation. For instance, in the case concerning *Pulau Ligitan and Pulau Sipadan*, the Court had to determine whether Article IV of the 1891 Convention between Great Britain and the Netherlands decided the sovereignty over the two islands. Taking into account the terms, object and purpose of the 1891 Convention, the Court did not find anything in the Convention to suggest that the parties intended to delimit the boundary between their possessions to the east of the islands of Borneo and Sebatik or to attribute sovereignty over any other island. Accordingly, the Court refused to consider that that boundary line extended to the sea.[41] In the *Territorial and Maritime Dispute (Nicaragua v. Colombia)* case, at the preliminary objections phase, the Court had to determine whether the 1928 Treaty between the parties 'settled', within the meaning of Article VI of the Pact of Bogotá, the question of the sovereignty over the San Andres Archipelago. The Court distinguished between the islands which were expressly mentioned in Article 1 of the 1928 Treaty, that is to say San Andrés, Providencia and Santa Catalina, on the one hand, from the 'other islands, islets and reefs forming part of the San Andrés Archipelago', on the other hand.[42] It held

---

[38] Ibid.

[39] Regarding treaty interpretation, see A. Remiro Brotóns, Chapter 14, The Law of Treaties, in this volume.

[40] *Minquiers and Ecrehos (France/United Kingdom) case, Judgment*, ICJ Reports 1953, p. 47 at 54.

[41] *Sovereignty over Pulau Ligitan and Pulau Sipadan (Indonesia/Malaysia), Judgment*, ICJ Reports 2002, p. 625 at 652–653, paras. 51–52.

[42] *Territorial and Maritime Dispute (Nicaragua v. Colombia), Preliminary Objections, Judgment*, ICJ Reports 2007, p. 832 at 863, para. 97 and 865, para. 104; For a similar reasoning, see *Minquiers and Ecrehos* at p. 54.

that the question could be considered as 'settled' only with regard to the islands expressly mentioned and attributed to Colombia by that provision of the 1928 Treaty.[43] However, at the merits phase, when the Court had to decide on the sovereignty over the other features, it did not interpret the scope of the meaning of the terms, 'the other islands, islets and reefs of the San Andrés archipelago' mentioned in the 1928 treaty.[44]

In some instances, a party to a territorial dispute may claim that the relevant treaty is null and void. The situation occurred in the above-mentioned case between Nicaragua and Colombia. Nicaragua declared in 1980 that the 1928 Treaty was null and void. At the preliminary objections stage, the Court held that the 1928 treaty was valid and in force in 1948, the year of the conclusion of the Pact of Bogota.[45] Subsidiarily, Nicaragua contended that the 1928 Treaty was terminated by a material breach. Nicaragua did not insist on these arguments at the merits stage.

In the *Territorial Dispute (Libyan Arab Jamahiriya/Chad)* case, the Court noted that the treaty, which was concluded in 1955, contained a clause stipulating that it was concluded for a period of twenty years and could be terminated by either party twenty years after its entry into force. For the Court, this clause did not have any impact on the boundary line agreed in the treaty. The Court observed that a boundary established by treaty had 'a legal life of its own' and that 'the continued existence of that boundary is not dependent upon the continuing life of the treaty under which the boundary is agreed'.[46] Indeed, the 1955 Treaty was applied for decades and neither party had declared it terminated before the submission of the case to the Court.

The leading case that allowed the Court to invoke the principle of stability of boundaries is the *Temple of Preah Vihear* case. In that case, the demarcation commission performed its task in the years immediately following the conclusion of the delimitation treaty. Several years after its distribution to the parties, Thailand invoked an alleged error in the map identifying the boundary as demarcated – which it held to be contradictory

---

[43] *Territorial and Maritime Dispute (Nicaragua v. Colombia), Judgment,* at p. 649, paras. 52–56.

[44] *Territorial and Maritime Dispute (Nicaragua v. Colombia),* Separate Opinion Judge Abraham at pp. 730–735 (criticising the approach of the Court).

[45] See *Territorial and Maritime Dispute (Nicaragua v. Colombia), Preliminary Objections, Judgment,* ICJ Reports 2007, p. 859, paras. 79–81.

[46] *Territorial Dispute (Libyan Arab Jamahiriya/Chad)* at 37, para. 73.

to the terms of the treaty. The Court explained that '[i]n general, when two countries establish a frontier between them, one of the primary objects is to achieve stability and finality. This is impossible if the line so established can, at any moment, and on the basis of a continuously available process, be called in question, and its rectification claimed, whenever any inaccuracy by reference to a clause in the parent treaty is discovered. Such a process could continue indefinitely, and finality would never be reached so long as possible errors still remained to be discovered. Such a frontier, so far from being stable, would be completely precarious'.[47]

Uti Possidetis Juris

The creation of a new state, whether through decolonisation, secession from, or dissolution of, an existing state, raises questions as to its boundaries. *Uti possidetis juris* is a rule of international law that serves to determine the boundaries of states following their accession to independence based on the principle of respect for the pre-existing administrative divisions or international delimitations decided by their predecessors. As the Chamber of the Court explained in *Burkina Faso/Mali*, the Latin genitive 'juris' serves to emphasise the 'pre-eminence accorded to legal title over effective possession as a basis of sovereignty'.[48] The Court has never referred to the so-called *uti possidetis de facto* as a title of territorial sovereignty.

Although the principle of *uti possidetis juris* was first applied in Latin America, the Court does not consider it as a regional rule of international law. For the Court, the principle of *uti possidetis juris* is a 'principle of general scope', 'a general principle, which is logically connected with the phenomenon of the obtaining of independence, wherever it occurs.'[49] In this respect, the Court does not see any opposition between the principle of *uti possidetis juris*, and the 'principle of the intangibility of frontiers inherited from colonization', which is often referred to in the African context. For the Court, it is the application of the principle of *uti possidetis juris* that gives rise to the respect for the intangibility of borders.[50]

The principle of *uti possidetis juris* requires the boundaries that existed before the accession to independence to be determined. Some

---

[47] *Temple of Preah Vihear (Cambodia v. Thailand), Merits*, ICJ Reports 1962, p. 6 at 34.
[48] *Frontier Dispute (Burkina Faso/Mali)* at 566, para. 23.   [49] Ibid at 565, para. 20.
[50] Ibid.

of these boundaries may arise from administrative divisions, whereas others may be based on international boundaries. The Court has used the principle *uti possidetis juris* in the frontier disputes between Burkina Faso and Mali, Burkina Faso and Niger, and Benin and Niger. The borders between the four countries are based on former administrative boundaries that were established by France when it was sovereign over these territories. In the case concerning Libya and Chad, in which the boundary line was established by the 1955 Treaty of Friendship and Good Neighbourliness concluded by France and Libya on 10 August 1955, the Court found no need to discuss the arguments of the parties based on the principle *uti possidetis juris*.[51] In the case concerning the island of Kasikili/Sedudu, the 1897 treaty between Great Britain and Germany was applicable.

The principle of *uti possidetis juris* has often required the Court to engage to a certain extent with colonial law when identifying the administrative limits existing before the accession to independence. It is well-known that domestic law is merely a 'fact' before international courts and tribunals.[52] In *Frontier Dispute (Burkina Faso/Mali)*, the Chamber of the Court explained the relevance of colonial law as a fact for the purpose of the application of *uti possidetis juris* as follows:

> The principle of *uti possidetis* freezes the territorial title; it stops the clock, but does not put back the hands. Hence international law does not effect any renvoi to the law established by the colonizing State, nor indeed to any legal rule unilaterally established by any State whatever; French law – especially legislation enacted by France for its colonies and *territoires d'outre-mer* – may play a role not in itself (as if there were a sort of continuum juris, a legal relay between such law and international law), but only as one factual element among others, or as evidence indicative of what has been called the 'colonial heritage', i.e., the 'photograph of the territory' at the critical date.[53]

One may infer from case law some guiding criteria on the use of colonial law by the Court. First, in determining the course of the relevant administrative divisions, the Court will take into account only those divisions that were established by competent domestic authorities. For this purpose, the

---

[51] *Territorial Dispute (Libyan Arab Jamahiriya/Chad)* at 38, para. 75.

[52] *Case concerning certain German interests in Polish Upper Silesia (Germany v. Poland)*, *Merits*, Judgment, PCIJ Series A No 7, p. 4 at 19.

[53] *Frontier Dispute (Burkina Faso/Mali)* at 568, para. 30.

Court may have to identify such authorities.[54] Second, the Court will also take into account any shared understanding among the competent domestic authorities on the course of the relevant administrative divisions, instead of trying to identify by itself what would be that course based on the correct interpretation of domestic law. In this respect, the Court seems to show deference to the interpretation and application by competent domestic authorities of the relevant domestic law.[55] Nonetheless, a mere error by domestic authorities when referring to the boundary as delimited by the relevant domestic law will not be granted weight in determining the course of the boundary line.[56] Third, when the title is not clear or its existence established, colonial *effectivités* (acts of exercise of state authority) may be used to identify the administrative divisions that existed at the moment of independence.[57] In some circumstances, this can also be the case for post-colonial *effectivités*. However, neither colonial nor post-colonial *effectivités* can by themselves displace such a title. Finally, reliance on the administrative divisions established by domestic law may in practice be inconclusive. This is the case when the boundary line in accordance with domestic law cannot be established or if colonial law cannot establish to which administrative division a territory belonged.[58] In the event that no other title is to be found, the Court will decide the dispute based on the balance of *effectivités*.[59]

Acquiescence

The Court has relied on acquiescence as a title of territorial sovereignty in two cases, namely in the *Temple of Preah Vihear (Cambodia* v. *Thailand)* case, and the case concerning *Sovereignty over Pedra Branca/Pulau Batu Puteh, Middle Rocks and South Ledge (Malaysia/Singapore)*. In *Malaysia/ Singapore*, the Court systematised its jurisprudence on acquiescence. The Court construed acquiescence as a tacit recognition whereby a State agrees to the passing of its title of territorial sovereignty to another State, or to its

[54] *Frontier Dispute (Benin/Niger), Judgment*, ICJ Reports 2005, p. 90 at 110–111, paras. 29–31; See also at 125, para. 65.
[55] *Frontier Dispute (Burkina Faso/Niger), Judgment, ICJ Reports 2013*, p. 44 at 75, para. 66.
[56] Ibid. at p. 79, para. 78; See also, *Frontier Dispute (Benin/Niger)* at 148, para. 140.
[57] *Frontier Dispute (Burkina Faso/Mali)* at 586, para. 63.
[58] *Land, Island and Maritime Frontier Dispute* at p. 351 at 559, para. 333.
[59] *Territorial and Maritime Dispute (Nicaragua* v. *Colombia), Judgment* at 651–652, paras. 65–66.

existence in favour of the latter. The Court explained that '[i]nternational law does not, in this matter, impose any particular form. Rather it places its emphasis on the parties' intentions'.[60]

In this respect, the Court considered that failure to protest against a display of territorial sovereignty may amount to acquiescence if the conduct of the other State called for a response,[61] taking into account the particular context in which the State that is alleged to have acquiesced to the loss of its sovereignty was during the relevant period.[62] Nonetheless, acquiescence should not be presumed lightly but should be established by sound evidence. For the Court, in light of the central importance in international law and relations of state sovereignty over territory and of the stability and certainty of that sovereignty, 'any passing of sovereignty over territory on the basis of the conduct of the parties, as set out above, must be manifested clearly and without any doubt by that conduct and the relevant facts. That is especially so if what may be involved, in the case of one of the parties, is in effect the abandonment of sovereignty over part of its territory.'[63] In *Sovereignty over Pedra Branca/Pulau Batu Puteh, Middle Rocks and South Ledge (Malaysia/Singapore)*, the Court referred to the practice of Malaysia and Singapore and their predecessors, especially the failure by Malaysia and Johor to protest against Great Britain and Singapore's sovereign conduct and assertion thereof on Pedra Branca/Pulau Batu Puteh. It concluded that by 1980, the critical date, sovereignty over Pedra Branca/Pulau Batu Puteh had passed to Singapore.[64]

---

[60] *Sovereignty over Pedra Branca/Pulau Batu Puteh, Middle Rocks and South Ledge* at 50, para. 120.

[61] Ibid. at 50–51, para. 121.

[62] Thus, in *Somalia* v. *Kenya*, a case that dealt with maritime delimitation and not territorial disputes, the Court was of the view that '[t]he jurisprudence relating to acquiescence and tacit agreement may be of assistance when examining whether there exists an agreement that is not in written form regarding the maritime boundary between two States' (para. 51). In this respect, it explained that it could not 'ignore the context of the civil war that afflicted Somalia, depriving it of a fully operational government and administration between 1991 and 2005. These circumstances were public and notorious .... This context needs to be taken into account in evaluating the extent to which Somalia was in a position to react to Kenya's claim during this period.' See, *Maritime Delimitation in the Indian Ocean (Somalia* v. *Kenya)*, ICJ Reports 2021, para. 79.

[63] *Sovereignty over Pedra Branca/Pulau Batu Puteh, Middle Rocks and South Ledge* at 51, para. 122.

[64] Ibid. at 96, para. 276.

IV The Identification by the Court of the Territorial Implications of Fundamental Principles of International Law

The fundamental principles of international law are to be found in the Charter of the United Nations, as interpreted and developed by Resolution 2625 containing 'The Declaration on Principles of International Law concerning Friendly Relations and Co-operation among States'. Three fundamental principles, namely the principle of equal rights and self-determination of peoples, the prohibition on the use of force in international law and the principle of the respect for territorial sovereignty, had significant effects on the legal framework applicable to the settlement of territorial disputes.

A The Right of Peoples to Self-Determination

The Charter does not clarify the territorial implications of the right of self-determination. It is through the practice of the General Assembly, interpreting the provisions of the Charter, that self-determination crystallised as a rule of customary international law. The Court provided the authoritative pronouncement establishing the right of self-determination as a principle of international law and defined the key elements necessary for its application.

In the *Namibia* advisory opinion, the Court clarified that the principle of self-determination was a principle of international law applicable to decolonisation based on the subsequent development of international law, which occurred through the Charter of the United Nations and by way of customary law.[65] In the *Chagos* advisory opinion, the Court found that resolution 1514 (XV) had 'a declaratory character with regard to the right to self-determination as a customary norm',[66] and confirmed its prior jurisprudence that 'respect for the right to self-determination is an obligation *erga omnes*'.[67]

---

[65] *Legal Consequences for States of the Continued Presence of South Africa in Namibia (South-West Africa) notwithstanding Security Council Resolution 276 (1970), Advisory Opinion*, ICJ Reports 1971, p. 16, at 31, paras. 52–53.

[66] *Legal Consequences of the Separation of the Chagos Archipelago from Mauritius in 1965* at 95, para. 152.

[67] Ibid. at 139, para. 180.

What characterises a human group as a 'people' enjoying the right of self-determination, including the right to choose between independence, free association or integration with an independent state, pursuant to Resolution 1541 (XV) of the General Assembly? Based on the practice of the General Assembly, the Court clarified in the *Western Sahara* advisory opinion that not all human groups constitute a 'people', within the meaning that international law attaches to this term.[68] For the Court, the 'right to independence' based on the right of self-determination belongs, pursuant to international law, only to 'the peoples of non-self-governing territories and peoples subject to alien subjugation, domination and exploitation.'[69]

As far as the territorial implications of the right of self-determination are concerned, the Court clarified that, even before their accession to independence, peoples hold sovereignty over their territory as a whole. As a result, 'any detachment by the administering Power of part of a non-self-governing territory, unless based on the freely expressed and genuine will of the people of the territory concerned, is contrary to the right to self-determination.'[70] By referring to former colonial powers as 'administering powers', the Court confirmed that '[t]he territory of a colony or other Non-Self-Governing Territory has, under the Charter, a status separate and distinct from the territory of the State administering it; and such separate and distinct status under the Charter shall exist until the people of the colony or Non-Self-Governing Territory have exercised their right of self-determination in accordance with the Charter, and particularly its purposes and principles'.[71]

B The Prohibition on the Use of Force[72]

Article 2(4) of the Charter provides that '[a]ll Members [of the United Nations] shall refrain in their international relations from the threat or use of force against the territorial integrity or political independence of

[68] *Western Sahara* at 33, para. 59; *Chagos* at para. 158.
[69] *Accordance with International Law of the Unilateral Declaration of Independence in Respect of Kosovo* at 436, para. 79.
[70] Ibid. at 134, para. 160.
[71] Resolution 2625 (XXV). Declaration on Principles of International Law concerning Friendly Relations and Co-operation among States in accordance with the Charter of the United Nations (A/RES/2625), 24 October 1970.
[72] See also A. Chehtman, Chapter 20, The Use of Force at the International Court of Justice.

any state, or in any other manner inconsistent with the Purposes of the United Nations.' The provision prohibits both the use of force, while reaffirming the customary international law rule calling for respect for the territorial integrity of States.

The Court reaffirmed the customary international law character of the principles regarding the use of force while detailing their territorial consequences. In the *Wall* advisory opinion, the Court, referring to its case law in *Military and Paramilitary Activities in and Against Nicaragua (Nicaragua v. United States)*,[73] noted that 'the principles as to the use of force incorporated in the Charter reflect customary international law ... [and that] the same is true of its corollary entailing the illegality of territorial acquisition resulting from the threat or use of force.'[74] This statement of the Court confirmed a determination already made in Resolution 2625 that *debellatio* and conquest cannot serve as titles to acquire territorial sovereignty in contemporary international law.[75] In *Costa Rica* v. *Nicaragua*, the Court noted that the use of force in a disputed territory could be characterised as unlawful irrespective of the subjective views of the parties on the validity of their claims. It noted '[t]he fact that Nicaragua considered that its activities were taking place on its own territory does not exclude the possibility of characterizing them as an unlawful use of force.'[76] This finding reinforces the principle in Resolution 2625 according to which, '[e]very State has the duty to refrain from the threat or use of force to violate the existing international boundaries of another State or as a means of solving international disputes, including territorial disputes and problems concerning frontiers of States.'[77]

C The Principle of Respect for Territorial Integrity

The Court has clarified the importance of the principle of territorial integrity and its relation to the principle of territorial sovereignty. In the *Corfu*

---

[73] *Military and Paramilitary Activities in and against Nicaragua* at 98–101, paras. 187–190.

[74] *Legal Consequences of the Construction of a Wall in the Occupied Palestinian Territory* at 171, para. 87.

[75] Resolution 2625 (XXV).

[76] *Certain Activities Carried Out by Nicaragua in the Border Area (Costa Rica v. Nicaragua) and Construction of a Road in Costa Rica along the San Juan River (Nicaragua v. Costa Rica), Judgment,* ICJ Reports 2015, p. 665 at 704, para. 97.

[77] Resolution 2625 (XXV).

Channel (UK v. Albania) case, the Court explained that '[b]etween independent States, respect for territorial sovereignty is an essential foundation of international relations'.[78] Some years later, the Court reaffirmed 'the duty of every State to respect the territorial sovereignty of others'.[79] In the *Kosovo* advisory opinion, the Court observed that 'the principle of territorial integrity is an important part of the international legal order'.[80] Both the Charter and Resolution 2625 refer only to the 'territorial integrity' of States, without mentioning 'territorial sovereignty'. In *Costa Rica* v. *Nicaragua*, Costa Rica requested the Court to find that Nicaragua breached both its territorial integrity and sovereignty. The Court found that by excavating three *caños* in Costa Rican territory, Nicaragua breached the latter's territorial sovereignty, but did not pronounce itself on the alleged breach of the principle of territorial integrity or the prohibition of the use of force. The Court found that having ascertained the breach of Costa Rica's territorial sovereignty by Nicaragua, it was not necessary to address the other claims.[81]

Concerning the scope of the principle of territorial integrity, in the *Kosovo* advisory opinion the Court was called to interpret state practice and determine whether the customary international law obligation bearing upon states to respect each other's territorial integrity applied also to secessionist movements. The Court distinguished in this respect the creation of states by peoples exercising their right to self-determination and the creation of states in other circumstances.[82] The exercise by peoples, within the meaning of international law, of their right to independence cannot be considered as an infringement to the territorial integrity of the administering power since the latter no longer possesses sovereignty over this territory.[83] By distinguishing the right to independence of peoples exercising their right to self-determination from claims to independence

---

[78] *Corfu Channel (United Kingdom v. Albania)*, Judgment, ICJ Reports 1949, p. 4 at 35.

[79] *Military and Paramilitary Activities in and against Nicaragua* at 111, and 128, para. 213 and paras. 251–252 respectively.

[80] *Accordance with International Law of the Unilateral Declaration of Independence in Respect of Kosovo* at 437, para. 80.

[81] *Certain Activities Carried Out by Nicaragua in the Border Area (Costa Rica v. Nicaragua) and Construction of a Road in Costa Rica along the San Juan River (Nicaragua v. Costa Rica)* at 703, para. 93.

[82] *Accordance with International Law of the Unilateral Declaration of Independence in Respect of Kosovo* at 436, para. 79.

[83] Ibid.

by secessionist movements, the Court seems to suggest that these movements do not have a right to independence under international law. Still,
the Court found that the principle of territorial integrity does not implicitly
prohibit unilateral declarations of independence. It noted that Resolution
2625 and the provisions of the Final Act of the Helsinki Conference
reaffirmed the principle of territorial integrity only in inter-State relations.
On this basis, the Court held that 'the scope of the principle of territorial
integrity is confined to the sphere of relations between States'.[84]
Strikingly, and notwithstanding its statement in the *Kosovo* advisory
opinion limiting the scope of application of the principle to inter-State
relations only, in the *Chagos* advisory opinion the Court extended, as noted
above, the scope of the respect for territorial integrity to non-self-
governing territories.

V The Court's Contribution to the Law Governing the Settlement of Territorial Disputes

The Court's contribution to the law governing the settlement of territorial
disputes is not only normative or practical; it is also conceptual. For the
purpose of the judicial settlement of territorial disputes, the Court crafted a
number of concepts that have now become legal terms of art in the field
(A). In addition, the Court devised a method for settling territorial disputes.
This method attaches consequences to Article 38 of the Statute which
defines the outer limits of the Court's jurisdiction (B) and gives preference
to titles of sovereignty over *effectivités* (C).

A Designing a Conceptual Framework

This chapter has already referred to some of the concepts devised by the
Court to decide territorial disputes, namely those of title and of *effectivités*.
Two other concepts are of critical importance, namely the critical date and
the intertemporal law rule.
  The Court was not the first adjudicatory body to articulate the inter-
temporal law rule. Its substance was well captured in 1928 by the sole

---

[84] Ibid. at 437, para. 98.

arbitrator Max Huber in the *Island of Palmas/Miangas (Netherlands/ United States of America)* case in the following words:

> As regards the question which of different legal systems prevailing at successive periods is to be applied in a particular case (the so-called intertemporal law), a distinction must be made between the creation of rights and the existence of rights. The same principle which subjects the act creative of a right to the law in force at the time the right arises, demands that the existence of the right, in other words its continued manifestation, shall follow the conditions required by the evolution of law.[85]

When dealing with the acquisition of territorial sovereignty by virtue of the agreements concluded with local political entities in the *Cameroon v. Nigeria* case, the Court noted that '[e]ven if this mode of acquisition does not reflect current international law, the principle of intertemporal law requires that the legal consequences of the treaties concluded at that time in the Niger delta be given effect today, in the present dispute'.[86] The Court was here applying the first aspect of the intertemporal law rule (the principle of contemporaneity), whereby the acquisition of sovereignty in the nineteenth century should be assessed in accordance with the rules of international law existing at that time. The Court applied the second aspect of the intertemporal law rule in the *Minquiers and Ecrehos* case. It noted that any feudal title of the Kings of France in respect of the Channel Islands has to be replaced by another title valid under contemporary international law, since feudalism is no longer in force.[87] The Court also applied the second aspect of the intertemporal law rule in the *Namibia* advisory opinion when it took into account the impact of the principle of self-determination on titles based on the mandates system created during the colonial period.[88]

The Court played a decisive role in establishing the concept of the critical date as a term of art in the settlement of territorial disputes since its first use by the Court in the *Minquiers and Ecrehos* case in 1953.[89]

---

[85] *Island of Palmas/Miangas* case *(Netherlands/USA)* II UNRIAA p. 829 at 845 (1928).

[86] *Land and Maritime Boundary between Cameroon and Nigeria* at 405, para. 205.

[87] *Minquiers and Ecrehos* at 56.

[88] *Legal Consequences for States of the Continued Presence of South Africa in Namibia (South-West Africa) notwithstanding Security Council Resolution 276 (1970)* at 31, para. 53.

[89] *Minquiers and Ecrehos* at 59–60.

As the Court stressed in the case concerning *Sovereignty over Pedra Branca/Pulau Batu Puteh, Middle Rocks and South Ledge (Malaysia/Singapore)*, '[i]ts significance lies in distinguishing between those acts à titre de souverain occurring prior to the date when the dispute crystallised, which should be taken into consideration for the purpose of establishing or ascertaining sovereignty, and those acts occurring after that date'.[90] In general, the date of the dispute is the critical date. Concretely, the critical date allows the Court not to 'take into consideration acts having taken place after the date on which the dispute between the Parties crystallised unless such acts are a normal continuation of prior acts and are not undertaken for the purpose of improving the legal position of the Party which relies on them'.[91]

B Clarifying the Implications of the Statute

When exercising its contentious jurisdiction under Article 38 of its Statute, the Court's function is to settle, in accordance with international law, disputes among states. Thus, the existence of a dispute is a fundamental requirement that the Court has to ascertain before exercising its jurisdiction over a case relating to territorial sovereignty. As a result, in the *Frontier dispute (Burkina Faso/Niger)*, the Court declined to exercise its contentious jurisdiction and to enshrine in the *dispositif* of its judgment a prior agreement of the parties on long stretches of their borders. The Court considered that it would be contradictory to its judicial integrity to do so.[92] In the *Northern Cameroons (Cameroon v. United Kingdom)* case, the Court considered that it would be contradictory to its judicial function to deliver a judgment on a territorial dispute when the legal interests that gave rise to the dispute had become moot.[93]

The question arose whether, under Article 38 of the Statute, parties to a dispute may, independently, or in connection with a dispute regarding the

---

[90] *Territorial and Maritime Dispute (Nicaragua v. Colombia), Judgment*, at 652, para. 67.

[91] *Sovereignty over Pulau Ligitan and Pulau Sipadan* at 682, para. 135.

[92] See, however, *Case of the Free Zones of Upper Savoy and the District of Gex, second phase, Order of 6 December 1930*, PCIJ Series A No 24, p. 4 at 14.

[93] *Northern Cameroons (Cameroon v. United Kingdom), Preliminary Objections, Judgment*, ICJ Reports 1963, p. 15 at pp. 33–34; See also the above-mentioned case, *Territorial and Maritime Dispute (Nicaragua v. Colombia)* at 649, paras. 52–56.

delimitation of their boundary, request the Court to demarcate it. In *Cameroon* v. *Nigeria*, the Court explained that 'the delimitation of a boundary consists in its "definition", whereas the demarcation of a boundary, which presupposes its prior delimitation, consists of operations marking it out on the ground'.[94] Due to the very practical nature of the tasks involved, it is doubtful whether the jurisdiction of the Court could extend to the demarcation of borders.[95] So far, the Court has never demarcated a border. It has only appointed experts for the demarcation when it was authorised to do so by the parties. The Chamber of the Court in the *Frontier Dispute (Burkina Faso/Mali)* case noted that 'there is nothing in the Statute of the Court nor in the settled jurisprudence to prevent the Chamber from exercising this power, the very purpose of which is to enable the Parties to achieve a final settlement of their dispute in implementation of the Judgment which it has delivered'.[96] The Court may, when exercising its power under Article 41 of the Statute to indicate provisional measures, draw itself a 'provisional demilitarized zone' binding on the parties to the dispute. The Court did it only once in order to ensure that 'no irreparable prejudice is caused to persons or property' in the relevant boundary area pending the delivery of its final judgment.[97] In previous cases, the Court directed only the parties to establish themselves the provisional demilitarised zone.[98]

Under Article 38 of the Statute, and as referred to in many *compromis* referring territorial disputes to the Court, its role is to decide disputes 'in accordance with international law'. As a result, the Court focused only on legal considerations when deciding territorial disputes and refused to engage with other factors. Thus, in the *Temple of Preah Vihear (Cambodia* v. *Thailand)*, the Court observed that '[t]he Parties have also

[94] *Land and Maritime Boundary between Cameroon and Nigeria (Cameroon* v. *Nigeria: Equatorial Guinea intervening), Judgment*, ICJ Reports 2002, p. 303 at 359, para. 84.
[95] *Case of the Free Zones of Upper Savoy and the District of Gex, Judgment of 7 June 1932,* Series A/B, PCIJ Reports, p. 96, at 168. See also, *Haya de la Torre Case (Colombia/Peru), Judgment*, ICJ Reports1951, p. 71 at 79.
[96] *Frontier Dispute (Burkina Faso/Mali), Nomination of Experts, Order*, ICJ Reports 1987, p. 7 at p. 8.
[97] *Request for Interpretation of the Judgment of 15 June 1962 in the Case concerning the Temple of Preah Vihear (Cambodia* v. *Thailand) (Cambodia* v. *Thailand), Provisional Measures,* ICJ Reports 2011, p. 552, paras. 61–62.
[98] See for instance, *Frontier Dispute (Burkina Faso* v. *Mali), Provisional Measures,* ICJ Reports 1986, p. 3 at 11–12, para. 32, point D of the *dispositif.*

relied on other arguments of a physical, historical, religious and archaeo-
logical character, but the Court is unable to regard them as *legally
decisive*'.[99] Similarly, the Court did not subscribe to the doctrine of natural
boundaries, and did not rely on natural features to determine the course of
a boundary unless the Parties themselves used natural features to define
their boundary. In *El Salvador/Honduras*, the Chamber of the Court
observed 'the predominance of local features, particularly rivers, in the
definition of the agreed sectors', and 'felt it right similarly to take some
account of the suitability of certain topographical features to provide an
identifiable and convenient boundary'. The Court clarified, however, that
by doing so, it was 'appealing not so much to any concept of "natural
frontiers"', but 'rather to a presumption underlying the boundaries on
which the *uti possidetis juris* operates', claiming that '[c]onsiderations of
this kind have been a factor in boundary-making everywhere'.[100] In the
*Land Boundary in the Northern Part of Isla Portillos (Costa Rica
v. Nicaragua)*, the 1858 Treaty fixed the boundary between Costa Rica
and Nicaragua along the right bank of the San Juan River. Accordingly,
the Court interpreted the terms of the Treaty to determine whether the 2010
caño that was excavated by Nicaragua formed part of the boundary and
concluded that it did not.[101] Subsequently, in its 2018 Judgment, the Court
had to determine, among others, whether there was a channel of the San
Juan River separating the Isla Portillos wetland from the coast. Based on
the reports of Court-appointed experts, the Court found that there was no
channel of the San Juan River separating the wetland from the coast. For
this purpose, the Court took into account the natural changes that intervened in the coastal configuration of the relevant boundary area.[102]

For the same reason, human considerations, while important for the
preservation of private rights, have not played any role in the settlement of
territorial disputes by the Court. Some parties have raised concerns
regarding the impact of the course of a boundary line over the population

---

[99] *Temple of Preah Vihear*, p. 16 (emphasis added).
[100] *Land, Island and Maritime Frontier Dispute* at p. 390, para. 46.
[101] *Certain Activities Carried Out by Nicaragua in the Border Area (Costa Rica v. Nicaragua)
and Construction of a Road in Costa Rica along the San Juan River (Nicaragua v. Costa
Rica)* at p. 703, paras. 89–92.
[102] *Maritime Delimitation in the Caribbean Sea and the Pacific Ocean (Costa Rica
v. Nicaragua) and Land Boundary in the Northern Part of Isla Portillos (Costa Rica
v. Nicaragua), Judgment,* ICJ Reports 2018, pp.167–168, para. 71.

inhabiting the disputed area. The Court has never taken these considerations into account to change the course of the boundary line. Thus, in *El Salvador/Honduras*, the Chamber of the Court noted that:

> The effect of the Chamber's Judgment will however not be that certain areas will 'become' part of Honduras; the Chamber's task is to declare what areas are, and what are not, already part of the one State and the other. If Salvadorians have settled in areas of Honduras, neither that fact, nor the consequences of the application of Honduran law to their properties, can affect the matter.[103]

In such cases, the Court invites the parties to take into account and to address these inconveniences through negotiations.[104] The Court clarified that its decision as to the sovereignty over the territory or the course of the boundary line does not have any impact on the property rights existing in the disputed territory.[105] Property rights that were acquired in good faith have to be respected by the state whose sovereignty over the dispute territory is declared by the Court. It goes without saying that human rights also must be respected.[106]

Article 38(2) of the Statute enables the Court to decide cases *ex aequo et bono* when it is so authorised by the parties. To date, this has never happened. Thus, in *Burkina Faso/Mali*, the Chamber of the Court stressed that 'the Chamber cannot decide *ex aequo et bono* in this case. Since the parties have not entrusted it with the task of carrying out an adjustment of their respective interests, it must also dismiss any possibility of resorting to equity *contra legem*.'[107] However, the Court may apply 'equity *infra legem*, that is, that form of equity which constitutes a method of interpretation of the law in force, and is one of its attributes'.[108] The Court relied on equity *infra legem* to take into account some social needs when the evidence available did not allow the Court to decide on the course of the boundary, as requested by the parties. In *Burkina Faso/Mali*, the Court drew the boundary line in such a way as to divide the pools in order to allow equal access to water in the arid border regions. In *Burkina Faso/Niger*, the Court

[103] *Land, Island and Maritime Frontier Dispute* at 419, para. 97.
[104] Ibid. at 400, para. 66; *Land and Maritime Boundary between Cameroon and Nigeria* at 373–374, para. 123. See also, *Croatia/Slovenia Arbitration*, PCA, 1, at 114, para. 357 (2017).
[105] *Frontier Dispute (Benin/Niger)* at pp. 141–142, para. 124.
[106] See *Land, Island and Maritime Frontier Dispute* at 400–401, para. 66; *Land and Maritime Boundary between Cameroon and Nigeria* at 452, para. 317.
[107] *Frontier Dispute (Burkina Faso/Mali)* at 567, para. 28.   [108] Ibid. at 567–568, para. 28.

made the boundary run in the middle of a non-navigable river, when no evidence allowed it to conclude that the river as a whole was attributed to one or the other party to the dispute. To make this decision, the Court took into account the 'requirement concerning access to water resources of all the people living in the riparian villages'.[109]

C Establishing a Clear and Coherent Methodology

Scholars proposed various concepts and doctrines to explain how territorial disputes should be settled. One such doctrinal construction assumed that the rules governing territorial disputes varied according to whether these disputes related to territorial disputes (disputes as to attribution of territory) or to frontier disputes (delimitation disputes).[110] For the Court, however, this distinction is irrelevant since 'in the great majority of cases ... the distinction outlined above is not so much a difference in kind but rather a difference of degree as to the way the operation in question is carried out. The effect of any delimitation, no matter how small the disputed area crossed by the line, is an apportionment of the areas of land lying on either side of the line.'[111] Accordingly, 'in both cases, a clarification is made of a given legal situation with declaratory effect from the date of the legal title upheld by the Court'.[112]

The Court's methodology for settling territorial disputes revolves around titles of territorial sovereignty and their relations with *effectivités*. The existence of a treaty applicable to the dispute operates as a *lex specialis*, the legal significance of which needs to be ascertained first by the Court before any further enquiry. When the Court finds that the parties concluded a valid treaty which settled the dispute, the legal enquiry by the Court focuses on determining the bearing of the treaty on the dispute. Accordingly, the Court may dismiss all other titles and arguments invoked by the parties. For example, in the case concerning *Libya/Chad*, the Court found that the dispute between the parties, 'whether described as a territorial dispute or a boundary dispute, is conclusively determined by a Treaty to which Libya is an original party and Chad a party in succession to

---

[109] *Frontier Dispute (Burkina Faso/Niger)* at 85, para. 101.
[110] See for instance, P. G. de Lapradelle, *La frontière: étude de droit international* (Les Editions internationales, 1928) at 140–143.
[111] *Frontier Dispute (Burkina Faso/Mali)* at 554, para. 17.   [112] Ibid.

France'.[113] Accordingly, the Court held that 'there is no need for the Court to explore matters which have been discussed at length before it, such as the principle *uti possidetis*, the applicability of the Declaration adopted by the Organization of African Unity at Cairo in 1964, the effectiveness of the occupation of the disputed areas in the past, the concepts of *terra nullius*, spheres of influence and of the hinterland doctrine, the rules of intertemporal law, or the history of the dispute as argued before the UN and the OAU'. For the Court, '[t]he 1955 Treaty completely determined the boundary between Libya and Chad'.[114] The situation would, of course, be different if the treaty concerned is declared invalid or if, for different reasons, it was never implemented and is no longer in force.

When there is no treaty deciding the dispute, the Court will examine the titles invoked by the parties to determine whether one of them grants sovereignty to a party. After establishing that a party holds a title of sovereignty over the territory, the Court may, if necessary, examine the subsequent conduct of the parties to determine whether the title that was established on a specific date has been transferred to the other party.

As well noted by Paul Reuter, '[a]ll territorial disputes, without exception, lead the judge to compare and assess titles, on the one hand, and facts of effective occupation, facts of effective exercise of sovereignty, on the other hand'.[115] Except for the instance where *effectivités* evidence an acquiescence, they cannot serve to trump an existing title of sovereignty. This is consistent with the Court's mandate to decide cases based on international law, and not merely on fiat. The Chamber of the Court articulated its understanding of the interaction between titles and *effectivités* in the *Burkina Faso/Mali* case, in a dictum that has since become a stalwart principle of its jurisprudence. It noted that:

> Where the act corresponds exactly to law, where effective administration is add-itional to the *uti possidetis juris*, the only role of *effectivité* is to confirm the exercise of the right derived from a legal title. Where the act does not correspond to the law, where the territory which is the subject of the dispute is effectively administered by a State other than the one possessing the legal title, preference should be given to the holder of the title. In the event that the *effectivité* does not

---

[113] *Territorial Dispute (Libyan Arab Jamahiriya/Chad)* at p. 38, para. 75. See also, *Territorial and Maritime Dispute (Nicaragua v. Colombia)*, Separate Opinion Judge Abraham, p. 730 at 730–731, paras. 1–4.

[114] Ibid. at 40, para. 76.

[115] *Temple of Preah Vihear (Cambodia v. Thailand) ICJ Pleadings* 1962, p. 522, at 545 (Paul Reuter).

co-exist with any legal title, it must invariably be taken into consideration. Finally, there are cases where the legal title is not capable of showing exactly the territorial expanse to which it relates. The *effectivité* can then play an essential role in showing how the title is interpreted in practice.[116]

Although the dictum was phrased in the context of the relations between colonial *effectivités* and title, the Court has consistently applied it to territorial disputes involving titles other than *uti possidetis*.[117] It has also been subsequently endorsed by the quasi-totality of arbitral tribunals dealing with territorial disputes, entrenching even further the leading role of the Court in the field.[118]

Applying this cornerstone principle of its jurisprudence, the Court has limited *effectivités* to an interpretative or a confirmatory role, except for instances in which no other title of territorial sovereignty exists. This was for example the case in *Pulau Ligitan and Sipadan*. In that case, the Court could not identify any other title for Indonesia or Malaysia. Accordingly, the Court weighed the *effectivités* produced by each Party and concluded that sovereignty over Pulau Ligitan and Sipadan belonged to Malaysia thanks to the strength of its *effectivités*, in that case measures taken to regulate and control the collecting of turtle eggs and the establishment of a bird reserve, compared to those adduced by Indonesia.[119]

The reaffirmation of the primacy of titles over *effectivités* places the focus more on recognised titles of territorial sovereignty under international law, instead of *effectivités*. Since territorial disputes are won and lost based on the existence of the title, instead of the sheer weight of *effectivités*, evidence in territorial disputes should focus more on proving the existence and expanse of the relevant title.

---

[116] *Frontier Dispute (Burkina Faso/Mali)* at 586–587, para. 63.

[117] *Land, Island and Maritime Frontier* at pp. 398–399, paras. 61–62; *Territorial Dispute (Libyan Arab Jamahiriya/Chad)* at 38, paras. 75–76; *Sovereignty over Pulau Ligitan and Pulau Sipadan* at 678, para. 126; *Land and Maritime Boundary* at 353, para. 68; *Frontier Dispute (Benin/Niger),* at 120, para. 47; and *Frontier Dispute (Burkina Faso/Niger)* at 79, para. 78; *Certain Activities Carried Out by Nicaragua in the Border Area (Costa Rica v. Nicaragua) and Construction of a Road in Costa Rica along the San Juan River (Nicaragua v. Costa Rica)* at 703, para. 89.

[118] See recently, *Crotia v. Slovenia*, p. 1 at 81–82, para. 262.

[119] See, *Sovereignty over Pulau Ligitan and Pulau Sipadan* at pp. 683–686, paras. 142–149. See also *Territorial and Maritime Dispute between Nicaragua and Honduras in the Caribbean Sea (Nicaragua v. Honduras), Judgment, ICJ Reports 2007,* p. 710, para. 165 and *Territorial and maritime dispute (Nicaragua v. Colombia), Judgment, ICJ Reports 2012,* p. 652, para. 66.

362 Marcelo Kohen and Mamadou Hébié

VI Conclusion

The law of territorial disputes is primarily the law as specified by the ICJ. The Court took advantage of its unique position on the international scene to reconstruct the contemporary understanding of the acquisition of titles to territorial sovereignty; to clarify the territorial implications of fundamental principles of international law; and, finally, to establish a clear and coherent method, based on law, for their settlement. The result of this undertaking is remarkable. By dismissing irrelevant doctrinal theories and by interpreting state practice to infer rules, the Court brought clarity and predictability in the settlement of territorial disputes. By choosing to focus on law, in a field where disputing parties make all kind of political, historical, religious and sociological arguments, the Court was able to bring some welcome rationality to the settlement of territorial disputes. In the same vein, the decision of the Court to give primacy to titles over *effectivités* contributes greatly to the maintenance of international peace and security since it reduces the need for states to assert through physical acts their claims over disputed territories, avoiding therefore the risk of confrontation. It is for this reason that the Court showed caution in relying upon acquiescence to displace an existing title of territorial sovereignty. The high evidentiary threshold required by the Court in *Pedra Branca/ Pulau Batu Puteh, Middle Rocks and South Ledge* to establish an acquiescence suggests that the principle that titles prevail over *effectivités* will not be altered so easily. The challenge therefore is that of the rigorous application of this framework in all territorial disputes submitted to the Court.

Further Reading

G Distefano, *L'ordre international entre légalité et effectivité: le titre juridique dans le contentieux territorial* (Pedone, 2002).

M. Hébié, *Souveraineté territoriale par traité: une étude des accords entre entités politiques locales et puissances coloniales* (PUF, 2015).

R. Jennings, *The Acquisition of Territory in International Law* (with a new introduction by M Kohen) (Manchester University Press, 2017).

M. G. Kohen, *Possession contestée et souveraineté territoriale* (Presses Universitaires de France, 1997).

M. G. Kohen and M. Hébié (eds.), *Research Handbook on Territorial Disputes in International Law* (Elgar, 2018).

Nilüfer Oral[*]

I Introduction

The *Corfu Channel (United Kingdom* v. *Albania)* case, filed in 1947, inaugurated the newly established International Court of Justice.[1] With the exception of multiple maritime boundary delimitation disputes, there have been very few law of the sea disputes on other issues in the case files of the Court since. To some extent, the emphasis on maritime boundaries is understandable given the history of the development of the law of the sea. From the time of the 1930 Hague Codification Conference until the adoption of the 1982 UN Convention on the Law of the Sea (1982 LOSC),[2] States struggled to reach agreement on the breadth of the territorial sea and to resolve the challenge of unilaterally declared expansive maritime zones.[3] Further attention was drawn to maritime boundaries with the 1945 Proclamation on the Continental Shelf by US President Truman, for the creation of a new and expansive maritime zone granting to the coastal State exclusive sovereignty rights to valuable natural resources.[4] Finally, after nine years of negotiations, the 1982 LOSC would resolve the outstanding matter of the breadth of the territorial sea,[5] and expand

[*] The author thanks Ms. Tutku Bektas (BA Oxford University/ LL.M NYU School of Law) for her invaluable assistance in preparing this chapter and Ms. Asli Korkmaz (LL.M candidate Queen Mary University of London) for her assistance.
[1] *Corfu Channel (United Kingdom* v. *Albania)* (Merits), ICJ Rep 1949, p. 4.
[2] Conference for the Codification of International Law, 13 March 1930, The Hague; United Nations Convention on the Law of the Sea (adopted 10 December 1982, entered into force 16 November 1994), 1833 UNTS 3 (UNCLOS).
[3] T. Treves, 'Historical Development of the Law of the Sea', *The Oxford Handbook of the Law of the Sea* (2015) 1.
[4] Proclamations 2667 and 2668, issued by US President Harry S. Truman on 28 September 1945 (10 Fed. Reg. 12303 and 10 Fed. Reg. 12304).
[5] UNCLOS, Art 3.

existing maritime zones beyond those established under the four 1958 Geneva Conventions.[6]

In addition to maritime zones, the 1982 LOSC also opened a new era for the law of the sea. It created new regimes for passage through straits and archipelagos, a unique access and benefit-sharing regime for seabed minerals under the Common Heritage of Mankind, a comprehensive framework of obligations and measures for protection of the marine environment and conservation of living resources, the first global framework for maritime scientific research, the transfer of marine technology, and importantly, an innovative regime for compulsory dispute settlement. Nonetheless, the diversity of cases relating to the law of the sea brought to the Court has been limited and not at all reflective of the 320 articles of the Convention.

This chapter will focus specifically on examining the key contributions of the Court to the development of the law of the sea since its establishment in four areas: maritime delimitation cases, the status of islands and rocks, navigational rights in straits and lastly, the conservation of natural resources. This chapter will explore how in the case of maritime delimitation the Court has played a very influential role in developing the principles and rules of international law in maritime boundary delimitation. By contrast, it has refrained from exercising its judicial prerogative of interpretation and clarification of the meaning of 'rocks' and 'islands' under Article 123 when requested to. In particular, the influence and contribution of the Court has been quite limited in navigational issues, as well as in relation to conservation and marine environmental issues despite the availability of compulsory dispute settlement options in Part XV and the possibility to select the Court under Article 287 of Part XV.

II Maritime Delimitation

A The Court's First Case and the Straight Baseline Method

The Court's first maritime boundary case was the dye for future cases where the Court would exercise its discretion and shape the international

---

[6] Convention on the Territorial Sea and Contiguous Zone (adopted 29 April 1958, entered into force 10 September 1964) 516 UNTS 205 (TSC); 1958 Convention on the High Seas (adopted 29 April 1958, entered into force 30 September 1962) 450 UNTS 11 (HSC); 1958 Convention on the Continental Shelf (adopted 29 April 1958, entered into force 10 June 1964) 450 UNTS 311 (CSC); 1958 Convention on Fishing and Conservation of the Living Resources of the High Seas (adopted 29 April 1958, entered into force 20 March 1966) 559 UNTS 285 (CFCLR).

rules and principles and maritime delimitation. In the 1951 *Anglo-Norwegian Fisheries* case the Court rejected the United Kingdom's challenge to Norway's use of straight baseline method as being contrary to international law.[7] Adopting a pragmatic approach, that would characterise its approach in future cases, the Court focused on geographic realities and found Norway's complex coastal geographical configuration to be relevant to justify application of the straight baseline method. The Court recognised that in the case of a deeply indented coast or a coast that is bordered by an archipelago 'the base-line becomes independent of the low-water mark, and can only be determined by means of a geometrical construction'.[8]

International principles and rules of maritime delimitation have been shaped by the jurisprudence of the Court since this first case. The Court's approach on straight baselines is directly reflected in Article 4 of the 1958 Geneva Convention on the Territorial Sea and Contiguous Zone and Article 7 of the 1982 LOSC.[9] Both allow for the drawing of straight baselines in cases of coastlines that are 'deeply indented and cut into, or if there is a fringe of islands along the coast in its immediate vicinity'. However, with the qualification that the line cannot 'depart to any appreciable extent from the general direction of the coast'. In addition, proximity is required so that 'the sea areas lying within the lines must be sufficiently closely linked to the land domain to be subject to the regime of internal waters'.[10] As remarked by authors this standard is vague enough to allow expansive interpretation and application of the straight baseline, which indeed has been the practice.[11] The Court later cautioned in the *Qatar* v. *Bahrain* case that the straight baseline method is to be used

---

[7] *Fisheries Case (United Kingdom v. Norway)* (Merits), ICJ Rep 1951, p. 116. By contrast Lowe and Tzanakopoulos question whether 'the decision indeed had any serious impact on the right to draw straight baselines which', the authors observe, 'was not really disputed, given that the UK was found to have acquiesced in the drawing of such baselines in that case'. *See* V. Lowe QC and A. Tzanakopoulos, 'The Development of the Law of the Sea by the International Court of Justice', *The Development of International Law by the International Court of Justice* (2013) 177-179. Tullio Treves states 'The impact of this judgment on the codification process and on the clarification of customary law is beyond doubt.' Treves, 'Historical Development of the Law of the Sea', 19.

[8] Ibid., 129.   [9] TSC, Art 4; UNCLOS, Art 7.   [10] Ibid.

[11] C. Schofield, 'Departures from the Coast: Trends in the Application of Territorial Sea Baselines under the Law of the Sea Convention' 27 *The International Journal of Marine and Coastal Law* (2012) 723-732 at 727; J. A. Roach, *Excessive maritime claims* (Brill, 2020); W. A. Qureshi, 'State Practices of Straight Baselines Institute Excessive Maritime Claims', 42 *Southern Illinois University Law Journal* (2018) 421-450.

restrictively as it is an exception to the normal rules of baselines.[12] However, this has not stopped States from expansive application of the straight baseline method given the significant amount of internal waters to be gained.

B Evolution of the Principles and Rules of International Law for Maritime Delimitation

The next set of delimitation cases decided by the Court were the landmark 1969 *North Sea Continental Shelf (Federal Republic of Germany* v. *Denmark; Federal Republic of Germany* v. *Netherlands)* cases.[13] These were also the first cases instituted subsequent to the adoption of the 1958 Continental Shelf Convention, and followed on the heels of the Second UN Conference on the Law of the Sea where States had failed to reach consensus on the breadth of the territorial sea.[14] This was a period when the state of international law concerning delimitation was still *de lege ferende*. The influence of this case was later described by the Chamber of the Court in the 1984 *Gulf of Maine (Canada* v. *United States of America)* case, as the 'judicial decision which has made the greatest contribution to the formation of customary law in this field'.[15] This observation is still valid over fifty years later with many of the Court's principles applied in subsequent cases. It is the decision that christened the primary role of 'equity' and 'equitable principles' for maritime delimitation.[16]

In the case, the Netherlands and Denmark sought application of the equidistance-special circumstances rule as codified under Article 6 of the 1958 Continental Shelf Convention. Germany, not a party to the 1958 Convention, opposed this and requested application of the 'just and

---

[12] *Maritime Delimitation and Territorial Questions between Qatar and Bahrain (Qatar* v. *Bahrain)* (Merits), ICJ Rep 2001, p. 97, para. 212.
[13] *North Sea Continental Shelf (Federal Republic of Germany* v. *Denmark; Federal Republic of Germany* v. *Netherlands)*, ICJ Rep 1969, p. 3.
[14] Second United Nations Conference on the Law of the Sea (UNCLOS II), 17 March–26 April 1960, Geneva, Switzerland.
[15] *Delimitation of the Maritime Boundary in the Gulf of Maine Area (Canada* v. *United States of America)* (Merits) ICJ Rep 1984, p. 246, para. 91.
[16] U. Leanza, 'International Courts and the Development of the International Law of the Sea on the Delimitation of the Continental Shelf', *International Courts and the Development of International Law* (2013) 281–290, 288.

equitable share' approach.[17] This division of views would foreshadow the division of States at the Third UN Conference on the Law of the Sea between the applications of equitable principles versus equidistance for maritime delimitation.[18] The Court determined that the 1958 Convention was inapplicable to the cases, and looked to the rules of customary international law. In a detailed examination of the history of Article 6 of the 1958 Convention, including the seminal work of the International Law Commission and State practice,[19] the Court concluded that the rule of equidistance-special circumstances for adjacent coasts under Article 6 of the 1958 Continental Shelf Convention had not crystallised any pre-existing or emerging rule of customary international law.[20] Instead, the Court pronounced as the guiding rule that 'delimitation is to be effected by agreement in accordance with equitable principles, and taking account of all the relevant circumstances, in such a way as to leave as much as possible to each party all those parts of the continental shelf that constitute a natural prolongation of its land territory into and under the sea, without encroachment on the natural prolongation of the land territory of the other'.[21] In its ruling the Court also stated that '[e]quity does not necessarily imply equality. There can never be any question of completely refashioning nature . . .'[22] Moreover, opening the door of judicial discretion the Court remarked, 'there is no legal limit to the considerations which States may take account of for the purpose of making sure that they apply equitable procedures'.[23] By rejecting a clear methodology of delimitation, such as what had been codified in Article 6, in favour of the vague contours of 'equitable principles', the Court set the course for opening a wide door of discretion for judicial law-making in the field of maritime delimitation.[24]

The rejection of the equidistance-special circumstance method of delimitation as a rule of customary international law was reaffirmed in subsequent cases such as in the 1984 *Gulf of Maine* case,[25] the 1985

---

[17] *North Sea Continental Shelf*, para. 15.

[18] P. Birnie, 'United Nations Convention on the Law of the Sea 1982 A Commentary, Vol IV', 16 *Marine Policy* (1992) 232–234; M. Lando, *Maritime Delimitation as a Judicial Process* (Cambridge University Press, 2019), 102.

[19] *North Sea Continental Shelf*, paras. 48–68.   [20] *North Sea Continental Shelf*, para. 69.

[21] *North Sea Continental Shelf*, para. 101.   [22] Ibid., para 91.   [23] Ibid.

[24] Lando, *Maritime Delimitation*.   [25] *Gulf of Maine*, para. 122.

Libya/Malta case,[26] the 1993 *Maritime Delimitation in the Area between Greenland and Jan Mayen* case,[27] which referred to the 1977 *Anglo-French Continental Shelf* case,[28] and the 2002 *Land and Maritime Boundary between Cameroon and Nigeria* case.[29] In the 1982 *Continental Shelf (Tunisia* v. *Libyan Arab Jamahiriya)* case, the Court, looking at the mixed nature of State practice and the drafting history of the 1982 LOSC, suggested that a combination of methods using equidistance and some other criteria could be employed based on the relevant circumstances in order to reach an equitable solution.[30] Such an example is seen in the 2007 *Territorial and Maritime Dispute between Nicaragua and Honduras in the Caribbean Sea* case[31] where the Court accorded a principal role to the bisector method of delimitation and not equidistance. Taking its customary pragmatic approach in face of geological realities, the Court found that the application of the bisector method was justified in cases where an unstable coast rendered the identification of a base point difficult.[32] Some authors point out, however, that the bisector line is seen as a simplified version of the equidistance line and is not an entirely distinct approach.[33] Nonetheless, the case represents

[26] *Continental Shelf (Libyan Arab Jamahiriya* v. *Malta)*, Judgment, ICJ Rep 1985, p. 13, para. 44.

[27] *Maritime Delimitation in the Area between Greenland and Jan Mayen (Denmark* v. *Norway)* (Merits) (Jan Mayen), ICJ Rep 1993, p. 38, paras. 45–46.

[28] Ibid., para. 46; *Anglo-French Continental Shelf cases (United Kingdom* v. *France)* (1977, 1978) 18 RIAA 3, para. 70.

[29] *Land and Maritime Boundary between Cameroon and Nigeria (Cameroon* v. *Nigeria: Equatorial Guinea intervening)* (Merits), ICJ Rep 2002, p. 303, para. 293, citing *Continental Shelf (Libyan Arab Jamahiriya* v. *Malta)*, para. 63: '[T]he equidistance method is not the only method applicable to the present dispute, and it does not even have the benefit of a presumption in its favour. Thus, under existing law, it must be demonstrated that the equidistance method leads to an equitable result in the case in question.'

[30] *Continental Shelf (Tunisia* v. *Libyan Arab Jamahiriya)* (Merits), ICJ Rep 1982, p. 18, para. 109.

[31] *Territorial and Maritime Dispute between Nicaragua and Honduras in the Caribbean Sea (Nicaragua* v. *Honduras)* (Judgment), ICJ Rep 2007, p. 659, paras. 278–280; C. G. Lathrop, 'Territorial and Maritime Dispute Between Nicaragua and Honduras in the Caribbean Sea (Nicaragua v. Honduras)' 102 *American Journal of International Law* (2008) 113–119.

[32] *Territorial and Maritime Dispute between Nicaragua and Honduras in the Caribbean Sea*, paras. 287–289. See also, *Gulf of Maine*, para. 195; *Continental Shelf (Tunisia* v. *Libyan Arab Jamahiriya)*, where equidistance could not be used for the second segment of the delimitation because the segment was to begin at a point not on any possible equidistance line; *see Delimitation of the maritime boundary between Guinea and Guinea-Bissau*, Award of 14 February 1985, 77 ILR 683–684, para. 108.

[33] See S. Fietta and R. Cleverly, *A Practitioner's Guide to Maritime Boundary Delimitation* (Oxford University Press, 2016). The authors conclude that '[t]he Court's judgment

an example of the pragmatic approach of the Court coupled with its broad discretionary powers in maritime delimitation.

The Court in its seminal *North Sea Continental Shelf* cases had also rejected the 'just and equitable share' approach argued by Germany as being incompatible with the fundamental rule that the rights of the coastal State over the continental shelf exist *ipso facto* and *ab initio*.[34] In this case, the Court famously proclaimed the now well-known principle that the *land dominates the sea*,[35] and 'is the legal source of the power which a State may exercise over territorial extensions to seaward'.[36] This is an example of a Court-fashioned principle that has been influential despite not having a basis in any treaty or State practice.

In the field of maritime delimitation, the Court has exercised ample judicial discretion relying on the abstract notion of equitable principles. Article 6 of the 1958 Convention does not mention equity in its methodology, yet the Court emphasised the role of equity and equitable principles in its decisions.[37] Another such example of the Court exercising discretion in fashioning the law of maritime delimitation is the appearance and disappearance of the principle of 'natural prolongation'. Despite not featuring in the 1958 Continental Shelf Convention, the Court invoked the concept of natural prolongation in the 1969 *North Sea Continental Shelf* cases, relying on the Truman Proclamation's notion that the continental shelf was an extension of the land naturally appurtenant to it.[38]

---

therefore confirms the primacy of the equidistance-based methodologies in modern maritime delimitation . . .'.

[34] *North Sea Continental Shelf*, para. 19.

[35] *North Sea Continental Shelf*, para. 96. This principle has been restated in subsequent cases of: *Gulf of Maine*, para. 157; *Aegean Sea Continental Shelf (Greece* v. *Turkey)*, ICJ Rep 1978, p. 3, para. 86; *Qatar* v. *Bahrain*, para. 185; *Territorial and Maritime Dispute between Nicaragua and Honduras in the Caribbean Sea*, paras. 113 and 126; *Maritime Delimitation in the Black Sea (Romania* v. *Ukraine)* (Merits), ICJ Rep 2009, p. 61, para. 77; *The Bay of Bengal Maritime Boundary Arbitration (Bangladesh* v. *India)* (PCA, Award of 7 July 2014), para. 279; *Continental Shelf (Tunisia* v. *Libyan Arab Jamahiriya)*, para. 73; *Dispute Concerning Delimitation of the Maritime Boundary Between Bangladesh and Myanmar in the Bay of Bengal (Bangladesh* v. *Myanmar)* (Judgment) ITLOS Reports 2012, p. 4, para. 185.

[36] *North Sea Continental Shelf*, para. 96.

[37] L. Delabie, 'The Role of Equity, Equitable Principles, and the Equitable Solution in Maritime Delimitation', *Maritime Boundary Delimitation: The Case Law* (2018) 145.

[38] *North Sea Continental Shelf*, paras. 47 and 101. The 1945 US Presidential Proclamation No. 2667, Policy of the United States with Respect to the Natural Resources of the Subsoil and Seabed of the Continental Shelf describing the continental shelf as 'an extension of the land mass of the coastal nation and thus naturally appurtenant to it . . .'.

Eventually, 'natural prolongation' found its way into Article 76(1) of the 1982 LOSC. However, with the *Tunisia/Libya* case the Court, for pragmatic reasons, abandoned the natural prolongation and instead applied the distance criterion that defines the EEZ of a coastal State.[39] Notably, the hints of this change did not come first from the ICJ but from the arbitral tribunal in the *Anglo-French Continental Shelf* case in 1977.[40] In that case, the Tribunal stated that the principle of natural prolongation of territory was not absolute and could be qualified in certain situations.[41] The EEZ, measured purely by distance criteria, would serve as that principal qualification[42] or simply because practically it was not possible geologically to determine the 'natural prolongation' of overlapping claims.[43]

The North Sea Continental Shelf cases also initiated the concept of relevant circumstances and set the stage for the primacy of geographical factors such as the presence of general configuration of the coasts of the parties, as well as the presence of any special or unusual features,[44] physical and geological structure, and natural resources, of the continental shelf areas involved unity of deposits,[45] reasonable proportionality of coastlines,[46] and any cut-off effect.[47] Subsequent cases also looked at non-geographical factors such as past conduct of the parties that involved past hydrocarbon licensing practice[48] and historic fishing rights.[49] These

---

[39] See also, H. J. Kim, 'Natural Prolongation: A Living Myth in the Regime of the Continental Shelf?' 45 *Ocean Development & International Law* (2014) 374–388.

[40] *Anglo-French Continental Shelf.*   [41] Ibid., paras. 192–193.

[42] *Continental Shelf*, para. 55; *Gulf of Maine*, paras. 185 and 61: 'the law applicable to the present dispute, [...], is based not on geological or geomorphological criteria, but on a criterion of distance from the Coast or, to use the traditional term, on the principle of adjacency as measured by distance'.

[43] *Continental Shelf (Tunisia v. Libyan Arab Jamahiriya). Gulf of Maine*, para. 45: 'neither party disputes the fact that there is nothing in this single sea-bed, lacking any marked elevations or depressions, to distinguish one part that might be considered as constituting the natural prolongation of the coasts of the United States from another part which could be regarded as the natural prolongation of the coasts of Canada'.

[44] *North Sea Continental Shelf*, para. 101.   [45] Ibid., para. 97.

[46] Ibid., para. 98. *See also Gulf of Maine* which introduced the term 'disproportionality'. Para. 185; *(Libya v. Malta)*; *Jan Mayen*; *Romania* v. *Ukraine*; *Territorial and Maritime Dispute (Nicaragua v. Colombia)*, Judgment, ICJ Rep 2012, p. 624; *Maritime Dispute (Peru v. Chile)*, Judgment, ICJ Rep 2014, p. 3; *Maritime Delimitation in the Caribbean Sea and the Pacific Ocean (Costa Rica v. Nicaragua)* and *Land Boundary in the Northern Part of Isla Portillos (Costa Rica v. Nicaragua)*, Judgment, ICJ Rep 2018, p. 139.

[47] *North Sea Continental Shelf*, para. 91.

[48] *Continental Shelf (Tunisia v. Libyan Arab Jamahiriya)*, para. 95.

[49] *Continental Shelf (Tunisia v. Libyan Arab Jamahiriya)*, para. 105.

factors are judicial creations. For example, as observed by Lando, 'Proportionality had no legal basis under international law at the time of North Sea Continental Shelf'.[50]

The Court's rejection of Article 6 was reflected in the 1982 LOSC which replaced the equidistance-special circumstances codified in the 1958 Continental Shelf Convention with the famously vague language in Article 83(1) that 'delimitation of the continental shelf between States with opposite or adjacent coasts shall be effected by agreement on the basis of international law [...] in order to achieve an equitable solution'.[51] This vague language resulted from the inability of States to reach consensus on whether maritime delimitation should be based on the equidistance-special circumstances approach, or by agreement and equitable principles.[52] The language in Article 83(1) was adopted *mutatis mutandis* in Article 74(1) for the EEZ.[53] As correctly observed by Jennings 'the concept of 'equitable result' leads to 'pure judicial discretion and a decision upon nothing more than the Court's subjective appreciation of what appears to be a fair compromise of the claims of either side'.[54] The Court in the 2001 *Maritime Delimitation and Territorial Questions between Qatar and Bahrain* case affirmed that the principles of maritime delimitation were enshrined in Articles 74 and 83 reflecting customary international law.[55] As noted by Kaye, the lack of consensus during the negotiations provided 'a unique opportunity to the ICJ and other international tribunals to frame the construction of a significant area of international law, largely without State interference'.[56] The Court had always possessed broad discretion to fashion its own methodology of delimitation guided by the vague rules of

---

[50] Lando, *Maritime Delimitation*, 258.   [51] UNCLOS, Art. 83(1).

[52] Third United Nations Conference on the Law of the Sea (UNCLOS III), 1973–1982; Official Records of the Third United Nations Conference on the Law of the Sea, Geneva, Switzerland, 24 April 1979, *Summary Record of the 57th Meeting*, para. 30: The Chair of Negotiation Group 7 expressed his doubt that none of the compromise provisions would 'offer a precise and definite answer to the question of delimitation criteria'.

[53] UNCLOS, Art. 74(1).

[54] R. Jennings, 'Equity and Equitable Principles' 42 *Annuaire Suisse de Droit International* (1986) 27–38, 31. *See also*, F. Olorundami, 'Objectivity versus Subjectivity in the Context of the ICJ's Three-stage Methodology of Maritime Boundary Delimitation' 32 *The International Journal of Marine and Coastal Law* (2017) 36–53.

[55] *Qatar v. Bahrain*.

[56] S. B. Kaye, 'Lessons Learned from the Gulf of Maine Case: The Development of Maritime Boundary Delimitation Jurisprudence since UNCLOS III' 14(1) *Ocean and Coastal Law Journal* (2008) 73, 74.

equitable principles, although this also raised criticisms of subjectivity and lack of predictability.[57] The somewhat abstract equitable principles offered little guidance as to defining an objective methodology for effecting delimitation between overlapping boundaries.[58] In time, the Court would eventually develop a more predictable methodology for delimitation of the continental shelf and the EEZ but never recognising any method as constituting a rule of customary international law.

C Consolidation of the Court's Delimitation Methodology: From a Two-Stage to Three-Stage Approach

In the 1984 *Gulf of Maine* case the Special Chamber of the Court intro-duced the first kernels of the two-stage procedure in maritime delimitation. Described as a 'practical method', the Chambers began with the drawing of a provisional delimitation line, followed by a determination of special circumstances that would require its correction.[59] In the 1985 *Continental Shelf (Libyan Arab Jamahiriya v. Malta)* case, the Court expressly identified the delimitation line as 'provisional' and explained: 'Were the Court to treat it as final, it would be conferring on the equi-distance method the status of being the only method the use of which is compulsory in the case of opposite coasts.'[60] However, the *Jan Mayen* case is recognised as when the ICJ expressly adopted the two-stage method-ology for maritime boundary delimitation: 'beginning with drawing pro-visional median line and then examining whether 'special circumstances' require any adjustment or shifting of that line'.[61] This method was followed in subsequent cases by the Court and other tribunals.[62]

---

[57] See T. M. Ndiaye, 'The Judge, Maritime Delimitation and the Grey Areas' 55 *Indian Journal of International Law* (2015) 493–533; A. Miron, 'A Practitioner's Guide to Maritime Boundary Delimitation Maritime Boundary Delimitation: The Case Law. Is It Consistent and Predictable?' 31 *European Journal of International Law* (2020) 372–377.

[58] See Y. Tanaka, *Predictability and Flexibility in the Law of Maritime Delimitation* (Hart, 2007).

[59] *Gulf of Maine*, paras. 215–217.

[60] *Continental Shelf (Libyan Arab Jamahiriya v. Malta)*, para. 63.

[61] *Jan Mayen*, p. 61, para. 51.

[62] *Cameroon v. Nigeria*, 231. See also Arbitration between Barbados and the Republic of Trinidad and Tobago (Decision) [2006] RIAA, Vol. XXVII, paras. 242 and 306; Arbitration between Guyana and Suriname (Award) [2008] ILM, Vol. 47, p. 116, at p. 213, para. 342; Second Stage of the Proceedings between Eritrea and Yemen *(Eritrea v. Yemen)* [1999]

The two-stage methodology eventually crystallised into the three-stage methodology in the 2009 *Maritime Delimitation in the Black Sea* and is well-accepted and used by courts and tribunals since.[63] The three-step methodology developed by the Court in the *Black Sea case* was applied subsequently in the 2012 *Nicaragua* v. *Columbia* case,[64] and also by ITLOS in the *Bay of Bengal case* between Bangladesh and Myanmar,[65] the *Ghana/Côte d'Ivoire* maritime delimitation case,[66] as well as by the arbitral Tribunal in the 2014 *Bay of Bengal* arbitration case between Bangladesh and India.[67] The reference to the three-step methodology developed by the Court in the *Black Sea Maritime Delimitation* case in these latter cases marks an important indication of coherence and consistency among the Court and different tribunals, countering previous concerns of possible fragmentation.[68] However, over the decades of evolution of the international law of maritime delimitation in the ICJ and in arbitral tribunals and more recently ITLOS, there is a consolidation of methodology.

In the first stage, after identifying the relevant (overlapping) coasts to be delimited, the Court draws a provisional delimitation line based on geometrically objective methods that are appropriate for the geography of the area to be delimited. For delimitation between adjacent coasts, an equidistance line will be drawn unless there are compelling reasons that make this unfeasible in the particular case; and for opposite coasts, the

---

XXII RIAA 335, 365–366; *Qatar* v. *Bahrain. See also* A. O. Elferink, T. Henriksen, and S. V. Busch, *Maritime Boundary Delimitation: The Case Law* (Cambridge University Press, 2018), 1–32: Alex Oude Elferink, Tore Henriksen and Signe Veierud Busch take the view that the three-stage approach was already used in the *Libya/Malta* and *Jan Mayen* cases.

[63] *Maritime Delimitation in the Black Sea*. See C. G. Lathrop, 'Maritime Delimitation in the Black Sea (*Romania* v. *Ukraine*)' 103(3) *American Journal of International Law* (2009) 543; N. Oral, 'Case concerning Maritime Delimitation in the Black Sea (*Romania* v. *Ukraine*) Judgment of 3 February 2009' 25 *International Journal of Marine and Coastal Law* (2010) 115. It has been applied in *Nicaragua* v. *Colombia*, paras. 190–193; *Maritime Dispute (Peru* v. *Chile)*, 240; and *Maritime Delimitation in the Caribbean Sea and the Pacific Ocean (Costa Rica* v. *Nicaragua)* and *Land Boundary in the Northern Part of Isla Portillos (Costa Rica* v. *Nicaragua)*, para. 135.

[64] *Territorial and Maritime Dispute (Nicaragua* v. *Colombia)*. The Court added an additional element to the third phase.

[65] *Bangladesh* v. *Myanmar*.   [66] Ibid.   [67] *Bangladesh* v. *India*, paras. 336–346.

[68] A. E. Boyle, 'Dispute Settlement and the Law of the Sea Convention: Problems of Fragmentation and Jurisdiction' 46 *International and Comparative Law Quarterly* (1997) 37–54.

provisional delimitation line will consist of a median line between the two coasts.[69] In the second stage, the Court considers whether there are factors calling for the adjustment or shifting of the provisional equidistance line in order to achieve an equitable result.[70] In the third stage, the Court determines whether there is any marked disproportion between the ratio of the respective coastal lengths and the ratio between the relevant maritime areas of each State by reference to the delimitation line.[71] Coastal disparity had been used as an equitable criteria in past cases, and was not new. The Court clarified it as the final step in determining whether adjustment of the provisional delimitation line was necessary in order to achieve an equitable result.

After some fifty years since the influential 1969 *North Sea Continental Shelf* cases, the Court has effectively recognised the equidistance method to be the principal method absent 'compelling' reasons otherwise, although some have queried the grounds for the Court giving priority to the equidistance method.[72] Nonetheless, the Court remains conservative in its identification and application of equitable criteria, especially for nongeographic reasons, to achieve an equitable result. The reason for this may lie in the Court's eloquent explanation in the *Libya/Malta* case of how it viewed the role of equity as '...*not abstract justice but justice according to the rule of law; which is to say that its application should display consistency and a degree of predictability; even though it looks with particularity to the peculiar circumstances of an instant case, it also looks beyond it to principles of more general application*'.[73] The goal of predictability and certainly would restrict the largesse of the Court in creating an expansive application of relevant circumstances to achieve an equitable result.

Over the years, the relevant circumstances taken into consideration by the Court entail both geographic and non-geographic factors. Geographic

---

[69] No legal consequences flow from the use of the terms 'median line' and 'equidistance line' since the method of delimitation is the same for both.

[70] *Maritime Delimitation in the Black Sea*, para. 120.

[71] *Maritime Delimitation in the Black Sea*, para. 122.

[72] J. Gao, 'A Note on the Nicaragua v. Colombia Case' 44 *Ocean Development & International Law* (2013) 219–234, 221. See also Lando, *Maritime Delimitation*, 27–28, for a discussion of critical views of the three-step methodology.

[73] *Continental Shelf (Libyan Arab Jamahiriya/Malta)*, para. 45.

factors include, presence of a peninsula,[74] proportionality,[75] presence of islands,[76] instability of the near shore coastal areas,[77] the enclosed nature of a sea,[78] concavity of the coast,[79] and cutting-off effect.[80] Non-geographic and socio-economic relevant circumstances have factored even less in the jurisprudence of the Court. Relevant factors considered, but not necessarily applied, by the Court include past conduct of the parties, such as hydrocarbon licensing practice,[81] historic fishing rights,[82] fishing activities,[83] oil and

[74] *Gulf of Maine*, para. 37 recognising prominent peninsula features such as Cape Cod and Nova Scotia coast could not be ignored and did constitute relevant circumstances. The ICJ relying on the *Gulf of Maine* case found that Nicoya Peninsula was a prominent part of Costa Rica's mainland and a relevant circumstance. *Maritime Delimitation in the Caribbean Sea and the Pacific Ocean (Costa Rica v. Nicaragua) and Land Boundary in the Northern Part of Isla Portillos (Costa Rica v. Nicaragua)*, Judgment, ICJ Rep 2018, p. 139, paras. 197–198.

[75] *North Sea Continental Shelf*, para. 98. There has not yet been a case in which international tribunals found that a boundary failed to satisfy the disproportionality test. *See* Lando, *Maritime Delimitation*, 247.

[76] *Continental Shelf (Tunisia v. Libyan Arab Jamahiriya)*, para. 79. The islands were accorded 'half effect' to avoid giving them excessive weight when drawing the delimitation line. Ibid., paras. 128–129; cf. *Land and Maritime Boundary between Cameroon and Nigeria*, para. 299; *Gulf of Maine*, para. 222; cf. *Maritime Delimitation in the Black Sea*, para. 178 The Corn Islands were accorded half effect and the equidistance line was adjusted in favour of Costa Rica in the Caribbean Sea in the case of *Maritime Delimitation in the Caribbean Sea and the Pacific Ocean (Costa Rica v. Nicaragua) and Land Boundary in the Northern Part of Isla Portillos*, paras. 153–154.

[77] The Court found the 'high instability and narrowness of the sandspit near the mouth of the San Juan River' and the 'instability of the sandbar separating Harbor Head Lagoon from the Caribbean Sea' to be a special circumstance relevant for delimitation of the territorial sea. *Maritime Delimitation in the Caribbean Sea and the Pacific Ocean (Costa Rica v. Nicaragua) and Land Boundary in the Northern Part of Isla Portillos (Costa Rica v. Nicaragua)*, Judgment, ICJ Rep 2018, p. 139; paras. 104–105.

[78] *Maritime Delimitation in the Black Sea*, para. 178.

[79] *Cameroon v. Nigeria: Equatorial Guinea intervening*, para. 297. However, the Court did not find the concavity of the Gulf of Guinea to be a relevant circumstance. ITLOS stated in the *Bangladesh v. Myanmar* delimitation case that 'concavity per se is not necessarily a relevant circumstance. However, when an equidistance line drawn between two States produces a cut-off effect on the maritime entitlement of one of those States, as a result of the concavity of the coast, then an adjustment of that line may be necessary in order to reach an equitable result.' Para. 292.

[80] *Gulf of Maine*, para. 222; *Maritime Delimitation in the Black Sea*, para. 201.

[81] *Continental Shelf (Tunisia v. Libyan Arab Jamahiriya)*, para. 95.

[82] *Continental Shelf (Tunisia v. Libyan Arab Jamahiriya)*, para. 105.

[83] *Maritime Delimitation in the Black Sea*, para. 198.

gas concessions,[84] possible third State claims,[85] existing delimitations already effected in the region,[86] security concerns,[87] naval patrols,[88] and economic disparity.[89] And, while not a relevant circumstance, the question of maritime boundaries based on tacit agreement was for the first time recognised by the Court in the *Peru* v. *Chile* case meeting the 'compelling evidence' standard set by the Court in the *Nicaragua and Honduras* case.[90]

The particularly cautious approach of the Court towards non-geographic relevant criteria was signalled early on in one of its well-known pronouncements from the *Gulf of Maine* case where the Chamber stated that fisheries activities or navigation, defence, petroleum exploration and exploitation, 'cannot be taken into account as a relevant circumstance' or equitable criterion unless 'likely to entail catastrophic repercussions for the livelihood and economic well-being of the population of the countries concerned'.[91] This set a very high threshold. Not surprisingly, the Court remains conservative in adjusting the provisional delimitation line based on non-geographic factors. The *Jan Mayen* case is among the few cases where the Court found the need for equitable access to natural resources (fisheries) as a special circumstance requiring adjustment.[92]

D Consideration of the Extended Continental Shelf

The 2012 *Territorial and Maritime Dispute (Nicaragua v. Columbia)* case was the first time the Court was requested to consider a claim regarding a State's (Nicaragua's) entitlement to a continental shelf extending beyond

---

[84] *Maritime Delimitation in the Black Sea*, para. 198. Cf, in *Cameroon* v. *Nigeria*, the Court did not consider the oil practice of the parties as a relevant circumstance: *Land and Maritime Boundary between Cameroon and Nigeria*, para. 304.

[85] *Continental Shelf (Libyan Arab Jamahiriya v. Malta)*, para. 68.

[86] *Maritime Delimitation in the Black Sea*, para. 178.

[87] *Maritime Delimitation in the Black Sea*, para. 204.

[88] *Maritime Delimitation in the Black Sea*, para. 198.

[89] *Continental Shelf (Tunisia v. Libyan Arab Jamahiriya)*; *Continental Shelf (Libyan Arab Jamahiriya v. Malta)*, para. 50.

[90] *Peru* v. *Chile*, paras. 237–258; *Bangladesh* v. *Myanmar*, paras. 100–118; *Tunisia* v. *Libya*, para. 118. ITLOS also rejected a tacit agreement for a maritime boundary in *Delimitation of the Maritime Boundary in the Atlantic Ocean (Ghana v. Côte d'Ivoire)*, Judgment, ITLOS Reports 2017, p. 4.

[91] *Gulf of Maine*, para. 237.   [92] *Jan Mayen*, para. 76.

200 nautical miles.[93] The Court, however, initially declined to address the matter on the grounds that such claims must first be reviewed by the Commission on the Limits of the Continental Shelf under Article 76 of the 1982 LOSC.[94] The deferral to the Commission by the Court stood in marked contrast to other decisions by arbitral tribunals. The Tribunal in the 2006 *Arbitration between Barbados and the Republic of Trinidad and Tobago* had concluded that it did have jurisdiction to delimit the maritime boundary of the continental shelf beyond 200 nautical miles, although it did not do so.[95] In 2012, ITLOS in the *Dispute Concerning Delimitation of the Maritime Boundary Between Bangladesh and Myanmar in the Bay of Bengal (Bangladesh* v. *Myanmar)* case,[96] found it had an obligation under the Convention to resolve a long-standing dispute that included delimitation of the continental shelf beyond 200 nautical miles and that this would not be encroaching upon the functions of the Commission.[97] Subsequently, in the second request made by Nicaragua, the Court, in somewhat of a *volte face*, decided it did have jurisdiction to delimit the continental shelf beyond 200 nm between Nicaragua and Columbia.[98] In this case, the Court decided that it did not have to wait for the report of the CLCC which was concerned only with the delineation of the outer limits of the continental shelf, and not delimitation. The Court took into account that Article 76(1) of UNCLOS expressly stated its provisions were without prejudice to the question of delimitation of the continental shelf between States with opposite or adjacent coasts.[99] The decision of the Court in the second case can be viewed as a reflection of the Court ensuring coherence among itself and other international tribunals thereby strengthening the predictability of international law in the field of maritime boundary delimitation and avoiding problems of fragmented decisions.

---

[93] *Nicaragua* v. *Colombia.* See J. Gao, 'A Note on the Nicaragua v. Colombia Case'.

[94] *Territorial and Maritime Dispute*, paras. 127–130. N. Grossman, 'International Decisions: Territorial and Maritime Dispute (Nicaragua v. Colombia)' 107(2) *American Journal of International Law* (2013) 396.

[95] *Trinidad and Tobago*, para. 217.   [96] *Bangladesh v, Myanmar.*

[97] Ibid. paras. 392–394. See also, *Ghana* v. *Côte d'Ivoire*, p. 4.

[98] Question of the Delimitation of the Continental Shelf between Nicaragua and Colombia beyond 200 Nautical Miles from the Nicaraguan Coast *(Nicaragua* v. *Colombia)*, Preliminary Objections, Judgment, ICJ Rep 2016, p. 100.

[99] Ibid., para. 110. The Court also rejected the other four preliminary objections made by Columbia.

III Islands, Rocks and Low Tide Elevation

The role, status and entitlements of low-tide elevations, islands and other offshore features, including artificial islands, have been a long-standing subject of international law.[100] During UNCLOS III there were differences of views, however, as to whether islands should be entitled to the full slate of maritime entitlements.[101,102] States held differing views in regard to the entitlements of islands. The vague language in Article 121 of the 1982 LOSC reflects a compromise in creating two categories of islands: those fully entitled to all maritime entitlements (Article 121(2)), and 'rocks which cannot sustain human habitation or economic life of their own'[103] not being entitled to an EEZ or continental shelf.[104] Despite the lively scholarly debate generated by this vague language,[105] the Court has shied away from directly identifying features under Article 121.

The *2001 Maritime Delimitation and Territorial Questions between Qatar and Bahrain (Qatar v. Bahrain)* case was the first occasion for the

---

[100] G. Gidel, *Le droit international public de la mer: le temps de paix. Tome III, La mer territoriale et la zone contiguë* (Duchemin, 1981); C. R. Symmons, *The Maritime Zones of Islands in International Law* (Martinus Nijhoff, 1979); J. Symonides 'The Legal Status of Islands in the New Law of the Sea' in H. Caminos (ed), *Law of the Sea* (Routledge, 2001) 115–134. For a legislative history of Part VIII of the 1982 Convention *see*, *The Law of the Sea: Regime of Islands Legislative History of Part VIII (Article 121) of the United Nations Convention on the Law of the Sea*, Office for Oceans Affairs and the Law of the Sea (United Nations, 1988). *See also*, B. Kwiatkowski and A. H. A. Soons, 'Entitlement to Maritime Areas of Rocks Which Cannot Sustain Human Habitation or Economic Life of Their Own' 21 *Netherlands Yearbook of International Law* (1990) 139; S. Murphy, 'International Law Relating to Islands' 386 *Collected Courses of the International Law Academy* (2017).

[101] For example, Japan, Greece, France, Venezuela, the United Kingdom, Brazil Portugal, Iran, Ecuador and Australia supported deletion of paragraph 3. See Y. Song, 'The Application of Article 121 of the Law of the Sea Convention to the Selected Geographical Features Situated in the Pacific Ocean' 9 *Chinese Journal of International Law* (2010) 663. *See also* S. N. Nandan and S. Rosenne (eds.), *United Nations Convention on the Law of the Sea: A Commentary*, Vol. III (Brill, 1995), 321–339. See Murphy, 'International Law Relating to Islands', 57–62. See also J. Charney, 'Rocks That Cannot Sustain Human Habitation' 93(4) *American Journal of International Law* (1999) 863, 866.

[102] Murphy, 'International Law Relating to Islands', 56–61; V. Prescott and C. Schofield, *Maritime Political Boundaries of the World* (Brill, 2004), 61–81.

[103] UNCLOS, Art. 121(3).   [104] UNCLOS, Art. 121.

[105] For example, Prescott and Schofield, *Maritime Political Boundaries of the World*, 61–63; J. R. V. Prescott, C. H. Schofield, J. Wu, and H. Zhang, *Maritime Political Boundaries of the World* (Brill, 2004), 19–37.

Court to examine Article 121.[106] The Court affirmed that 'islands, regardless of their size, in this respect enjoy the same status, and therefore generate the same maritime rights, as other land territory' and that Article 121(2) UNCLOS codifies customary international law.[107] However, the Court did not clarify the meaning of Article 121(3) but in dicta confirmed as customary international law that a low-tide elevation does not generate a territorial sea of its own but that it could 'be used as the baseline for measuring the breadth of the territorial sea if it is situated wholly or partly at a distance not exceeding the breadth of the territorial sea from the mainland or an island', as codified in Article 13 of the 1982 LOSC as customary law.[108]

In the 2009 *Maritime Delimitation in the Black Sea (Romania v. Ukraine)* case,[109] the Court avoided addressing Ukraine's position that Serpent's Island was entitled to all maritime zones by simply excluding the use of Serpent's Island as a relevant circumstance.[110] Lastly, in the 2012 *Territorial and Maritime Dispute (Nicaragua v. Colombia)*[111] case as agreed by the parties,[112] the Court affirmed the customary international law status of Article 121.[113] Nevertheless, the Court did not directly address whether specific maritime features in the case were rocks under Article 121(3). The Court did, however, provide some guidance. Citing the 2001 *Maritime Delimitation and Territorial Questions between Qatar and Bahrain* case, the Court reaffirmed the 'long-standing principle' that 'islands, regardless of their size ... enjoy the same status, and therefore generate the same maritime rights, as other land territory' and further that a 'comparatively small island may give an entitlement to a considerable maritime area'.[114] Second, the Court further brought some clarification to the meaning of 'naturally formed land', by stating that '[i]nternational law defines an island by reference to whether it is "naturally formed" and whether it is above water at high tide, not by reference to its geological composition.'[115]

[106] *Qatar* v. *Bahrain.*
[107] *Qatar* v. *Bahrain*, para. 185, recalled in *Nicaragua* v. *Honduras*, para. 113.
[108] *Qatar* v. *Bahrain*, para. 201. Also known as the 'leapfrog' rule.
[109] *Maritime Delimitation in the Black Sea*, paras. 180 and 184. See J. M. Van Dyke, 'The Romania v. Ukraine Decision and Its Effect on East Asian Maritime Delimitations' 15 *Ocean and Coastal Law Journal* (2010) 261.
[110] *Maritime Delimitation in the Black Sea*, para. 187.
[111] *Territorial and Maritime Dispute.*   [112] Ibid., para. 138.   [113] Ibid., para. 139.
[114] Ibid., paras. 139 and 176.   [115] Ibid., para. 37.

Importantly, in a very rare instance the Court actually expressly classified one feature (Quitasueño) to be a rock under Article 121(3).[116]

The first detailed examination of Article 121(3), however, was provided by the arbitral tribunal in the 2016 *South China Sea Arbitration (Philippines* v. *China)* brought by the Philippines against China under the compulsory dispute settlement provisions of the 1982 LOSC pursuant to Annex VII as the default procedure under Article 287(5).[117] In that case, the Tribunal made detailed assessments of the features in question finding none of them to be fully entitled islands under Article 121(2).[118] Much ink has been spilled on this award which China has rejected.[119] It is interesting to speculate if both parties at the time of ratifying the Convention had selected the Court under Article 287(1)(b) how different the outcome might have been in view of the Court's historical reluctance to delve into the details of Article 121(3).

IV Navigational Rights and Straits

Innocent passage rights of vessels including warships are recognised as an accepted rule of international law. As observed by the 1930 Hague Codification Conference, that a 'Coastal State will not forbid the innocent passage of foreign warships through its territorial sea is but to recognise existing practice'.[120] The 1949 *Corfu Channel* case concerned the sinking

[116] Ibid., para. 238.

[117] *The South China Sea Arbitration (Republic of the Philippines* v. *People's Republic of China)* PCA Case No. 2013-19, UNCLOS, Award, 12 July 2016.

[118] Ibid., pp. 175, 259.

[119] See N. Klein, 'The South China Sea Arbitration: Toward an International Legal Order in the Oceans, written by Yoshifumi Tanaka' 36 *The International Journal of Marine and Coastal Law* (2020) 187–192; 'The South China Sea Arbitration Awards: A Critical Study' 17 *Chinese Journal of International Law* (2018) 207–748.

[120] 'Report of The Second Committee', Conference for The Codification of International Law, The Hague, 1930, League Of Nations Doc C.230.M.117.1930.V, Art 4. In general see, H. Caminos, 'The Legal Regime of Straits in the 1982 United Nations Convention on the Law of the Sea' 205 *Recueil Des Cours* (1987) 9, 20; J. A. de Yturriaga, *Straits Used For International Navigation: A Spanish Perspective* (Springer, 1991); B. B. Jia, *The Regime of Straits in International Law* (Clarendon Press, 1998); A. G. Lopez Martin, *International Straits: Concept, Classification and Rules of Passage* (Springer, 2010); H. Caminos and V. P. Cogliati-Bantz, *The Legal Regime of Straits: Contemporary Challenges and Solutions* (Cambridge University Press, 2014); D. D. Caron and N. Oral, *Navigating Straits: Challenges for International Law* (Brill, 2014), 11–32; N. Oral, 'Navigating the Oceans:

of two British navy destroyers after hitting mines while passing through the Corfu Channel.[121] Albania claimed that the United Kingdom had violated its sovereignty by not seeking prior authorisation for passage through its territorial waters, whereas the United Kingdom claimed innocent passage rights for its warships in times of peace through international straits, as well as territorial waters. In its well-known pronouncement, the Court declared, 'that States, in time of peace, have a right to send their warships through straits used for international navigation between two parts of the high seas, provided that the passage is innocent'.[122]

There were two key issues: the criteria that made a strait subject to innocent passage rights and, second, the criteria to assess 'innocent passage'. On the first, the Court stated that the 'decisive criterion' in defining a strait in which innocent passage rights apply was not the volume of foreign ship traffic but rather 'its geographical situation as connecting two parts of the high seas and the fact of its being used for international navigation.[123] The Court considered the Corfu Channel as an international strait 'through which passage cannot be prohibited by a coastal State in time of peace'.[124] On the second, the Court looked at objective factors as to the manner of passage and not subjective intent, as argued by Albania, and concluded that passage was consistent with innocent passage.[125]

The Court did not define the meaning of innocent passage. It could have made reference to the work of the 1930 Hague Codification Conference, which provided the early kernels of the current definition of innocent passage as that which is 'not prejudicial to the peace, good order or security of the coastal State'. The *Corfu Channel* case judgment was reflected in Article 16(4) of the 1958 Convention on the Territorial Sea and Contiguous Zone.[126] It is interesting to note that the Articles concerning the Law of the Sea, as adopted by the International Law Commission in 1956, contradicted the judgment of the Court in the *Corfu Channel* case, as

---

Old and New Challenges for the Law of the Sea for Straits Used for International Navigation' 46 *Ecology Law Quarterly* (2019) 163.

[121] *Corfu Channel.*   [122] *Corfu Channel*, p. 28 (Emphasis in original).

[123] *Corfu Channel*, p. 28.

[124] *Corfu Channel*, pp. 29–30. The Court did not address the question of the right of a State to send warships in time of peace through territorial waters.

[125] *Corfu Channel*, pp. 30–32.

[126] TSC, Art. 16(4) 'There shall be no suspension of the innocent passage of foreign ships through straits which are used for international navigation between one part of the high seas and another part of the high seas or the territorial sea of a foreign State.'

Article 24 provided that the coastal State could make the passage of warships through the territorial sea subject to its prior authorisation.[127] The *Corfu Channel* case, while considered a landmark case,[128] nonetheless, had limited impact on the development of the modern law of the sea on passage rights and for straits used in international navigation.[129] A new and more complex regime of straits passage was introduced under Part III of the 1982 LOSC.[130]

The next opportunity to address navigational rights through straits was presented to the Court in the 1991 *Passage through the Great Belt (Finland v. Denmark)* case.[131] Finland brought an application to the Court with a request for a provisional measures order against Denmark's plan to construct a high-level suspension bridge in the Great Belt, claiming that the bridge would prevent all ships from exercising their rights of free passage. The case only went as far as a hearing on provisional measures, where the Court denied Finland's request finding there was no 'urgency' and prejudice to rights that would justify a provisional order.[132] The case on the merits was discontinued the following year.[133]

The last pronouncement by the Court on innocent passage was its dicta in 2001 *Maritime Delimitation and Territorial Questions between Qatar and Bahrain (Qatar v. Bahrain)* case where the Court reaffirmed that the vessels of the State of Qatar enjoy innocent passage rights under customary international law in the territorial sea of Bahrain separating the Hawar Islands from the other Bahraini territory.[134]

V Marine Natural Resources and Conservation

The Court has not had many opportunities to address questions of international law pertaining to the protection of marine natural resources. The

---

[127] International Law Commission, 'Articles concerning the Law of the Sea with Commentaries' (1956) II *Yearbook of the International Law Commission*. Initially the Commission followed the judgment of the Court but later took a very different position.

[128] Jia, *The Regime of Straits in International Law*, 1.   [129] Part III UNCLOS.

[130] Part III UNCLOS.

[131] *Passage through the Great Belt (Finland v. Denmark)* (Provisional Measures), ICJ Rep 1991, p. 12.

[132] Ibid.

[133] *Passage through the Great Belt (Finland v. Denmark)* (Order), ICJ Rep 1992, p. 348.

[134] *Qatar v. Bahrain*, para. 223.

earliest instance where the Court addressed the question of conservation interests was in the 1974 *Fisheries Jurisdiction (United Kingdom v. Iceland; Federal Republic of Germany v. Iceland)* cases.[135] Germany and the United Kingdom challenged Iceland's unilateral extension of an 'exclusive fishery zone' to fifty nautical miles stretching into areas that were high seas.[136] It is one of the early cases where the Court expressed concern for conservation of natural resources, even though it ultimately found that Iceland's unilaterally established exclusive fisheries zone was unlawful.[137] The Court, controversially at the time, recognised the existence of a right of preferential access for coastal states to fisheries under customary law, especially in the case of coastal States with special dependence on coastal fisheries.[138] The Court stated that 'the former laissez-faire treatment of the living resources of the sea in the high seas has been replaced by a recognition of a duty to have due regard to the rights of other States and the needs of conservation for the benefit of all . . .'.[139]

However, the decision was criticised,[140] and, as observed by Lowe and Tzanakopoulos, had little impact, and was eventually subsumed by the emergence of the regime of the EEZ. By contrast, Treves characterises the decision as an example 'in which judicial decisions became intertwined with codification processes[141] crystalising as customary international law the concept of an exclusive fisheries zone up to 12 nm and the preferential rights of fishing in adjacent waters in favour of the coastal State in a situation of special dependence on its coastal fisheries'.[142] The case may

---

[135] *Fisheries Jurisdiction (United Kingdom v. Iceland)* (Merits), ICJ Rep 1974, p. 3; *Fisheries Jurisdiction (Federal Republic of Germany v. Iceland)* (Merits), ICJ Rep 1974, p. 175. See also R. R. Churchill, 'The Fisheries Jurisdiction Cases: The Contribution of the International Court of Justice to the Debate on Coastal States' Fisheries Rights' 24 *ICLQ* (1975) 82.

[136] Iceland did not appear contesting the jurisdiction of the Court.

[137] *Fisheries Jurisdiction (United Kingdom v. Iceland)*, para. 79. *Fisheries Jurisdiction (Federal Republic of Germany v. Iceland)*, para. 77.

[138] *Fisheries Jurisdiction (Federal Republic of Germany v. Iceland)*, para. 50; *Fisheries Jurisdiction (United Kingdom v. Iceland)*, para. 58. See Churchill, 'The Fisheries Jurisdiction Cases'.

[139] *Fisheries Jurisdiction (Federal Republic of Germany v. Iceland)*, para. 64; *Fisheries Jurisdiction (United Kingdom v. Iceland)*, para. 72.

[140] Churchill critically noted the Court failed to provide any detail as to the essential characteristics of such a zone or how it differed from coastal State preferential rights. Churchill, 'The Fisheries Jurisdiction Cases', 87.

[141] Treves, 'Historical Development of the Law of the Sea', 21.

[142] Treves, 'Historical Development of the Law of the Sea', 21.

have had less impact then the jurisprudence of the Court on maritime boundary delimitation, nonetheless, it stands as an early indicator of the Court's interest to promote conservation issues.

The 1998 *Fisheries Jurisdiction (Spain* v. *Canada)* case might have been a very interesting follow-up case to the 1974 *Fisheries Jurisdiction* cases, as it also involved questions of opposability against third States of fisheries conservation regulations in the high seas and the right to fish in the high seas.[143] However, the Court found it lacked jurisdiction.

The first case that directly involves conservation was brought to the Court under the 1946 International Whaling Convention in the *Whaling in the Antarctic (Australia* v. *Japan)* case with New Zealand intervening. While there have been cases brought before international tribunals involving the marine environment,[144] to date, the Court has not entertained a case arising under Part XII of the 1982 LOSC for the protection and preservation of the marine environment.

In the *Whaling case*, Australia and New Zealand challenged the lawfulness of Japan's whale research program (JARPA II) which allowed for the exceptional killing of whales for purposes of scientific research under the exception provided under Article VIII(1) of the International Whaling Convention, otherwise prohibited by the moratorium in the Southern Ocean.[145] One of the issues raised by Australia involved defining 'scientific research'.[146] To the disappointment of some scholars the Court decided it was unnecessary to offer a general definition of scientific research. Instead, the Court determined that lethal sampling of whales under JARPA II could 'broadly be characterised as scientific research', and consequently there

---

[143] *Fisheries Jurisdiction (Spain* v. *Canada)* (Decision on the Jurisdiction), ICJ Rep 1998, p. 432, para. 23.

[144] For example, *the Southern Bluefin Tuna (New Zealand* v. *Japan; Australia* v. *Japan)* (Provisional Measures), Order of 27 August 1999, 3 ITLOS Reports 1999, 280; *the MOX Plant (Ireland* v. *United Kingdom) (Provisional Measures)*, Order of 3 December 2001, 5 ITLOS Reports 2001, 89; *Case concerning Land Reclamation by Singapore in and around the Straits of Johor (Malaysia* v. *Singapore)* (Provisional Measures), Order of 8 October 2003, 7 ITLOS Reports 2003, 10. See also, H. Tuerk, 'The Contribution of the International Tribunal for the Law of the Sea to International Law' 26 *Penn State International Law Review* (2007) 289; J. Xiaoyi and Z. Jianwei, 'Marine Environment and the International Tribunal for the Law of the Sea: Twenty Years' Practices and Prospects' 5 *China Legal Science* (2017) 84.

[145] *Whaling in the Antarctic (Australia* v. *Japan: New Zealand intervening)* (Merits), ICJ Rep 2014, p. 226.

[146] Ibid., para. 74.

was no need to examine 'generally the concept of "scientific research"'.[147] The Court ultimately decided the case in favour of Australia, finding that the design and implementation of the programme were not reasonable in relation to achieving its stated objectives[148] and decided that Japan was required to revoke any authorisation, permit or licence granted under the program.[149]

This was an important first foray by the Court into the less familiar arena of marine conservation. The Court's hesitation to enter into the murky waters of defining scientific research is understandable given the Court being a legal body and not a scientific one. Still, there was disappointment expressed by some scholars with the Court's reluctance in giving guidance on the meaning of 'scientific research'.[150] Some commented that this would have improved common understanding of marine scientific research in Part XV and Part XIII of the 1982 LOSC, other law of the sea treaties and recent developments.[151] The issue is not theoretical as differentiation between marine scientific research and other activities, such as commercial activities, is becoming increasingly important. This was demonstrated by the controversial case of marine geoengineering activities[152] and, more recently, in relation to access and benefit sharing of marine genetic resources in areas beyond national jurisdiction, currently under negotiation for a new international legally binding instrument on the conservation and sustainable use of marine biodiversity of areas beyond national jurisdiction.[153]

---

[147] Ibid., para. 127.   [148] Ibid., para. 227.   [149] Ibid., para. 227.

[150] A. Telesetsky, D. K. Anton, and T. Koivurova, 'ICJ's Decision in Australia v. Japan: Giving up the Spear or Refining the Scientific Design?' 45 *Ocean Development & International Law* (2014) 328–340.

[151] J. J. Smith, 'Evolving to Conservation?: The International Court's Decision in the Australia/Japan Whaling Case' 45 *Ocean Development & International Law* (2014) 301–327.

[152] S. Broder, '12 International Governance of Ocean Fertilization and other Marine Geoengineering Activities' *Ocean Law and Policy* (2017) 307.

[153] UNGA Res 72/249 (24 December 2018) UN Doc A/RES/72/249. International legally binding instrument under the United Nations Convention on the Law of the Sea on the conservation and sustainable use of marine biological diversity of areas beyond national jurisdiction, dated 24 December 2018. See M. Rabone, H. Harden-Davies, J. E. Collins, S. Zajderman, W. Appeltans, G. Droege, A. Brandt, L. Pardo-Lopez, T. G. Dahlgren, A. G. Glover, T. Horton, 'Access to Marine Genetic Resources (MGR): Raising Awareness of Best-Practice Through a New Agreement for Biodiversity Beyond National Jurisdiction (BBNJ)' 6 *Frontiers in Marine Science* (2019) 520; R. Blasiak, J. B. Jouffray, C. C. Wabnitz, E. Sundström and H. Österblom, 'Corporate Control and Global Governance of Marine

Part XV of the LOSC offers an invaluable tool for States to bring cases concerning the marine environment to the Court. However, there are certain issues, beginning first with the procedural hurdle that both States must have selected the Court under Article 287(1)(b), otherwise, the default option of Annex VII kicks in. In addition, the Court has not built up a robust jurisprudence on disputes concerning conservation issues. In addition, while the recent *Whaling* case and even the earlier 1974 *Fisheries Jurisdiction*, coupled with the Court's previous decisions and advisory opinions in cases involving protection of the environment[154] do indicate the Court is favourable towards these issues, the procedural impediments make future prospects for such cases being brought under the 1982 LOSC somewhat limited.

VI Conclusion

In this short overview of the contribution of the Court to the development of the law of the sea since 1947 the following observations can be made. First, the vast majority of its cases have been on maritime boundary delimitation. In these cases, the Court has mapped its own methodology and approach, sometimes at odds with codified provisions. As observed by authors, because of the vague provisions of the 1982 LOSC, maritime delimitation is also known as 'judge-made law'.[155] In the case of the Court, this started early in cases where it chose not to apply Article 6 of the 1958 Continental Shelf Convention. Since the 1969 *North Sea Continental Shelf* cases the Court has consistently declined to recognise any one method of delimitation as representing a rule of customary international law, except for Article 15 on delimitation of the territorial sea.[156] Indeed, Article 74 for the EEZ and Article 83 for the continental shelf

---

Genetic Resources' 4(6) *Science Advances* (2018), available at https://advances .sciencemag.org/content/advances/4/6/eaar5237.full.pdf.

[154] Recent examples include the Court's decisions recognising as a rule of customary international law the obligation of States to conduct environmental impact assessments. See also *Pulp Mills (Argentina v. Uruguay)* (Provisional Measures) ICJ Rep 2006, p. 113. Other well-known cases of the Court include *Gabcikovo-Nagymaros Project (Hungary/Slovakia)*, Judgment, ICJ Rep 1997, p. 7. See also D. Bodansky, Chapter 17, International Environmental Law.

[155] Elferink, Henriksen and Busch, *Maritime Boundary Delimitation: The Case Law*, 3.

[156] *Qatar v. Bahrain*, para. 176. In *Qatar v. Bahrain*, the ICJ declared Article 15 to be part of customary international law.

[reflect what was articulated by] the Court in the 1969 *North Sea Continental Shelf* cases, that 'delimitation is to be effected by agreement in accordance with equitable principles, and taking account of all the relevant circumstances ...'[157] In addition, despite the express mention of *natural prolongation* in Article 76(1) the Court eliminated this concept from its methodology as a criterion and instead applied the distance criteria.

Nonetheless, over many years and cases, the Court's methodology has become established with the three-stage approach, where having identified the relevant coasts, the Court first commences with the drawing of a provisional line, second examines any factors calling for the adjustment or shifting of the provisional equidistance line in order to achieve an equitable result and, third, determines if there is any marked disproportion between respective coastal lengths of the relevant maritime areas of each coastal State. The Court has also proven to be extremely reluctant to adjust the provisional line for socio-economic circumstances in order to achieve an equitable result. The conservative approach of the Court has limited the scope of factors that are considered as equitable circumstances, leading to greater predictability.

The second observation concerns the reluctance of the Court to clarify the meaning of Article 121. There has been a great deal of scholarly ink spilled on Article 121, but despite the opportunities availed to the Court, it has consistently avoided providing guidance. Moreover, the importance of understanding Article 121 has taken on new importance because of sea level rise from climate change and its possible consequences on the legal status of inhabited islands, an issue currently studied by the International Law Commission.[158] This has left the matter open for other tribunals, as was the case in the *South China Sea* arbitration case.

The third observation is the notable lack of cases on non-maritime delimitation law of the sea issues, such as protection of the marine environment or navigation. Since 1947, the *Corfu Channel case* remains as the only instance the Court has been engaged in that involves navigation issues related to the law of the sea.[159] This might partly be explained by

---

[157] *Qatar* v. *Bahrain.*

[158] See A/CN.4/740, *First issues paper by Bogdan Aurescu and Nilüfer Oral, Co-Chairs of the Study Group on sea-level rise in relation to international law* (2020).

[159] The Court also addressed passage rights in straits in dicta in the *Maritime Delimitation and Territorial Questions Between Qatar and Bahrain.*

cases going to ITLOS, but these cases have principally been provisional measure or prompt release cases. It is beyond the scope of this chapter to explain what the reasons may be for the lack of diversity of cases involving law of the sea, but it is notable that most of the cases filed pursuant to the compulsory dispute settlement provisions of Article 287 of the 1982 LOSC come either before ITLOS (usually provisional measures) or Annex VII arbitral tribunals under Article 287. Some notable examples include, the 2016 *South China Sea arbitration (Philippines v. China)*,[160] and the *Chagos Marine Protected Area arbitration (Mauritius v. United Kingdom)*,[161] 2014 *Arctic Sunrise arbitration (Netherlands v. Russia)*,[162] and even the recent '*Enrica Lexie*' *Incident arbitration (Italy v. India)*.[163]

---

[160] *The South China Sea Arbitration.*
[161] *Chagos Marine Protected Area Arbitration, Mauritius* v. *United Kingdom*, Final Award, PCA Case No. 2011-03, 18 March 2015.
[162] *The Arctic Sunrise Arbitration, Netherlands* v. *Russia*, Award on the Merits, PCA Case No. 2014-02, 14 August 2015.
[163] *The 'Enrica Lexie' Incident arbitration, The Italian Republic* v. *The Republic of India*, Provisional Measures, PCA Case No. 2015-28, 29 April 2016.

International Environmental Law 17

Daniel Bodansky

I Introduction

The contribution of the International Court of Justice to international environmental law has been comparatively modest. Since it first emerged in the early twentieth century, international environmental law has developed primarily through negotiations among States rather than judicial decisions. Although the increasing judicialisation of international law[1] in recent decades has included an uptick in environmental litigation, most of this litigation has taken place in specialised tribunals such as the regional human rights courts, the International Tribunal for the Law of the Sea, and the World Trade Organization's Dispute Settlement Mechanism, not the International Court of Justice.[2] Today, even on the most generous accounting, the 'environmental' decisions of the Court still number in the single digits and, for the most part, have taken a rather conservative approach, lending the Court's authority to well-established principles rather than breaking new ground.

To the extent the Court's jurisprudence has contributed to international environmental law, its contributions have taken several forms:

- *Articulating foundational principles* – Until the 1990s, the Court contributed to international environmental law only indirectly, by embracing the foundational concepts of *sic utere tuo* in *Corfu Channel* and obligations *erga omnes* in *Barcelona Traction*.
- *Acting as a gatekeeper for customary international law* – Beginning with its *Nuclear Weapons Advisory Opinion* in 1996, the Court has lent

---

[1] A. Føllesdal and G. Ulfstein (eds.), *The Judicialization of International Law: A Mixed Blessing?* (Oxford University Press, 2018).

[2] For excellent summaries of the cases, see the annual surveys of international environmental litigation by James Harrison in the *Journal of Environmental Law*.

its weight to claims about the customary international law status of widely recognised rules such as the duty to prevent significant trans-boundary pollution and the duty to undertake environmental impact assessments. In doing so, the Court has served as the 'gate-keeper and guardian' of general international law, as Jorge Viñuales puts it.[3]

- *Elaborating existing principles* – In the last decade, in *Pulp Mills* and *Costa Rica* v. *Nicaragua*, the Court has begun to play a more creative role – for example, holding that the duty of due diligence entails procedural duties to assess, notify, and consult.

- *Interpreting environmental agreements* – In the *Japanese Whaling* case, the Court interpreted the International Whaling Convention's exemption for scientific whaling.

- *Valuing environmental harms* – Recently, the Court's first monetary award of environmental damages in *Costa Rica* v. *Nicaragua* discussed the methodology of environmental damage valuation.

- *Incorporating environmental considerations into other areas of international law* – Finally, apart from contributing to international environmental law as a distinct field, the Court has helped diffuse environmental considerations into other areas of international law, including international humanitarian law in its *Nuclear Weapons Advisory Opinion* (where the Court said that environmental damage should be included in necessity and proportionality analysis) and the law of State responsibility in the *Gabčikovo-Nagymaros Project* case (where the Court acknowledged that damage to the environment could create a state of ecological necessity that would excuse an otherwise wrongful act).

This chapter proceeds as follows. Section II reviews the substantive contributions of the ICJ to both customary and treaty law relating to the environment. Section III then assesses the role and limits of the ICJ as an actor in the international environmental law process, including in resolving disputes, developing international environmental law, and influencing the behaviour of States. Section IV concludes with brief observations about the future role of the Court.

---

[3] J. E. Viñuales, 'The Contribution of the International Court of Justice to the Development of International Environmental Law: An Assessment', 32 *Fordham International Law Journal* (2008) 232, 258.

II Substantive Contributions

International environmental law is a comparatively young field, with broad, open-textured principles such as the harm prevention principle, inter-generational equity, and sustainable development. As such, one might expect it to provide 'fertile ground' for judicial interpretation and influence.[4] In actuality, however, the overall contribution of the Court's jurisprudence to international environmental law has been modest. Malgosia Fitzmaurice characterised it in 2013 as a 'poor relative' compared to the Court's jurisprudence on other areas of international law such as diplomatic protection,[5] and the same is true today.

The Court's environmental jurisprudence, broadly conceived, includes ten cases, including:

- four contentious cases, three of which focused primarily on customary international law (*Gabčikovo-Nagymaros*, *Pulp Mills*, and *Costa Rica v. Nicaragua)* and one on a multilateral environmental agreement (*Japanese Whaling*),
- three cases that did not yield decisions on the merits, either because the Court dismissed them on preliminary grounds (*Nuclear Tests*) or because the parties settled (*Certain Phosphate Lands* and *Aerial Herbicide Spraying*),
- two cases that did not involve international environmental law directly but contributed indirectly to its foundations (*Corfu Channel* and *Barcelona Traction*), and
- one advisory opinion (*Nuclear Weapons).*

To the extent these cases have contributed to the substance of international environmental law, they have played a bigger role with respect to custom than treaties, and their contribution has primarily been to lend the

---

[4] C. J. Tams, 'The Development of International Law by the International Court of Justice', in *Decisions of the ICJ as Sources of International Law*, Gaetano Morelli Lecture Series (International and European Papers Publishing, 2018), p. 63 at 93–99.

[5] M. Fitzmaurice, 'The International Court of Justice and International Environmental Law', in C. J. Tams and J. Sloan (eds.), *The Development of International Law by the International Court of Justice* (Oxford University Press, 2013), p. 353. Ronald Bettauer goes further, characterising the Court's contribution as 'marginal'. R. J. Bettauer, 'International Environmental Law-Making and the International Court of Justice: Remarks', 105 *American Society of International Law Proceedings* (2011) 61, 65.

Court's de facto authority to rules that were already well established in soft law instruments and treaties – for example, the duty to prevent and the duty to conduct environmental impact assessments – rather than to progressively develop the law.[6] One of the few intellectual innovations of the Court has been to draw the 'functional link' between substantive and procedural duties – in particular, by suggesting that the substantive duty of due diligence entails procedural duties such as prior assessment.

A Duty to Prevent

Perhaps the Court's most important substantive contribution has been to confirm, and to some degree clarify, the duty to prevent significant transboundary pollution,[7] which has been called the 'cornerstone' of international environmental law.[8] The duty to prevent was first articulated in the *Trail Smelter* arbitration, which observed that 'no State has the right to use or permit the use of its territory in such a manner as to cause injury ... in or to the territory of another or the properties or persons therein, when the case is of serious consequence'.[9] It was broadened to encompass pollution of the global commons in Principle 21 of the 1972 Stockholm Declaration on the Human Environment, which provides:

States have, in accordance with the Charter of the United Nations and the principles of international law, the sovereign right to exploit their own resources pursuant to their own environmental policies, and the responsibility to ensure that activities within their jurisdiction or control do not cause damage to the environment of other States or of areas beyond the limits of national jurisdiction.[10]

---

[6] See Viñuales, 'The Contribution of the International Court of Justice', 258 (main role of Court 'arguably not that of a ground-breaking body but rather that of a stock-taking institution').

[7] *See generally* M. Jervan, *The Prohibition of Transboundary Environmental Harm: An Analysis of the Contribution of the International Court of Justice to the Development of the No-Harm Rule*, Pluricourts Research Paper No. 14–17 (2014).

[8] G. Handl, 'Transboundary Impacts', in D. Bodansky, J. Brunnée and E. Hey (eds.), *The Oxford Handbook of International Environmental Law* (Oxford University Press, 2007), p. 531 at 548.

[9] Trail Smelter Case (*US* v. *Canada*), (1941) 3 UN Rep. Int'l Arbitral Awards 1905 at 1965.

[10] Stockholm Declaration on the Human Environment, 5–16 June 1972, UN Doc. A/CONF.48/14/Rev.1. Principle 21 was reiterated in Principle 2 of the 1992 Rio Declaration, with the addition of the words 'and developmental' before 'policies'. Rio Declaration on Environment and Development, 3–14 June 1992, UN Doc. A/CONF.151/26 (vol. 1).

The ICJ has considered the duty to prevent in five cases: *Corfu Channel,* the *Nuclear Tests* case, the *Nuclear Weapons Advisory Opinion, Pulp Mills,* and *Costa Rica* v. *Nicaragua.*

- In *Corfu Channel,* the Court recognised the principle of *sic utere tuo ut alienum laedas* (use your property in such a manner as not to injure that of another) as one of the 'general and well-recognised principles' of international law,[11] although it formulated the duty as a requirement not to 'knowingly' allow one's territory to be used contrary to the rights of other States, rather than as a due diligence obligation, as it is now usually understood in international environmental law.
- The 1973 *Nuclear Tests* case was the first ICJ case that raised environmental issues directly. Although the Court dismissed the case as moot before reaching the merits,[12] its interim measures order implicitly recognised that international law may limit activities that cause transboundary pollution by calling on France to avoid nuclear tests that caused radioactive fallout in Australia.[13]
- In its *Nuclear Weapons Advisory Opinion,* the Court made its first significant statement regarding international environmental law, confirming that the duty to prevent, as formulated in the Stockholm and Rio Declarations, is now 'part of the corpus of international law relating to the environment'[14] – an opinion that many regard as settling the legal status of the duty to prevent.[15]

[11] Corfu Channel Case (*United Kingdom* v. *Albania*), Judgment, ICJ Reports 1949, p. 4, 22.
[12] Nuclear Tests I (*Australia* v. *France*), Judgment of 20 December, ICJ Reports 1974, p. 253. New Zealand joined the case, claiming that the obligations of France were *erga omnes*. New Zealand attempted to revive the case in 1995, when France began a program of underground nuclear testing, but the Court dismissed New Zealand's petition for lack of jurisdiction and never reached the merits. Nuclear Tests II (*New Zealand* v. *France*), Order of 22 September, ICJ Reports 1995, p. 288.
[13] Nuclear Tests (*Australia* v. *France*), Interim Protection Order, ICJ Reports 1973, p. 99, 106. Judge Petrén dissented from the Court's provisional measures order in part because he believed that atmospheric tests of nuclear weapons are not governed by international law, but instead belong to 'a highly political domain where the norms concerning their international legality or illegality are still at the gestation phase'. Ibid., Separate Opinion of Judge Petrén, p. 126.
[14] Legality of the Threat or Use of Nuclear Weapons, Advisory Opinion of 8 July, ICJ Reports 1996, p. 226, 241–242, para. 29.
[15] See, e.g., P. Sands and J. Peel, *Principles of International Environmental Law* (3rd ed., Cambridge University Press, 2012), pp. 195–196 ('Following the ICJ's 1996 Advisory Opinion ... there can be *no question* but that Principle 21 reflects a rule of customary international law ...') (emphasis added).

- In *Pulp Mills*, the Court interpreted the duty to prevent as an obligation 'to act with due diligence' that entails both 'the adoption of appropriate rules and measures' as well as exercising 'a certain level of vigilance in their enforcement'.[16] It further found that due diligence has procedural as well as substantive elements. In particular, it entails undertaking an environmental impact assessment when there is a risk that a proposed industrial activity may cause significant transboundary harm.[17] Although *Pulp Mills* was decided on the basis of a bilateral treaty between Argentina and Uruguay rather than general international law, it is perhaps the Court's most important environmental case to date because of its extensive discussion of the duty to prevent and the related duty to perform environmental impact assessments of activities that risk significant transboundary harm.[18]

- Finally, in *Costa Rica* v. *Nicaragua*, the Court considered whether either Nicaragua or Costa Rica had breached the substantive duty to prevent transboundary harm. In brief, the Court reiterated its conclusions in *Pulp Mills* that States have a duty under customary international law to use due diligence to prevent significant transboundary harm, to conduct environmental impact assessments of activities that risk causing significant harm to other States, and to notify and consult with potentially affected States.[19] The Court concluded that Costa Rica violated its duty to conduct an environmental impact assessment of its planned road activity, and that Nicaragua was responsible for the environmental damage to Costa Rica caused by its illegal construction of a canal in the territory of Costa Rica. In a subsequent decision in 2018, the Court awarded compensation to Costa Rica based on a lengthy analysis of environmental damages valuation.[20]

---

[16] Pulp Mills on the River Uruguay (*Argentina* v. *Uruguay*), Judgment of 20 April, ICJ Reports 2010, p. 14, 79, para. 197.

[17] Ibid., p. 83, para. 204.

[18] After a lengthy review of Uruguay's actions, the Court concluded that Uruguay had breached various procedural obligations under the bilateral treaty with Argentina, but that there was 'no conclusive evidence' showing a failure to exercise due diligence. Ibid., pp. 101, 106, paras. 265, 282(1).

[19] Certain Activities Carried Out by Nicaragua in the Border Area (*Costa Rica* v. *Nicaragua*) and Construction of a Road in Costa Rica along the San Juan River (*Nicaragua* v. *Costa Rica*), Judgment of 16 December, ICJ Reports 2015, p. 665, 706–707, para. 104.

[20] Certain Activities Carried Out by Nicaragua in the Border Area (*Costa Rica* v. *Nicaragua*), Judgment on Compensation of 2 February, ICJ Reports 2018, p. 15.

In its jurisprudence on the duty to prevent, the Court was initially unclear as to the source of the duty, characterizing it as part of the 'corpus of international law' without specifying whether it is a treaty rule, custom, or a general principle.[21] But the Court subsequently clarified in *Pulp Mills* that it regarded the duty to prevent as a 'customary rule' – although it cited no State practice or *opinio juris* in support of this conclusion.[22]

In contrast, the Court's jurisprudence remains unclear about the content of the duty to prevent.[23] Two issues are central. First, is the duty to prevent an obligation of result, an obligation of conduct, or some combination of the two? Second, if it is an obligation of conduct, what is the required standard of care?

The *Trail Smelter* arbitration and Principle 21 arguably formulated the duty to prevent as an obligation of result – that is, to prevent significant transboundary pollution – which would make States strictly liable if significant pollution occurred. But the International Law Commission (ILC), in its Draft Articles on Prevention of Transboundary Harm, interpreted the duty to prevent as an obligation of conduct – namely, to take 'all appropriate measures' to prevent or at least minimise significant transboundary harm, an obligation that the ILC characterised as one of 'due diligence'.[24]

The Court is unclear which approach it adopts. On the one hand, in *Pulp Mills*, it described the duty to prevent as a duty of conduct, namely, to act with due diligence.[25] But, in practice, the Court also looks to results, finding in *Costa Rica* v. *Nicaragua* that the duty to prevent had not been violated because neither Costa Rica nor Nicaragua proved that it had

---

[21] Nuclear Weapons Advisory Opinion, p. 242, para. 29.

[22] Pulp Mills, Judgment, p. 55, para. 101.

[23] In her Hague lectures on procedural and substantive obligations in international environmental law, Jutta Brunnée charitably remarked that the Court's opinions show that the harm prevention rule is 'far more complex than one might have imagined'. J. Brunnée, 'Procedure and Substance in International Environmental Law', 405 *Collected Courses of the Academy of International Law* (2020) 75, 117. But whether it is actually more complex or whether the Court's opinions have made it so is open to question.

[24] International Law Commission, Draft Articles on Prevention of Transboundary Harm from Hazardous Activities, art. 3, comments 7 and 8, Report of the International Law Commission on the Work of Its 53rd Session, p. 154.

[25] Pulp Mills, Judgment, p. 97, para. 197; quoted approvingly in *Costa Rica* v. *Nicaragua*, Judgment, p. 711, para. 118.

suffered significant transboundary harm.[26] Moreover, the Court left open the possibility that causing transboundary harm is not just a necessary condition for violating the duty to prevent, but also a sufficient condition, saying that it did not need to decide whether Nicaragua was required to pay compensation regardless of fault,[27] as Costa Rica argued, because Costa Rica had failed to prove any harm. This suggests that the Court views the duty to prevent not as an obligation of conduct, but either as an obligation involving both conduct (due diligence) and results (no harm), or simply as an obligation of result (if Costa Rica was correct that harm by itself would have been a basis for compensation, even if Nicaragua had acted diligently).

The Court's jurisprudence also engenders confusion because it fails to acknowledge the differences between the standards of conduct it articulates. In a single paragraph in *Pulp Mills*,[28] the Court put forward three apparently different formulations of the duty to prevent, without any discussion of their relationship. First, it said that the duty to prevent has its 'origins' in due diligence. Then, it quoted the principle articulated in *Corfu Channel*, which requires knowledge of the transboundary threat. Finally, it concluded that a State is 'thus' obliged to use 'all means at its disposal' to avoid activities causing transboundary harm, apparently in the belief that due diligence entails using 'all means' at one's disposal, regardless of cost, rather than those that are reasonable under the circumstances. The result is significant confusion about what the duty to prevent, as an obligation of conduct, actually entails.

B Procedural Duties: Environmental Impact Assessment, Notice, and Consultation

In *Pulp Mills* and *Costa Rica* v. *Nicaragua*, the Court also discussed the procedural duties of States relating to transboundary pollution and their relation to the 'substantive' duty to prevent. In *Pulp Mills*, it found that the practice of undertaking an environmental impact assessment when a 'proposed industrial activity may have a significant adverse impact in a

---

[26] *Costa Rica* v. *Nicaragua*, Judgment, p. 712, para. 120 (Costa Rica failed to prove transboundary harm); ibid. p. 737, para. 217 (Nicaragua failed to prove transboundary harm).

[27] Ibid., pp. 711–712, paras. 117–118.   [28] Pulp Mills, Judgment, pp. 55–56, para. 101.

transboundary context' has 'gained so much acceptance among States that it may now be considered a requirement under general international law' and is an element of due diligence.[29] However, in the Court's view, international law allows States to determine in their domestic legislation the 'scope and content' of the assessment, rather than specifying these itself.[30] In *Costa Rica* v. *Nicaragua*, the Court went on to say that, if the environmental impact assessment 'confirms' that a planned activity has a risk of significant transboundary harm, then the State has an obligation to notify and consult with the potentially affected State.[31]

The Court in *Pulp Mills* and *Costa Rica* v. *Nicaragua* clearly believed that the procedural duties to undertake an environmental impact assessment and to notify and consult with potentially affected States are entailed by the duty to use due diligence.[32] But, arguably, it also concluded that States have an independent procedural obligation to undertake an environment impact assessment,[33] although individual judges expressed different opinions on this question.[34]

In any event, to the extent the duty to undertake an environmental impact assessment is an independent procedural obligation, it does little work, since international law does not 'specify the scope and content' of

---

[29] Ibid., p. 83, para. 204.   [30] Ibid., p. 83, para. 205.

[31] *Costa Rica* v. *Nicaragua*, Judgment, p. 724, para. 168. In her separate opinion, Judge Donoghue expressed skepticism that the duties to consult and notify are customary obligations, saying that they do 'not emerge obviously from ... State practice and *opinio juris*'. *Costa Rica* v. *Nicaragua*, Separate Opinion of Judge Donoghue, ICJ Reports 2015, p. 782, 787, para. 17.

[32] *Pulp Mill*, Judgment, p. 83, para. 204; *Costa Rica* v. *Nicaragua*, Judgment, pp. 706–707, para. 104.

[33] In discussing the duty to undertake an environmental impact assessment, the Court first said that the practice of environmental impacts assessments 'has gained so much acceptance among States that it may now be considered a requirement under general international law'. It then went on to say, '*moreover*, due diligence ... would not be considered to be exercised' if a State did not undertake an environmental impact assessment. *Pulp Mills*, p. 83, para. 204 (emphasis added).

[34] In his separate opinion in *Costa Rica* v. *Nicaragua*, Judge Dugard specifically found that the duty to conduct an environmental impact assessment is an 'independent obligation', not simply an aspect of due diligence. *Costa Rica* v. *Nicaragua*, Separate Opinion of Judge Dugard, ICJ Reports 2015, p. 842, 845, para. 9. In contrast, Judge Donoghue expressed doubt as to whether there was sufficient State practice and *opinio juris* to establish a customary obligation and argued that environmental impact assessments should be understood as a possible element of due diligence. *Costa Rica* v. *Nicaragua*, Separate Opinion of Judge Donoghue, p. 786, para. 13.

assessments.[35] In contrast, as an aspect of the duty of due diligence, the environmental impact assessment requirement appears more fulsome. Indeed, in *Pulp Mills*, the Court engaged in an extensive review of the Uruguayan environmental assessment to determine whether it met the standard of due diligence. The Court also found that international law governs the timing of assessments, asserting that they must be undertaken both prior to a project's initiation as well as throughout the project's lifetime (as a continuing obligation to monitor the effects of the project on the environment).[36] In *Costa Rica* v. *Nicaragua*, the Court applied this test, concluding that Costa Rica breached its obligation under general international law to carry out an environmental impact assessment prior to constructing a road in the border region.[37]

C Protection of the Global Commons

Although *Barcelona Traction* involved an investment rather than an environmental dispute, it complements *Corfu Channel*'s focus on transboundary harms by articulating the concept of obligations *erga omnes* – that is, obligations owed not bilaterally between States but to the international community as a whole – a concept that lays the foundation for protection of the global commons.[38] The Court's list of examples in *Barcelona Traction* of obligations *erga omnes* did not include any environmental obligations, but obligations to protect global commons such as the atmosphere and the high seas would appear excellent candidates for *erga omnes*

---

[35] *Pulp Mills*, Judgment, pp. 83–84, para. 205. In reaching this conclusion, the Court declined to apply the requirements set forth in the 1991 Espoo Convention on Environmental Impact Assessment in a Transboundary Context or the 1987 UNEP Goals and Principles of Environmental Impact Assessment, presumably on the basis that they have not become customary international law.

[36] Ibid.   [37] *Costa Rica* v. *Nicaragua*, Judgment, p. 723, para. 162.

[38] Barcelona Traction, Light and Power Company (*Belgium* v. *Spain*), Judgment of 5 February, ICJ Reports 1970, p. 3. *Barcelona Traction* involved a claim by Belgium against Spain on behalf of Belgian investors in a Canadian company. The Court ultimately dismissed the case on the ground that Belgium lacked standing to bring a case for injuries to a Canadian company. In reaching this conclusion, the Court contrasted obligations owed bilaterally between States with obligations *erga omnes* – that is, obligations owed to the international community as a whole.

status, since by their nature they involve the interests of the international community generally, not individual States.

D Precautionary Approach

The precautionary principle has become a staple of international environmental discourse, if not law. But it has received little attention from the Court.[39] In contrast to the duty to prevent and the duty to undertake environmental impact assessments, the Court has not opined about whether the precautionary principle is part of general international law, as opposed to specific treaties. In *Gabčikovo-Nagymaros*, Hungary raised the precautionary principle,[40] but the Court did not discuss it, other than to note that the parties agreed on the need to take precautionary measures.[41] In *Japanese Whaling*, New Zealand again raised the precautionary principle, arguing that it entails reversing the burden of proof.[42] But, again, the Court did not address New Zealand's arguments. Thus far, the only case in which the Court has discussed the precautionary principle is *Pulp Mills*, where it referred to precaution as an 'approach' rather than a principle, and said that, whatever else the approach might mean, 'it does not follow that it operates as a reversal of the burden of proof'.[43]

In contrast to the Court's reserve, individual judges have been more expansive. For example, Judge Trindade discussed precaution at length in his separate opinion in *Pulp Mills*,[44] largely in philosophical rather than legal terms, viewing it as interrelated with the duty to prevent and

[39] One commentator calls the ICJ's cases that address the precautionary principle a 'near miss', a 'tangential touching', and a 'feeble pat'. D. E. VanderZwaag, 'The ICJ, ITLOS, and the Precautionary Principle: Paltry Progressions, Jurisprudential Jousting', 35 *University of Hawaii Law Review* (2013) 617, 620.

[40] Gabčikovo-Nagymaros Project (*Hungary* v. *Slovakia*), Judgment of 25 September, ICJ Reports 1997, p. 7, 62, para. 97.

[41] Ibid., p. 68, para. 113. *See* J. Howley, 'The Gabčikovo-Nagymaros Case: The Influence of the International Court of Justice on the Law of Sustainable Development', 2 *Queensland Law Student Review* (2009) 1, 12 (noting that the majority failed 'to ever expressly mention, let alone address the status or possible application of the precautionary principle').

[42] Whaling in the Antarctic (*Australia* v. *Japan*), Judgment of 31 March, ICJ Reports 2014, p. 226, 241, para. 27.

[43] Pulp Mills, Judgment, p. 71, para. 164.

[44] Pulp Mills, Separate Opinion of Judge Trindade, ICJ Reports 2010, p. 135, 159–170, paras. 62–92.

expressing exasperation that the Court 'has so far had so much precaution with the precautionary principle'.[45]

E Sustainable Development

Sustainable development is perhaps the only environmental norm more frequently invoked by commentators than the precautionary principle. But, like the precautionary principle, the Court has mentioned it only in passing and has done little to elaborate its meaning. In *Gabčíkovo-Nagymaros*, the Court noted that the 'need to reconcile economic develop- ment with protection of the environment is aptly expressed in the concept of sustainable development', but left it up to the parties to find 'an agreed solution' for a joint management regime.[46] In *Pulp Mills*, the Court's Provisional Measures Order provided that use of the River Uruguay should allow for sustainable development and that 'from this point of view account must be taken of the need to safeguard the continued conservation of the river environment and the rights of economic development of the riparian States',[47] but did not provide any additional elaboration of the concept of sustainable development either in the order or in its final judgment.[48]

As with the precautionary principle, individual judges – most notably, Judge Weeramantry – have not been so circumspect. In his separate opinion in *Gabčíkovo-Nagymaros*, he discussed at length the history and philosoph- ical basis of the concept of sustainable development, including its antece- dents in civilisations around the world.[49] In his view, sustainable development is 'more than a mere concept'; it is 'a principle with normative value which is crucial to the determination of this case'.[50] He went on to say that the principle of sustainable development is 'a part of modern inter- national law by reason not only of its inescapable logical necessity, but also by reason of its wide and general acceptance by the global community'.[51]

---

[45] Ibid., p. 161, para. 67.   [46] Gabčíkovo-Nagymaros, p. 78, paras. 140–141.
[47] Pulp Mills, Provisional Measures Order of 13 July, ICJ Reports 2006, p. 113, 133, para. 80.
[48] Pulp Mills, Judgment, p. 75, para. 177.
[49] Gabčíkovo-Nagymaros Project, Separate Opinion of Judge Weeramantry, ICJ Reports 1997, p. 7, 88–111.
[50] Ibid., p. 85.
[51] Ibid., p. 95; *see also* Pulp Mills, Separate Opinion of Judge Trindade, p. 187, para. 139 (noting 'strong reasons' for recognising sustainable development as 'a guiding general principle').

F Valuation of Environmental Damage

The Court's decision on compensation in *Costa Rica* v. *Nicaragua* was its first award of environmental damages. Importantly, the Court held that compensation is due not only for damage to the injured State, but for damage 'to the environment, in and of itself'.[52] In valuing environmental damages, Nicaragua proposed using the approach of the UN Compensation Commission for assessing damages resulting from Iraq's illegal invasion and occupation of Kuwait, while Costa Rica proposed using an 'ecosystem services' approach.[53] The Court found that international law does not 'prescribe any specific method of valuation' and should take into account 'the specific circumstances and characteristics of each case'.[54] In practice, the Court started from Nicaragua's calculation of damages using Costa Rica's ecosystem services approach, and then made an adjustment to account for 'shortcomings' that the Court identified in Nicaragua's analysis – an approach perhaps intended to satisfy both sides by incorporating elements of their calculations,[55] but resulting in an award much closer to Nicaragua's valuation than to Costa Rica's.[56] In her separate opinion, Judge Donoghue noted that the value of 'pure' environmental damages is 'inevitably an approximation based on just and reasonable inferences'.[57]

G Interpretations of Multilateral Environmental Agreements

Because multilateral environmental agreements generally create their own compliance systems rather than provide for compulsory dispute settlement by the Court, the ICJ has had only two opportunities to interpret multilateral environmental agreements, in both cases because the parties had

[52] Certain Activities Carried Out by Nicaragua in the Border Area (*Costa Rica* v. *Nicaragua*), Compensation Judgment, ICJ Reports 2018, p. 15, 28, para. 41.

[53] Ibid., p. 29, para. 45. The two approaches yielded widely disparate results. Costa Rica claimed that it suffered nearly US $2.9 million in environmental damage, while Nicaragua argued that Costa Rica was entitled only to replacement costs, which it valued at US $ 27,000–35,000. Ibid., p. 32, paras. 57–58.

[54] Ibid., p. 31, para. 52.   [55] Ibid., pp. 38–39, paras. 86–87.

[56] Nicaragua calculated Costa Rica's environmental damages as $84,296, in contrast to Costa Rica's valuation of $2,880,746. Ibid., pp. 32, 38, paras. 57, 84. The Court awarded environmental damages of $120,000, only about 4 per cent of Costa Rica's claim. Ibid., p. 39, para. 86.

[57] *Costa Rica* v. *Nicaragua*, Compensation Award, Separate Opinion of Judge Donoghue ICJ Reports 2018, p. 85, 94, para. 32.

accepted the Court's compulsory jurisdiction under the Optional Clause of the ICJ Statute. In only one of these cases, *Japanese Whaling*, the Court found a violation.[58] Australia brought the case in 2010, contending that the taking of whales by Japan pursuant to its 'scientific' whaling program did not qualify for the scientific research exemption provided in Article VIII(1) of the International Whaling Convention.[59] The Court's decision turned on the relatively narrow question of whether Japan's program was 'for purposes of scientific research', rather than on the program's consistency with the object and purpose of the Whaling Convention more generally. The Court held that, although Article VIII(1) gives parties discretion in designing scientific research programs, it establishes an objective standard that requires that a program's 'design and implementation [be] reasonable in relation to its stated scientific objectives'.[60] Applying this reasonableness standard, the Court decided by a 12-4 vote that the Japanese program was not 'for purposes of scientific research', did not therefore qualify for the Article VIII exemption, and hence violated Japan's obligations under the Schedule to the Convention.

H Implications for Other Areas of International Law

Finally, two opinions of the Court have incorporated environmental considerations into other areas of international law. In its *Nuclear Weapons Advisory Opinion*, the Court concluded that States must take environmental effects 'into account when assessing what is necessary and proportionate in the pursuit of legitimate military objectives'.[61] And, in the *Gabčikovo-Nagymaros Project* case, the ICJ agreed with Hungary that a grave danger to the environment could create a 'state of ecological necessity'[62] and thereby be a ground precluding international

---

[58] Whaling in the Antarctic, p. 299, para. 247. In the other case, *Costa Rica* v. *Nicaragua*, the Court found that neither the Ramsar Wetlands Convention nor a Central American wildlife conservation agreement created an obligation on Costa Rica or Nicaragua to notify and consult. *Costa Rica* v. *Nicaragua*, Judgment, pp. 709–710, para. 110–111; ibid., p. 725, para. 172.

[59] International Convention for the Regulation of Whaling, Washington, DC, 2 December 1946, in force 10 November 1948, 161 UNTS 72.

[60] Whaling in the Antarctic, p. 258, para. 88.

[61] Nuclear Weapons Advisory Opinion, p. 242, para. 30.

[62] Gabčikovo-Nagymaros Project, p. 35, para. 40.

wrongfulness under the law of State responsibility,[63] although it ultimately concluded that Hungary had not established that the environmental dangers posed by the Danube project were sufficiently certain and imminent to justify backing out of the project.[64] The Court further held that developments in environmental knowledge did not entitle Hungary to terminate its treaty commitments to Slovakia under the doctrine of *rebus sic standibus*.[65] The Court did, however, conclude that the dam project's impact on the environment is a key issue, that environmental damage is often irreversible and cannot be addressed through reparations, and that the parties should consider environmental factors in negotiating a joint operational regime going forward.[66]

III Assessing the Court's Impact

In assessing the Court's impact on international environmental law, it is useful to distinguish three types of impacts: resolving disputes, contributing to the development of international environmental law, and influencing State behaviour.

A Resolving Disputes

In theory, the Court's primary function is to resolve disputes between States. But it has had little opportunity to do so, since States have submitted only seven environmental disputes to the Court in its seventy-five-year history. These have mostly depended on compulsory jurisdiction under the Optional Clause of the Court's Statute (*Nuclear Tests, Certain Phosphate Lands*,[67] and *Japanese Whaling*) or on a regional or bilateral treaty (*Aerial Herbicide Spraying*,[68] *Pulp Mills* and *Costa Rica* v. *Nicaragua*), since multilateral environmental agreements do not give the Court compulsory

---

[63] ILC Draft Articles on State Responsibility, art. 25(1) (necessity as a circumstance precluding wrongfulness of an act not in conformity with international law).

[64] Gabčikovo-Nagymaros Project, p. 45, para. 57.   [65] Ibid., pp. 64–65, para. 104.

[66] Ibid., pp. 77–78, para. 140.

[67] Certain Phosphate Lands in Nauru (*Nauru* v. *Australia*), Application Instituting Proceedings, 19 May 1989, (1989) ICJ General List No. 80, p. 5.

[68] Aerial Herbicide Spraying (*Ecuador* v. *Colombia*), Application Instituting Proceedings, 28 March 2008 (2008), ICJ General List No. 138, p. 6, para. 7.

jurisdiction to hear disputes and States have mutually agreed to refer a dispute to the Court only once, in the *Gabčikovo-Nagymaros Project* case.

In 1993, the ICJ established a Chamber for Environmental Matters, composed of seven judges, in the hope this would be a more attractive forum for States than the full Court. But in its thirteen-year existence, States submitted no cases to the Chamber, and it was finally discontinued in 2006.[69]

In lieu of compulsory dispute settlement by the Court, multilateral environmental agreements generally channel compliance issues to specialised compliance procedures that are more political than judicial in character,[70] focusing on promoting future compliance rather than on adjudicating past violations.[71] Notably, only one case has been decided thus far pursuant to the dispute settlement provision of a multilateral environmental agreement, the *MOX Plant* case, which was brought by Ireland against the UK in 2001 under the Convention for the Protection of the Marine Environment of the North-East Atlantic[72] and was decided by an arbitral tribunal, not the ICJ.[73]

To the extent the Court has heard environmental disputes, it has served largely as a stimulus rather than an alternative to negotiations. In two cases – *Aerial Herbicide Spraying* and *Certain Phosphate Lands* – the States involved decided to resolve their disputes diplomatically, through a negotiated settlement, and the cases were ultimately dismissed.[74] In another case – *Gabčikovo-Nagymaros* – the Court ordered the parties to negotiate in good faith a joint management regime under their bilateral agreement. The only environmental disputes that the Court 'resolved' on its own were *Costa Rica* v. *Nicaragua* and *Japanese Whaling*, and, in the latter

---

[69] The reluctance of States to use judicial dispute resolution has been long-standing. See R. B. Bilder, 'The Settlement of Disputes in the Field of International Law of the Environment', 144 *Recueil des Cours* (1975) 140, 228.

[70] M. Koskenniemi, 'Breach of Treaty or Non-Compliance? Reflections on the Enforcement of the Montreal Protocol', 3 *Yearbook of International Environmental Law* (1993) 123.

[71] J. Klabbers, 'Compliance Procedures', in Bodansky et al., *Oxford Handbook*, p. 995.

[72] Convention for the Protection of the Marine Environment of the North-East Atlantic, 22 September 1992, in force 25 March 1998, 32 ILM 1069.

[73] Dispute relating to the MOX plant at Sellafield (Ireland v U.K.), Award of July 2, 2003, in B. Macmahon (ed.), *The OSPAR Arbitration Award of 2003* (T.M.C. Asser Press, 2009).

[74] Certain Phosphate Lands in Nauru (*Nauru* v. *Australia*), Order of 13 September, ICJ Reports 1993, p. 322 (removing case from list); Aerial Herbicide Spraying (*Ecuador* v. *Colombia*), Order of 13 September, ICJ Reports 2013, p. 278 (removing case from list).

case, its judgment left Japan free to develop a new research program that satisfied the requirements of the Article VIII exemption.

The predilection to resolve environmental disputes through political rather than judicial processes seems to be a feature not a bug of international environmental law. Several factors may help account for it:

- Complex global problems such as climate change – which affect and are affected by the entire international community – are not easily susceptible to bilateral dispute resolution. The concept of obligations *erga omnes* addresses one issue: standing. But many difficult issues remain, including causation.
- The Court's 'notorious difficulty dealing with complex facts'[75] further limits its capacity to resolve environmental disputes, which are often quite technical.
- Finally, negotiations and non-compliance procedures allow States to retain greater control over the outcome of disputes and are, in any event, non-binding.

B Developing International Environmental Law

The Court has also had only a modest impact on the substantive content of international environmental law, most of which is the product of negotiations among States and is reflected in treaties. The Court plays only a nominal role in the treaty process both *ex ante* and *ex post. Ex ante,* the Court's decisions have little discernable influence on States in the intensely political process of negotiating agreements. *Ex post,* multilateral environmental agreements do not give the Court compulsory jurisdiction to interpret or apply them, so the Court has had very few opportunities to do so. Instead, States prefer to interpret and develop agreements through their subsequent practice – for example, by means of decisions, amendments, or additional agreements.

States generally prefer negotiation to adjudication as a means of developing the law for the same kinds of reasons discussed above in relation to dispute settlement:

---

[75] Bettauer, 'International Environmental Law-Making', 63.

- Negotiations allow States to determine the content of the law, a factor that is perhaps even more important in the environmental realm than in other areas of international law because of the close connection between international and domestic policy and the resulting potential for international rules to impinge on national sovereignty.
- Environmental problems such as climate change, protection of the stratospheric ozone layer, and conservation of biological diversity involve complex policy decisions and trade-offs that States prefer to address through a legislative rather than a judicial process.
- Negotiations allow States to establish specialised institutional arrangements to help implement and adapt the rules, as circumstances change.

The Court's decision in *Japanese Whaling*, in which it simply announced – with no clear explanation – a 'reasonableness' standard for assessing whether permits are issued for purposes of scientific research, may reinforce the wariness of some States to give the Court a greater role in elaborating treaty law.

To the extent the Court plays a significant role in the development of international environmental law, it is mostly with respect to customary law, where the Court serves as a 'material' source of international law, helping to shape the *opinio juris* of the international legal community. For example, when the Court found in its *Nuclear Weapons Advisory Opinion* that the duty to prevent is part of the 'corpus' of international law, its pronouncement was taken by commentators as dispositive.[76] The same is true of the Court's opinions about due diligence,[77] environmental impact assessment,[78] and a variety of other issues.

---

[76] See, e.g., Sands and Peel, *Principles*, pp. 195–196 ('Following the ICJ's 1996 Advisory Opinion ... there can be *no question* but that Principle 21 reflects a rule of customary international law ...') (emphasis added); P.-M. Dupuy and J. E. Viñuales, *International Environmental Law* (Cambridge University Press, 2015), p. 57 (Principle 21 'only became part of positive international law' when ICJ recognised it in *Nuclear Weapons Advisory Opinion*).

[77] An example of the ICJ's influence with judges can be seen in the ITLOS Advisory Opinion on Responsibilities and Obligations of States Sponsoring Persons and Entities with Respect to Activities in the Area, Case No. 17, ITLOS (Seabed Dispute Chamber), Advisory Opinion of 1 February 2011, para. 110–111 (citing ICJ *Pulp Mills* judgment in deciding that the obligation 'to ensure' in UNCLOS Article 139(1) is an obligation of due diligence).

[78] See, for example, Sands and Peel, *Principles*, p. 622 (citing ICJ decisions in *Gabčíikovo-Nagymaros* and *Pulp Mills* as showing 'the extent to which the concept of environmental assessment has developed and become established').

Because the Court's opinions, in theory, have no precedential effect, there is no formal difference between its pronouncements about international environmental law in contentious cases versus advisory opinions, or in *ratio decidendi* versus *obiter dictum*. Indeed, one of the leading treatises on international environmental law cites the *Nuclear Weapons Advisory Opinion* more frequently than any other case.[79]

The basis of the Court's de facto authority is not altogether clear, since its decisions not only have no formal precedential effect; they generally provide little evidence or reasoning to support their conclusions.[80] Sometimes the Court simply announces a rule as part of 'general' international law, without identifying its source.[81] When the Court does find a rule to be part of customary international law, it generally cites no State practice or *opinio juris* in support. For example, in *Pulp Mills*, it stated that the practice of undertaking environmental impact assessments when there is a risk of significant transboundary harm has 'gained so much acceptance among States' that it is now 'a requirement under general international law'. But the Court did not refer to any evidence that States generally undertake assessments of potential transboundary harms or that, when they do so, it is out of a sense of international legal obligation. For this reason, Judge Donoghue, in her separate opinion in *Costa Rica* v. *Nicaragua*, took issue with the Court's approach to customary international law, noting that 'the Court is ... ill equipped to conduct its own survey of the laws and practices of various States'.[82]

In any event, the Court has taken quite a conservative approach to customary international law, preferring to confirm the customary status of established principles rather than progressively developing inchoate ones. For example, in *Gabčikovo-Nagymaros*, the Court merely referenced the need to balance economic development and environmental protection and admonished the parties to take environmental considerations into

---

[79] Dupuy and Viñuales, *International Environmental Law*, p. lxvii (citing *Nuclear Weapons* twenty-one times, as compared to sixteen citations of the next most cited case, *Pulp Mills*).

[80] For an interesting theoretical discussion, see H. G. Cohen, 'Theorizing Precedent in International Law', in A. Bianchi, D. Peat and M. Windsor (eds.), *Interpretation in International Law* (Oxford University Press, 2015), p. 268 at 270.

[81] In *Costa Rica* v. *Nicaragua*, it was left to Judges Donoghue and Dugard, in their separate opinions, to clarify that 'general international law' means customary international law. *Costa Rica* v. *Nicaragua*, Separate Opinion of Judge Donoghue, p. 782, para. 2; Separate Opinion of Judge Dugard, p. 848, para. 16.

[82] Ibid., Separate Opinion of Judge Donoghue, p. 787, para. 18.

account, rather than attempting to do so itself. In *Pulp Mills*, it refused to apply the precautionary principle. And, in its compensation award in *Costa Rica* v. *Nicaragua*, it took a limited view of the amount of compensable damages. As a result, even in the area of customary law, the Court has played less of a role in shaping the law than other judicial bodies such as the International Tribunal for the Law of the Sea and the European Court of Human Rights.[83]

In contrast, some individual judges have taken a more expansive view of the role of the Court in progressively developing the law. For example, in *Costa Rica* v. *Nicaragua*, Judge Bhandari editorialised that international environmental law is 'lamentably silent' on the exact contents of environmental impact assessments.[84] Although he claimed to be 'acutely aware' that the Court cannot impose a regional treaty on the world, he then proceeded to outline minimum standards for environmental impact assessments that reflected his 'affinity toward the ambitious approach taken in the Espoo Convention'.[85] Later, in the damages phase of the case, he made even less pretence of interpreting and applying existing law. Rather, he wrote, the Court should 'develop the law of international responsibility beyond its traditional limits by elaborating on the issue of punitive or exemplary damages', because '[p]reserving and protecting the natural environment *ought* to be one of the supreme obligations under international law in the twenty-first century'.[86] Whether individual opinions such as this, however, play a significant role in developing international environmental law is questionable. Separate opinions and dissents lack the institutional authority of the Court. Instead, they depend for their influence on the quality and insightfulness of their reasoning, like the work of scholars.

---

[83] Dupuy and Viñuales, *International Environmental Law*, pp. 63–64 (contrasting ICJ approach with European Court of Human Rights and the International Tribunal for the Law of the Sea); ibid., p. 249 (contrasting 'neutral' stance of ICJ towards international environmental law with 'more generous reception' by other tribunals such as the European Court of Human Rights and the International Tribunal for the Law of the Sea).

[84] *Costa Rica* v. *Nicaragua*, Judgment, Separate Opinion of Judge Bhandari, ICJ Reports 2017, p. 790, 806, para. 47.

[85] Ibid., p. 801, para. 32; ibid., p. 803, para. 41.

[86] *Costa Rica* v. *Nicaragua*, Compensation Award, Separate Opinion of Judge Bhandari, ICJ Reports 2018, p. 96, 102, paras. 17–18 (emphasis added).

C Behaviour of States

The most important potential impact of the Court would be on the actual behaviour of States. But this impact is, at present, difficult to assess. The Court's impact on legal development can be measured, at least in part, by indicators such as citations by other courts and scholars. By comparison, there are no clear means to measure the ICJ's impact on State behaviour. Do more States actually undertake environmental assessments in response to *Pulp Mills*? Do they exercise greater diligence in attempting to prevent significant transboundary pollution? In contrast to multilateral environmental agreements, which typically establish reporting obligations that produce information about whether States are complying with their obligations, there is no general reporting system in international environmental law like the system of Universal Periodic Review for human rights.[87] As a result, the only readily available information about the impact of an ICJ decision is whether the parties to the case themselves comply, not whether a decision has a wider effect on State behaviour.

IV Conclusion

Negotiation and adjudication tend to represent alternative ways of addressing environmental problems.[88] Throughout most of its history, international environmental law has developed primarily through negotiations. But the pace of the Court's environmental decision-making has increased in recent years. Arguably, its three most important environmental cases have all been decided in the last decade. If negotiations fail to deliver acceptable results, frustrated States may well turn to the ICJ in the hope that it will provide a sympathetic forum. In that event, the ICJ will have more opportunities to contribute actively to the development of international environmental law than it has had to date. Whether it chooses to do so, however, is an open question, given the modesty of its past jurisprudence.

---

[87] Office of the UN High Commissioner for Human Rights, 'Basic Facts about the UPR', www .ohchr.org/EN/HRBodies/UPR/Pages/BasicFacts.aspx.

[88] D. Bodansky, 'Adjudication vs. Negotiation in Protecting Environmental Commons', 41 *University of Hawai'i Law Review* (2019) 260.

Further Reading

D. Bodansky, 'Adjudication vs. Negotiation in Protecting Environmental Commons', 41 *University of Hawai'i Law Review* (2019) 260.

M. Fitzmaurice, 'The International Court of Justice and International Environmental Law', in C. J. Tams and J. Sloan (eds.), *The Development of International Law by the International Court of Justice* (Oxford University Press), 2013, p. 353.

I. E. Kornfeld, 'Are International Courts the Best Adjudicators of Environmental Disputes?', in L. C. Paddock, R. L. Glicksman and N. S. Bryner (eds.), *Encyclopedia of Environmental Law vol. II* (Elgar, 2016), p. 441.

T. Stephens, *International Courts and Environmental Protection* (Cambridge University Press, 2009).

J. E. Viñuales, 'The Contribution of the International Court of Justice to the Development of International Environmental Law: An Assessment', 32 *Fordham International Law Journal* (2008) 232.

The Law of State Responsibility 18

Federica Paddeu

I Introduction

According to Article 36(2) of the Statute of the International Court of Justice ('ICJ' or 'Court'), the Court has jurisdiction in all legal disputes concerning, among others, 'the existence of any fact which, if established, would constitute a breach of an international obligation' and 'the nature or extent of the reparation to be made for the breach of an international obligation'.[1] The Court has, in short, jurisdiction over matters of State responsibility for the breach of international obligations.

The law of State responsibility is set out in the Articles on the Responsibility of States for Internationally Wrongful Acts ('ARSIWA' or 'Articles'), which were adopted by the International Law Commission ('ILC') and 'noted' by the United Nations General Assembly in 2001.[2] For the most part, the provisions in ARSIWA are customary in character and discussions as to the future status of this instrument, and whether there should be a treaty on State responsibility, are ongoing.[3] The law of State responsibility regulates three broad areas. First, it contains rules for the determination of the existence of an internationally wrongful act of the State, including rules on the attribution of conduct to the State,[4] on the breach of international obligations,[5] the circumstances in which a

My thanks to the editors of the book, as well as to Adam Brown and Nefeli Poulopati, two of my students at Queens' College, for their useful comments on earlier drafts of this chapter.

[1] Regarding the jurisdiction of the Court, see Jean-Marc Thouvenin, Chapter 6, The Jurisdiction of the Court.

[2] Articles on the Responsibility of States for Internationally Wrongful Acts, annexed to UNGA Res 56/83 (12 December 2001) GAOR 56th Session Supp 49 vol 1, 499, and Commentary.

[3] For an overview, see: F. Paddeu, 'To Convene or Not to Convene? The Future Status of the Articles on State Responsibility: Recent Developments' 21 *Max Planck Yearbook UN Law* (2017) 83.

[4] Articles 4–11 ARSIWA.   [5] Articles 12–15 ARSIWA.

State is responsible in connection with the wrongful act of another State,[6] and rules concerning defences.[7] Second, the law of State responsibility regulates the consequences arising from the commission of an internationally wrongful act, namely on the content of the responsibility of a State for the violation of its international obligations. These consequences include the broad categories of cessation and reparation (in its three forms of restitution, compensation and satisfaction),[8] as well as the regime of consequences arising from the serious violation of peremptory rules of international law.[9] Third, it also regulates questions concerning the implementation of State responsibility, and in particular the standing to invoke the responsibility of a State for an internationally wrongful act,[10] and certain measures of enforcement such as countermeasures.[11]

Since its establishment in 1945 and until the end of 2020, 151 cases have been filed before the Court.[12] By subject-matter, these can be divided into three main categories: (i) cases involving responsibility; (ii) cases involving territory, land or maritime delimitation; and (iii) a residual category of cases that are not clearly about either responsibility or territory/boundaries.[13] Of these 151 cases, at least 91 have involved claims about State responsibility.[14] In addition, matters of responsibility have also arisen in at least fourteen cases from categories (ii) and (iii).[15] Thus, States have occasionally claimed reparation for the breach of international law in

---

[6] Articles 16–19 ARSIWA.

[7] Referred to as 'circumstances precluding wrongfulness' in ARSIWA, see Chapter V of Part One, Articles 20–27, of ARSIWA.

[8] Articles 28–39 ARSIWA.   [9] Articles 40 and 41 ARSIWA.

[10] Articles 42 and 48 ARSIWA.   [11] Articles 49–54 ARSIWA.

[12] Cases not added to the Court's list are not included in this number. Joined cases have been counted as a single case. The data in this chapter refers to the period 1945–2020. No cases introduced after this period have been taken into account for these purposes.

[13] J. Crawford, 'The International Court of Justice and the Law of State Responsibility' in C. J. Tams and J. Sloane (eds.), *The Development of International Law by the International Court of Justice* (Oxford University Press, 2013), 85.

[14] For present purposes, a case 'involving State responsibility' is one in which the applicant alleges a breach by the respondent of an international obligation and requests some form of reparation.

[15] The classification of cases into categories (i) and (iii), especially when they involve questions of responsibility, requires some degree of evaluation. By way of example, I have included the ICAO council cases against Qatar in the third category because the dispute is an appeal against a decision of the ICAO Council. Nevertheless, I have counted these cases as involving issues of responsibility as the Court was called upon to assess claims about countermeasures and the scope of the ICAO Council's jurisdiction to assess these matters.

relation to territorial disputes (either due to the unlawful occupation of territory that is found to be theirs, or to activities about those territories),[16] and included claims in connection with the violation of rights, the determination or existence of which was the main subject matter of the dispute.[17] Taking these into account, then, issues of responsibility have been raised in 105 out of 151 cases before the Court – this is just over two thirds of the cases before the Court (about 70 per cent). Questions of State responsibility have also arisen, if less frequently, in requests for advisory opinions.[18]

In this sizeable case-law, the Court has greatly contributed both to developing and settling the law of State responsibility.[19] This chapter provides an overview of some of these developments, and considers the question of State responsibility before the Court in three (roughly) chronological steps, each addressing a different theme. First, it looks at the past and considers the contribution of the Court to the development of the law of responsibility and, in particular, its codification by the ILC in the ARSIWA adopted in 2001 (Section II). Second, it turns to the present, focusing on the ICJ's attitude towards ARSIWA, as expressed in its judgments since 2001 (Section III). Third, it looks to the future and addresses one of the main challenges facing the Court in this field: that of 'multilateral' disputes before the Court (Section IV).

---

[16] E.g., *Land and Maritime Boundary between Cameroon and Nigeria (Cameroon v. Nigeria: Equatorial Guinea intervening)* ICJ Rep 2002, p. 303.

[17] E.g., *Obligation to Negotiate Access to the Pacific Ocean (Bolivia v. Chile), Judgment*, ICJ Rep 2018, p. 507, paras. 13–14.

[18] On which, see F. L. Bordin, 'State Responsibility in Advisory Proceedings: Thoughts on Judicial Propriety and Multilateralism in the *Chagos* Opinion' in T. Burri and J. Trinidad (eds.), *Decolonization and the International Court of Justice: New Directions from the Chagos Advisory Opinion* (Cambridge University Press, 2021) 95.

[19] See, among others, R. Higgins, 'Issues of State Responsibility before the International Court of Justice' in M. Fitzmaurice and D. Sarooshi (eds.), *Issues of State Responsibility before International Judicial Institutions* (Bloomsbury, 2004), 1; I. Brownlie, 'State Responsibility and the International Court of Justice' in M. Fitzmaurice and D. Sarooshi (eds.), *Issues of State Responsibility before International Judicial Institutions* (Bloomsbury, 2004), 11; S. Villalpando, 'Le codificateur et le juge face à la responsabilité internationale de l'Etat: interaction entre la CDI et la CIJ dans la détermination des règles secondaires' 55 *AFDI* (2009) 39; A. Pellet, 'Some Remarks on the Recent Case Law of the International Court of Justice on Responsibility Issues' in P. Kovács (ed.), *International Law: A Quiet Strength. Miscellanea in Memoriam Géza Herczegh* (Pázmány Press, 2011), 111; Crawford, 'The International Court of Justice'; C. Tams, 'Law-Making in Complex Processes: The World Court and the Modern Law of State Responsibility' in C. Chinkin and F. Baetens (eds.), *Sovereignty, Statehood and State Responsibility: Essays in Honour of James Crawford* (Cambridge University Press, 2015), 287.

II Past: The ICJ and the Development of the Law of State Responsibility

The law of State responsibility, said Professor Alain Pellet, is 'essentially judge made'.[20] Whether or not one agrees with the full extent of this statement, two things are undeniable: (i) that the law of State responsibility is particularly receptive to judicial development, and (ii) that the present law of State responsibility owes much to judicial development and, in particular, to development by the ICJ and its predecessor, the Permanent Court of International Justice ('PCIJ').[21] Indeed, the Articles are based 'on case law precedents, to a far greater extent than on State practice and doctrine',[22] and many of these case law precedents were referred to by the ILC during its work on responsibility and now feature in the Commentary to (almost all of) the ARSIWA provisions.[23]

There are three main stages in the development of the law of responsibility, often overlapping: (A) laying of foundations; (B) codification and systematisation; and, (C) endorsement and refinement of ARSIWA. The ICJ has contributed to each of these stages, though in different degrees.

A Laying of Foundations

The first stage was dominated by the PCIJ, which laid down some of the basic principles of responsibility, such as the autonomy of international responsibility from internal law;[24] the focus on wrongfulness and its consequences, primarily in bilateral settings;[25] and the concept of reparation and its content.[26] The ICJ built on this significant tradition of

---

[20] Pellet, 'Some Remarks', 112.   [21] See, e.g., Tams, 'Law-Making', 304.

[22] P. Daillier, 'The Development of the Law of Responsibility through the Case Law' in J. Crawford et al. (eds.), *The Law of International Responsibility* (Oxford University Press, 2010), 41.

[23] Daillier notes that the references to international decisions are absent from the commentaries of the following Articles only: Art 18 (coercion); Arts 19, 28 and 46, on plurality of injured States; Arts 53 (termination of countermeasures) and 54 (measures taken by States other than the injured State); and Art 56 (questions not regulated by the Articles): 'Development', 41.

[24] E.g., *The SS 'Wimbledon'* (1923) PCIJ, Series A No 01, 15, 29–30; *The SS 'Lotus'* (1927) PCIJ, Series A No 10, 3, 24.

[25] E.g., *Phosphates in Morocco* (1938) PCIJ, Series A/B No 74, 10, 28.

[26] E.g., *Factory at Chorzów (Merits)* (1928) PCIJ, Series A No 17, 3, 29, 47.

cases of the PCIJ, and itself made some significant contributions to the foundational aspects of the law of responsibility. Most importantly, the ICJ clarified that the system of responsibility was unitary, applicable to both treaty and customary rules;[27] that while primarily bilateral, responsibility could arise also in multilateral settings;[28] and that responsibility applied to international organisations.[29]

B Codification and Systematisation

The second stage was dominated by the ILC, which for four decades worked on the codification and systematisation of the law of responsibility, with the ICJ taking on a 'supporting' role.[30] Indeed, an important feature of this stage was the dialogue established between the ILC and the ICJ, manifested in multiple ways and which involved both foundational principles as well as the detail of certain rules or principles of responsibility.

First, many cases brought before the ICJ in this period raised novel issues which were subsequently taken up by the ILC. For example, the acknowledgement and adoption attribution rule was set out in *Tehran Hostages*,[31] and subsequently adopted by the ILC.[32] Likewise, the notion of *erga omnes* obligations, now reflected in ARSIWA Article 48 on the standing of States other than the injured State to invoke responsibility, was articulated in *Barcelona Traction*.[33] In many of these instances, the ILC seemed to go beyond what the ICJ had actually said.[34] But this was inevitable given the different roles of these two bodies. The ICJ was deciding specific (and complex) disputes, whereas the ILC had to lay down general and abstract rules applicable to all manner of situations. As James Crawford has noted, formulating such abstract rules, even if working from

---

[27] *Gabčíkovo-Nagymaros Project (Hungary/Slovakia)*, ICJ Rep 1997, p. 7, para. 47.

[28] *Barcelona Traction, Light and Power Company, Limited, Judgment* (1970) ICJ Rep 3, paras. 33–34.

[29] *Reparation for Injuries Suffered in the Service of the United Nations, Advisory Opinion*, ICJ Rep 1949, pp. 174, 179–180.

[30] This section draws on Christian Tams' analysis in: 'Law-Making', 289ff.

[31] *United States Diplomatic and Consular Staff in Tehran*, ICJ Rep 1980, p. 3, para. 74.

[32] ARS Article 11.   [33] *Barcelona Traction*, paras. 33–34.

[34] For an overview: Villalpando, 'Le codificateur', 44–47.

existing precedents in case law or practice, involved, to some extent, 'inventing' them.[35]

Second, the ICJ also gave its *imprimatur* to rules developed by the ILC. Thus, in *Nicaragua*, the Court endorsed the rule on attribution of conduct of *de facto* organs,[36] adopted by the ILC as draft Article 8(a), albeit without mentioning this provision.[37] It also endorsed the defences of necessity and countermeasures in *Gabčíkovo-Nagymaros*.[38] Third, the ICJ contributed to the clarification of certain rules included in the draft Articles. For example, in *Gabčíkovo-Nagymaros* it clarified the relation between countermeasures and VCLT Article 60,[39] and introduced the notion of a 'commensurate response' in the context of countermeasures.[40]

The ILC-ICJ dialogue has been criticised from the standpoint of the (formal) doctrine of sources.[41] Judicial decisions are not a source of international law, they are only 'subsidiary means' for the determination of rules of law.[42] And yet, on many occasions, the ICJ's *imprimatur* of certain ILC draft Articles was sufficient to override the objections and concerns raised by States. The leading example in this regard is the plea of necessity. States' opinions were split roughly equally on the desirability of this provision, when it was adopted on first reading by the ILC,[43] such that when the *Gabčíkovo-Nagymaros* dispute came to the Court 'it was very much an open question whether the defence would be accepted'.[44] Only a few years earlier, the Tribunal in *Rainbow Warrior* had rejected the argument that necessity was a customary rule.[45] The ICJ endorsed the customary status of the plea in

---

[35] Crawford, 'The International Court of Justice', 74.

[36] *Military and Paramilitary Activities in and Against Nicaragua (Nicaragua v. United States of America)*, ICJ Rep 1986, p. 14, para. 109.

[37] ILC, Report of the Commission on the work of its twenty-sixth session, UN Doc A/9610/Rev.1, ILC Yearbook 1974, vol II(1), 277.

[38] *Gabčíkovo-Nagymaros*, para. 51 (necessity), para. 83 (countermeasures).

[39] *Gabčíkovo-Nagymaros*, para. 105.   [40] *Gabčíkovo-Nagymaros*, para. 85.

[41] See, e.g., J. D'Aspremont, 'Canonical Cross-Referencing in the Making of the Law of International Responsibility' in S. Forlati et al. (eds.), *The Gabčíkovo-Nagymaros Judgment and its Contribution to the Development of International Law* (Brill, 2020), 40. Regarding sources, see Jean d'Aspremont, Chapter 8, The International Court of Justice as the Master of the Sources.

[42] ICJ Statute, Art 38(1)(d).

[43] For an overview, see F. Paddeu, *Justification and Excuse in International Law: Concept and Theory of General Defences* (Cambridge University Press, 2018), 398–401.

[44] Crawford, 'The International Court of Justice', 81.

[45] *Rainbow Warrior (New Zealand v. France)* (1990) 20 RIAA 215.

Gabčíkovo-Nagymaros. When the ILC revisited the defence on second reading, it was able to rely on the ICJ's holding to set aside any outstanding controversies about whether necessity was customary.[46] This way of proceeding was described by Santiago Villalpando as an 'autocatalytic process', and in more negative terms as a 'normative Ponzi scheme'.[47]

In a broader systemic perspective, however, this dialogue was valuable. The codification of the law of responsibility had historically been difficult and unsuccessful. The adoption of ARSIWA was the culmination of efforts started more than a century earlier.[48] The failures and difficulties of most of these efforts have usually been explained away as the result of a codificatory approach focused on damage to aliens and their property. Yet, after codification turned its focus to 'secondary rules' only, the ILC still laboured for four decades before completing ARSIWA, suggesting that, perhaps, it was the subject of responsibility, regardless of approach, which was difficult to codify.[49] The ingenious idea of distinguishing primary and secondary rules, with its technical undertones and the illusion of separability between obligation and responsibility, hides the reality that this conceptual separation is not possible because secondary rules depend, and determine the scope of, primary rules.[50] It also obscures the fact that States codify secondary rules with an eye to how they will affect their obligations under primary rules. Given this context, the ILC's codification task would have been all the more arduous had the ICJ not shown its support for this project: the Court supported many of the ILC's choices and, in so doing, vested the ILC's work with authority from its early stages. Crucially, moreover, States have been largely content with this way of proceeding[51] and, it may be added, with ARSIWA more generally,[52]

---

[46] D. Bodansky and J. Crook, 'Symposium: The ILC's State Responsibility Articles: Introduction and Overview' (2002) 96 *AJIL* 773, 788.

[47] S. Villalpando, 'On the International Court of Justice and the Determination of Rules of Law' 26 *LJIL* (2013) 243, 248.

[48] On which see L. Laithier, 'Private Codification Efforts' in J. Crawford et al. (eds), *The Law of International Responsibility* (Oxford University Press, 2010), 61; C. Bories, 'The Hague Conference of 1930' in J. Crawford et al. (eds.), *The Law of International Responsibility* (Oxford University Press, 2010), 69.

[49] F. Paddeu, 'To Convene', 121–123.

[50] G. Gaja, 'Primary and Secondary Rules in the International Law of State Responsibility' 97 *Rivista di diritto internazionale* (2014) 981.

[51] S. Villalpando, 'Determination', 249.

[52] For an overview of State comments on ARSIWA since their adoption, see: F. Paddeu, 'To Convene', 101–107.

allaying some of the concerns voiced over the 'autocatalytic' process's compatibility with the doctrine of sources.

C Endorsement and Refinement

An important side-effect of the ILC's codification of the law of responsibility was that of constraining the ICJ as an agent of legal development in this field of international law. Once the ILC joined the law of responsibility 'scene', the ICJ began to operate within what Christian Tams has termed the ILC's 'master plan', and this limited the Court's ability to lay down broad and foundational principles of responsibility.[53] But this did not mean that the ICJ became less influential. There are, indeed, 222 references to the case law of the Court in the ARSIWA Commentary.[54]

The Court continues to play an important role in the consolidation and refinement of the rules in ARSIWA, even after their adoption in 2001. The rules in ARSIWA are stated in broad and abstract terms so as to ensure the generality of their application. In applying them to specific (and often complex cases), the ICJ has thus contributed to fleshing them out. This has sometimes involved the consolidation of certain rules. For example, the ICJ endorsed the ILC's approach to Article 4 (on attribution of conduct by State organs) and Article 8 (on attribution of private conduct under instructions of, or directed or controlled by, the State) in *Bosnian Genocide*,[55] rejecting the lower threshold of 'overall control' developed in the case law of the International Criminal Tribunal for Yugoslavia.[56] It has also sometimes expanded the scope of certain rules, as in the case of Article 16 on aid and assistance which, as held in *Bosnian Genocide*, applies also when the assistance is given to a non-State actor.[57]

The ICJ does not always endorse the ILC's choices, though it rarely contradicts the Commission expressly. In *Croatian Genocide*, the Court withheld judgment on the customary status of Article 10(2), on attribution of conduct of successful secessionist movements, a matter over which the

---

[53] C. Tams, 'Law-Making', 297.   [54] S. Villalpando, 'Determination', 247.

[55] *Application of the Convention on the Prevention and Punishment of the Crime of Genocide (Bosnia and Herzegovina v. Serbia and Montenegro)*, ICJ Rep 2007, p. 43, paras. 402–406.

[56] *Prosecutor v. Tadić, Appeal Chamber of the UN International Criminal Tribunal for the former Yugoslavia* IT-94-1-A, Judgment, 2 October 1995, para. 115ff.

[57] *Bosnian Genocide*, para. 420.

parties disagreed.[58] Other times, such departures are less explicit. For example, the Court has been skeptical about assurances and guarantees of non-repetition. While not dismissing ARSIWA Article 30(b) (it has never even cited it), the Court never finds that assurances are needed in fact in the circumstances.[59]

The ICJ both participated in the making of the substance of ARSIWA, as well as in the vesting of this document with the authority it has today.[60] The ILC's Articles have indeed not only codified the law of State responsibility, but also 'encoded' the way in which international actors think about responsibility.[61]

III Present: The ICJ and the Articles on State Responsibility

One interesting feature of the ICJ's engagement with this body of law is that it rarely, if ever, provides evidence of the positive law basis of responsibility rules. Historically, the Court relied 'on its own authority to sustain its findings of law' in this field.[62] From the 1990s onwards, the Court began to make reference to the ILC's work as authority for the responsibility rules it applied. As noted above, in this way, the Court greatly contributed to vesting the ARSIWA with authority.[63] One would thus be justified in assuming that, since their adoption, references to ARSIWA had become routine in ICJ judgments. But this is not the case.

Since 2001, the Court has issued decisions on jurisdiction, merits, or advisory opinions in sixty-nine cases.[64] The Court addressed, or referred

---

[58] *Application of the Convention on the Prevention and Punishment of the Crime of Genocide (Croatia v. Serbia), Judgment,* ICJ Rep 2015, p. 3, para. 105.

[59] For an overview of the adoption of ARSIWA Art 30(b) and the Court's approach to guarantees of non-repetition, see J. Crawford, *State Responsibility: The General Part* (Cambridge University Press, 2013), 469–475.

[60] On this see F. L. Bordin, 'Reflections of Customary International Law: The Authority of Codification Conventions and the ILC Draft Articles in International Law' 63 *ICLQ* (2014) 535.

[61] Crawford, 'The International Court of Justice', 81. See also Paddeu and Tams, 'Dithering, Trickling Down, and Encoding: Concluding Thoughts on the 'ILC Articles at 20' Symposium', *EJIL:Talk!* (9 August 2021) available at: www.ejiltalk.org/dithering-trickling-down-and-encoding-concluding-thoughts-on-the-ilc-articles-at-20-symposium/.

[62] Villalpando, 'Determination', 245.   [63] See references at fn 69.

[64] Joined cases that resulted in the same decision have been counted as one case. The data is up to date as at the end of 2020.

to, issues or rules of State responsibility in at least thirty-seven of these decisions, including twenty-one merits,[65] two compensation,[66] twelve preliminary objections judgments,[67] and two advisory opinions.[68] Overall, only twelve of these contain references to ARSIWA (seven merits

---

[65] *LaGrand (Germany v. USA)*, ICJ Rep 2001, p. 466; *Cameroon v. Nigeria; Arrest Warrant of 11 April 2002 (DRC v. Belgium)*, ICJ Rep 2002, p. 3; *Oil Platforms (Islamic Republic of Iran v. United States of America)* ICJ Rep 2003, p. 161; *Case Concerning Avena and other Mexican Nationals (Mexico v. United States of America)* ICJ Rep 2004, p. 12; *Armed Activities on the Territory of the Congo (DRC v. Uganda)*, ICJ Rep 2005, p. 168; *Bosnian Genocide; Certain Questions of Mutual Assistance in Criminal Matters (Djibouti v. France)*, Judgment ICJ Rep 2008, p. 177; *Navigational and Related Rights (Costa Rica v. Nicaragua)*, ICJ Rep 2009, p. 213; *Case Concerning Pulp Mills on the River Uruguay (Argentina v. Uruguay)*, ICJ Rep 2010, p. 14; *Case Concerning Ahmadou Sadio Diallo, Merits, Judgment*, ICJ Rep 2010, p. 639; *Application of the Interim Accord of 13 September 1995 (FYR Macedonia v. Greece)*, ICJ Rep 2011, p. 644; *Jurisdictional Immunities of the State (Germany v. Italy: Greece intervening)*, ICJ Rep 2012, p. 99; *Questions Relating to the Obligation to Prosecute or Extradite (Belgium v. Senegal)*, Judgment, ICJ Rep 2012, p. 422; *Whaling in the Antarctic (Australia v. Japan: New Zealand intervening), Judgment*, ICJ Rep 2014, p. 226; *Croatian Genocide; Certain Activities Carried out by Nicaragua in the Border Area (Costa Rica v. Nicaragua) and Construction of a Road in Costa Rica along the San Juan River (Nicaragua v. Costa Rica), Judgment*, ICJ Rep 2015, p. 665; *Jadhav Case (India v. Pakistan), Judgment*, ICJ Rep 2019, p. 418; *Appeal Relating to the Jurisdiction of the ICAO Council Under Article 84 of the Convention on International Civil Aviation (Bahrain, Egypt, Saudi Arabia and United Arab Emirates v. Qatar)* ICJ, Judgment 14 July 2020; *Appeal Relating to the Jurisdiction of the ICAO Council Under Article II, Section 2, of the 1944 International Air Services Transit Agreement (Bahrain, Egypt and United Arab Emirates v. Qatar)* (2020) ICJ, Judgment 14 July 2020; *Immunities and Criminal Proceedings (Equatorial Guinea v. France), Merits* (2020) ICJ, Judgment 11 December 2020.

[66] *Case Concerning Ahmadou Sadio Diallo (Guinea v. DRC), Compensation, Judgmen*, ICJ Rep 2012, p. 324; *Certain Activities Carried out by Nicaragua in the Border Area (Costa Rica v. Nicaragua), Compensation, Judgment*, ICJ Rep 2018, p. 15.

[67] In the eight judgments in *Legality of Use of Force*, against Belgium (para. 128), Canada (para. 115), France (para. 115), Germany (para. 114), Italy (para. 115), Netherlands (para. 127), Portugal (para. 118), and the UK (para. 114); *Armed Activities on the Territory of the Congo (New Application: 2002) (Democratic Republic of the Congo v. Rwanda)*, Jurisdiction and Admissibility, ICJ Rep 2006, p. 6, para. 127; *Obligations Concerning Negotiations Relating to the Cessation of the Nuclear Arms Race and to Nuclear Disarmament (Marshall Islands v. India), Jurisdiction and Admissibility, Judgment*, ICJ Rep 2016, p. 255, para. 42; *Obligations Concerning Negotiations Relating to the Cessation of the Nuclear Arms Race and to Nuclear Disarmament (Marshall Islands v. United Kingdom), Jurisdiction and Admissibility, Judgment*, ICJ Rep 2016, p. 833, para. 45; *Application of the International Convention for the Suppression of the Financing of Terrorism and of the Internatioanl Convention on the Elimination of All Forms of Racial Discrimination (Ukraine v. Russian Federation), Preliminary Objections*, ICJ Rep 2019, p. 558, paras. 44, 152.

[68] *Legal Consequences of the Construction of a Wall in the Occupied Palestinian Territory*, ICJ Rep 2004, p. 136; *Legal Consequences of the Separation of the Chagos Archipelago from Mauritius in 1965, Advisory Opinion*, ICJ Rep 2019, 95.

judgments, three jurisdiction judgments, and two advisory opinions).[69] This number is surprising both in terms of the overall number of ICJ judgments addressing questions of responsibility in this period, and more generally. According to data compiled by the UN Secretariat, between January 2001 and January 2019, the Articles had been referred to in 204 decisions by international courts, tribunals and other bodies.[70] Overall, the Court has referred to at least twenty-two Articles in its decisions.[71]

The Court's approach to citing authorities for the rules of State responsibility it applies is, indeed, quite varied. Notable examples include the *Bosnian Genocide* case, which references at least ten ARSIWA provisions,[72] and *DRC* v. *Uganda*,[73] *Pulp Mills*,[74] and *Germany* v. *Italy*,[75] each containing four references. The Court has relied on ARSIWA provisions which reflect well-established rules, such as Article 1 (the general principle of responsibility),[76] and Articles 4 and 8,[77] but *also* on provisions which

---

[69] *Palestinian Wall*; *DRC* v. *Uganda*; *Bosnian Genocide*; *Pulp Mills*; *Germany* v. *Italy*; *Diallo (Compensation)*; *Croatian Genocide*; *Marshall Islands* v. *India*; *Marshall Islands* v. *UK*; *Certain Activities (Compensation)*; *Chagos*; *Ukraine* v. *Russia (Preliminary Objections)*.

[70] The Secretariat lists a total of 249 decisions: UN Secretariat, Responsibility of States for internationally wrongful acts: Compilation of decisions of international courts, tribunals and other bodies, UN Doc A/71/80/Add.1, 20 June 2017, at para. 5 (163 cases); UN Secretariat, Responsibility of States for internationally wrongful acts: Compilation of decisions of international courts, tribunals and other bodies, UN Doc A/74/83, 23 April 2019, at para. 5 (86 further cases). However, 45 of these contain references to the draft articles adopted on first reading, before 2001: UN Secretariat, Responsibility of States for internationally wrongful acts: Compilation of decisions of international courts, tribunals and other bodies, UN Doc A/62/62, para. 5, and Annex I. Note also that the UN Secretariat uses the term 'decision' very broadly in these analyses, and has included decisions on jurisdiction and admissibility, merits, annulment proceedings, and advisory opinions, in its list.

[71] Not including references in the judgment to Articles cited by the parties in their pleadings, the Court has referred in its reasoning to the following Articles: 1, 3, 4, 5, 6, 8, 9, 10, 11, 14, 16, 25, 30, 31, 34, 35, 36, 37, 38, 41, 45, 58. It has indirectly referred to Article 44 as well: in *Ukraine* v. *Russia (Preliminary Objections)* the Court cited the commentary to Article 44 in support of the proposition that the local remedies rule (codified in Art 44(2)) is part of customary law.

[72] *Bosnian Genocide*, referring to articles: 4 (paras. 385, 388, 414), 5 (para. 414), 6 (para. 414), 8 (paras. 398, 401, 407, 414), 9 (para. 414), 11 (para. 414), 14 (para. 431), 16 (para. 420), 31 (para. 460), and 36 (para. 460).

[73] *DRC* v. *Uganda*, para. 160 (Arts 4, 5, and 8), para. 293 (referring to Commentary to Art 45).

[74] *Pulp Mills*, referring to 'Articles 34 to 37' (para. 273).

[75] *Germany* v. *Italy*, Arts 13 (para. 58), 30 (para. 137), 35 (para. 137), and 41 (para. 93).

[76] *Chagos*, para. 177.

[77] E.g., *Bosnian Genocide*, at paras. 385 (Article 4) and para. 398 (Article 8).

represented progressive development of international law by the ILC and which were controversial among States. Thus, the Court endorsed, and even expanded the scope of, Article 16 on aid and assistance in *Bosnian Genocide*,[78] and in *Germany* v. *Italy* it referred to – admittedly only in *obiter* – the provision in Article 41 on the consequences of serious violations of *jus cogens*.[79] Further, as already noted in respect of Article 10(2), the Court does not always refer to the ILC Articles with approval.[80]

In many cases, the Court has instead cited its own (and the PCIJ's) past case law as authority for responsibility rules. For instance, after finding it had no jurisdiction in the *Legality of Use of Force* cases, the Court reminded parties that they remained responsible for acts attributable to them in breach of the rights of other States (codified in ARSIWA Article 1), citing past case law in support of this principle.[81] Likewise, it referred to its own case law as authority for the obligation to cease a continuing wrongful act (ARSIWA Article 30(a)) in *Palestinian Wall*,[82] and referred to the PCIJ's judgments in *Chorzów Factory* in its statement of the principle of reparation (ARSIWA Article 31) in *Avena*,[83] *Palestinian Wall*,[84] *Diallo*,[85] and *Jadhav*.[86] In *Croatian Genocide*, it relied on *DRC* v. *Uganda* as authority for the attribution rule on *ultra vires* acts of State organs (ARSIWA Article 7).[87] In some further cases, it has relied on rules in other areas of international law. In *Pulp Mills*, for example, it cited VCLT Article 27 for the principle that a State cannot shield behind its domestic law as exoneration for the violation of international law (ARSIWA Article 3),[88] and in *DRC* v. *Uganda*, it relied on IHL in relation to attribution of *ultra vires* acts of their organs (ARSIWA Article 7).[89]

Sometimes, the Court has cited both its past case-law and the ILC Articles. In *Chagos*, it supported the basic principle that all internationally wrongful acts of a State engage its responsibility by reference to Article 1 ARSIWA and its judgments in *Corfu Channel* and *Gabčíkovo-Nagymaros*;[90] in

---

[78] *Bosnian Genocide*, para. 420.   [79] *Germany* v. *Italy*, para. 93.
[80] *Croatian Genocide*, para. 105.
[81] See, e.g., *Legality of Use of Force*, against Belgium (para. 128), Canada (para. 115), France (para. 115), Germany (para. 114), Italy (para. 115), Netherlands (para. 127), Portugal (para. 118), and the UK (para. 114).
[82] *Palestinian Wall*, para. 150.   [83] *Avena*, para. 119.   [84] *Palestinian Wall*, para. 152.
[85] *Diallo (Merits)*, para. 161.   [86] *Jadhav*, para. 138.   [87] *Croatian Genocide*, para. 449.
[88] *Pulp Mills*, para. 121.   [89] *DRC* v. *Uganda*, para. 214.   [90] *Chagos*, para. 177.

Palestinian Wall, it referred to both Article 25 and *Gabčíkovo-Nagymaros* in relation to the defence of necessity.[91]

Other times, it has cited nothing at all. In *DRC v. Rwanda*, the Court omitted any authorities when it reminded the parties that, irrespective of its jurisdiction over the case, they remained responsible for acts attributable to them in violation of international law.[92] In *Navigational Rights*,[93] *Whaling*,[94] and *Certain Activities*,[95] the Court considered the violation of obligations by States and their consequences without referring to the source of, or indeed any authorities for, the responsibility rules applied.

To an extent, the Court's approach to citing ARSIWA is simply erratic. For instance, mentions of ARSIWA have not increased over time, at least not in a significant way, in line with the Articles' increased use and authority among other international courts and tribunals. ARSIWA were mentioned in three of ten merits judgments in the period 2001–2010, and four of eleven in the period 2011–2020.[96] Likewise, ICJ references to ARSIWA seem unrelated to the parties' reliance on the Articles in their pleadings. A technical report prepared by the UN Secretariat shows that up to 2017 ARSIWA were referred to in 370 pleadings of parties to cases before the Court as compared to, over the same period, eighteen references in judgments of the Court.[97]

There are, nevertheless, two identifiable (if weak) trends in the Court's approach towards citing ARSIWA. First, in respect of reparations, the Court has tended not to follow the provisions in Part Two of ARSIWA preferring, instead, to rely on its past case law.[98] Indeed, it has referred to provisions on reparations in only five judgments.[99] This may be due to two main factors: first, the practical difficulties involved in questions of reparation, especially compensation, and, second, the wish to create a

---

[91] *Palestinian Wall*, para. 140.   [92] *DRC v. Rwanda*, para. 127.

[93] *Navigational Rights*, 266–268.   [94] *Whaling*, 293–296 (breach), 298 (remedies).

[95] *Certain Activities*, 716–718 (reparations owed to Costa Rica), 738–740 (reparations owed to Nicaragua).

[96] The eleven cases which mention ARSIWA are temporally distributed as follows: 2004: *Palestinian Wall*; 2005: *DRC v. Uganda*; 2007: *Bosnian Genocide*; 2010: *Pulp Mills*; 2012: *Germany v. Italy; Diallo (Compensation)*; 2015: *Croatian Genocide*; 2016: *Marshall Islands (RMI v. UK; RMI v. India)*; 2018: *Certain Activities (Compensation)*; 2019: *Chagos*.

[97] The period includes both pre- and post-2001 decisions, and ends in January 2017.

[98] D'Aspremont, 'Canonical Cross-Referencing', 38–39.

[99] *Bosnian Genocide*, para. 460; *Pulp Mills*, para. 273; *Germany v. Italy*, para. 137; *Diallo (compensation)*, para. 49; *Certain activities (compensation)*, para. 151.

legal environment which favours a 'conciliation of the parties' positions'.[100] The rules on reparations were indeed developed in the context of injuries to aliens and diplomatic protection claims, so they may not facilitate conciliation in disputes involving, for example, serious human rights violations or violations of the rules concerning the use of force between States.[101]

Second, the Court has tended *not* to cite controversial provisions of ARSIWA. Thus, the Court has applied in substance the rules in ARSIWA Articles 48 (*Belgium* v. *Senegal*[102] and *Whaling*)[103] and 41 (*Palestinian Wall*)[104] without mentioning either provision. The omission in *Palestinian Wall* is especially noteworthy, given that the Court referred to other provisions of ARSIWA in that same decision.[105] To confound things, however, the Court does on occasion mention controversial provisions: Article 41, for example, is expressly referred to in *Germany* v. *Italy*.[106] And sometimes it does not mention provisions relating to long-settled rules of State responsibility, such as the basic principle of responsibility enshrined in Article 1. So while there may be a tendency not to refer to controversial provisions of ARSIWA, not all omissions of ARSIWA references in the Court's judgments are due to the controversial nature of the relevant rule.

What, then, to make of the Court's practice in citing ARSIWA? At a general level, perhaps not too much should be made of it. Whether the Court cites (or does not) this or that provision, does not detract from the fact that, as a whole, the Court has endorsed the Articles: its analyses of State responsibility – whether relying expressly on ARSIWA or not – follow the structure and concepts laid down in the Articles. The Court follows, to borrow Tams' expression, the ILC's 'master plan'.[107] At a more specific level, in respect of the understanding or status of each individual rule of responsibility applied by the Court, two lessons can be learned. First, that in light of the Court's overall practice on citing ARSIWA, no firm conclusions should be reached on the basis of the Court's mention of, or omission to mention, provisions in ARSIWA. Second, that in assessing the Court's views on any given rule (including its interpretation and its

---

[100] Villalpando, 'Le codificateur', 59.   [101] Ibid.   [102] *Belgium* v. *Senegal*, paras. 64–70.
[103] *Whaling*, 343.   [104] *Palestinian Wall*, paras. 159–160.
[105] *Palestinian Wall*, para. 140.   [106] *Germany* v. *Italy*, para. 93.
[107] Tams, 'Law-Making', 297.

customary status), each judgment must be taken on its own and its import understood. This will require a careful reading of the judgment, alongside the opinions of the judges and the pleadings of the parties 'in light of the general debates in the legal scholarship of our times'.[108]

IV Future: Multilateral Disputes in Bilateral Settings

One of the most difficult challenges for the Court in the years ahead will be to adapt to claims involving the breach of multilateral obligations,[109] namely claims for the breach of obligations established for the protection of the interests of a group of States, or of the international community as a whole, brought by a State which is not injured by the relevant breach. The recent *Rohingya Genocide* case provides a good illustration of this type of community interest litigation: the case was brought against Myanmar by The Gambia, a State whose rights have not been directly injured by Myanmar's actions against the Rohingya population. The Gambia's standing is based on its legal interest in compliance with the obligations under the Genocide Convention, to which both Myanmar and The Gambia are parties.[110] At the time of writing, the Maldives,[111] and Canada and the Netherlands,[112] all States who are not injured or specially affected by Myanmar's alleged breach of the Genocide Convention, had expressed their desire to intervene in the proceedings.

The Court's *dictum* on the concept of *erga omnes* obligations in *Barcelona Traction* is one of its most influential in the field of State

---

[108] Villalpando, 'Determination', 251.

[109] Used here in the sense of: J. Crawford, 'Multilateral Rights and Obligations in International Law' 319 *Collected Courses of the Academy of International Law* (2006) 325, 331.

[110] Application instituting proceedings and request for provisional measures (*The Gambia v. Myanmar*), 11 November 2019, ICJ, paras. 123–127, at: www.icj-cij.org/public/files/case-related/178/178-20191111-APP-01-00-EN.pdf.

[111] See: www.foreign.gov.mv/index.php/en/mediacentre/news/5483-the-republic-of-maldives-to-file-declaration-of-intervention-in-support-of-the-rohingya-people,-at-the-international-court-of-justice.

[112] See: www.government.nl/documents/diplomatic-statements/2020/09/02/joint-statement-of-canada-and-the-kingdom-of-the-netherlands-regarding-intention-to-intervene-in-the-gambia-v.-myanmar-case-at-the-international-court-of-justice.

responsibility.[113] Article 48 of the Articles, which translated this concept into the language of responsibility, is an example of progressive development by the ILC; one of those instances in which the Commission, working from a concise formulation in a judgment of the Court, essentially 'invented' a rule broadening that concise formulation into an abstract and general legal proposition. Article 48 and the idea of community interest litigation that it generated was controversial, and there remain States that would wish to exclude this provision from an eventual treaty on State responsibility.[114]

Despite the controversies, the Court appears to have accepted this idea, even if it has not, to date, mentioned Article 48 in its judgments. The first clear case involving the breach of a multilateral obligation before the Court was *Belgium* v. *Senegal*, in which the Court accepted Belgium's standing to demand compliance by Senegal with its obligations under the Torture Convention despite Senegal's objections.[115] Later, in *Whaling*, the Court did not even address the issue of standing, taking for granted Australia's standing to claim against Japan under the Whaling Convention.[116] The Court has also accepted The Gambia's standing to demand compliance with the Genocide Convention from Myanmar in the *Rohingya Genocide* case.[117]

While accepting the idea, the essentially bilateralist character of ICJ procedure has presented some difficulties. The Court's case law has clarified that *erga omnes* obligations do not override the jurisdictional limitations and other procedural requirements for bringing cases before the Court. Claims involving multilateral obligations must be made to fit into this bilateralist mold. The Court has thus clarified that there must be a jurisdictional basis for the claim in question.[118] It has also clarified that the *erga omnes* character of the obligation allegedly breached cannot exclude

---

[113] On which see C. Tams and A. Tzanakopoulos, '*Barcelona Traction* at 40: The ICJ as an Agent of Legal Development' 23 *LJIL* (2010) 784.

[114] See F. Paddeu, 'To Convene', 105–106.   [115] *Belgium* v. *Senegal*, paras. 64–70.

[116] *Whaling*, 343. For an informative contextual explanation of this judgment see, C. Tams, 'Roads Not Taken, Opportunities Missed: Procedural and Jurisdictional Questions Sidestepped in the *Whaling* Judgment' in M. Fitzmaurice and D. Tamada (eds.), *Whaling in the Antarctic: The Significance and the Implications of the ICJ Judgment* (Brill, 2016), 201–211.

[117] *Application of the Convention on the Prevention and Punishment of the Crime of Genocide (The Gambia* v. *Myanmar), Preliminary Objections*, ICJ Order of 22 July 2022.

[118] *Bosnian Genocide*, para. 147.

the requirement of the existence of a dispute,[119] the applicability of the necessary-third-party rule,[120] the requirements for the indication of provisional measures,[121] or the admissibility requirements for intervention by a third party.[122] It has, however, excluded the applicability of the nationality of claims rule (in Article 44(a) of the ILC Articles) to claims involving *erga omnes partes* obligations: insofar as claims for alleged breaches of these obligations 'derive from the common interest of all States parties in compliance with these obligations', they are 'therefore not limited to the State of nationality of the alleged victims'.[123]

The extent to which these requirements are compatible with, or facilitative of, multilateral disputes has often been doubted.[124] On occasion, as in the recent *Marshall Islands* cases, the Court's application of its requirements has given the impression of a Court ready to seize on technicality and formalism to avoid the merits of the dispute. Scholars have worried whether, when viewed against the context of the attack on multilateralism and multilateral institutions in the past few years,[125] the Court's choice to dismiss claims on the basis of a failure to comply with formalistic requirements does not reflect a lingering ambivalence towards multilateralism and, worse still, could be seen as the Court backpedalling on its earlier support for the 'legally progressive regime' of Article 48.[126] While it is not possible to know the Court's motivations, it must not be overlooked that this recent case law has not called into question the standing of non-injured States in relation to multilateral obligations: the principle stands, despite the recognition of limitations to its implementation.[127]

---

[119] *Marshall Islands.*   [120] *East Timor (Portugal v. Australia)* (1995) ICJ Rep 90.

[121] *Rohingya Genocide,* ICJ Order of 23 January 2020.

[122] *Whaling in the Antarctic (Australia v. Japan), Declaration of Intervention of New Zealand,* Order of 6 February 2013, (2013) ICJ Rep 3.

[123] *Application of the Convention on the Prevention and Punishment of the Crime of Genocide (The Gambia v. Myanmar), Preliminary Objections,* para. 109.

[124] For criticism of the Court's application of the third-party rule in *East Timor,* see: Crawford, 'Responsibility for Breaches of Communitarian Norms: An Appraisal of Article 48 of the ILC Articles on Responsibility of States for Wrongful Acts' in Fastenrath et al. (eds.), *From Bilateralism to Community Interest: Essays in Honour of Bruno Simma* (Oxford University Press, 2011), 231.

[125] On which see: J. Crawford, 'Current Political Discourse Concerning International law' 81 *Modern LR* (2018) 1.

[126] Bordin, 'Advisory Proceedings', 110.

[127] See Y. Tanaka, 'Reflections on *Locus Standi* in Response to a Breach of Obligations *Erga Omnes Partes*: A Comparative Analysis of the *Whaling in the Antarctic* and *South China Sea* Cases' 17 *Law & Prac Intl Cts & Tribunals* (2018) 527, 541–542.

At a deeper level, its engagement with multilateral disputes has on occasion revealed a Court unable to 'see' the multilateral character of the dispute as well as the multilateral character of the underlying relations.[128] To be sure, the ICJ must look at these disputes through the bilateralist-tinted lens of its procedure, but it must also be conscious of the distortions this can cause. While multilateral disputes must be shoehorned into a bilateral process, the Court must avoid treating these disputes *as if* they were bilateral in character. The Court must not allow the form to distort the substance, but rather adapt the form to the substance.[129] The Court has already had occasion to explain how some of its jurisdictional and other requirements apply to multilateral disputes though, as noted, not always suitably. But many procedural issues remain to be addressed, including the extent to which the rule on exhaustion of local remedies applies to applications by States other than the injured State; participation of non-State actors as *amici curiae*; whether the character of the obligation breached affects the burden and standard of proof, or the Court's fact-finding powers and, in particular, its powers to 'obtain evidence of co-responsible parties who are not parties to the dispute' before the Court; and the application of the *res judicata* principle in respect of injured States, and other non-injured States.[130] The Court has had occasion to contend with some of these issues already. In its advisory jurisdiction the Court has, for example, managed the participation of, and submissions by, large numbers of States, which may assist in cases with multiple applicants or multiple interveners. It has also considered questions of evidence in respect of violations of *erga omnes* obligations, and addressed participation by non-State actors. While there are important differences between contentious and advisory jurisdiction, the Court could nevertheless valuably draw from its experience in advisory proceedings in adapting its procedures to multilateral disputes.

In revisiting old issues and addressing new ones, the Court will need to strike a careful balance between adapting its procedures to multilateral disputes, and avoid antagonising existing and potential respondent States,

---

[128] *Marshall Islands*, Crawford diss op, para. 20.

[129] *Marshall Islands*, Crawford diss op, para. 21.

[130] A. Nollkaemper, 'International Adjudication of Global Public Goods: The Intersection of Substance and Procedure' 23 *EJIL* (2012) 769, 779. See ibid for references to relevant scholarship on each of these aspects. See also: P. Urs, 'Obligations *Erga Omnes* and the Question of Standing Before the International Court of Justice' 34(2) *LJIL* (2021) 505.

as this might lead them to withdraw from its jurisdiction and thereby undermine the justification for the recognition of standing of all States in respect of *erga omnes* obligations in the first place: to fill the enforcement gap.[131]

V Conclusion

State responsibility is an ever-present subject before the Court: two thirds of the Court's cases in the period 1945–2020 have involved questions of State responsibility. Throughout its history, the Court has greatly contributed to the development of this area of international law by laying its foundational principles, and by consolidating and refining its rules. While the ICJ's function as an agent of legal development in this field has been constrained by the ILC's Articles on State Responsibility, the Court remains an important player. The Court has, through its case law, assisted in fleshing out the abstract and broad rules of responsibility. It also has contributed to vesting ARSIWA with the authority they have today and, as such, to the 'encoding' of the law of State responsibility: the Articles are far from perfect, but they have the merit of having synthesised and systematised in a way that is largely acceptable to States one of the most 'elusive, unsettled and intractable'[132] areas of international law. The Court retains an important role in the growth and development of this area of international law, in particular in respect of community interest litigation for the enforcement of *erga omnes* obligations.

Further Reading

F. L. Bordin, 'State Responsibility in Advisory Proceedings: Thoughts on Judicial Propriety and Multilateralism in the *Chagos* Opinion' in T. Burri and J. Trinidad (eds.), *Decolonization and the International Court of Justice: New Directions from the Chagos Advisory Opinion* (Cambridge University Press, 2021) 95.

---

[131] By way of example, both Japan after *Whaling* and the UK after *Marshall Islands* limited their acceptance of the jurisdiction of the Court, see Tanaka, 'Reflections', 542.

[132] R. Jennings, 'Recent Developments in the International Law Commission: Its Relation to the Sources of International Law' 13 *ICLQ* (1964) 385, 396.

J. Crawford, 'The International Court of Justice and the Law of State Responsibility' in C. J. Tams and R. D. Sloane (eds.), *The Development of International Law by the International Court of Justice* (Oxford University Press, 2013) 71.

R. Higgins, 'Issues of State Responsibility before the International Court of Justice' in M. Fitzmaurice and D. Sarooshi (eds.), *Issues of State Responsibility before International Judicial Institutions* (Bloomsbury, 2004) 1.

C. J. Tams, 'Law-Making in Complex Processes: The World Court and the Modern Law of State Responsibility' in C. M. Chinkin and F. Baetens (eds.), *Sovereignty, Statehood and State Responsibility: Essays in Honour of James Crawford* (Cambridge University Press, 2015) 287.

P. Urs, 'Obligations *Erga Omnes* and the Question of Standing Before the International Court of Justice' 34(2) *Leiden Journal of International Law* (2021) 505.

Jurisdictional Immunities 19

Roger O'Keefe

I Introduction

The ICJ did not rule on the scope of the jurisdictional immunities owed by one State to another under international law until 2002,[1] when it rendered its judgment in the *Arrest Warrant* case.[2] Since then, it has been called on to consider the jurisdictional immunities applicable between States in six other cases,[3] although in only three of these has any issue of immunities proceeded to the merits.[4] The ICJ's pronouncements on interstate jurisdictional immunities were not, however, its first forays into jurisdictional

---

[1] The obligation of the host State to ensure the inviolability of the persons of foreign diplomatic agents, as distinct from their immunity from the jurisdiction of its courts, was previously at issue in *United States Diplomatic and Consular Staff in Tehran (United States of America* v. *Islamic Republic of Iran), Judgment*, ICJ Reports 1980, p. 3, especially at pp. 30–33, paras. 62–68 and pp. 35–37, paras. 76–80, but the Court was not required to rule on any controverted aspect of this inviolability. For what is nonetheless a relevant dictum by the Court in this case, see Section II.C.

[2] See *Arrest Warrant of 11 April 2000 (Democratic Republic of the Congo* v. *Belgium), Judgment*, ICJ Reports 2002, p. 3.

[3] In addition to the cases cited n. 4, see *Certain Criminal Proceedings in France (Republic of the Congo* v. *France), Provisional Measure, Order of 17 June 2003*, ICJ Reports 2003, p. 102, where it was unnecessary for the ICJ to determine the scope of the immunities at issue in the case, which was removed from the Court's list in 2010 before oral argument on the merits; *Questions relating to the Seizure and Retention of Certain Documents and Data (Timor-Leste* v. *Australia), Provisional Measures, Order of 3 March 2014*, ICJ Reports 2014, p. 147 at pp. 152–153, paras. 24–28, by necessary implication dismissing as implausible the applicant's arguments as to the alleged immunity and inviolability of what it alleged to be its property; *Certain Iranian Assets (Islamic Republic of Iran* v. *United States of America), Preliminary Objections, Judgment*, ICJ Reports 2019, p. 7, where the Court ruled that it lacked jurisdiction over the issues of immunity raised by the applicant. As to the last, see Philippa Webb, Chapter 10, 'The ICJ and Other Courts and Tribunals: Integration and Fragmentation', pp. [2–3].

[4] See *Certain Questions of Mutual Assistance in Criminal Matters (Djibouti* v. *France), Judgment*, ICJ Reports 2008, p. 177; *Jurisdictional Immunities of the State (Germany* v. *Italy: Greece intervening), Judgment*, ICJ Reports 2012, p. 99. In *Immunities and Criminal Proceedings (Equatorial Guinea* v. *France), Preliminary Objections, Judgment*,

immunities as such. The Court had already delivered advisory opinions, in 1989 and 1999, on aspects of the jurisdictional immunities owed by member States to the United Nations.[5]

What the ICJ has said on these different occasions has affirmed basic aspects of the international law of jurisdictional immunities, elucidated a few more specific points, and variously crystallised, consolidated, and catalysed the further development of important customary rules on controversial issues in relation to civil and criminal proceedings respectively. In the process, the Court has reasserted in the interstate context an orthodox, some might say conservative vision of the role of jurisdictional immunities in the international legal order in the face of challenges to it.

II The Court's Case-Law

A Basic Aspects of the Law of Jurisdictional Immunities

In a rejection of the isolated but persistent view[6] that a State's grant to another State of immunity from the jurisdiction of its courts is no more than a matter of comity and as such discretionary, the ICJ has underlined that a State is obliged by customary international law to accord the immunity *ratione materiae* known as State immunity to another State, in

ICJ Reports 2018, p. 292, the Court, ruling that it lacked jurisdiction over most of the issues of immunity raised by the applicant, held that it enjoyed jurisdiction in relation to the inviolability and immunity from attachment of certain putative diplomatic premises. See also Philippa Webb, Chapter 10, 'The ICJ and Other Courts and Tribunals: Integration and Fragmentation', p. [2]. In the event, the Court's judgment on the merits did not deal with any question of inviolability or immunity as such but solely with whether the premises formed part of the premises of the diplomatic mission, which the Court held they did not. See *Immunities and Criminal Proceedings (Equatorial Guinea v. France), Judgment*, ICJ Reports 2020, p. 300.

[5] See *Applicability of Article VI, Section 22, of the Convention on the Privileges and Immunities of the United Nations, Advisory Opinion*, ICJ Reports 1989, p. 177; *Difference Relating to Immunity from Legal Process of a Special Rapporteur of the Commission on Human Rights, Advisory Opinion*, ICJ Reports 1999, p. 62.

[6] See e.g., *Verlinden BV v. Central Bank of Nigeria*, 461 US 480, 486 (1983), *Dole Food Co. v. Patrickson*, 538 US 468, 479 (2003), and *Republic of Austria v. Altmann*, 541 US 677, 689, 696 (2004), although it is unclear whether the 'comity' referred to is between the USA and foreign States or between the US judiciary and the US executive; *Democratic Republic of the Congo v. FG Hemisphere Associates LLC (No. 1)*, 147 ILR 376 at 451, para. 228 and 452, para. 231 (2011).

respect of both the State itself in its different guises and its property, and that the other State conversely enjoys a right under customary international law to such immunity.[7] In the process, the Court has endorsed the classical position that State immunity, which it has said occupies 'an important place in international law and international relations', derives 'from the principle of sovereign equality of States', which it has described as 'one of the fundamental principles of the international legal order'.[8] The ICJ has equally made clear that a State is obliged by customary international law to accord a more plenary immunity *ratione personae* from the jurisdiction of its courts and inviolability from measures of personal constraint to certain officials who represent another State in its international relations and that the other State conversely enjoys a right under customary international law to see those officials benefit from this immunity and inviolability.[9] As explained by the Court, this broader immunity *ratione personae* and inviolability is founded on the pragmatic need 'to ensure the effective performance' by those officials 'of their functions on behalf of their respective States'.[10]

The ICJ has repeatedly affirmed the purely procedural nature of the jurisdictional immunities required by international law.[11] In relation to State immunity, the Court has stressed that the rules on immunity 'are confined to determining whether or not the courts of one State may exercise jurisdiction in respect of another State' and 'do not bear upon the question whether the conduct in respect of which the proceedings are brought was lawful or unlawful'.[12] In the context of the immunity of State officials from foreign criminal jurisdiction, it has underlined that '[i]mmunity from criminal jurisdiction and individual criminal responsibility are quite separate concepts', the first 'procedural in nature', the second 'a question of substantive law', so that jurisdictional immunity 'may well bar prosecution for a certain period or for certain offences' but

---

[7] *Jurisdictional Immunities* at p. 123, para. 56.

[8] Ibid. at para. 57. See also *Immunities and Criminal Proceedings* at p. 321, para. 93 and ibid., joint diss. op. Xue, Sebutinde, Robinson and Kateka at pp. 346–348, paras. 17 and 23–25.

[9] See *Arrest Warrant* at pp. 20–30, paras. 51–71; *Certain Questions of Mutual Assistance* at pp. 236–244, paras. 170–197.

[10] *Arrest Warrant* at p. 21, para. 53. See also, more generally, ibid. at pp. 21–22, paras. 53–55.

[11] See ibid. at p. 25, para. 60; *Jurisdictional Immunities* at pp. 124–125, paras. 58 and 60, p. 140, para. 93, and p. 143, para. 100.

[12] *Jurisdictional Immunities* at p. 140, para. 93. See similarly ibid. at p. 125, para. 60.

'cannot exonerate the person to whom it applies from all criminal responsibility'.[13] Similarly, the Court has noted that the immunity from legal process of an official or agent of the United Nations 'is distinct from the issue of compensation for any damages incurred as a result of acts performed by the United Nations [as such] or by its [officials or] agents acting in their official capacity'.[14]

A corollary of the procedural nature of jurisdictional immunities emphasised by the ICJ is the necessarily preliminary character of any question as to their applicability.[15] In the words of the Court, immunity issues 'must be decided expeditiously *in limine litis*'.[16] That is, 'national courts have to determine questions of immunity at the outset of the proceedings, before consideration of the merits'.[17]

B State Immunity from Civil Jurisdiction

Immunity from Proceedings for Death or Personal Injury

In *Jurisdictional Immunities*, the ICJ was asked to rule on the existence of a customary 'territorial tort' exception to State immunity from foreign civil proceedings, an exception posited in the only two treaties on State immunity and in the national law of a wide range of States in respect of claims alleging acts by another State occasioning death or personal injury or damage to or loss of tangible property in the territory of the forum State.[18] In the event, the Court did not decide 'whether there is in customary international law a "[territorial] tort exception" to State immunity applicable to *acta jure imperii* in general'[19] but instead restricted its ruling to proceedings in respect of acts performed by another State's armed forces and State organs working in cooperation with them in the territory of the forum State in the course of conducting an armed conflict.[20] On the basis

---

[13] *Arrest Warrant* at p. 25, para. 60.
[14] *Immunity from Legal Process of a Special Rapporteur* at p. 88, para. 66.
[15] See ibid. at para. 63; *Jurisdictional Immunities* at p. 136, para. 82.
[16] *Immunity from Legal Process of a Special Rapporteur* at p. 88, para. 63.
[17] *Jurisdictional Immunities* at p. 145, para. 106. See also ibid. at p. 136, para. 82.
[18] For the two treaty provisions, see United Nations Convention on Jurisdictional Immunities of States and Their Property, New York, 2 December 2004, not in force, UN doc. A/RES/59/38, Annex (16 December 2004), Art. 12; European Convention on State Immunity, Basel, 16 May 1972, in force 11 June 1976, 1495 UNTS 182, Art. 11.
[19] *Jurisdictional Immunities* at pp. 127–128, para. 65.   [20] Ibid. at p. 128, para. 65.

of an analysis of State practice and *opinio juris*, it held that 'customary international law continues to require that a State be accorded immunity in proceedings for torts allegedly committed on the territory of another State by its armed forces and other organs of State in the course of conducting an armed conflict'.[21] Additionally, although not required to decide the point, the Court ventured the further view, not confined to armed conflict, that various national judicial decisions and a judgment of a Grand Chamber of the European Court of Human Rights suggested 'that a State is entitled to immunity in respect of *acta jure imperii* committed by its armed forces on the territory of another State'.[22]

The ICJ was also called on in *Jurisdictional Immunities* to decide the controversial question whether there existed an exception to State immunity from foreign civil proceedings where the claimant alleged serious violations of international humanitarian law or international human rights law or of peremptory norms of general international law (*jus cogens*). It prefaced its analysis with the observation, premised on the preliminary character of the question of jurisdictional immunity, that 'the proposition that the availability of immunity will be to some extent dependent upon the gravity of the unlawful act presents a logical problem', insofar as, '[i]f immunity were to be dependent upon the State actually having committed a serious violation of international human rights law or the law of armed conflict, then it would become necessary for the national court to hold an enquiry into the merits in order to determine whether it had jurisdiction'.[23] Proceeding to examine 'a substantial body of State practice', the Court concluded that 'customary international law does not treat a State's entitlement to immunity as dependent on the gravity of the act of which it is accused or the peremptory nature of the rule which it is alleged to have violated'.[24] Nor, in the eyes of the Court, was there any logical conflict 'between a rule, or rules, of *jus cogens* and the rule of customary

---

[21] Ibid. at p. 135, para. 78.
[22] Ibid. at p. 132, para. 72, citing, among others, *McElhinney* v. *Ireland*, ECHR Reports 2001-XI, p. 39.
[23] Ibid. at p. 136, para. 82.
[24] Ibid. at p. 137, para. 84. See also ibid. at p. 142, para. 97. The Court emphasised (ibid. at p. 139, para. 91) that it was 'addressing only the immunity of the State itself from the jurisdiction of courts of other States', since 'the question whether, and if so to what extent, immunity might apply in criminal proceedings against an official of the State [was] not in issue'.

international law which requires one State to accord immunity to another'.[25] Since the rules governing State immunity were 'confined to determining whether or not the courts of one State may exercise jurisdiction in respect of another State' and did 'not bear upon the question whether the conduct in respect of which the proceedings are brought was lawful or unlawful', 'recognizing the immunity of a foreign State in accordance with international law [did] not amount to recognizing as lawful a situation created by the breach of a *jus cogens* rule ... or [to] rendering aid or assistance in maintaining that situation'.[26] 'To the extent', furthermore, 'that it [was] argued that no rule which is not of the status of *jus cogens* may be applied if to do so would hinder the enforcement of a *jus cogens* rule, even in the absence of a direct conflict', the Court saw 'no basis for such a proposition'.[27] It equally found 'no basis' in State practice to suggest 'that international law makes the entitlement of a State to immunity dependent upon the existence of effective alternative means of securing redress'.[28]

Immunity from Proceedings for Recognition and Enforcement of a Foreign Judgment

The ICJ has clarified in the context of State immunity from civil jurisdiction that proceedings in the courts of a State for the recognition and enforcement – or, more precisely, for the recognition and declaration as enforceable – of a foreign judgment rendered against another State implicate that other State's immunity from jurisdiction *stricto sensu* (or, synonymously, its immunity from proceedings), rather than the immunity of that State's property from post-judgment measures of constraint like attachment and execution.[29] Moreover, such proceedings are to be treated for immunity purposes as a claim initiated against that other State in the forum State in respect of the matter adjudicated in the foreign judgment.[30]

---

[25] Ibid. at p. 140, para. 93.

[26] Ibid. at p. 141, para. 94, referring to Articles on Responsibility of States for Internationally Wrongful Acts, GA res. 56/83, 12 December 2001, Annex, Art. 41.

[27] Ibid. at para. 95. The Court noted (ibid. at pp. 141–142, para. 96) that the argument that '*jus cogens* displac[es] the law of State immunity' had been rejected by a range of national courts and by the European Court of Human Rights (see *Al-Adsani* v. *United Kingdom*, 123 ILR 24 at 42, para. 61 and 43, para. 66 (2011); *Kalogeropoulou* v. *Greece and Germany*, 129 ILR 537 at 546 and 547 (2002)) and was not reflected in national legislation.

[28] *Jurisdictional Immunities* at p. 143, para. 101.   [29] Ibid. at p. 150, para. 124.

[30] Ibid. at p. 151, paras. 128–129.

As such, they implicate the other State's immunity from proceedings in the same way as would have proceedings in the forum State on the merits of the claim.[31]

Immunity from Measures of Constraint against State Property

The ICJ has affirmed as a matter of customary international law that, while they are both manifestations of State immunity, a State's immunity from any order by a foreign court granting some measure of constraint, such as arrest, attachment or execution, against its property in connection with judicial proceedings is distinct from and more plenary than its immunity from foreign proceedings themselves.[32] The rules governing the one, the Court has explained, must be applied separately from the rules governing the other.[33]

When it comes to immunity specifically from post-judgment measures of constraint, such as attachment and execution, against the property of another State, the Court – as well as affirming customary exceptions in respect of express consent and consent implied by that other State's allocation of the property for the satisfaction of the claim at issue – has held that a customary exception to immunity exists where the property in question is 'in use for an activity not pursuing government non-commercial purposes'.[34] In stating, moreover, that, for this so-called 'commercial activity' exception to apply, the property 'must be in use' for such an activity, the Court appears necessarily to have excluded the alternative

---

[31] Ibid. at pp. 151–152, para. 130.   [32] Ibid. at p. 146, para. 113.

[33] Ibid. at p. 147, para. 113. Even more fundamentally, the Court has arguably implicitly affirmed that a State's jurisdictional immunity in respect of its property pertains strictly to the amenability of State property to pre-judgment and post-judgment measures of constraint in connection with judicial proceedings and does not serve to prohibit the seizure and retention of State property prior to the initiation of judicial proceedings or unconnected with them. See *Seizure and Retention of Certain Documents and Data* at p. 153, para. 28, seeming by implication to dismiss as implausible the argument of Timor-Leste, advanced in the oral pleadings and recalled ibid. at p. 152, para. 24, that State immunity served to render internationally wrongful Australia's seizure and retention of documents and data belonging to Timor-Leste, although query the precise import of the words 'at least'. Insofar, moreover, as the seizure and retention of State property prior to the initiation of judicial proceedings or unconnected with them may implicate the legally separate question of the property's inviolability, the Court has also arguably implicitly affirmed that no general inviolability of State property can plausibly be said to exist under international law. See ibid. at p. 153, para. 28, seeming by implication to accept Australia's argument to this effect recalled ibid. at p. 152, para. 25.

[34] *Jurisdictional Immunities* at p. 148, para. 118.

limb of the exception as formulated in Article 19(c) of the United Nations
Convention on Jurisdictional Immunities of States and Their Property
2004, to which the Court referred,[35] as well as in the legislation of some
States, which permits post-judgment measures of constraint where
the property of the other State, although not currently in such use, is
intended for it.[36]

C The Immunity of State Officials from Foreign Criminal Jurisdiction

Immunity *Ratione Personae* and Inviolability

In *Arrest Warrant*, the ICJ ruled that a State was obliged to accord the
serving minister for foreign affairs of another State absolute immunity
ratione personae from the criminal jurisdiction of its courts and to inviolability from measures of personal constraint such as arrest.[37] Although the
Court presented its conclusion as one of customary international law,[38] it
adduced no State practice or *opinio juris*, instead arguing teleologically
and analogically. The immunities that as a matter of customary international law served to protect ministers for foreign affairs did so, the
Court reasoned, 'to ensure the effective performance of their functions
on behalf of their respective States'.[39] 'In the performance of these functions', the Court continued, a minister for foreign affairs, like a diplomat,
'is frequently required to travel internationally, and thus must be in a
position freely to do so whenever the need should arise'.[40] '[A]ccordingly',
it concluded, 'the functions of a Minister for Foreign Affairs are such that,
throughout the duration of his or her office, he or she when abroad enjoys
full immunity from criminal jurisdiction and inviolability'.[41] This immunity and inviolability were without regard, the Court specified, to the
capacity, public or private, in which the impugned acts were performed
or, indeed, to whether they were performed during or prior to the minister's

---

[35] See ibid. at para. 116.
[36] Although the Court expressly considered it unnecessary to decide whether all of Art. 19 of
the 2004 UN Convention was consonant with current customary international law (ibid. at
para. 117), its statement that State property 'must be in use' for an activity not pursuing
governmental non-commercial purposes (ibid. at para. 118), which it described as a
'condition that has to be satisfied before any measure of constraint may be taken against
property belonging to a foreign State' (ibid.), is incompatible with the alternative that the
property may instead be merely intended for such use.
[37] *Arrest Warrant* at p. 22, para. 54.   [38] See ibid. at pp. 21–22, paras. 52 and 53.
[39] Ibid. at p. 21, para. 53.   [40] Ibid.   [41] Ibid. at p. 22, para. 54.

term of office.[42] Nor could any distinction be drawn between official and private visits to foreign States.[43] While the Court noted, moreover, that it was called on to address the immunity and inviolability only of a minister for foreign affairs,[44] it nonetheless alluded to the implicitly cognate immunity and inviolability from which heads of State and heads of government were protected under international law[45] and highlighted in passing the analogous representative capacities under international law of all three officials, which were taken to speak for the State solely by virtue of their office.[46] Nor did the Court say that other officers of State did not benefit from absolute immunity *ratione personae* and from inviolability. Indeed, it considered it 'firmly established' that 'certain holders of high-ranking office in a State', of which the head of State, head of government, and minister for foreign affairs were cited as examples, 'enjoy immunities from jurisdiction in other States'.[47] It subsequently specified, however, in *Certain Questions of Mutual Assistance* that at least a senior prosecuting magistrate and the head of national security did not benefit under customary international law from immunity *ratione personae* from foreign criminal jurisdiction,[48] affirming at the same time that a serving head of State did.[49]

What was ultimately at issue in *Arrest Warrant* was the contested question whether an exception existed under customary international law to immunity *ratione personae* from foreign criminal jurisdiction and to inviolability from foreign measures of personal constraint when the allegations against a minister for foreign affairs were of war crimes and crimes against humanity. In the event, having avowedly 'carefully examined State practice', the Court declared itself 'unable to deduce ... that there exists under customary international law any form of exception to the rule according immunity from criminal jurisdiction and inviolability to incumbent Ministers for Foreign Affairs ... where they are suspected of having committed war crimes and crimes against humanity'.[50] It added that, 'although various international conventions on the prevention and punishment of certain serious crimes impose on States obligations of

---

[42] Ibid. at para. 55.   [43] Ibid.   [44] Ibid. at p. 21, para. 51.   [45] See ibid.
[46] See ibid. at para. 53.   [47] Ibid. at para. 51.
[48] *Certain Questions of Mutual Assistance* at pp. 243–244, para. 194.
[49] Ibid. at pp. 236–237, para. 170 and p. 238, para. 174.
[50] *Arrest Warrant* at p. 24, para. 58.

prosecution or extradition [and] requir[e] them to extend their criminal jurisdiction, [this] in no way affects immunities under customary international law', which 'remain opposable before the courts of a foreign State, even where those courts exercise such a jurisdiction under these conventions'.[51] Furthermore, in a subsequent dictum in *Jurisdictional Immunities*, the Court recalled its judgment in *Arrest Warrant* as one where, 'albeit without express reference to the concept of *jus cogens*', it effectively held that 'the fact that a Minister for Foreign Affairs was accused of criminal violations of rules which undoubtedly possess the character of *jus cogens* did not deprive the Democratic Republic of the Congo of the entitlement which it possessed as a matter of customary international law to demand immunity on his behalf'.[52]

As to what is barred by immunity *ratione personae* and inviolability, the ICJ asserted in *Arrest Warrant*, without distinguishing between the two, that 'immunity and ... inviolability protect the individual concerned against any act of authority of another State which would hinder him or her in the performance of his or her duties'.[53] This statement was reiterated and applied to a head of State in *Certain Questions of Mutual Assistance*,[54] where the Court continued that 'the determining factor in assessing whether or not there has been an attack on the immunity' – by which it meant both the immunity from jurisdiction and the inviolability[55] – 'of the Head of State lies in the subjection of the latter to a constraining act of authority'.[56] Applying this later dictum, the Court ruled in the second case that a foreign criminal court's issue, in relation to a State official, of a summons to appear as witness did not violate the immunity from jurisdiction or inviolability owed in respect of that official when the summons represented not a measure of constraint but merely an invitation to testify that the official could freely accept or decline.[57] This was *a fortiori* so as regards a summons that expressly sought the official's consent.[58] As specifically regards inviolability from measures of personal constraint, the Court had previously taken pains to point out that a State's observance

[51] Ibid. at p. 25, para. 59.
[52] *Jurisdictional Immunities* at p. 141, para. 95, citing *Arrest Warrant* at p. 24, para. 58 and p. 33, para. 78.
[53] *Arrest Warrant* at p. 22, para. 54.
[54] See *Certain Questions of Mutual Assistance* at p. 237, para. 170.
[55] Ibid., see the sentence immediately prior to para. 170   [56] Ibid.
[57] See ibid. at para. 171.   [58] See ibid. at p. 240, para. 179.

of its obligation to ensure this inviolability did not imply that a beneficiary 'caught in the act of committing an assault or other offence may not, on occasion, be briefly arrested by the police of the receiving State in order to prevent the commission of the particular crime'.[59]

Immunity *Ratione Materiae*

The ICJ has implicitly affirmed that the immunity *ratione materiae* from foreign criminal jurisdiction from which all serving and former State officials benefit under customary international law is a manifestation of State immunity – in other words, of the immunity from the jurisdiction of foreign courts of the official's State itself, of which the official, when acting in that capacity, comprises an organ.[60]

More concretely, the Court in *Arrest Warrant*, although not required to address the issue, went out of its way to refer in a fleeting dictum to the scope of the customary immunity *ratione materiae* from which serving and former State officials benefit, explaining that 'one State may try a former Minister for Foreign Affairs of another State in respect of acts committed prior or subsequent to his or her period of office, as well as in respect of acts committed during that period of office in a private capacity'.[61] In so putting it, the Court necessarily implied *a contrario* that, in contrast to the situation in relation to civil proceedings, the State immunity that may serve to bar foreign criminal proceedings against any current or former State official is not circumscribed by the distinction between those acts performed in an official capacity which can be characterised as exercises of sovereign authority (*acta jure imperii*) and those acts which, although performed in an official capacity, are the sort of thing a private person could do (*acta jure gestionis*), insofar as the distinction could have logical purchase in the criminal context in the first place. Rather, it extends to all acts performed by State officials in their official or 'public' capacity, meaning in their capacity as State officials.[62] The Court's dictum also

---

[59] *United States Diplomatic and Consular Staff in Tehran* at p. 40, para. 86.

[60] See *Certain Questions of Mutual Assistance* at p. 242, para. 188 and p. 243, paras. 191 and 193; *Jurisdictional Immunities* at p. 139, para. 91.

[61] *Arrest Warrant* at p. 25, para. 61.

[62] The same was implied in *Certain Questions of Mutual Assistance* at p. 243, para. 141, where the Court 'observe[d] that it ha[d] not been "concretely verified" before it that the acts which were the subject of the summonses as *témoins assistés* issued by France were indeed acts within the scope of [the officials'] duties as organs of State'.

necessarily implies that immunity *ratione materiae* remains available as a bar to the foreign prosecution of a serving or former State official for an international crime allegedly committed by that official in anything other than a private capacity.[63]

D The Immunity of Experts on Mission for the United Nations

The ICJ has had two occasions on which to interpret and apply Article VI, section 22 of the Convention on the Privileges and Immunities of the United Nations 1946. Section 22 provides, with respect to experts – other than officials of the Organisation – performing missions for the United Nations, for what the provision's chapeau refers to as 'such . . . immunities as are necessary for the independent exercise of their functions during the period of their missions, including the time spent on journeys in connec-tion with their missions'.[64] More specifically, it provides for the immunity of such experts from all judicial process 'in respect of words spoken or written and acts done by them in the course of the performance of their mission' and for their inviolability from arrest and detention.[65]

The Court has held that the decisive factor in determining whether a person who does not have the status of a UN official is to be considered an expert on mission for the UN within the meaning of section 22 is whether 'they have been entrusted with a mission by the United Nations';[66] that the word 'mission' refers to the 'tasks entrusted to' an expert, 'whether or not they involve travel',[67] so that section 22 'is

---

[63] Recall also the Court's earlier pronouncement in *Arrest Warrant* at p. 25, para. 59, in which it stressed that, 'although various international conventions on the prevention and pun-ishment of certain serious crimes impose on States obligations of prosecution or extradi-tion [and] require[e] them to extend their criminal jurisdiction', this 'in no way affects immunities under customary international law', which 'remain opposable before the courts of a foreign State, even where those courts exercise such a jurisdiction under these conventions' – the reference to 'immunities under customary international law' not being restricted to the immunity *ratione personae* of a serving minister for foreign affairs at issue in the case.
[64] Convention on Privileges and Immunities of the United Nations, New York, 13 February 1946, in force 17 September 1946, 1 UNTS 15, corrigendum 90 UNTS 327, Art. VI, s. 22.
[65] Ibid., Art. VI, s. 22(b) and (a) respectively, the latter using the term 'immunity' for inviolability.
[66] *Immunity from Legal Process of a Special Rapporteur* at p. 83, para. 43. See also *Applicability of Article VI, Section 22* at p. 196, para. 52.
[67] *Applicability of Article VI, Section 22* at p. 195, para. 49.

applicable to every expert on mission, whether or not he travels';[68] and that the immunity and inviolability from which experts on mission for the UN benefit by virtue of section 22 is opposable to their State of nationality and, where it differs, to their State of residency.[69] The Court has also noted the 'pivotal role' played by the UN Secretary-General in determining whether, on the facts of any case, words spoken or written or acts done by an expert on mission for the UN were in the course of the performance of the latter's mission, thereby requiring the grant of immunity from all judicial process.[70] Notification to a member State of the Secretary-General's finding that particular words spoken or written or acts done by an expert were in the course of the performance of his or her mission creates, according to the Court, 'a presumption which can only be set aside for the most compelling reasons and is thus to be given the greatest weight by national courts'.[71]

In a dictum equally applicable as a matter of logic to all forms of immunity from foreign judicial proceedings, the Court has stated that the immunity from judicial process from which experts on mission for the UN benefit requires that they be held harmless for any costs imposed on them by a foreign court.[72]

III The Court's Impact

The ICJ was a latecomer to the international law of jurisdictional immunities. In the interstate context, the general contours of the customary international law of State immunity from foreign civil jurisdiction had developed over centuries, with the more recent evolution from the absolute to the restrictive doctrine being driven both by unilateral moves on the part of national courts and legislatures and by States' contributions and reactions to more coordinated, international efforts, public and private, towards the progressive development and eventual binding codification of

---

[68] Ibid. at para. 50. See also ibid. at p. 196, para. 52.

[69] Ibid. at pp. 195–196, paras. 51–52, excepting where that State has entered a valid reservation to Art. VI, s. 22. See also *Immunity from Legal Process of a Special Rapporteur* at p. 84, para. 46, noting the agreement on this point of all participants in the proceedings.

[70] *Immunity from Legal Process of a Special Rapporteur* at p. 84, para. 50.

[71] Ibid. at p. 87, para. 61.   [72] Ibid. at p. 88, para. 64.

a new international law of State immunity.[73] To these developments the Court has simply lent its imprimatur, in effect setting the seal on the emergent rules and in the process usefully clarifying certain points. The same goes, *mutatis mutandis*, for the Court's pronouncements on the Convention on the Privileges and Immunities of the United Nations, even if the history of this multilateral treaty is very different.

In contrast, in relation to foreign civil proceedings against States specifically for alleged violations of international humanitarian or human rights law and in particular of *jus cogens*, the ICJ was called on to adjudicate against the backdrop of a divided body of State practice,[74] effectively placing it in the position of final arbiter of a controverted question of customary international law. In this context, its ruling in *Jurisdictional Immunities*, while prefigured by the European Court of Human Rights and the majority of preceding decisions in national courts,[75] has been decisive, drawing a line under the matter in terms of positive international law.[76] As

---

[73] See, generally, G. Hafner, 'Historical Background to the Convention', in R. O'Keefe and C. J. Tams (eds.), *The United Nations Convention on Jurisdictional Immunities of States and Their Property: A Commentary* (Oxford University Press, 2013), p. 1; H. Fox and P. Webb, *The Law of State Immunity*, revised and updated 3rd ed. (Oxford University Press, 2015), chaps. 6 and 9; Y. Xiaodong, *State Immunity in International Law* (Cambridge University Press, 2012), chap. 1. As for the particular immunities from which serving and former diplomats, consuls, heads of State, and members of special missions benefit under international law, their genesis and the shaping of their basic contours similarly owe nothing to the Court, being the products of largely the same processes as gave rise to the modern law of State immunity. That said, the Court's reconceptualisation of head-of-State immunity in *Arrest Warrant* as akin to diplomatic immunity, including in the pragmatic reasons that underpin it, rather than as an instantiation of State immunity, has significant implications, in particular for the content of head-of-State immunity from civil proceedings. See R. O'Keefe, 'Article 3', in O'Keefe and Tams, *The United Nations Convention*, p. 73 at pp. 84–88.

[74] See R. O'Keefe, 'Jurisdictional Immunities', in C. J. Tams and J. Sloan (eds.), *The Development of International Law by the International Court of Justice* (Oxford University Press, 2013) 107 at pp. 137–140.

[75] See *Al-Adsani* at 42, para. 61 and 43, para. 66 and *Kalogeropoulou* at 547, as well as the national case-law cited in O'Keefe, 'Jurisdictional Immunities', p. 137.

[76] See O'Keefe, 'Jurisdictional Immunities', pp. 144–146, as well as *Jones* v. *United Kingdom*, 168 ILR 369 at 425–426 (2014), *Li* v. *Zhou and Attorney General of the Commonwealth*, 168 ILR 437 at 463–464, paras. 54–55 and 469, paras. 74–75 (2014), *Estate of Kazemi* v. *Islamic Republic of Iran*, 159 ILR 299 at 344–345, paras. 154–155 and 157 (2014), and *Federal Republic of Germany* v. *Philipp*, Case No. 19-351, Opinion, 3 February 2021, slip opinion at 10–11 (US Supreme Court). But cf., as a matter of Italian constitutional law, *Judgment No. 238/2014*, 168 ILR 529 (2014); and, as a matter of South Korean constitutional law, Case No. 2016 Ga-Hap 505092, Judgment, 8 January 2021 (Seoul Central District Court).

regards the uncodified immunity *ratione personae* of certain State officials from foreign criminal jurisdiction, particularly in respect of allegations of international crimes, the ICJ was drawn into the controversy while State practice was still sparse,[77] enabling it in *Arrest Warrant* actively to shape the emerging law, including eventually via the subsequent work – triggered in no small part and strongly influenced by the Court – of the International Law Commission. Even if the Court was pushing at an open door, it is still largely in response to its ruling and dicta in *Arrest Warrant* that it was rapidly accepted by States as a matter of customary international law not only that a State's head of State, head of government, and minister for foreign affairs benefit from absolute immunity *ratione personae* from foreign criminal jurisdiction and from inviolability from foreign measures of personal constraint[78] but also that no exception exists in this regard in relation to allegations of international crimes, including those that the forum State is obliged by treaty to prosecute.[79] At the same time, the Court's reference to holders of 'high-ranking office' and its repeated assimilation of ministers for foreign affairs to heads of State and heads of government has been taken as a cue by States that the beneficiaries under uncodified customary international law of immunity *ratione personae* from criminal jurisdiction and of inviolability are few.[80]

More generally and fundamentally, the judgments in *Arrest Warrant* and *Jurisdictional Immunities* have been influential in turning the political tide of what was touted Whig–historically as the inevitability of the

---

[77] See O'Keefe, 'Jurisdictional Immunities', pp. 115–116 and 120–121.

[78] See ibid., pp. 117–118. See also draft art. 3 of the draft articles on immunity of State officials from foreign criminal jurisdiction provisionally adopted so far by the International Law Commission (ILC), *Report of the International Law Commission, Sixty-ninth session (1 May–2 June and 3 July–4 August 2017)*, UN doc. A/72/10, p. 175, para. 140; *Prosecutor v. Al-Bashir*, ICC-02/05-01/09-397-Corr, Appeals Chamber, Judgment in the Jordan Referral re Al-Bashir Appeal, 6 May 2019 at para. 101 (head of State).

[79] See O'Keefe, 'Jurisdictional Immunities', pp. 122–123, as well as *Minister of Justice and Constitutional Development* v. *Southern African Litigation Centre* (867/15) [2016] ZASCA 17 at paras. 67–84. See also draft art. 4(2) of the draft articles on immunity of State officials from foreign criminal jurisdiction provisionally adopted so far by the ILC, *Report of the International Law Commission, Sixty-ninth session*, p. 175, para. 140.

[80] See O'Keefe, 'Jurisdictional Immunities', pp. 119–120. Indeed, draft art. 3 of the draft articles on immunity of State officials from foreign criminal jurisdiction provisionally adopted so far by the ILC limits their number to the head of State, head of government, and minister for foreign affairs, although the divided reaction to this of States in the Sixth Committee of the UN General Assembly indicates that a consensus is yet to emerge as to whether customary international law is so restrictive.

abrogation of the immunity of serving and former State officials from foreign criminal proceedings for alleged international crimes and of State immunity from foreign civil proceedings for alleged violations of international humanitarian or human rights law and more specifically *jus cogens*. Although in reality the occasional reformist statute or judgment of a national court always belied the preponderance of States' support for the status quo, the temper of the millennial times led many activists, scholars, and activist scholars from the mid-1990s to imagine that the fusty old international law of sovereign equality and of the sacrosanctity of a State's representatives abroad would give way in national courts before long to a new international law of accountability, individual and State, for violations of rules of international law for the protection of the human person. The ICJ's judgment in *Arrest Warrant*, with its insistence on the necessity of the unencumbered conduct of diplomacy regardless of the international character of the crimes alleged, threw cold water on this assumption. The Court's later judgment in *Jurisdictional Immunities*, capping a line of judicial State practice and international jurisprudence founded on strict respect for the sovereign equality of States whatever the putative internationally wrongful acts, did so perhaps even more. This vindication of the classical paradigm of the place of jurisdictional immunities in the international legal order has been seized on since by many States, especially non-western ones, to oppose any unilateralist and most multilateralist progressive development of the international law of jurisdictional immunities insofar as it might serve to expose them and their representatives to greater risk of foreign judicial proceedings, in particular in western courts. While various important aspects of these immunities remain unsettled,[81] the ICJ has considerably strengthened the hand of the orthodox majority.

IV Conclusion

The ICJ has variously restated, elaborated, and stimulated the evolution of the international law of jurisdictional immunities, affirming in the process

---

[81] Among these is whether immunity *ratione materiae* remains available as a bar to the foreign prosecution of a serving or former State official for an international crime allegedly committed by that official in an official capacity, as touched on by the Court in *Arrest Warrant* at p. 25, para. 61. See Section II.C.

a traditional vision of interstate relations based on free channels of intercourse and mutual non-interference. Its pronouncements have been valuable and in varied measure influential, both doctrinally and politically. Although coming late to the game, in the field of immunities the Court has proved a major player.

Further Reading

J. Foakes, *The Position of Heads of State and Senior Officials in International Law* (Oxford University Press, 2014).

H. Fox and P. Webb, *The Law of State Immunity*, revised and updated 3rd edn (Oxford University Press, 2015).

R. O'Keefe, 'Jurisdictional Immunities' in C. J. Tams and J. Sloan (eds.), *The Development of International Law by the International Court of Justice* (Oxford University Press, 2013) 107.

R. O'Keefe and C. J. Tams (eds.), *The United Nations Convention on Jurisdictional Immunities of States and Their Property: A Commentary* (Oxford University Press, 2013).

A. Orakhelashvili (ed.), *Research Handbook on Jurisdiction and Immunities in International Law* (Edward Elgar Publishing, 2015).

A. Peters, E. Lagrange, S. Oeter and C. Tomuschat (eds.), *Immunities in the Age of Global Constitutionalism* (Brill, 2014).

T. Ruys and N. Angelet (eds.), *The Cambridge Handbook of Immunities and International Law* (Cambridge University Press, 2019).

V. Volpe, A. Peters and S. Battini (eds.), *Remedies against Immunity? Reconciling International and Domestic Law after the Italian Constitutional Court's Sentenza 238/2014* (Berlin: Springer, 2021).

Y. Xiaodong, *State Immunity in International Law* (Cambridge University Press, 2012).

20 The Use of Force

Alejandro Chehtman

I Introduction

This chapter presents a succinct overview of the main contributions of the International Court of Justice (ICJ) to the use of force. It centrally addresses the opinions of the Court on a number of key issues, such as the prohibition to use force and its potential exceptions, most notably the law on individual and collective self-defence. It seeks to identify the main conceptualisations, inconsistencies, disagreements, and limitations of the Court's opinions, as well as their evolution over the years. It ultimately argues that although the initial influence of the Court was substantial, it has faded significantly over the years as the unfortunate outcome of the of what seems a conscious, even strategic decision of its judges.

A good way to start our analysis is to look at some descriptive statistics. The ICJ made explicit reference to use of force or military operations in thirteen contentious cases and four advisory cases.[1] These issues were brought to the Court in twenty-one further contentious cases on which it did not arrive at a decision on the merits.[2] The bulk of the relevant legal propositions on the use of force, however, stems from only six cases (four contentious and two advisory proceedings): the *Corfu Channel* case, the *Nicaragua* case, the *Oil Platforms* case, the *Armed Activities* case, and the Advisory Opinions on *Nuclear Weapons* and on the *Construction of the*

Thanks to Francisco Quintana, Justina Uriburu and to the editors of this volume for comments and suggestions to a previous version of this chapter. Clara Damianovich and Patricio López Turconi provided excellent research assistance. All mistakes are my own.

[1] The ICJ also gave two advisory opinions on UN peace operations which directly relate to the use of force, *Reparations from Injuries Suffered in the Service of the United Nations* (1949), and the case on *Certain Expenses of the United Nations (Article 17, paragraph 2, of the Charter)* (1962).

[2] These cases amount to a significant 25 per cent of the contentious cases brought before the ICJ, and about 15 per cent of the advisory opinions.

Wall. Significantly, in its contentious case-law the Court never found that a concrete resort to force satisfied the requirements of permissible use of force under international law, and it often indicated that conduct under its scrutiny failed to satisfy more than one of those requirements. In all these decisions it ultimately upheld (explicit or implicitly) the prohibition on the use of force.

Voting patterns are also eloquent. Cases were generally decided by a significant majority: of the ninety-three relevant votes, seventy-five judges voted with the majority (80.65 per cent), while a modest eighteen issued dissenting opinions (19.35 per cent).[3] Admittedly, there has been less agreement on the specific legal reasoning as of the seventy-five majority votes, twenty-eight were issued as separate opinions (37.3 per cent). This indicates more agreement on the outcome of the case than on the concrete legal reasoning.

With regards to participation in the proceedings, a significant majority of the bench and legal counsel arguing before the Court had studied or taught in the Global North, even when they were not native from those countries.[4] Furthermore, these cases were overwhelmingly argued and decided by men: of the total ninety-three votes and opinions, eighty-nine were issued by males whereas only four were issued by a (single) woman (4 per cent);[5] of the 184 counsel arguing before the Court, only 8 were women (4 per cent), they all appeared in Advisory proceedings, and only 5 argued orally before the Court. This picture confirms the persistence of Chinkin's 1992 observation concerning the 'invisibility of women in determining the legality or otherwise of any international use of force',[6] as well as Heathcote's concern with the entrenchment of gendered assumptions into the relationship of law and violence.[7]

Let us move to the law. Section II focuses on the prohibition of the use of force under international law in the ICJ's case law. Section III concentrates

---

[3] Given the composition of the Court it is virtually impossible to have unanimous decisions.

[4] Data on file with author. For a recent study documenting these and other imbalances, see S. Kumar and C. Rose, 'A Study of Lawyers Appearing before the International Court of Justice 1999–2012' 25(3) EJIL (2014), 893–917.

[5] On the composition of the Court, see further K. Keith, 'The Role of an ICJ Judge', Chapter 2 of this volume.

[6] C. Chinkin, 'A Gendered Perspective to the International Use of Force' 12*Australian Yearbook of International Law* (1992) 280.

[7] G. Heathcote, *The Law on the Use of Force: A Feminist Analysis* (Routledge, 2012).

on the dicta of the Court regarding self-defence, which is arguably where most of the action is. Section IV assesses other possible exceptions to the prohibition to use force. Section V concludes by offering a brief assessment of the Court's influence in this area.

II The Prohibition of the Use or Threat of Use of Force

The Court famously argued that the rule in Article 2(4) prohibiting the use or threat of force under international law is a 'cardinal principle'[8] and one of the cornerstones of the international legal system.[9] It has also claimed that it is 'unhesitantly' part of customary international law,[10] and most likely a rule of *jus cogens*.[11] By considering that the Friendly Relations Declaration (1970) reflected customary international law, the ICJ extended the obligations emanating from this provision not only to the members of the UN, as explicitly stated in Article 2(4), but to 'every State'. Although there are still areas of obscurity, ambiguity and vagueness, the Court has construed this prohibition in arguably the broadest possible terms available considering the textual constraints.

First, it has suggested that violating this rule does not require a substantial gravity threshold. In the *Corfu Channel* case, the ICJ condemned the British assembling a large number of warships in the territorial waters of another State even though no physical harm to persons or property resulted from it. Admittedly, it only implicitly stated that it violated the prohibition on the use of force, as any such finding was not within the Court's jurisdiction (para. 33–34). Yet the case was important to provide support to the newly established Charter regime.[12] In *Armed Activities*, the Court further characterised Uganda's unlawful military occupation of part

---

[8] *Nicaragua*, Merits, para. 190.

[9] See also Dissenting Opinion of Elaraby in *Oil Platforms*, p. 134.

[10] E.g., ILC, 'Reports of the Commission to the General Assembly', (1966-II) YBILC, 247.

[11] In *Nicaragua*, the Court approvingly cited the opinion of the ILC to that effect (Merits, para. 190). In the *Kosovo* advisory opinion, it illustrated the existence of peremptory norms by reference to the unlawful use of force in the context of discussing the scope of *jus cogens* norms (para. 81). This proposition was subscribed by several individual votes in, e.g., *Oil Platforms* (Elaraby, Diss, op., 291), *Nicaragua* (Singh and Sette-Camara, Sep. ops., 153 and 199, respectively), and *Oil Platforms* (Simma and Kooijmans, Sep ops., paras. 9 and 44, respectively).

[12] See, e.g., the opening statements of Alvarez' Separate Opinion (p. 39).

of the territory of the DRC as a violation of the principle of non-use of force (para. 345).[13]

Second, in *Corfu Channel* the Court rejected the argument by the UK that the rule in article 2(4) covered only actions that threatened the territorial integrity or the political independence of a foreign State.[14] In a famous passage the Court stated that it 'can only regard the *alleged* right of intervention [invoked by the UK] as the manifestation of a policy of force, such as has, in the past, given rise to most serious abuses and such as cannot, whatever be the present defects in international organisation find a place in international law' (para. 35, emphasis added).[15] The Court thereby rejected the proposition that international law only prohibited 'aggressive' uses of force, while it allowed for other forms of non-aggressive military action.

Third, the Court argued that the prohibition to use force not only covers direct action by States, but also indirect action executed through non-state armed groups. In *Nicaragua* it considered the arming and training of non-state actors fighting on the territory of another State against its armed forces covered by the prohibition to use force, and only excepted the 'mere supply of funds' from the prohibition (para. 228). It relied for this on the 1970 Friendly Relations Declaration duty to 'refrain from organizing or encouraging the organization of irregular forces or armed bands ... [and] the duty to refrain from organizing, instigating, assisting or participating in acts of civil strife or terrorist act in another State'.[16] In *Armed Activities*, the Court considered this rule declaratory of customary international law and indicated that it also prohibited the mere toleration or acquiescence of non-state actors which carry out trans-boundary armed action (para. 300).

Finally, the majority of the Court rejected the view that it was barred from adjudicating on this issue pending a Security Council decision, thereby stating unequivocally that disputes regarding the use of force are 'inherently justiciable'.[17] In *Nicaragua* the USA had argued that '[t]he

---

[13] Kooijmans disagreed. He suggested that the occupation 'should not have been characterised in a direct sense as a violation of the principle of the non-use of force' (Sep. Op, para. 56).

[14] *Corfu Channel* case, UK Oral Statement of 12 Nov 1948, 296.

[15] The USA tried a similar line of argument to show that their response was defensive in the *Oil Platforms* case with as little success (Counter memorial, para. 4.03).

[16] UN Doc A/RES/2625 (1970).

[17] T. Ruys, *'Armed Attack' and Article 51 of the UN Charter* (Cambridge University Press, 2010) 1.

precise language of Article 51 leaves no room for a judicial determination to terminate a resort to armed force in the midst of on-going armed conflict, which necessarily involves the exercise of the inherent right of self-defence by one or more of the parties to the conflict'.[18] It also suggested that, by contrast, 'Article 51 permits only the Security Council to take action with respect to claims of self-defence, and a judgment on the question by the Court would constitute an entry in the field of competence reserved to the Council.'[19] Schwebel, the American Judge in the Court, held that, while these disputes were in principle justiciable, there was a temporary exception in situations of continuing use of force, where the facts were disputed and unclear, and where the Court was in no position to reach a reliable ('final') judgment (p. 284–296). The majority was unmoved.

Nonetheless, this expansive understanding of the prohibition to the use of force is limited in three important ways. First, it only prohibits force by States in their 'international relations'. Namely, it prohibits neither force exercised by non-state actors, nor force exercised by a State within its own borders against its own population. Second, it covers only 'armed' force, rather than any other form of economic or political coercion. Finally, the Court adopted a more limited understanding of the prohibition of *threats* of force, compared to actual uses of force. In the *Nuclear Weapons* advisory opinion it held that the legality of a threat depended on whether using force would be ultimately legal. To illustrate, it declared that this would not comprise threats 'to secure territory from another State, or to cause it to follow or not follow certain political or economic paths' (para. 47). It further indicated that unlawful actions were limited to cases of a 'signaled intention to use force if certain events occur' or a 'stated readiness' to do so, requiring a kind of subjective element that in practice would be extremely difficult to prove. Indeed, in the *Corfu Channel* case it rejected Albania's contention that the UK had displayed an unnecessarily large force with the intention to exercise political pressure over it (para. 35). Similarly, in *Nicaragua* the Court refrained to consider US troop movements in Honduran regions, as well as the deployment of vessels off the Nicaraguan coast a forbidden threat of force (para. 227).

[18] Counter memorial, para. 455.
[19] Counter-Memorial of the USA (17th August 1984), para. 516. The Government of Nicaragua had brought the situation to the attention of the UNSC thirteen times between 1982 and 1988.

III Self-Defence

Arguably, the most sensitive part of the Court's case-law in this area concerns the law on self-defence. To begin, the Court in *Nicaragua* explicitly stated the rules on self-defence are provided both in the UN Charter and in customary international law, as per the recognition of an inherent right in Article 51 of the Charter (para. 193). The Court further considered that '[o]n a number of points, the areas governed by the two sources of law do not exactly overlap, and the substantive rules in which they are framed are not identical in content' (para. 175). It is unlikely that this means that there are contradictions between the treaty and customary regimes. The better view is that, as the Court observed, 'the United Nations Charter . . . by no means covers the whole area of regulation of the use of force in international relations' (para. 176).

Self-defence *ratione materiae*. Under Article 51, the right to self-defence is triggered 'if an armed attack occurs'. In *Nicaragua* the Court claimed that '[t]here appears now to be general agreement on the nature of the acts which can be treated as constituting armed attacks' (para. 195). Furthermore it assimilated it, albeit in passing or through references to pronouncements by the USA and El Salvador, with the notion of aggression (paras. 163–165).[20] Answering this question, it stated, requires distinguishing 'the most grave forms of the use of force (those constituting an armed attack) from other less grave forms' (para. 191). This means, rather conclusively, that the notion of 'armed attack' is different from (that is, more demanding than) the concept of 'prohibited use of force' under Article 2(4).[21] However, the ICJ never clearly stated where the line should be drawn between acts that trigger the right to use force in self-defence, and those which – although they violate the prohibition to use force – do not.

---

[20] See also the separate opinions of judges Elaraby and Simma in *Armed Activities* (paras. 8–20 and 3, respectively) and A. Haque, 'The United Nations Charter at 75: Between Force and Self-Defense (parts I and II)', available at www.justsecurity.org.

[21] As Kress points out, a further distinction is that an armed attack cannot be conducted indirectly. Namely, whereas the mere 'arming and training by a State of non-state actors fighting the government of another State on the latter's territory' constitutes a form of (prohibited) use of force, it does not amount to an armed attack for the purposes of permissible self-defence. C. Kress, 'The International Court of Justice and the "Principle of Non-Use of Force"', in M. Weller, *The Oxford Handbook of The Use of Force in International Law* (Oxford University Press, 2015) 584.

In *Nicaragua* the Court famously set the bar quite high by describing an armed attack as

The sending by or on behalf of a State of armed bands, groups, irregulars or mercenaries, which carry out acts of armed force against another State of such gravity as to amount to the acts listed above, or its substantial involvement therein. (para. 195)[22]

Among such acts are 'the invasion of attack of the territory of another State, or any military occupation', 'bombardment of the territory of another State', blockade of ports or coasts by armed forces, an attack of the land, sea or air forces or marine and air fleets of another State, among others.

By contrast, in *Oil Platforms* it significantly lowered the bar by claiming that it 'could not rule out the possibility that the mining of a single military vessel might be sufficient to bring into play the "inherent right of self-defence"' (para. 72). Even if the attack in question had been particularly severe (the ship was incapacitated and it almost sank), the contrast with the *Nicaragua* standard is striking.[23] The Court further clarified that 'the burden of proof of the acts showing the existence of such an attack rests with the State that claims to be acting in self-defence' (para. 57). Many commentators have complained that the standard of proof required has hardly received any attention by the Court.[24]

Furthermore, in *Oil Platforms* the Court implied that the threshold relevant to permissible defensive force could be satisfied through a 'cumulative' series of small attacks (para. 64). This proposition cuts through the arguments of both parties. Iran had claimed that the question of whether an armed attack had taken place should be answered by reference to 'each single incident which occurred'.[25] The USA, in turn, had protested that 'Iran's arguments are, without exception, designed to fit neatly into its stealthy, one-by-one method of attack'.[26] Simma explicitly opined that, 'to begin with', no iterated or continued pattern of attacks from Iran against

---

[22] As defined in the UNGA Resolution 3314 on the Definition of Aggression (XXIX) (1974), Article 3(g).

[23] See D. Crist, *The Twilight War: The Secrete History of America's Thirty-Year Conflict with Iran* (Penguin, 2012), chap. 17.

[24] E.g., Ruys, *'Armed Attack' and Article 51 of the UN Charter*, 546.

[25] Reply and Defence to Counter-Claim submitted by Iran, at para. 7.22.

[26] Rejoinder submitted by the USA, 23 March 2001, at para. 5.33.

the USA had taken place (para. 14). In any event, the majority of the Court implicitly confirmed the possibility of a cumulative series of acts amounting to an armed attack in the *Armed Activities* case (para. 146).

A separate question is whether defensive force could be lawful against threats that do not reach the required level of gravity, that is, outside of article 51. The Court disapproved of the possibility of permissible forcible countermeasures in the *Corfu Channel* case (p. 35). Yet in *Nicaragua* it explicitly raised the issue only to leave it unanswered (paras. 210/249). In his dissent, Schwebel further claimed that 'if an armed attack occurs' in the Charter should not be read 'if and only if', indicating that it was a sufficient but not a necessary condition for lawful defensive force (para. 173). As a result, *Nicaragua* has been criticised both for adopting a high threshold for the concept of an armed attack and for opening the door to lawful armed countermeasures.[27]

In *Oil Platforms*, by contrast, the Court preferred not to entertain the possibility of lawful armed countermeasures though, as indicated, perhaps at the expense of significantly lowering the scale and intensity threshold of an armed attack as previously established in *Nicaragua*. In his Separate opinion Simma insisted in distinguishing between 'full-scale self-defence' and 'proportionate defensive measures'. He argued that

> we may encounter also a lower level of hostile military action, not reaching the threshold of an 'armed attack' within the meaning of Article 51 ... Against such hostile acts, a State may of course defend itself, but only within a more limited range and quality of responses ... and bound to necessity, proportionality and immediacy in time in a particularly strict way. (para. 13)

The Court ultimately rejected the possibility of lawful armed countermeasures in the *Armed activities* case, when it explicitly stated that the Charter 'does not allow the use of force by a State to protect perceived security interests beyond' the parameters of Article 51 (para. 148).

Finally, the Court has addressed whether resort to force in self-defence is permitted *before* the armed attack has materialised, that is, whether anticipatory, pre-emptive or preventive self-defence would be lawful. This has been one of the most contentious issues in the recent law on the use of force. In *Nicaragua*, the Court stated that it would express 'no view on this

---

[27] See, e.g., J. L. Hardgrove, 'The Nicaragua Judgment and the Future of the Law of Force and Self-Defense', 81(1) *AJIL* (1987), 139.

issue' in light of the fact that 'issue of the lawfulness of a response to the imminent threat of armed attack [had] not been raised' (para. 194). In *Armed Activities*, it suggested that 'Article 51 of the Charter may justify a use of force in self-defence only within the strict confines there laid down. It does not allow the use of force to protect perceived security interests beyond these parameters' (para. 148).[28] This statement has been interpreted as firmly rejecting the lawfulness of self-defence against a non-imminent threat, though not necessarily vis-à-vis imminent ones.[29] In effect, the latter issue had not been part of the controversy between the parties in the merits stage of the proceedings. Although Uganda did mention being under threat by the DRC, it never explicitly invoked a right to anticipatory self-defence.[30]

Self-defence *ratione personae*. The central issue here is whether non-state armed groups can carry out armed attacks and trigger a State's right to self-defence.[31] This is another of the most sensitive questions in contemporary debates on the use of force. In *Nicaragua* the Court argued that an armed attack can involve 'the sending by or on behalf of a State' of irregular forces, or the State's 'substantial involvement therein' (para. 195). It thereby acknowledged that such attack need not be conducted by *de jure* organs of the State. Yet, the Court seem to have required that the acts be attributed to a State.[32] The Court stated that even if the participation of the United States was

preponderant or decisive, in the financing organizing, training, supplying and equipping of the contras, the selection of its military or paramilitary targets, and the planning of the whole of its operation, [it was] still insufficient in itself . . . for the purpose of attributing to the United States the acts committed by the contras in the course of their military or paramilitary operations in Nicaragua (para. 115).

---

[28] See also Simma's Separate Opinion in *Armed Activities* drawing a line before pre-emptive use of force or the so-called 'Bush Doctrine' (paras. 7–11).

[29] E.g., Ruys, *'Armed Attack' and Article 51 of the UN Charter*, 338. This proposition, though, leaves significant room for debate as to how we should interpret imminence in this context.

[30] See, respectively, Counter Memorial (21 April 2001), 331 and Oral pleadings (12 April 2005), CR 2005/3, para. 35.

[31] See also D. Tladi, Chapter 3, The Role of the International Court of Justice in the Development of International Law, pp. [11–12].

[32] On attribution at the ICJ, see Chapter 18, F. Paddeu's contribution, 'The Law of State Responsibility', to this volume.

For this to obtain, the USA would have to have 'directed or enforced the perpetration of the acts'.[33] In the *Oil Platforms* case, the Court again required that the USA show that it had suffered attacks 'for which Iran was responsible' (para. 51).[34] This means that the majority opinion stuck to the claim that an armed attack can only be conducted by a State.

However, Article 3(g) of the Definition of Aggression (cited above), on which the Court relied, also covers situations of 'substantial involvement' of the State, that is, a standard short of attribution. In *Nicaragua* the majority of the Court took a very narrow understanding of this possibility, ultimately equating it to attribution. Schwebel in his dissent took a diametrically opposite view by somewhat implausibly interpreting the terms 'substantial involvement' by reference to 'acts of armed force', rather than in the 'sending by or on behalf of a State' (para. 166).[35] Yet he was on firmer grounds when he argued that the provision of arms, training and other forms of assistance should be qualified as 'substantial involvement' in terms of Article 3(g). Commentators have argued that the majority's interpretation was consistent with existing practice at the time.[36]

Nevertheless, the Court has since muddled its position on whether, or under what conditions non-state armed groups can carry out an armed attack. In the *Wall* advisory opinion, it argued that

Article 51 ... recognizes the existence of an inherent right of self-defence in the case of an armed attack by a State against another State. However, Israel does not claim that the attacks against it are imputable to a foreign State. The Court also notes that Israel exercises control in the Occupied Palestinian Territory and that, as Israel itself states, the threat which it regards as justifying the construction of the wall originates within, and not, outside this territory. (para. 139)

On these bases the Court distinguished the situation being assessed from that which underpinned Security Council Resolutions 1368(2001) and

---

[33] Jennings disagreed, though more on whether the standard had been fulfilled than on the standard itself. He claimed that 'to say that the provision of arms, coupled with "logistical or other support" is not an armed attack is going much too far', since '[l]ogistical support may itself be crucial' (para. 543).

[34] K. N. Trapp, 'Of Dissonance and Silence. State Responsibility in the Bosnia Genocide Case', 62 *Neth. Int Law Rev* (2015), 250.

[35] Knof and Kress have indicated that the French version of the text speaks even more clearly against Schwebel's interpretation (cited in J. Kammerhofer, 'The US Intervention in Nicaragua: 1981–88', in T. Ruys et al., *The Use of Force in International Law: A Case-Based Approach* (Oxford University Press, 2018)).

[36] See, e.g., C. Gray, *International Law and The Use of Force* (2018), 130.

1373(2001), passed in the aftermath of the 9/11 attacks, and which explicitly made reference to the USA's legitimate recourse to self-defence. There is wide agreement in the specialised literature that this statement could hardly be less clear. Yet the separate and dissenting opinions in this case suggest that the majority was not too far away from the *Nicaragua* holding. Higgins and Buergenthal each argued that the requirement that an armed attack be conducted by a State was not provided in Article 51 of the Charter, but rather the result of the Court's dicta in *Nicaragua* (para. 33 and para. 6, respectively). Yet Higgins admitted that this proposition 'is to be regarded as a statement of the law as it now stands'. Although deferential to the majority's position stating that armed attacks had to come from another State, Kooijmans cautiously stated that UNSC resolutions introduced a 'completely new element' vis-à-vis acts of international terrorism, the legal implications of which 'cannot as yet be assessed but which [mark] undeniably a new approach' (para. 35).

In *Armed Activities*, neither the DRC nor Uganda claimed that attacks by non-state actors could trigger the right to self-defence under Article 51: while Uganda admittedly took a looser view concerning state involvement, the DRC defended a more traditional approach requiring substantial and active involvement.[37] Yet Brownlie (arguing for Uganda) suggested that 'there is a separate, a super-added standard of responsibility, according to which a failure to control the activities of armed bands, creates a susceptibility to action in self-defence by neighbouring States'.[38] The majority of the Court claimed that it had 'no need to respond to the contentions of the parties as to whether and under what conditions contemporary international law provides for a right of self-defence against large-scale attacks by irregular forces' (para. 147). In his Separate Opinion, Kooijmans interpreted this statement as a refusal to answer 'the question as to the kind of action a victim State is entitled to take if the armed operation by irregulars ... would have been classified as an armed attack rather than as a mere frontier incident had [it] been carried out by regular armed forces' (para. 26). Citing his previous Separate Opinion in the *Wall* case, he insisted that Article 51 says 'nothing that this armed attack must come from another State even if this has been the generally accepted

---

[37] Mémoire de la Republique Démocratique du Congo, 6 July 2000, 517 (my translation). Both parties argued by reference to the provision of Article 3(g) of the Definition of Aggression.

[38] Monday 18 April 2005, CR 2005/7, para. 80.

interpretation for more than 50 years' (para. 28.). Simma concurred citing favourable reactions to the use of force against terrorist groups after 9/11 (paras. 7–11). But they still represented a small minority in the Court.

Necessity and proportionality. These requirements are not mentioned in Article 51 of the Charter. In *Nicaragua* the Court, however, recognised that there is a 'specific rule whereby self-defence would warrant only measures which are proportional to the armed attack and necessary to respond to it, a rule well established in customary international law' (para. 176).[39] It further suggested that failing to fulfill these requirements could 'constitute an additional ground of wrongfulness' (para. 237).

Two main dicta provide sufficient guidance as to the Court's understanding of necessity. In *Nicaragua* the Court reasoned that insofar the 'major offensive of the armed opposition against the Government of El Salvador had been completely repulsed … it was possible to eliminate the danger to the Salvadorian Government without the United States embarking on activities in and against Nicaragua' (para. 237). On this basis, it concluded that the requirement of necessity had not been met. In *Oil Platforms*, the Court observed that US forces 'attacked the R-4 platform as a "target of opportunity"', suggesting again that the USA had not even provided indications that the targets were connected to the harm they had suffered (para. 76).[40] Simma further indicated that the 'Iranian oil platforms and their possible non-commercial activities during the Gulf War were too remote from these incidents (in every sense of this word)' (para. 14). We may thereby conclude that, according to the Court, to satisfy necessity the defensive acts ultimately need to be capable of thwarting, stopping or preventing the threat from materialising, which essentially constituted one of the main arguments articulated by Iran in *Oil Platforms*.[41] Furthermore, the Court added that the analysis of necessity must be 'strict and objective, leaving no room for any "measure of discretion"' (para. 73).[42]

---

[39] Although the Caroline incident was explicitly invoked by different parties, the Court did not make any explicit reference to it.

[40] This observation can be read as a general consideration regarding the burden of proof, but it responded to the US allegation that the exercise of 'the right of self-defence be evaluated in light of the information available to the victim … at the time the measures were taken.' Rejoinder submitted by the USA, at para. 5.13.

[41] See, e.g., Memorial (paras. 4.21–4.38).

[42] In its Rejoinder in *Armed Activities*, Uganda advocated that a State acting in self-defence should 'benefit of a margin of appreciation in relation to the dimensions of the perceived threat and the means of dealing with that threat effectively.' (at para. 284).

By contrast, the Court has failed to provide a consistent understanding of the requirement of proportionality, perhaps in line with competing approaches to this principle in the literature.[43] In some cases, the Court seemingly adopted the 'quantitative' understanding of proportionality which compares the harm that will be caused by the defensive action against the harm that has been inflicted and will be prevented.[44] In *Nicaragua*, the Court compared the scale of US activities vis-à-vis Nicaragua against the latter's aid to Salvadorian armed opposition groups (para. 327). In *Oil Platforms*, the Court added that the proportionality of a defensive action must be assessed not against a particular deed 'in isolation' but against the scale of 'the whole operation' (para. 77). It indicated that

[a]s a response to the mining, by an unidentified agency, of a single United States warship, which was severely damaged but not sunk, and without loss of life, neither 'Operation Praying Mantis' as a whole, nor even that part of it that destroyed the Salman and Nasr platforms, can be regarded, in the circumstances of this case, as a proportionate use of force in self-defence. (para. 77)

Kooijmans favoured a similar understanding in the *Wall* advisory opinion. He argued that '[t]he route chosen for the construction of the wall and the ensuing disturbing consequences for the inhabitants of the Occupied Palestinian Territory are manifestly disproportionate to the interests which Israel seeks to protect' (para. 34). In the *Nuclear Weapons* advisory opinion, the Court had clarified that this type of analysis must include all types of harms, including environmental ones (para. 30). By contrast, it indicated that potential or indirect risks arising from the use of force in terms of the probability of escalation of the conflict should only 'be born in mind' (para. 43).

---

[43] See, e.g., J. Gardam, *Necessity, Proportionality and the Use of Force by States* (Cambridge University Press, 2004).

[44] This was the understanding of proportionality defended by the USA in its Counter-Memorial and Counter-Claim (paras. 3.42 and ff.). Incorporating past harms ('sunk costs') to the proportionality analysis of defensive action, which is standardly forward-looking, is conceptually problematic. This was already stated by the British Law Officers in 1839 in the context of the Caroline affair, when they argued that 'the grounds on which we consider the conduct of the British Authorities to be justified, is that it was absolutely necessary as a means of precaution *for the future* and not a measure of retaliation for the past.' (A. D. McNair (ed.), *International Law Opinions* Vol 2, 228; emphasis in the original). Admittedly, it may be defended on policy (consequentialist) grounds, given that it provides greater certainty and predictability, avoiding speculation of harms that have not yet occurred.

In *Armed Activities* the Court switched to what is often called the functional understanding of proportionality, which considers disproportionate any harm not necessary to achieve the aims of the defensive force.[45] Just after arguing that there was no armed attack that would justify resorting to force in self-defence, the Court could not 'fail to observe, however, that the taking of airports and towns many hundreds of kilometers from Uganda's border would not seem proportionate to the series of transborder attacks it claimed had given rise to the right of self-defence, nor to be necessary to that end' (para. 147). Influential scholars have argued that the functional approach has gained significant support in the specialised literature,[46] and some further suggest that the dicta of the court in defence of the quantitative approach are favoured by the particular facts of the cases at hand.[47] The fact remains, though, that the Court seems to have been far more favourable to the quantitative than to the functional view of proportionality.

This is hardly a purely conceptual or a doctrinal issue. The former understanding has been standardly defended by States claiming that they had been victims of unlawful resort to force (Nicaragua in *Nicaragua*[48], Iran in the *Oil Platforms* case,[49] DRC in *Armed activities*,[50] and Palestine[51] in the *Wall* advisory opinion,) whereas the latter was advocated by countries defending their right to use force in self-defence (e.g., the USA in *Oil Platforms*, Uganda in *Armed Activities*[52], Israel in the *Wall* advisory opinion).[53] Professor Bothe as Agent of Iran in the *Oil Platforms* case put

[45] For criticism, see A. Chehtman, 'The *ad bellum* Challenge of Drones: Recalibrating Permissible Use of Force', 28(1) *EJIL* (2017), 195.
[46] See, e.g., Ruys, *'Armed Attack' and Article 51 of the UN Charter*, 112 and notes.
[47] See, e.g., C. Tams, 'Necessity and Proportionality', in L. van den Herik and N. Schrijver (eds.), *Counter-Terrorism Strategies in a Fragmented International Legal Order* (Cambridge University Press, 2013) 373.
[48] Albeit mixing the two, *Nicaragua* ultimately relied on the other (see statements by Prof Chaye Oral Arguments on the Merits at p. 187).
[49] Although it initially relied on Ago's functional standard, Iran subsequently adopted a quantitative approach comparing the US response with 'the first use of force'. Reply and defence to Counter-Claim, 10/3/1999, at para. 7.62.
[50] See, e.g., Reply of the DRC (29/5/2002), at para. 3.159.
[51] Written Statement in the *Wall* advisory opinion, para. 530.
[52] Making reference to the 'long-term absence of any, or of any effective, State administration in Eastern Congo' as a 'decisive circumstance' (Rejoinder 6/12/2002, at paras. 282–283).
[53] Written Statement of the Government in the Wall advisory Opinion, chapter 8.3.

it clearly: 'it may well be that powerful nations feel more comfortable with a broader legal option to use military force'.[54]

Reporting to the UN Security Council. In *Nicaragua*, the Court noted that it is 'clear' that 'a procedure so closely dependent on the content of a treaty commitment and of the institutions established by it' cannot be a condition of the lawfulness of the use of force (para. 200).[55] Yet it also suggested that 'the absence of a report may be one of the factors indicating whether the State in question was itself convinced that it was acting in self-defence' (para. 200). The Court further pointed out that this was the position the USA had adopted in the Security Council in relation to the 1979 Soviet invasion in Afghanistan (para. 235). In *Armed Activities*, the Court indeed noted that 'Uganda did not report to the Security Council events that it had regarded as requiring to act in self-defence' (para. 145). By contrast, the Court never explicitly addressed the requirement under Article 51 of the Charter indicating self-defensive action cannot be impaired 'until the Security Council has taken the measures necessary to maintain international peace and security'. Eloquently, though, in the *Nuclear Weapons* advisory opinion the Court cited Article 51 almost in full while ignoring this specific provision (para. 44).

Collective self-defence. The ICJ has noted that the existence of an armed attack against a third country is a necessary but not a sufficient condition for collective self-defence to arise. Additional requirements have been defended either on principled grounds, such as respect for the right to self-determination, as well as on the basis of a concern for the strategic abuse of this right by States acting exclusively in their self-interest. Accordingly, the Court in *Nicaragua* required first a 'request by the State which is the victim of the alleged attack' (para. 199), noting that 'if the victim wishes another State to come to its help in the exercise of the right to collective self-defence, it will normally make an express request to that effect' (para. 232).[56] The second additional condition stipulated in *Nicaragua* is that the 'State for whose benefit this right is used will have

---

[54] Oral proceedings, verbatim record 2003/7, para. 19.

[55] Schwebel observed that 'the international community at large, as represented by the Security Council, has an interest in the maintenance of international peace and security which should not be pre-empted by the failure of a State to report its defensive measures to the Security Council' (Dissenting op., 227).

[56] Despite the fact that this requirement has been criticised, Ruys notes that it is generally supported by customary practice (*'Armed Attack' and Article 51 of the UN Charter*, 89).

declared itself to be the victim of an armed attack'. The reason for to permit 'another State to exercise the right of collective self-defence on the basis of its own assessment of the situation' (para. 194). In his Dissenting opinion, Jennings objected to this dictum considering it 'somewhat formalistic', and specifically doubting that the fact a State 'declared' itself to be the victim of an armed attack was a necessary 'requirement' for its lawfulness (p. 534). Going further, Schwebel questioned 'where is it written that, where one State covertly promotes the subversion of another by multiple means tantamount to an armed attack, the latter may not informally and quietly seek foreign assistance?' (para. 191). In *Oil Platforms* the Court only required that the State which requests the assistance 'regards' itself as the victim of an armed attack (para. 51).

IV Other Exceptions to the Prohibition to Use Force

This section briefly covers the other existing and potential exceptions to the prohibition to use force. We shall survey the Court's analysis of state consent, UN Security Council authorisation, humanitarian and pro-democratic interventions, and protection of nationals.

The Court has acknowledged that military actions with the consent of the territorial State are not in breach of the prohibition to use force. In *Nicaragua* the Court suggested that that intervention by a foreign state would be 'allowable at the request of the government of a state', yet it rejected the possibility that intervention could be allowed at the request of the opposition (para. 246).[57] Notably, the Court cited no limitations to the right to request military assistance by the Government.[58] In *Armed Activities* it further clarified that consent could be provided and withdrawn both explicitly and implicitly, given that 'no formalities would have been required' (para. 51). It also stated that it could be limited in any way the consenting State sees fit, including in terms of temporal scope, 'geographic

---

[57] Of course, this is more complicated. See, e.g., E. Lieblich, 'Why Can't We Agree When Governments Can Consent to External Intervention? A Theoretical Inquiry', *Journal on the Use of Force and International Law* 7(2020), 5.

[58] But see F. Paddeu, 'Military Assistance on Request and General Reasons against Force: Consent as a Defence to the Prohibition of Force,' 7 *Journal on the Use of Force and International Law* (2020) 227.

location' and the relevant 'objectives' to be pursued, and that it can be withdrawn at any time and for any reason (para. 52).

Although arguably at the core of the collective security system put in place through the UN Charter, the ICJ has not concerned itself much with the authorisation to use force by the UN Security Council. In *Certain Expenses of the United Nations*, the Court merely stated that 'it cannot be said that the Charter has left the Security Council impotent in the face of an emergency situation when agreements under Article 43 have not been concluded' (para. 167). Furthermore, in the *Nuclear Weapons* advisory opinion, the Court made it clear that 'a lawful use of force is envisaged in Article 42 [of the UN Charter], whereby the Security Council may take military enforcement measures in conformity with Chapter VII' (para. 38).

The Court never decided on the merits of a case involving a claim of humanitarian intervention or any other form of protection of a State's nationals against their own government. Yet, as in other contexts, it has provided some limited guidance on the matter. In *Nicaragua*, the Court recognised that 'while the United States might form its own appraisal of the situation as to respect for human rights in *Nicaragua*, the use of force could not be the appropriate method to monitor or ensure such respect' (para. 268). The so-called Reagan Doctrine, which advocated the containment of the spread of socialism through support to so-called freedom fighters, was also effectively (if only implicitly) criticised. Namely, the Court rejected 'the creation of a new rule opening up a right of intervention by one State against another on the ground that the latter has opted for some particular ideology or political system' (para. 263). Furthermore, it also held that there was no general right of intervention on behalf of insurgent groups in foreign states. It recognised the existence of a number of instances of such intervention, but concluded they were not relevant to the case at hand, which was not about the process of decolonisation (para. 206).[59] By contrast, it stated that intervention in civil strife was allowable only at the request of the government (para. 246). Permitting intervention at the request of the opposition 'would permit any State to intervene at any moment in the internal affairs of another State' (para. 246).

---

[59] On this point, Schwebel complained that 'to say that [he] dissent[ed] from the Court's Judgment is to understate the depths of [his] differences with it.' (Diss. Op., page 266). This question of law is largely moot at the present time.

Notably, the Court's precise finding is far narrower, and thereby qualifies this general proposition. That is, the Court argued that 'the protection
of human rights ... cannot be compatible with the mining of ports, the
destruction of oil installations, or again with the training, arming and
equipping of the *contras*' (para. 268). Yet, part of the reason for this was
that it 'cannot in any event be reconciled with the legal strategy of the
respondent State, which is based on the right of collective self-defence'
(para. 268). In the *Genocide Case*, the Court recognised the duty of states to
prevent a genocide even beyond its borders, yet it explicitly recognised
that it 'may only act within the limits permitted by international law'
(para. 437).

In the case concerning NATO bombings of Serbia, it was only able to
indicate it was 'profoundly concerned with the use of force in Yugoslavia',
adding that 'such use raises very serious issues of international law'.[60]
Only Belgium invoked a permission to use force to 'prevent a humanitarian
catastrophe', though it justified it on grounds of necessity as provided in
Art. 33 of the ILC's Articles on State Responsibility.[61] The UK, more
cautiously, merely highlighted that NATO action sought to prevent
'the systematic and intolerable violence being waged against an entire
population'.[62] In summary, as Neff has observed, the Court carefully
declined to provide any encouragement to supporters of humanitarian
intervention although it has held back from making a definitive general
pronouncement on the question.[63]

Finally, the Court addressed the issue of protection of nationals abroad
only obliquely in the *Tehran Hostages* case, as it was not raised 'before the
Court' (para. 94). President Carter had invoked Article 51 and the USA's
right 'to protect and rescue its citizens where the government of the
territory in which they are located is unwilling or unable to protect
them'.[64] Yet the Court only expressed 'its concern' regarding the 'incursion
into the territory of Iran made by the United States military units' in order
to liberate the hostages held by Iran, despite the fact that a ruling on the

---

[60] Order (2 June 1999), 17.   [61] Belgian Pleadings, at CR99/15.

[62] Cited in G. Simpson, *Great Powers and Outlaw States* (2004), 204.

[63] C. Neff, *War and the Law of Nations* (2005), 361–362. This issue was brought up explicitly
by Belgium in the *Case Concerning Legality of Use of Force* in 1999, but the Court
concluded it lacked jurisdiction to adjudicate the case.

[64] Cited in . Forteau and A. S. Ying Xiu, 'The US Hostage Rescue Operation in Iran:1980', in
Ruys et al. *The Use of Force in International Law*, 306.

legality of the operation was beyond its jurisdiction (paras. 93–94). It further noted that it felt 'bound to observe that an operation undertaken in those circumstances, for whatever motive, is of a kind calculated to undermine respect for judicial process in international relations' given that in its previous order it had indicated that 'no action was to be taken by either party which might aggravate the tension between the two countries' (paras. 93–94). But it did not condemn the incident in any stronger language.

V The ICJ and Its Fading Influence

The Court's general approach can be read in connection to a fundamental concern with defending a meaningful prohibition of the use of force as the cornerstone of the UN Charter, and arguably of international law more broadly.[65] In Elaraby's words, 'this fundamental principle draws a distinction between a post-Charter era of law-abiding, civilised community of nations and the pre-Charter era when the strong and powerful States were not restrained from attacking the weak at will and with impunity'.[66] As many scholars have suggested, the rulings of the Court have been decisive in consolidating the 'revolutionary' Charter regime – and its reflection in customary international law – as the exclusive locus of legal regulation of the use of force.[67] This is of major significance, particularly against the background of concerns for the premature death of Article 2(4).[68] Furthermore, the strong commitment for a restrictive understanding of the conditions of lawful self-defence may be interpreted as an attempt to counter the concern that 'growing reliance on self-defence as a justification for using force ... threatens to make self-defence the exception that swallows the rule against war'.[69] This is especially relevant since international legal justification is the language in which States ultimately argue

---

[65] *Armed Activities*, para. 148.   [66] Dissenting op. *Oil Platforms*, p. 134.

[67] See, dissenting opinion of Schwebel in *Nicaragua* (admissibility), para. 88, Dissenting op. Jennings, *Nicaragua* (merits), page 530 ff, Separate opinion of President Singh, 151 and ff, and Separate op. of Ago, para. 6. See also, C. Tams, 'The Use of Force against Terrorists' 20 (2) *EJIL* (2009) 363.

[68] T. Franck, 'Who Killed Article 2(4)? or: Changing Norms Governing the Use of Force by States', 64(5) *AJIL* (1970) 809.

[69] O. Hathaway and S. Shapiro, *The Internationalists: How a Radical Plan to Outlaw War Remade the World* (Simon & Schuster, 2017) 416.

for the legitimacy of their military actions, to the exclusion of almost any other consideration.[70]

The impact of its initial case-law can hardly be overstated. The seminal *Nicaragua* decision set 'the rules' of the game in terms of the debates concerning the scope of the prohibition to use force under both the Charter and customary international law, as well as the main criteria to lawfully resort to individual and collective self-defence. However, in its more recent case-law the Court failed to give any guidance on what probably are the most hotly contested issues in this area, such as the required scale and intensity of an armed attack, the permissibility of anticipatory defensive force, and the use of force against cross-border violence by non-state actors (not attributable to a State). The reaction by the Court to this new context, as illustrated by its post-2001 case-law, shows substantial uneasiness 'combining an ostensible reaffirmation of the *Nicaragua* threshold with a smoke screen of ambiguity'.[71] A number of commentators, and even of judges within the Court, have complained about the 'missed opportunities' to clarify these aspects of the law.[72]

This reluctance can only be perceived as a deliberate, indeed strategic decision by the justices. However, it has resulted in the influence of the Court fading in this area of the law. For one, the Court's case-law has been remarkably absent in contemporary doctrinal discussions concerning resort to force against non-state actors.[73] Furthermore, the legal and analytical framework the Court authoritatively contributed to establish is currently under significant pressure. On the one hand, the UN Security Council seems to be challenging the general framework advocated by the Court in favour of more informal, flexible standards.[74] On the other hand, the UN Human Rights Committee has questioned the State-centric logic of the Court's approach by recognising that certain

---

[70] I. Hurd, *How to Do Things with International Law* (Princeton University Press, 2018) 73.

[71] Ruys, *'Armed Attack' and Article 51 of the UN Charter*, 487.

[72] J. Green, 'The Great African War and the Intervention by Uganda and Rwanda in the Democratic Republic of Congo', in Ruys et al., *The Use of Force in International Law*, 593. See also, Elaraby in *Oil Platforms*, p. 295 and Kooijmans and Simma in *Armed activities* at para. 25, 35 and para. 8, respectively.

[73] To give just one example, see J. Brunnée and S. Toope, 'Self-Defence against Non-State Actors: Are Powerful States Willing but Unable to Change International Law?', 67 *ICLQ* (2018), 263–283, making only a passing reference to the Court's case-law.

[74] See, e.g., M. Hakimi, 'Jus ad Bellum's Regulatory Form' 112 *AJIL* (2018) 151.

violations of the *jus ad bellum* violate the human right to life.[75] Under this understanding, human rights courts may be called upon to adjudicate on *jus ad bellum* issues.[76] Finally, these developments arise in a context where the central concern with outlawing the resort to force seems increasingly displaced by the concern with preventing atrocity.[77] It may be this is inevitable when the separation between war and peace becomes increasingly blurry as a result of the consolidation of new patterns of violence in the world.

VI Conclusion

The ICJ played a central role in consolidating and developing the UN Charter's framework on the use of force.[78] This role is best captured in the Court's broad interpretation of the prohibition on the use of force and its restraining treatment of the requirements of self-defence. More recently the Court has been criticised for avoiding to squarely address some of the most urgent, controversial issues in this regime. The majority of the ICJ admittedly failed to articulate a cogent position with regards to key developments post 9/11. Nevertheless, it may be doubted whether the Court is in the best position to move the current situation forward. I have referred to several developments occurring before the UN Security Council, the Human Rights Committee, the ILC, to which we may add the International Criminal Court. But the ICJ may have already suggested a more promising way forward. Namely, the use that the ICJ has made of GA Resolutions 2625 and 3314 has proven both balanced and influential. Despite lacking any formal norm-creating powers, it may be that the Court sees the UN General Assembly as a promising institutional setting in which these issues should be addressed.

[75] See, UN Human Rights Committee, General Comment 36 (2018), UN Doc. CCPR/C/GC/36, 30.
[76] *Georgia v. Russia (II)*, Judgment of 21 January 2021, para. 26–31.
[77] See, e.g., R. Liss, 'Crimes Against the Sovereign Order: Rethinking International Criminal Justice' 113(4) *AJIL* (2019) 727, and S. Moyn, 'From Aggression to Atrocity: Rethinking the History of International Criminal Law', in KJ Heller et al., *The Oxford Handbook of International Criminal Law* (Oxford University Press, 2010).
[78] See Giladi & Shany, 'Assessing the Effectiveness of the International Court of Justice', Chapter 5 of this volume.

Further Reading

J. Brunnée and S. Toope, 'Self-Defence against Non-State Actors: Are Powerful States Willing but Unable to Change International Law?', 67 *ICLQ* (2018) 263.

T. Dannembaum, *The Crime of Aggression, Humanity, and the Soldier* (Cambridge University Press, 2018).

C. Gray, *International Law and The Use of Force* (4th ed., Oxford University Press, 2018).

G. Heathcote, *The Law on the Use of Force: A Feminist Analysis* (Routledge, 2012).

T. Ruys, *'Armed Attack' and Article 51 of the UN Charter* (CUP, 2010).

21 International Organisations Law

Jan Klabbers

I Introduction

The ICJ has not contributed much to the formation or development of international organisations law, nor could it have done so. The ICJ's main task, after all, is to settle disputes; it is not a law-making or law-developing agency. In this light, it is no coincidence that a leading academic contribution on the topic can only discuss the ICJ's work on international organisations in terms of treaty interpretation: the ICJ, on this view, can only help develop law through a more or less legitimate exercise of interpretation of the constituent treaties of international organisations and related legal instruments.[1]

But there are other reasons why the ICJ's role has been limited. To some extent, parts of the law were already in place by the time the ICJ started its work, having been developed to some extent by its predecessor, the PCIJ and by academic writings.[2] Another reason is that the ICJ has only intermittently addressed the law of international organisations, being dependent on what parties in disputes bring to it or, on occasion, what it is asked to render an advisory opinion about. Third, many of the relevant decisions and opinions of the ICJ address one single organisation: the UN. And the UN is highly a-typical, being the only universal organisation of general jurisdiction. It is also the organisation of which the ICJ is a principal organ.

---

[1] E. Lauterpacht, 'The Development of the Law of International Organizations by the Decisions of International Tribunals', 152 *Collected Courses of the Academy of International Law* (1976) 377. Naturally, sometimes issues before the Court can be framed as issues of interpretation and not much more: see e.g., *Applicability of the Obligation to Arbitrate under* section 21 *of the United Nations Headquarters Agreement of 26 June 1947*, advisory opinion, ICJ Rep. 1988, p. 12; *Applicability of Article VI, section 22, of the Convention on the Privileges and Immunities of the United Nations*, ICJ Rep. 1989, p. 177.

[2] For an overview, see J. Klabbers, 'The Life and Times of the Law of International Organizations', 70 *Nordic Journal of International Law* (2001) 287.

Put differently, the ICJ says little about organisations such as the World Health Organization or the International Civil Aviation Organization, and next to nothing about the vast majority of international organisations. Hence, not too much of general applicability should be expected.[3]

Most fundamental, the ICJ's approach reflects the general ambivalence of classic international law when it comes to international institutions – it may even be questioned whether there exists something like 'international organisations law' to begin with.[4] International law is often still taught as the result of interactions between independent, sovereign States; notwithstanding institutionalisation, and notwithstanding the emergence of human rights law and international criminal law, international law is still by and large conceptualised as State-centric, as some kind of private law between public entities.[5] And in such a setting there is little room for entities, actors and agents that do not fit the existing epistemic categories. If the proverbial man with a hammer sees nails everywhere, so the international lawyer (and her colleague studying international politics) sees States everywhere – and in such a setting, international organisations typically are reduced to creatures set up by States and for the benefit of States.

And yet, there is occasionally also an awareness that international organisations are conceptually highly ambivalent creatures. While generally considered creatures of, and agents for, their member States, they are sometimes also seen as autonomous from those same member States. But even when considered actors in their own right, the State always shines through – whether at issue are the powers of organisations, the treaties they conclude, or their accountability, or even their general level of activity.[6] Organisations are evaluated both for being indolent and for

---

[3] Sloan and Hernandez limit their analysis to a discussion of the ICJ's role in the development of UN law. See J. Sloan and G. Hernandez, 'The Role of the International Court of Justice in the Development of the Institutional Law of the United Nations', in C. Tams and J. Sloan (eds.), *The Development of International Law by the International Court of Justice* (Oxford University Press, 2013) 197.

[4] Elsewhere I have suggested that international organisations law collapses into the law of each individual organisation, with their external relations being governed by general international law. See J. Klabbers, 'The Paradox of International Institutional Law', 5 *International Organizations Law Review* (2008) 151.

[5] But see M. Ruffert and C. Walter, *Institutionalisiertes Völkerrecht* (Munich: Beck, 2009) or, in translation, *Institutionalized International Law* (Hart, 2015).

[6] The leading monograph is C. M. Brölmann, *The Institutional Veil in Public International Law: International Organisations and the Law of Treaties* (Hart, 2007).

overreach, depending on which conception is employed at any given moment; likewise, they can act as independent actors, but also be seen as fora for inter-State negotiations, the latter confirmed by the ICJ as recently as 2020.[7] Both conceptions are equally plausible,[8] but the Court usually falls back on the State-centric conception, and given its position as a court in a State-centric legal order where the State enjoys epistemic priority, it could hardly be otherwise.

Notwithstanding the above, the ICJ has developed the law on implied powers, and has said sensible things about checks and balances. But arguably its most important contribution has been to sketch the limits of the law of international organisations or, rather, of its underlying operating system. If the case law of the ICJ makes one thing abundantly clear, it is that the traditional view of international organisations, as agents of their member States, is extremely limited: the main contribution of the ICJ has been to make the limits of international organisations law visible. That is, to be sure, a worthy contribution: the Court has clearly struggled to come to terms with international organisations, and its lack of success merely reflects the underlying ambivalences in the legal framework.

International organisations embody three different types of legal dynamics, and this trichotomy will inform the discussion below.[9] The first dynamic is that of the relationship between the organisation and its member States; the second involves the the organisation and its internal matters (relations between organs, relations with staff), while the third concerns the relations between the organisation and the world around it (non-members, other organisations, private individuals and companies). One of the problems the ICJ has encountered is that those three dynamics cannot be treated in the same way: the legal position of a third party is different from that of a member State, and likewise, relations between

---

[7] See, e.g., *Appeal Relating to the Jurisdiction of the ICAO Council Under Article II*, section 2, *of the 1944 International Air Services Transit Agreement (Bahrain, Egypt and United Arab Emirates v. Qatar)*, ICJ, judgment of 14 July 2020.

[8] Jan Klabbers, 'Two Concepts of International Organization', 2 *International Organizations Law Review* (2005) 277.

[9] For fuller statements, see J. Klabbers, 'The EJIL Foreword: The Transformation of International Organizations Law', 26 *European Journal of International Law* (2015) 9; and J. Klabbers, 'Theorising International Organisations', in A. Orford and F. Hoffmann (eds.), *The Oxford Handbook of the Theory of International Law* (Oxford University Press, 2016), 618.

organs cannot be analysed solely in terms of what the member States may have had in mind.

I will leave several broad topics unconsidered. These include the opinions spelling out the law relating to advisory opinions,[10] and the cases in which the ICJ functions as an appellate civil service tribunal. The former has little to do with the law as it relates to international organisations, but is better classified as part of the ICJ's own procedural environment, with much hinging on the interpretation of Article 65 UN Charter.[11] And much the same actually applies to the latter: as the 2012 *IFAD* opinion[12] makes clear, the ICJ is (rightly) very concerned about the imbalance in procedural rights whenever it addresses civil service complaints, but has rarely used the occasion to develop further the law as it relates to organisations themselves and their position in the global legal order.

II International Organisations and Their Members

It has long been unclear what exactly makes for an international organisation and, related, whether and under what circumstances such organisations can be considered as possessing international legal personality. The ICJ was confronted with the question in 1949, when asked whether the new UN organisation had the competence to present claims under international law. It held in the affirmative, having started its discussion by an analysis of the personality of the UN under international law. This discussion, however, was awkward: the Court took for granted that the UN was indeed an international organisation but without discussing any criteria

---

[10] Seminal is K. Keith, *The Extent of the Advisory Jurisdiction of the International Court of Justice* (Sijthoff, 1971). Related, I will not address the Court's pronouncements on a possible role for regional organisations in dispute settlement; the Court has repeatedly noted that such a role has no bearing on the Court's jurisdiction. See, e.g., *Military and Paramilitary Activities in and against Nicaragua (Nicaragua v. USA)*, jurisdiction and admissibility, ICJ Rep. 1984, p. 392 (paras 107–108), and *Case Concerning the Land and Maritime Boundary between Cameroon and Nigeria (Cameroon v. Nigeria)*, preliminary objections, ICJ Rep. 1998, p. 275, paras. 67–68.

[11] See, e.g., *Western Sahara* (advisory opinion), ICJ Rep. 1975, p. 12; *Legal Consequences of the Construction of a Wall in the Occupied Palestinian Territory*, advisory opinion, ICJ Rep. 2004, p. 136.

[12] See *Judgment No. 2867 of the Administrative Tribual of the International Labour Organization upon a Complaint Filed Against the International Fund for Agricultural Development*, advisory Opinion, ICJ Rep. 2012, p. 10.

for 'organisationhood', and then proceeded by discussing the particular reasons why the UN would possess international legal personality. This, it felt, derived from an inductive analysis of some of its activities, including the possibility of concluding treaties, mentioning the 1946 Convention on Privileges and Immunities of the UN as an example: 'It is difficult to see how such a convention could operate except upon the international plane and as between parties possessing international personality.'[13] That would have been a compelling point, except for one thing: the UN is not – and never has been – a party to that Convention. The UN is a beneficiary, clearly, but that is not quite the same.[14]

The Court proceeded by discussing whether the legal personality of the UN was 'objective', that is, opposable to all (including non-member States), and found that this was indeed the case. Importantly though, this objective personality was based on the specific characteristics of the UN. The Court's sole argument was that the UN was set up by fifty States, at the time 'representing the vast majority of the members of the international community'. Those States had the power to 'bring into being an entity possessing objective international personality, and not merely personality recognized by them alone'.[15] The argument can be extrapolated perhaps to all universal international organisations – perhaps here the same logic could apply. But surely, it cannot apply to regional organisations, or organisations of otherwise limited membership.[16]

On the other hand, this may seriously overestimate the relevance of objective personality. In practice (and perhaps, admittedly, as a political and unintended consequence of *Reparation*), the personality of organisations is rarely questioned by non-members, and quite possibly what the Court aimed for in *Reparation* was a concept of 'presumptive personality', open in principle to rebuttal but rarely actually rebutted.[17]

---

[13] *Reparation for Injuries Suffered in the Service of the United Nations*, advisory opinion, ICJ Rep 1949, p. 174, at 179.

[14] The Convention moreover creates some obligations for the UN and the Secretary-General, e.g., to waive immunity when appropriate and to assist in the proper administration of justice.

[15] *Reparation*, 185.

[16] Truly universal organisations do not need 'objective' personality vis-à-vis States, as they have few or no non-member States.

[17] J. Klabbers, *An Introduction to International Organizations Law* (3rd ed. Cambridge University Press, 2015) 46–50.

The Court has made clear, without being explicit, that it is perfectly possible for two States to set up an international organisation: the river commission set up by Uruguay and Argentina (CARU) is considered an international organisation in *Pulp Mills*.[18] What is more (and of greater relevance), at no point did the Court in *Pulp Mills* investigate whether the resulting creature was intended to be an international organisation, or rather something else (whatever that something else might be). Confronted with a more or less permanent entity embodying cooperation between States, it presumed the entity must be an international organisation.[19]

The Court has often viewed international organisations as collections of States instead of autonomous creatures. In some circumstances, this was inevitable: since only States can be parties in proceedings before the court, the former Yugoslavia had to express its displeasure with NATO by starting proceedings against ten individual NATO member States, and the Court could only address matters in State-centric terms. The result is slightly alienating: at no point is mention made of State action being conducted through NATO.[20]

A more active State-centrism emerges from the *FYROM* case.[21] FYROM, the Former Yugoslav Republic of Macedonia, had suggested, amongst other things, that a decision taken unanimously by NATO was attributable to its individual member States, instead of being attributable to NATO, but the Court rejected this way of framing the issue. Instead, so the Court held, the question was solely whether one of the member States in question (that is, Greece) had violated a bilaterally agreed-upon obligation towards FYROM.[22] Framing the issue in this way was conceptually astute: it entailed that decision-making within NATO remained outside the Court's purview, and allowed the Court to focus solely on Greece's behaviour. Still, by framing the issue in strictly bilateral terms, the Court reinforced the view

---

[18] *Pulp Mills on the River Uruguay* (*Argentina* v. *Uruguay*), ICJ Rep. 2010, p. 14.

[19] This may have implications for discussions of entities such as the OSCE, ostensibly not intended to be an international organisation within the meaning of international law. On the latter, see M. Steinbrück Platise, C. Moser and A. Peters (eds.), *The Legal Framework of the OSCE* (Cambridge University Press, 2019).

[20] See, e.g., *Legality of Use of Force* (*Yugoslavia* v. *Belgium*), ICJ Rep. 1999, p. 124. All ten cases were quickly dismissed, mostly for want of jurisdiction.

[21] See Sofia Barros, *Governance as Responsibility: Member States as Human Rights Protectors in International Financial Institutions* (Cambridge University Press, 2019).

[22] *Application of the Interim Accord of 13 September 1995* (*FYROM* v. *Greece*), ICJ Rep. 2011, p. 644, para. 42.

that organisations are but gatherings of States, are driven by States, and are vehicles for States, effectively ignoring the institutional component.[23] And so as to demonstrate the usefulness of ambivalence of the law, a year and a half earlier the same Court had stressed the institutional component in its opinion on the independence of Kosovo. When tasked with the interpretation of a Security Council resolution, the Court noted that the Security Council is not so much a gathering of States as it is 'a single, collective organ', and the eventual text of a resolution 'represents the view of the Security Council as a body'.[24] The structural ambivalence between organisation and members, in other words, provides the Court with considerable leeway in terms of framing issues – and therewith outcomes.

Closely related to isssues of existence and personality is the question of the powers of organisations: the usual *topos* holds that it is through its power that the organisation manifests its existence and personality.[25] The Permanent Court of International Justice already developed this idea, but not without some hesitation: after a string of cases suggesting that what the International Labour Organisation could do was largely a matter of treaty interpretation, by the mid-1920s the PCIJ started to realise that a different approach might be needed. It launched the idea, discussing the powers of the Danube Commission, that these competences derived from express grants from the member States: conferred powers.[26] This was rapidly followed by the realization that such conferred powers cannot always answer any contingency, and need to be accompanied by implied powers, powers then conceptualised as those powers needed to give effect to express powers.[27] Simply put: the power to walk the dog would imply a power to put the dog on its leash.

This simple but effective framework was disturbed in *Reparation*. The Court here did not ask whether the power to bring a claim could be implied

---

[23] In 2018, the two States agreed on the issue of Macedonia's name, which had clouded relations since its independence; FYROM is now known as the Republic of North Macedonia.

[24] *Accordance with International Law of the Unilateral Declaration of Independence with respect to Kosovo*, advisory opinion, ICJ Rep 2010, 403, para. 94.

[25] V. Engström, *Constructing the Powers of International Institutions* (Martinus Nijhoff, 2012).

[26] *Jurisdiction of the European Commission of the Danube between Galatz and Braila*, advisory opinion, PCIJ, 1926, Series B, no. 14.

[27] *Interpretation of the Greco-Turkish Agreement of December 1st, 1926*, advisory opinion, PCIJ, 1928, Series B, no. 16.

from any existing power conferred upon the UN (such would have been impossible to find), but instead whether the power could be considered necessary for the effective functioning of the organisation.[28] And that proved a dramatic broadening: after all, it is usually not that difficult to suggest that a particular activity, although not envisaged in the constituent instrument, may nonetheless be considered necessary for the organisation's effective functioning. The underlying reasoning connects means to ends, and does so in the knowledge that means can be infinite, and their success in achieving the ends can rarely be predicted in advance. So, effectively, all that is required is that a plausible case can be made in favour of a particular activity as functionally necessary, and especially where supported by a majority of members, few will argue that the ends do not justify the (implied) means.

Additionally, however, the ICJ has repeatedly underlined that even implied powers, despite not being rendered expressly, nonetheless originate 'by necessary intendment', or are 'conferred' on the organisation. The line of reasoning is questionable. Surely, if a power were intended, it would have been granted explicitly. But the rhetoric serves to save face: this way, member States can ingeniously justify their non-opposition to a particular activity under reference to such power having already been accepted at an earlier date, by an earlier government, at the time when that earlier government joined the organisation. The pattern is consistent: the ICJ has repeatedly made use of its implied powers doctrine, and consistently maintained that implied powers arise by necessary intendment.

Beyond this, the Court has occasionally added some extras. In *Effect of Awards*, justifying the creation of an administrative tribunal at the UN, it relied in part on implied powers, but also invoked the UN's general mandate: it would be awkward for an organisation set up to foster international justice to deny the possibility of justice to its own employees.[29] The Court must have considered adding the argument to be necessary, as critics of the administrative tribunal could have pointed out that the costs associated with staff compensation and the fact that not even the tribunal's general task was envisaged in the Charter, might have made an

---

[28] *Reparation*, 182–183.
[29] *Effect of Awards of Compensation made by the United Nations Administrative Tribunal*, advisory opinion, ICJ Rep. 1954, p. 47.

implied powers argument on its own less than persuasive.[30] What the Court could not predict, however, is that the same argument has a flipside: organisations might be held responsible for not living up to their mandate, as was the case when the UN refused to act during the Rwandan genocide.[31]

In *Certain Expenses*, dealing with the financial fall-out of the first peacekeeping missions authorised by the General Assembly, the Court refused to be drawn into a competence struggle between the Assembly and the Security Council, and again came up with a broad, open-ended construction.[32] Even if an organ exceeds its own powers, the activity concerned may still be within the scope of the organisation's overall powers, and at any rate, each organ is to be judge of its own competence. That was useful for the UN as a whole, no doubt: the message was that the UN can hardly do wrong. As Bowett once held, the Court's answer was 'entirely predictable' and not very helpful, in that it 'made virtually no difference to the entrenched positions of the opponents of the powers assumed by the General Assembly'.[33] That said, the Court has made clear that the practice of UN organs can come to affect the distribution of powers between those organs. In the 2004 *Wall* opinion, it referred to the 'accepted practice' of the General Assembly to address matters of peace and security as being relevant in determining whether the Assembly had exceeded its powers.[34]

The Court tried a different approach in the 1996 *WHA Opinion* where, aided by the circumstance of two near-identical requests for an advisory opinion, it assimilated the relation between the UN and its specialised

---

[30] Put differently: it is difficult to argue that offering remedies to staff members in labour disputes somehow contributes to the maintenance of peace and security – something additional might be needed.

[31] For an argument to this effect, see J. Klabbers, 'Reflections on Role Responsibility: The Responsibility of International Organizations for Failing to Act', 28 *European Journal of International Law* (2017) 1133.

[32] *Certain Expenses of the United Nations (Article 17, Paragraph 2, of the Charter)*, advisory opinion, ICJ Rep. 1962, p. 151.

[33] D. W. Bowett, 'The Court's Role in Relation to International Organizations', in Vaughan Lowe and Malgosia Fitzmaurice (eds.), *Fifty Years of the International Court of Justice* (Cambridge University Press, 1996), 181, at 185. Note, however, that Bowett may have had an axe to grind, having just been passed over as nominee for a seat on the Court. See C. Jennings, *Robbie: The Life of Sir Robert Jennings* (Matador, 2019), at 472.

[34] *Construction of a Wall*, para. 28.

agencies in terms borrowed from domestic governance structures.[35] In this scheme, the UN General Assembly (the other organ asking for an advisory opinion) would be like a ministry of general affairs, assisted by more specialised ministries: the specialised agencies. And in this scheme of things, the powers of those agencies would owe something to the idea of 'speciality': not quite the same as implied powers, but more something along the lines of specialised powers. *In casu*, the powers of the WHO and its Assembly would have to be read against this general scheme, which entailed that the powers of the World Health Assembly depended not only on the WHO Constitution, but also on the UN Charter. This now proved to be an untenable proposition, impossible to reconcile with the basic structure of the international legal order. Afer all, agreement between States are not supposed to affect third parties: every treaty, every constitution even, is *res inter alios acta* – a thing between the parties.[36] The Court made a valiant attempt to break through this system, but eventually could not do so plausibly. It is no surprise that the idea disappeared about as quickly as it has surfaced, even if the term 'speciality' is sometimes still used; but if and when it is used, it is used as synonymous to implied powers, different from how the Court itself conceptualised it in its *WHA Opinion*.

The Court has been careful to maintain the proposition that the steps member States should take following its decisions and advisory opinions, are best left to those States themselves;[37] all the Court can do is to suggest how international obligation should be understood, or find whether international legal obligations have been violated, and inform member States accordingly.[38] In doing so, however, it sometimes gives legal effect to organisational instruments. In *Chagos*, e.g., it construed a string of (ostensibly non-binding) General Assembly resolutions as providing contents to the principle of self-determination. The Court did not endorse a broad concept of self-determination, but having found the General Assembly

---

[35] *Legality of the Use by a State of Nuclear Weapons in Armed Conflict*, advisory opinion, ICJ Rep. 1996, p. 66.
[36] J. Klabbers, 'Global Governance at the ICJ: Re-reading the WHA Opinion', 13 *Max Planck Yearbook of United Nations Law* (2009) 1.
[37] *Kosovo* opinion, para. 44.
[38] Even with respect to determinations of whether acts fall within the scope of the function of international officials, the Court has suggested that the organisation's opinion is not by definition the final word: it can be asset aside if there are "compelling reasons" to do so. See *Difference Relating to Immunity from Legal Process of a Special Rapporteur of the Commission of Human Rights*, advisory opnion, ICJ Rep. 1999, p. 62, para. 61.

competent to address decolonization, it treated the relevant General Assembly resolutions as giving effect to the Assembly's role in the decolonization process.[39]

III Internal Affairs

Much of what the Court has said on internal matters within organisations has drawn inspiration from domestic public law doctrines relating to separation of powers or checks and balances, and it could hardly be otherwise. This already became clear in *Admissions II*. It was asked whether the General Assembly could decide on admission without, as Article 4 of the Charter has it, a recommendation by the Security Council.[40] The Court felt this could not be allowed; to hold otherwise 'would be to deprive the Security Council of an important power which has been entrusted to it by the Charter'.[41] The upshot was that the Charter had created a system of checks and balances, which could not be disturbed.

Still, this is about as far as the Court has gone. In *Certain Expenses*, the ICJ declined to divide the proper sphere of competence of the Security Council and General Assembly with any precision, merely suggesting that in first instance, each organ is itself responsible for delimiting its proper sphere of action when it comes to matters of peace and security. It accepted that the Charter assigns 'primary responsibility' to the Council, but that was about as far as it was willing to go. The Court did much the same in several opinions on the validity of ICAO Council decisions, effectively limiting itself to a procedural and marginal review of the contested decisions.[42]

The Court has also been extremely reluctant to pronounce itself on judicial review, in particular on the question whether the Court itself would

[39] The dilemma: if self-determination encompasses more than decolonization, then the Court could not have given the same force to General Assembly instruments. For commentary, see J. Klabbers, 'Shrinking Self-Determination: The Chagos Opinion of the International Court of Justice', 8 *ESIL Reflections* (2019).

[40] It had earlier discussed the substantive equirements for admission, in *Conditions of Admission of a State to Membership in the United Nations (Article 4 of the Charter)*, ICJ Rep. 1948, p. 57.

[41] *Competence of the General Assembly for the Admission of a State to the United Nations*, advisory opinion, ICJ Rep. 1950, p. 4, at 9.

[42] Already in the early 1970s in *Appeal Relating to the Jurisdiction of the ICAO Council (India v. Pakistan)*, ICJ Rep. 1952, p. 46.

have the power to review Security Council acts. A proposal to that effect had been defeated during the drafting process of the UN Charter, and in various cases the Court tried to duck the bullet, never more so than in *Lockerbie*. At issue was the legality of Security Council sanctions imposed on Libya for its refusal to hand over suspects of terrorist activities. Libya argued, not unreasonably, that there is no general obligation under international law to hand over individuals, much less one's own nationals, and accordingly, the sanctions amounted to a violation of Libya's rights under the Montreal Convention.[43] Thus, the sanctions should be quashed – surely, the Council cannot be allowed to violate the rights of States under international law.

The counter-argument was that the Charter itself imposes no limits on what the Security Council can do: its discretion is nigh-on unlimited and consequently, beyond judicial review. The Court's dilemma was clear. It could not afford to impose limits on the Security Council, for if the Council would subsequently ignore the Court, the entire system would be in crisis. It also could not afford to approve of the Council's acts, for in that case too, the entire system would be in crisis – the Council's legislative blank check would then be confirmed. As a result, the Court very effectively did nothing. In 1992, it refused to offer Libya interim relief. A mere six years later it found it had jurisdiction to decide the case (it could hardly have found otherwise), but was clearly not in a hurry, and some years later the case, still undecided, was removed from the roll at the parties' request.

The Court was internally highly divided over *Lockerbie*, with quite a few judges having some sympathy for Libya's position. In those circumstances, it may well be politically wise (if legally unsatisfactory) to adopt a conciliatory course, something the politically most astute among the judges realised all too well.[44] In those cases, on the other hand, where the Court could approve Security Council action, it has been less reluctant to engage in judicial review – it could do so without jeopardizing the international legal order. Thus, in *Namibia*, it found that the Council's decision-making

---

[43] The Convention contains the *aut dedere, aut judicare* principle, and thus creates the possibility for States to resort to prosecution rather than extradition.

[44] In his brief separate opinion to the order on interim relief, Judge Lachs frames the issue not as one of judicial review, but as one of concurrent jurisdiction between two UN organs, and the need to act harmoniously between them.

practice, while departing from the Charter, was nonetheless justified as a 'general practice of the organisation', after South Africa had argued that since the Charter procedure was not followed, the resulting decisions had to be annulled.[45]

Indeed, generally the Court has been reluctant to step in the shoes of political organs. If in the various ICAO cases it limited itself to checking for manifest errors in decision-making,[46] in *IMCO Maritime Safety Committee* it endorsed a close, textual reading of the constituent instrument. It was asked to ascertain whether the term 'largest ship owning nations' has to be given a literal meaning, or rather a functional meaning in light of IMCO's functions, which include safety at sea. Conservatively perhaps, it advocated the former, therewith approving the initial IMCO Assembly decision to include Panama and Liberia as members of the Maritime Safety Committee, the maritime equivalent of having the fox guard the henhouse.[47]

IV The External World

The ICJ has struggled on various occasion with determining the position of international organisations as international actors, quite apart from considerations about legal personality as discussed above. Perhaps its boldest attempt resides in the dispositif of its 1971 *Namibia* opinion. Having been asked to determine what the consequences are for States of the various resolutions adopted by the Security Council condemning South Africa's administration over what is now Namibia, and imposing sanctions, the

---

[45] See *Legal Consequences for States of the Continued Presence of South Africa in Namibia (South-West Africa) Notwithstanding Security Council Resolution 276 (1970)*, advisory opinion, ICJ Rep. 1971, p. 16, para. 22. In *Bosnia*, moreover, it could hold that a request to declare a Security Council resolution invalid fell outside the scope of an action for interim measures of protection: see *Case Concerning Application of the Convention on the Prevention and Punishment of the Crime of Genocide (Bosnia and Herzegovina v. Yugoslavia (Serbia and Montenegro))*, further request for the indication of provisional measures, ICJ Rep. 1993, p. 325.

[46] See e.g., the 1972 *India* v. *Pakistan* case, and the recent *Qatar* decisions.

[47] See *Constitution of the Maritime Safety Committee of the Inter-Governmental Maritime Consultative Organisation*, advisory opinion, ICJ Rep. 1960, p. 150. The literature often proposes a more expansive, teleological interpretation: see, e.g., T. Sato, *Evolving Constitutions of International Organizations* (Martinus Nijhoff, 1996).

Court held that it was 'incumbent' on non-member States of the UN to assist the UN in the action it had taken in respect of Namibia.[48] Put differently: non-member States, so the Court held, would be obligated to give effect to binding UN action. The point has remained under-illuminated, partly perhaps because while four judges voted against, the judges issuing a dissenting opinion had bigger fish to fry. Even so, the point once again struck at the heart of conceptions about the international legal order. If based on State sovereignty, then the UN simply cannot exercise legal authority over non-members, and no obligations arising under the Charter can be 'incumbent' on non-members. At most, the UN can kindly request, in accordance with Article 2(6) of the UN Charter, those non-members' assistance. It can ask, but not order. A possible justification could reside in the theory of the *erga omnes* obligation, launched some time earlier, and this is likely precisely what the ICJ had in mind. If so, however, and whatever its merits, the obligation would have to stem from considerations extraneous to the UN Charter, and thus would shed little light on UN law, much less international organisations law.[49]

The most sobering opinion of the Court involving international organ-isations is its 1980 opinion in the *WHO/Egypt* case. At issue was whether the WHO could unilaterally terminate its headquarters agreement with Egypt after the latter had made itself unpopular by concluding a peace agreement with Israel. Some of the individual judges felt this was a question solely about the scope of the WHO's powers. The majority, however, realised the issue was not about WHO powers, but about the position of the WHO in the international legal order. Egypt, true enough, was a member State, and could thus, in that capacity, be considered as having consented to the WHO's lawful activities. On the other hand though, in addition to being a member State, Egypt was also a treaty partner, and as such protected by the *pacta sunt servanda* rule. The headquarters agreement was a treaty like any treaty, subject to the work-ings of the law of treaties. That one side happened to be an international organisation could take nothing away from that construction, nor that the

---

[48] See *Legal Consequences for States of the Continued Presence of South Africa in Namibia (South-West Africa) Notwithstanding Security Council Resolution 276 (1970)*, advisory opinion, ICJ Rep. 1971, p. 16, para. 133(3).

[49] J. Klabbers, 'The Scope of International Law: Erga Omnes Obligations and the Turn to Morality', in M. Tupamäki (ed.), *Liber Amicorum Bengt Broms* (ILA, 1999), 149.

treaty partner also had a different capacity as member State. The Court realised there was no way out, and that the rights of Egypt qua treaty partner would have to be respected. If not, the consequences would be dire: who would want to do business with organisations if *pacta* would only be *servanda* as long as the organisation would be happy with them? Allowing this to happen, the Court must have thought, can only create havoc: no State, no private actor, would wish to be subjected to such a one-sided regime.

In other words, in its *WHO/Egypt* opinion, the Court ran into the limits of the law of international organisations. Traditionally, organisations had been conceived, rightly or (more likely) wrongly, as only involving their member States: outward radiation, whether towards third States or even individuals within member States, was not anticipated. The Court managed to circumvent the problem in 1949 in *Reparation*, by suggesting that the UN had international legal personality (despite the absence of a clause to that effect in the Charter) and, what is more, the sort of personality that is opposable to the outside world. This allowed the UN (though not necessarily any other organisation) to bring claims against the outside world. But confronted with the reverse situation (a claim coming from the outside, that is Egypt) and towards a different organisation (the WHO), the Court could no longer escape – it could only draw the conclusion that the law, as it stood, had reached its limits. It noted, somewhat in passing, that international organisations are subjected to international law, whether in the form of treaties they are parties to or in the form of 'general rules of international law', but doing so also entailed that the organisation's freedom and autonomy from the international legal order were limited, regardless (and this is the important point) of what the member States had agreed upon among themselves. Liberating the organisation from its members (necessary, ironically, to allow organisations to function effectively) went hand in hand with limiting the organisation by recognizing the authority of international law.

V To Conclude

The Court's main contribution to the law of international organisations has been to confirm many of the ambivalences inherent in the latter, as well as the limits of what the law, as traditionally conceived, can do. That is not to be sniffed at: courts can only work with the materials before them and within the parameters of the legal framework in which they are embedded. In the case of international law, that framework was largely developed in the late nineteenth and early twentieth century, based on insights and understandings that were then generally accepted. Against such a background, the surprising thing is not that the Court managed to contribute little to the development of the law of international organisations, but rather that it managed to contribute anything at all.

Further Reading

S. Barros, *Governance as Responsibility: Member States as Human Rights Protectors in International Financial Institutions* (Cambridge University Press, 2019).

D. W. Bowett, 'The Court's Role in Relation to International Organizations', in V. Lowe and M. Fitzmaurice (eds.), *Fifty Years of the International Court of Justice* (Cambridge University Press, 1996), 181.

C. M. Brölmann, *The Institutional Veil in Public International Law: International Organisations and the Law of Treaties* (Hart, 2007).

V. Engström, *Constructing the Powers of International Institutions* (Martinus Nijhoff, 2012).

J. Klabbers, *An Introduction to International Organizations Law* (3rd ed., Cambridge University Press, 2015).

J. Klabbers, 'The EJIL Foreword: The Transformation of International Organizations Law', 26 *European Journal of International Law* (2015) 9.

E. Lauterpacht, 'The Development of the Law of International Organizations by the Decisions of International Tribunals', 152 *Collected Courses of the Academy of International Law* (1976) 377.

T. Sato, *Evolving Constitutions of International Organizations* (Martinus Nijhoff, 1996).

J. Sloan and G. Hernandez, 'The Role of the International Court of Justice in the Development of the Institutional Law of the United Nations', in C. Tams and J. Sloan (eds.), *The Development of International Law by the International Court of Justice* (Oxford University Press, 2013) 197.

22 Human Rights

Carlos Espósito

The jurisdiction of the International Court of Justice is general and broad. International human rights, as a fundamental part of international law, are in principle a source of law applicable by the Court. The Court, however, is not a specialised human rights tribunal Court. Moreover, a more modest role of the Court in the field of human rights is also restricted by several structural and normative limitations to the Court's role in the interpretation and application of international human rights. The exclusive clients of the Court's contentious jurisdiction are States and individuals do not have standing before the Court: therefore, human rights issues are not the most common business of the Court. The lawyers who generally appear before the Court are traditional public international lawyers, not specialised human rights lawyers. The exclusive nature of the Court's institutional legal structure and the reluctance of the States to accept the jurisdiction of the Court in human rights treaties have significant influence on the rather scant jurisprudence of the Court regarding the interpretation and application of human rights.

This chapter will first describe the institutional reasons that explain the restricted and scarce role of the World Court on human rights – that is, its contentious jurisdiction is limited to inter-State dispute settlement and the lack of standing for individuals before the Court. It will also deal with normative burdens stemming from the human rights system and the lack of will of the States to give the Court the authority to solve the disputes concerning the interpretation and application of human rights treaties. The second part will consider the impact that the international law of human rights has already had in the advisory opinions and judgments of the Court, and it will assess the actual contribution of the Court to the protection and promotion of human rights. I argue that the structural limitations

Thanks to Jessica Almqvist and Kate Parlett for helpful comments.

have not impeded the Court from making important contributions to human rights even if the limitations continue to be felt in the case law. A brief conclusion considers the role of the Court in the protection and promotion of human rights, its potential and its limits.

I Not a Human Rights Court: Structural Disengagement and Legal Tribes

The disengagement of the International Court of Justice with human rights may be described as a consequence of the institutional design of the World Court. Human rights did not even exist as legal international rights at the time of the conception of the Statute of the Permanent Court of International Justice,[1] prepared by the Advisory Committee of Jurists in 1920, which remained significantly the same after the adoption of the Statute of the Permanent Court of International Justice in 1945.[2] The Charter of the United Nations introduced a new conception of the Court as the principal judicial organ of the Organization,[3] and affirmed the purpose to 'achieve international co-operation in [...] promoting and encouraging respect for human rights and for fundamental freedoms for all without distinction as to race, sex, language, or religion', and the obligation 'to promote universal respect for and observance of human rights and fundamental freedoms for all, without distinction as to race, sex, language or religion'.[4] These most relevant provisions, which became the seed of a

---

[1] For several reasons, including that for this author international human rights become legal rights after 1945, this survey will not engage with the jurisprudence of the PCIJ, which arguably contributed to the field of human rights by considering private rights and the treatment of aliens in its judgments and advisory opinions. See S. M. Schwebel, 'The Treatment of Human Rights and of Aliens in the International Court of Justice', in V. Lowe and M. Fitzmaurice (eds.), *Fifty Years of the International Court of Justice. Essays in Honour of Sir Robert Jennings* (Cambridge University Press, 1996) 327, at 327–329.

[2] Advisory Committee of Jurists, Documents Presented to the Committee Relating to Existing Plans for the Establishment of a Permanent Court of International Justice (1920). See O. Spiermann, 'Historical Introduction', in A. Zimmermann and Tams (eds.), *The Statute of the International Court of Justice. A Commentary* (3rd ed. Oxford University Press, 2019) pp. 92–116.

[3] Art. 7 UN Charter. See V. Gowlland-Debbas and M. Forteau, 'Article 7 UN Charter', in *The Statute of the International Court of Justice. A Commentary*, 135.

[4] Articles 1(3) and 55 UN Charter, respectively. For an early study of these clauses in connection with Court, see E. Schwelb, 'The International Court of Justice and the Human Rights Clauses of the Charter', 66 *American Journal of International Law* (1972) 337.

universal system of promotion and protection of human rights, did not at that time affect substantially the original idea of the Court as an *inter-State dispute settlement body* that admits only States as parties in cases before the Court, as provided by Article 34(1) of the Statute.[5]

The strict limitations on the contentious jurisdiction of the Court reflects the conception of international law in the 1920s, with its most exclusive notion of international legal personality only reserved to States.[6] The State-only approach of the Statute has been the object of an intense criticism from both scholars and judges of the Court.[7] Already in 1950, Hersch Lauterpacht affirmed that the formulation of Article 34 of the Statute must 'be regarded as out of keeping with the needs and tendencies of international law', and urged its amendment to extend the access to the Court to individuals with the consent of States.[8] He suggested a new wording for Article 34: 'The Court shall have jurisdiction: (1) in disputes between States; (2) in disputes between States and private and public bodies or private individuals in cases in which States have consented, in advance or by special agreement, to appear as defendants before the Court'.[9] An authoritative commentator of the law and practice of the Court, Shabtai Rosenne, also rejected the 'States only' condition as 'the most out of tune of the requirements of modern international law'.[10]

International courts of a general character, such as the European Court of Justice, are accessible to individuals and allow individual suits against States under certain circumstances. Some scholars have suggested that the ICJ should follow such experiences.[11] Most of the criticism of Article 34,

---

[5] On Art. 34 of the Statute, see R. Kolb, *The International Court of Justice* (Hart 2013) 259 ff.

[6] See, e.g., the famous *S.S. Lotus (France v. Turkey)*, 1927 PCIJ Ser. A, No. 10, at p. 18 ('International law governs relations between independent States'). The ICJ expanded the concept of subjects of international law to international organisations already in its 1949 advisory opinion on the *Reparation for Injuries Suffered in the Service of the United Nations 11 April 1949*, ICJ Reports 1949, p. 174, at 179.

[7] Including judges Sir Robert Jennings and Sir Gerald Fitzmaurice, and the Institute de Droit International. See P.-M. Dupuy and C Hoss, Article 34, *The Statute of the International Court of Justice. A Commentary*, pp. 18–25.

[8] H. Lauterpacht, *International Law and Human Rights* (Stevens & Sons Ltd., 1950, reprinted by Archon Books in 1968) pp. 56–60.

[9] Ibid., p. 58.

[10] S. Rosenne, *The Law and Practice of the International Court* (Kluwer, 1965) 268.

[11] M. W. Janis, 'Individuals and the International Court', in in A. S. Muller, D. Raic, and J. Thuransky (eds.), *The International Court of Justice; Its Future Role after Fifty Years* (Kluwer Law International, The Hague, 1997). For Janis, '[o]pening the jurisdiction

however, has been directed towards the absence of standing for international organisations in contentious cases, not individuals as natural legal persons.[12] Notwithstanding these criticisms and proposals, the crude reality is that Court's contentious jurisdiction is still limited to States only, and the lack of standing for individuals in contentious cases before the Court is clearly an essential limitation on its role in human rights law. Even if granting individuals a right to be parties in cases before the Court were practically possible,[13] there seems to be little or no State support for the idea of expanding the jurisdiction of the Court in this direction[14] and transforming it into a human rights tribunal or a sort of world court of human rights.[15]

Not all can be blamed on history, though. Some qualitative credit for the narrow role of the Court in the protection and development of human rights must be ascribed to the stakeholders. Indeed, the preservation of the structural disengagement presented above may also be explained on the basis of certain tribal attitudes and cultural preconceptions of the legal and political actors involved in the business of solving disputes of an international character and who, with or without reasonable basis, do not see the World Court as a favourable forum for the effective protection of human rights. These impediments to a stronger human rights role for the Court stem from

of the ICJ to individuals is probably the best and perhaps the only means for ensuring its effective utilization' (at 209).

[12] For a general work on the position of the individual in the international legal system, see K. Parlett, *The Individual in the International Legal System. Continuity and Change in International Law* (Cambridge, 2010). For specific study on access of individuals to international justice, see A. A. Cançado Trindade, *The Access of Individuals to International Justice* (Oxford University Press, 2011).

[13] Some authors even doubt the practicality of admitting international organisations as parties in cases before the Court. See, e.g., Kolb, *The International Court of Justice* at 279.

[14] Simma refers to a proposal by the United Kingdom to 'invest the ICJ with the power to give advisory opinions on human rights which could then be submitted for action to the General Assembly. The view was "demolished" in subsequent discussion.' B. Simma, 'Human Rights before the International Court of Justice: Community Interest Coming to Life', in C. J. Tams and J. Sloan (eds.), *The Development of International Law by the International Court of Justice* (Oxford University Press, 2013) 303, fn 6.

[15] For a proposal to create a universal court of human rights, see J. Kozma, M. Nowak and M. Scheinin, *A World Court of Human Rights: Consolidated Statute and Commentary* (2010). See also M. Nowak, 'Eight Reasons Why We Need a World Court of Human Rights', in G. Alfredsson et al. (eds.), *International Human Rights Monitoring Mechanisms* (Martinus Nijhoff, 2009) 697; M. Nowak, 'The Need for a World Court of Human Right', 7 *Hum. Rts. L. Rev.* (2007) 251.

the lack of will of the States to give the Court authority to resolve the disputes concerning the interpretation and application of human rights treaties, and the access to the universal human rights system itself.

The contentious jurisdiction of the Court in cases involving human rights occurs only when States express consent through special agreements, declarations recognising the compulsory jurisdiction of the Court under Article 36 (2) of the Statute,[16] or compromissory clauses included in human rights treaties and conventions. This consent is not frequently given with respect to human rights. Article 36(2) declarations do not abound, and all of them have reservations.[17] Regarding human rights, the salient example is the *Diallo* case,[18] in which Guinea relied on Article 36(2) to establish the jurisdiction of the Court in a case brought by way of diplomatic protection[19] involving the responsibility of the Democratic Republic of Congo under the International Covenant on Civil and Political Rights, and the African Charter on Human and People's Rights. Compromissory clauses accepting the jurisdiction of the Court in human rights treaties are also rare. States limit the role of the Court as an interpreter of human rights because of the scarcity of human rights treaties, and the lack of international humanitarian law instruments, that confer jurisdiction on the Court.[20] Moreover, of the very few human rights treaties that do provide for disputes to be referred to the Court,[21] only the Genocide Convention does it

---

[16] See J. M. Touvenin on jurisdiction, Chapter 6 in this volume.

[17] For a list of declarations recognising the jurisdiction of the Court as compulsory, see www .icj-cij.org/en/declarations.

[18] *Ahmadou Sadio Diallo* (*Republic of Guinea* v. *Democratic Republic of the Congo*), Preliminary Objections, ICJ Reports 2007, p. 596, para. 32.

[19] See K. Parlett, 'Diplomatic Protection and the International Court of Justice', in C. J. Tams and J. Sloan (eds.), *The Development of International Law by the International Court of Justice* (Oxford University Press, 2013), pp. 87–106.

[20] J. Crawford and A. Keene, 'Interpretation of the Human Rights Treaties by the International Court of Justice', 24 (7)*The International Journal of Human Rights* (2020) 935, at 936. On the Court and humanitarian law see C. Kress, 'The International Court of Justice and the Law of Armed Conflicts', in C. J. Tams and J. Sloan (eds.), *The Development of International Law by the International Court of Justice* (Oxford University Press, 2013) 264.

[21] See Convention on the Prevention and Punishment of the Crime of Genocide, 78 UNTS 277 (signed in Paris, 9 February 1948, entered into force 12 January 1951), Art. IX; Convention on the Political Rights of Women, 193 UNTS 135 (signed in New York, 31 March 1953, entered into force 7 July 1954); the International Convention on the Elimination of All Forms of Racial Discrimination, 660 UNTS 195 (signed in New York, 7 March 1996, entered into force 4 January 1969), Art. 22; the Convention on the Elimination of All Forms of Discrimination against Women, 1349 UNTS 13 (signed in New York, 18 December 1979,

unconditionally,[22] the rest having strict conditions that operate as obstacles to the jurisdiction of the Court. This was the case, for example, in *Georgia* v. *Russia*.[23] The Court held in her judgment that Georgia did not attempt to fulfil the prior obligation to negotiate as provided in Article 22 of CERD[24] as a precondition to the exercise of the jurisdiction of the Court, and therefore upheld the preliminary objection raised by the Russian Federation.[25] Some judges in the minority criticised this conclusion as too formalistic, when the case demanded a realistic and substantive approach.[26] Judge Cançado Trindade, consistently with his theoretical approach to international law,[27] went further in his critique, disapproving of the arguments and the interpretation of the majority of the Court, among other things, for their conception of 'the fundamental principle of consent',[28] and for not taking

entered into force 3 September 1981), Art. 29; and the Convention against Torture and Other Cruel, Inhuman or Degrading Treatment or Punishment, 1465 UNTS 85 (signed in New York, 10 December 1984, entered into force 26 June 1987), Art. 30; International Convention for the Protection of All Persons from Enforced Disappearance, 2716 UNTS 3 (signed in New York, 20 December 2006), Art 42 (1).

[22] Article IX of the Genocide Convention provides that: 'Disputes between the Contracting Parties relating to the interpretation, application or fulfilment of the present Convention, including those relating to the responsibility of a State for genocide or for any of the other acts enumerated in article III, shall be submitted to the International Court of Justice at the request of any of the parties to the dispute'.

[23] *Application of the International Convention on the Elimination of All Forms of Racial Discrimination (Georgia* v. *Russian Federation)* (Preliminary Objections), ICJ Reports 2011, p. 70, paras. 122–184.

[24] Art. 22 CERD provides that: 'Any dispute between two or more States Parties with respect to the interpretation or application of this Convention, which is not settled by negotiation or by the procedures expressly provided for in this Convention, shall, at the request of any of the parties to the dispute, be referred to the International Court of Justice for decision, unless the disputants agree to another mode of settlement'.

[25] Cf. *Application of the International Convention on the Elimination of All Forms of Racial Discrimination (Azerbaijan* v. *Armenia),* Order of 7 December 2021, para. 40, affirming its *prima facie* jurisdiction; and *Application of the International Convention on the Elimination of All Forms of Racial Discrimination (Qatar* v. *United Arab Emirates), Provisional Measures, Order of 23 July 2018, ICJ Reports 2018 (II)*, p. 419, para. 41 affirming its *prima facie* jurisdiction.

[26] *Application of the International Convention on the Elimination of All Forms of Racial Discrimination.* Joint Dissenting Opinion of President Owada, Judges Simma, Donoghue, and Judge ad hoc Gaja.

[27] For instance, A. A. Cançado Trindade, *International Law for Humankind Towards a New Jus Gentium* (3rd rev. ed., Brill, 2020).

[28] *Application of the International Convention on the Elimination of All Forms of Racial Discrimination*, para. 110.

seriously the basic rationale of human rights treaties and the need to interpret them as living instruments.[29]

Fundamentally, these jurisdictional and structural limitations have a direct influence in the way in which human rights treaties are interpreted by the Court, because the Court does not use and is not willing to use consistently typical human rights modes of interpretation.[30] This interpretive controversy is connected to another limitation that the Court may find when dealing with compromissory clauses in human rights treaties, because such treaties, in principle, also admit reservations, which may lead the Court to find that it does not have jurisdiction, as happened with Rwanda's reservations to certain human rights treaties in the *Armed Activities* case.[31] This conclusion was adopted notwithstanding the hierarchy of the international rights and obligations involved in this case – *erga omnes* obligations or peremptory norms.[32]

The access to the universal human rights system may also be a factor for the limited role of the Court in human rights. The institutions of the human rights system are best equipped to deal with human rights claims whether at regional human rights courts, such as the European Court of Human Rights or the Inter-American Court of Human Rights, or at the numerous United Nations Charter bodies[33] and treaty bodies[34] dealing with a diverse range of human rights claims. It can be argued that the human rights system fosters a sort of tribal approach that would accentuate the focus of international human rights lawyers in their strategies and practices, leaving the International Court of Justice out because of its limitations and classical approach to international law. This strategy is explicitly acknowledged by some human rights lawyers, who would suggest that the lesser

---

[29] *Application of the International Convention on the Elimination of All Forms of Racial Discrimination.* Dissenting Opinion of Judge Cançado Trindade.

[30] For a somewhat different view, see Crawford and Keene, 'Interpretation of the Human Rights', 947.

[31] Armed Activities on the Territory of the Congo (New Application: 2002) (*Democratic Republic of the Congo* v. *Rwanda*), Jurisdiction and Admissibility, Judgment, ICJ Reports 2006, p. 6.

[32] See *infra* Section II of this chapter.

[33] See, e.g., M. Kothari, 'From Commission to the Council: Evolution of the UN Charter Bodies', D. Shelton (ed.), *The Oxford Handbook of Human Rights* (Oxford University Press, 2013) 587.

[34] See, e.g., N. Rodley, 'The Role and Impact of Treaty Bodies', D. Shelton (ed.), *The Oxford Handbook of Human Rights* (Oxford University Press, 2013) 621.

role of the Court on this field is beneficial from the perspective of human rights, 'given the tendencies towards a relatively conservative and State-oriented position of the Court'.[35]

II Human Rights Find a Way: Incorporation of International Human Rights in the Case Law of the Court

The structural, normative and cultural limitations discussed in the previous part clearly indicate that the position of the Court will never be that of a specialised human rights tribunal. This does not mean that the Court is prevented from playing a significant role in the interpretation and application of human rights. On the contrary, there are robust reasons that support a relevant role for the Court in human rights. On the one hand, the structure, based on consent and the 'states only' conception, has its cracks. One may be found in the advisory jurisdiction[36] of the Court. Advisory proceedings do not depend on the consent of States: 'no State, whether a Member of the United Nations or not, can prevent the giving of an Advisory Opinion which the United Nations considers to be desirable in order to obtain enlightenment as to the course of action it should take'.[37] Moreover, the Court openly recognises that '[t]he mere fact that it is not the rights of States which are in issue in the proceedings cannot suffice to deprive the Court of a competence expressly conferred on it by its Statute'.[38]

The history of the Court, on the other hand, demonstrates that there is an evolution in the manner in which the Court deals with human right issues. Judge Simma refers to this evolution as going from hesitation and restraint to a potential qualitative gap in the caselaw of the Court.[39] Indeed, a further evolution is possible on many important levels, including the fight for human rights at the levels of advocacy and theory, because human

---

[35] J. Grimheden, 'The International Court of Justice: Monitoring Human Rights', in Gudmundur Alfredsson et al. (eds.), *International Monitoring Mechanisms: Essays in Honour of Jacob Th. Möller* (2nd rev. ed., Martinus Nijhoff, 2009) 249, at 249–250.

[36] On the advisory jurisdiction of the Court see J. M. Touvenin, Chapter 6, this volume. See generally P. d'Argent, 'Article 65', in *The Statute of the International Court of Justice. A Commentary*, 1783, with an updated bibliography.

[37] *Interpretation of the Peace Treaties*, Advisory Opinion, ICJ Reports 1950, p. 65, at 71.

[38] *Application for Review of Judgement No. 158 of the United Nations Administrative Tribunal* (Advisory Opinion), ICJ Reports 1973, p. 16, para. 14.

[39] B. Simma, 'Human Rights before the International Court of Justice: Community Interest Coming to Life', 303–317.

rights law is part of the province of international law, and the jurisdiction of the Court does not have limits *ratione materiae.* The Court already has a relevant role in the incorporation of human rights into its own jurisprudence through many and diverse ways. This process has been brilliantly described by Judge Simma as judicial mainstreaming[40] of human rights which occurs when the Court integrates 'this branch of the law into both the fabric of general international law and its various other branches'.[41] The means for the incorporation of human rights into general international law are varied. They include the clarification of the human rights nature of certain treaty obligations,[42] contributions to specific areas of treaty law in relation to human rights,[43] or the elucidation of concepts such as 'jus cogens' norms and 'erga omnes obligations', which may prove particularly helpful for the interpretation and enforcement of human rights. Mainstreaming, however, also denotes a normative position about the proper role of the Court regarding human rights, which might not be wholly satisfactory for those who support a stronger view of the value of human rights in international law. In any case, modest and limited as it might be, there is a significant contribution to the development of human rights by the Court through a substantial incorporation of these rights into general international law. The following paragraphs discuss two central instances of actual or potential contributions by the Court to the promotion and protection of human rights, and their limits.[44]

A The Art of Interpretation

The first such instance concerns treaty interpretation, a key element of the judicial practice of the Court.[45] In order to examine the actual and

[40] B. Simma, 'Mainstreaming Human Rights: The Contribution of the International Court of Justice', 3(1) *Journal of International Dispute Settlement* (2012) 7.

[41] B. Simma, 'Human Rights before the International Court of Justice: Community Interest Coming to Life', 323–324.

[42] For example, the obligations of States under Article 36, para. 1, of the Vienna Convention on Consular Relations in *LaGrand (Germany* v. *United States of America)*, ICJ Reports 2001, 466; *Avena and Other Mexican Nationals (Mexico* v. *United States of America)*, ICJ Reports 2007, 12; *Jadhav (India* v. *Pakistan), Judgment, ICJ Reports 2019*, p. 418.

[43] For instance, on reservation to treaties, *Reservations to the Convention on the Prevention and Punishment of the Crime of Genocide* (Advisory Opinion), ICJ Reports 1951, 15.

[44] For comprehensive studies, see the Further Reading section of this chapter.

[45] See Remiro, Chapter 14 in this volume. For a specific analysis, see Crawford and Keene, 'Interpretation of the Human Rights'.

potential contribution of the Court to human rights, one must start by offering an answer to the dilemma of specialisation of human rights treaty interpretation.[46] Are general courts, such as the International Court of Justice, valid interpreters of human rights treaties? Or is it the case that only specialised human rights courts can validly interpret treaties providing for the protection of human rights? This dilemma presupposes a regime of specialised rules of interpretation for human rights treaties as an exception to the general rule established by Articles 31–33 of the Vienna Convention on the Law of Treaties,[47] which is applied by the Court as reflecting customary international law.[48]

I share the view of the authors who defend the flexible nature of the interpretation regime established by the VCLT. In that sense, for example, Gardiner believes that 'the Vienna rules are more in the nature of principles

---

[46] See M. Waibel, 'Uniformity versus Specialization (2): A Uniform Regime of Treaty Interpretation?' in C. Tams and others (eds.), *Research Handbook on the Law of Treaties* (Elgar, 2014) 375.

[47] B. Çali, 'Specialized Rules of Treaty Interpretation', in D. B. Hollis (ed.), *Oxford Guide to Treaties* (2nd ed., 2020), 504.

[48] For example, *Arbitral Award of 31 July 1989 (Guinea Bissau v. Senegal)*, Judgment, ICJ Reports 1991, p. 53, para. 48; *Territorial Dispute (Libyan Arab Jamahiriya/ Chad)*, Judgment, ICJ Reports 1994, pp. 21–22, para. 41; *LaGrand (Germany v. United States of America)*, Judgment, ICJ Reports 2001, p. 501, para. 99; *Sovereignty over Pulau Ligitan and Pulau Sipadan (Indonesia/Malaysia)*, Judgment, ICJ Reports 2002, p. 645, para. 37; *Legal Consequences of the Construction of a Wall in Occupied Palestinian Territory*, Advisory Opinion, ICJ Reports 2004, p. 174, para. 94; *Avena and Other Mexican Nationals (Mexico v. United States of America)*, Judgment, ICJ Reports 2004, p. 48, para. 83; *Application of the Convention on the Prevention and Punishment of the Crime of Genocide (Bosnia and Herzegovina v. Serbia and Montenegro)*, Judgment, ICJ Reports 2007 (I), pp. 109–110, para. 160; *Dispute Regarding Navigational and Related Rights (Costa Rica v. Nicaragua)*, Judgment, ICJ Reports 2009, p. 213, para. 47. See M. Forteau, 'Les techniques interpretative de la Cour International de Justice', *Revue Général de Droit International Public* (2011) 399ff. (who speaks of a perfect orthodoxy to describe the interpretive practice of the Court: 'il existe une symbiose parfaite entre les règles d'interprétations définies aux articles 31 à 33 de la convention de Vienne sur le droit des traités et la jurispudence de la Cour'.); S. Torres-Bernárdez, 'Interpretation of Treaties by the International Court of Justice following the Adoption of the 1969 Vienna Convention on the Law of Treaties', in G. Hafner et al. (eds.), *Liber Amicorum: Professor Ignaz Seidl-Hohenveldern: In Honour of His 80th Birthday* (Kluwer, 1998), 721. See generally R. K. Gardiner, 'The Vienna Convention Rules of Treaty Interpretation', in D. B. Hollis (ed.), *Oxford Guide to Treaties* (2nd ed., Oxford University Press, 2020) 488, with a fine list of recommended readings, including his book R. K. Gardiner, *Treaty Interpretation* (2nd ed. Oxford University Press, 2015). Also U. Linderfalk, *On the Interpretation of Treaties: The Modern International Law as Expressed in the 1969 Vienna Convention on the Law of Treaties* (Springer, 2007).

and indications of admissible material. They reveal a quite loose structure for developing interpretations, rather than a straightjacket or formulaic set of requirements.'[49]

The exegesis of Article 31(1) VCLT reveals a compromise between these two extremes with a certain preference for a qualified textuality,[50] but it is not restrictive. On the contrary, it is a flexible toolbox, including an ample set of interpretative methods. Article 31 reads: 'A treaty shall be interpreted in good faith in accordance with the ordinary meaning to be given to the terms of the treaty in their context and in the light of its object and purpose.' The textual, contextual and teleological method of interpretation are all included in the rule. There are jurists who understand the rule as setting a lexical priority to the interpretation of the ordinary words of the text. This approach has its appeal based on the qualified textuality, but it is not uncontroversial in theory and practice. The explanation of the general rule of interpretation by the International Law Commission expresses a preference for a holistic approach:

The Commission, by heading the article 'General rule of interpretation' in the singular and by underlining the connexion between paragraphs 1 and 2 and again between paragraph 3 and the two previous paragraphs, intended to indicate that the application of the means of interpretation in the article would be a single combined operation. All the various elements, as they were present in any given case, would be thrown into the crucible, and their interaction would give the legally relevant interpretation. Thus, Article 27 [now 31] is entitled 'General *rule* of interpretation' in the singular, not 'General *rules'* in the plural, because the Commission desired to emphasize that the process of interpretation is a unity and that the provisions of the article form a single, closely integrated rule.[51]

---

[49] Gardiner, *Treaty Interpretation*, 477.
[50] The ILC recognises that 'the text must be presumed to be the authentic expression of the intentions of the parties; and that, in consequence, the starting point of interpretation is the elucidation of the meaning of the text, not an investigation *ab initio* into the intentions of the parties'. YBILC (1966) vol II, 220. The Court starts with the text. See, for example, *Territorial Dispute (Libyan Arab Jamahiriya/Chad), Judgment, ICJ Reports 1994*, p. 22, para. 41 ('[i]nterpretation must be based above all upon the text of the treaty'). See J.-M. Sorel, V. Boré Eveno, 'Article 31', in Olivier Corten, Pierre Klein (eds.), *The Vienna Conventions on the Law of Treaties*, vol. 1 (2011 Oxford University Press), 803. In connection with the topic of this chapter, see the analysis by Waibel, 'Uniformity Versus Specialization (2): A Uniform Regime of Treaty Interpretation?', pp. 380 ss.
[51] YBILC (1966) vol II, 219 (emphasis in original).

The crucible is the melting pot in which text, context and the object and purpose of the treaty are thrown to produce the appropriate meaning for a given interpretation. The European Court of Human Rights backed the holistic approach in the famous *Golder* case when it said that 'the process of interpretation of a treaty is a unity' and that the general rule of Article 31 'places on the same footing the various elements enumerated in the four paragraphs of the Article.'[52] Of course, this process of interpretation allows for a wide range of possibilities depending on the precision of the legal texts being interpreted and the nature of the obligations concerned. However, as Çali has persuasively showed, 'there does not seem to be evidence to suggest that the crucible approach cannot accommodate the interpretive challenges of human rights treaty provisions',[53] including specific rules of interpretation associated with the principle of effectiveness.[54]

So, if the ICJ is not restricted by the general rule of interpretation as set by the VCLT, how has it performed regarding interpretations of human rights treaties? The truth is that the Court, due to the jurisdictional limitations explained in the previous part, has not had many possibilities of interpreting human rights treaties *per se*. In many cases, as Simma has pointed out, the references to human rights by the Court 'appeared in more or less incidental ways'.[55] More recently, however, the Court has dealt with violations of human rights substantively. The salient judgments of the Court based on jurisdictional clauses of human rights

---

[52] *Golder* v. *United Kingdom* (App No 4451/ 70) (1975) 1 EHRR 524, at para. 530. Later the Court also supported a qualified textuality in *Witold Litwa* v. *Poland*, 33 EHRR (2001) 1267: '[T]he sequence in which those elements are listed in Article 31 of the Vienna Convention regulates, however, the order which the process of interpretation of the treaty should follow. That process must start from ascertaining the ordinary meaning of the terms of a treaty – in their context and in the light of its object and purpose, as laid down in paragraph 1 of Article 31' (paras. 58–59).

[53] Çali, 'Specialized Rules of Treaty Interpretation', 511, citing M. Fitzmaurice, 'Interpretation of Human Rights Treaties', in D. Shelton (ed.), *The Oxford Handbook of International Human Rights Law* (Oxford University Press, 2015) 739.

[54] Cf. G. Letsas, 'Strasbourg's Interpretive Ethic: Lessons for the International Lawyer' 21 *EJIL* (2010) 509: 'the VCLT has played very little role in the ECHR case law and [...] the Court's interpretive ethic has been very dismissive of originalism and literal interpretation' (512). See generally S. Touzé, 'Les techniques interprétatives des organes de protection de droits de l'homme', *Revue Général de Droit International Public* (2011–2012) 517.

[55] B. Simma, 'Human Rights Before the International Court of Justice: Community Interest Coming to Life', 304–305.

treaties are those connected to the Genocide Convention,[56] the *Diallo*[57] and *Armed Activities*[58]cases. The Diallo case is particularly important because it is the first judgment in which the Court unanimously found that 'in respect of the circumstances in which Mr. Diallo was expelled from Congolese territory on 31 January 1996, the Democratic Republic of the Congo violated Article 13 of the International Covenant on Civil and Political Rights and Article 12, paragraph 4, of the African Charter on Human and Peoples' Rights; and that 'in respect of the circumstances in which Mr. Diallo was arrested and detained in 1995–1996 with a view to his expulsion, the Democratic Republic of the Congo violated Article 9, paragraphs 1 and 2, of the International Covenant on Civil and Political Rights and Article 6 of the African Charter on Human and Peoples' Rights'.[59] Judge Cançado Trindade has referred to this case-law as 'the advent of a new era of international adjudication of human rights cases by the ICJ'.[60]

---

[56] *Application of the Convention on the Prevention and Punishment of the Crime of Genocide (Bosnia and Herzegovina v. Yugoslavia)* (Preliminary Objections), ICJ Reports 1996, p. 595; *Application of the Convention on the Prevention and Punishment of the Crime of Genocide (Bosnia and Herzegovina v. Serbia and Montenegro)* (Merits), ICJ Reports 2007, p. 43.

[57] *Ahmadou Sadio Diallo (Republic of Guinea v. Democratic Republic of the Congo)* (Merits), ICJ Reports 2010, p. 639.

[58] *Armed Activities on the Territory of the Congo (New Application: 2002) (Democratic Republic of the Congo v. Rwanda)* (Jurisdiction and Admissibility), ICJ Reports 2002, p. 6.

[59] *Ahmadou Sadio Diallo,* para. 165 (2)(3). The Court also found that 'by not informing Mr. Diallo without delay, upon his detention in 1995–1996, of his rights under Article 36, paragraph 1 *(b)*, of the Vienna Convention on Consular Relations, the Democratic Republic of the Congo violated the obligations incumbent upon it under that sub- paragraph'. In the understanding of the Court, however, this is not a proper human rights violation but just an individual right. The Court had the opportunity both in *LaGrand* (para. 78) and *Avena* (para. 124) to recognise such right as a human right, but contrary to the arguments of Germany and Mexico, respectively, did not consider it necessary or appropriate in accordance with the text, context and object of the Vienna Convention on Consular Relations of 1963. Cf. Inter-American Court of Human Rights, Advisory Opinion OC-16/99, 1 October 1999, requested by the United Mexican States, on the *'the right to information on consular assistance in the framework of the guarantees of the due process of law'.* 'See B. Simma and C. Hoppe, 'From LaGrand and Avena to Medellin: A Rocky Road Toward Implementation', *Tulane Journal of International and Comparative Law* (2005) 7, at p. 13 (arguing that Mexico's position asking for a broad recognition of a fundamental human right backfired as the Court did not find support for such a pledge in the text or the object and purpose of the treaty). See also Chapter 10 by P. Webb in this volume.

[60] Separate Opinion of Judge A. A. Cançado Trindade, ICJ Reports 2010 (II), pp. 807–811, paras. 232–245.

The goal of the chapter is not to conduct a detailed analysis of these cases;[61] my point here is to consider more generally if the Court has shown indices of an interpretative practice fit to deal with human rights cases. My answer is a qualified yes. Given the structural limits of the Court – having States as its primary clients, not individuals – the Court has demonstrated that it is able and in certain occasions willing to apply principles and methods associated with (but not exclusive to) the interpretation of human rights – such as teleological, effective, purposive or evolutive interpretation. For instance, in its practice beyond human rights treaties, the Court has held that narrow interpretations of conventional rights are not necessarily mandatory when they involve limitations of sovereignty,[62] that treaties should be interpreted 'within the framework of the entire legal system prevailing at the time of the interpretation',[63] and that words may 'be understood to have the meaning they bear on each occasion on which the Treaty is to be applied, and not necessarily their original meaning'.[64] The Court, therefore, is not impeded by the rules of interpretation and may use an actual and potential relevant voice in the conversation on human rights and the narrative on the humanisation of international law. Salient examples may be found in the Court's references to *human values*, a willingness to reaffirm human rights and its *scope of application*, and in

---

[61] For such analysis see Crawford and A Keene, 'Interpretation of the Human Rights'.

[62] Dispute Regarding Navigational and Related Rights (*Costa Rica* v. *Nicaragua*), Judgment, ICJ Reports 2009, p. 213, para. 48: 'the Court is not convinced by Nicaragua's argument that Costa Rica's right of free navigation should be interpreted narrowly because it represents a limitation of the sovereignty over the river conferred by the Treaty on Nicaragua, that being the most important principle set forth by Article VI'.

[63] *Legal Consequences for States of the Continued Presence of South Africa in Namibia (South-West Africa) notwithstanding Security Council Resolution 276* (Advisory Opinion) ICJ Reports 1970, p. 16, para. 53. On systematic integration see *Oil Platforms case (Iran* v. *United States of America)*, Merits, Judgment of 6 November 2003, ICJ Reports 2003, p. 161, para. 41.

[64] Dispute Regarding Navigational and Related Rights (*Costa Rica* v. *Nicaragua*), Judgment, ICJ Reports 2009, p. 213, para. 70: 'the terms by which the extent of Costa Rica's right of free navigation has been defined, including in particular the term "comercio", must be understood to have the meaning they bear on each occasion on which the Treaty is to be applied, and not necessarily their original meaning'. Cf. *Whaling in the Antarctic (Australia* v. *Japan*; New Zealand intervening), Judgment, ICJ Reports 2014, p. 226, where the Court did not take a truly evolutionary approach. On these methods of interpretation in international law: E. Bjorge, *The Evolutionary Interpretation of Treaties* (Oxford University Press 2014); G. Abi-Saab, K. Keith, G. Marceau, C. Marquet (eds.), *Evolutionary Interpretation and International Law* (Bloomsbury Academic, 2019).

a predisposition to *dialogue* with specialised institutions and tribunals using and relying on their interpretation of human rights.

Values

The Court has recognised human values as key to its function of law ascertaining. In the judgment on the merits of its first contentious case, the *Corfu Channel*, the Court referred to the general and well-recognised principle of 'elementary considerations of humanity'[65] as one basis for determining the consuetudinary nature of certain rules of international and humanitarian law – in that case, the notification of the existence of minefields in the territorial sea of Albania, and the warning of imminent dangers for approaching British warships. The application of this principle resonates in other judgments of the Court, as it occurs in the *Diallo* case, where the Court acknowledged the right to be treated with humanity and dignity, and not be subjected to torture or other cruel, inhuman or degrading treatment as provided for in Articles 7, and 10, paragraph 1, of the Covenant, Article 5 of the African Charter, adding that: 'There is no doubt, moreover, that the prohibition of inhuman and degrading treatment is among the rules of general international law which are binding on States in all circumstances, even apart from any treaty commitments.'[66]

This kind of language was also present in the advisory opinion on the *Reservations to the Genocide Convention*. The Court investigated the object of the Convention affirming that '[t]he Convention was manifestly adopted for a purely humanitarian and civilizing purpose'.[67] The Court acknowledged that the treaty under consideration was of a special nature:

[i]n such a convention the contracting States do not have any interests of their own; they merely have, one and all, a common interest, namely, the accomplishment of those high purposes which are the *raison d'être* of the convention. Consequently, in a convention of this type one cannot speak of individual advantages or disadvantages to States, or of the maintenance of a perfect contractual

[65] *Corfu Channel Case (United Kingdom of Great* Britain and Northern *Ireland* v. *Albania)* (Merits) ICJ Reports 1949, p. 4, 22. 'Such obligations are based, not on the Hague Convention of 1907, No. VTII, which is applicable in time of war, but on certain general and well-recognised principles, namely: elementary considerations of humanity, even more exacting in peace than in war [..]'.
[66] *Ahmadou Sadio Diallo*, para. 87.
[67] *Reservations to the Convention on the Prevention and Punishment of the Crime of Genocide* (Advisory Opinion), ICJ Reports 1951, p. 15, at p. 23.

balance between rights and duties. The high ideals which inspired the Convention provide, by virtue of the common will of the parties, the foundation and measure of all its provisions.[68]

Scope

In a number of relatively recent cases, the Court has interpreted broadly the scope of application of human rights and humanitarian law treaties.[69] The advisory opinion on the *Legal Consequences of the Construction of a Wall in the Occupied Palestinian Territory* is particularly relevant[70] The Court, taking into account the 'object and purpose of the International Covenant on Civil and Political Rights',[71] and the practice of the Human Rights Committee, considered that the International Covenant on Civil and Political Rights was applicable in respect of acts done by a State in the exercise of its jurisdiction outside its own territory.[72] The Court arrived to the same conclusion in the case of the scope of application of the Covenant on Economic, Social and Cultural Rights, which does not have a provision on jurisdiction, and the Convention on the Rights of the Child of 20 November 1989, applicable therefore within the Occupied Palestinian

---

[68] This approach based on the special object of the treaty was fundamental in other cases concerning the prohibition of genocide: *Application of the Convention on the Prevention and Punishment of the Crime of Genocide (Bosnia and Herzegovina v. Yugoslavia)* (Preliminary Objections), ICJ Reports 1996, p. 595, para. 31; *Application of the Convention on the Prevention and Punishment of the Crime of Genocide (Bosnia and Herzegovina v. Serbia and Montenegro)* (Merits) ICJ Reports 2007, p. 43, para. 161. See also *Armed Activities on the Territory of the Congo (New Application: 2002) (Democratic Republic of the Congo v. Rwanda)* (Jurisdiction and Admissibility) ICJ Reports 2002, p. 6, para. 64. Cf. *Legality of the Threat or Use of Nuclear Weapons*, Advisory Opinion, ICJ Reports 1996, p. 226, para. 26.

[69] R. Wilde, 'Human Rights beyond Borders at the World Court: The Significance of the International Court of Justice's Jurisprudence on the Extraterritorial Application of International Human Rights Law Treaties', 12(4) *Chinese Journal of International Law* (2013), 639. Wilde finds a basis for these developments in a statement by Court in the Namibia Advisory Opinion, where the Court found that South Africa was accountable for any violations of the rights of the people of Namibia: 'Physical control of a territory, and not sovereignty or legitimacy of title, is the basis of State liability for acts affecting other States.' Legal Consequences for States of the Continued Presence of South Africa in Namibia (South-West Africa) Notwithstanding Security Council Resolution 276 (1970), Advisory Opinion, ICJ Reports 1971, para. 118. See generally M. Milavović, *Extraterritorial Application of Human Rights Teaties* (Oxford University Press, 2011).

[70] *Legal Consequences of the Construction of a Wall in the Occupied Palestinian Territory*, ICJ Reports 2004, p. 136, paras. 107–113.

[71] *Wall*, para. 109.   [72] *Wall*, para. 111.

Territory.[73] The protection, in the view of the Court, does not cease in cases of armed conflict, clarifying also the relationship between international human rights law and humanitarian law.[74] In *Armed Activities,* the Court relied on its findings on the Wall advisory opinion to reaffirm that international human rights and humanitarian law instruments are applicable 'in respect of acts done by a State in the exercise of its jurisdiction outside its own territory, particularly in occupied territories'.[75] The Court has applied the same understanding of the extraterritorial scope of human rights treaty obligations to the Convention on the Elimination of all Forms of Racial Discrimination[76] as well as to the Genocide Convention, which the Court considers not limited by territory, but applicable to a State 'wherever it may be acting or may be able to act' in order to comply with its obligations under the Convention.[77]

Dialogue

The *Diallo* case is fundamental from the human rights perspective not only because the Court declared a violation of human rights, but also for strongly relying on interpretation of human rights by specialised organs.[78] Indeed, with reference to the interpretation of a regional instrument for the protection of human rights, the Court acknowledged that 'it must take due account of the interpretation of that instrument adopted by the independent bodies which have been specifically created, if such has been the case,

---

[73] *Wall,* paras. 112–113.

[74] 'The protection offered by human rights conventions does not cease in case of armed conflict, save through the effect of provisions for derogation of the kind to be found in Article 4 of the International Covenant on Civil and Political Rights. As regards the relationship between international humanitarian law and human rights law, there are thus three possible situations: some rights may be exclusively matters of international humanitarian law; others may be exclusively matters of human rights law; yet others may be matters of both these branches of international law.' *Wall,* p. 178, para. 106.

[75] *Armed Activities on the Territory of the Congo (Democratic Republic of the Congo* v. *Uganda)* (Merits) ICJ Reports 2005, p. 168, para. 216.

[76] *Application of the International Convention on the Elimination of All Forms of Racial Discrimination (Georgia* v. *Russia)* (Provisional Measures), ICJ Reports 2008, p. 353, paras. 108–109.

[77] *Croatia* v. *Serbia,* para. 183.

[78] Previous references by the Court to the practice of human rights organs include *Questions relating to the Obligation to Prosecute or Extradite (Belgium* v. *Senegal), Judgment,* ICJ Reports 2012, p. 422, para. 101, citing to decisions of the Committee against Torture, and *Wall,* para. 109, referring to the 'constant practice of the Human Rights Committee'.

to monitor the sound application of the treaty in question'.[79] Moreover, in a well-known paragraph concerning the interpretation of the Covenant, the Court held that:

Although the Court is in no way obliged, in the exercise of its judicial functions, to model its own interpretation of the Covenant on that of the Committee, it believes that it should ascribe great weight to the interpretation adopted by this independent body that was established specifically to supervise the application of that treaty. The point here is to achieve the necessary clarity and the essential consistency of international law, as well as legal security, to which both the individuals with guaranteed rights and the States obliged to comply with treaty obligations are entitled.[80]

This position has been welcomed as a basis for an improved dialogue between the Court and the human rights treaty bodies. The wording of this paragraph is ambivalent: it affirms the autonomy of the Court as interpreter of the Covenant and at the same time ascribes a great weight to the interpretation of the Committee for the sake of clarity, consistency, and legal security. The 'great weight' of the Committee's interpretation was tested in the case concerning the *Application of the International Convention on the Elimination of All Forms of Racial Discrimination (Qatar v. United Arab Emirates)*[81] as Qatar not only started proceedings before the Court but also parallel inter-State proceedings before the CERD Committee.[82] The Court, in its judgment, differs from the interpretation of the CERD Committee regarding the meaning of the term 'national origin' in Article 1, paragraph 1, of the Convention.[83] For the Court, national origin refers to a birth attribute and does not encompass current nationalities, '[c]onsequently, the measures complained of by Qatar in the present case as part of its first claim, which are based on the current nationality of its citizens, do not fall within the scope *ratione materia* of CERD'.[84] This

[79] Ibid., para. 67.   [80] *Guinea* v. *Congo* (Merits), para. 66.
[81] *Application of the International Convention on the Elimination of All Forms of Racial Discrimination (Qatar* v. *United Arab Emirates, Judgment,* ICJ Reports 2021 (n.d.).
[82] CERD C/99/4, 27 August 2019, Admissibility of the Inter-State Communication Submitted by Qatar against the United Arab Emirates.
[83] CERD General Recommendation XXX on Discrimination Against Non-Citizens, *Adopted on 1 October 2002.*
[84] *Application of the International Convention on the Elimination of All Forms of Racial Discrimination,* para. 105. From the point of view of strategic litigation, Qatar arguably benefited from the recourse to the Court as it indicated provisional measures in favour of Qatar in 2018. See *Application of the International Convention on the Elimination of All Forms of Racial Discrimination (Qatar* v. *United Arab Emirates), Provisional Measures,*

outcome can be read as a win for the Court's autonomy and a loss for consistency.[85] However, a true dialogue in this international context must assume that there are no final interpreters and that reasonable disagreement on treaty interpretation is inevitable for many different causes.[86] Some may argue that the professional background of the members of the Court may lead to a pro-state bias compared to human right judges' antecedents. There is truth in this statement, but there are also signals of change as some of the present judges of the Court have been members of regional human rights courts (Cançado Trindade), members of the Human Rights Commission (Iwasawa) or champions of women's rights in international law (Charlesworth).

B Community Concerns

The second instance of contributions by the Court to the promotion and protection of human rights deals with the development of certain normative concepts most relevant to human rights, that is, *erga omnes* obligations and *jus cogens*, and its consequences. Both *erga omnes* obligations and *jus cogens* are based on global community interests[87] and implicate a broader discussion on the conception and hierarchy of international law.[88] Be that as it may, such concepts take seriously into account values that belong not to any particular State but to the international community as a whole. The role of the Court in the development of each of these concepts

---

Order of 23 July 2018. A reference to the protection of human rights through provisional measures may be found in D. Švarc Pipan. 'The Contribution of the International Court of Justice to the Promotion and Protection of Human Rights' in A. Follesdal and G. Ulfstain (eds.), *The Judicialization of International Law* (Oxford University Press, 2018) 209 at 225–226.

[85] See the dissenting opinions of Judge Bhandari and Judge Robinson in *Application of the International Convention on the Elimination of All Forms of Racial Discrimination*. They both criticise the majority of the Court for not taking seriously the 'great weight' that the Diallo's judgment ascribed to the interpretations' by the CERD Committee. Bandhari even called the CERD Committee 'the guardian of the Convention' (para. 21).

[86] J. Pauwelyn and M. Elsig, 'The Politics of Treaty Interpretation' in J. L. Dunoff and M. A. Pollack (eds.), *Interdisciplinary Perspectives on International Law and International Relations* (Cambridge University Press, 2012) 445.

[87] B. Simma, 'From Bilateralism to Community Interest in International Law' 250 *Collected Courses of the Hague Academy of International Law* (1994).

[88] D. Shelton, 'International Law and Relative Normativity' in M. Evans (ed.), *International Law* (Oxford University Press, 2009) 159.

differs: it introduced *erga omnes* obligations in 1970, and only recognised *jus cogens* thirty-six years after in 2006.

The Court initiated the concept of *erga omnes* obligations in an *obiter dictum* in its judgment of 5 February 1970 concerning the *Barcelona Traction* case. The Court distinguished between mere reciprocal obligations and 'obligations of a State toward the international community as a whole'. They 'are the concern of all States' and 'all States can be held to have a legal interest in their protection'.[89] The Court did not offer practical proof for such normative distinction,[90] but only gave examples of *erga omnes* obligations, including 'from the outlawing of acts of aggression, and of genocide, as also from the principles and rules concerning the basic rights of the human person, including protection from slavery and racial discrimination'.[91] Since then, the category is generally accepted in international law and the Court has made numerous references to these obligations in its judgments and advisory opinions, that is, to the *erga omnes* character of the rights and obligations enshrined by the Genocide Convention,[92] the obligations under the Convention against Torture[93] or the obligation to respect the right of self-determination.[94]

---

[89] *Barcelona Traction, Light and Power Company, Limited (Belgium* v. *Spain)* (Second Phase), ICJ Reports 1970, p. 3, para. 33. For an authoritative definition, see Institut de Droit International 'Resolution on Obligations *erga omnes* in International Law', Annuaire IDI vol 71(2) (2005), pp. 286–9. See M. Ragazzi, *The Concept of International Obligations Erga omnes* (Clarendon Press, 1997); C. J. Tams, *Enforcing Obligations erga omnes in International Law* (Cambridge University Press 2005); S. Villalpando, *L'émergence de la communauté internationale dans la responsabilité des Etats* (Presses Universitaires de France, 2005).

[90] See D. Tadli, Chapter 3, in this volume.

[91] *Barcelona Traction, Light and Power Company, Limited (Belgium* v. *Spain)* (Second Phase), ICJ Reports 1970, p. 3, para. 34.

[92] *Application of the Convention on the Prevention and Punishment of the Crime of Genocide (Bosnia and Herzegovina* v. *Serbia and Montenegro), Preliminary Objections, Judgment of 11 July 1996, ICJ Reports 1996 (II)*, p. 616, para. 31; *Application of the Convention on the Prevention and Punishment of the Crime of Genocide (Croatia* v. *Serbia), Judgment of 3 February 2015, ICJ Reports 2015*, p. 47, para. 87.

[93] *Questions relating to the Obligation to Prosecute or Extradite (Belgium* v. *Senegal), Judgment, ICJ Reports 2012 (II)*, p. 450, para. 69.

[94] *East Timor (Portugal* v. *Australia), Judgment, ICJ Reports 1995*, p. 90, para. 29; *Wall*, para. 155; *Legal Consequences of the Separation of the Chagos Archipelago from Mauritius in 1965, Advisory Opinion, ICJ Reports 2019*, p. 95, para. 180: 'Since respect for the right to self-determination is an obligation *erga omnes*, all States have a legal interest in protecting that right.'

The notion of *jus cogens*, peremptory norms of general international law, was discussed by the International Law Commission and incorporated in Article 53 of the Vienna Convention of the Law of Treaties of 1969 as a norm 'accepted and recognised by the international community of States as a whole as a norm from which no derogation is permitted and which can be modified only by a subsequent norm of general international law having the same character'.[95] Members of the Court referred to *jus cogens* norms in their dissenting opinions before and after the adoption of the Vienna Convention on the Law of Treaties,[96] but the Court itself did not give support to the notion until recently.[97] The Court first acknowledged *jus cogens* as such in its judgment in *Armed Activities* where the Court clearly identified the prohibition of genocide as a peremptory norm of international law.[98] Afterwards, the Court has affirmed the nature of *jus*

---

[95] See generally R. Kolb, *Peremptory International Law: Jus Cogens. A General Inventory* (Hart, 2015); A. Orakhelashvili, *Peremptory Norms in International Law* (Oxford University Press, 2006); C. Tomuschat and J. M. Thouvenin (eds.), *The Fundamental Rules of the International Legal Order: Jus Cogens and Obligations Erga Omnes* (Martinus Nijhoff, 2006). For a relevant current discussion on *jus cogens*, see D. Tladi (ed.) *Peremptory Norms of General international Law (Jus Cogens): Disputations and Disquisitions* (Brill, 2021). See also ILC, Peremptory norms of general international law (*jus cogens*) Text of the draft conclusions and draft annex provisionally adopted by the Drafting Committee on first reading, 24 May 2019, A/CN.4/L.936.

[96] Judge *ad hoc* Fernandes in his dissenting opinion in the *Right of Passage over Indian Territory (Portugal v. India), Merits, Judgment, ICJ Reports 1960*, p. 135 ('rules of *ius cogens*, over which no special practice can prevail'); and Judge Tanaka in his dissenting opinion in the *South-West Africa (Ethiopia v. South Africa; Liberia v. South Africa), Second Phase, Judgment, ICJ Reports 1966*, p. 298 ('surely the law concerning the protection of human rights may be considered to belong to the *jus cogens*').

[97] Judge *ad hoc* Dugard said in his Separate Opinion that the Court 'carefully and deliberately avoided endorsing the notion of *jus cogens* despite the many opportunities it had to do so'. Other courts and tribunals have been more open to support the notion of jus cogens, e.g., Inter-American Court of Human Rights, *Case of Goiburú et al. v. Paraguay*, Judgment of 22 September 2006 (Merits, Reparations and Costs), para. 84. See A. A. Cançado Trindade, 'Enforced Disappearances of Persons as a Violation of *Jus Cogens*: The Contribution of the Jurisprudence of the Inter-American Court of Human Rights', *Nordic Journal of International Law* 81 (2012), pp. 507–536.

[98] *Armed Activities on the Territory of the Congo (Democratic Republic of the Congo v. Rwanda), ICJ Reports 2006*, p. 6, para. 64 ('assuredly the case with regard to the prohibition of genocide'). See also *Application of the Convention on the Prevention and Punishment of the Crime of Genocide (Bosnia and Herzegovina v. Serbia and Montenegro), Judgment of 26 February 2007, ICJ Reports 2007 (I)*, p. 111, para. 161; *Application of the Convention on the Prevention and Punishment of the Crime of Genocide (Croatia v. Serbia), Judgment, ICJ Reports 2015 (I)*, pp. 45–47, paras. 85–88.

cogens of crimes against humanity and war crimes,[99] and the prohibition of torture.[100]

The observance and enforcement of these norms concern the most basic human values and, in principle, are not stopped by domestic frontiers; their realm is the international community as a whole. Therefore, the potential of these normative distinctions for human rights law is immense. However, the practice of the Court also reveals the limits of these notions. Indeed, the Court has opted for a rather narrow interpretation of *erga omnes* obligations and *jus cogens* when confronted with normative conflicts between them and the consent of States or secondary rules of international law.[101] In the case concerning *East Timor* the Court accepted the 'irreproachable' *erga omnes* character of the right of peoples to self-determination, but held that

> the *erga omnes* character of a norm and the rule of consent to jurisdiction are two different things. Whatever the nature of the obligations invoked, the Court could not rule on the lawfulness of the conduct of a State when its judgment would imply an evaluation of the lawfulness of the conduct of another State which is not a party to the case. Where this is so, the Court cannot act, even if the right in question is a right *erga omnes*.[102]

The Court affirmed that '[t]he same applies to the relationship between peremptory norms of general international law *(jus cogens)* and the establishment of the Court's jurisdiction'. For the Court, *jus cogens* cannot provide a basis of jurisdiction by itself; the Court's Statute requires the consent of the parties to establish its jurisdiction over a dispute.[103]

[99] *Jurisdictional Immunities of the State (Germany v. Italy: Greece intervening), Judgment,* ICJ Reports 2012, p. 99, para. 93.

[100] *Arrest Warrant of 11 April 2000 (Democratic Republic of the Congo v. Belgium)* (Judgment) ICJ Reports 2002, p. 3, para. 12.

[101] See J. Vidmar, 'Norm Conflicts and Hierarchy in International Law: Towards a Vertical International Legal System' in E. De Wet and J. Vidmar (eds.), *Hierarchy in International Law: The Place of Human Rights* (Oxford University Press, 2012) 13, at 33–40 (arguing that 'the operation of the peremptory character may be limited to the so-called "negative obligations" of states').

[102] *East Timor (Portugal v. Australia), Judgment,* ICJ Reports 1995, p. 102, para. 29. In Armed Activities, again, the Court said that 'the mere fact that rights and obligations *erga omnes* or peremptory norms of general international law *(jus cogens)* are at issue in a dispute cannot in itself constitute an exception to the principle that its jurisdiction always depends on the consent of the parties'. *Armed Activities on the Territory of the Congo (Democratic Republic of the Congo v. Rwanda), ICJ Reports 2006,* p. 6, para. 64.

[103] *Armed Activities on the Territory of the Congo (Democratic Republic of the Congo v. Rwanda), ICJ Reports 2006,* p. 6, para. 64.

Recognising such an exception, in the words of Dugard, is 'a bridge too far' for the Court as it would amount to engaging in law-making beyond its legitimate judicial function. 'Only States can amend Article 36 of the Court's Statute.'[104]

The Court has dealt with other situations of rules based on State sovereignty limiting and controlling the effects of peremptory norms of international law in cases where the parties alleged exceptions to the principles of immunity from criminal and civil jurisdiction. The Court rejected such exceptions. In the *Arrest Warrant* case, the Court, without making express reference to *jus cogens*, examined State practice, international instruments, and the decisions of international criminal tribunals to conclude that it was unable to deduce from them 'that there exists under customary international law any form of exception to the rule according immunity from criminal jurisdiction and inviolability to incumbent Ministers for Foreign Affairs, where they are suspected of having committed war crimes or crimes against humanity'.[105] In the *jurisdictional immunities* case the Court confirmed the same approach by denying any exception to the applicability of the customary international law on State immunity. For the Court, *jus cogens* and jurisdictional immunities are essentially two different kind of rules, substantive and procedural, which cannot conflict:

> A *jus cogens* rule is one from which no derogation is permitted but the rules which determine the scope and extent of jurisdiction and when that jurisdiction may be exercised do not derogate from those substantive rules which possess *jus cogens* status, nor is there anything inherent in the concept of *jus cogens* which would require their modification or would displace their application.[106]

These arguments reflect a persistent ambivalence between State consent and community values in international law, with the Court showing a preference in these cases for a cautious State-centric approach to the

---

[104] Judge ad hoc Dugard, Separate Opinion, *Armed Activities on the Territory of the Congo (Democratic Republic of the Congo v. Rwanda), ICJ Reports 2006*, p. 86, para. 13.

[105] *Arrest Warrant of 11 April 2000 (Democratic Republic of the Congo v. Belgium), Judgment,* ICJ Reports 2002, p. 3, para. 58.

[106] *Jurisdictional Immunities of the State (Germany v. Italy: Greece intervening), Judgment, ICJ Reports 2012*, p. 99, para. 95. See Chapter 19 by R. O'Keefe in this volume. Cf. Dissenting Opinion of Judge Cançado Trindade, ibid., p. 179 ss. Cf. also C. Espósito, 'Jus Cogens and Jurisdictional Immunities of States at the International Court of Justice: A Conflict Does Exist', 21 *Italian Yearbook of International Law* (2011) 161.

progressive development of international law in matters affecting the basic principles of the international law and the stability of international relations.

A window of opportunity has been open for an enriched role of the Court in the protection of human rights by the broadening of legal standing which came along with the incorporation of the notions of *erga omnes* obligations into the system by the Articles on State responsibility for international wrongful acts (ARSIWA).[107] Contrary to what the Court said in *South-West Africa*,[108] now States which are not directly injured by violations of obligations *erga omnes partes* have legal standing before the Court. Article 48(1) ARSIWA provides that:

Any State other than an injured State is entitled to invoke the responsibility of another State in accordance with paragraph 2 if: (a) the obligation breached is owed to a group of States including that State, and is established for the protection of a collective interest of the group; or (b) the obligation breached is owed to the international community as a whole.

This Article was not expressly mentioned in the *Obligation to Prosecute or Extradite* case, but was in the spirit of the wording of the Court when it construed the obligations to prosecute or extradite the former President of Chad, Hissène Habré, arising from the Convention against Torture and Other Cruel, Inhuman or Degrading Treatment or Punishment as obligations *erga omnes*, therefore acknowledging Belgium's standing to bring the case against Senegal. The Court held that:

[t]he common interest in compliance with the relevant obligations under the Convention against Torture implies the entitlement of each State party to the Convention to make a claim concerning the cessation of an alleged breach by another State party. If a special interest were required for that purpose, in many cases no State would be in the position to make such a claim. It follows that any State party to the Convention may invoke the responsibility of another State party with a view to ascertaining the alleged failure to comply with its obligations *erga*

---

[107] On the humanisation of state responsibility, see T. Meron, *The Humanization of International Law* (Brill, 2006) chapter 4, pp. 248–306.

[108] *South-West Africa* (Ethiopia *and Liberia* v. *South Africa)*, Second Phase, International Court of Justice, Judgment of 18 July 1966, ICJ Rep. 6, para. 88: 'although a right of this kind may be known to certain municipal systems of law, it is not known to international law as it stands at present: nor is the Court able to regard it as imported by the "general principles of law" referred to in Article 38, paragraph 1(c), of its Statute'.

omnes partes, such as those under Article 6, paragraph 2, and Article 7, paragraph 1, of the Convention, and to bring that failure to an end.[109]

With a similar approach, in *The Gambia* v. *Myanmar,* the Court rejected Myanmar's objection that only specially affected parties can legitimately invoke responsibility for the violation of obligations under the Genocide Convention.[110] The Court recalled its Advisory Opinion on *Reservations to the Convention on the Prevention and Punishment of the Crime of Genocide* and the judgment on the *Obligation to Prosecute or Extradite* to affirm the 'common interest' in achieving the high purposes of the Convention[111] and the *erga omnes* character of the obligations involved to conclude that 'The Gambia has *prima facie* standing to submit to it the dispute with Myanmar on the basis of alleged violations of obligations under the Genocide Convention.'[112] Furthermore, the Court held that 'there is a real and imminent risk of irreparable prejudice to the rights invoked by The Gambia',[113] and indicated provisional measures to protect the rights of the members of the Rohingya group in the territory of Myanmar.[114] Thus confirming also the important role of the indication of provisional measures for the protection of human rights.[115]

III Conclusion

Although the International Court of Justice will never be a specialised human rights court, conceiving an enhanced, more significant, human

---

[109] *Questions relating to the Obligation to Prosecute or Extradite,* para. 69.

[110] *Application of the Convention on the Prevention and Punishment of the Crime of Genocide (The Gambia* v. *Myanmar), Provisional Measures, Order of 23 January 2020, ICJ Reports 2020,* p. 3, paras. 39–42.

[111] See fn 68.   [112] *The Gambia* v. *Myanmar,* para. 42.

[113] *The Gambia* v. *Myanmar,* para. 75.   [114] *The Gambia* v. *Myanmar,* para. 86.

[115] See fn 84. Also, Separate Opinion of Judge Cançado Trindade, *Application of the International Convention for the Suppression of the Financing of Terrorism and of the International Convention on the Elimination of All Forms of Racial Discrimination (Ukraine* v. *Russian Federation),* Provisional Measures, Order of 19 April 2017, ICJ Reports 2017, p. 185, para. 86: 'Human beings in vulnerability are the ultimate beneficiaries of provisional measures of protection, endowed nowadays with a truly *tutelary* character, as true jurisdictional guarantees of preventive character.' Also cited in his separate opinion appended to the *The Gambia* v. *Myanmar,* para. 64.

rights role for the Court is desirable and possible.[116] This chapter has argued that structural disengagement in the sense of allowing only states to litigate before the Court does not impede substantial incorporation which depends on other factors, such as the changing attitudes of the ICJ judges and lawyers before the court. Recent cases, such as the Chagos advisory opinion and The Gambia claim against Myammar in order to protect the Rohingyas, show an increased relevance of strategic human rights litigation before the Court, and perhaps a signal that human rights advocates have widened their playfield to include the Court.[117] There are of course some unavoidable obstacles, such as the limitations on the right of access to the Court, which 'colours the entirety of its activities',[118] and cultural barriers, such as the tribal tendencies towards segregating the human rights practice from other fields of the law. One may also encounter a certain mistrust of the Court by human rights lawyers due to its traditional State-centric positions.

The Court, however, has recognised and advanced global community values through interpretation and has used normative tools to improve the chances of both giving relevance to fundamental norms of human rights and humanitarian law, and, in the expression of judge Simma, mainstreaming human rights within general international law.[119] Regarding interpretation, the extensive practice of the Court, including both human rights treaties and other treaties, reveals that it is not unable to apply interpretive techniques which have been generally associated with human rights courts and tribunals, such as the effectiveness rule and the evolutive interpretation. Moreover, the Court has contributed to clarifying the scope of human rights, and has opened itself to a dialogue with other courts and

---

[116] See B. Çali, Z. Elibol and L. McGregor, 'The International Court of Justice as an Integrator, Developer and Globaliser of International Human Rights Law', in M. Sheinin (ed.), *Human Rights Norms in 'Other' International Courts* (Cambridge University Press, 2019) 62.

[117] See J. Almqvist, 'La Corte Internacional de Justicia como foro para el litigio estratégico de derechos humanos', in S. Torrecuadrada García-Lozano (ed.), *Los nuevos retos de la Corte Internacional de Justicia* (Kluwer, 2021) 215 (underlying that human rights courts also allow inter-State litigation so the phenomenon is not entirely new for human rights advocates). Regarding the ECHR case load, see for example, ECHR, *Azerbaijan* v. *Armenia* (N° 47319/20), application of 15 January 2021; ECHR, *Armenia* v. *Azerbaijan* (N° 42521/20), application of 1 February 2021; *The Netherlands* v. *Russia* (N° 28525/20) application of 10 July 2020.

[118] R. Kolb, *The International Court of Justice*, p. 269.

[119] B. Simma, 'Mainstreaming Human Rights: The Contribution of the International Court of Justice'.

tribunals, and with human rights organs with a view to establish the appropriate meaning of human rights treaty provisions.

The findings of the Court can both contribute to the actual protection of human rights, even in cases in which, admittedly, the legal problem before the Court is just a tiny part of a major conflict, and 'have a positive ripple effect for the enforcement of human rights, beyond [it]s own case law'.[120] The increasing number of inter-State human rights litigation[121] and prospective challenging requests for advisory opinions, including the announced legal question on the effects of sea-level rise for small islands[122] and its connection with the human right to a healthy environment,[123] will certainly give the Court additional opportunities to 'contribute to a human-ised law of nations'.[124]

Further Reading

B. Çali, Z. Elibol and L. McGregor, 'The International Court of Justice as an Integrator, Developer and Globaliser of International Human Rights Law', in M. Sheinin (ed.), *Human Rights Norms in 'Other' International Courts* (Cambridge University Press, 2019) 62.

J. Crawford and A. Keene (2020) Interpretation of the Human Rights Treaties by the International Court of Justice, 24 (7) *The International Journal of Human Rights* 935.

B. Simma, 'Human Rights Before the International Court of Justice: Community Interest Coming to Life?' in C. J. Tams and J. Sloan (eds.), *The Development of International Law by the International Court of Justice* (Oxford University Press, 2013) 301.

S. Sivakumaran, 'The International Court of Justice and Human Rights' in S. Joseph and A. McBeth (eds.) *Research Handbook on International Human Rights Law* (Elgar, 2010) 299.

---

[120] G. Zyberi, 'Enforcing Human Rights Through the International Court of Justice: Between Idealism and Realism,' in N. Rodley and T. Van Ho (eds.), *Research Handbook on Human Rights Institutions and Enforcement* (Elgar, 2018) 24.

[121] See, e.g., the cases mentioned in fn. 117.

[122] British Institute of International and Comparative Law, '*Rising Sea Levels: A Matter for the ICJ?*' (11 March 2021) <www.biicl.org/events/11468/webinar-series-rising-sea-levels-promoting-climate- justice-through-international-law>. On the protection of the environment and the ICJ, see Chapter 17 by Daniel Bodansky in this volume.

[123] A/HRC/RES/48/13, The human right to a clean, healthy, and sustainable environment, adopted on 8 October 2021.

[124] A. Cançado Trindade, Separate Opinion, *Application of the International Convention on the Elimination of All Forms of Racial Discrimination*, para. 28.

D. Svarc Pipan. 'The Contribution of the International Court of Justice to the Promotion and Protection of Human Rights' in A. Follesdal and G. Ulfstain eds., *The Judicialization of International Law* (Oxford University Press, 2018) 209.

R. Wilde, 'Human Rights beyond Borders at the World Court: The Significance of the International Court of Justice's Jurisprudence on the Extraterritorial Application of International Human Rights Law Treaties', 12(4) *Chinese Journal of International Law* (2013), 639.

G. Zyberi, *The Humanitarian Face of the International Court of Justice* (Intersentia, 2008).

Index

Made in United States
North Haven, CT
11 February 2024

48578527R10300